THE MULTILINGUAL DICTIONARY OF PRINTING AND PUBLISHING

"THE MULTILINGUAL DICTIONARY OF PRINTING AND PUBLISHING"

Dr. Alan Isaacs, editor

FREDERICK MULLER LIMITED,
LONDON

THE MULTILINGUAL DICTIONARY OF PRINTING AND PUBLISHING

First published in Great Britain by
Frederick Muller Limited, London, NW2 6LE.
Published in the USA by Facts On File, Inc.,
New York.

ISBN 0-584-95569-3

Printed in the United States of America

A

aba da sobrecapa *(f)* Pt
De Umschlagklappe *(f)*
En jacket flap
Es solapa de la cubierta *(f)*
Fr rabat de la jaquette *(m)*
It risvolto della sovracopertina *(m)*

abbozzo *(m)* n It
De Skizze *(f)*
En rough
Es boceto *(m)*
Fr croquis *(m)*
Pt esboço *(m)*

abbreviation n En
De Abkürzung *(f)*
Es abreviatura *(f)*
Fr abréviation *(f)*
It abbreviazione *(f)*
Pt abreviatura *(f)*

abbreviazione *(f)* n It
De Abkürzung *(f)*
En abbreviation
Es abreviatura *(f)*
Fr abréviation *(f)*
Pt abreviatura *(f)*

Abdeckband *(n)* n De
En masking tape
Es cinta para enmascarar *(f)*
Fr bande de masquage *(f)*
It nastro per mascheratura *(m)*
Pt fita de mascarar *(f)*

abdecken vb De
En mask
Es enmascarar
Fr oblitérer
It mascherare
Pt mascarar

Abdecken *(n)* n De
En blocking out
Es enmienda con sobreimpresión *(f)*
Fr oblitération *(f)*
It mascheratura con vernice coprente *(f)*
Pt cobrimento *(m)*

Abdeckung *(f)* n De
En masking
Es enmascarado *(m)*
Fr masquage *(m)*
It mascheratura *(f)*
Pt máscara *(f)*

abgedroschen adj De
En hackneyed
Es común
Fr stéréotypé
It comune
Pt vulgar

Abkommen *(n)* n De
En agreement
Es acuerdo *(m)*
Fr accord *(m)*
It accordo *(m)*
Pt acordo *(m)*

Abkürzung *(f)* n De
En abbreviation
Es abreviatura *(f)*
Fr abréviation *(f)*
It abbreviazione *(f)*
Pt abreviatura *(f)*

Ableimung *(f)* n De
En delamination
Es delaminación *(f)*
Fr séparation des plis *(f)*
It separazione degli strati *(f)*
Pt deslaminação *(f)*

abondamment illustré Fr
De großzügig illustriert
En lavishly illustrated
Es profusamente ilustrado
It riccamente illustrato
Pt profusamente ilustrado

Abpressen *(n)* n De
En backing; pressing
Es formación de cajos; prensado *(f m)*
Fr endossure; pressage *(f m)*
It rinforzo; stiratura *(m f)*
Pt colocação de lombada; compressão *(f)*

abréviation *(f)* n Fr
De Abkürzung *(f)*
En abbreviation

Es abreviatura *(f)*
It abbreviazione *(f)*
Pt abreviatura *(f)*

abreviatura *(f)* n Es, Pt
De Abkürzung *(f)*
En abbreviation
Fr abréviation *(f)*
It abbreviazione *(f)*

abrir parágrafo Pt
De einrücken
En indent
Es sangrar
Fr renforcer
It dentellare

abschreiben vb De
En copy
Es copiar
Fr copier
It copiare
Pt copiar

Abschrift *(f)* n De
En copy
Es original *(m)*
Fr copie *(f)*
It copia *(f)*
Pt cópia *(f)*

Abstand *(m)* n De
En spacing
Es espaciado *(m)*
Fr espacement *(m)*
It spaziatura *(f)*
Pt espaçamento *(m)*

Abtaster *(m)* n De
En scanner
Es explorador *(m)*
Fr analyseur électronique *(m)*
It scanner *(m)*
Pt dispositivo explorador *(m)*

Abteilung *(f)* n De
En division
Es división *(f)*
Fr division *(f)*
It divisione *(f)*
Pt divisão *(f)*

Abziehapparat *(m)* n De
En proofing press
Es prensa sacapruebas *(f)*
Fr presse pour tirer les épreuves *(f)*

It tirabozze *(m)*
Pt prensa para tirar provas *(f)*

Abzug *(m)* n De
En proof
Es prueba *(f)*
Fr épreuve *(f)*
It bozza *(f)*
Pt prova *(f)*

acabado *(m)* n Es
De Ausrüstung *(f)*
En finish
Fr apprêt *(m)*
It appretto *(m)*
Pt acabamento *(m)*

acabado antiguo *(m)* Es
De Antik-Ausrüstung *(f)*
En antique finish
Fr apprêt à l'antique *(m)*
It appretto tipo antico *(m)*
Pt acabamento antigo *(m)*

acabado en seco *(m)* Es
De Blindbearbeitung *(f)*
En blind finishing
Fr gaufrage à sec *(m)*
It finitura cieca *(f)*
Pt acabamento cego *(m)*

acabamento *(m)* n Pt
De Ausrüstung *(f)*
En finish
Es acabado *(m)*
Fr apprêt *(m)*
It appretto *(m)*

acabamento antigo *(m)* Pt
De Antik-Ausrüstung *(f)*
En antique finish
Es acabado antiguo *(m)*
Fr apprêt à l'antique *(m)*
It appretto tipo antico *(m)*

acabamento cego *(m)* Pt
De Blindbearbeitung *(f)*
En blind finishing
Es acabado en seco *(m)*
Fr gaufrage à sec *(m)*
It finitura cieca *(f)*

academic books En
De akademische Bücher
(pl)
Es libros académicos (m
pl)
Fr livres d'étude (m pl)
It libri accademici (m
pl)
Pt livros académicos (m
pl)

acção (f) n Pt
De Aktie (f)
En share
Es acción (f)
Fr action (f)
It azione (f)

accent n En; Fr (m)
De Akzent (m)
Es acento (m)
It accento (m)
Pt acento (m)

accent aigu (m) Fr
De Akut (m)
En acute accent
Es acento agudo (m)
It accento acuto (m)
Pt acento agudo (m)

accent circonflexe (m)
Fr
De Zirkumflex (m)
En circumflex
Es acento circunflejo
(m)
It accento circonflesso
(m)
Pt acento circunflexo
(m)

accent flottant (m) Fr
De Schwebender Akzent
(m)
En floating accent
Es acento postizo (m)
It accento fluttuante
(m)
Pt acento flutuante (m)

accent grave (m) Fr
De Gravis (m)
En grave accent
Es acento grave (m)
It accento grave (m)
Pt acento grave (m)

accento (m) n It
De Akzent (m)
En accent

Es acento (m)
Fr accent (m)
Pt acento (m)

accento acuto (m) It
De Akut (m)
En acute accent
Es acento agudo (m)
Fr accent aigu (m)
Pt acento agudo (m)

accento circonflesso
(m) It
De Zirkumflex (m)
En circumflex
Es acento circunflejo
(m)
Fr accent circonflexe
(m)
Pt acento circunflexo
(m)

accento fluttuante (m) It
De Schwebender Akzent
(m)
En floating accent
Es acento postizo (m)
Fr accent flottant (m)
Pt acento flutuante (m)

accento grave (m) It
De Gravis (m)
En grave accent
Es acento grave (m)
Fr accent grave (m)
Pt acento grave (m)

access time En
De Zugriffzeit (f)
Es tiempo de acceso (m)
Fr temps d'accès (m)
It tempo di accesso (m)
Pt tempo de acesso (m)

acción (f) n Es
De Aktie (f)
En share
Fr action (f)
It azione (f)
Pt acção (f)

accionista (m) n Es, Pt
De Aktionär (m)
En shareholder
Fr actionnaire (m)
It azionista (m/f)

accord (m) n Fr
De Abkommen (n)
En agreement

Es acuerdo (m)
It accordo (m)
Pt acordo (m)

accordo (m) n It
De Abkommen (n)
En agreement
Es acuerdo (m)
Fr accord (m)
Pt acordo (m)

accordo coll'autore (m)
It
De Verfasservertrag (m)
En author's agreement
Es contrato de autor (m)
Fr contrat d'auteur (m)
Pt acordo do autor (m)

accumulateur (m) n Fr
De Akkumulator (m)
En accumulator
Es acumulador (m)
It accumulatore (m)
Pt acumulador (m)

accumulator n En
De Akkumulator (m)
Es acumulador (m)
Fr accumulateur (m)
It accumulatore (m)
Pt acumulador (m)

accumulatore (m) n It
De Akkumulator (m)
En accumulator
Es acumulador (m)
Fr accumulateur (m)
Pt acumulador (m)

acento (m) n Es, Pt
De Akzent (m)
En accent
Fr accent (m)
It accento (m)

acento agudo (m) Es, Pt
De Akut (m)
En acute accent
Fr accent aigu (m)
It accento acuto (m)

acento circunflejo (m)
Es
De Zirkumflex (m)
En circumflex
Fr accent circonflexe
(m)
It accento circonflesso
(m)

Pt acento circunflexo
(m)

acento circunflexo (m)
Pt
De Zirkumflex (m)
En circumflex
Es acento circunflejo
(m)
Fr accent circonflexe
(m)
It accento circonflesso
(m)

acento flutuante (m) Pt
De Schwebender Akzent
(m)
En floating accent
Es acento postizo (m)
Fr accent flottant (m)
It accento fluttuante
(m)

acento grave (m) Es, Pt
De Gravis (m)
En grave accent
Fr accent grave (m)
It accento grave (m)

acento postizo (m) Es
De Schwebender Akzent
(m)
En floating accent
Fr accent flottant (m)
It accento fluttuante
(m)
Pt acento flutuante (m)

acidatura (f) n It
De Ätzphase (f)
En bite (platemaking)
Es mordido (m)
Fr larron (m)
Pt mordente (m)

acid-free adj En
De säurefrei
Es exento de ácido
Fr sans acide
It privo di acidi
Pt isento de ácido

acid-resist adj En
De säurebeständig
Es resistente al ácido
Fr résistant à l'acide
It resistente agli acidi
Pt resistente contra
ácidos

acknowledgments *pl n*
En
De Anerkennung *(f)*
Es agradecimientos *(m pl)*
Fr remerciements *(m pl)*
It ringraziamenti *(m pl)*
Pt agradecimentos *(m pl)*

a colori It
Am in full color
De in voller Farbe
En in full colour
Es a todo color
Fr en couleurs
Pt a toda a cor

acondicionamiento *(m) n* Es
De Konditionierung *(f)*
En conditioning (of paper)
Fr conditionnement *(m)*
It stagionatura *(f)*
Pt condicionamento *(m)*

acordo *(m) n* Pt
De Abkommen *(n)*
En agreement
Es acuerdo *(m)*
Fr accord *(m)*
It accordo *(m)*

acordo do autor *(m)* Pt
De Verfasservertrag *(m)*
En author's agreement
Es contrato de autor *(m)*
Fr contrat d'auteur *(m)*
It accordo coll'autore *(m)*

acotación *(f) n* Es
De Anmerkung *(f)*
En annotation
Fr annotation *(f)*
It annotazione *(f)*
Pt anotação *(f)*

acquaforte *(m) n* It
De Mezzotintoverfahren *(n)*
En mezzotint
Es grabado mezzotinto *(m)*
Fr mezzo-tinto *(m)*
Pt meia-tinta *(f)*

acquafortista raffinata *(f)* It
De Feinätzung *(f)*

En fine etching
Es aguafuerte fina *(f)*
Fr gravure à l'eau-forte très mordancé *(m)*
Pt gravado fino *(m)*

acquatinta *(f) n* It
De Aquatinta *(f)*
En aquatint
Es acuatinta *(f)*
Fr aquatinte *(f)*
Pt aqua-tinta *(f)*

action *(f) n* Fr
De Aktie *(f)*
En share
Es acción *(f)*
It azione *(f)*
Pt acção *(f)*

actionnaire *(m) n* Fr
De Aktionär *(m)*
En shareholder
Es accionista *(m)*
It azionista *(m/f)*
Pt accionista *(m)*

acto de recorrer *(m)* Pt
De Umbrechen *(n)*
En over-running
Es recorrido *(m)*
Fr remaniement *(m)*
It rimaneggiamento *(m)*

actualizado *adj* Es, Pt
De überarbeitet
En updated
Fr mis à jour
It aggiornato

actualizar *vb* Es, Pt
De überarbeiten
En update
Fr mettre à jour
It aggiornare

acuatinta *(f) n* Es
De Aquatinta *(f)*
En aquatint
Fr aquatinte *(f)*
It acquatinta *(f)*
Pt aqua-tinta *(f)*

acuatono *(m) n* Es
De Aquaton-Verfahren *(n)*
En aquatone
Fr aquatone *(m)*
It aquatone *(m)*
Pt aquatone *(m)*

acuerdo *(m) n* Es
De Abkommen *(n)*
En agreement
Fr accord *(m)*
It accordo *(m)*
Pt acordo *(m)*

acumulador *(m) n* Es, Pt
De Akkumulator *(m)*
En accumulator
Fr accumulateur *(m)*
It accumulatore *(m)*

acuñado *(m) n* Es
De Schließen *(n)*
En locking-up
Fr serrage *(m)*
It serramento *(m)*
Pt enramado *(m)*

acuñado de material de escritorio *(m)* Es
De Briefpapier-Binden *(n)*
En stationery binding
Fr reliure papeterie *(f)*
It rilegatura da cartoleria *(f)*
Pt encadernação para escritório *(f)*

acuñado tipográfico *(m)* Es
De Buchdruck-Binden *(n)*
En letterpress binding
Fr reliure imprimerie *(f)*
It legatura da tipografia *(f)*
Pt encadernação tipográfica *(f)*

acute accent En
De Akut *(m)*
Es acento agudo *(m)*
Fr accent aigu *(m)*
It accento acuto *(m)*
Pt acento agudo *(m)*

adaptar al inglés Es
De anglisieren
En Anglicize
Fr angliciser
It anglicizzare
Pt anglificar

addenda *(m) n* Fr
De Anhang *(m)*
En addendum
Es adición *(f)*

It addendo *(m)*
Pt adenda *(m)*

addendo *(m) n* It
De Anhang *(m)*
En addendum
Es adición *(f)*
Fr addenda *(m)*
Pt adenda *(m)*

addendum *n* En
De Anhang *(m)*
Es adición *(f)*
Fr addenda *(m)*
It addendo *(m)*
Pt adenda *(m)*

address (computer) *n* En
De Adresse *(f)*
Es dirección *(f)*
Fr adresse *(f)*
It indirizzo *(m)*
Pt endereço *(m)*

adenda *(m) n* Pt
De Anhang *(m)*
En addendum
Es adición *(f)*
Fr addenda *(m)*
It addendo *(m)*

adiantamento *(m) n* Pt
De Vorschuß *(m)*
En advance
Es anticipo *(m)*
Fr avance *(f)*
It anticipo *(m)*

adiantamento sobre direitos de autor *(m)* Pt
De Tantiemenvorschuß *(m)*
En advance against royalties
Es anticipo sobre derechos de autor *(m)*
Fr avance sur les droits d'auteur *(f)*
It anticipo sui diritti di licenza *(m)*

adición *(f) n* Es
De Anhang *(m)*
En addendum
Fr addenda *(m)*
It addendo *(m)*
Pt adenda *(m)*

adjoint *(m)* Fr
De persönlicher
Assistent *(m)*
En personal assistant
Es ayudante personal
(m)
It assistente personale
(m)
Pt ajudante pessoal *(m)*

**administrateur
directeur** *(m)* Fr
De leitende
Führungskraft *(f)*
En chief executive
Es jefe ejecutivo *(m)*
It direttore generale *(m)*
Pt executivo principal
(m)

adornos de imprenta *(m
pl)* Es
De Typenornamente *(pl)*
En printer's ornaments
Fr vignette typo *(f)*
It ornamenti dello
stampatore *(m pl)*
Pt ornamentações de
impressão *(f pl)*

Adreßbuch *(n)* n De
En directory
Es directorio *(m)*
Fr annuaire *(m)*
It annuario *(m)*
Pt anuário *(m)*

adresse *(f)* n Fr
De Adresse *(f)*
En address (computer)
Es dirección *(f)*
It indirizzo *(m)*
Pt endereço *(m)*

Adresse *(f)* n De
En address (computer)
Es dirección *(f)*
Fr adresse *(f)*
It indirizzo *(m)*
Pt endereço *(m)*

advance n En
De Vorschuß *(m)*
Es anticipo *(m)*
Fr avance *(f)*
It anticipo *(m)*
Pt adiantamento *(m)*

**advance against
royalties** En

De Tantiemenvorschuß
(m)
Es anticipo sobre
derechos de autor
(m)
Fr avance sur les droits
d'auteur *(f)*
It anticipo sui diritti di
licenza *(m)*
Pt adiantamento sobre
direitos de autor *(m)*

advance copies *pl* n En
De Vorausexemplare *(pl)*
Es ejemplares para
reseña *(m pl)*
Fr exemplaires de
lancement *(m pl)*
It copie in anteprima *(f
pl)*
Pt provas tipográficas *(f
pl)*

advanced sprocket feed
En
De Führungsloch-
Vorschub *(m)*
Es arrastre por rueda
dentada *(m)*
Fr perforation
d'entraînement *(f)*
It alimentazione a
tamburo dentato
avanzato *(f)*
Pt alimentação
avançada do carreto
(f)

advance sheets *pl* n En
De Aushängebogen *(pl)*
Es hojas por adelantado
(f pl)
Fr bonnes feuilles *(f pl)*
It fogli in anticipo *(m pl)*
Pt folhas tipográficas *(f
pl)*

advertise *vb* En
De werben
Es anunciar
Fr faire de la publicité
pour
It pubblicizzare
Pt anunciar

advertisement n En
De Anzeige *(f)*
Es anuncio *(m)*
Fr annonce *(f)*
It annuncio
pubblicitario *(m)*
Pt anúncio *(m)*

advertising n En
De Werbung *(f)*
Es publicidad *(f)*
Fr publicité *(f)*
It pubblicità *(f)*
Pt publicidade *(f)*

advertising agency En
De Werbeagentur *(f)*
Es agencia publicitaria
(f)
Fr agence de publicité
(f)
It agenzia pubblicitaria
(f)
Pt agência de
publicidade *(f)*

aerografo *(m)* n It
De Aerograph *(m)*
En aerograph
Es aerógrafo *(m)*
Fr aérographe *(m)*
Pt aerograma *(m)*

aerógrafo *(m)* n Es
De Aerograph *(m)*
En aerograph
Fr aérographe *(m)*
It aerografo *(m)*
Pt aerograma *(m)*

aerograma *(m)* n Pt
De Aerograph *(m)*
En aerograph
Es aerógrafo *(m)*
Fr aérographe *(m)*
It aerografo *(m)*

aerograph n En
De Aerograph *(m)*
Es aerógrafo *(m)*
Fr aérographe *(m)*
It aerografo *(m)*
Pt aerograma *(m)*

Aerograph *(m)* n De
En aerograph
Es aerógrafo *(m)*
Fr aérographe *(m)*
It aerografo *(m)*
Pt aerograma *(m)*

aérographe *(m)* n Fr
De Aerograph *(m)*
En aerograph
Es aerógrafo *(m)*
It aerografo *(m)*
Pt aerograma *(m)*

affiche *(f)* n Fr
De Poster *(n)*
En poster
Es cartel *(m)*
It manifesto *(m)*
Pt cartaz *(m)*

agarrador *(m)* n Pt
De Greifer *(m)*
En gripper
Es pinza *(f)*
Fr pince *(f)*
It pinza *(f)*

agemcia editorial *(f)* Es
De Redaktionsagentur *(f)*
En editorial agency
Fr agence de rédaction
(f)
It agenzia editoriale *(f)*
Pt agência editorial *(f)*

agence *(f)* n Fr
De Agentur *(f)*
En agency
Es agencia *(f)*
It agenzia *(f)*
Pt agência *(f)*

agence de publicité *(f)*
Fr
De Werbeagentur *(f)*
En advertising agency
Es agencia publicitaria
(f)
It agenzia pubblicitaria
(f)
Pt agência de
publicidade *(f)*

agence de rédaction *(f)*
Fr
De Redaktionsagentur *(f)*
En editorial agency
Es agemcia editorial *(f)*
It agenzia editoriale *(f)*
Pt agência editorial *(f)*

agencia *(f)* n Es
De Agentur *(f)*
En agency
Fr agence *(f)*
It agenzia *(f)*
Pt agência *(f)*

agência *(f)* n Pt
De Agentur *(f)*
En agency
Es agencia *(f)*
Fr agence *(f)*
It agenzia *(f)*

agência de publicidade
(f) Pt
De Werbeagentur (f)
En advertising agency
Es agencia publicitaria
(f)
Fr agence de publicité
(f)
It agenzia pubblicitaria
(f)

agência editorial (f) Pt
De Redaktionsagentur (f)
En editorial agency
Es agemcia editorial (f)
Fr agence de rédaction
(f)
It agenzia editoriale (f)

agencia publicitaria (f)
Es
De Werbeagentur (f)
En advertising agency
Fr agence de publicité
(f)
It agenzia pubblicitaria
(f)
Pt agência de
publicidade (f)

agency n En
De Agentur (f)
Es agencia (f)
Fr agence (f)
It agenzia (f)
Pt agência (f)

agent n En; Fr (m)
De Handelnder (m)
Es agente (m)
It agente (m)
Pt agente (m)

agente (m) n Es, It, Pt
De Handelnder (m)
En agent
Fr agent (m)

agente expedidor (m)
Es, Pt
De Spediteur (m)
En forwarding agent
Fr transitaire (m)
It spedizioniere (m)

agente letterario (m) It
De Literatur-Agentur (f)
En literary agent
Es agente literario (m)
Fr agent littéraire (m)
Pt agente literário (m)

agente literario (m) Es
De Literatur-Agentur (f)
En literary agent
Fr agent littéraire (m)
It agente letterario (m)
Pt agente literário (m)

agente literário (m) Pt
De Literatur-Agentur (f)
En literary agent
Es agente literario (m)
Fr agent littéraire (m)
It agente letterario (m)

agent littéraire (m) Fr
De Literatur-Agentur (f)
En literary agent
Es agente literario (m)
It agente letterario (m)
Pt agente literário (m)

Agentur (f) n De
En agency
Es agencia (f)
Fr agence (f)
It agenzia (f)
Pt agência (f)

agenzia (f) n It
De Agentur (f)
En agency
Es agencia (f)
Fr agence (f)
Pt agência (f)

agenzia editoriale (f) It
De Redaktionsagentur (f)
En editorial agency
Es agemcia editorial (f)
Fr agence de rédaction
(f)
Pt agência editorial (f)

agenzia pubblicitaria (f)
It
De Werbeagentur (f)
En advertising agency
Es agencia publicitaria
(f)
Fr agence de publicité
(f)
Pt agência de
publicidade (f)

aggiornare vb It
De überarbeiten
En update
Es actualizar
Fr mettre à jour
Pt actualizar

aggiornato adj It
De überarbeitet
En updated
Es actualizado
Fr mis à jour
Pt actualizado

**aggiustamento di
originali** (m) It
De Texteinpassung (f)
En copy-fitting
Es ajuste de originales
(m)
Fr montage du texte (m)
Pt ajustamento do
original (m)

agotado adj Es
De vergriffen;
ausverkauft
En out of print; sold out
Fr épuisé; liquidé
It esaurito
Pt esgotado

agradecimentos (m pl)
Pt
De Anerkennung (f)
En acknowledgments pl
n
Es agradecimientos (m
pl)
Fr remerciements (m pl)
It ringraziamenti (m pl)

agradecimientos (m pl)
Es
De Anerkennung (f)
En acknowledgments pl
n
Fr remerciements (m pl)
It ringraziamenti (m pl)
Pt agradecimentos (m
pl)

a grana grossa (f) It
De grober Raster (m)
En coarse screen
Es trama gruesa (f)
Fr trame à gros grains
(f)
Pt retícula grossa (f)

agrandi adj Fr
De vergrößert
En blown up
Es ampliado
It ingrandito
Pt ampliado

agrandir vb Fr
De vergrößern
En enlarge
Es ampliar
It ingrandire
Pt ampliar

agrandisseur (m) n Fr
De Vergrößerungsgerät
(n)
En enlarger
Es ampliadora (f)
It ingranditore (m)
Pt ampliadora (f)

agrandisseur photo (m)
Fr
De photographisches
Vergrößerungsgerät
(n)
En photographic
enlarger
Es ampliadora
fotográfica (f)
It ingranditore
fotografico (m)
Pt ampliador fotográfico
(m)

agreement n En
De Abkommen (n)
Es acuerdo (m)
Fr accord (m)
It accordo (m)
Pt acordo (m)

aguada (f) n Es
De Gouachegemälde (n)
En gouache
Fr gouache (f)
It guazzo (m)
Pt guache (f)

aguafuerte fina (f) Es
De Feinätzung (f)
En fine etching
Fr gravure à l'eau-forte
très mordancé (m)
It acquafortista
raffinata (f)
Pt gravado fino (m)

airbrush n En
De Retuschierapparat
(m)
Es pistola pulverizadora
(f)
Fr pinceau
pneumatique (m)
It polverizzatrice ad aria
compressa (f)

Pt pistola pulverizadora
(f)

air courier En
De Luftkurier *(m)*
Es estafeta aérea *(f)*
Fr courrier aérien *(m)*
It corriere aereo *(m)*
Pt mensageiro aéreo
(m)

air-dried *adj* En
De luftgetrocknet
Es secado al aire
Fr séché à l'air
It essiccata ad aria
Pt seco ao ar

airfreight *n* En
De Luftfracht *(f)*
Es flete aéreo *(m)*
Fr fret aérien *(m)*
It trasporto merci per
via aerea *(m)*
Pt frete aéreo *(m)*

ajourner *vb* Fr
De aufschieben
En shelve
Es postergar
indefinidamente
It porre in disparte
Pt arquivar

**ajudante de
investigação** *(m)* Pt
De Forschungs-
Assistent *(m)*
En research assistant
Es ayudante de
investigación *(m)*
Fr assistant des
recherches *(m)*
It assistente di ricerca
(m)

ajudante de vendedor
(m) Pt
De Verkäufer *(m)*
En sales assistant
Es ayudante de ventas
(m)
Fr commis *(m)*
It commesso *(m)*

ajudante editorial *(m)* Pt
De Redaktionsassistent
(m)
En editorial assistant
Es ayudante de editorial
(m)

Fr secrétaire de
rédaction *(m)*
It assistente editoriale
(m)

ajudante pessoal *(m)* Pt
De persönlicher
Assistent *(m)*
En personal assistant
Es ayudante personal
(m)
Fr adjoint *(m)*
It assistente personale
(m)

ajustadora *(f)* *n* Pt
De Sammler *(m)*
En assembler
Es elevador reunidor *(m)*
Fr assembleur *(m)*
It raccoglitore *(m)*

ajustamento do original
(m) Pt
De Texteinpassung *(f)*
En copy-fitting
Es ajuste de originales
(m)
Fr montage du texte *(m)*
It aggiustamento di
originali *(m)*

ajuste de originales *(m)*
Es
De Texteinpassung *(f)*
En copy-fitting
Fr montage du texte *(m)*
It aggiustamento di
originali *(m)*
Pt ajustamento do
original *(m)*

akademische Bücher
(pl) De
En academic books
Es libros académicos *(m
pl)*
Fr livres d'étude *(m pl)*
It libri accademici *(m
pl)*
Pt livros académicos *(m
pl)*

Akkumulator *(m)* *n* De
En accumulator
Es acumulador *(m)*
Fr accumulateur *(m)*
It accumulatore *(m)*
Pt acumulador *(m)*

Aktie *(f)* *n* De
En share
Es acción *(f)*
Fr action *(f)*
It azione *(f)*
Pt acção *(f)*

Aktienpapier *(n)* *n* De
En loan paper
Es papel para
documentos *(m)*
Fr papier pour titres *(m)*
It carta per valori *(f)*
Pt papel de empréstimo
(m)

Aktionär *(m)* *n* De
En shareholder
Es accionista *(m)*
Fr actionnaire *(m)*
It azionista *(m/f)*
Pt accionista *(m)*

aktuell *adj* De
En newsworthy
Es de interés
periodístico
Fr d'intérêt
journalistique
It che fa notizia
Pt digno de ser
publicado

Akut *(m)* *n* De
En acute accent
Es acento agudo *(m)*
Fr accent aigu *(m)*
It accento acuto *(m)*
Pt acento agudo *(m)*

Akzent *(m)* *n* De
En accent
Es acento *(m)*
Fr accent *(m)*
It accento *(m)*
Pt acento *(m)*

Akzidenzdrucker *(m)* *n*
De
En jobbing printer
Es impresor a
remiendos *(m)*
Fr imprimeur de travaux
de ville *(m)*
It stampatore
comerciale *(m)*
Pt impressor comercial
(m)

albumen plate En
De Albuminplatte *(f)*
Es plancha offset a la
albúmina *(f)*
Fr procédé à l'albumine
(m)
It lastra all'albumina *(f)*
Pt chapa de albumina *(f)*

Albuminplatte *(f)* *n* De
En albumen plate
Es plancha offset a la
albúmina *(f)*
Fr procédé à l'albumine
(m)
It lastra all'albumina *(f)*
Pt chapa de albumina *(f)*

alcograbado *(m)* *n* Es
De Alko-Tiefdruck *(m)*
En alcogravure
Fr alcogravure *(f)*
It alcoincisione *(f)*
Pt alcogravura *(f)*

alcogravura *(f)* *n* Pt
De Alko-Tiefdruck *(m)*
En alcogravure
Es alcograbado *(m)*
Fr alcogravure *(f)*
It alcoincisione *(f)*

alcogravure *n* En; Fr *(f)*
De Alko-Tiefdruck *(m)*
Es alcograbado *(m)*
It alcoincisione *(f)*
Pt alcogravura *(f)*

alcoincisione *(f)* *n* It
De Alko-Tiefdruck *(m)*
En alcogravure
Es alcograbado *(m)*
Fr alcogravure *(f)*
Pt alcogravura *(f)*

aleación *(f)* *n* Es
De Legierung *(f)*
En alloy
Fr alliage *(m)*
It lega *(f)*
Pt liga *(f)*

aleta dianteira *(f)* Pt
De vordere
Umschlagklappe *(f)*
En front flap
Es solapa delantera *(f)*
Fr rabat avant *(m)*
It risvolto anteriore *(m)*

alfa *(m)* n Fr
De Esparto *(n)*
En esparto grass
Es esparto *(m)*
It sparto *(m)*
Pt esparto *(m)*

alfabeto cirílico *(m)* Es,
Pt
De kyrillisches Alphabet
(n)
En cyrillic alphabet
Fr alphabet cyrillique
(m)
It alfabeto cirillico *(m)*

alfabeto cirillico *(m)* It
De kyrillisches Alphabet
(n)
En cyrillic alphabet
Es alfabeto cirílico *(m)*
Fr alphabet cyrillique
(m)
Pt alfabeto cirílico *(m)*

alfabeto fonético
internacional *(m)* Es
De internationales
Phonetik-Alphabet *(n)*
En international
phonetic alphabet
(IPA)
Fr alphabet phonétique
international *(m)*
It alfabeto fonetico
internazionale *(m)*
Pt alfabeto fonético
international *(m)*

alfabeto fonetico
internazionale *(m)*
It
De internationales
Phonetik-Alphabet *(n)*
En international
phonetic alphabet
(IPA)
Es alfabeto fonético
internacional *(m)*
Fr alphabet phonétique
international *(m)*
Pt alfabeto fonético
international *(m)*

alfabeto fonético
international *(m)* Pt
De internationales
Phonetik-Alphabet *(n)*
En international
phonetic alphabet
(IPA)

Es alfabeto fonético
internacional *(m)*
Fr alphabet phonétique
international *(m)*
It alfabeto fonetico
internazionale *(m)*

alfabeto romano *(m)* Es,
Pt
De römisches Alphabet
(n)
En roman alphabet
Fr alphabet romain *(m)*
It alfabeto romano
tondo *(m)*

alfabeto romano tondo
(m) It
De römisches Alphabet
(n)
En roman alphabet
Es alfabeto romano *(m)*
Fr alphabet romain *(m)*
Pt alfabeto romano *(m)*

alignement *(m)* n Fr
De Ausrichtung *(f)*
En alignment
Es alineación *(f)*
It allineamento *(m)*
Pt alinhamento *(m)*

aligner à droite Fr
De rechts in Linie
bringen
En range right
Es alinear al margen
derecho
It allineare
verticalmente a
destra
Pt explorar direita

aligner à gauche Fr
De links in Linie bringen
En range left
Es alinear al margen
izquierdo
It allineare
verticalmente a
sinistra
Pt explorar esquerda

alignment n En
De Ausrichtung *(f)*
Es alineación *(f)*
Fr alignement *(m)*
It allineamento *(m)*
Pt alinhamento *(m)*

alimentação avançada
do carreto *(f)* Pt
De Führungsloch-
Vorschub *(m)*
En advanced sprocket
feed
Es arrastre por rueda
dentada *(m)*
Fr perforation
d'entraînement *(f)*
It alimentazione a
tamburo dentato
avanzato *(f)*

alimentador *(m)* n Es
De Einleger *(m)*
En feeder
Fr margeur *(m)*
It alimentatore *(m)*
Pt alimentadora *(f)*

alimentadora *(f)* n Pt
De Einleger *(m)*
En feeder
Es alimentador *(m)*
Fr margeur *(m)*
It alimentatore *(m)*

alimentador automático
(m) Es, Pt
De automatischer
Einleger *(m)*
En automatic feeder
Fr margeur
automatique *(m)*
It alimentatore
automatico *(f)*

alimentador de folhas
de avanço
contínuo *(m)* Pt
De Schuppenanleger *(m)*
En stream feeder
Es ponepliegos de
avance continuo *(m)*
Fr margeur à nappe *(m)*
It alimentatore di fogli a
avanzamento
continuo *(m)*

alimentador por sucção
(m) Pt
De Sauganleger *(m)*
En suction feeder
Es ponepliegos de soplo
(m)
Fr margeur
automatique à
aspiration *(m)*
It alimentatore ad
aspirazione *(m)*

alimentatore *(m)* n It
De Einleger *(m)*
En feeder
Es alimentador *(m)*
Fr margeur *(m)*
Pt alimentadora *(f)*

alimentatore ad
aspirazione *(m)* It
De Sauganleger *(m)*
En suction feeder
Es ponepliegos de soplo
(m)
Fr margeur
automatique à
aspiration *(m)*
Pt alimentador por
sucção *(m)*

alimentatore
automatico *(f)* It
De automatischer
Einleger *(m)*
En automatic feeder
Es alimentador
automático *(m)*
Fr margeur
automatique *(m)*
Pt alimentador
automático *(m)*

alimentatore di fogli a
avanzamento
continuo *(m)* It
De Schuppenanleger *(m)*
En stream feeder
Es ponepliegos de
avance continuo *(m)*
Fr margeur à nappe *(m)*
Pt alimentador de folhas
de avanço contínuo
(m)

alimentazione a
tamburo dentato
avanzato *(f)* It
De Führungsloch-
Vorschub *(m)*
En advanced sprocket
feed
Es arrastre por rueda
dentada *(m)*
Fr perforation
d'entraînement *(f)*
Pt alimentação
avançada do carreto
(f)

alinéa *(m)* n Fr
De Paragraph *(m)*
En paragraph
Es párrafo *(m)*

It paragrafo *(m)*
Pt parágrafo *(m)*

alineación *(f) n* Es
De Ausrichtung *(f)*
En alignment
Fr alignement *(m)*
It allineamento *(m)*
Pt alinhamento *(m)*

alinear *vb* Es
De ausrichten
En line up
Fr parangonner
It allineare
Pt alinhar

alinear al margen derecho Es
De rechts in Linie bringen
En range right
Fr aligner à droite
It allineare verticalmente a destra
Pt explorar direita

alinear al margen izquierdo Es
De links in Linie bringen
En range left
Fr aligner à gauche
It allineare verticalmente a sinistra
Pt explorar esquerda

alinhamento *(m) n* Pt
De Ausrichtung *(f)*
En alignment
Es alineación *(f)*
Fr alignement *(m)*
It allineamento *(m)*

alinhar *vb* Pt
De ausrichten
En line up
Es alinear
Fr parangonner
It allineare

a livello It
De glatt
En flush
Es a ras
Fr ras
Pt nivelado

Alko-Tiefdruck *(m) n* De
En alcogravure
Es alcograbado *(m)*
Fr alcogravure *(f)*
It alcoincisione *(f)*
Pt alcogravura *(f)*

alle Rechte vorbehalten De
En all rights reserved
Es reservados todos los derechos
Fr tous droits réservés
It tutti i diritti riservati
Pt todos os direitos reservados

alliage *(m) n* Fr
De Legierung *(f)*
En alloy
Es aleación *(f)*
It lega *(f)*
Pt liga *(f)*

allineamento *(m) n* It
De Ausrichtung *(f)*
En alignment
Es alineación *(f)*
Fr alignement *(m)*
Pt alinhamento *(m)*

allineare *vb* It
De ausrichten
En line up
Es alinear
Fr parangonner
Pt alinhar

allineare verticalmente a destra It
De rechts in Linie bringen
En range right
Es alinear al margen derecho
Fr aligner à droite
Pt explorar direita

allineare verticalmente a sinistra It
De links in Linie bringen
En range left
Es alinear al margen izquierdo
Fr aligner à gauche
Pt explorar esquerda

alloy *n* En
De Legierung *(f)*
Es aleación *(f)*
Fr alliage *(m)*

It lega *(f)*
Pt liga *(f)*

all-rag paper En
De Vollhadernpapier *(n)*
Es papel de hilo puro *(m)*
Fr papier pur chiffon *(m)*
It carta di cenci *(f)*
Pt papel inteiramente de trapos *(m)*

all rights reserved En
De alle Rechte vorbehalten
Es reservados todos los derechos
Fr tous droits réservés
It tutti i diritti riservati
Pt todos os direitos reservados

almacén *(m) n* Es
De Lagerhaus *(n)*
En warehouse
Fr entrepôt *(m)*
It magazzino *(m)*
Pt armazém *(m)*

almacenamiento *(m) n* Es
De Speicherung *(f)*
En storage
Fr stockage *(m)*
It immagazzinaggio *(m)*
Pt armazenamento *(m)*

almacenar *vb* Es
De lagern
En store
Fr entreposer
It immagazzinare
Pt armazenar

almacenes *(m pl)* Es
De Speicherungsmöglichkeiten *(pl)*
En storage facilities
Fr entrepôts *(m pl)*
It servizi di immagazzinaggio *(m pl)*
Pt instalações de armazenamento *(f pl)*

almanac *n* En
De Almanach *(m)*
Es almanaque *(m)*
Fr almanach *(m)*
It almanacco *(m)*
Pt almanaque *(m)*

almanacco *(m) n* It
De Almanach *(m)*
En almanac
Es almanaque *(m)*
Fr almanach *(m)*
Pt almanaque *(m)*

almanach *(m) n* Fr
De Almanach *(m)*
En almanac
Es almanaque *(m)*
It almanacco *(m)*
Pt almanaque *(m)*

Almanach *(m) n* De
En almanac
Es almanaque *(m)*
Fr almanach *(m)*
It almanacco *(m)*
Pt almanaque *(m)*

almanaque *(m) n* Es, Pt
De Almanach *(m)*
En almanac
Fr almanach *(m)*
It almanacco *(m)*

almoço de trabalho *(m)* Pt
De geschäftliches Mittagessen *(n)*
En working lunch
Es comida de trabajo *(f)*
Fr déjeuner de travail *(m)*
It pranzo di lavoro *(m)*

alphabet cyrillique *(m)* Fr
De kyrillisches Alphabet *(n)*
En cyrillic alphabet
Es alfabeto cirílico *(m)*
It alfabeto cirillico *(m)*
Pt alfabeto cirílico *(m)*

alphabet phonétique international *(m)* Fr
De internationales Phonetik-Alphabet *(n)*
En international phonetic alphabet (IPA)
Es alfabeto fonético internacional *(m)*
It alfabeto fonetico internazionale *(m)*
Pt alfabeto fonético international *(m)*

alphabet romain (m) Fr
De römisches Alphabet (n)
En roman alphabet
Es alfabeto romano (m)
It alfabeto romano tondo (m)
Pt alfabeto romano (m)

alta cassa It
De Oberkasten (m)
En upper case
Es caja alta (f)
Fr haut de casse (m)
Pt caixa alta (f)

alte luci (f pl) It
De Lichter (pl)
En highlights pl n
Es blancos (m pl)
Fr grandes lumières (f pl)
Pt partes claras (f pl)

alternate title En
De Untertitel (m)
Es subtítulo (m)
Fr sous-titre (m)
It titolo alternato (m)
Pt título alternativo (m)

altezza tipografica (f) It
De Schrifthöhe (f)
En type height
Es altura del tipo (f)
Fr hauteur de caractère (f)
Pt altura de tipo (f)

altura del tipo (f) Es
De Schrifthöhe (f)
En type height
Fr hauteur de caractère (f)
It altezza tipografica (f)
Pt altura de tipo (f)

altura de tipo (f) Pt
De Schrifthöhe (f)
En type height
Es altura del tipo (f)
Fr hauteur de caractère (f)
It altezza tipografica (f)

Aluminiumfarbe (f) n De
Am aluminum ink
En aluminium ink
Es tinta plateada (f)
Fr encre métallique (f)

It inchiostro all'alluminio (m)
Pt tinta de alumínio (f)

aluminium ink En
Am aluminum ink
De Aluminiumfarbe (f)
Es tinta plateada (f)
Fr encre métallique (f)
It inchiostro all'alluminio (m)
Pt tinta de alumínio (f)

aluminum ink Am
De Aluminiumfarbe (f)
En aluminium ink
Es tinta plateada (f)
Fr encre métallique (f)
It inchiostro all'alluminio (m)
Pt tinta de alumínio (f)

alza bajo el tipo (f) Es
De Unterlage (f)
En underlay
Fr hausse (f)
It alzo (m)
Pt calço (m)

alzado (m) n Es
De Zusammentragung (f)
En collating
Fr assemblage (m)
It raccoglitura (f)
Pt revisão (f)

alza mecánica (f) Es
De mechanische Zurichtung (f)
En mechanical overlay
Fr mise en train mécanique (f)
It sovrapposizione meccanica (f)
Pt corte mecânico (m)

alza mecánica de tiza (f) Es
De Kreidezurichten (n)
En chalk overlay
Fr papier baryté (m)
It carta gessata (f)
Pt calço de giz (f)

alzar vb Es
De vergleichen
En collate
Fr assembler
It collazionare
Pt rever

alzo (m) n It
De Unterlage (f)
En underlay
Es alza bajo el tipo (f)
Fr hausse (f)
Pt calço (m)

amadurecer vb Pt
De ausreifen
En mature
Es madurar
Fr conditionner
It stagionare

à maintenir Fr
De Stehen lassen
En stet
Es vale lo tachado
It vive
Pt stet

amanuense (m) n Es, It
De Amanuensis (m)
En amanuensis
Fr copiste (m/f)
Pt copista (m/f)

amanuensis n En
De Amanuensis (m)
Es amanuense (m)
Fr copiste (m/f)
It amanuense (m)
Pt copista (m/f)

Amanuensis (m) n De
En amanuensis
Es amanuense (m)
Fr copiste (m/f)
It amanuense (m)
Pt copista (m/f)

amarelo para policromia (m) Pt
De Verfahrensgelb (n)
En process yellow
Es amarillo de tricromía (m)
Fr jaune d'impression couleur (m)
It giallo di tricromia (m)

amarillo de tricromía (m) Es
De Verfahrensgelb (n)
En process yellow
Fr jaune d'impression couleur (m)
It giallo di tricromia (m)
Pt amarelo para policromia (m)

amartillamiento (m) n Es
De Kräuseln (n)
En cockling
Fr gondolage (m)
It arricciatura (f)
Pt enrugamento (m)

ambigüedad (f) n Es
De Zweideutigkeit (f)
En ambiguity
Fr ambiguïté (f)
It ambiguità (f)
Pt ambiguidade (f)

ambiguidade (f) n Pt
De Zweideutigkeit (f)
En ambiguity
Es ambigüedad (f)
Fr ambiguïté (f)
It ambiguità (f)

ambiguità (f) n It
De Zweideutigkeit (f)
En ambiguity
Es ambigüedad (f)
Fr ambiguïté (f)
Pt ambiguidade (f)

ambiguïté (f) n Fr
De Zweideutigkeit (f)
En ambiguity
Es ambigüedad (f)
It ambiguità (f)
Pt ambiguidade (f)

ambiguity n En
De Zweideutigkeit (f)
Es ambigüedad (f)
Fr ambiguïté (f)
It ambiguità (f)
Pt ambiguidade (f)

American cloth En
De Wachstuch (n)
Es hule (m)
Fr moleskine (f)
It tela cerata (f)
Pt pano americano (m)

américaniser vb Fr
De amerikanisieren
En Americanize
Es americanizar
It americanizzare
Pt americanizar

Americanism n En
De Amerikanismus (m)
Es americanismo (m)
Fr américanisme (m)

It americanismo *(m)*
Pt americanismo *(m)*

américanisme *(m) n* Fr
De Amerikanismus *(m)*
En Americanism
Es americanismo *(m)*
It americanismo *(m)*
Pt americanismo *(m)*

americanismo *(m) n* Es,
It, Pt
De Amerikanismus *(m)*
En Americanism
Fr américanisme *(m)*

americanizar *vb* Es, Pt
De amerikanisieren
En Americanize
Fr américaniser
It americanizzare

Americanize *vb* En
De amerikanisieren
Es americanizar
Fr américaniser
It americanizzare
Pt americanizar

americanizzare *vb* It
De amerikanisieren
En Americanize
Es americanizar
Fr américaniser
Pt americanizar

American spelling En
De amerikanische
  Schreibweise *(f)*
Es deletreo americano
  (m)
Fr orthographe
  américaine *(f)*
It ortografia americana
  (f)
Pt ortografia americana
  (f)

American usage En
De amerikanischer
  Sprachgebrauch *(m)*
Es uso americano *(m)*
Fr usage américain *(m)*
It uso americano *(m)*
Pt costume americano
  (m)

**amerikanischer
  Sprachgebrauch**
  (m) De

En American usage
Es uso americano *(m)*
Fr usage américain *(m)*
It uso americano *(m)*
Pt costume americano
  (m)

**amerikanische
  Schreibweise** *(f)* De
En American spelling
Es deletreo americano
  (m)
Fr orthographe
  américaine *(f)*
It ortografia americana
  (f)
Pt ortografia americana
  (f)

amerikanisieren *vb* De
En Americanize
Es americanizar
Fr américaniser
It americanizzare
Pt americanizar

Amerikanismus *(m) n* De
En Americanism
Es americanismo *(m)*
Fr américanisme *(m)*
It americanismo *(m)*
Pt americanismo *(m)*

ammassamento *(m) n* It
De Pelzen *(n)*
En piling
Es espesamiento *(m)*
Fr encrassement *(m)*
Pt espessamento de
  tinta *(m)*

**amministratore
  delegato** *(m)* It
De Geschäftsführender
  Direktor *(m)*
En managing director
Es director gerente *(m)*
Fr directeur général *(m)*
Pt director geral *(m)*

ampersand *n* En
De Und-Zeichen *(n)*
Es y abreviada *(f)*
Fr et commercial *(m)*
It congiunzione
  commerciale *(f)*
Pt e comercial *(f)*

ampliado *adj* Es, Pt
De vergrößert
En blown up

Fr agrandi
It ingrandito

ampliadora *(f) n* Es, Pt
De Vergrößerungsgerät
  (n)
En enlarger
Fr agrandisseur *(m)*
It ingranditore *(m)*

ampliadora fotográfica
  (f) Es
De photographisches
  Vergrößerungsgerät
  (n)
En photographic
  enlarger
Fr agrandisseur photo
  (m)
It ingranditore
  fotografico *(m)*
Pt ampliador fotográfico
  (m)

ampliador fotográfico
  (m) Pt
De photographisches
  Vergrößerungsgerät
  (n)
En photographic
  enlarger
Es ampliadora
  fotográfica *(f)*
Fr agrandisseur photo
  (m)
It ingranditore
  fotografico *(m)*

ampliar *vb* Es, Pt
De vergrößern
En enlarge
Fr agrandir
It ingrandire

amplitud *(f) n* Es
De Seitenzahl *(f)*
En extent
Fr nombre de pages *(m)*
It estensione *(m)*
Pt extensão *(f)*

ampolla *(f) n* Es
De Schnalle *(f)*
En blister (on paper)
Fr cloque *(f)*
It bolla *(f)*
Pt bolha *(f)*

anachronism *n* En
De Anachronismus *(m)*
Es anacronismo *(m)*

Fr anachronisme *(m)*
It anacronismo *(m)*
Pt anacronismo *(m)*

anachronisme *(m) n* Fr
De Anachronismus *(m)*
En anachronism
Es anacronismo *(m)*
It anacronismo *(m)*
Pt anacronismo *(m)*

Anachronismus *(m) n* De
En anachronism
Es anacronismo *(m)*
Fr anachronisme *(m)*
It anacronismo *(m)*
Pt anacronismo *(m)*

anacronismo *(m) n* Es, It,
  Pt
De Anachronismus *(m)*
En anachronism
Fr anachronisme *(m)*

analista de sistemas *(m)*
  Es, Pt
De Systemanalytiker *(m)*
En systems analyst
Fr analyste de systèmes
  (m/f)
It analista di sistema
  (m/f)

analista di sistema *(m/f)*
  It
De Systemanalytiker *(m)*
En systems analyst
Es analista de sistemas
  (m)
Fr analyste de systèmes
  (m/f)
Pt analista de sistemas
  (m)

analyse de marché *(f)* Fr
De Marktforschung *(f)*
En market research
Es investigación del
  mercado *(f)*
It ricerca di mercato *(f)*
Pt investigação do
  mercado *(f)*

analyseur électronique
  (m) Fr
De Abtaster *(m)*
En scanner
Es explorador *(m)*
It scanner *(m)*
Pt dispositivo
  explorador *(m)*

analyste de systèmes
(m/f) Fr
De Systemanalytiker *(m)*
En systems analyst
Es analista de sistemas
(m)
It analista di sistema
(m/f)
Pt analista de sistemas
(m)

ancho del lomo *(m)* Es
De Rückendicke *(f)*
En spine width
Fr largeur du dos *(f)*
It larghezza del dorso *(f)*
Pt largura de lombada
(f)

Andrucken *(n)* n De
En proofing
Es tirada de pruebas *(f)*
Fr tirage d'épreuves *(m)*
It tiratura di prova *(f)*
Pt tiragem de provas *(f)*

Anerkennung *(f)* De
En acknowledgments;
credits *pl* n
Es agradecimientos;
créditos *(m pl)*
Fr remerciements *(m pl)*
It ringraziamenti *(m pl)*
Pt agradecimentos;
créditos *(m pl)*

Anführungszeichen *(pl)*
n De
En quotation marks
Es comillas *(f pl)*
Fr guillemets *(m pl)*
It virgolette *(f pl)*
Pt aspas *(f pl)*

Angebot *(n)* n De
En quotation (estimate)
Es cotización *(f)*
Fr prix coté *(m)*
It quotazione *(f)*
Pt cotação *(f)*

Angestellter *(m)* n De
En employee
Es empleado *(m)*
Fr employé *(m)*
It dipendente *(m)*
Pt empregado *(m)*

angliciser *vb* Fr
De anglisieren
En Anglicize

Es adaptar al inglés
It anglicizzare
Pt anglificar

anglicisme *(m)* n Fr
De Anglizismus *(m)*
En Briticism
Es anglicismo *(m)*
It anglicismo *(m)*
Pt briticismo *(m)*

anglicismo *(m)* n Es, It
De Anglizismus *(m)*
En Briticism
Fr anglicisme *(m)*
Pt briticismo *(m)*

Anglicize *vb* En
De anglisieren
Es adaptar al inglés
Fr angliciser
It anglicizzare
Pt anglificar

anglicizzare *vb* It
De anglisieren
En Anglicize
Es adaptar al inglés
Fr angliciser
Pt anglificar

anglificar *vb* Pt
De anglisieren
En Anglicize
Es adaptar al inglés
Fr angliciser
It anglicizzare

anglisieren *vb* De
En Anglicize
Es adaptar al inglés
Fr angliciser
It anglicizzare
Pt anglificar

Anglizismus *(m)* n De
En Briticism
Es anglicismo *(m)*
Fr anglicisme *(m)*
It anglicismo *(m)*
Pt briticismo *(m)*

Anhang *(m)* n De
En addendum; appendix
Es adición; apéndice *(f
m)*
Fr addenda; appendice
(m)
It addendo; appendice
(m f)

Pt adenda; apêndice
(m)

anhängen *vb* De
En run on (typesetting)
Es componer sin punto y
aparte
Fr suivre sans alinéa
It scrivere a testo
continuo
Pt compor seguido

anilado *adj* Pt
De azuriertes
En azured
Es azurado
Fr azuré
It azzurrato

aniline ink En
De Anilinfarbe *(f)*
Es tinta de anilina *(f)*
Fr encre à l'aniline *(f)*
It inchiostro all'anilina
(m)
Pt tinta de anilina *(f)*

Anilinfarbe *(f)* n De
En aniline ink
Es tinta de anilina *(f)*
Fr encre à l'aniline *(f)*
It inchiostro all'anilina
(m)
Pt tinta de anilina *(f)*

animal sizing En
De Tierleimbindung *(f)*
Es cola animal *(f)*
Fr collage animal *(m)*
It colla animale *(f)*
Pt cola animal *(f)*

Anlagekanten *(pl)* De
En feed edges *pl* n
Es orillas de entrada *(f
pl)*
Fr côté des marges *(m)*
It margini di entrata *(m
pl)*
Pt bordos de entrada *(m
pl)*

Anmerkung *(f)* n De
En annotation
Es acotación *(f)*
Fr annotation *(f)*
It annotazione *(f)*
Pt anotação *(f)*

Anmerkungen *(pl)* De
En notes *pl* n
Es notas *(f pl)*
Fr notes *(f pl)*
It note *(f pl)*
Pt notas *(f pl)*

annonce *(f)* n Fr
De Anzeige *(f)*
En advertisement
Es anuncio *(m)*
It annuncio
pubblicitario *(m)*
Pt anúncio *(m)*

annotateur d'un texte
(m) Fr
De Manuskriptredakteur
(m)
En copy-editor
Es corrector de
originales *(m)*
It correttore di originali
(m)
Pt revisor do original *(m)*

annotation n En; Fr *(f)*
De Anmerkung *(f)*
Es acotación *(f)*
It annotazione *(f)*
Pt anotação *(f)*

annotazione *(f)* n It
De Anmerkung *(f)*
En annotation
Es acotación *(f)*
Fr annotation *(f)*
Pt anotação *(f)*

annoter *vb* Fr
De auszeichnen
En mark up (copy)
Es marcar
It contrassegnare
Pt marcar

annuaire *(m)* n Fr
De Adreβbuch;
Jahrbuch *(n)*
En directory; year book
Es anuario; directorio
(m)
It annuario *(m)*
Pt anuário *(m)*

annual conference En
De Jahreskonferenz *(f)*
Es conferencia anual *(f)*
Fr congrès annuel *(m)*

It conferenza annuale *(f)*
Pt conferência anual *(f)*

annuario *(m) n* It
De Adreβbuch;
    Jahrbuch *(n)*
En directory; year book
Es anuario; directorio
    (m)
Fr annuaire *(m)*
Pt anuário *(m)*

annuncio pubblicitario
    (m) It
De Anzeige *(f)*
En advertisement
Es anuncio *(m)*
Fr annonce *(f)*
Pt anúncio *(m)*

anotação *(f) n* Pt
De Anmerkung *(f)*
En annotation
Es acotación *(f)*
Fr annotation *(f)*
It annotazione *(f)*

Anschluβstücke *(pl)* De
En borders *pl n*
Es marcos *(m pl)*
Fr vignettes *(f pl)*
It margini *(m pl)*
Pt bordas *(f pl)*

anteportada *(f) n* Es, Pt
De Innentitel *(m)*
En half title
Fr faux-titre *(m)*
It titolo abbreviato *(m)*

anthologie *(f) n* Fr
De Anthologie *(f)*
En anthology
Es antología *(f)*
It antologia *(f)*
Pt antologia *(f)*

Anthologie *(f) n* De
En anthology
Es antología *(f)*
Fr anthologie *(f)*
It antologia *(f)*
Pt antologia *(f)*

anthology *n* En
De Anthologie *(f)*
Es antología *(f)*
Fr anthologie *(f)*

It antologia *(f)*
Pt antologia *(f)*

anticipo *(m) n* Es, It
De Vorschuβ *(m)*
En advance
Fr avance *(f)*
Pt adiantamento *(m)*

**anticipo sobre derechos
    de autor** *(m)* Es
De Tantiemenvorschuβ
    (m)
En advance against
    royalties
Fr avance sur les droits
    d'auteur *(f)*
It anticipo sui diritti di
    licenza *(m)*
Pt adiantamento sobre
    direitos de autor *(m)*

**anticipo sui diritti di
    licenza** *(m)* It
De Tantiemenvorschuβ
    (m)
En advance against
    royalties
Es anticipo sobre
    derechos de autor
    (m)
Fr avance sur les droits
    d'auteur *(f)*
Pt adiantamento sobre
    direitos de autor *(m)*

anticuado *adj* Es
De veraltet
En out of date
Fr périmé
It superato
Pt desactualizado

anthologie *(f) n* Fr
De Anthologie *(f)*
En anthology
Es antología *(f)*
It antologia *(f)*
Pt antologia *(f)*

It antologia *(f)*
Pt antologia *(f)*

Antik-Ausrüstung *(f)* De
En antique finish
Es acabado antiguo *(m)*
Fr apprêt à l'antique *(m)*
It appretto tipo antico
    (m)
Pt acabamento antigo
    (m)

Antikdruckpapier *(n) n*
    De
En antique wove
Es papel avitelado
    antiguo *(m)*
Fr vélin à l'antique *(m)*
It carta retinata tipo
    antico *(f)*
Pt tecido estilo antigo
    (m)

antiquarian books En
De antiquarische Bücher
    (pl)
Es libros antiguos *(m pl)*
Fr livres anciens *(m pl)*
It libri antichi *(m pl)*
Pt livros de antiquário
    (m pl)

antiquarische Bücher
    (pl) De
En antiquarian books
Es libros antiguos *(m pl)*
Fr livres anciens *(m pl)*
It libri antichi *(m pl)*
Pt livros de antiquário
    (m pl)

antique finish En
De Antik-Ausrüstung *(f)*
Es acabado antiguo *(m)*
Fr apprêt à l'antique *(m)*
It appretto tipo antico
    (m)
Pt acabamento antigo
    (m)

antique wove En
De Antikdruckpapier *(n)*
Es papel avitelado
    antiguo *(m)*
Fr vélin à l'antique *(m)*
It carta retinata tipo
    antico *(f)*
Pt tecido estilo antigo
    (m)

antologia *(f) n* It, Pt
De Anthologie *(f)*
En anthology
Es antología *(f)*
Fr anthologie *(f)*

antología *(f) n* Es
De Anthologie *(f)*
En anthology
Fr anthologie *(f)*
It antologia *(f)*
Pt antologia *(f)*

antonimo *(m) n* It
De Antonym *(n)*
En antonym
Es antónimo *(m)*
Fr antonyme *(m)*
Pt antónimo *(m)*

antónimo *(m) n* Es, Pt
De Antonym *(n)*
En antonym

Fr antonyme *(m)*
It antonimo *(m)*

antonym *n* En
De Antonym *(n)*
Es antónimo *(m)*
Fr antonyme *(m)*
It antonimo *(m)*
Pt antónimo *(m)*

Antonym *(n) n* De
En antonym
Es antónimo *(m)*
Fr antonyme *(m)*
It antonimo *(m)*
Pt antónimo *(m)*

antonyme *(m) n* Fr
De Antonym *(n)*
En antonym
Es antónimo *(m)*
It antonimo *(m)*
Pt antónimo *(m)*

anuario *(m) n* Es
De Jahrbuch *(n)*
En year book
Fr annuaire *(m)*
It annuario *(m)*
Pt anuário *(m)*

anuário *(m) n* Pt
De Adresbuch; Jahrbuch
    (n)
En directory; year book
Es anuario; directorio
    (m)
Fr annuaire *(m)*
It annuario *(m)*

anunciar *vb* Es, Pt
De werben
En advertise
Fr faire de la publicité
    pour
It pubblicizzare

anuncio *(m) n* Es
De Anzeige *(f)*
En advertisement
Fr annonce *(f)*
It annuncio
    pubblicitario *(m)*
Pt anúncio *(m)*

anúncio *(m) n* Pt
De Anzeige *(f)*
En advertisement
Es anuncio *(m)*
Fr annonce *(f)*

It annuncio
pubblicitario *(m)*

anúncio em majúsculas e ilustrado *(m)* Pt
De Displaywerbung *(f)*
En display
advertisement
Es anuncio publicitario
(m)
Fr grande annonce *(f)*
It inserzione
pubblicitaria *(f)*

anuncio publicitario *(m)*
Es
De Displaywerbung *(f)*
En display
advertisement
Fr grande annonce *(f)*
It inserzione
pubblicitaria *(f)*
Pt anúncio em
majúsculas e
ilustrado *(m)*

Anzeige *(f)* n De
En advertisement
Es anuncio *(m)*
Fr annonce *(f)*
It annuncio
pubblicitario *(m)*
Pt anúncio *(m)*

apagar *vb* Pt
De streichen; löschen
En delete; erase
Es suprimir; borrar
Fr rayer; effacer
It cassare

aparagem *(f)* n Pt
De Beschneiden *(n)*
En trimming
Es recorte *(m)*
Fr rognage *(m)*
It rifilatura *(f)*

aparar *vb* Pt
De beschneiden
En trim
Es cortar
Fr ébarber
It rifilare

apéndice *(m)* n Es
De Anhang *(m)*
En appendix
Fr appendice *(m)*
It appendice *(f)*
Pt apêndice *(m)*

apêndice *(m)* n Pt
De Anhang *(m)*
En appendix
Es apéndice *(m)*
Fr appendice *(m)*
It appendice *(f)*

Apfelsinenschalen-Effekt *(m)* De
En orange-peel effect
Es efecto de piel de
naranja *(m)*
Fr effet pelure d'orange
(m)
It effetto a buccia
d'arancia *(m)*
Pt efeito casca de
laranja *(m)*

aplat *(m)* n Fr
De Tonplatte *(f)*
En flat-tint plate
Es clisé de media tinta
(m)
It lastra a tinta opaca *(f)*
Pt chapa de meia-tinta
(f)

à-plat *adj* Fr
De kompreβ
En solid
Es desinterlineado
It sterlineato
Pt maciço

apoio *(m)* n Pt
De Widerdruck *(m)*
En backing-up
Es respaldado *(m)*
Fr mettant en retiration
(f)
It supporto *(m)*

apóstrofe *(f)* n Pt
De Apostroph *(m)*
En apostrophe
Es apóstrofo *(m)*
Fr apostrophe *(f)*
It apostrofo *(m)*

apostrofo *(m)* n It
De Apostroph *(m)*
En apostrophe
Es apóstrofo *(m)*
Fr apostrophe *(f)*
Pt apóstrofe *(f)*

apóstrofo *(m)* n Es
De Apostroph *(m)*
En apostrophe
Fr apostrophe *(f)*

It apostrofo *(m)*
Pt apóstrofe *(f)*

Apostroph *(m)* n De
En apostrophe
Es apóstrofo *(m)*
Fr apostrophe *(f)*
It apostrofo *(m)*
Pt apóstrofe *(f)*

apostrophe n En; Fr *(f)*
De Apostroph *(m)*
Es apóstrofo *(m)*
It apostrofo *(m)*
Pt apóstrofe *(f)*

**appareil
photomécanique**
(m) Fr
De Reproduktionsgerät
(n)
En process camera
Es cámara fotomecánica
(f)
It macchina fotografica
per riproduzioni
fotomeccaniche *(f)*
Pt câmara de
processamento *(f)*

appendice n Fr *(m)*; It *(f)*
De Anhang *(m)*
En appendix
Es apéndice *(m)*
Pt apêndice *(m)*

appendix n En
De Anhang *(m)*
Es apéndice *(m)*
Fr appendice *(m)*
It appendice *(f)*
Pt apêndice *(m)*

apprêt *(m)* n Fr
De Ausrüstung *(f)*
En finish
Es acabado *(m)*
It appretto *(m)*
Pt acabamento *(m)*

apprêt à l'antique *(m)* Fr
De Antik-Ausrüstung *(f)*
En antique finish
Es acabado antiguo *(m)*
It appretto tipo antico
(m)
Pt acabamento antigo
(m)

appretto *(m)* n It
De Ausrüstung *(f)*
En finish
Es acabado *(m)*
Fr apprêt *(m)*
Pt acabamento *(m)*

appretto tipo antico *(m)*
It
De Antik-Ausrüstung *(f)*
En antique finish
Es acabado antiguo *(m)*
Fr apprêt à l'antique *(m)*
Pt acabamento antigo
(m)

aquatint n En
De Aquatinta *(f)*
Es acuatinta *(f)*
Fr aquatinte *(f)*
It acquatinta *(f)*
Pt aqua-tinta *(f)*

aqua-tinta *(f)* n Pt
De Aquatinta *(f)*
En aquatint
Es acuatinta *(f)*
Fr aquatinte *(f)*
It acquatinta *(f)*

Aquatinta *(f)* n De
En aquatint
Es acuatinta *(f)*
Fr aquatinte *(f)*
It acquatinta *(f)*
Pt aqua-tinta *(f)*

aquatinte *(f)* n Fr
De Aquatinta *(f)*
En aquatint
Es acuatinta *(f)*
It acquatinta *(f)*
Pt aqua-tinta *(f)*

aquatone n En; Fr, It, Pt
(m)
De Aquaton-Verfahren
(n)
Es acuatono *(m)*

Aquaton-Verfahren *(n)* n
De
En aquatone
Es acuatono *(m)*
Fr aquatone *(m)*
It aquatone *(m)*
Pt aquatone *(m)*

arabic numerals En
De arabische Ziffern (pl)
Es números arábigos (m pl)
Fr chiffres arabes (m pl)
It numeri arabi (m pl)
Pt numeros árabes (m pl)

arabische Ziffern (pl) De
En arabic numerals
Es números arábigos (m pl)
Fr chiffres arabes (m pl)
It numeri arabi (m pl)
Pt numeros árabes (m pl)

a ras Es
De glatt
En flush
Fr ras
It a livello
Pt nivelado

Arbeit (f) n De
En work
Es trabajo (m)
Fr travail (m)
It lavoro (m)
Pt trabalho (m)

Arbeitgeber (m) n De
En employer
Es patrón (m)
Fr employeur (m)
It datore di lavoro (m)
Pt entidade patronal (f)

Arbeitgeber-Arbeitnehmer-Beziehungen (pl) De
Am labor relations
En labour relations
Es relaciones laborales (f pl)
Fr relations syndicales (f pl)
It relazioni di lavoro (f pl)
Pt relações laborais (f pl)

arbeitsintensive Aufträge (pl) De
Am labor-intensive work
En labour-intensive work
Es trabajo intensivo de mano de obra (m)
Fr travail à forte main-d'oeuvre (m)

It lavoro ad alto contenuto di mano d'opera (m)
Pt trabalho com muita mão de obra (m)

Arbeitsplan (m) n De
En schedule
Es plano (m)
Fr prévisions (f pl)
It orario (m)
Pt plano (m)

árbol (m) n Es
De Stiel (m)
En shank
Fr tige (f)
It gambo (m)
Pt árvore (f)

archivio dati (m) It
De Datenablage (f)
En data file
Es fichero de datos (m)
Fr fichier de données (m)
Pt arquivo de dados (m)

armazém (m) n Pt
De Lagerhaus (n)
En warehouse
Es almacén (m)
Fr entrepôt (m)
It magazzino (m)

armazenamento (m) n Pt
De Speicherung (f)
En storage
Es almacenamiento (m)
Fr stockage (m)
It immagazzinaggio (m)

armazenar vb Pt
De lagern
En store
Es almacenar
Fr entreposer
It immagazzinare

armazenista (m) n Pt
De Großhändler (m)
En wholesaler
Es mayorista (m)
Fr grossiste (m)
It grossista (m)

arquivar vb Pt
De aufschieben
En shelve

Es postergar indefinidamente
Fr ajourner
It porre in disparte

arquivo de dados (m) Pt
De Datenablage (f)
En data file
Es fichero de datos (m)
Fr fichier de données (m)
It archivio dati (m)

arrachage (m) n Fr
De Rupfen (n)
En plucking
Es picado (m)
It strappatura (f)
Pt picado (m)

arranjo preliminar (m) Pt
De Vorzurichtung (f)
En pre-makeready
Es arreglo preliminar (m)
Fr pré-mise en train (f)
It preavviamento (m)

arrastre por rueda dentada (m) Es
De Führungsloch-Vorschub (m)
En advanced sprocket feed
Fr perforation d'entraînement (f)
It alimentazione a tamburo dentato avanzato (f)
Pt alimentação avançada do carreto (f)

arreglo preliminar (m) Es
De Vorzurichtung (f)
En pre-makeready
Fr pré-mise en train (f)
It preavviamento (m)
Pt arranjo preliminar (m)

arricciatura (f) n It
De Kräuseln (n)
En cockling
Es amartillamiento (m)
Fr gondolage (m)
Pt enrugamento (m)

art board En
De Kunstdruckkarton (m)
Es tablero de dibujo (m)
Fr carte couchée (f)

It cartone da disegno (m)
Pt prancha de arte (f)

art books pl n En
De Kunstbücher (pl)
Es libros de arte (m pl)
Fr livres d'art (m pl)
It libri d'arte (m pl)
Pt livros de arte (m pl)

art canvas En
De Mattkunstgewebe (n)
Es tela de arte (f)
Fr toile pour reliure (f)
It tela d'arte (f)
Pt tela de arte (f)

art director En
De künstlerischer Leiter (m)
Es director gráfico (m)
Fr directeur artistique (m)
It direttore artistico (m)
Pt director artístico (m)

arte da sobrecapa (m) Pt
De Umschlag-Satzmontage (f)
En jacket artwork
Es trabajo artístico de la sobrecubierta (m)
Fr illustration de la jaquette (f)
It menabò per sovracopertina (m)

arte dell'incisione (f) It
De Gravierung (f)
En engraving (process)
Es grabado (proceso) (m)
Fr gravure (f)
Pt gravura (processo) (f)

art editor En
De Kunst-Redakteur (m)
Es redactor gráfico (m)
Fr rédacteur artistique (m)
It editore artistico (m)
Pt editor artístico (m)

artesano (m) n Es
De Handwerker (m)
En craftsman
Fr artisan (m)
It artigiano (m)
Pt artesão (m)

artesão *(m)* n Pt
De Handwerker *(m)*
En craftsman
Es artesano *(m)*
Fr artisan *(m)*
It artigiano *(m)*

article n En; Fr *(m)*
De Artikel; Eintrag *(m)*
Es artículo *(m)*
It articolo; voce *(m f)*
Pt artigo; entrada *(m f)*

articolo *(m)* n It
De Artikel *(m)*
En article
Es artículo *(m)*
Fr article *(m)*
Pt artigo *(m)*

artículo *(m)* n Es
De Artikel; Eintrag *(m)*
En article; entry
Fr article; entrée *(m f)*
It articolo; voce *(m f)*
Pt artigo; entrada *(m f)*

artigiano *(m)* n It
De Handwerker *(m)*
En craftsman
Es artesano *(m)*
Fr artisan *(m)*
Pt artesão *(m)*

artigo *(m)* n Pt
De Artikel *(m)*
En article
Es artículo *(m)*
Fr article *(m)*
It articolo *(m)*

arti grafiche *(f pl)* It
De graphisches
   Gewerbe *(n)*
En graphics *pl* n
Es gráfica *(f)*
Fr graphique *(f)*
Pt gráfica *(f)*

Artikel *(m)* n De
En article
Es artículo *(m)*
Fr article *(m)*
It articolo *(m)*
Pt artigo *(m)*

artisan *(m)* n Fr
De Handwerker *(m)*
En craftsman
Es artesano *(m)*

It artigiano *(m)*
Pt artesão *(m)*

artist n En
De Künstler *(m)*
Es artista *(m)*
Fr artiste *(m)*
It artista *(m)*
Pt artista *(m/f)*

artista *(m)* n Es, It, Pt
De Künstler *(m)*
En artist
Fr artiste *(m)*

artiste *(m)* n Fr
De Künstler *(m)*
En artist
Es artista *(m)*
It artista *(m)*
Pt artista *(m/f)*

artist's materials *pl* n En
De Kunstmaterialien *(pl)*
Es materiales de
   dibujante *(m pl)*
Fr fournitures de dessin
   (f pl)
It materiale d'arte *(m)*
Pt materiais do artista
   (m pl)

arts and crafts books *pl*
   n En
De Kunstgewerbebücher
   (pl)
Es libros de artes y
   oficios *(m pl)*
Fr livres artisanaux *(m
   pl)*
It libri d'arte e
   d'artigianato *(m pl)*
Pt livros de artes e
   ofícios *(m pl)*

árvore *(f)* n Pt
De Stiel *(m)*
En shank
Es árbol *(m)*
Fr tige *(f)*
It gambo *(m)*

ascendantes *(f pl)* Fr
De Buchstaben-
   Oberlänge *(n pl)*
En ascenders (of letter)
   pl n
Es palos altos *(m pl)*
It lettere ascendenti *(f
   pl)*
Pt ascendentes *(f pl)*

ascendentes *(f pl)* Pt
De Buchstaben-
   Oberlänge *(n pl)*
En ascenders (of letter)
   pl n
Es palos altos *(m pl)*
Fr ascendantes *(f pl)*
It lettere ascendenti *(f
   pl)*

ascenders (of letter) *pl* n
   En
De Buchstaben-
   Oberlänge *(n pl)*
Es palos altos *(m pl)*
Fr ascendantes *(f pl)*
It lettere ascendenti *(f
   pl)*
Pt ascendentes *(f pl)*

asentadores *(m pl)* Es
De Bestoßhobel *(pl)*
En planes *pl* n
Fr rabots *(m pl)*
It pialle *(f pl)*
Pt niveladores *(m pl)*

aspas *(f pl)* n Pt
De Anführungszeichen
   (pl)
En quotation marks
Es comillas *(f pl)*
Fr guillemets *(m pl)*
It virgolette *(f pl)*

assemblage *(m)* n Fr
De Zusammentragung;
   Zusammentragen *(f
   n)*
En collating; gathering
Es alzado; recogida *(m f)*
It raccoglitura; raccolta
   (f)
Pt revisão; reunião *(f)*

assembler n En
De Sammler *(m)*
Es elevador reunidor *(m)*
Fr assembleur *(m)*
It raccoglitore *(m)*
Pt ajustadora *(f)*

assembler *vb* Fr
De vergleichen
En collate
Es alzar
It collazionare
Pt rever

assembleur *(m)* n Fr
De Sammler *(m)*
En assembler
Es elevador reunidor *(m)*
It raccoglitore *(m)*
Pt ajustadora *(f)*

assinatura *(f)* Pt
De Signatur *(f)*
En signature (of a book)
Es signatura *(f)*
Fr signature *(f)*
It segnatura *(f)*

assistant de production
   (m) Fr
De Produktionsassistent
   (m)
En production assistant
Es ayudante de
   producción *(m)*
It assistente di
   produzione *(m)*
Pt assistente de
   produção *(m)*

**assistant des
   recherches** *(m)* Fr
De Forschungs-
   Assistent *(m)*
En research assistant
Es ayudante de
   investigación *(m)*
It assistente di ricerca
   (m)
Pt ajudante de
   investigação *(m)*

assistant editor En
De stellvertretender
   Redakteur *(m)*
Es redactor adjunto *(m)*
Fr rédacteur adjoint *(m)*
It assistente editore *(m)*
Pt editor adjunto *(m)*

assistente de produção
   (m) Pt
De Produktionsassistent
   (m)
En production assistant
Es ayudante de
   producción *(m)*
Fr assistant de
   production *(m)*
It assistente di
   produzione *(m)*

**assistente di
   produzione** *(m)* It
De Produktionsassistent
   (m)

En production assistant
Es ayudante de
producción *(m)*
Fr assistant de
production *(m)*
Pt assistente de
produção *(m)*

assistente di ricerca *(m)*
It
De Forschungs-
Assistent *(m)*
En research assistant
Es ayudante de
investigación *(m)*
Fr assistant des
recherches *(m)*
Pt ajudante de
investigação *(m)*

assistente editore *(m)* It
De stellvertretender
Redakteur *(m)*
En assistant editor
Es redactor adjunto *(m)*
Fr rédacteur adjoint *(m)*
Pt editor adjunto *(m)*

assistente editoriale *(m)*
It
De Redaktionsassistent
(m)
En editorial assistant
Es ayudante de editorial
(m)
Fr secrétaire de
rédaction *(m)*
Pt ajudante editorial *(m)*

assistente personale *(m)*
It
De persönlicher
Assistent *(m)*
En personal assistant
Es ayudante personal
(m)
Fr adjoint *(m)*
Pt ajudante pessoal *(m)*

assortiment *(m)* Fr
De Schriftgarnitur *(f)*
En sorts *pl n*
Es suertes *(f pl)*
It rappezzi *(m pl)*
Pt sortes *(f pl)*

asterisco *(m) n* Es, It, Pt
De Sternchen *(n)*
En asterisk
Fr astérisque *(m)*

asterisk *n* En
De Sternchen *(n)*
Es asterisco *(n)*
Fr astérisque *(m)*
It asterisco *(m)*
Pt asterisco *(m)*

astérisque *(m) n* Fr
De Sternchen *(n)*
En asterisk
Es asterisco *(m)*
It asterisco *(m)*
Pt asterisco *(m)*

astuccio del libro *(m)* It
De Schuber *(m)*
En slip case
Es estuche *(m)*
Fr étui *(m)*
Pt estojo de livro *(m)*

atelier *(m) n* Fr
De Fabrik *(f)*
En shop (in industry)
Es taller *(m)*
It officina *(f)*
Pt oficina *(f)*

atelier de composition
(m) Fr
De Setzerei *(f)*
En composing room
Es sala de composición
(f)
It sala composizione *(f)*
Pt sala de composição
(f)

atelier de reliure *(m)* Fr
De Buchbinderei *(f)*
En bindery
Es taller de
encuadernación *(f)*
It legatoria *(f)*
Pt oficina de
encadernação *(f)*

atelier d'imprimerie *(m)*
Fr
De Pressesaal *(m)*
En press room
Es sala de máquinas *(f)*
It sala stampa *(f)*
Pt sala de imprensa *(f)*

atlante *(m) n* It
De Atlas *(m)*
En atlas
Es atlas *(m)*
Fr atlas *(m)*
Pt atlas *(m)*

atlas *n* En; Es, Fr, Pt *(m)*
De Atlas *(m)*
It atlante *(m)*

Atlas *(m) n* De
En atlas
Es atlas *(m)*
Fr atlas *(m)*
It atlante *(m)*
Pt atlas *(m)*

a toda a cor Pt
Am in full color
De in voller Farbe
En in full colour
Es a todo color
Fr en couleurs
It a colori

a todo color Es
Am in full color
De in voller Farbe
En in full colour
Fr en couleurs
It a colori
Pt a toda a cor

attrezzi da rilegatore *(m pl)* It
De Buchbinder-
Werkzeuge *(pl)*
En binder´s tools
Es herramientas de
encuadernación *(f pl)*
Fr outils de reliure *(m pl)*
Pt ferramenta de
encadernação *(f)*

Ätzphase *(f) n* De
En bite (platemaking)
Es mordido *(m)*
Fr larron *(m)*
It acidatura *(f)*
Pt mordente *(m)*

Ätzpigmentpapier *(n) n*
De
En carbon tissue
Es papel pigmento *(m)*
Fr papier au carbone
(n)
It carta al carbone *(f)*
Pt tecido carbono *(m)*

Auflage *(f) n* De
En impression
Es tirada *(f)*
Fr tirage *(m)*
It tiratura *(f)*
Pt tiragem *(m)*

aufschieben *vb* De
En shelve
Es postergar
indefinidamente
Fr ajourner
It porre in disparte
Pt arquivar

Aufstoßen *(n) n* De
En knocking-up (of
paper)
Es emparejamiento de
hojas *(m)*
Fr taquage des feuilles
(m)
It uniformazione di
foglie *(f)*
Pt empilhamento de
folhas *(m)*

Auftragsvertreter *(m) n*
De
En commission
representative
Es representante a
comisión *(m)*
Fr représentant chargé
des commandes *(m)*
It rappresentante
commissione *(m)*
Pt representante à
comissão *(m)*

**Auftragvergabe-
Redakteur** *(m)* De
En commissioning editor
Es editor por encargo
(m)
Fr rédacteur chargé des
commandes *(m)*
It redattore
commissioni *(m)*
Pt editor que
encomenda a obra
(m)

augmentation *(f) n* Fr
De Hinaufsetzung *(f)*
En mark-up (of prices)
Es aumento *(m)*
It prezzatura *(f)*
Pt aumento *(m)*

augmenter *vb* Fr
De hinaufsetzen
En mark up (price)
Es aumentar
It aumentare (il prezzo)
Pt aumentar

aumentar vb Es, Pt
De hinaufsetzen
En mark up (price)
Fr augmenter
It aumentare (il prezzo)

aumentare (il prezzo) vb
It
De hinaufsetzen
En mark up (price)
Es aumentar
Fr augmenter
Pt aumentar

aumento (m) n Es, Pt
De Hinaufsetzung (f)
En mark-up (of prices)
Fr augmentation (f)
It prezzatura (f)

Ausdruck (m) n De
En printout
Es vaciado a la
    impresora (m)
Fr sortie d'imprimante
    (f)
It printout (m)
Pt impressão em
    positivo directo (f)

ausdrucken vb De
En print out
Es imprimir (por
    ordenador)
Fr sortir
It stampare (per
    elaboratore)
Pt imprimir em positivo
    directo

auseinandertragen vb
    De
En decollate
Es separar hojas
Fr déliasser
It decollare
Pt decapitar

Ausfallszeit (f) n De
En down time
Es tiempo muerto (m)
Fr période d'arrêt (f)
It tempo passivo (m)
Pt tempo de paragem
    (m)

Ausführpunkte (pl) De
En leaders pl n
Es filetes puntillados (m
    pl)

Fr points de conduite
    (m pl)
It puntini (m pl)
Pt pontos de reticência
    (m pl)

Ausgabe (f) n De
En edition
Es edición (f)
Fr édition (f)
It edizione (f)
Pt edição (f)

Aushängebogen (pl) De
En advance sheets pl n
Es hojas por adelantado
    (f pl)
Fr bonnes feuilles (f pl)
It fogli in anticipo (m pl)
Pt folhas tipográficas (f
    pl)

**Auslandsrecht-
    Abteilung** (f) De
En foreign-rights
    department
Es departamento de
    derechos en el
    extranjero (m)
Fr service des droits à
    l'étranger (m)
It reparto diritti esteri
    (m)
Pt departamento de
    direitos estrangeiros
    (m)

Auslandsrechte (pl) De
En foreign rights
Es derechos en el
    extranjero (m pl)
Fr droits à l'étranger (m
    pl)
It diritti esteri (m pl)
Pt direitos estrangeiros
    (m pl)

Auslandsrecht-Leiter
    (m) De
En foreign-rights
    manager
Es director de derechos
    en el extranjero (m)
Fr directeur des droits à
    l'étranger (m)
It dirigente diritti esteri
    (m)
Pt director dos direitos
    estrangeiros (m)

Auslandsumsätze (pl)
    De
En foreign sales pl n
Es ventas extranjeras (f
    pl)
Fr ventes à l'étranger (f
    pl)
It servizio vendite
    estero (m)
Pt vendas no
    estrangeiro (f pl)

Auslassungszeichen (n)
    n De
En caret mark
Es signo de
    intercalación (m)
Fr renvoi de marge (m)
It segno di rimando (m)
Pt sinal de intercalar (m)

ausreifen vb De
En mature
Es madurar
Fr conditionner
It stagionare
Pt amadurecer

ausrichten vb De
En line up
Es alinear
Fr parangonner
It allineare
Pt alinhar

Ausrichtung (f) n De
En alignment
Es alineación (f)
Fr alignement (m)
It allineamento (m)
Pt alinhamento (m)

Ausrufungszeichen (n) n
    De
En exclamation mark
Es signo de admiración
    (m)
Fr point d'exclamation
    (m)
It punto esclamativo
    (m)
Pt ponto de exclamação
    (m)

Ausrüstung (f) n De
En finish
Es acabado (m)
Fr apprêt (m)
It appretto (m)
Pt acabamento (m)

Ausschlußstück (m) n
    De
En space
Es espacio (m)
Fr espace (m)
It spazio (m)
Pt espaço (m)

Außenarbeit (n) n De
En outwork
Es trabajo externo (m)
Fr travail à domicile (m)
It lavoro esterno (m)
Pt trabalho externo (m)

Aussprache (f) n De
En pronunciation
Es pronunciación (f)
Fr prononciation (f)
It pronuncia (f)
Pt pronunciação (f)

ausstellen vb De
En display
Es exhibir
Fr exhiber
It mostrare
Pt exibir

Aussteller (m) n De
En exhibitor
Es expositor (m)
Fr exposant (m)
It espositore (m)
Pt expositor (m)

austauschen vb De
En transpose
Es trasponer
Fr transposer
It trasporre
Pt transpor

ausverkauft adj De
En sold out
Es agotado
Fr liquidé
It esaurito
Pt esgotado

auszeichnen vb De
En mark up (copy)
Es marcar
Fr annoter
It contrassegnare
Pt marcar

Auszeichnungssatz (m)
    n De
En display type

Es tipos titulares *(m pl)*
Fr caractères vedettes *(m pl)*
It caratteri di titolo *(m pl)*
Pt tipos de maiúscula *(m pl)*

auteur *(m) n* Fr
De Verfasser *(m)*
En author
Es autor *(m)*
It autore *(m)*
Pt autor *(m)*

auteur de l'index *(m)* Fr
De Indexierer *(m)*
En indexer
Es indexador *(m)*
It compilatore di un indice *(m)*
Pt indiciador *(m)*

author *n* En
De Verfasser *(m)*
Es autor *(m)*
Fr auteur *(m)*
It autore *(m)*
Pt autor *(m)*

authoritative *adj* En
De autoritativ
Es autorizado
Fr de source sure
It autorevole
Pt autoritativo

author promotion tour En
De Verfasser-Werbetour *(f)*
Es viaje de promoción del autor *(m)*
Fr voyage promotionnel d'auteur *(m)*
It itinerario promozionale dell'autore *(m)*
Pt viagem de promoção de autor *(f)*

author's agreement En
De Verfasservertrag *(m)*
Es contrato de autor *(m)*
Fr contrat d'auteur *(m)*
It accordo coll'autore *(m)*
Pt acordo do autor *(m)*

author's corrections *pl n* En
De Autorkorrekturen *(pl)*
Es correcciones de autor *(f pl)*
Fr corrections de l'auteur *(f pl)*
It correzioni dell'autore *(f pl)*
Pt correcções do autor *(f pl)*

author's free copies *pl n* En
De Autorexemplare *(pl)*
Es ejemplares de obsequio del autor *(m pl)*
Fr exemplaires gratuits pour l'auteur *(m pl)*
It copie gratuite dell'autore *(f pl)*
Pt exemplares grátis para o autor *(m pl)*

author's proof En
De Autor-Korrekturabzug *(m)*
Es prueba de autor *(f)*
Fr épreuve d'auteur *(f)*
It bozza dell'autore *(f)*
Pt prova do autor *(f)*

autobiografia *(f) n* It, Pt
De Autobiographie *(f)*
En autobiography
Es autobiografía *(f)*
Fr autobiographie *(f)*

autobiografía *(f) n* Es
De Autobiographie *(f)*
En autobiography
Fr autobiographie *(f)*
It autobiografia *(f)*
Pt autobiografia *(f)*

autobiographie *(f) n* Fr
De Autobiographie *(f)*
En autobiography
Es autobiografía *(f)*
It autobiografia *(f)*
Pt autobiografia *(f)*

Autobiographie *(f) n* De
En autobiography
Es autobiografía *(f)*
Fr autobiographie *(f)*
It autobiografia *(f)*
Pt autobiografia *(f)*

autobiography *n* En
De Autobiographie *(f)*
Es autobiografía *(f)*
Fr autobiographie *(f)*
It autobiografia *(f)*
Pt autobiografia *(f)*

autograbado *(m) n* Es
De Autotiefdruck *(m)*
En autogravure
Fr autogravure *(f)*
It autorotocalcografia *(f)*
Pt autogravura *(f)*

autógrafar *vb* Pt
De signieren
En autograph
Es firmar
Fr signer
It autografare

autografare *vb* It
De signieren
En autograph
Es firmar
Fr signer
Pt autógrafar

autograph *vb* En
De signieren
Es firmar
Fr signer
It autografare
Pt autógrafar

autographic transfer En
De autographischer Transferdruck *(m)*
Es transferencia autográfica *(f)*
Fr procédé autographique *(m)*
It trasferimento autografico *(m)*
Pt transferência autográfica *(f)*

autographie *(f) n* Fr
De Steinauto *(f)*
En autolithography
Es autolitografía *(f)*
It autolitografia *(f)*
Pt autolitografia *(f)*

autographischer Transferdruck *(m)* De
En autographic transfer
Es transferencia autográfica *(f)*

autobiography *n* En
De Autobiographie *(f)*
Es autobiografía *(f)*
Fr autobiographie *(f)*
It autobiografia *(f)*
Pt autobiografia *(f)*

autogravura *(f) n* Pt
De Autotiefdruck *(m)*
En autogravure
Es autograbado *(m)*
Fr autogravure *(f)*
It autorctocalcografia *(f)*

autogravure *n* En; Fr *(f)*
De Autotiefdruck *(m)*
Es autograbado *(m)*
It autorotocalcografia *(f)*
Pt autogravura *(f)*

autolithography *n* En
De Steinauto *(f)*
Es autolitografía *(f)*
Fr autographie *(f)*
It autolitografia *(f)*
Pt autolitografia *(f)*

autolitografia *(f) n* It, Pt
De Steinauto *(f)*
En autolithography
Es autolitografía *(f)*
Fr autographie *(f)*

autolitografía *(f) n* Es
De Steinauto *(f)*
En autolithography
Fr autographie *(f)*
It autolitografia *(f)*
Pt autolitografia *(f)*

automatic data processing (ADP) En
De automatische Datenverarbeitung *(f)*
Es proceso automático de datos *(m)*
Fr traitement automatique de l'information *(m)*
It processazione automatica dati *(f)*
Pt tratamento automático de dados *(m)*

automatic feeder En
De automatischer Einleger *(m)*

Es alimentador
automático (m)
Fr margeur
automatique (m)
It alimentatore
automatico (f)
Pt alimentador
automático (m)

automatic pile delivery
En
De automatischer
Stapelausleger (m)
Es receptor automático
de pila de pliegos (m)
Fr distribution
automatique des
piles (f)
It avanzamento
automatico di pile (f)
Pt entrega automática
de pilhas (f)

**automatische
Datenverarbeitung**
(f) De
En automatic data
processing (ADP)
Es proceso automático
de datos (m)
Fr traitement
automatique de
l'information (m)
It processazione
automatica dati (f)
Pt tratamento
automático de dados
(m)

automatischer Einleger
(m) De
En automatic feeder
Es alimentador
automático (m)
Fr margeur
automatique (m)
It alimentatore
automatico (f)
Pt alimentador
automático (m)

**automatischer
Stapelausleger** (m)
De
En automatic pile
delivery
Es receptor automático
de pila de pliegos (m)
Fr distribution
automatique des
piles (f)
It avanzamento
automatico di pile (f)

Pt entrega automática
de pilhas (f)

Automobilbücher (n) De
En automotive books pl
n
Es libros sobre el
automóvil (m pl)
Fr livres sur
l'automobile (m pl)
It libri automobilistici
(m pl)
Pt livros automotores
(m pl)

automotive books pl n
En
De Automobilbücher (n)
Es libros sobre el
automóvil (m pl)
Fr livres sur
l'automobile (m pl)
It libri automobilistici
(m pl)
Pt livros automotores
(m pl)

autor (m) n Es, Pt
De Verfasser (m)
En author
Fr auteur (m)
It autore (m)

autor de esboço (m) Pt
Am draftsman
De Zeichner (m)
En draughtsman
Es delineante (m)
Fr dessinateur-
concepteur (m)
It disegnatore (m)

autore (m) n It
De Verfasser (m)
En author
Es autor (m)
Fr auteur (m)
Pt autor (m)

autorevole adj It
De autoritativ
En authoritative
Es autorizado
Fr de source sure
Pt autoritativo

Autorexemplare (pl) De
En author's free copies
pl n
Es ejemplares de

obsequio del autor
(m pl)
Fr exemplaires gratuits
pour l'auteur (m pl)
It copie gratuite
dell'autore (f pl)
Pt exemplares grátis
para o autor (m pl)

autoritativ adj De
En authoritative
Es autorizado
Fr de source sure
It autorevole
Pt autoritativo

autoritativo adj Pt
De autoritativ
En authoritative
Es autorizado
Fr de source sure
It autorevole

autorizado adj Es
De autoritativ
En authoritative
Fr de source sure
It autorevole
Pt autoritativo

Autor-Korrekturabzug
(m) De
En author's proof
Es prueba de autor (f)
Fr épreuve d'auteur (f)
It bozza dell'autore (f)
Pt prova do autor (f)

Autorkorrekturen (pl)
De
En author's corrections
pl n
Es correcciones de
autor (f pl)
Fr corrections de
l'auteur (f pl)
It correzioni dell'autore
(f pl)
Pt correcções do autor
(f pl)

autorotocalcografia (f) n
It
De Autotiefdruck (m)
En autogravure
Es autograbado (m)
Fr autogravure (f)
Pt autogravura (f)

Autotiefdruck (m) n De
En autogravure
Es autograbado (m)
Fr autogravure (f)
It autorotocalcografia
(f)
Pt autogravura (f)

autotipia (f) n Es, Pt
De Halbton (m)
En halftone
Fr simili (f)
It mezzatinta (f)

autumn list En
De Herbstliste (f)
Es catálogo de otoño
(m)
Fr catalogue de la
rentrée (m)
It elenco d'autunno (m)
Pt lista de outono (f)

autumn publication En
De Herbstausgabe (f)
Es publicación de otoño
(f)
Fr parution de la rentrée
(f)
It pubblicazione
d'autunno (f)
Pt publicação de outono
(f)

avance (f) n Fr
De Vorschuβ (m)
En advance
Es anticipo (m)
It anticipo (m)
Pt adiantamento (m)

**avance sur les droits
d'auteur** (f) Fr
De Tantiemenvorschuβ
(m)
En advance against
royalties
Es anticipo sobre
derechos de autor
(m)
It anticipo sui diritti di
licenza (m)
Pt adiantamento sobre
direitos de autor (m)

avant-propos (m) n Fr
De Vorwort
En foreword
Es proemio (m)
It proemio (m)
Pt proémio (m)

**avanzamento
automatico di pile**
(f) It
De automatischer
Stapelausleger (m)
En automatic pile
delivery
Es receptor automático
de pila de pliegos (m)
Fr distribution
automatique des
piles (f)
Pt entrega automática
de pilhas (f)

ayudante de editorial
(m) Es
De Redaktionsassistent
(m)
En editorial assistant
Fr secrétaire de
rédaction (m)
It assistente editoriale
(m)
Pt ajudante editorial (m)

**ayudante de
investigación** (m)
Es
De Forschungs-
Assistent (m)
En research assistant
Fr assistant des
recherches (m)
It assistente di ricerca
(m)
Pt ajudante de
investigação (m)

ayudante de producción
(m) Es
De Produktionsassistent
(m)
En production assistant
Fr assistant de
production (m)
It assistente di
produzione (m)
Pt assistente de
produção (m)

ayudante de ventas (m)
Es
De Verkäufer (m)
En sales assistant
Fr commis (m)
It commesso (m)
Pt ajudante de
vendedor (m)

ayudante personal (m)
Es
De persönlicher
Assistent (m)
En personal assistant
Fr adjoint (m)
It assistente personale
(m)
Pt ajudante pessoal (m)

azione (f) n It
De Aktie (f)
En share
Es acción (f)
Fr action (f)
Pt acção (f)

azionista (m/f) n It
De Aktionär (m)
En shareholder
Es accionista (m)
Fr actionnaire (m)
Pt accionista (m)

azul celeste avitelado
(m) Es
De Azur-Velinpapier (n)
En azure wove
Fr vélin azur (m)
It carta retinata azzura
(f)
Pt tecido anilado (m)

azul de tricromía (m) Es
De Verfahrensblau (n)
En process blue
Fr bleu d'impression
couleur (m)
It azzurro di tricromia
(m)
Pt azul para policromia
(m)

azul para policromia (m)
Pt
De Verfahrensblau (n)
En process blue
Es azul de tricromía (m)
Fr bleu d'impression
couleur (m)
It azzurro di tricromia
(m)

azul verdoso (m) Es
De Cyan (n)
En cyan
Fr cyan (m)
It ciano (m)
Pt cianogénio (m)

azurado adj Es
De azuriertes
En azured
Fr azuré
It azzurrato
Pt anilado

azuré adj Fr
De azuriertes
En azured
Es azurado
It azzurrato
Pt anilado

azured adj En
De azuriertes
Es azurado
Fr azuré
It azzurrato
Pt anilado

azure wove En
De Azur-Velinpapier (n)
Es azul celeste avitelado
(m)
Fr vélin azur (m)
It carta retinata azzura
(f)
Pt tecido anilado (m)

azuriertes adj De
En azured
Es azurado
Fr azuré
It azzurrato
Pt anilado

Azur-Velinpapier (n) De
En azure wove
Es azul celeste avitelado
(m)
Fr vélin azur (m)
It carta retinata azzura
(f)
Pt tecido anilado (m)

azzurrato adj It
De azuriertes
En azured
Es azurado
Fr azuré
Pt anilado

azzurro di tricromia (m)
It
De Verfahrensblau (n)
En process blue
Es azul de tricromía (m)
Fr bleu d'impression
couleur (m)

Pt azul para policromia
(m)

B

back flap En
De hintere
Umschlagklappe (f)
Es solapa posterior (f)
Fr rabat arrière (m)
It risvolto di retro (m)
Pt contracapa (f)

backing n En
De Abpressen (n)
Es formación de cajos (f)
Fr endossure (f)
It rinforzo (m)
Pt colocação de
lombada (f)

backing pages pl n En
De Rückseiten (pl)
Es páginas de lomo (f pl)
Fr pages de garde (f pl)
It pagine di rinforzo (f
pl)
Pt páginas de lombada
(f pl)

backing-up n En
De Widerdruck (m)
Es respaldado (m)
Fr mettant en retiration
(f)
It supporto (m)
Pt apoio (m)

back lining En
De Buchrücken-
Fütterung (f)
Es contralomo (m)
Fr garniture du dos (f)
It fodera di costa (f)
Pt forro de lombada (m)

bad copy En
De schlechtes
Manuskript (n)
Es original malo (m)
Fr mauvaise copie (f)
It copia illeggibile (f)
Pt exemplar ilegível (m)

balconista *(m)* n Pt
De Gewerkschafts-
  Betriebsobmann *(m)*
En shop steward
Es dirigente obrero *(m)*
Fr délégué d´atelier *(m)*
It delegato di fabbrica
  (m)

banca dei dati *(f)* It
De Datenbank *(f)*
En data bank
Es banco de datos *(m)*
Fr banque de données
  (f)
Pt banco de dados *(m)*

bancarotta *(f)* n It
De Bankerott *(m)*
En bankruptcy
Es bancarrota *(f)*
Fr faillite *(f)*
Pt falência *(f)*

bancarrota *(f)* n Es
De Bankerott *(m)*
En bankruptcy
Fr faillite *(f)*
It bancarotta *(f)*
Pt falência *(f)*

banco de dados *(m)* Pt
De Datenbank *(f)*
En data bank
Es banco de datos *(m)*
Fr banque de données
  (f)
It banca dei dati *(f)*

banco de datos *(m)* Es
De Datenbank *(f)*
En data bank
Fr banque de données
  (f)
It banca dei dati *(f)*
Pt banco de dados *(m)*

banco tipografico *(m)* It
De Form; Schließplatte
  (f)
En imposing surface;
  stone (letterpress
  composition)
Es superficie de
  imposición *(f)*
Fr marbre de serrage
  (m)
Pt superfície de
  imposição *(f)*

bande de masquage *(f)*
  Fr
De Abdeckband *(n)*
En masking tape
Es cinta para
  enmascarar *(f)*
It nastro per
  mascheratura *(m)*
Pt fita de mascarar *(f)*

bande de papier *(f)* Fr
De Lochstreifen *(m)*
En paper tape
Es cinta de papel *(f)*
It nastro di carta *(m)*
Pt fita de papel *(f)*

bande magnétique *(f)* Fr
De Magnetband *(n)*
En magnetic tape
Es cinta magnética *(f)*
It nastro magnetico *(m)*
Pt fita magnética *(f)*

bande perforée *(f)* Fr
De Lochstreifen *(m)*
En punched paper tape
Es cinta perforada *(f)*
It nastro di carta
  perforato *(m)*
Pt fita de papel
  perfurado *(f)*

bandes des couleurs *(f
  pl)* Fr
Am color bars *pl n*
De Farbstreifen *(pl)*
En colour bars *pl n*
Es franjas de color *(f pl)*
It barre di colore *(f pl)*
Pt franjas de cor *(f pl)*

Bankerott *(m)* n De
En bankruptcy
Es bancarrota *(f)*
Fr faillite *(f)*
It bancarotta *(f)*
Pt falência *(f)*

Bankerotteur *(m)* n De
En bankrupt
Es quebrado *(m)*
Fr failli *(m)*
It fallito *(m)*
Pt falido *(m)*

bankerott machen De
En bankrupt
Es quebrar
Fr mettre en faillite

It far bancarotta
Pt falir

bankrupt *vb* En
De bankerott machen
Es quebrar
Fr mettre en faillite
It far bancarotta
Pt falir

bankrupt *n* En
De Bankerotteur *(m)*
Es quebrado *(m)*
Fr failli *(m)*
It fallito *(m)*
Pt falido *(m)*

bankruptcy *n* En
De Bankerott *(m)*
Es bancarrota *(f)*
Fr faillite *(f)*
It bancarotta *(f)*
Pt falência *(f)*

banque de données *(f)*
  Fr
De Datenbank *(f)*
En data bank
Es banco de datos *(m)*
It banca dei dati *(f)*
Pt banco de dados *(m)*

barba *(f)* n Es, Pt
De Büttenrand *(m)*
En deckle edge
Fr barbe *(f)*
It zazzera *(f)*

barbe *(f)* n Fr
De Büttenrand *(m)*
En deckle edge
Es barba *(f)*
It zazzera *(f)*
Pt barba *(f)*

Bargeldfluß *(m)* n De
En cash flow
Es flujo de caja *(m)*
Fr cash-flow *(m)*
It movimento di cassa
  (m)
Pt movimento em
  dinheiro *(m)*

barniz *(m)* n Es
De Lack *(m)*
En varnish
Fr vernis *(m)*
It vernice *(f)*
Pt verniz *(m)*

barre di colore *(f pl)* It
Am color bars *pl n*
De Farbstreifen *(pl)*
En colour bars *pl n*
Es franjas de color *(f pl)*
Fr bandes des couleurs
  (f pl)
Pt franjas de cor *(f pl)*

bas de caisse *(m)* Fr
De Unterkasten *(m)*
En lower case
Es caja baja *(f)*
It bassa cassa *(f)*
Pt caixa baixa *(f)*

**base de venda ou
  devolução** *(f)* Pt
De Kauf oder Rückgabe
  (m)
En sale-or-return basis
Es base de ventas o
  devoluciones *(f)*
Fr vente avec possibilité
  de rendre *(f)*
It base venduto o reso
  (f)

**base de ventas o
  devoluciones** *(f)* Es
De Kauf oder Rückgabe
  (m)
En sale-or-return basis
Fr vente avec possibilité
  de rendre *(f)*
It base venduto o reso
  (f)
Pt base de venda ou
  devolução *(f)*

base venduto o reso *(f)*
  It
De Kauf oder Rückgabe
  (m)
En sale-or-return basis
Es base de ventas o
  devoluciones *(f)*
Fr vente avec possibilité
  de rendre *(f)*
Pt base de venda ou
  devolução *(f)*

bassa cassa *(f)* It
De Unterkasten *(m)*
En lower case
Es caja baja *(f)*
Fr bas de caisse *(m)*
Pt caixa baixa *(f)*

Bastardkegel *(m)* n De
En bastard size
Es tamaño bastardo *(m)*

Fr format bâtard *(m)*
It dimensione
   irregolare *(f)*
Pt tamanho bastardo
   (m)

bastard size En
De Bastardkegel *(m)*
Es tamaño bastardo *(m)*
Fr format bâtard *(m)*
It dimensione
   irregolare *(f)*
Pt tamanho bastardo
   (m)

bastone *(m) n* It
De Grotesk-Schrifttyp
   (m)
En sans-serif typeface
Es tipo sin remate *(m)*
Fr caractère antique
   (sans empâtement)
   (m)
Pt olho de tipo sem
   remate *(m)*

batido *(m) n* Es
De Mahlung *(f)*
En beating
   (papermaking)
Fr raffinage *(m)*
It raffinamento *(m)*
Pt batimento *(m)*

batidora *(f) n* Es
De Mahlmaschine *(f)*
En beating machine
Fr pilon *(m)*
It raffinatrice *(f)*
Pt máquina de bater *(f)*

batimento *(m) n* Pt
De Mahlung *(f)*
En beating
   (papermaking)
Es batido *(m)*
Fr raffinage *(m)*
It raffinamento *(m)*

battered type En
De Defekt *(m)*
Es carácter estropeo *(m)*
Fr caractère
   endommagé *(m)*
It carattere avariato *(m)*
Pt carácter defeituoso
   (m)

battitura *(f) n* It
De Granierung *(f)*
En stippling

Es punteado *(m)*
Fr grisé *(m)*
Pt ponteado *(m)*

beard (of letter) *n* En
De Kopf (type) *(m)*
Es relieve *(m)*
Fr talus *(m)*
It bianco alla base *(m)*
Pt relevo *(m)*

beating (papermaking) *n*
   En
De Mahlung *(f)*
Es batido *(m)*
Fr raffinage *(m)*
It raffinamento *(m)*
Pt batimento *(m)*

beating machine En
De Mahlmaschine *(f)*
Es batidora *(f)*
Fr pilon *(m)*
It raffinatrice *(f)*
Pt máquina de bater *(f)*

becquet *(m) n* Fr
De Deckblatt *(n)*
En overlay (on artwork,
   etc.)
Es superponible *(m)*
It sovrapposizione *(f)*
Pt coberta *(f)*

bed (printing machine) *n*
   En
De Druckkarren *(m)*
Es platina *(f)*
Fr marbre *(m)*
It piano *(m)*
Pt mesa *(f)*

Bedingungen *(pl)* De
En terms (of agreement,
   etc.) *pl n*
Es condiciones *(f pl)*
Fr conditions *(f pl)*
It condizioni *(f pl)*
Pt condições *(m pl)*

Begriffszeichen *(n) n* De
En ideogram
Es ideograma *(m)*
Fr idéogramme *(m)*
It ideogramma *(m)*
Pt ideograma *(m)*

beletrística *(f)* Pt
De Schöne Literatur *(f)*
En belles-lettres *pl n*

Es bellas letras *(f pl)*
Fr belles-lettres *(f pl)*
It belle lettere *(f pl)*

belichten *vb* De
En expose
Es exponer
Fr exposer
It esporre
Pt expor

Belichtung *(f) n* De
En exposure
   (photographic)
Es exposición *(f)*
Fr pose *(f)*
It posa *(f)*
Pt exposição *(f)*

bellas letras *(f pl)* Es
De Schöne Literatur *(f)*
En belles-lettres *pl n*
Fr belles-lettres *(f pl)*
It belle lettere *(f pl)*
Pt beletrística *(f)*

belle lettere *(f pl)* It
De Schöne Literatur *(f)*
En belles-lettres *pl n*
Es bellas letras *(f pl)*
Fr belles-lettres *(f pl)*
Pt beletrística *(f)*

belle page *(f)* Fr
De rechte Seite *(f)*
En right-hand page
Es página derecha *(f)*
It pagina di destra *(f)*
Pt página da direita *(f)*

belles-lettres *pl n* En; Fr
   (f pl)
De Schöne Literatur *(f)*
Es bellas letras *(f pl)*
It belle lettere *(f pl)*
Pt beletrística *(f)*

bénéfices *(m pl)* Fr
De Einnahmen *(pl)*
En earnings *pl n*
Es beneficios *(m pl)*
It entrate *(f pl)*
Pt rendimentos *(m pl)*

beneficios *(m pl)* Es
De Einnahmen *(pl)*
En earnings *pl n*
Fr bénéfices *(m pl)*
It entrate *(f pl)*
Pt rendimentos *(m pl)*

berechnen *vb* De
En cast off
Es calibrar la
   composición
Fr calibrer un texte
It equilibrare la
   composizione
Pt calibrar a
   composição

Bericht *(m) n* De
En report
Es informe *(m)*
Fr reportage *(m)*
It relazione *(f)*
Pt relatório *(m)*

berichten *vb* De
En report
Es informar
Fr faire un reportage
It relazionare
Pt informar

Berichterstatter *(m) n*
   De
En reporter
Es reportero *(m)*
Fr reporter *(m)*
It cronista *(m)*
Pt reporter *(m)*

Berstwiderstand *(m) n*
   De
En bursting strength
Es resistencia al
   reventamiento *(f)*
Fr résistance à
   l'éclatement *(f)*
It resistenza alla rottura
   (f)
Pt resistência ao
   arrebentamento *(f)*

beschneiden *vb* De
En trim
Es cortar
Fr ébarber
It rifilare
Pt aparar

Beschneiden *(n) n* De
En trimming
Es recorte *(m)*
Fr rognage *(m)*
It rifilatura *(f)*
Pt aparagem *(f)*

Beschnittgröße *(f) n* De
En trimmed page size

Es tamaño de página
   cortada *(m)*
Fr format fini *(m)*
It dimensioni di pagina
   rifilata *(f pl)*
Pt tamanho de página
   aparada *(m)*

Beschnitt-
   Markierungen *(pl)*
   n De
En trim marks
Es marcas de recorte *(f
   pl)*
Fr repères de rognage
   (m pl)
It segni per rifilatura *(m
   pl)*
Pt marcas de aparar *(f
   pl)*

Bestoßhobel *(pl)* De
En planes *pl n*
Es asentadores *(m pl)*
Fr rabots *(m pl)*
It pialle *(f pl)*
Pt niveladores *(m pl)*

Betragender *(m) n* De
En contributor
Es contribuidor *(m)*
Fr collaborateur *(m)*
It collaboratore *(m)*
Pt contribuidor *(m)*

Betriebsredakteur *(m) n*
   De
En managing editor
Es jefe de redacción *(m)*
Fr chef de la rédaction
   (m)
It capo redattore *(m)*
Pt chefe de redacção
   (m)

bevel *n* En
De Konus *(m)*
Es bisel *(m)*
Fr biseau *(m)*
It smusso *(m)*
Pt chanfro *(m)*

bewegliche Schrift *(f)*
   De
En movable type
Es tipos movibles *(m pl)*
Fr caractères mobiles
   (m pl)
It carattere mobile *(m)*
Pt tipo móvel *(m)*

Bezeichnung *(f) n* De
En term
Es término *(m)*
Fr terme *(m)*
It termine *(m)*
Pt termo *(m)*

Bezeichnungen *(pl)* De
En labels (on diagram) *pl
   n*
Es rótulos *(m pl)*
Fr étiquettes *(f pl)*
It etichette *(f pl)*
Pt legendas *(f pl)*

bianco alla base *(m)* It
De Kopf (type) *(m)*
En beard (of letter)
Es relieve *(m)*
Fr talus *(m)*
Pt relevo *(m)*

bianco trasparente *(m)* It
De Transparentweiß *(n)*
En transparent white
Es blanco transparente
   (m)
Fr blanc transparent *(m)*
Pt branco transparente
   (m)

bibbia *(f) n* It
De Bibel *(f)*
En bible
Es biblia *(f)*
Fr bible *(f)*
Pt bíblia *(f)*

Bibel *(f) n* De
En bible
Es biblia *(f)*
Fr bible *(f)*
It bibbia *(f)*
Pt bíblia *(f)*

Bibel(druck)papier *(n) n*
   De
En bible paper
Es papel biblia *(m)*
Fr papier bible *(m)*
It carta bibbia *(f)*
Pt papel bíblia *(m)*

bible *n* En; Fr *(f)*
De Bibel *(f)*
Es biblia *(f)*
It bibbia *(f)*
Pt bíblia *(f)*

bible paper En
De Bibel(druck)papier *(n)*
Es papel biblia *(m)*
Fr papier bible *(m)*
It carta bibbia *(f)*
Pt papel bíblia *(m)*

biblia *(f) n* Es
De Bibel *(f)*
En bible
Fr bible *(f)*
It bibbia *(f)*
Pt bíblia *(f)*

bíblia *(f) n* Pt
De Bibel *(f)*
En bible
Es biblia *(f)*
Fr bible *(f)*
It bibbia *(f)*

bibliografia *(f) n* It, Pt
De Literaturverzeichnis
   (n)
En bibliography
Es bibliografía *(f)*
Fr bibliographie *(f)*

bibliografía *(f) n* Es
De Literaturverzeichnis
   (n)
En bibliography
Fr bibliographie *(f)*
It bibliografia *(f)*
Pt bibliografia *(f)*

bibliographie *(f) n* Fr
De Literaturverzeichnis
   (n)
En bibliography
Es bibliografía *(f)*
It bibliografia *(f)*
Pt bibliografia *(f)*

bibliography *n* En
De Literaturverzeichnis
   (n)
Es bibliografía *(f)*
Fr bibliographie *(f)*
It bibliografia *(f)*
Pt bibliografia *(f)*

biblioteca *(f) n* Es, It, Pt
De Bibliothek *(f)*
En library
Fr bibliothèque *(f)*

biblioteca de colegio *(f)*
   Es
De Schulbücherei *(f)*

En school library
Fr bibliothèque scolaire
   (f)
It biblioteca scolastica
   (f)
Pt biblioteca escolar *(f)*

biblioteca de consulta
   (f) Es, Pt
De Nachschlagewerk-
   Bücherei *(f)*
En reference library
Fr bibliothèque
   d´ouvrages de
   référence *(f)*
It biblioteca di
   consultazione *(f)*

biblioteca de
   universidad *(f)* Es
De Universitätsbücherei
   (f)
En university library
Fr bibliothèque
   universitaire *(f)*
It biblioteca
   universitaria *(f)*
Pt biblioteca
   universitária *(f)*

biblioteca di
   consultazione *(f)* It
De Nachschlagewerk-
   Bücherei *(f)*
En reference library
Es biblioteca de
   consulta *(f)*
Fr bibliothèque
   d´ouvrages de
   référence *(f)*
Pt biblioteca de
   consulta *(f)*

biblioteca escolar *(f)* Pt
De Schulbücherei *(f)*
En school library
Es biblioteca de colegio
   (f)
Fr bibliothèque scolaire
   (f)
It biblioteca scolastica
   (f)

biblioteca pubblica *(f)* It
De öffentliche Bibliothek
   (f)
En public library
Es biblioteca pública *(f)*
Fr bibliothèque
   publique *(f)*
Pt biblioteca pública *(f)*

biblioteca pública *(f)* Es, Pt
De öffentliche Bibliothek *(f)*
En public library
Fr bibliothèque publique *(f)*
It biblioteca pubblica *(f)*

bibliotecario *(m) n* Es, It
De Bibliothekar *(m)*
En librarian
Fr bibliothécaire *(m/f)*
Pt bibliotecário *(m)*

bibliotecário *(m) n* Pt
De Bibliothekar *(m)*
En librarian
Es bibliotecario *(m)*
Fr bibliothécaire *(m/f)*
It bibliotecario *(m)*

biblioteca scolastica *(f)* It
De Schulbücherei *(f)*
En school library
Es biblioteca de colegio *(f)*
Fr bibliothèque scolaire *(f)*
Pt biblioteca escolar *(f)*

biblioteca universitaria *(f)* It
De Universitätsbücherei *(f)*
En university library
Es biblioteca de universidad *(f)*
Fr bibliothèque universitaire *(f)*
Pt biblioteca universitária *(f)*

biblioteca universitária *(f)* Pt
De Universitätsbücherei *(f)*
En university library
Es biblioteca de universidad *(f)*
Fr bibliothèque universitaire *(f)*
It biblioteca universitaria *(f)*

bibliothécaire *(m/f) n* Fr
De Bibliothekar *(m)*
En librarian
Es bibliotecario *(m)*
It bibliotecario *(m)*
Pt bibliotecário *(m)*

Bibliothek *(f) n* De
En library
Es biblioteca *(f)*
Fr bibliothèque *(f)*
It biblioteca *(f)*
Pt biblioteca *(f)*

Bibliothekar *(m) n* De
En librarian
Es bibliotecario *(m)*
Fr bibliothécaire *(m,'f)*
It bibliotecario *(m)*
Pt bibliotecário *(m)*

bibliothèque *(f) n* Fr
De Bibliothek *(f)*
En library
Es biblioteca *(f)*
It biblioteca *(f)*
Pt biblioteca *(f)*

bibliothèque d'ouvrages de référence *(f)* Fr
De Nachschlagewerk-Bücherei *(f)*
En reference library
Es biblioteca de consulta *(f)*
It biblioteca di consultazione *(f)*
Pt biblioteca de consulta *(f)*

bibliothèque publique *(f)* Fr
De öffentliche Bibliothek *(f)*
En public library
Es biblioteca pública *(f)*
It biblioteca pubblica *(f)*
Pt biblioteca pública *(f)*

bibliothèque scolaire *(f)* Fr
De Schulbücherei *(f)*
En school library
Es biblioteca de colegio *(f)*
It biblioteca scolastica *(f)*
Pt biblioteca escolar *(f)*

bibliothèque universitaire *(f)* Fr
De Universitätsbücherei *(f)*
En university library
Es biblioteca de universidad *(f)*
It biblioteca universitaria *(f)*
Pt biblioteca universitária *(f)*

bichromie *(f) n* Fr
Am two-color printing
De Zweifarbendruck *(m)*
En two-colour printing
Es impresión bicolor *(f)*
It stampa a due colori *(f)*
Pt impressão a duas cores *(f)*

bigliettino da visita *(m)* It
De Visitenkarte *(f)*
En business card
Es tarjeta comercial *(f)*
Fr carte de visite professionnelle *(f)*
Pt cartão de visita profissional *(m)*

bigotillo *(m) n* Es
De Serif *(m)*
En serif
Fr empâtement *(m)*
It terminazione *(f)*
Pt remate *(m)*

Bild *(n) n* De
En image; picture
Es imagen *(f)*
Fr dessin; image *(m f)*
It immagine; figura *(f)*
Pt imagem *(f)*

Bildschärfe *(f) n* De
En definition (photography)
Es claridad *(f)*
Fr netteté *(f)*
It nitidezza *(f)*
Pt nitidez *(f)*

Bildunterschrift *(f) n* De
En caption
Es encabezamiento *(m)*
Fr inscription *(f)*
It didascalia *(f)*
Pt epígrafe *(f)*

bilingual dictionary En
De zweisprachiges Wörterbuch *(n)*
Es diccionario bilingüe *(m)*
Fr dictionnaire bilingue *(m)*
It dizionario bilingue *(m)*
Pt biblioteca universitária *(f)*
Pt dicionário bilíngue *(m)*

bind *vb* En
De binden
Es encuadernar
Fr relier
It rilegare
Pt encadernar

Bindemaschine *(f) n* De
En binding machine
Es encuadernadora *(f)*
Fr machine à relier *(f)*
It macchina legatrice *(f)*
Pt encadernadora *(f)*

binden *vb* De
En bind
Es encuadernar
Fr relier
It rilegare
Pt encadernar

binder *n* En
De Buchbinder *(m)*
Es encuadernador *(m)*
Fr relieur *(m)*
It rilegatore *(m)*
Pt encadernador *(m)*

binder's dummy En
De Buchbinder-blindband *(n)*
Es molde de estampación *(m)*
Fr maquette de la reliure *(f)*
It menabò del rilegatore *(m)*
Pt maqueta de encadernação *(f)*

binder's tools En
De Buchbinder-Werkzeuge *(pl)*
Es herramientas de encuadernación *(f pl)*
Fr outils de reliure *(m pl)*
It attrezzi da rilegatore *(m pl)*
Pt ferramenta de encadernação *(f)*

bindery *n* En
De Buchbinderei *(f)*
Es taller de encuadernación *(f)*
Fr atelier de reliure *(m)*
It legatoria *(f)*

Pt oficina de
   encadernação (f)

Bindestrich (m) n De
En hyphen
Es guión (m)
Fr trait d'union (m)
It trattino di unione (m)
Pt traço de união (m)

binding machine En
De Bindemaschine (f)
Es encuadernadora (f)
Fr machine à relier (f)
It macchina legatrice (f)
Pt encadernadora (f)

biografia (f) n It, Pt
De Biographie (f)
En biography
Es biografía (f)
Fr biographie (f)

biografía (f) n Es
De Biographie (f)
En biography
Fr biographie (f)
It biografia (f)
Pt biografia (f)

biografo (m) n It
De Biograph (m)
En biographer
Es biógrafo (m)
Fr biographe (m)
Pt biógrafo (m)

biógrafo (m) n Es, Pt
De Biograph (m)
En biographer
Fr biographe (m)
It biografo (m)

Biograph (m) n De
En biographer
Es biógrafo (m)
Fr biographe (m)
It biografo (m)
Pt biógrafo (m)

biographe (m) n Fr
De Biograph (m)
En biographer
Es biógrafo (m)
It biografo (m)
Pt biógrafo (m)

biographer n En
De Biograph (m)
Es biógrafo (m)

Fr biographe (m)
It biografo (m)
Pt biógrafo (m)

biographical note En
De biographische
   Anmerkung (f)
Es nota biográfica (f)
Fr note biographique (f)
It nota biografica (f)
Pt nota biográfica (f)

biographie (f) n Fr
De Biographie (f)
En biography
Es biografía (f)
It biografia (f)
Pt biografia (f)

Biographie (f) n De
En biography
Es biografía (f)
Fr biographie (f)
It biografia (f)
Pt biografia (f)

**biographische
   Anmerkung** (f) De
En biographical note
Es nota biográfica (f)
Fr note biographique (f)
It nota biografica (f)
Pt nota biográfica (f)

biography n En
De Biographie (f)
Es biografía (f)
Fr biographie (f)
It biografia (f)
Pt biografia (f)

biseau (m) n Fr
De Konus (m)
En bevel
Es bisel (m)
It smusso (m)
Pt chanfro (m)

bisel (m) n Es
De Konus (m)
En bevel
Fr biseau (m)
It smusso (m)
Pt chanfro (m)

bisturí (m) n Pt
De Skalpell (n)
En scalpel
Es escalpelo (m)
Fr scalpel (m)

It bisturi ad un solo
   taglio (m)

bisturi ad un solo taglio
   (m) It
De Skalpell (n)
En scalpel
Es escalpelo (m)
Fr scalpel (m)
Pt bisturí (m)

bite (platemaking) n En
De Atzphase (f)
Es mordido (m)
Fr larron (m)
It acidatura (f)
Pt mordente (m)

black (trade unionism) vb
   En
De boykottieren
Es boicotear
Fr boycotter
It boicottare
Pt boicotar

**black-and-white
   illustration** En
De Schwarzweiß-
   illustration (f)
Es ilustración en blanco
   y negro (f)
Fr illustration en noir et
   blanc (f)
It illustrazione in bianco
   e nero (f)
Pt ilustração a branco e
   negro (f)

black plate En
De Schwarzplatte (f)
Es plancha negra (f)
Fr cliché en noir (m)
It lastra nera (f)
Pt chapa preta (f)

blanchiment (m) n Fr
De Bleichen (n)
En bleaching
Es blanqueo (m)
It imbianchimento (m)
Pt branqueamento (m)

blanco (m) n Es
De Seitekopf (m)
En head (of page)
Fr tête (f)
It testata (f)
Pt cabeçalho (m)

blancos (m pl) Es
De Lichter (pl)
En highlights pl n
Fr grandes lumières (f
   pl)
It alte luci (f pl)
Pt partes claras (f pl)

blanco transparente (m)
   Es
De Transparentweiß (n)
En transparent white
Fr blanc transparent (m)
It bianco trasparente
   (m)
Pt branco transparente
   (m)

blanc transparent (m) Fr
De Transparentweiß (n)
En transparent white
Es blanco transparente
   (m)
It bianco trasparente
   (m)
Pt branco transparente
   (m)

blanket (offset litho) n En
De Drucktuch (n)
Es mantilla (f)
Fr décharge (f)
It caucciù (m): tessuto
   gommato (m)
Pt feltro (m)

blank page En
De Vakantseite (f)
Es página en blanco (f)
Fr page blanche (f)
It pagina bianca (f)
Pt página em branco (f)

blanqueo (m) n Es
De Bleichen (n)
En bleaching
Fr blanchiment (m)
It imbianchimento (m)
Pt branqueamento (m)

Blatt (n) n De
En leaf
Es hoja (f)
Fr feuillet (m)
It foglio (m)
Pt folha (f)

blaue Linien (pl) De
En feints pl n
Es rayas en azul (f pl)

Fr règles en bleu clair *(f pl)*
It righi finti *(m pl)*
Pt linhas pautadas a azul-claro *(f pl)*

Blaupause *(f) n* De
En blueprint
Es cianotipo *(m)*
Fr bleu *(m)*
It cianografia *(f)*
Pt cianotipo *(m)*

bleaching *n* En
De Bleichen *(n)*
Es blanqueo *(m)*
Fr blanchiment *(m)*
It imbianchimento *(m)*
Pt branqueamento *(m)*

bleed *vb* En
De randlos drucken
Es correrse la tinta
Fr rogner
It refilare
Pt ressumbrar

Blei *(n) n* De
En lead (metal)
Es plomo *(m)*
Fr plomb *(m)*
It piombo *(m)*
Pt chumbo *(m)*

Bleichen *(n) n* De
En bleaching
Es blanqueo *(m)*
Fr blanchiment *(m)*
It imbianchimento *(m)*
Pt branqueamento *(m)*

Bleiform *(f) n* De
Am lead mold
En lead mould
Es molde de plomo *(m)*
Fr empreinte sur plomb *(f)*
It stampo di piombo *(m)*
Pt molde de chumbo *(m)*

Bleistiftzeichnung *(f) n* De
En pencil drawing
Es dibujo a lápiz *(m)*
Fr dessin au crayon *(m)*
It disegno a matita *(m)*
Pt desenho a lápis *(m)*

blemish *n* En
De Fehler *(m)*
Es imperfección *(f)*
Fr défaut *(m)*
It imperfezione *(f)*
Pt mancha *(f)*

bleu *(m) n* Fr
De Blaupause *(f)*
En blueprint
Es cianotipo *(m)*
It cianografia *(f)*
Pt cianotipo *(m)*

bleu d'impression couleur *(m)* Fr
De Verfahrensblau *(n)*
En process blue
Es azul de tricromía *(m)*
It azzurro di tricromia *(m)*
Pt azul para policromia *(m)*

Blindband *(m) n* De
En dummy; mock-up
Es maqueta *(f)*
Fr maquette *(f)*
It menabò *(m)*
Pt maquete *(f)*

Blindbearbeitung *(f) n* De
En blind finishing
Es acabado en seco *(m)*
Fr gaufrage à sec *(m)*
It finitura cieca *(f)*
Pt acabamento cego *(m)*

blind embossing En
De Blindprägung *(f)*
Es gofrado *(m)*
Fr dorure à froid *(f)*
It goffratura cieca *(f)*
Pt gravação em alto relevo cego *(f)*

blind finishing En
De Blindbearbeitung *(f)*
Es acabado en seco *(m)*
Fr gaufrage à sec *(m)*
It finitura cieca *(f)*
Pt acabamento cego *(m)*

blind keyboard En
De Blindtastatur *(f)*
Es teclado ciego *(m)*
Fr clavier aveugle *(m)*

It tastiera cieca *(f)*
Pt teclado cego *(m)*

Blindprägung *(f) n* De
En blind embossing
Es gofrado *(m)*
Fr dorure à froid *(f)*
It goffratura cieca *(f)*
Pt gravação em alto relevo cego *(f)*

Blindtastatur *(f) n* De
En blind keyboard
Es teclado ciego *(m)*
Fr clavier aveugle *(m)*
It tastiera cieca *(f)*
Pt teclado cego *(m)*

blister (on paper) *n* En
De Schnalle *(f)*
Es ampolla *(f)*
Fr cloque *(f)*
It bolla *(f)*
Pt bolha *(f)*

block *n* En
De Klischee *(n)*
Es placa impresora *(f)*
Fr cliché *(m)*
It cliché *(m)*
Pt cliché *(f)*

blocking out En
De Abdecken *(n)*
Es enmienda con sobreimpresión *(f)*
Fr oblitération *(f)*
It mascheratura con vernice coprente *(f)*
Pt cobrimento *(m)*

blockmaker *n* En
De Klischeeanstalt *(f)*
Es grabador *(m)*
Fr photograveur *(m)*
It zincografo *(m)*
Pt gravador *(m)*

blocos de vinheta *(m pl)* Pt
De Gelegenheitsvignetta *(f)*
En vignetted blocks *pl n*
Es fotograbados esfumados *(m pl)*
Fr simili dégradée *(f)*
It clichés à vignette *(m pl)*

blocos duplicados *(m pl)* Pt
De Duplikatklischees *(pl)*
En duplicate blocks *pl n*
Es bloques duplicados *(m pl)*
Fr cliché en double *(m)*
It cliché duplicati *(m pl)*

bloques duplicados *(m pl)* Es
De Duplikatklischees *(pl)*
En duplicate blocks *pl n*
Fr cliché en double *(m)*
It cliché duplicati *(m pl)*
Pt blocos duplicados *(m pl)*

blotting paper En
De Löschpapier *(n)*
Es papel secante *(m)*
Fr papier buvard *(m)*
It carta assorbente *(f)*
Pt papel mataborrão *(m)*

blown up En
De vergrößert
Es ampliado
Fr agrandi
It ingrandito
Pt ampliado

blueprint *n* En
De Blaupause *(f)*
Es cianotipo *(m)*
Fr bleu *(m)*
It cianografia *(f)*
Pt cianotipo *(m)*

Blumenornament *(n) n* De
En fleuron
Es florón *(m)*
Fr fleuron *(m)*
It fleuron *(m)*
Pt floreta *(f)*

blurb *n* En
De Reklamestreifen *(m)*
Es bombo *(m)*
Fr manchette publicitaire *(f)*
It soffietto editoriale *(m)*
Pt sinopse *(f)*

blurred edges En
De unscharfe Kanten *(pl)*
Es bordes borrosos *(m pl)*
Fr bords abîmés *(m pl)*

It   bordi sfocati *(m pl)*
Pt   bordos borrados *(m pl)*

board-glazed paper En
De   kartoniertes Glanzpapier *(n)*
Es   papel satinado *(m)*
Fr   papier satiné *(m)*
It   cartone satinato *(m)*
Pt   papel acetinado *(m)*

board of directors En
De   Vorstand *(m)*
Es   consejo de administración *(m)*
Fr   direction générale *(f)*
It   comitato direttivo *(m)*
Pt   conselho de administração *(m)*

bobina *(f) n* Es, It, Pt
De   Spule *(f)*
En   reel
Fr   bobine *(f)*

bobine *(f) n* Fr
De   Spule *(f)*
En   reel
Es   bobina *(f)*
It   bobina *(f)*
Pt   bobina *(f)*

bocaxim *(m) n* Pt
De   Buckram *(m)*
En   buckram
Es   bucarán *(m)*
Fr   bougran *(m)*
It   tela da fusto *(f)*

boceto *(m) n* Es
De   Skizze *(f)*
En   rough
Fr   croquis *(m)*
It   abbozzo *(m)*
Pt   esboço *(m)*

body size (of type) En
De   Kegelgröße *(f)*
Es   tamaño del tipo *(m)*
Fr   corps d´un caractère *(m)*
It   corpo del carattere *(m)*
Pt   tamanho de corpo *(m)*

Bogendruck *(m)* De
En   sheet-fed printing
Es   impresión de hojas *(f)*

Fr   impression à machine à feuilles *(f)*
It   stampa a fogli *(f)*
Pt   impressão de folhas *(f)*

bogenkalander-bearbeitetes Papier *(n)* De
En   plate-finished paper
Es   papel satinado a plancha *(m)*
Fr   papier laminé à la plaque *(m)*
It   carta rifinita *(f)*
Pt   papel lustrado à prancha *(m)*

boicotar *vb* Pt
De   boykottieren
En   black (trade unionism)
Es   boicotear
Fr   boycotter
It   boicottare

boicotear *vb* Es
De   boykottieren
En   black (trade unionism)
Fr   boycotter
It   boicottare
Pt   boicotar

boicottare *vb* It
De   boykottieren
En   black (trade unionism)
Es   boicotear
Fr   boycotter
Pt   boicotar

boîte lumineuse *(f)* Fr
De   Leuchtkasten *(m)*
En   light box
Es   caja de luz *(f)*
It   cassa luminosa *(f)*
Pt   caixa de luz *(f)*

bold *adj* En
De   fett
Es   negrita
Fr   mi-gras
It   neretto
Pt   negrito

boldface type En
De   fetter Schrifttyp *(m)*
Es   tipo negrilla *(m)*
Fr   caractères gras *(m pl)*

It   carattere in neretto *(m)*
Pt   tipo cheio *(m)*

boletín informativo *(m)* Es
De   Presseveröffentlichung *(f)*
En   press release
Fr   communiqué de presse *(m)*
It   comunicato stampa *(m)*
Pt   comunicado de imprensa *(f)*

bolha *(f) n* Pt
De   Schnalle *(f)*
En   blister (on paper)
Es   ampolla *(f)*
Fr   cloque *(f)*
It   bolla *(f)*

bolla *(f) n* It
De   Schnalle *(f)*
En   blister (on paper)
Es   ampolla *(f)*
Fr   cloque *(f)*
Pt   bolha *(f)*

bombo *(m) n* Es
De   Reklamestreifen *(m)*
En   blurb
Fr   manchette publicitaire *(f)*
It   soffietto editoriale *(m)*
Pt   sinopse *(f)*

bon à tirer *(m)* Fr
De   letzte Korrektur *(f)*
En   press proof
Es   prueba de prensa *(f)*
It   bozza di stampa *(f)*
Pt   prova de imprensa *(f)*

bonded ink En
De   gebundene Farbe *(f)*
Es   tinta adherida *(f)*
Fr   encre liée *(f)*
It   inchiostro aderente *(m)*
Pt   tinta aglutinada *(f)*

bond paper En
De   Schreibmaschinenpapier *(n)*
Es   papel bond *(m)*
Fr   papier coquille *(m)*
It   carta bond *(f)*
Pt   papel bond *(m)*

bonnes feuilles *(f pl)* Fr
De   Aushängebogen *(pl)*
En   advance sheets *pl n*
Es   hojas por adelantado *(f pl)*
It   fogli in anticipo *(m pl)*
Pt   folhas tipográficas *(f pl)*

bon usage *(m)* Fr
De   Formalgebrauch *(m)*
En   formal usage
Es   uso formal *(m)*
It   uso formale *(m)*
Pt   utilização formal *(f)*

book *n* En
De   Buch *(n)*
Es   libro *(m)*
Fr   livre *(m)*
It   libro *(m)*
Pt   livro *(m)*

bookbinding *n* En
De   Buchbinden *(n)*
Es   encuadernación de libros *(f)*
Fr   reliure *(f)*
It   rilegatura *(f)*
Pt   encadernação *(f)*

book club En
De   Buchclub *(m)*
Es   club del libro *(m)*
Fr   club du livre *(m)*
It   club del libro *(m)*
Pt   clube de leitores *(m)*

book-club edition En
De   Buchclub-Auflage *(f)*
Es   edición de club del libro *(f)*
Fr   édition club du livre *(f)*
It   edizione club del libro *(f)*
Pt   edição de club de leitores *(f)*

book fair En
De   Büchermesse *(f)*
Es   feria del libro *(f)*
Fr   foire du livre *(f)*
It   fiera del libro *(m)*
Pt   feira do livro *(f)*

booklet *n* En
De   Heft *(n)*
Es   opúsculo *(m)*
Fr   plaquette *(f)*

It libretto *(m)*
Pt folheto *(m)*

bookplate *n* En
De Bücherzeichen *(n)*
Es ex libris *(m)*
Fr ex-libris *(m)*
It ex-libris *(m)*
Pt ex-libris *(m)*

bookseller *n* En
De Buchhändler *(m)*
Es vendedor de libros *(m)*
Fr libraire *(m)*
It libraio *(m)*
Pt livreiro *(m)*

bookselling *n* En
De Buchverkauf *(m)*
Es venta de libros *(f)*
Fr commerce de librairie *(m)*
It vendita di libri *(f)*
Pt venda de livros *(f)*

book shop En
De Buchladen *(m)*
Es librería *(f)*
Fr librairie *(f)*
It libreria *(f)*
Pt livraria *(f)*

book sizes *pl n* En
De Büchergrößen *(pl)*
Es tamaños de libros *(m pl)*
Fr formats des livres *(m pl)*
It formati di libri *(m pl)*
Pt formatos de livros *(m pl)*

book trade En
De Buchhandel *(m)*
Es comercio del libro *(m)*
Fr commerce des livres *(m)*
It commercio librario *(m)*
Pt comércio de livros *(m)*

bordas *(f pl)* Pt
De Anschlusstücke *(pl)*
En borders *pl n*
Es marcos *(m pl)*
Fr vignettes *(f pl)*
It margini *(m pl)*

borders *pl n* En
De Anschlußstücke *(pl)*
Es marcos *(m pl)*
Fr vignettes *(f pl)*
It margini *(m pl)*
Pt bordas *(f pl)*

bordes borrosos *(m pl)* Es
De unscharfe Kanten *(pl)*
En blurred edges
Fr bords abîmés *(m pl)*
It bordi sfocati *(m pl)*
Pt bordos borrados *(m pl)*

bordi sfocati *(m pl)* It
De unscharfe Kanten *(pl)*
En blurred edges
Es bordes borrosos *(m pl)*
Fr bords abîmés *(m pl)*
Pt bordos borrados *(m pl)*

bordo anteriore *(m)* It
De Schnitt *(m)*
En fore edge
Es canto *(m)*
Fr gouttière *(f)*
Pt canto dianteiro *(m)*

bordos borrados *(m pl)* Pt
De unscharfe Kanten *(pl)*
En blurred edges
Es bordes borrosos *(m pl)*
Fr bords abîmés *(m pl)*
It bordi sfocati *(m pl)*

bordos de entrada *(m pl)* Pt
De Anlagekanten *(pl)*
En feed edges *pl n*
Es orillas de entrada *(f pl)*
Fr côté des marges *(m)*
It margini di entrata *(m pl)*

bords abîmés *(m pl)* Fr
De unscharfe Kanten *(pl)*
En blurred edges
Es bordes borrosos *(m pl)*
It bordi sfocati *(m pl)*
Pt bordos borrados *(m pl)*

borrador *(m)* n Es
De Entwurf *(m)*
En draft
Fr ébauche *(f)*
It minuta *(f)*
Pt rascunho *(m)*

borrar *vb* Es
De löschen
En erase
Fr effacer
It cassare
Pt apagar

bougran *(m)* n Fr
De Buckram *(m)*
En buckram
Es bucarán *(m)*
It tela da fusto *(f)*
Pt bocaxim *(m)*

bound books En
De gebundene Bücher *(pl)*
Es libros encuadernados *(m pl)*
Fr livres reliés *(m pl)*
It libri rilegati *(m pl)*
Pt livros encadernados *(m pl)*

boutique *(f)* n Fr
De Laden *(m)*
En shop (retail)
Es tienda *(f)*
It negozio *(m)*
Pt loja *(f)*

box rule En
De Linieneinfassung *(f)*
Es filete de marco *(m)*
Fr filet d'encadrement latéral *(m)*
It filleto di cornice *(m)*
Pt filete de requadro *(m)*

boycotter *vb* Fr
De boykottieren
En black (trade unionism)
Es boicotear
It boicottare
Pt boicotar

boykottieren *vb* De
En black (trade unionism)
Es boicotear
Fr boycotter
It boicottare
Pt boicotar

bozza *(f)* n It
De Abzug *(m)*
En proof
Es prueba *(f)*
Fr épreuve *(f)*
Pt prova *(f)*

bozza a colori *(f)* It
Am color proof
De Farbabzug *(m)*
En colour proof
Es prueba en colores *(f)*
Fr épreuve couleurs *(f)*
Pt prova a cores *(f)*

bozza dell'autore *(f)* It
De Autor-Korrekturabzug *(m)*
En author's proof
Es prueba de autor *(f)*
Fr épreuve d'auteur *(f)*
Pt prova do autor *(f)*

bozza di stampa *(f)* It
De letzte Korrektur *(f)*
En press proof
Es prueba de prensa *(f)*
Fr bon à tirer *(m)*
Pt prova de imprensa *(f)*

bozza impaginata *(f)* It
De Korrektur *(f)*
En page proof
Es prueba de página *(f)*
Fr épreuve en pages *(f)*
Pt prova de página *(f)*

bozza in colonna *(f)* It
De Korrekturfahne *(f)*
En galley proof
Es prueba de galeradas *(f)*
Fr épreuve en placard *(f)*
Pt prova de galé *(f)*

bozza nitida *(f)* It
De sauberer Abzug *(m)*
En clean proof
Es prueba limpia *(f)*
Fr épreuve au net *(f)*
Pt prova limpa *(f)*

bozze corrette *(f pl)* It
De revidierter Abzug *(m)*
En revised proofs
Es pruebas corregidas *(f pl)*
Fr épreuves de révision *(f pl)*
Pt provas revistas *(f pl)*

bozze progressive *(f pl)*
It
De Farbandrucke *(pl)*
En progressive proofs
Es pruebas de gama *(f pl)*
Fr épreuves-gammes *(f pl)*
Pt provas progressivas *(f pl)*

branco transparente *(m)*
Pt
De Transparentweiß *(n)*
En transparent white
Es blanco transparente *(m)*
Fr blanc transparent *(m)*
It bianco trasparente *(m)*

branqueamento *(m) n* Pt
De Bleichen *(n)*
En bleaching
Es blanqueo *(m)*
Fr blanchiment *(m)*
It imbianchimento *(m)*

brass (binder's) *n* En
De Messingreglette *(f)*
Es latón *(m)*
Fr laiton *(m)*
It ottone *(m)*
Pt latão *(m)*

brayer *n* En
De Farbreiber *(m)*
Es rodillo batidor *(m)*
Fr rouleau à main *(m)*
It rullo inchiostratore a mano *(m)*
Pt rolo de mão *(m)*

breach of contract En
De Vertragsbruch *(m)*
Es incumplimiento de contrato *(m)*
Fr rupture de contrat *(f)*
It violazione di contratto *(f)*
Pt quebra de contrato *(f)*

break-even point En
De Nutzschwelle *(f)*
Es punto de equilibrio *(m)*
Fr seuil de rentabilité *(m)*
It punto di pareggio *(m)*
Pt ponto de equilíbrio *(m)*

breaking strength (of paper) En
De Reißfestigkeit *(f)*
Es resistencia a la rotura *(f)*
Fr résistance à la rupture *(f)*
It resistenza allo sfilacciamento *(f)*
Pt resistência à rotura *(f)*

breiter Schrifttyp *(m)* De
En expanded typeface
Es tipo de ojo ancho *(m)*
Fr oeil plus grand que la normale *(m)*
It carattere largo (m)
Pt tipo de olho largo *(m)*

Briefpapier *(n) n* De
En stationery
Es efectos de escritorio *(m pl)*
Fr papeterie de détail *(f)*
It cartoleria *(f)*
Pt papel e artigos de escritório *(m)*

Briefpapier-Binden *(n)* De
En stationery binding
Es acuñado de material de escritorio *(m)*
Fr reliure papeterie *(f)*
It rilegatura da cartoleria *(f)*
Pt encadernação para escritório *(f)*

Briticism *n* En
De Anglizismus *(m)*
Es anglicismo *(m)*
Fr anglicisme *(m)*
It anglicismo *(m)*
Pt briticismo *(m)*

briticismo *(m) n* Pt
De Anglizismus *(m)*
En Briticism
Es anglicismo *(m)*
Fr anglicisme *(m)*
It anglicismo *(m)*

britischer Sprachgebrauch *(m)* De
En British usage
Es uso británico *(m)*
Fr usage anglais *(m)*
It uso britannico *(m)*
Pt costume británico *(m)*

britische Schreibweise *(f)* De
En British spelling
Es deletreo británico *(m)*
Fr orthographe anglaise *(f)*
It ortografia britannica *(f)*
Pt ortografia britânica *(f)*

British spelling En
De britische Schreibweise *(f)*
Es deletreo británico *(m)*
Fr orthographe anglaise *(f)*
It ortografia britannica *(f)*
Pt ortografia britânica *(f)*

British usage En
De britischer Sprachgebrauch *(m)*
Es uso británico *(m)*
Fr usage anglais *(m)*
It uso britannico *(m)*
Pt costume británico *(m)*

brochura *(f) n* Pt
De Broschüre *(f)*
En brochure
Es folleto *(m)*
Fr brochure *(f)*
It opuscolo *(m)*

brochure *n* En; Fr *(f)*
De Broschüre *(f)*
Es folleto *(m)*
It opuscolo *(m)*
Pt brochura *(f)*

broke (papermaking) *n* En
De Defektbogen *(m)*
Es papel roto *(m)*
Fr cassés *(m pl)*
It cascame di carta *(m)*
Pt empastelado *(m)*

brometo *(m) n* Pt
De Bromsilberabzug *(m)*
En bromide
Es bromuro *(m)*
Fr papier au bromure *(m)*
It copia al bromuro *(f)*

bromide *n* En
De Bromsilberabzug *(m)*
Es bromuro *(m)*

Fr papier au bromure *(m)*
It copia al bromuro *(f)*
Pt brometo *(m)*

Bromsilberabzug *(m) n* De
En bromide
Es bromuro *(m)*
Fr papier au bromure *(m)*
It copia al bromuro *(f)*
Pt brometo *(m)*

bromuro *(m) n* Es
De Bromsilberabzug *(m)*
En bromide
Fr papier au bromure *(m)*
It copia al bromuro *(f)*
Pt brometo *(m)*

bronceado *(m) n* Es
De Bronzieren *(n)*
En bronzing (printing)
Fr métallisation *(f)*
It bronzatura *(f)*
Pt bronzeamento *(m)*

bronzatura *(f) n* It
De Bronzieren *(n)*
En bronzing (printing)
Es bronceado *(m)*
Fr métallisation *(f)*
Pt bronzeamento *(m)*

bronzeamento *(m) n* Pt
De Bronzieren *(n)*
En bronzing (printing)
Es bronceado *(m)*
Fr métallisation *(f)*
It bronzatura *(f)*

Bronzedrucktinten *(pl)* De
En metallic inks
Es tintas metálicas *(f pl)*
Fr encres métalliques *(f pl)*
It inchiostri metallici *(m pl)*
Pt tintas metálicas *(f pl)*

Bronzieren *(n) n* De
En bronzing (printing)
Es bronceado *(m)*
Fr métallisation *(f)*
It bronzatura *(f)*
Pt bronzeamento *(m)*

bronzing (printing) *n* En
De Bronzieren *(n)*
Es bronceado *(m)*
Fr métallisation *(f)*
It bronzatura *(f)*
Pt bronzeamento *(m)*

Broschüre *(f) n* De
En brochure
Es folleto *(m)*
Fr brochure *(f)*
It opuscolo *(m)*
Pt brochura *(f)*

brunissage *(m) n* Fr
De Polieren *(n)*
En burnishing
Es fileteado *(m)*
It brunitura *(f)*
Pt lustro *(m)*

brunitura *(f) n* It
De Polieren *(n)*
En burnishing
Es fileteado *(m)*
Fr brunissage *(m)*
Pt lustro *(m)*

brush-coated paper En
De bürstengestrichenes
Papier *(n)*
Es papel estucado a
brocha *(m)*
Fr papier couché à la
brosse *(m)*
It carta coperta a
spazzola *(f)*
Pt papel revestido com
pincel *(m)*

bucarán *(m) n* Es
De Buckram *(m)*
En buckram
Fr bougran *(m)*
It tela da fusto *(f)*
Pt bocaxim *(m)*

Buch *(n) n* De
En book
Es libro *(m)*
Fr livre *(m)*
It libro *(m)*
Pt livro *(m)*

Buch (25 Bogen) *(n) n* De
En quire
Es mano de papel *(f)*
Fr main de papier *(f)*
It mazzetta di 24 fogli
(f)
Pt caderno de papel *(f)*

**Buchband mit engem
  Lederrücken** *(n)* De
En quarter-bound book
Es libro encuadernado a
cuarta piel *(m)*
Fr demi-reliure *(f)*
It libro rilegato con
dorso in pelle *(m)*
Pt livro in quarto *(m)*

Buchbinden *(n) n* De
En bookbinding
Es encuadernación de
libros *(f)*
Fr reliure *(f)*
It rilegatura *(f)*
Pt encadernação *(f)*

Buchbinder *(m) n* De
En binder
Es encuadernador *(m)*
Fr relieur *(m)*
It rilegatore *(m)*
Pt encadernador *(m)*

Buchbinder-blindband
  (n) De
En binder's dummy
Es molde de
estampación *(m)*
Fr maquette de la
reliure *(f)*
It menabò del
rilegatore *(m)*
Pt maqueta de
encadernação *(f)*

Buchbinderei *(f) n* De
En bindery
Es taller de
encuadernación *(f)*
Fr atelier de reliure *(m)*
It legatoria *(f)*
Pt oficina de
encadernação *(f)*

Buchbinder-Werkzeuge
  (pl) De
En binder's tools
Es herramientas de
encuadernación *(f pl)*
Fr outils de reliure *(m pl)*
It attrezzi da rilegatore
(m pl)
Pt ferramenta de
encadernação *(f)*

Buchclub *(m) n* De
En book club
Es club del libro *(m)*
Fr club du livre *(m)*

It club del libro *(m)*
Pt clube de leitores *(m)*

Buchclub-Auflage *(f)* De
En book-club edition
Es edición de club del
libro *(f)*
Fr édition club du livre
(f)
It edizione club del libro
(f)
Pt edição de club de
leitores *(f)*

Buchdeckel *(m) n* De
En case (bookbinding)
Es tapas *(f)*
Fr couverture *(f)*
It custodia *(f)*
Pt capa separada *(f)*

Buchdruck *(m) n* De
En letterpress printing
Es impresión tipográfica
(f)
Fr impression
typographique *(f)*
It stampa tipografica *(f)*
Pt impressão tipográfica
(f)

Buchdruck-Binden *(n)*
  De
En letterpress binding
Es acuñado tipográfico
(m)
Fr reliure imprimerie *(f)*
It legatura da tipografia
(f)
Pt encadernação
tipográfica *(f)*

Büchergrößen *(pl)* De
En book sizes *pl n*
Es tamaños de libros *(m
pl)*
Fr formats des livres *(m
pl)*
It formati di libri *(m pl)*
Pt formatos de livros *(m
pl)*

Büchermesse *(f) n* De
En book fair
Es feria del libro *(f)*
Fr foire du livre *(f)*
It fiera del libro *(m)*
Pt feira do livro *(f)*

Bücherzeichen *(n) n* De
En bookplate
Es ex libris *(m)*
Fr ex-libris *(m)*
It ex-libris *(m)*
Pt ex-libris *(m)*

Buchhandel *(m) n* De
En book trade
Es comercio del libro
(m)
Fr commerce des livres
(m)
It commercio librario
(m)
Pt comércio de livros
(m)

Buchhändler *(m) n* De
En bookseller
Es vendedor de libros
(m)
Fr libraire *(m)*
It libraio *(m)*
Pt livreiro *(m)*

Buchladen *(m) n* De
En book shop
Es librería *(f)*
Fr librairie *(f)*
It libreria *(f)*
Pt livraria *(f)*

**Buch mit
  Bibliothek-Einband**
  (n) De
En library-bound book
Es libro encuadernado
para biblioteca *(m)*
Fr reliure bibliothèque
publique *(f)*
It libro rilegato per
biblioteca *(m)*
Pt livro encadernado
para biblioteca *(m)*

**Buch mit festem
  Rücken** *(n)* De
En fixed back book
Es libro de lomo fijo *(m)*
Fr livre à dos fixe *(m)*
It libro a costa fissa *(m)*
Pt livro de lombada fixa
(m)

**Buch mit flachen
  Rücken** *(n)* De
En flat-back book
Es libro de lomo liso *(m)*
Fr livre à dos plat *(m)*
It libro a costa piatta
(m)

Pt livro de lombada
plana *(m)*

Buchrücken-Fütterung
(f) n De
En back lining
Es contralomo *(m)*
Fr garniture du dos *(f)*
It fodera di costa *(f)*
Pt forro de lombada *(m)*

Buchstabe *(m) n* De
En letter
Es letra *(f)*
Fr lettre *(f)*
It lettera *(f)*
Pt letra *(f)*

Buchstabenabstand *(m)*
n De
En letter spacing
Es espaciado entre
letras *(m)*
Fr espacement entre
caractère *(m)*
It spaziatura tra le
lettere *(f)*
Pt espaço entre letras
(m)

Buchstabenindex *(m) n*
De
En tab index
Es índice de pestañas
(m)
Fr index à touche *(m)*
It indice a striscettine
(m)
Pt índice de pestanas
(m)

Buchstaben-Oberlänge
(n pl) De
En ascenders (of letter)
pl n
Es palos altos *(m pl)*
Fr ascendantes *(f pl)*
It lettere ascendenti *(f
pl)*
Pt ascendentes *(f pl)*

Buchstabensatz *(m) n*
De
En character set
Es juego de caracteres
(m)
Fr jeu de caractères *(m)*
It gioco di caratteri *(m)*
Pt jogo de caracteres
(m)

buchstabieren *vb* De
En spell
Es deletrear
Fr épeler
It sillabare
Pt soletrar

Buchstabierung *(f) n* De
En spelling
Es deletreo *(m)*
Fr épellation *(f)*
It compitazione *(f)*
Pt soletração *(f)*

Buchverkauf *(m) n* De
En bookselling
Es venta de libros *(f)*
Fr commerce de
librairie *(f)*
It vendita di libri *(f)*
Pt venda de livros *(f)*

buckram *n* En
De Buckram *(m)*
Es bucarán *(m)*
Fr bougran *(m)*
It tela da fusto *(f)*
Pt bocaxim *(m)*

Buckram *(m) n* De
En buckram
Es bucarán *(m)*
Fr bougran *(m)*
It tela da fusto *(f)*
Pt bocaxim *(m)*

bulk (of paper) *n* En
De Papierdicke *(f)*
Es cuerpo de papel *(m)*
Fr épaisseur de papier
(m)
It grossezza di carta *(f)*
Pt grossura do papel *(f)*

bulk (of a book) *n* En
De Masse *(f)*
Es grueso de libro *(m)*
Fr épaisseur d'un livre
(f)
It grossezza del libro *(f)*
Pt espessura dum livro
(f)

bulked dummy En
De richtige dickes
Blindband *(n)*
Es maqueta realzada *(f)*
Fr maquette garnie *(f)*
It menabò di grossezza
preciso *(m)*

Pt maquete engrossada
(f)

bundling machine En
De Packmaschine *(f)*
Es prensadora-
embaladora de
pliegos *(f)*
Fr machine à emballer
(f)
It macchina per rotoli
(f)
Pt máquina de prensar e
formar fascículos *(f)*

burbujas *(f pl)* Es
De Nadellöcher *(pl)*
En pinholes *pl n*
Fr perforation des
négatifs *(f)*
It mancanza di densità
(f)
Pt furos *(m pl)*

burnishing *n* En
De Polieren *(n)*
Es fileteado *(m)*
Fr brunissage *(m)*
It brunitura *(f)*
Pt lustro *(m)*

bürstengestrichenes
Papier *(n)* De
En brush-coated paper
Es papel estucado a
brocha *(m)*
Fr papier couché à la
brosse *(m)*
It carta coperta a
spazzola *(f)*
Pt papel revestido com
pincel *(m)*

bursting strength En
De Berstwiderstand *(m)*
Es resistencia al
reventamiento *(f)*
Fr résistance à
l'éclatement *(f)*
It resistenza alla rottura
(f)
Pt resistência ao
arrebentamento *(f)*

business card En
De Visitenkarte *(f)*
Es tarjeta comercial *(f)*
Fr carte de visite
professionnelle *(f)*
It bigliettino da visita
(m)

Pt cartão de visita
profissional *(m)*

Büttenrand *(m) n* De
En deckle edge
Es barba *(f)*
Fr barbe *(f)*
It zazzera *(f)*
Pt barba *(f)*

Büttenwerkdruckpapier
(n) n De
Am mold-made paper
En mould-made paper
Es papel de tina *(m)*
Fr papier moyen âge
(m)
It carta formata a mano
(f)
Pt papel moldado *(m)*

C

cabeçalho *(m) n* Pt
De Seitekopf *(m)*
En head (of page)
Es blanco *(m)*
Fr tête *(f)*
It testata *(f)*

cabecera *(f) n* Es
De Kapitelband *(m)*
En headband
Fr tranchefile *(f)*
It capitello *(m)*
Pt friso *(m)*

caccia di notizie *(f)* It
De Zeitungsrahmen *(m)*
En news chase
Es rama de noticias *(f)*
Fr châssis à journal *(m)*
Pt rama de notícias *(f)*

caderno de papel *(f)* Pt
De Buch (25 Bogen) *(n)*
En quire
Es mano de papel *(f)*
Fr main de papier *(f)*
It mazzetta di 24 fogli
(f)

cadrat *(m)* *n* Fr
De Quadrat *(n)*
En quad
Es cuadrado *(m)*
It quadrato *(m)*
Pt quadrado *(m)*

cadratin *(m)* *n* Fr
De Geviert *(n)*
En em
Es cuadratín *(m)*
It riga *(f)*
Pt quadratim *(m)*

cahier *(m)* *n* Fr
De Druckbogen *(m)*
En section
Es pliego *(m)*
It sezione *(f)*
Pt secção *(f)*

caixa *(f)* *n* Pt
De Setzkasten *(m)*
En case (typesetting)
Es caja *(f)*
Fr casse *(f)*
It cassa tipografica *(f)*

caixa alta *(f)* Pt
De Oberkasten *(m)*
En upper case
Es caja alta *(f)*
Fr haut de casse *(m)*
It alta cassa *(f)*

caixa baixa *(f)* Pt
De Unterkasten *(m)*
En lower case
Es caja baja *(f)*
Fr bas de caisse *(m)*
It bassa cassa *(f)*

caixa de luz *(f)* Pt
De Leuchtkasten *(m)*
En light box
Es caja de luz *(f)*
Fr boîte lumineuse *(f)*
It cassa luminosa *(f)*

caixilho de vácuo *(m)* Pt
De Vakuumrahmen *(m)*
En vacuum frame
Es prensa al vacío *(f)*
Fr chassis pneumatique *(m)*
It telaio a vuoto *(m)*

caja *(f)* *n* Es
De Setzkasten *(m)*
En case (typesetting)

Fr casse *(f)*
It cassa tipografica *(f)*
Pt caixa *(f)*

caja alta *(f)* Es
De Oberkasten *(m)*
En upper case
Fr haut de casse *(m)*
It alta cassa *(f)*
Pt caixa alta *(f)*

caja baja *(f)* Es
De Unterkasten *(m)*
En lower case
Fr bas de caisse *(m)*
It bassa cassa *(f)*
Pt caixa baixa *(f)*

caja de luz *(f)* Es
De Leuchtkasten *(m)*
En light box
Fr boîte lumineuse *(f)*
It cassa luminosa *(f)*
Pt caixa de luz *(f)*

calandra *(f)* *n* It, Pt
De Kalander *(m)*
En calender
Es calandria *(f)*
Fr calandre finisseuse *(f)*

calandratura a caldo *(f)* It
De Warmwalzen *(n)*
En hot rolling
Es entintado en caliente *(m)*
Fr laminage à chaud *(m)*
Pt laminação a quente *(f)*

calandre finisseuse *(f)* Fr
De Kalander *(m)*
En calender
Es calandria *(f)*
It calandra *(f)*
Pt calandra *(f)*

calandria *(f)* *n* Es
De Kalander *(m)*
En calender
Fr calandre finisseuse *(f)*
It calandra *(f)*
Pt calandra *(f)*

càlcário da Bavária *(m)* Pt
De Stein *(m)*
En stone (lithography)
Es piedra *(f)*

Fr pierre calcaire *(f)*
It pietra litografica *(f)*

calço *(m)* *n* Pt
De Unterlage *(f)*
En underlay
Es alza bajo el tipo *(f)*
Fr hausse *(f)*
It alzo *(m)*

calço de giz *(f)* Pt
De Kreidezurichten *(n)*
En chalk overlay
Es alza mecánica de tiza *(f)*
Fr papier baryté *(m)*
It carta gessata *(f)*

calculateur numérique *(m)* Fr
De Digitalcomputer *(m)*
En digital computer
Es ordenador digital *(m)*
It elaboratore digitale *(m)*
Pt computador digital *(m)*

calender *n* En
De Kalander *(m)*
Es calandria *(f)*
Fr calandre finisseuse *(f)*
It calandra *(f)*
Pt calandra *(f)*

calendered paper En
De kalandriertes Papier *(n)*
Es papel caladrando *(m)*
Fr papier calandré *(m)*
It carta calandrata *(f)*
Pt papel calandrado *(m)*

calendrier des parutions *(m)* Fr
Am publishing program
De Veröffentlichungs-programm *(n)*
En publishing programme
Es programa de publicaciones *(m)*
It programma editoriale *(m)*
Pt programa de edição *(m)*

calfbound *adj* En
De gebunden in Kalbleder

Es encuadernado en piel de becerro
Fr relié en veau
It rilegato in pelle
Pt encadernado a carneira

calibrar a composição Pt
De berechnen
En cast off
Es calibrar la composición
Fr calibrer un texte
It equilibrare la composizione

calibrar la composición Es
De berechnen
En cast off
Fr calibrer un texte
It equilibrare la composizione
Pt calibrar a composição

calibrer un texte Fr
De berechnen
En cast off
Es calibrar la composición
It equilibrare la composizione
Pt calibrar a composição

calle *(f)* *n* Es
De weiser Streifen im Satz *(m)*
En river
Fr rue *(f)*
It spaziatura difettosa *(f)*
Pt espaço defeituoso *(m)*

câmara de processamento *(f)* Pt
De Reproduktionsgerät *(n)*
En process camera
Es cámara fotomecánica *(f)*
Fr appareil photomécanique *(m)*
It macchina fotografica per riproduzioni fotomeccaniche *(f)*

câmara escura *(f)* Pt
De Dunkelkammer *(f)*
En darkroom
Es cuarto oscuro *(m)*
Fr chambre noire *(f)*
It camera oscura *(f)*

cámara fotomecánica *(f)*
Es
De Reproduktionsgerät *(n)*
En process camera
Fr appareil photomécanique *(m)*
It macchina fotografica per riproduzioni fotomeccaniche *(f)*
Pt câmara de processamento *(f)*

camera oscura *(f)* It
De Dunkelkammer *(f)*
En darkroom
Es cuarto oscuro *(m)*
Fr chambre noire *(f)*
Pt câmara escura *(f)*

camera-ready copy En
De kamerafertige Vorlage *(f)*
Es original preparado para la cámara *(m)*
Fr copie prête à photographier *(f)*
It copia pronta per fotografia *(f)*
Pt exemplar pronto para a máquina fotográfica *(m)*

camisa *(f) n* Es
De Umschlag *(m)*
En jacket
Fr jaquette *(f)*
It sovracopertina *(f)*
Pt sobrecapa *(f)*

campagna di vendita *(f)*
It
De Verkaufskampagne *(f)*
En sales campaign
Es campaña de ventas *(f)*
Fr campagne de vente *(f)*
Pt campanha comercial *(f)*

campagna promozionale *(f)* It
De Werbekampagne *(f)*

En promotional campaign
Es campaña de promoción *(f)*
Fr campagne publicitaire *(f)*
Pt campanha de promoção *(f)*

campagne de vente *(f)*
Fr
De Verkaufskampagne *(f)*
En sales campaign
Es campaña de ventas *(f)*
It campagna di vendita *(f)*
Pt campanha comercial *(f)*

campagne publicitaire *(f)* Fr
De Werbekampagne *(f)*
En promotional campaign
Es campaña de promoción *(f)*
It campagna promozionale *(f)*
Pt campanha de promoção *(f)*

campaña de promoción *(f)* Es
De Werbekampagne *(f)*
En promotional campaign
Fr campagne publicitaire *(f)*
It campagna promozionale *(f)*
Pt campanha de promoção *(f)*

campaña de ventas *(f)* Es
De Verkaufskampagne *(f)*
En sales campaign
Fr campagne de vente *(f)*
It campagna di vendita *(f)*
Pt campanha comercial *(f)*

campanha comercial *(f)*
Pt
De Verkaufskampagne *(f)*
En sales campaign
Es campaña de ventas *(f)*
Fr campagne de vente *(f)*

campagna di vendita *(f)*

campanha de promoção *(f)* Pt
De Werbekampagne *(f)*
En promotional campaign
Es campaña de promoción *(f)*
Fr campagne publicitaire *(f)*
It campagna promozionale *(f)*

campione *(m) n* It
De Muster *(n)*
En swatch
Es muestrario *(m)*
Fr échantillon *(m)*
Pt mostruário *(m)*

canal *(m) n* Es, Pt
De Kanal *(m)*
En channel
Fr rainure *(f)*
It canale *(m)*

canal de tinta *(m)* Pt
De Farbkanal *(m)*
En ink duct
Es tintero de la prensa *(m)*
Fr encrier *(m)*
It condotto per inchiostro *(m)*

canale *(m) n* It
De Kanal *(m)*
En channel
Es canal *(m)*
Fr rainure *(f)*
Pt canal *(m)*

cancellare *vb* It
De streichen
En delete
Es suprimir
Fr rayer
Pt apagar

cancellatura *(f) n* It
De Streichung *(f)*
En deletion
Es supresión *(f)*
Fr suppression *(f)*
Pt eliminação *(f)*

cancelled matter En
De gestrichener Text *(m)*
Es composición suprimida *(f)*
Fr texte annulé *(m)*
It testo annullato *(m)*
Pt matéria cancelada *(f)*

canto *(m) n* Es
De Schnitt *(m)*
En fore edge
Fr gouttière *(f)*
It bordo anteriore *(m)*
Pt canto dianteiro *(m)*

canto dianteiro *(m)* Pt
De Schnitt *(m)*
En fore edge
Es canto *(m)*
Fr gouttière *(f)*
It bordo anteriore *(m)*

canvas (bookbinders') *n*
En
De Mattgewebe *(n)*
Es lona *(f)*
Fr toile *(f)*
It tela *(f)*
Pt tela *(f)*

caolín *(m) n* Es
De Kaolin *(n)*
En china clay
Fr kaolin *(m)*
It caolino *(m)*
Pt caolino *(m)*

caolino *(m) n* It, Pt
De Kaolin *(n)*
En china clay
Es caolín *(m)*
Fr kaolin *(m)*

capa separada *(f)* Pt
De Buchdeckel *(m)*
En case (bookbinding)
Es tapas *(f)*
Fr couverture *(f)*
It custodia *(f)*

capitals (caps) *pl n* En
De Großbuchstaben *(pl)*
Es mayúsculas *(f pl)*
Fr majuscules *(f pl)*
It maiuscole *(f pl)*
Pt maiusculas *(f pl)*

capitello *(m) n* It
De Kapitelband *(m)*
En headband

Es cabecera *(f)*
Fr tranchefile *(f)*
Pt friso *(m)*

capitolo *(m) n* It
De Kapitel *(n)*
En chapter
Es capítulo *(m)*
Fr chapitre *(m)*
Pt capítulo *(m)*

capítulo *(m) n* Es, Pt
De Kapitel *(n)*
En chapter
Fr chapitre *(m)*
It capitolo *(m)*

capo redattore *(m)* It
De Betriebsredakteur
(m)
En managing editor
Es jefe de redacción *(m)*
Fr chef de la rédaction
(m)
Pt chefe de redacção
(m)

captação de dados *(f)* Pt
De Datenerfassung *(f)*
En data capture
Es toma de datos *(f)*
Fr saisie de données *(f)*
It cattura dei dati *(f)*

caption *n* En
De Bildunterschrift *(f)*
Es encabezamiento *(m)*
Fr inscription *(f)*
It didascalia *(f)*
Pt epígrafe *(f)*

carácter *(m) n* Es, Pt
De Schriftzeichen *(n)*
En character
Fr caractère *(m)*
It carattere *(m)*

carácter defeituoso *(m)*
Pt
De Defekt *(m)*
En battered type
Es carácter estropeo *(m)*
Fr caractère
endommagé *(m)*
It carattere avariato *(m)*

caractère *(m) n* Fr
De Schriftzeichen *(n)*
En character
Es carácter *(m)*

It carattere *(m)*
Pt carácter *(m)*

caractère antique (sans
empâtement) *(m)* Fr
De Grotesk-Schrifttyp
(m)
En sans-serif typeface
Es tipo sin remate *(m)*
It bastone *(m)*
Pt olho de tipo sem
remate *(m)*

**caractère de bas de
caisse** *(m)* Fr
De kleiner Buchstabe
(m)
En lower-case letter
Es minúscula *(f)*
It minuscola *(f)*
Pt minúscula *(f)*

caractère d'imprimerie
(m) Fr
De Schrift *(f)*
En type
Es tipo *(m)*
It carattere tipografico
(m)
Pt tipo *(m)*

caractère effilé *(m)* Fr
De schmaler Schrifttyp
(m)
En condensed typeface
Es tipo estrecho *(m)*
It carattere allungato
(m)
Pt estilo de tipo
condensado *(m)*

caractère endommagé
(m) Fr
De Defekt *(m)*
En battered type
Es carácter estropeo *(m)*
It carattere avariato *(m)*
Pt carácter defeituoso
(m)

caractère mi-gras *(m)* Fr
De halbfetter Satz *(m)*
En semi-bold type
Es seminegrilla *(f)*
It carattere
semi-grassetto *(m)*
Pt tipo semi-negro *(m)*

caractères conservés *(m
pl)* Fr
De guter Satz *(m)*

En standing type
Es composición
levantada *(f)*
It carattere eretto *(m)*
Pt composição
levantada *(f)*

caractères gras *(m pl)* Fr
De fetter Schrifttyp *(m)*
En boldface type
Es tipo negrilla *(m)*
It carattere in neretto
(m)
Pt tipo cheio *(m)*

caracteres inferiores *(m
pl)* Pt
De tiefstehende
Buchstaben *(pl)*
En inferior characters
Es subíndices *(m pl)*
Fr petites lettres
inférieures *(f pl)*
It caratteri inferiori *(m
pl)*

caractères mobiles *(m
pl)* Fr
De bewegliche Schrift *(f)*
En movable type
Es tipos movibles *(m pl)*
It carattere mobile *(m)*
Pt tipo móvel *(m)*

caracteres pi *(m pl)* Es,
Pt
De Handsatz-
Schrifttypen *(pl)*
En pi characters
Fr figures spéciales *(f pl)*
It caratteri pi *(m pl)*

caractères supérieurs
(m pl) Fr
De hochstehende
Buchstaben *(pl)*
En superior characters
Es exponentes *(m pl)*
It caratteri superiori *(m
pl)*
Pt caracteres superiores
(m pl)

caracteres superiores
(m pl) Pt
De hochstehende
Buchstaben *(pl)*
En superior characters
Es exponentes *(m pl)*
Fr caractères supérieurs
(m pl)

It caratteri superiori *(m
pl)*

carácter estropeo *(m)* Es
De Defekt *(m)*
En battered type
Fr caractère
endommagé *(m)*
It carattere avariato *(m)*
Pt carácter defeituoso
(m)

caractères vedettes *(m
pl)* Fr
De Auszeichnungssatz
(m)
En display type
Es tipos titulares *(m pl)*
It caratteri di titolo *(m
pl)*
Pt tipos de maiúscula
(m pl)

caractéristiques *(f pl) n*
Fr
De Spezifikation *(f)*
En specification
Es especificación *(f)*
It specifiche *(f pl)*
Pt especificação *(f)*

cara interior *(f)* Es
De Siebseite *(f)*
En wire side
Fr côté toilé *(m)*
It lato tela *(m)*
Pt lado da tela *(m)*

carattere *(m) n* It
De Schriftzeichen *(n)*
En character
Es carácter *(m)*
Fr caractère *(m)*
Pt carácter *(m)*

carattere allungato *(m)*
It
De schmaler Schrifttyp
(m)
En condensed typeface
Es tipo estrecho *(m)*
Fr caractère effilé *(m)*
Pt estilo de tipo
condensado *(m)*

carattere avariato *(m)* It
De Defekt *(m)*
En battered type
Es carácter estropeo *(m)*
Fr caractère
endommagé *(m)*

Pt carácter defeituoso
(m)

carattere elzeviro (m) It
De Mediäval (n)
En old face
Es estilo antiguo (m)
Fr elzévir (m)
Pt tipo de estilo antigo
(m)

carattere eretto (m) It
De guter Satz (m)
En standing type
Es composición
levantada (f)
Fr caractères conservés
(m pl)
Pt composição
levantada (f)

carattere in neretto (m)
It
De fetter Schrifttyp (m)
En boldface type
Es tipo negrilla (m)
Fr caractères gras (m pl)
Pt tipo cheio (m)

carattere largo (m) It
De breiter Schrifttyp (m)
En expanded typeface
Es tipo de ojo ancho (m)
Fr oeil plus grand que la
normale (m)
Pt tipo de olho largo (m)

carattere mobile (m) It
De bewegliche Schrift (f)
En movable type
Es tipos movibles (m pl)
Fr caractères mobiles
(m pl)
Pt tipo móvel (m)

carattere moderno (m) It
De moderner Schrifttyp
(m)
En modern face
Es tipo moderno (m)
Fr didone (f)
Pt olho moderno (m)

carattere romano tondo
(m) It
De römische Schrift (f)
En roman type
Es tipo redondo (m)
Fr romain (m)
Pt tipo romano (m)

carattere sbagliato (m) It
De falscher Schrifttyp
(m)
En wrong typeface
Es ojo de tipo incorrecto
(m)
Fr lettre d'un autre oeil
(f)
Pt olho de tipo errado
(m)

**carattere
semi-grassetto** (m)
It
De halbfetter Satz (m)
En semi-bold type
Es seminegrilla (f)
Fr caractère mi-gras (m)
Pt tipo semi-negro (m)

carattere tipografico (m)
n It
De Schrift (f)
En type
Es tipo (m)
Fr caractère
d'imprimerie (m)
Pt tipo (m)

caratteri corsivi (m pl) It
De Kursivdruck (m)
En italics pl n
Es cursivas (f pl)
Fr italiques (m pl)
Pt itálico (m)

caratteri di titolo (m pl)
It
De Auszeichnungssatz
(m)
En display type
Es tipos titulares (m pl)
Fr caractères vedettes
(m pl)
Pt tipos de maiúscula
(m pl)

caratteri inferiori (m pl)
It
De tiefstehende
Buchstaben (pl)
En inferior characters
Es subíndices (m pl)
Fr petites lettres
inférieures (f pl)
Pt caracteres inferiores
(m pl)

caratteri pi (m pl) It
De Handsatz-
Schrifttypen (pl)
En pi characters

Es caracteres pi (m pl)
Fr figures spéciales (f pl)
Pt caracteres pi (m pl)

caratteri superiori (m pl)
It
De hochstehende
Buchstaben (pl)
En superior characters
Es exponentes (m pl)
Fr caractères supérieurs
(m pl)
Pt caracteres superiores
(m pl)

carbon tissue En
De Ätzpigmentpapier (n)
Es papel pigmento (m)
Fr papier au carbone
(m)
It carta al carbone (f)
Pt tecido carbono (m)

cardboard n En
De Karton (m)
Es cartulina (f)
Fr carton (m)
It cartone (m)
Pt cartão (m)

caret mark En
De Auslassungszeichen
(n)
Es signo de
intercalación (m)
Fr renvoi de marge (m)
It segno di rimando (m)
Pt sinal de intercalar (m)

carga (f) n Pt
De Füllerstoff (m)
En filler
Es material de carga (m)
Fr charge (f)
It carica (f)

carica (f) n It
De Füllerstoff (m)
En filler
Es material de carga (m)
Fr charge (f)
Pt carga (f)

caricatore (m) n It
De Schriftlager (n)
En magazine (matrix
store)
Es depósito (m)
Fr magasin (m)
Pt depósito (m)

carta (f) n It
De Papier (n)
En paper
Es papel (m)
Fr papier (m)
Pt papel (m)

carta (f) n Pt
De Tabelle (f)
En chart
Es diagrama (m)
Fr diagramme (m)
It tabella (f)

carta a grana corta (f) It
De kurzkörniges Papier
(n)
En short-grain paper
Es papel de fibra corta
(m)
Fr papier à fibres
courtes (m)
Pt papel de grão curto
(m)

carta a grana lunga (f) It
De langkörniges Papier
(n)
En long-grain paper
Es papel plegado al hilo
(m)
Fr papier sens machine
sur longueur (m)
Pt papel de grão
comprido (m)

carta al carbone (f) It
De Ätzpigmentpapier (n)
En carbon tissue
Es papel pigmento (m)
Fr papier au carbone
(m)
Pt tecido carbono (m)

carta al cromo (f) It
De Chromopapier (n)
En chromo paper
Es papel para
cromolitografía (m)
Fr papier chromo (m)
Pt papel cromo (m)

carta altobrillante (f) It
De Gussgestrichenes
Papier (n)
En cast-coated paper
Es papel de respaldo
esmaltado (m)
Fr papier couché
chrome superbrillant
(m)

Pt papel estereotipado
 (m)

carta a mano *(f)* It
De Handbütten *(n)*
En handmade paper
Es papel hecho a mano
 (m)
Fr papier cuve *(m)*
Pt papel feito à mão *(m)*

carta assorbente *(f)* It
De Löschpapier *(n)*
En blotting paper
Es papel secante *(m)*
Fr papier buvard *(m)*
Pt papel mataborrão *(m)*

carta bibbia *(f)* It
De Bibel(druck)papier *(n)*
En bible paper
Es papel biblia *(m)*
Fr papier bible *(m)*
Pt papel bíblia *(m)*

carta bond *(f)* It
De Schreibmaschinen-
 papier *(n)*
En bond paper
Es papel bond *(m)*
Fr papier coquille *(m)*
Pt papel bond *(m)*

carta calandrata *(f)* It
De kalandriertes Papier
 (n)
En calendered paper
Es papel caladrando *(m)*
Fr papier calandré *(m)*
Pt papel calandrado *(m)*

carta colorata *(f)* It
De getöntes Papier *(n)*
En tinted paper
Es papel coloreado *(m)*
Fr papier de couleur *(m)*
Pt papel colorido *(m)*

carta coperta a spazzola
 (f) It
De bürstengestrichenes
 Papier *(n)*
En brush-coated paper
Es papel estucado a
 brocha *(m)*
Fr papier couché à la
 brosse *(m)*
Pt papel revestido com
 pincel *(m)*

carta da disegno *(f)* It
De Kartuschenpapier *(n)*
En cartridge paper
Es papel para cartuchos
 (m)
Fr papier cartouche *(m)*
Pt papel cartucho *(m)*

carta da giornale *(f)* It
De Rotationsdruckpapier
 (n)
En newsprint
Es papel periódico *(m)*
Fr papier-journal *(m)*
Pt papel para jornal *(m)*

carta da grafici *(f)* It
De Registrierpapier *(n)*
En chart paper
Es papel gráfico *(m)*
Fr papier pour
 graphiques *(m)*
Pt papel de mapa *(m)*

carta da lucidi *(f)* It
De Pauspapier *(n)*
En tracing paper
Es papel de calcar *(m)*
Fr papier calque *(m)*
Pt papel de cópia *(m)*

carta di cenci *(f)* It
De Vollhadernpapier *(n)*
En all-rag paper
Es papel de hilo puro
 (m)
Fr papier pur chiffon *(m)*
Pt papel inteiramente
 de trapos *(m)*

carta di stracci *(f)* It
De Hadernpapier *(n)*
En rag paper
Es papel de trapos *(m)*
Fr papier de chiffon *(m)*
Pt papel de trapos *(m)*

carta duplex *(f)* It
De Duplexpapier *(n)*
En duplex paper
Es cartón duplo *(m)*
Fr papier duplex *(m)*
Pt papel duplex *(m)*

**carta duplex con anima
 di tela** *(f)* It
Am cloth-centered paper
De Papier mit Stoffmitte
 (n)
En cloth-centred paper

Es papel duplex con
 alma de lino *(m)*
Fr papier entre deux
 toiles *(m)*
Pt papel centrado em
 tela *(m)*

carta finita a macchina
 (f) It
De maschinenglattes
 Papier *(n)*
En machine-finished
 paper
Es papel acabado a
 máquina *(m)*
Fr papier apprêté sur
 machine *(m)*
Pt papel acabado à
 máquina *(m)*

carta formata a mano *(f)*
 It
Am mold-made paper
De Büttenwerkdruck-
 papier
 (n)
En mould-made paper
Es papel de tina *(m)*
Fr papier moyen âge
 (m)
Pt papel moldado *(m)*

carta gessata *(f)* It
De Kreidezurichten *(n)*
En chalk overlay
Es alza mecánica de tiza
 (f)
Fr papier baryté *(m*
Pt calço de giz *(f*

**carta imbozzimata in
 tino** *(f)* It
De oberflächengeleimtes
 Papier *(n)*
En tub-sized paper
Es papel encolado en
 tina *(m)*
Fr papier collé à la cuve
 (m)
Pt papel encolado em
 tina *(m)*

carta kraft *(f)* It
De Kraftpapier *(n)*
En kraft paper
Es papel kraft *(m)*
Fr papier Kraft *(m)*
Pt papel kraft *(m)*

carta kraft union *(f)* It
De Kraftverbundpapier
 (n)

En kraft union paper
Es papel kraft union *(m)*
Fr papier kraft
 doublé-bitumé *(m)*
Pt papel kraft union *(m)*

**carta lisciata a
 macchina** *(f)* It
De maschinenglattes
 Papier *(n)*
En mill-finished paper
Es papel calandrado *(m)*
Fr papier apprêté
 machine *(m)*
Pt papel de acabamento
 à máquina *(m)*

carta lucida *(f)* It
De Glanzpapier *(n)*
En glazed paper
Es papel lustroso *(m)*
Fr papier glacé *(m)*
Pt papel lustrado *(m)*

carta marmorizzata *(f)* It
De Marmorpapier *(n)*
En marbled paper
Es papel jaspeado *(m)*
Fr papier marbré *(m)*
Pt papel jaspeado *(m)*

carta millimetrata *(f)* It
De Koordinatenpapier
 (n)
En grid paper
Es papel milimétrico *(m)*
Fr papier millimétrique
 (m)
Pt papel milimétrico *(m)*

**carta molto
 imbozzimada** *(f)* It
De Hartleimpapier *(n)*
En hard-sized paper
Es papel de encolado
 duro *(m)*
Fr papier très collé *(m)*
Pt papel de
 encolamento duro
 (m)

carta non imbozzimata
 (f) It
De ungeleimtes Papier
 (n)
En waterleaf
Es papel no encolado
 (m)
Fr papier non collé *(m)*
Pt papel absorvente *(m)*

cartâo *(m)* n Pt
De Karton *(m)*
En cardboard
Es cartulina *(f)*
Fr carton *(m)*
It cartone *(m)*

cartâo amarelo *(m)* Pt
De Strohkarton *(m)*
En strawboard
Es cartón paja *(m)*
Fr carton paille *(m)*
It cartone-paglia *(m)*

carta oblunga *(f)* It
De Langformat-Papier
(n)
En oblong paper
Es papel apaisado *(m)*
Fr format à l'italienne
(m)
Pt papel alongado *(m)*

cartâo de polpa *(m)* Pt
De Zellstoff-Karton *(m)*
En pulp board
Es cartón de pasta *(m)*
Fr carton-pâte *(m)*
It cartone di pasta di
legno *(m)*

cartâo de trapos *(m)* Pt
De Hadernkarton *(m)*
En rag board
Es cartón de trapos *(m)*
Fr carton chiffon *(m)*
It cartone di stracci *(m)*

**cartâo de visita
profissional** *(m)* Pt
De Visitenkarte *(f)*
En business card
Es tarjeta comercial *(f)*
Fr carte de visite
professionnelle *(f)*
It bigliettino da visita
(m)

cartâo grosso *(m)* Pt
De Pappdeckel *(m)*
En mill board
Es cartón grueso *(m)*
Fr carton gris à reliure
(m)
It cartone forte *(m)*

cartâo marfim *(m)* Pt
De Elfenbeinkarton *(m)*
En ivory board
Es cartulina marfil *(f)*

Fr carton invoire *(m)*
It cartone avorio *(m)*

carta patinata *(f)* It
De gestrichenes Papier
(n)
En coated paper; art
paper
Es papel cuché *(m)*
Fr papier couché *(m)*
Pt papel revestido *(m)*

**carta patinata a
macchina** *(f)* It
De maschinen-
gestrichenes Papier
(n)
En machine-coated
paper
Es papel estucado a
máquina *(m)*
Fr papier couché
machine *(m)*
Pt papel revestido à
máquina *(m)*

carta patinata opaca *(f)*
It
De Mattkunstdruck-
papier *(n)*
En matt art paper
Es papel cuché mate
(m)
Fr papier couché mat
(m)
Pt papel artístico mate
(m)

cartapecora *(f)* n It
De Velinpapier *(n)*
En vellum
Es vitela *(f)*
Fr vélin *(m)*
Pt velino *(m)*

carta per copertine *(f)* It
De Umschlagpapier *(n)*
En cover paper
Es papel para cubiertas
(m)
Fr papier à couverture
(m)
Pt papel de cobertura
(m)

carta per duplicatori *(f)*
It
De Vervielfältigungs-
papier *(n)*
En manifold paper
Es papel de copias *(m)*

Fr papier pour formules
(m)
Pt papel de cópias *(m)*

carta per valori *(f)* It
De Aktienpapier *(n)*
En loan paper
Es papel para
documentos *(m)*
Fr papier pour titres *(m)*
Pt papel de empréstimo
(m)

carta piuma *(f)* It
De Federleichtpapier *(n)*
En featherweight paper
Es papel ligero *(m)*
Fr papier bouffant *(m)*
Pt papel peso pena *(m)*

carta protocollo *(f)* It
De Folioformat *(n)*
En foolscap
Es papel de oficio *(m)*
Fr papier ministre *(m)*
Pt papel ministro *(m)*

carta quadrettata *(f)* It
De kariertes Papier *(n)*
En quadrille
Es cuadrícula *(f)*
Fr papier quadrillé *(m)*
Pt papel quadriculado
(m)

carta retinata *(f)* It
De Velinpapier *(n)*
En wove paper
Es papel avitelado *(m)*
Fr papier vélin *(m)*
Pt papel tecido *(m)*

carta retinata azzura *(f)*
It
De Azur-Velinpapier *(n)*
En azure wove
Es azul celeste avitelado
(m)
Fr vélin azur *(m)*
Pt tecido anilado *(m)*

**carta retinata tipo
antico** *(f)* It
De Antikdruckpapier *(n)*
En antique wove
Es papel avitelado
antiguo *(m)*
Fr vélin à l'antique *(m)*
Pt tecido estilo antigo
(m)

carta rifinita *(f)* It
De bogenkalander-
bearbeitetes Papier
(n)
En plate-finished paper
Es papel satinado a
plancha *(m)*
Fr papier laminé à la
plaque *(m)*
Pt papel lustrado à
prancha *(m)*

carta rivestita in tela *(f)*
It
De stoffüberzogenes
Papier *(n)*
En cloth-lined paper
Es papel forrado de tela
(m)
Fr papier entoilé une
face *(m)*
Pt papel forrado a tela
(m)

carta seccata all'aria *(f)*
It
De Lufttrokkenes Papier
(n)
En loft-dried paper
Es papel secado al aire
(m)
Fr papier séché à l'air
(m)
Pt papel secado ao ar
(m)

carta smaltata *(f)* It
De Hochglanzpapier *(n)*
En enamel paper
Es papel esmaltado *(m)*
Fr papier émaillé *(m)*
Pt papel esmalte *(m)*

carta supercalandrata *(f)*
It
De Illustrations-
druckpapier *(m)*
En super-calendered
paper
Es papel
supercalandrado *(m)*
Fr papier supercalandré
(m)
Pt papel
supercalandrado *(m)*

**carta tagliata a
macchina** *(f)* It
De Maschinengröβe *(f)*
En engine-sized paper
Es papel encolado a
máquina *(m)*

Fr papier collé en pâte
(m)
Pt papel encolado à
máquina (m)

carta traslucida (f) It
De Dünndruckpapier (n)
En onion-skin paper
Es papel cebolla (m)
Fr papier pelure (m)
Pt papel cebola (m)

carta velina (f) It
De Seidenpapier (n)
En tissue paper
Es papel de seda (m)
Fr papier mousseline
(m)
Pt papel de seda (m)

carta vergata (f) It
De Vergépapier (n)
En laid paper
Es papel verjurado (m)
Fr papier vergé (m)
Pt papel vergé (m)

carta vergata crema (f) It
De mattgelbes geripptes
Papier (n)
En cream laid paper
Es papel verjurado
crema (m)
Fr papier vergé pâle (m)
Pt papel rugoso (m)

cartaz (m) n Pt
De Poster (n)
En poster
Es cartel (m)
Fr affiche (f)
It manifesto (m)

carte (f) n Fr
De Karte (f)
En map
Es mapa (m)
It mappa (f)
Pt mapa (m)

carte couchée (f) Fr
De Kunstdruckkarton (m)
En art board
Es tablero de dibujo (m)
It cartone da disegno
(m)
Pt prancha de arte (f)

**carte de visite
professionnelle** (f)
Fr
De Visitenkarte (f)
En business card
Es tarjeta comercial (f)
It bigliettino da visita
(m)
Pt cartão de visita
profissional (m)

cartel (m) n Es
De Poster (n)
En poster
Fr affiche (f)
It manifesto (m)
Pt cartaz (m)

carte magnétique (f) Fr
De Magnetkarte (f)
En magnetic card
Es ficha magnética (f)
It scheda magnetica (f)
Pt ficha magnética (f)

carte perforée (f) Fr
De Lochkarte (f)
En punched card
Es tarjeta perforada (f)
It scheda perforata (f)
Pt ficha perfurada (f)

cartiera (f) n It
De Papierfabrik (f)
En paper mill
Es fábrica de papel (f)
Fr fabrique de papier (f)
Pt fábrica de papel (f)

cartoleria (f) n It
De Briefpapier (n)
En stationery
Es efectos de escritorio
(m pl)
Fr papeterie de détail (f)
Pt papel e artigos de
escritório (m)

carton (m) n Fr
De Karton (m)
En cardboard; board
Es cartulina; cartón (f m)
It cartone (m)
Pt cartão; cartonado
(m)

cartonados a carneira
(m pl) Pt
De Lederfaserpappen
(pl)
En leather boards

Es cartones de cuero (m
pl)
Fr carton simili cuir (m)
It cartoni uso cuoio (m
pl)

carton chiffon (m) Fr
De Hadernkarton (m)
En rag board
Es cartón de trapos (m)
It cartone di stracci (m)
Pt cartão de trapos (m)

carton contre-collé (m)
Fr
De Pappe (f)
En pasteboard
Es cartón de varias
capas (m)
It cartone accoppiato
(m)
Pt papelão (m)

cartón de pasta (m) Es
De Zellstoff-Karton (m)
En pulp board
Fr carton-pâte (m)
It cartone di pasta di
legno (m)
Pt cartão de polpa (m)

cartón de trapos (m) Es
De Hadernkarton (m)
En rag board
Fr carton chiffon (m)
It cartone di stracci (m)
Pt cartão de trapos (m)

cartón de varias capas
(m) Es
De Pappe (f)
En pasteboard
Fr carton contre-collé
(m)
It cartone accoppiato
(m)
Pt papelão (m)

cartón duplo (m) Es
De Duplexpapier (n)
En duplex paper
Fr papier duplex (m)
It carta duplex (f)
Pt papel duplex (m)

cartone (m) n It
De Karton (m)
En cardboard; board
Es cartulina; cartón (f m)
Fr carton (m)

Pt cartão; cartonado
(m)

cartone accoppiato (m)
It
De Pappe (f)
En pasteboard
Es cartón de varias
capas (m)
Fr carton contre-collé
(m)
Pt papelão (m)

cartone avorio (m) It
De Elfenbeinkarton (m)
En ivory board
Es cartulina marfil (f)
Fr carton invoire (m)
Pt cartão marfim (m)

cartone da disegno (m)
It
De Kunstdruckkarton (m)
En art board
Es tablero de dibujo (m)
Fr carte couchée (f)
Pt prancha de arte (f)

**cartone di pasta di
legno** (m) It
De Zellstoff-Karton (m)
En pulp board
Es cartón de pasta (m)
Fr carton-pâte (m)
Pt cartão de polpa (m)

cartone di stracci (m) It
De Hadernkarton (m)
En rag board
Es cartón de trapos (m)
Fr carton chiffon (m)
Pt cartão de trapos (m)

cartone forte (m) It
De Pappdeckel (m)
En mill board
Es cartón grueso (m)
Fr carton gris à reliure
(m)
Pt cartão grosso (m)

cartone-paglia (m) n It
De Strohkarton (m)
En strawboard
Es cartón paja (m)
Fr carton paille (m)
Pt cartão amarelo (m)

cartone satinato (m) It
De kartoniertes
Glanzpapier (n)
En board-glazed paper
Es papel satinado (m)
Fr papier satiné (m)
Pt papel acetinado (m)

cartones de cuero (m pl)
Es
De Lederfaserpappen
(pl)
En leather boards
Fr carton simili cuir (m)
It cartoni uso cuoio (m
pl)
Pt cartonados a carneira
(m pl)

carton gris à reliure (m)
Fr
De Pappdeckel (m)
En mill board
Es cartón grueso (m)
It cartone forte (m)
Pt cartão grosso (m)

cartón grueso (m) Es
De Pappdeckel (m)
En mill board
Fr carton gris à reliure
(m)
It cartone forte (m)
Pt cartão grosso (m)

carton invoire (m) Fr
De Elfenbeinkarton (m)
En ivory board
Es cartulina marfil (f)
It cartone avorio (m)
Pt cartão marfim (m)

cartoni uso cuoio (m pl)
It
De Lederfaserpappen
(pl)
En leather boards
Es cartones de cuero (m
pl)
Fr carton simili cuir (m)
Pt cartonados a carneira
(m pl)

cartonnage (m) n Fr
De Einhängen (n)
En casing-in
Es metido en tapas (m)
It messa in custodia (f)
Pt colocação em capa
separada (f)

carton paille (m) Fr
De Strohkarton (m)
En strawboard
Es cartón paja (m)
It cartone-paglia (m)
Pt cartão amarelo (m)

cartón paja (m) Es
De Strohkarton (m)
En strawboard
Fr carton paille (m)
It cartone-paglia (m)
Pt cartão amarelo (m)

carton-pâte (m) Fr
De Zellstoff-Karton (m)
En pulp board
Es cartón de pasta (m)
It cartone di pasta di
legno (m)
Pt cartão de polpa (m)

carton simili cuir (m) Fr
De Lederfaserpappen
(pl)
En leather boards
Es cartones de cuero (m
pl)
It cartoni uso cuoio (m
pl)
Pt cartonados a carneira
(m pl)

cartridge paper En
De Kartuschenpapier (n)
Es papel para cartuchos
(m)
Fr papier cartouche (m)
It carta da disegno (f)
Pt papel cartucho (m)

cartulina (f) n Es
De Karton (m)
En cardboard
Fr carton (m)
It cartone (m)
Pt cartão (m)

cartulina marfil (f) Es
De Elfenbeinkarton (m)
En ivory board
Fr carton invoire (m)
It cartone avorio (m)
Pt cartão marfim (m)

casa editorial (f) Es, Pt
De Verlag (m)
En publisher (company)
Fr maison d'édition (f)
It casa editrice (f)

casa editrice (f) It
De Verlag (m)
En publisher (company)
Es casa editorial (f)
Fr maison d'édition (f)
Pt casa editorial (f)

casas comerciais (f pl) Pt
De Druckbetriebe (pl)
En trade houses pl n
Es casas comerciales (f
pl)
Fr maisons
commerciales (f pl)
It case commerciali (f
pl)

casas comerciales (f pl)
Es
De Druckbetriebe (pl)
En trade houses pl n
Fr maisons
commerciales (f pl)
It case commerciali (f
pl)
Pt casas comerciais (f
pl)

casa tipográfica (f) Pt
De Druckerei (f)
En printing house
Es imprenta (casa) (f)
Fr imprimerie (maison)
(f)
It stabilimento
tipografico (m)

cascame di carta (m) It
De Defektbogen (m)
En broke (papermaking)
Es papel roto (m)
Fr cassés (m pl)
Pt empastelado (m)

case (bookbinding) n En
De Buchdeckel (m)
Es tapas (f)
Fr couverture (f)
It custodia (f)
Pt capa separada (f)

case (typesetting) n En
De Setzkasten (m)
Es caja (f)
Fr casse (f)
It cassa tipografica (f)
Pt caixa (f)

case commerciali (f pl) It
De Druckbetriebe (pl)
En trade houses pl n

Es casas comerciales (f
pl)
Fr maisons
commerciales (f pl)
Pt casas comerciais (f
pl)

cash flow En
De Bargeldfluß (m)
Es flujo de caja (m)
Fr cash-flow (m)
It movimento di cassa
(m)
Pt movimento em
dinheiro (m)

cash-flow (m) n Fr
De Bargeldfluß (m)
En cash flow
Es flujo de caja (m)
It movimento di cassa
(m)
Pt movimento em
dinheiro (m)

casing-in n En
De Einhängen (n)
Es metido en tapas (m)
Fr cartonnage (m)
It messa in custodia (f)
Pt colocação em capa
separada (f)

cassa luminosa (f) It
De Leuchtkasten (m)
En light box
Es caja de luz (f)
Fr boîte lumineuse (f)
Pt caixa de luz (f)

cassare vb It
De löschen
En erase
Es borrar
Fr effacer
Pt apagar

cassa tipografica (f) It
De Setzkasten (m)
En case (typesetting)
Es caja (f)
Fr casse (f)
Pt caixa (f)

casse (f) n Fr
De Setzkasten (m)
En case (typesetting)
Es caja (f)
It cassa tipografica (f)
Pt caixa (f)

cassés *(m pl)* n Fr
De Defektbogen *(m)*
En broke (papermaking)
Es papel roto *(m)*
It cascame di carta *(m)*
Pt empastelado *(m)*

cast-coated paper En
De Gussgestrichenes Papier *(n)*
Es papel de respaldo esmaltado *(m)*
Fr papier couché chrome superbrillant *(m)*
It carta altobrillante *(f)*
Pt papel estereotipado *(m)*

casting n En
De Gießen *(n)*
Es fusión *(f)*
Fr coulée *(f)*
It fusione *(f)*
Pt fusão *(f)*

cast off En
De berechnen
Es calibrar la composición
Fr calibrer un texte
It equilibrare la composizione
Pt calibrar a composição

catalog n Am
De Katalog *(m)*
En catalogue
Es catálogo *(m)*
Fr catalogue *(m)*
It catalogo *(m)*
Pt catálogo *(m)*

catalogo *(m)* n It
Am catalog
De Katalog *(m)*
En catalogue
Es catálogo *(m)*
Fr catalogue *(m)*
Pt catálogo *(m)*

catálogo *(m)* n Es, Pt
Am catalog
De Katalog *(m)*
En catalogue
Fr catalogue *(m)*
It catalogo *(m)*

catálogo de novelas *(m)* Es
De Romanliteratur-Liste *(f)*
En fiction list
Fr catalogue des romans *(m)*
It elenco di narrativa *(m)*
Pt lista de ficção *(f)*

catálogo de otoño *(m)* Es
De Herbstliste *(f)*
En autumn list
Fr catalogue de la rentrée *(m)*
It elenco d'autunno *(m)*
Pt lista de outono *(f)*

catálogo de primavera *(m)* Es
De Frühjahrsliste *(f)*
En spring list
Fr catalogue de printemps *(m)*
It elenco di primavera *(m)*
Pt lista de Primavera *(f)*

catalogue n En; Fr *(f)*
Am catalog
De Katalog *(m)*
Es catálogo *(m)*
It catalogo *(m)*
Pt catálogo *(m)*

catalogue de la rentrée *(m)* Fr
De Herbstliste *(f)*
En autumn list
Es catálogo de otoño *(m)*
It elenco d'autunno *(m)*
Pt lista de outono *(f)*

catalogue de printemps *(m)* Fr
De Frühjahrsliste *(f)*
En spring list
Es catálogo de primavera *(m)*
It elenco di primavera *(m)*
Pt lista de Primavera *(f)*

catalogue des romans *(m)* Fr
De Romanliteratur-Liste *(f)*
En fiction list
Es catálogo de novelas *(m)*

It elenco di narrativa *(m)*
Pt lista de ficção *(f)*

cattura dei dati *(f)* It
De Datenerfassung *(f)*
En data capture
Es toma de datos *(f)*
Fr saisie de données *(f)*
Pt captação de dados *(f)*

caucciù *(m)* *(m)* n It
De Drucktuch *(n)*
En blanket (offset litho)
Es mantilla *(f)*
Fr décharge *(f)*
Pt feltro *(m)*

cediglia *(f)* n It
De Cedille *(f)*
En cedilla
Es cedilla *(f)*
Fr cédille *(f)*
Pt cedilha *(f)*

cedilha *(f)* n Pt
De Cedille *(f)*
En cedilla
Es cedilla *(f)*
Fr cédille *(f)*
It cediglia *(f)*

cedilla n En; Es *(f)*
De Cedille *(f)*
Fr cédille *(f)*
It cediglia *(f)*
Pt cedilha *(f)*

Cedille *(f)* n De
En cedilla
Es cedilla *(f)*
Fr cédille *(f)*
It cediglia *(f)*
Pt cedilha *(f)*

cédille *(f)* n Fr
De Cedille *(f)*
En cedilla
Es cedilla *(f)*
It cediglia *(f)*
Pt cedilha *(f)*

cellulosa *(f)* n It
De Zellulose *(f)*
En cellulose
Es celulosa *(f)*
Fr cellulose *(f)*
Pt celulose *(f)*

cellulose n En; Fr *(f)*
De Zellulose *(f)*
Es celulosa *(f)*
It cellulosa *(f)*
Pt celulose *(f)*

celulosa *(f)* n Es
De Zellulose *(f)*
En cellulose
Fr cellulose *(f)*
It cellulosa *(f)*
Pt celulose *(f)*

celulose *(f)* n Pt
De Zellulose *(f)*
En cellulose
Es celulosa *(f)*
Fr cellulose *(f)*
It cellulosa *(f)*

center vb Am
De zentrieren
En centre (typesetting)
Es centrar
Fr centrer
It centrare
Pt centrar

centrar vb Es, Pt
Am center
De zentrieren
En centre (typesetting)
Fr centrer
It centrare

centrare vb It
Am center
De zentrieren
En centre (typesetting)
Es centrar
Fr centrer
Pt centrar

centre (typesetting) vb En
Am center
De zentrieren
Es centrar
Fr centrer
It centrare
Pt centrar

centrer vb Fr
Am center
De zentrieren
En centre (typesetting)
Es centrar
It centrare
Pt centrar

cerotipia (f) n Es, Pt
De Wachsgravieren (n)
En wax engraving
Fr électrotype par
dessin sur métal
paraffiné (m)
It incisione a cera (f)

chairman n En
De Vorsitzender (m)
Es presidente (m)
Fr président (m)
It presidente (m)
Pt presidente (m)

chaïking n En
De Kalkschleier (m)
Es desintegración en
polvo (f)
Fr poudrage (m)
It sfarinamento (m)
Pt descascamento (m)

chalk overlay En
De Kreidezurichten (n)
Es alza mecánica de tiza
(f)
Fr papier baryté (m)
It carta gessata (f)
Pt calço de giz (f)

chambre noire (f) Fr
De Dunkelkammer (f)
En darkroom
Es cuarto oscuro (m)
It camera oscura (f)
Pt câmara escura (f)

chanfro (m) n Pt
De Konus (m)
En bevel
Es bisel (m)
Fr biseau (m)
It smusso (m)

channel n En
De Kanal (m)
Es canal (m)
Fr rainure (f)
It canale (m)
Pt canal (m)

chapa de albumina (f) Pt
De Albuminplatte (f)
En albumen plate
Es plancha offset a la
albúmina (f)
Fr procédé à l'albumine
(m)
It lastra all'albumina (f)

**chapa de impressão
fotopolimérica** (f)
Pt
De Photopolymer-
Druckplatte (f)
En photopolymer
printing plate
Es placa impresora de
polimerización
fotoquímica (f)
Fr plaque
photopolymère (f)
It lastra da stampa ai
fotopolimeri (f)

chapa de meia-tinta (f)
Pt
De Tonplatte (f)
En flat-tint plate
Es clisé de media tinta
(m)
Fr aplat (m)
It lastra a tinta opaca (f)

**chapa litográfica de
gravação funda** (f)
Pt
De Tiefdruck-Offsetplatte
(f)
En deep-etch litho plate
Es plancha al
hueco-offset (f)
Fr offset en creux (m)
It lastra litografica a
incisione profonda (f)

chapa molhada (f) Pt
De feuchte Platte (f)
En wet plate
Es placa húmeda (f)
Fr plaque humide (f)
It lastra al collodio (f)

chapa preta (f) Pt
De Schwarzplatte (f)
En black plate
Es plancha negra (f)
Fr cliché en noir (m)
It lastra nera (f)

chapitre (m) n Fr
De Kapitel (n)
En chapter
Es capítulo (m)
It capitolo (m)
Pt capítulo (m)

chapter n En
De Kapitel (n)
Es capítulo (m)
Fr chapitre (m)

It capitolo (m)
Pt capítulo (m)

chapter heading En
De Kapitelüberschrift (f)
Es encabezamiento de
capítulo (m)
Fr tête de chapitre (f)
It titolo del capitolo (m)
Pt título do capítulo (m)

character n En
De Schriftzeichen (n)
Es carácter (m)
Fr caractère (m)
It carattere (m)
Pt carácter (m)

character set En
De Buchstabensatz (m)
Es juego de caracteres
(m)
Fr jeu de caractères (m)
It gioco di caratteri (m)
Pt jogo de caracteres
(m)

charge (f) n Fr
De Füllerstoff (m)
En filler
Es material de carga (m)
It carica (f)
Pt carga (f)

chart n En
De Tabelle (f)
Es diagrama (m)
Fr diagramme (m)
It tabella (f)
Pt carta (m)

chart paper En
De Registrierpapier (n)
Es papel gráfico (m)
Fr papier pour
graphiques (m)
It carta da grafici (f)
Pt papel de mapa (m)

chase (letterpress) n En
De Rahmen (m)
Es rama (f)
Fr châssis (m)
It telaio (m)
Pt rama (f)

châssis (m) n Fr
De Rahmen (m)
En chase (letterpress)
Es rama (f)

It telaio (m)
Pt rama (f)

châssis à journal (m) Fr
De Zeitungsrahmen (m)
En news chase
Es rama de noticias (f)
It caccia di notizie (f)
Pt rama de notícias (f)

châssis de pliage (m) Fr
De Falzrahmen (m)
En folding chase
Es rama dúplex (f)
It telaio di piegafoglio
(m)
Pt rama duplex (f)

châssis machine (m) Fr
De Maschinenrahmen
(m)
En machine chase
Es rama de máquina (f)
It telaio di forma chiusa
(m)
Pt rama de máquina (f)

chassis pneumatique
(m) Fr
De Vakuumrahmen (m)
En vacuum frame
Es prensa al vacío (f)
It telaio a vuoto (m)
Pt caixilho de vácuo (m)

check vb En
De überprüfen
Es comprobar
Fr vérifier
It verificare
Pt verificar

che fa notizia It
De aktuell
En newsworthy
Es de interés
periodístico
Fr d'intérêt
journalistique
Pt digno de ser
publicado

chef de la rédaction (m)
Fr
De Betriebsredakteur
(m)
En managing editor
Es jefe de redacción (m)
It capo redattore (m)
Pt chefe de redacção
(m)

chef des ventes *(m)* Fr
De Verkaufsleiter *(m)*
En sales manager
Es jefe de ventas *(m)*
It direttore vendite *(m)*
Pt gerente de vendas
(m)

chefe de redacção *(m)*
Pt
De Betriebsredakteur
(m)
En managing editor
Es jefe de redacción *(m)*
Fr chef de la rédaction
(m)
It capo redattore *(m)*

Chefredakteur *(m) n* De
En editorial director
Es director de editorial
(m)
Fr directeur de la
rédaction *(m)*
It direttore editoriale
(m)
Pt director editorial *(m)*

Chemiegraphie *(f) n* De
En process engraving
Es fotograbado *(m)*
Fr photogravure *(f)*
It zincografia *(f)*
Pt fototipogravura *(f)*

chief executive En
De leitende
Führungskraft *(f)*
Es jefe ejecutivo *(m)*
Fr administrateur
directeur *(m)*
It direttore generale *(m)*
Pt executivo principal
(m)

chiffre *(m) n* Fr
De Stelle *(f)*
En digit
Es dígito *(m)*
It cifra *(f)*
Pt dígito *(m)*

chiffre d'affaires *(m)* Fr
De Umsatz *(m)*
En turnover
Es cifra de negocios *(f)*
It fatturato *(m)*
Pt movimento *(m)*

chiffres arabes *(m pl)* Fr
De arabische Ziffern *(pl)*
En arabic numerals
Es números arábigos *(m
pl)*
It numeri arabi *(m pl)*
Pt numeros árabes *(m
pl)*

chiffres romains *(m pl)*
Fr
De römische Zahlen *(pl)*
En roman numerals
Es números romanos *(m
pl)*
It numeri romani *(m pl)*
Pt números romanos *(m
pl)*

children's books *pl n* En
De Kinderbücher *(pl)*
Es libros para niños *(m
pl)*
Fr livres pour enfants *(m
pl)*
It libri per bambini *(m
pl)*
Pt livros infantís *(m pl)*

china clay En
De Kaolin *(n)*
Es caolín *(m)*
Fr kaolin *(m)*
It caolino *(m)*
Pt caolino *(m)*

chomage partiel *(m)* Fr
De Entlassung *(f)*
En redundancy
Es redundancia *(f)*
It ridondanza *(f)*
Pt redundância *(f)*

chromo paper En
De Chromopapier *(n)*
Es papel para
cromolitografía *(m)*
Fr papier chromo *(m)*
It carta al cromo *(f)*
Pt papel cromo *(m)*

Chromopapier *(n) n* De
En chromo paper
Es papel para
cromolitografía *(m)*
Fr papier chromo *(m)*
It carta al cromo *(f)*
Pt papel cromo *(m)*

chumbo *(m) n* Pt
De Blei *(n)*
En lead (metal)
Es plomo *(m)*
Fr plomb *(m)*
It piombo *(m)*

ciano *(m) n* It
De Cyan *(n)*
En cyan
Es azul verdoso *(m)*
Fr cyan *(m)*
Pt cianogénio *(m)*

cianogénio *(m) n* Pt
De Cyan *(n)*
En cyan
Es azul verdoso *(m)*
Fr cyan *(m)*
It ciano *(m)*

cianografia *(f) n* It
De Blaupause *(f)*
En blueprint
Es cianotipo *(m)*
Fr bleu *(m)*
Pt cianotipo *(m)*

cianotipo *(m) n* Es, Pt
De Blaupause *(f)*
En blueprint
Fr bleu *(m)*
It cianografia *(f)*

cicero *n* En; It *(m)*
De Cicero *(f)*
Es cícero *(m)*
Fr cicéro *(m)*
Pt cícero *(m)*

Cicero *(f) n* De
En cicero
Es cícero *(m)*
Fr cicéro *(m)*
It cicero *(m)*
Pt cícero *(m)*

cícero *(m) n* Es, Pt
De Cicero *(f)*
En cicero
Fr cicéro *(m)*
It cicero *(m)*

cicéro *(m) n* Fr
De Cicero *(f)*
En cicero
Es cícero *(m)*
It cicero *(m)*
Pt cícero *(m)*

ciencia *(f) n* Es
De Wissenschaft *(f)*
En science
Fr science *(f)*
It scienza *(f)*
Pt ciência *(f)*

ciência *(f) n* Pt
De Wissenschaft *(f)*
En science
Es ciencia *(f)*
Fr science *(f)*
It scienza *(f)*

ciencia-ficción *(f) n* Es
De Science-fiction *(f)*
En science fiction
Fr science-fiction *(f)*
It fantascienza *(f)*
Pt ficção científica *(f)*

cifra *(f) n* It
De Stelle *(f)*
En digit
Es dígito *(m)*
Fr chiffre *(m)*
Pt dígito *(m)*

cifra de negocios *(f)* Es
De Umsatz *(m)*
En turnover
Fr chiffre d'affaires *(m)*
It fatturato *(m)*
Pt movimento *(m)*

cilindro *(m) n* It
De Walze *(f)*
En roller
Es rodillo *(m)*
Fr rouleau
(d'impression) *(m)*
Pt rolo (de impressão)
(m)

cilindro à filigrana *(m)* It
De Egoutteur *(m)*
En dandy roll
Es rodillo afiligranador
(m)
Fr rouleau égoutteur
(m)
Pt rolo filigranador *(m)*

cinta de papel *(f)* Es
De Lochstreifen *(m)*
En paper tape
Fr bande de papier *(f)*
It nastro di carta *(m)*
Pt fita de papel *(f)*

cinta magnética *(f)* Es
De Magnetband *(n)*
En magnetic tape
Fr bande magnétique *(f)*
It nastro magnetico *(m)*
Pt fita magnética *(f)*

cinta para enmascarar
(f) Es
De Abdeckband *(n)*
En masking tape
Fr bande de masquage
(f)
It nastro per
mascheratura *(m)*
Pt fita de mascarar *(f)*

cinta perforada *(f)* Es
De Lochstreifen *(m)*
En punched paper tape
Fr bande perforée *(f)*
It nastro di carta
perforato *(m)*
Pt fita de papel
perfurado *(f)*

circumflex *n* En
De Zirkumflex *(m)*
Es acento circunflejo
(m)
Fr accent circonflexe
(m)
It accento circonflesso
(m)
Pt acento circunflexo
(m)

cita *(f)* *n* Es
De Zitat *(n)*
En quotation (extract)
Fr citation *(f)*
It citazione *(f)*
Pt citação *(f)*

citação *(f)* *n* Pt
De Zitat *(n)*
En quotation (extract)
Es cita *(f)*
Fr citation *(f)*
It citazione *(f)*

citar *vb* Es, Pt
De zitieren
En quote (an extract)
Fr citer
It citare tra virgolette

citare tra virgolette It
De zitieren
En quote (an extract)
Es citar

Fr citer
Pt citar

citation *(f)* *n* Fr
De Zitat *(n)*
En quotation (extract)
Es cita *(f)*
It citazione *(f)*
Pt citação *(f)*

citazione *(f)* *n* It
De Zitat *(n)*
En quotation (extract)
Es cita *(f)*
Fr citation *(f)*
Pt citação *(f)*

citer *vb* Fr
De zitieren
En quote (an extract)
Es citar
It citare tra virgolette
Pt citar

claridad *(f)* *n* Es
De Bildschärfe *(f)*
En definition
(photography)
Fr netteté *(f)*
It nitidezza *(f)*
Pt nitidez *(f)*

clásicos *(m pl)* Es
De klassische Werke *(pl)*
En classics *pl n*
Fr classiques *(m pl)*
It classici *(m pl)*
Pt clássicos *(m pl)*

classici *(m pl)* It
De klassische Werke *(pl)*
En classics *pl n*
Es clásicos *(m pl)*
Fr classiques *(m pl)*
Pt clássicos *(m pl)*

clássicos *(m pl)* Pt
De klassische Werke *(pl)*
En classics *pl n*
Es clásicos *(m pl)*
Fr classiques *(m pl)*
It classici *(m pl)*

classics *pl n* En
De klassische Werke *(pl)*
Es clásicos *(m pl)*
Fr classiques *(m pl)*
It classici *(m pl)*
Pt clássicos *(m pl)*

classiques *(m pl)* Fr
De klassische Werke *(pl)*
En classics *pl n*
Es clásicos *(m pl)*
It classici *(m pl)*
Pt clássicos *(m pl)*

cláusula *(f)* *n* Es
De Satz *(m)*
En sentence
Fr phrase *(f)*
It frase *(f)*
Pt frase *(f)*

clavier *(m)* *n* Fr
De Tastatur *(m)*
En keyboard
Es teclado *(m)*
It tastiera *(f)*
Pt teclado *(m)*

clavier aveugle *(m)* Fr
De Blindtastatur *(f)*
En blind keyboard
Es teclado ciego *(m)*
It tastiera cieca *(f)*
Pt teclado cego *(m)*

claviste *(m)* *n* Fr
De Tastatur-Setzer *(m)*
En keyboarder
Es operador de teclado
(m)
It operatore di tastiera
(m)
Pt mecanotipista *(m)*

clean copy En
De sauberer Text *(m)*
Es original limpio *(m)*
Fr copie au net *(f)*
It copia nitida *(f)*
Pt exemplar a limpo *(m)*

clean proof En
De sauberer Abzug *(m)*
Es prueba limpia *(f)*
Fr épreuve au net *(f)*
It bozza nitida *(f)*
Pt prova limpa *(f)*

clichage *(m)* *n* Fr
De Kopieren *(n)*
En platemaking
Es preparación de
planchas *(f)*
It preparazione delle
matrici *(f)*
Pt preparação de
estampas *(f)*

cliché *(m)* *n* Fr, It, Pt
De Klischee *(n)*
En block
Es placa impresora *(f)*

cliché a tratto *(m)* It
De Strichätzung *(f)*
En line block
Es fotograbado de línea
(m)
Fr cliché au trait *(m)*
Pt placa de estereotipia
(f)

cliché au trait *(m)* Fr
De Strichätzung *(f)*
En line block
Es fotograbado de línea
(m)
It cliché a tratto *(m)*
Pt placa de estereotipia
(f)

cliché duplicati *(m pl)* It
De Duplikatklischees *(pl)*
En duplicate blocks *pl n*
Es bloques duplicados
(m pl)
Fr cliché en double *(m)*
Pt blocos duplicados *(m
pl)*

cliché en double *(m)* Fr
De Duplikatklischees *(pl)*
En duplicate blocks *pl n*
Es bloques duplicados
(m pl)
It cliché duplicati *(m pl)*
Pt blocos duplicados *(m
pl)*

cliché en noir *(m)* Fr
De Schwarzplatte *(f)*
En black plate
Es plancha negra *(f)*
It lastra nera *(f)*
Pt chapa preta *(f)*

clicherie *(f)* *n* Fr
De Schriftgießerei *(f)*
En type foundry
Es fundición de tipos *(f)*
It fonderia di caratteri
(f)
Pt fundição de tipos
(casa) *(f)*

clichés à vignette *(m pl)*
It
De Gelegenheitsvignetta
(f)

En vignetted blocks *pl n*
Es fotograbados esfumados *(m pl)*
Fr simili dégradée *(f)*
Pt blocos de vinheta *(m pl)*

cliché sin contrastes *(m)* Es
De flaches Negativ *(n)*
En flat negative
Fr négatif sans contraste *(m)*
It negativo senza contrasti *(m)*
Pt negativo plano *(m)*

client *n* En; Fr *(m)*
De Kunde *(m)*
Es cliente *(m)*
It cliente *(m)*
Pt cliente *(m)*

cliente *(m) n* Es, It, Pt
De Kunde *(m)*
En client
Fr client *(m)*

clisé de media tinta *(m)* Es
De Tonplatte *(f)*
En flat-tint plate
Fr aplat *(m)*
It lastra a tinta opaca *(f)*
Pt chapa de meia-tinta *(f)*

cloque *(f) n* Fr
De Schnalle *(f)*
En blister (on paper)
Es ampolla *(f)*
It bolla *(f)*
Pt bolha *(f)*

cloth-bound book En
De Leinenbandbuch *(n)*
Es libro encuadernado en tela *(m)*
Fr livre relié pleine toile *(m)*
It libro rilegato in tela *(m)*
Pt livro encadernado em tela *(m)*

cloth-centered paper Am
De Papier mit Stoffmitte *(n)*
En cloth-centred paper

Es papel duplex con alma de lino *(m)*
Fr papier entre deux toiles *(m)*
It carta duplex con anima di tela *(f)*
Pt papel centrado em tela *(m)*

cloth-centred paper En
Am cloth-centered paper
De Papier mit Stoffmitte *(n)*
Es papel duplex con alma de lino *(m)*
Fr papier entre deux toiles *(m)*
It carta duplex con anima di tela *(f)*
Pt papel centrado em tela *(m)*

cloth-lined paper En
De stoffüberzogenes Papier *(n)*
Es papel forrado de tela *(m)*
Fr papier entoilé une face *(m)*
It carta rivestita in tela *(f)*
Pt papel forrado a tela *(m)*

club del libro *(m)* Es, It
De Buchclub *(m)*
En book club
Fr club du livre *(m)*
Pt clube de leitores *(m)*

club du livre *(m)* Fr
De Buchclub *(m)*
En book club
Es club del libro *(m)*
It club del libro *(m)*
Pt clube de leitores *(m)*

clube de leitores *(m)* Pt
De Buchclub *(m)*
En book club
Es club del libro *(m)*
Fr club du livre *(m)*
It club del libro *(m)*

coarse screen En
De grober Raster *(m)*
Es trama gruesa *(f)*
Fr trame à gros grains *(f)*
It a grana grossa *(f)*
Pt retícula grossa *(f)*

coated paper En
De gestrichenes Papier *(n)*
Es papel cuché *(m)*
Fr papier couché *(m)*
It carta patinata *(f)*
Pt papel revestido *(m)*

coating *n* En
De Streichen *(n)*
Es revestimiento *(m)*
Fr couchage du papier *(m)*
It rivestimento *(m)*
Pt revestimento *(m)*

coberta *(f) n* Pt
De Deckblatt *(n)*
En overlay (on artwork, etc.)
Es superponible *(m)*
Fr becquet *(m)*
It sovrapposizione *(f)*

cobrimento *(m) n* Pt
De Abdecken *(n)*
En blocking out
Es enmienda con sobreimpresión *(f)*
Fr oblitération *(f)*
It mascheratura con vernice coprente *(f)*

cobrir as despesas Pt
De die Kosten decken
En cover one's costs
Es cubrir los gastos propios
Fr couvrir ses dépenses
It coprire i costi

cockling *n* En
De Kräuseln *(n)*
Es amartillamiento *(m)*
Fr gondolage *(m)*
It arricciatura *(f)*
Pt enrugamento *(m)*

code (computing) *n* En; Fr *(m)*
De Code *(m)*
Es código *(m)*
It codice *(m)*
Pt código *(m)*

Code *(m) n* De
En code (computing)
Es código *(m)*
Fr code *(m)*
It codice *(m)*
Pt código *(m)*

codice *(m) n* It
De Code *(m)*
En code (computing)
Es código *(m)*
Fr code *(m)*
Pt código *(m)*

código *(m) n* Es, Pt
De Code *(m)*
En code (computing)
Fr code *(m)*
It codice *(m)*

coedição *(f) n* Pt
De gemeinsame Ausgabe *(f)*
En co-edition
Es coedición *(f)*
Fr co-édition *(f)*
It coedizione *(m)*

coedição internacional *(f)* Pt
De internationale Gemeinschafts-Ausgabe *(f)*
En international co-edition
Es coedición internacional *(f)*
Fr co-édition internationale *(f)*
It coedizione internazionale *(f)*

coedición *(f) n* Es
De gemeinsame Ausgabe *(f)*
En co-edition
Fr co-édition *(f)*
It coedizione *(m)*
Pt coedição *(f)*

coedición internacional *(f)* Es
De internationale Gemeinschafts-Ausgabe *(f)*
En international co-edition
Fr co-édition internationale *(f)*
It coedizione internazionale *(f)*
Pt coedição internacional *(f)*

co-éditeur *(m) n* Fr
De Verleger einer gemeinsamen Ausgabe *(m)*
En co-edition publisher

Es editorial de
coediciones (f)
It editore di coedizione
(m)
Pt editorial de coedição
(f)

co-edition n En
De gemeinsame
Ausgabe (f)
Es coedición (f)
Fr co-édition (f)
It coedizione (m)
Pt coedição (f)

co-édition (f) n Fr
De gemeinsame
Ausgabe (f)
En co-edition
Es coedición (f)
It coedizione (m)
Pt coedição (f)

**co-édition
internationale** (f) Fr
De internationale
Gemeinschafts-
Ausgabe (f)
En international
co-edition
Es coedición
internacional (f)
It coedizione
internazionale (f)
Pt coedição
internacional (f)

co-edition publisher En
De Verleger einer
gemeinsamen
Ausgabe (m)
Es editorial de
coediciones (f)
Fr co-éditeur (m)
It editore di coedizione
(m)
Pt editorial de coedição
(f)

coedizione (m) n It
De gemeinsame
Ausgabe (f)
En co-edition
Es coedición (f)
Fr co-édition (f)
Pt coedição (f)

**coedizione
internazionale** (f) It
De internationale
Gemeinschafts-
Ausgabe (f)

En international
co-edition
Es coedición
internacional (f)
Fr co-édition
internationale (f)
Pt coedição
internacional (f)

coin (m) n Fr
De Keil (m)
En quoin
Es cuña (f)
It serraforme (m)
Pt cunha (f)

cola (f) n Pt
De Kleister (m)
En paste
Es engrudo (m)
Fr colle (f)
It colla (f)

cola animal (f) Es, Pt
De Tierleimbindung (f)
En animal sizing
Fr collage animal (m)
It colla animale (f)

colaborador anónimo
(m) Pt
De Schattenautor (m)
En ghost writer
Es escritor fantasma (m)
Fr nègre (m)
It collaboratore
anonimo (m)

cold-set adj En
De kalttrocknend
Es solidificardo en frio
Fr seché à froid
It solidificato a freddo
(f)
Pt secado a frio (f)

coleção (f) n Pt
De Sammlung (f)
En collection
Es colección (f)
Fr recueil (m)
It collezione (f)

colección (f) n Es
De Sammlung (f)
En collection
Fr recueil (m)
It collezione (f)
Pt coleção (f)

colis (m) n Fr
De Paket (n)
En package
Es paquete (m)
It pacco (m)
Pt pacote (m)

colla (f) n It
De Kleister (m)
En paste
Es engrudo (m)
Fr colle (f)
Pt cola (f)

colla animale (f) It
De Tierleimbindung (f)
En animal sizing
Es cola animal (f)
Fr collage animal (m)
Pt cola animal (f)

collaborateur (m) n Fr
De Betragender (m)
En contributor
Es contribuidor (m)
It collaboratore (m)
Pt contribuidor (m)

collaboratore (m) n It
De Betragender (m)
En contributor
Es contribuidor (m)
Fr collaborateur (m)
Pt contribuidor (m)

collaboratore anonimo
(m) It
De Schattenautor (m)
En ghost writer
Es escritor fantasma (m)
Fr nègre (m)
Pt colaborador anónimo
(m)

collage (m) n Fr
De Klebeumbruch (m)
En paste-up
Es montaje (m)
It incollatura (f)
Pt montagem (f)

collage animal (m) Fr
De Tierleimbindung (f)
En animal sizing
Es cola animal (f)
It colla animale (f)
Pt cola animal (f)

collaggio (m) n It
De Leimung (f)
En sizing
Es encolado (m)
Fr encollage (m)
Pt encolamento (m)

collate vb En
De vergleichen
Es alzar
Fr assembler
It collazionare
Pt rever

collating n En
De Zusammentragung (f)
Es alzado (m)
Fr assemblage (m)
It raccoglitura (f)
Pt revisão (f)

collating marks pl n En
De Kollationierzeichen
(pl)
Es señales escalonadas
de alzado (f pl)
Fr repères
d'assemblage (m pl)
It segni di raccoglitura
(m pl)
Pt marcas de revisão (f
pl)

collazionare vb It
De vergleichen
En collate
Es alzar
Fr assembler
Pt rever

colle (f) n Fr
De Kleister (m)
En paste
Es engrudo (m)
It colla (f)
Pt cola (f)

collected works En
De gesammelten Werke
(pl)
Es obras reunidas (f pl)
Fr recueil des oeuvres
(m pl)
It raccolta di opere (f pl)
Pt compilação de obras
(f)

collection n En
De Sammlung (f)
Es colección (f)
Fr recueil (m)

It collezione (f)
Pt coleção (f)

collegarsi vb It
De in Kontakt stehen
En liaise
Es enlazar
Fr garder contact
Pt ligar

collezione (f) n It
De Sammlung (f)
En collection
Es colección (f)
Fr recueil (m)
Pt coleção (f)

collotipia (f) n It
De Lichtdruck (m)
En collotype
Es colotipia (f)
Fr phototype (m)
Pt colotipo (m)

collotype n En
De Lichtdruck (m)
Es colotipia (f)
Fr phototype (m)
It collotipia (f)
Pt colotipo (m)

colocação de lombada
      (f) Pt
De Abpressen (n)
En backing
Es formación de cajos (f)
Fr endossure (f)
It rinforzo (m)

colocação de sobrecapa
      (f) Pt
De Klebenindung (f)
En wrappering
Es sobrecubierta (f)
Fr emballage (m)
It mettitura le
      sovracopertine (f)

colocação de um traço
      de união (f) Pt
De Trennung (f)
En hyphenation
Es separación con
      guiones (f)
Fr coupure (f)
It legatura con trattino
      (f)

colocação em capa
      separada (f) Pt
De Einhängen (n)
En casing-in
Es metido en tapas (m)
Fr cartonnage (m)
It messa in custodia (f)

colofón (m) n Es
De Signet (n)
En colophon
Fr colophon (m)
It colofone (m)
Pt colofónio (m)

colofone (m) n It
De Signet (n)
En colophon
Es colofón (m)
Fr colophon (m)
Pt colofónio (m)

colofónio (m) n Pt
De Signet (n)
En colophon
Es colofón (m)
Fr colophon (m)
It colofone (m)

colon n En
De Doppelpunkt (m)
Es dos puntos (m)
Fr deux-points (m)
It doppiopunto (m)
Pt dois pontos (m)

colonna (f) n It
De Spalte (f)
En column (of text)
Es columna (f)
Fr colonne (f)
Pt coluna (f)

colonne (f) n Fr
De Spalte (f)
En column (of text)
Es columna (f)
It colonna (f)
Pt coluna (f)

colophon n En; Fr (m)
De Signet (n)
Es colofón (m)
It colofone (m)
Pt colofónio (m)

coloration mécanique (f)
      Fr
De mechanische Töne
      (pl)

En mechanical tints
Es fondos grisados (m
      pl)
It colori di gradazioni
      chiare ottenuti
      meccanicamente (m
      pl)
Pt lâminas de acinzentar
      (f pl)

color bars pl n Am
De Farbstreifen (pl)
En colour bars
Es franjas de color (f pl)
Fr bandes des couleurs
      (f pl)
It barre di colore (f pl)
Pt franjas de cor (f pl)

color correction Am
De Farbkorrektur (f)
En colour correction
Es rectificación
      cromática (f)
Fr correction des
      couleurs (f)
It correzione di colore
      (f)
Pt correcção de cor (f)

colores para policromía
      (m pl) Es
Am process colors
De Verfahrensfarben (pl)
En process colours
Fr polychromie (f)
It colori per policromia
      (m pl)
Pt cores para policromia
      (f pl)

colori di gradazioni
      chiare ottenuti
      meccanicamente
      (m pl) It
De mechanische Töne
      (pl)
En mechanical tints
Es fondos grisados (m
      pl)
Fr coloration
      mécanique (f)
Pt lâminas de acinzentar
      (f pl)

color illustration Am
De Farbillustration (f)
En colour illustration
Es ilustración en color (f)
Fr illustration en
      couleurs (f)

It illustrazione a colori
      (f)
Pt ilustração a cores (f)

colori per policromia (m
      pl) It
Am process colors
De Verfahrensfarben (pl)
En process colours
Es colores para
      policromía (m pl)
Fr polychromie (f)
Pt cores para policromia
      (f pl)

color photograph Am
De Farbphoto (n)
En colour photograph
Es fotografía en colores
      (f)
Fr photographie en
      couleurs (f)
It fotografia a colori (f)
Pt fotografia a cores (f)

color plates pl n Am
De Farbtafeln (pl)
En colour plates
Es láminas en color (f pl)
Fr planches en couleurs
      (f pl)
It tavole a colori (f pl)
Pt páginas a cores (f pl)

color proof Am
De Farbabzug (m)
En colour proof
Es prueba en colores (f)
Fr épreuve couleurs (f)
It bozza a colori (f)
Pt prova a cores (f)

color separation Am
De Farbtrennung (f)
En colour separation
Es selección
      fotomecánica de
      colores (f)
Fr séparation des
      couleurs (f)
It selezione di colore (f)
Pt separação de cores
      (f)

color supplement Am
De Farbbeilage (f)
En colour supplement
Es suplemento en color
      (m)
Fr supplément en
      couleurs (m)

It   supplemento a colori
(m)
Pt   suplemento a cores
(m)

colotipia *(f) n* Es
De   Lichtdruck *(m)*
En   collotype
Fr   phototype *(m)*
It   collotipia *(f)*
Pt   colotipo *(m)*

colotipo *(m) n* Pt
De   Lichtdruck *(m)*
En   collotype
Es   colotipia *(f)*
Fr   phototype *(m)*
It   collotipia *(f)*

colour bars *pl n* En
Am color bars
De   Farbstreifen *(pl)*
Es   franjas de color *(f pl)*
Fr   bandes des couleurs
(f pl)
It   barre di colore *(f pl)*
Pt   franjas de cor *(f pl)*

colour correction En
Am color correction
De   Farbkorrektur *(f)*
Es   rectificación
cromática *(f)*
Fr   correction des
couleurs *(f)*
It   correzione di colore
(f)
Pt   correcção de cor *(f)*

colour illustration En
Am color illustration
De   Farbillustration *(f)*
Es   ilustración en color *(f)*
Fr   illustration en
couleurs *(f)*
It   illustrazione a colori
(f)
Pt   ilustração a cores *(f)*

colour photograph En
Am color photograph
De   Farbphoto *(n)*
Es   fotografía en colores
(f)
Fr   photographie en
couleurs *(f)*
It   fotografia a colori *(f)*
Pt   fotografia a cores *(f)*

colour plates *pl n* En
Am color plates
De   Farbtafeln *(pl)*
Es   láminas en color *(f pl)*
Fr   planches en couleurs
(f pl)
It   tavole a colori *(f pl)*
Pt   páginas a cores *(f pl)*

colour proof En
Am color proof
De   Farbabzug *(m)*
Es   prueba en colores *(f)*
Fr   épreuve couleurs *(f)*
It   bozza a colori *(f)*
Pt   prova a cores *(f)*

colour separation En
Am color separation
De   Farbtrennung *(f)*
Es   selección
fotomecánica de
colores *(f)*
Fr   séparation des
couleurs *(f)*
It   selezione di colore *(f)*
Pt   separação de cores
(f)

colour supplement En
Am color supplement
De   Farbbeilage *(f)*
Es   suplemento en color
(m)
Fr   supplément en
couleurs *(m)*
It   supplemento a colori
(m)
Pt   suplemento a cores
(m)

column (of text) *n* En
De   Spalte *(f)*
Es   columna *(f)*
Fr   colonne *(f)*
It   colonna *(f)*
Pt   coluna *(f)*

columna *(f) n* Es
De   Spalte *(f)*
En   column (of text)
Fr   colonne *(f)*
It   colonna *(f)*
Pt   coluna *(f)*

coluna *(f) n* Pt
De   Spalte *(f)*
En   column (of text)
Es   columna *(f)*
Fr   colonne *(f)*
It   colonna *(f)*

coma *(f) n* Es
De   Komma *(n)*
En   comma
Fr   virgule *(f)*
It   virgola *(f)*
Pt   vírgula *(f)*

comércio *(m) n* Pt
De   Handel *(m)*
En   trade
Es   oficio *(m)*
Fr   commerce *(m)*
It   commercio *(m)*

comércio de livros *(m)*
Pt
De   Buchhandel *(m)*
En   book trade
Es   comercio del libro
(m)
Fr   commerce des livres
(m)
It   commercio librario
(m)

comercio del libro *(m)* Es
De   Buchhandel *(m)*
En   book trade
Fr   commerce des livres
(m)
It   commercio librario
(m)
Pt   comércio de livros
(m)

comida de trabajo *(f)* Es
De   geschäftliches
Mittagessen *(n)*
En   working lunch
Fr   déjeuner de travail
(m)
It   pranzo di lavoro *(m)*
Pt   almoço de trabalho
(m)

comillas *(f pl) n* Es
De   Anführungszeichen
(pl)
En   quotation marks
Fr   guillemets *(m pl)*
It   virgolette *(f pl)*
Pt   aspas *(f pl)*

comissão *(f) n* Pt
De   Kommission *(f)*
En   commission
Es   encargo *(m)*
Fr   commission *(f)*
It   commissione *(f)*

comitato direttivo *(m)* It
De   Vorstand *(m)*
En   board of directors
Es   consejo de
administración *(m)*
Fr   direction générale *(f)*
Pt   conselho de
administração *(m)*

comma *n* En
De   Komma *(n)*
Es   coma *(f)*
Fr   virgule *(f)*
It   virgola *(f)*
Pt   vírgula *(f)*

commander *vb* Fr
De   in Auftrag geben
En   commission
Es   encargar
It   commissionare
Pt   encomendar

commedia *(f) n* It
De   Stück *(n)*
En   play
Es   obra dramática *(f)*
Fr   pièce de théâtre *(f)*
Pt   peça *(f)*

commerce *(m) n* Fr
De   Handel *(m)*
En   trade
Es   oficio *(m)*
It   commercio *(m)*
Pt   comércio *(m)*

commerce de gros *(m)*
Fr
De   Großhandelsvertrieb
(m)
En   wholesale
distribution
Es   distribución al por
mayor *(f)*
It   distribuzione
all'ingrosso *(f)*
Pt   distribuição por
atacado *(f)*

commerce de l'édition
(m) Fr
De   Verlagswesen *(n)*
En   publishing
Es   editorial *(f)*
It   editoria *(f)*
Pt   negocio de
publicação *(m)*

commerce de librairie
(m) Fr
De Buchverkauf (m)
En bookselling
Es venta de libros (f)
It vendita di libri (f)
Pt venda de livros (f)

commerce des livres (m)
Fr
De Buchhandel (m)
En book trade
Es comercio del libro
(m)
It commercio librario
(m)
Pt comércio de livros
(m)

commercio (m) n It
De Handel (m)
En trade
Es oficio (m)
Fr commerce (m)
Pt comércio (m)

commercio librario (m) It
De Buchhandel (m)
En book trade
Es comercio del libro
(m)
Fr commerce des livres
(m)
Pt comércio de livros
(m)

commesso (m) n It
De Verkäufer (m)
En sales assistant
Es ayudante de ventas
(m)
Fr commis (m)
Pt ajudante de
vendedor (m)

commis (m) n Fr
De Verkäufer (m)
En sales assistant
Es ayudante de ventas
(m)
It commesso (m)
Pt ajudante de
vendedor (m)

commission vb En
De in Auftrag geben
Es encargar
Fr commander
It commissionare
Pt encomendar

commission n En; Fr (f)
De Kommission (f)
Es encargo (m)
It commissione (f)
Pt comissão (f)

commissionare vb It
De in Auftrag geben
En commission
Es encargar
Fr commander
Pt encomendar

commissione (f) n It
De Kommission (f)
En commission
Es encargo (m)
Fr commission (f)
Pt comissão (f)

commissioning editor
En
De Auftragvergabe-
Redakteur (m)
Es editor por encargo
(m)
Fr rédacteur chargé des
commandes (m)
It redattore
commissioni (m)
Pt editor que
encomenda a obra
(m)

**commission
representative** En
De Auftragsvertreter (m)
Es representante a
comisión (m)
Fr représentant chargé
des commandes (m)
It rappresentante
commissione (m)
Pt representante à
comissão (m)

communiqué de presse
(m) Fr
De Pressever-
öffentlichung (f)
En press release
Es boletín informativo
(m)
It comunicato stampa
(m)
Pt comunicado de
imprensa (f)

compaginação (f) n Pt
De Satzumbruch (m)
En make-up
Es compaginación (f)

Fr montage (m)
It impaginatura (f)

compaginación (f) n Es
De Satzumbruch (m)
En make-up
Fr montage (m)
It impaginatura (f)
Pt compaginação (f)

compaginar vb Es, Pt
De umbrechen
En make up
Fr mettre en pages
It compaginare

compaginare vb It
De umbrechen
En make up
Es compaginar
Fr mettre en pages
Pt compaginar

companhia de serviços
(f) Pt
De Dienstleitungsfirma
(f)
En service company
Es compañía de
servicios (f)
Fr entretien (m)
It società di servizio (f)

compañía de servicios
(f) Es
De Dienstleitungsfirma
(f)
En service company
Fr entretien (m)
It società di servizio (f)
Pt companhia de
serviços (f)

**compañía
empaquetadora** (f)
Es
De Verpackungsfirma (f)
En packaging company
Fr entreprise de
l´emballage (f)
It società
confezionamento (m)
Pt sociedade
empacotadora (f)

compatibile adj It
De kompatibel
En compatible (of
computer systems)
Es compatible

Fr compatible
Pt compatível

compatibilidad (f) n Es
De Kompatibiltät (f)
En compatibility (of
computer systems)
Fr compatibilité (f)
It compatibilità (f)
Pt compatibilidade (f)

compatibilidade (f) n Pt
De Kompatibiltät (f)
En compatibility (of
computer systems)
Es compatibilidad (f)
Fr compatibilité (f)
It compatibilità (f)

compatibilità (f) n It
De Kompatibiltät (f)
En compatibility (of
computer systems)
Es compatibilidad (f)
Fr compatibilité (f)
Pt compatibilidade (f)

compatibilité (f) n Fr
De Kompatibiltät (f)
En compatibility (of
computer systems)
Es compatibilidad (f)
It compatibilità (f)
Pt compatibilidade (f)

compatibility (of
computer systems) n
En
De Kompatibiltät (f)
Es compatibilidad (f)
Fr compatibilité (f)
It compatibilità (f)
Pt compatibilidade (f)

compatible (of computer
systems) adj En, Es,
Fr
De kompatibel
It compatibile
Pt compatível

compatível adj Pt
De kompatibel
En compatible (of
computer systems)
Es compatible
Fr compatible
It compatibile

compendio *(m)* *n* Es
De Handbuch *(n)*
En handbook
Fr guide-âne *(m)*
It manualetto *(m)*
Pt compêndio *(m)*

compêndio *(m)* *n* Pt
De Handbuch *(n)*
En handbook
Es compendio *(m)*
Fr guide-âne *(m)*
It manualetto *(m)*

compilação de obras *(f)*
Pt
De gesammelten Werke *(pl)*
En collected works
Es obras reunidas *(f pl)*
Fr recueil des œuvres *(m pl)*
It raccolta di opere *(f pl)*

compilatore di un indice *(m)* It
De Indexierer *(m)*
En indexer
Es indexador *(m)*
Fr auteur de l'index *(m)*
Pt indiciador *(m)*

compitazione *(f)* *n* It
De Buchstrabierung *(f)*
En spelling
Es deletreo *(m)*
Fr épellation *(f)*
Pt soletração *(f)*

completamente encadernado Pt
De voll gebunden
En fully bound
Es totalmente encuadernado
Fr reliure pleine
It completamente rilegato

completamente rilegato It
De voll gebunden
En fully bound
Es totalmente encuadernado
Fr reliure pleine
Pt completamente encadernado

complete works En
De sämtliche Werke *(pl)*
Es obras completas *(f pl)*
Fr oeuvres complètes *(f pl)*
It opera completa *(f)*
Pt obras completas *(f pl)*

complimentary copy En
De Gratisexemplar *(n)*
Es ejemplar de obsequio *(m)*
Fr exemplaire en hommage *(m)*
It copia omaggio *(f)*
Pt exemplar de oferta *(m)*

componer *vb* Es
De setzen
En compose
Fr composer
It comporre
Pt compor

componer de nuevo Es
De neu setzen
En reset
Fr remanier
It riazzerare
Pt tornar a compor

componer sin punto y aparte Es
De anhängen
En run on (typesetting)
Fr suivre sans alinéa
It scrivere a testo continuo
Pt compor seguido

compor *vb* Pt
De setzen
En compose
Es componer
Fr composer
It comporre

comporre *vb* It
De setzen
En compose
Es componer
Fr composer
Pt compor

compor seguido Pt
De anhängen
En run on (typesetting)
Es componer sin punto y aparte
Fr suivre sans alinéa

It scrivere a testo continuo

compose *vb* En
De setzen
Es componer
Fr composer
It comporre
Pt compor

composé à l'américaine Fr
De glatt zurichten
En cut flush
Es cortado a ras
It tagliato a filo
Pt recorte raso

composer *vb* Fr
De setzen
En compose
Es componer
It comporre
Pt compor

composeuse *(f)* *n* Fr
De Setzmaschine *(f)*
En composing machine; typesetting machine
Es máquina de componer; máquina de composición *(f)*
It compositrice *(f)*
Pt máquina de composição; compositora de tipos *(f)*

composição *(f)* *n* Pt
De Setzen *(n)*
En composition
Es composición *(f)*
Fr composition *(f)*
It composizione *(f)*

composição com máquina de escrever *(f)* Pt
De Schreibmaschinen-Satz *(m)*
En typewriter composition
Es composición mecanográfica *(f)*
Fr composition à la machine à écrire *(f)*
It composizione su macchina da scrivere *(f)*

composição de linhas *(f)*
Pt
De Zeilensatz *(m)*
En line composition
Es composición por líneas *(f)*
Fr photogravure typographique *(f)*
It composizione della linea *(f)*

composição de tipos *(f)*
Pt
De Schriftsatz *(m)*
En typesetting
Es composición tipográfica *(f)*
Fr composition typographique *(f)*
It composizione tipografica *(f)*

composição de tipos de metal quente *(f)* Pt
De Maschinensatz *(m)*
En hot-metal typesetting
Es composición metálica en caliente *(f)*
Fr composition chaude *(f)*
It composizione a metallo caldo *(f)*

composição levantada *(f)* Pt
De guter Satz *(m)*
En standing type
Es composición levantada *(f)*
Fr caractères conservés *(m pl)*
It carattere eretto *(m)*

composição manual *(f)*
Pt
De Handsatz *(m)*
En hand setting
Es composición a mano *(f)*
Fr composition manuelle *(f)*
It composizione a mano *(f)*

composição mecânica *(f)* Pt
De mechanischer Satz *(m)*
En mechanical composition

Es composición
mecánica (f)
Fr composition
mécanique (f)
It composizione
meccanica (f)

**composição tipográfica
por computador** (f)
Pt
De Computersatz (m)
En computer typesetting
Es composición
tipográfica con
ordenador (f)
Fr composition
automatisée (f)
It composizione
computerizzata (f)

composición (f) n Es
De Setzen (n)
En composition
Fr composition (f)
It composizione (f)
Pt composição (f)

composición a mano (f)
Es
De Handsatz (m)
En hand setting
Fr composition
manuelle (f)
It composizione a
mano (f)
Pt composição manual
(f)

**composición
fotomecánica** (f) Es
De Photosatz (m)
En phototypesetting;
photocomposition
Fr photocomposition (f)
It fotocomposizione (f)
Pt fotocomposição (f)

composición levantada
(f) Es
De guter Satz (m)
En standing type
Fr caractères conservés
(m pl)
It carattere eretto (m)
Pt composição
levantada (f)

composición mecánica
(f) Es
De mechanischer Satz
(m)

En mechanical
composition
Fr composition
mécanique (f)
It composizione
meccanica (f)
Pt composição
mecânica (f)

**composición
mecanográfica** (f)
Es
De Schreibmaschinen-
Satz (m)
En typewriter
composition
Fr composition à la
machine à écrire (f)
It composizione su
macchina da scrivere
(f)
Pt composição com
máquina de escrever
(f)

**composición
mecanotipíca** (f) Es
De Schriftguβ (m)
En typecasting
Fr fonte de caractères
(f)
It fusione dei caratteri
(f)
Pt fundição de tipos
(processo) (f)

**composición metálica
en caliente** (f) Es
De Maschinensatz (m)
En hot-metal typesetting
Fr composition chaude
(f)
It composizione a
metallo caldo (f)
Pt composição de tipos
de metal quente (f)

composición por líneas
(f) Es
De Zeilensatz (m)
En line composition
Fr photogravure
typographique (f)
It composizione della
linea (f)
Pt composição de
linhas (f)

composición suprimida
(f) Es
De gestrichener Text (m)
En cancelled matter

Fr texte annulé (m)
It testo annullato (m)
Pt matéria cancelada (f)

**composición
tipográfica** (f) Es
De Schriftsatz (m)
En typesetting
Fr composition
typographique (f)
It composizione
tipografica (f)
Pt composição de tipos
(f)

**composición
tipográfica con
ordenador** (f) Es
De Computersatz (m)
En computer typesetting
Fr composition
automatisée (f)
It composizione
computerizzata (f)
Pt composição
tipográfica por
computador (f)

composing machine En
De Setzmaschine (f)
Es máquina de
componer (f)
Fr composeuse (f)
It compositrice (f)
Pt máquina de
composição (f)

composing room En
De Setzerei (f)
Es sala de composición
(f)
Fr atelier de
composition (m)
It sala composizione (f)
Pt sala de composição
(f)

composition n En; Fr (f)
De Setsen (n)
Es composición (f)
It composizione (f)
Pt composição (f)

**composition à la
machine à écrire** (f)
Fr
De Schreibmaschinen-
Satz (m)
En typewriter
composition
Es composición
mecanográfica (f)

It composizione su
macchina da scrivere
(f)
Pt composição com
máquina de escrever
(f)

**composition
automatisée** (f) Fr
De Computersatz (m)
En computer typesetting
Es composición
tipográfica con
ordenador (f)
It composizione
computerizzata (f)
Pt composição
tipográfica por
computador (f)

composition chaude (f)
Fr
De Maschinensatz (m)
En hot-metal typesetting
Es composición
metálica en caliente (f)
It composizione a
metallo caldo (f)
Pt composição de tipos
de metal quente (f)

composition en drapeau
(f) Fr
De Schrägsatz (m)
En unjustified text
Es texto sin justificar (m)
It testo non giustificato
(m)
Pt texto não justificado
(m)

composition manuelle
(f) Fr
De Handsatz (m)
En hand setting
Es composición a mano
(f)
It composizione a
mano (f)
Pt composição manual
(f)

composition mécanique
(f) Fr
De mechanischer Satz
(m)
En mechanical
composition
Es composición
mecánica (f)

It composizione
meccanica *(f)*
Pt composição
mecânica *(f)*

**composition
typographique** *(f)*
Fr
De Schriftsatz *(m)*
En typesetting
Es composición
tipográfica *(f)*
It composizione
tipografica *(f)*
Pt composição de tipos
(f)

compositor *n* En; Es, Pt
(m)
De Setzer *(m)*
Fr typographe *(m)*
It compositore *(m)*

compositora de tipos *(f)*
Pt
De Setzmaschine *(f)*
En typesetting machine;
composing machine
Es máquina de
composición;
máquina de
componer *(f)*
Fr machine à
composer;
composeuse *(f)*
It compositrice *(f)*

compositore *(m)* *n* It
De Setzer *(m)*
En compositor
Es compositor *(m)*
Fr typographe *(m)*
Pt compositor *(m)*

compositoria *(f)* *n* It
De Schriftsetzerei *(f)*
En typesetter (company)
Es taller de composición
(m)
Fr maison de
composition *(f)*
Pt empresa de
composição *(f)*

compositrice *(f)* *n* It
De Setzmaschine *(f)*
En typesetting machine;
composing machine
Es máquina de
composición;
máquina de
componer *(f)*

Fr machine à
composer;
composeuse *(f)*
Pt compositora de
tipos; máquina de
composição *(f)*

composizione *(f)* *n* It
De Setzen *(n)*
En composition
Es composición *(f)*
Fr composition *(f)*
Pt composição *(f)*

composizione a mano *(f)*
It
De Handsatz *(m)*
En hand setting
Es composición a mano
(f)
Fr composition
manuelle *(f)*
Pt composição manual
(f)

**composizione a metallo
caldo** *(f)* It
De Maschinensatz *(m)*
En hot-metal typesetting
Es composición
metálica en caliente
(f)
Fr composition chaude
(f)
Pt composição de tipos
de metal quente *(f)*

**composizione
computerizzata** *(f)*
It
De Computersatz *(m)*
En computer typesetting
Es composición
tipográfica con
ordenador *(f)*
Fr composition
automatisée *(f)*
Pt composição
tipográfica por
computador *(f)*

**composizione della
linea** *(f)* It
De Zeilensatz *(m)*
En line composition
Es composición por
líneas *(f)*
Fr photogravure
typographique *(f)*
Pt composição de
linhas *(f)*

**composizione
meccanica** *(f)* It
De mechanischer Satz
(m)
En mechanical
composition
Es composición
mecánica *(f)*
Fr composition
mécanique *(f)*
Pt composição
mecânica *(f)*

**composizione
sovrastante** *(f)* It
De überlanger Satz *(m)*
En overmatter
Es material sobrante *(m)*
Fr surimpression *(f)*
Pt matéria que sobra *(f)*

**composizione su
macchina da
scrivere** *(f)* It
De Schreibmaschinen-
Satz *(m)*
En typewriter
composition
Es composición
mecanográfica *(f)*
Fr composition à la
machine à écrire *(f)*
Pt composição com
máquina de escrever
(f)

**composizione
tipografica** *(f)* It
De Schriftsatz *(m)*
En typesetting
Es composición
tipográfica *(f)*
Fr composition
typographique *(f)*
Pt composição de tipos
(f)

compressão *(f)* *n* Pt
De Abpressen *(n)*
En pressing
Es prensado *(m)*
Fr pressage *(m)*
It stiratura *(f)*

comprobar *vb* Es
De überprüfen
En check
Fr vérifier
It verificare
Pt verificar

computador *(m)* *n* Pt
De Computer *(m)*
En computer
Es ordenador *(m)*
Fr ordinateur *(m)*
It computer *(m)*

computador digital *(m)*
Pt
De Digitalcomputer *(m)*
En digital computer
Es ordenador digital *(m)*
Fr calculateur
numérique *(m)*
It elaboratore digitale
(m)

computer *n* En; It *(m)*
De Computer *(m)*
Es ordenador *(m)*
Fr ordinateur *(m)*
Pt computador *(m)*

Computer *(m)* *n* De
En computer
Es ordenador *(m)*
Fr ordinateur *(m)*
It computer *(m)*
Pt computador *(m)*

Computersatz *(m)* *n* De
En computer typesetting
Es composición
tipográfica con
ordenador *(f)*
Fr composition
automatisée *(f)*
It composizione
computerizzata *(f)*
Pt composição
tipográfica por
computador *(f)*

computer typesetting
En
De Computersatz *(m)*
Es composición
tipográfica con
ordenador *(f)*
Fr composition
automatisée *(f)*
It composizione
computerizzata *(f)*
Pt composição
tipográfica por
computador *(f)*

común *adj* Es
De abgedroschen
En hackneyed
Fr stéréotypé

It comune
Pt vulgar

comune *adj* It
De abgedroschen
En hackneyed
Es común
Fr stéréotypé
Pt vulgar

**comunicado de
imprensa** *(f)* Pt
De Presseveröffentlichung *(f)*
En press release
Es boletín informativo
(m)
Fr communiqué de
presse *(m)*
It comunicato stampa
(m)

comunicato stampa *(m)*
It
De Presseveröffentlichung *(f)*
En press release
Es boletín informativo
(m)
Fr communiqué de
presse *(m)*
Pt comunicado de
imprensa *(f)*

con bordi dorati It
De mit Goldschnitt
En gilt-edged
Es de cortes dorados
Fr doré sur tranche
Pt dourado nas beiras

concepire *vb* It
De entwerfen
En design
Es diseñar
Fr concevoir
Pt desenhar

**concepteur
typographique** *(m)*
Fr
De Satzgestalter *(m)*
En typographic designer
Es diseñador tipográfico
(m)
It disegnatore
tipografico *(m)*
Pt desenhador
tipográfico *(m)*

**conception de la
jaquette** *(f)* Fr
De Umschlagentwurf
(m)
En jacket design
Es diseño de la
sobrecubierta *(m)*
It disegno della
sovracopertina *(m)*
Pt desenho da
sobrecapa *(m)*

concevoir *vb* Fr
De entwerfen
En design
Es diseñar
It concepire
Pt desenhar

concise dictionary En
De Kurzwörterbuch *(n)*
Es diccionario abreviado
(m)
Fr dictionnaire abrégé
(m)
It dizionario conciso
(m)
Pt dicionário conciso
(m)

condensed typeface En
De schmaler Schrifttyp
(m)
Es tipo estrecho *(m)*
Fr caractère effilé *(m)*
It carattere allungato
(m)
Pt estilo de tipo
condensado *(m)*

condicionamento *(m)* *n*
Pt
De Konditionierung *(f)*
En conditioning (of
paper)
Es acondicionamiento
(m)
Fr conditionnement *(m)*
It stagionatura *(f)*

condiciones *(f pl)* Es
De Bedingungen *(pl)*
En terms (of agreement,
etc.) *pl n*
Fr conditions *(f pl)*
It condizioni *(f pl)*
Pt condições *(m pl)*

condições *(m pl)* Pt
De Bedingungen *(pl)*
En terms (of agreement,
etc.) *pl n*

Es condiciones *(f pl)*
Fr conditions *(f pl)*
It condizioni *(f pl)*

conditioning (of paper) *n*
En
De Konditionierung *(f)*
Es acondicionamiento
(m)
Fr conditionnement *(m)*
It stagionatura *(f)*
Pt condicionamento *(m)*

conditionnement *(m)* *n*
Fr
De Konditionierung *(f)*
En conditioning (of
paper)
Es acondicionamiento
(m)
It stagionatura *(f)*
Pt condicionamento *(m)*

conditionner *vb* Fr
De ausreifen
En mature
Es madurar
It stagionare
Pt amadurecer

conditions *(f pl)* Fr
De Bedingungen *(pl)*
En terms (of agreement,
etc.) *pl n*
Es condiciones *(f pl)*
It condizioni *(f pl)*
Pt condições *(m pl)*

condizioni *(f pl)* It
De Bedingungen *(pl)*
En terms (of agreement,
etc.) *pl n*
Es condiciones *(f pl)*
Fr conditions *(f pl)*
Pt condições *(m pl)*

condotto per inchiostro
(m) It
De Farbkanal *(m)*
En ink duct
Es tintero de la prensa
(m)
Fr encrier *(m)*
Pt canal de tinta *(m)*

conducteur de machine
(m) Fr
De Maschinenmeister
(m)
En machine minder
Es prensista *(m)*

It macchinista *(m)*
Pt tratador da máquina
(m)

conférence de presse *(f)*
Fr
De Pressekonferenz *(f)*
En press conference
Es conferencia de
prensa *(f)*
It conferenza stampa *(f)*
Pt conferência de
imprensa *(f)*

conferencia anual *(f)* Es
De Jahreskonferenz *(f)*
En annual conference
Fr congrès annuel *(m)*
It conferenza annuale
(f)
Pt conferência anual *(f)*

conferência anual *(f)* Pt
De Jahreskonferenz *(f)*
En annual conference
Es conferencia anual *(f)*
Fr congrès annuel *(m)*
It conferenza annuale
(f)

**conferência de
imprensa** *(f)* Pt
De Pressekonferenz *(f)*
En press conference
Es conferencia de
prensa *(f)*
Fr conférence de presse
(f)
It conferenza stampa *(f)*

conferencia de prensa
(f) Es
De Pressekonferenz *(f)*
En press conference
Fr conférence de presse
(f)
It conferenza stampa *(f)*
Pt conferência de
imprensa *(f)*

conferencia de ventas
(f) Es
De Verkaufskonferenz *(f)*
En sales conference
Fr réunion de vente *(f)*
It conferenza di vendita
(f)
Pt conferência de
vendedores *(f)*

conferência de vendedores *(f)* Pt
De Verkaufskonferenz *(f)*
En sales conference
Es conferencia de ventas *(f)*
Fr réunion de vente *(f)*
It conferenza di vendita *(f)*

conferenza annuale *(f)* It
De Jahreskonferenz *(f)*
En annual conference
Es conferencia anual *(f)*
Fr congrès annuel *(m)*
Pt conferência anual *(f)*

conferenza di vendita *(f)* It
De Verkaufskonferenz *(f)*
En sales conference
Es conferencia de ventas *(f)*
Fr réunion de vente *(f)*
Pt conferência de vendedores *(f)*

conferenza stampa *(f)* It
De Pressekonferenz *(f)*
En press conference
Es conferencia de prensa *(f)*
Fr conférence de presse *(f)*
Pt conferência de imprensa *(f)*

confezionamento a restringimento *(m)* It
De Schrumpfverpackung *(f)*
En shrink-wrapping
Es envoltura por contracción *(f)*
Fr emballage serré *(m)*
Pt embalagem de encolher *(f)*

confrontare coll'original It
De mit dem Manuskript vergleichen
En read against copy
Es leer a la vista del original
Fr corriger avec copie
Pt ler comparando com a cópia

congiunzione commerciale *(f)* It
De Und-Zeichen *(n)*
En ampersand
Es y abreviada *(f)*
Fr et commercial *(m)*
Pt e comercial *(f)*

congrès annuel *(m)* Fr
De Jahreskonferenz *(f)*
En annual conference
Es conferencia anual *(f)*
It conferenza annuale *(f)*
Pt conferência anual *(f)*

consejo de administración *(m)* Es
De Vorstand *(m)*
En board of directors
Fr direction générale *(f)*
It comitato direttivo *(m)*
Pt conselho de administração *(m)*

conselho de administração *(m)* Pt
De Vorstand *(m)*
En board of directors
Es consejo de administración *(m)*
Fr direction générale *(f)*
It comitato direttivo *(m)*

consignes de conception *(f pl)* Fr
De Stilmuster *(n)*
En style guide
Es guía del estilo *(f)*
It guida di stile *(f)*
Pt guia de estilo *(m)*

contact print En
De Kontaktdruck *(m)*
Es copia por contacto *(f)*
Fr tirage contact *(m)*
It stampa a contatto *(f)*
Pt prova por contacto *(f)*

contact screen En
De Kontaktraster *(m)*
Es retícula de contacto *(f)*
Fr écran de contact *(m)*
It retino a contatto *(m)*
Pt retícula de contacto *(f)*

contents page En
De Inhaltsseite *(f)*
Es página de índice *(f)*
Fr page des matières *(f)*
It pagina indice *(f)*
Pt página de índice *(f)*

continuar a imprimir Pt
De fortdrucken
En run on (printing)
Es proseguir la tirada
Fr faire des tirages supplémentaires
It imprimir una super-tiratura *(f)*

continuous tone En
De kontinuerlich Ton *(m)*
Es tono continuo *(m)*
Fr ton en continu *(m)*
It tono continuo *(m)*
Pt tom contínuo *(m)*

contracapa *(f)* n Pt
De hintere Umschlagklappe *(f)*
En back flap
Es solapa posterior *(f)*
Fr rabat arrière *(m)*
It risvolto di retro *(m)*

contract n En
De Vertrag *(m)*
Es contrato *(m)*
Fr contrat *(m)*
It contratto *(m)*
Pt contrato *(m)*

contralomo *(m)* n Es
De Buchrücken-Fütterung *(f)*
En back lining
Fr garniture du dos *(f)*
It fodera di costa *(f)*
Pt forro de lombada *(m)*

contrassegnare vb It
De auszeichnen
En mark up (copy)
Es marcar
Fr annoter
Pt marcar

contrat *(m)* n Fr
De Vertrag *(m)*
En contract
Es contrato *(m)*
It contratto *(m)*
Pt contrato *(m)*

contrat d'auteur *(m)* Fr
De Verfasservertrag *(m)*
En author's agreement
Es contrato de autor *(m)*
It accordo coll'autore *(m)*
Pt acordo do autor *(m)*

contrato *(m)* n Es, Pt
De Vertrag *(m)*
En contract
Fr contrat *(m)*
It contratto *(m)*

contrato de autor *(m)* Es
De Verfasservertrag *(m)*
En author's agreement
Fr contrat d'auteur *(m)*
It accordo coll'autore *(m)*
Pt acordo do autor *(m)*

contratto *(m)* n It
De Vertrag *(m)*
En contract
Es contrato *(m)*
Fr contrat *(m)*
Pt contrato *(m)*

contrecollage sous pression *(m)* Fr
De Glanzfolien-kaschierung *(f)*
En laminating
Es laminación *(f)*
It laminazione *(f)*
Pt laminação *(f)*

contrefaçon *(f)* n Fr
De Verletzung des Copyright *(f)*
En infringement of copyright
Es violación de los derechos de autor *(f)*
It violazione di copyright *(f)*
Pt infracção de um copyright *(f)*

contribuidor *(m)* n Es, Pt
De Betragender *(m)*
En contributor
Fr collaborateur *(m)*
It collaboratore *(m)*

contributor n En
De Betragender *(m)*
Es contribuidor *(m)*
Fr collaborateur *(m)*

It collaboratore *(m)*
Pt contribuidor *(m)*

cookery book En
De Kochbuch *(n)*
Es libro de cocina *(m)*
Fr livre de cuisine *(m)*
It libro di cucina *(m)*
Pt livro de cozinha *(m)*

copia *(f)* n It
De Abschrift *(f)*
En copy
Es original *(m)*
Fr copie *(f)*
Pt cópia *(f)*

cópia *(f)* n Pt
De Abschrift *(f)*
En copy
Es original *(m)*
Fr copie *(f)*
It copia *(f)*

copia al bromuro *(f)* It
De Bromsilberabzug *(m)*
En bromide
Es bromuro *(m)*
Fr papier au bromure
(m)
Pt brometo *(m)*

copia di recensione *(f)* It
De Rezensions-Exemplar
(n)
En review copy
Es ejemplar para reseña
(m)
Fr exemplaire de service
de presse *(m)*
Pt exemplar para
resenha *(m)*

copia illeggibile *(f)* It
De schlechtes
Manuskript *(n)*
En bad copy
Es original malo *(m)*
Fr mauvaise copie *(f)*
Pt exemplar ilegível *(m)*

copialettere *(f)* n It
De Vervielfältigungs-
maschine *(f)*
En duplicator
Es duplicadora *(f)*
Fr duplicateur *(m)*
Pt duplicadora *(f)*

copia molto emendata
(f) It
De stark revidiertes
Manuskript *(n)*
En heavily edited copy
Es ejemplar mucho
enmendada *(m)*
Fr texte très corrigé *(m)*
Pt exemplar muito
corrigido *(m)*

copia nitida *(f)* It
De sauberer Text *(m)*
En clean copy
Es original limpio *(m)*
Fr copie au net *(f)*
Pt exemplar a limpo *(m)*

copia omaggio *(f)* It
De Gratisexemplar *(n)*
En complimentary copy
Es ejemplar de obsequio
(m)
Fr exemplaire en
hommage *(m)*
Pt exemplar de oferta
(m)

copia por contacto *(f)* Es
De Kontaktdruck *(m)*
En contact print
Fr tirage contact *(m)*
It stampa a contatto *(f)*
Pt prova por contacto *(f)*

**copia pronta per
fotografia** *(f)* It
De kamerafertige
Vorlage *(f)*
En camera-ready copy
Es original preparado
para la cámara *(m)*
Fr copie prête à
photographier *(f)*
Pt exemplar pronto para
a máquina
fotográfica *(m)*

copiar *vb* Es, Pt
De abschreiben
En copy
Fr copier
It copiare

copiare *vb* It
De abschreiben
En copy
Es copiar
Fr copier
Pt copiar

copie *(f)* n Fr
De Abschrift *(f)*
En copy
Es original *(m)*
It copia *(f)*
Pt cópia *(f)*

copie au net *(f)* Fr
De sauberer Text *(m)*
En clean copy
Es original limpio *(m)*
It copia nitida *(f)*
Pt exemplar a limpo *(m)*

**copie gratuite
dell'autore** *(f pl)* It
De Autorexemplare *(pl)*
En author's free copies
pl n
Es ejemplares de
obsequio del autor
(m pl)
Fr exemplaires gratuits
pour l'auteur *(m pl)*
Pt exemplares grátis
para o autor *(m pl)*

copie in anteprima *(f pl)*
It
De Vorausexemplare *(pl)*
En advance copies *pl* n
Es ejemplares para
reseña *(m pl)*
Fr exemplaires de
lancement *(m pl)*
Pt provas tipográficas *(f
pl)*

**copie prête à
photographier** *(f)* Fr
De kamerafertige
Vorlage *(f)*
En camera-ready copy
Es original preparado
para la cámara *(m)*
It copia pronta per
fotografia *(f)*
Pt exemplar pronto para
a máquina
fotográfica *(m)*

copier *vb* Fr
De abschreiben
En copy
Es copiar
It copiare
Pt copiar

copista *(m/f)* n Pt
De Amanuensis *(m)*
En amanuensis
Es amanuense *(m)*

Fr copiste *(m/f)*
It amanuense *(m)*

copiste *(m/f)* n Fr
De Amanuensis *(m)*
En amanuensis
Es amanuense *(m)*
It amanuense *(m)*
Pt copista *(m/f)*

copper-plate printing En
De Kupferdruck *(m)*
Es impresión en hueco
(f)
Fr gravure sur cuivre *(f)*
It stampa a calcografia
(f)
Pt impressão com
chapa de cobre *(f)*

coprire i costi It
De die Kosten decken
En cover one's costs
Es cubrir los gastos
propios
Fr couvrir ses dépenses
Pt cobrir as despesas

copy *vb* En
De abschreiben
Es copiar
Fr copier
It copiare
Pt copiar

copy n En
De Abschrift *(f)*
Es original *(m)*
Fr copie *(f)*
It copia *(f)*
Pt cópia *(f)*

copy-edit *vb* En
De Manuskript
revidieren
Es corregir originales
Fr éditer un texte
It correggere originali
Pt editar

copy-editing n En
De Manuskriptrevision *(f)*
Es corrección de
originales *(f)*
Fr préparation d'un
texte *(f)*
It correzione di originali
(f)
Pt revisão do original *(f)*

copy-editor *n* En
De Manuskriptredakteur
(m)
Es corrector de
originales *(m)*
Fr annotateur d'un texte
(m)
It correttore di originali
(m)
Pt revisor do original *(m)*

copy-fitting *n* En
De Texteinpassung *(f)*
Es ajuste de originales
(m)
Fr montage du texte *(m)*
It aggiustamento di
originali *(m)*
Pt ajustamento do
original *(m)*

copyright *n* En; Fr, It, Pt
(m)
De Copyright *(n)*
Es propiedad literaria *(f)*

Copyright *(n) n* De
En copyright
Es propiedad literaria *(f)*
Fr copyright *(m)*
It copyright *(m)*
Pt copyright *(m)*

copywriter *n* En
De Texter *(m)*
Es redactor de textos
publicitarios *(m)*
Fr rédacteur-
concepteur
publicitaire *(m)*
It redattore
pubblicitario *(m)*
Pt redactor de textos
publicidades *(m)*

coquille *(f) n* Fr
De Setzfehler *(m)*
En literal
Es error de imprenta *(m)*
It errore di stampa *(m)*
Pt errata literal *(f)*

cording *n* En
De Verschnüren *(n)*
Es encordonado *(m)*
Fr nerf *(m)*
It imputaggio *(m)*
Pt encordoamento *(m)*

cores para policromia *(f
pl)* Pt
Am process colors
De Verfahrensfarben *(pl)*
En process colours
Es colores para
policromía *(m pl)*
Fr polychromie *(f)*
It colori per policromia
(m pl)

corpo *(m) n* It
De Punktgröβe *(f)*
En point size
Es cuerpo del tipo *(m)*
Fr corps *(m)*
Pt tamanho de ponto
(m)

corpo del carattere *(m)*
It
De Kegelgröβe *(f)*
En body size (of type)
Es tamaño del tipo *(m)*
Fr corps d'un caractère
(m)
Pt tamanho de corpo
(m)

corps *(m) n* Fr
De Punktgröβe *(f)*
En point size
Es cuerpo del tipo *(m)*
It corpo *(m)*
Pt tamanho de ponto
(m)

corps d'un caractère *(m)*
Fr
De Kegelgröβe *(f)*
En body size (of type)
Es tamaño del tipo *(m)*
It corpo del carattere
(m)
Pt tamanho de corpo
(m)

correcção de cor *(f)* Pt
Am color correction
De Farbkorrektur *(f)*
En colour correction
Es rectificación
cromática *(f)*
Fr correction des
couleurs *(f)*
It correzione di colore
(f)

corrección de originales
(f) Es
De Manuskriptrevision *(f)*
En copy-editing

Fr préparation d'un
texte *(f)*
It correzione di originali
(f)
Pt revisão do original *(f)*

corrección de pruebas
(f) Es
De Korrekturlesen *(n)*
En proofreading
Fr correction
d'épreuves *(f)*
It correzione di bozze *(f)*
Pt revisão de provas *(f)*

correcciones *(f pl)* Es
De Korrekturen *(pl)*
En corrections *pl n*
Fr corrections *(f pl)*
It correzioni *(f pl)*
Pt correcções *(f pl)*

correcciones de autor *(f
pl)* Es
De Autorkorrekturen *(pl)*
En author's corrections
pl n
Fr corrections de
l'auteur *(f pl)*
It correzioni dell'autore
(f pl)
Pt correcções do autor
(f pl)

correcções *(f pl)* Pt
De Korrekturen *(pl)*
En corrections *pl n*
Es correcciones *(f pl)*
Fr corrections *(f pl)*
It correzioni *(f pl)*

correcções do autor *(f
pl)* Pt
De Autorkorrekturen *(pl)*
En author's corrections
pl n
Es correcciones de
autor *(f pl)*
Fr corrections de
l'auteur *(f pl)*
It correzioni dell'autore
(f pl)

correct *vb* En
De korrigieren
Es corregir
Fr corriger
It correggere
Pt corrigir

correcteur d'épreuves
(m) Fr
De Korrekturleser *(m)*
En proofreader
Es corrector de pruebas
(m)
It correttore di bozze
(m)
Pt revisor de provas *(m)*

correction d'épreuves
(f) Fr
De Korrekturlesen *(n)*
En proofreading
Es corrección de
pruebas *(f)*
It correzione di bozze *(f)*
Pt revisão de provas *(f)*

correction des couleurs
(f) Fr
Am color correction
De Farbkorrektur *(f)*
En colour correction
Es rectificación
cromática *(f)*
It correzione di colore
(f)
Pt correcção de cor *(f)*

corrections *pl n* En; Fr *(f)*
De Korrekturen *(pl)*
Es correcciones *(f pl)*
It correzioni *(f pl)*
Pt correcções *(f pl)*

corrections de l'auteur
(f pl) Fr
De Autorkorrekturen *(pl)*
En author's corrections
pl n
Es correcciones de
autor *(f pl)*
It correzioni dell'autore
(f pl)
Pt correcções do autor
(f pl)

corrector *(m) n* Es
De Zweiter Redakteur
(m)
En subeditor
Fr secrétaire de la
rédaction *(m)*
It redattore aggiunto
(m)
Pt redactor auxiliar *(m)*

corrector de imprenta
(m) Es
De Druckerei-
Korrekturleser *(m)*

En printer's reader
Fr corrigeur (m)
It correttore di bozze da stampa (m)
Pt leitor de tipografia (m)

corrector de originales (m) Es
De Manuskriptredakteur (m)
En copy-editor
Fr annotateur d'un texte (m)
It correttore di originali (m)
Pt revisor do original (m)

corrector de pruebas (m) Es
De Korrekturleser (m)
En proofreader
Fr correcteur d'épreuves (m)
It correttore di bozze (m)
Pt revisor de provas (m)

correggere vb It
De korrigieren
En correct
Es corregir
Fr corriger
Pt corrigir

correggere le bozze It
De korrekturlesen
En proofread
Es corregir pruebas
Fr corriger les épreuves
Pt rever provas

correggere originali It
De Manuskript revidieren
En copy-edit
Es corregir originales
Fr éditer un texte
Pt editar

corregir vb Es
De korrigieren
En correct
Fr corriger
It correggere
Pt corrigir

corregir originales Es
De Manuskript revidieren
En copy-edit

Fr éditer un texte
It correggere originali
Pt editar

corregir pruebas Es
De korrekturlesen
En proofread
Fr corriger les épreuves
It correggere le bozze
Pt rever provas

correio (m) n Pt
De Post (f)
En mail
Es correo (m)
Fr courrier (m)
It posta (f)

correo (m) n Es
De Post (f)
En mail
Fr courrier (m)
It posta (f)
Pt correio (m)

correrse la tinta Es
De randlos drucken
En bleed
Fr rogner
It refilare
Pt ressumbrar

correttore di bozze (m) It
De Korrekturleser (m)
En proofreader
Es corrector de pruebas (m)
Fr correcteur d'épreuves
Pt revisor de provas (m)

correttore di bozze da stampa (m) It
De Druckerei-Korrekturleser (m)
En printer's reader
Es corrector de imprenta (m)
Fr corrigeur (m)
Pt leitor de tipografia (m)

correttore di originali (m) It
De Manuskriptredakteur (m)
En copy-editor
Es corrector de originales (m)

Fr annotateur d'un texte (m)
Pt revisor do original (m)

correzione di bozze (f) It
De Korrekturlesen (n)
En proofreading
Es corrección de pruebas (f)
Fr correction d'épreuves (f)
Pt revisão de provas (f)

correzione di colore (f) It
Am color correction
De Farbkorrektur (f)
En colour correction
Es rectificación cromática (f)
Fr correction des couleurs (f)
Pt correcção de cor (f)

correzione di originali (f) It
De Manuskriptrevision (f)
En copy-editing
Es corrección de originales (f)
Fr préparation d'un texte (f)
Pt revisão do original (f)

correzioni (f pl) It
De Korrekturen (pl)
En corrections pl n
Es correcciones (f pl)
Fr corrections (f pl)
Pt correcções (f pl)

correzioni dell'autore (f pl) It
De Autorkorrekturen (pl)
En author's corrections pl n
Es correcciones de autor (f pl)
Fr corrections de l'auteur (f pl)
Pt correcções do autor (f pl)

corriere aereo (m) It
De Luftkurier (m)
En air courier
Es estafeta aérea (f)
Fr courrier aérien (m)
Pt mensageiro aéreo (m)

corriger vb Fr
De korrigieren
En correct
Es corregir
It correggere
Pt corrigir

corriger avec copie Fr
De mit dem Manuskript vergleichen
En read against copy
Es leer a la vista del original
It confrontare coll'original
Pt ler comparando com a cópia

corriger les épreuves Fr
De korrekturlesen
En proofread
Es corregir pruebas
It correggere le bozze
Pt rever provas

corrigeur (m) n Fr
De Druckerei-Korrekturleser (m)
En printer's reader
Es corrector de imprenta (m)
It correttore di bozze da stampa (m)
Pt leitor de tipografia (m)

corrigir vb Pt
De korrigieren
En correct
Es corregir
Fr corriger
It correggere

cortado a ras Es
De glatt zurichten
En cut flush
Fr composé à l'américaine
It tagliato a filo
Pt recorte raso

cortar vb Es
De beschneiden
En trim
Fr ébarber
It rifilare
Pt aparar

corte mecânico (m) Pt
De mechanische Zurichtung (f)

En mechanical overlay
Es alza mecánica (f)
Fr mise en train
   mécanique (f)
It sovrapposizione
   meccanica (f)

cortesía (f) n Es
De Respektblatt (n)
En flyleaf
Fr feuille de garde (f)
It risguardo (m)
Pt folha em branco (f)

corte transversal (m) Pt
De Querschnitt (m)
En cross section
Es sección transversal (f)
Fr vue en coupe (f)
It sezione trasversale (f)

coser por fora (m) Pt
De Holländern (n)
En oversewing
Es cosido por el plano
   (m)
Fr point hollandais (m)
It cucitura a punto
   saltato (f)

cosido a galápago (m) Es
De Sattelheftung (f)
En saddle stitching
Fr couture dans le pli (f)
It cucitura in piega (f)
Pt costura com
   grampos (f)

cosido con alambre (m)
   Es
De Drahtheftung (f)
En wire stitching
Fr couture métallique (f)
It cucitura a punti
   metallici (f)
Pt costura com arame
   (f)

cosido pela lombada (m)
   Pt
De Querheftung (f)
En side-stitching
Es cosido por el costado
   (m)
Fr couture de côté (f)
It cucitura laterale (f)

cosido por el costado
   (m) Es
De Querheftung (f)
En side-stitching

Fr couture de côté (f)
It cucitura laterale (f)
Pt cosido pela lombada
   (m)

cosido por el plano (m)
   Es
De Holländern (n)
En oversewing
Fr point hollandais (m)
It cucitura a punto
   saltato (f)
Pt coser por fora (m)

costes de fabricación (m
   pl) Es
De Herstellungskosten
   (pl)
En manufacturing costs
Fr coût de fabrication
   (m)
It costi di lavorazione
   (m pl)
Pt custos de produção
   (m pl)

coste unitario (m) Es
De Einheitskosten (pl)
En unit cost
Fr coût unitaire (m)
It costo unitario (m)
Pt custo unitário (m)

**costi di
   immagazzinaggio**
   (m pl) It
De Lagerkosten (pl)
En warehousing costs
Es gastos de almacén
   (m pl)
Fr frais
   d'emmagasinage (m
   pl)
Pt custos de armazém
   (m pl)

costi di lavorazione (m
   pl) It
De Herstellungskosten
   (pl)
En manufacturing costs
Es costes de fabricación
   (m pl)
Fr coût de fabrication
   (m)
Pt custos de produção
   (m pl)

costi di spedizione (m
   pl) It
De Verschiffungskosten
   (pl)

En shipping costs
Es gastos de envío (m
   pl)
Fr frais d'expédition (m
   pl)
Pt custos de envio (m
   pl)

costi di trasporto (m pl)
   It
De Transportkosten (pl)
En transport costs
Es gastos de transporte
   (m pl)
Fr frais de transport (m
   pl)
Pt custos de transporte
   (m pl)

**cost, insurance, and
   freight** (c.i.f.) En
De Kosten,
   Versicherung, und
   Fracht
Es costo, seguro, y flete
Fr coût, assurance, et
   fret (c.a.f.)
It costo, assicurazione,
   e nolo
Pt custo, seguro, e frete

**costo, assicurazione, e
   nolo** It
De Kosten,
   Versicherung, und
   Fracht
En cost, insurance, and
   freight (c.i.f.)
Es costo, seguro, y flete
Fr coût, assurance, et
   fret (c.a.f.)
Pt custo, seguro, e frete

costo, seguro, y flete Es
De Kosten,
   Versicherung, und
   Fracht
En cost, insurance, and
   freight (c.i.f.)
Fr coût, assurance, et
   fret (c.a.f.)
It costo, assicurazione,
   e nolo
Pt custo, seguro, e frete

costo unitario (m) It
De Einheitskosten (pl)
En unit cost
Es coste unitario (m)
Fr coût unitaire (m)
Pt custo unitário (m)

costume americano (m)
   Pt
De amerikanischer
   Sprachgebrauch (m)
En American usage
Es uso americano (m)
Fr usage américain (m)
It uso americano (m)

costume britânico (m) Pt
De britischer
   Sprachgebrauch (m)
En British usage
Es uso británico (m)
Fr usage anglais (m)
It uso britannico (m)

costura com arame (f) Pt
De Drahtheftung (f)
En wire stitching
Es cosido con alambre
   (m)
Fr couture métallique (f)
It cucitura a punti
   metallici (f)

costura com grampos (f)
   Pt
De Sattelheftung (f)
En saddle stitching
Es cosido a galápago
   (m)
Fr couture dans le pli (f)
It cucitura in piega (f)

cotação (f) n Pt
De Angebot (n)
En quotation (estimate)
Es cotización (f)
Fr prix coté (m)
It quotazione (f)

cotar vb Pt
De ein Angebot
   unterbreiten
En quote (a price)
Es cotizar
Fr mentionner
It dare le quotazioni

côté de deux (m) Fr
De innere Form (f)
En inner forme
Es plana interior (f)
It forma interna (f)
Pt forma interior (f)

côté des marges (m) Fr
De Anlagekanten (pl)
En feed edges pl n

Es orillas de entrada (f
pl)
It margini di entrata (m
pl)
Pt bordos de entrada (m
pl)

côté des pinces (m) Fr
De Greifkanten (f)
En gripper edge
Es orilla de entrada (f)
It lato pinza (m)
Pt margem dianteira (f)

**côté émulsion vers le
bas** (m) Fr
De Emulsionsseite unten
(f)
En emulsion-side down
Es lado de la emulsión
hacia abajo (m)
It lato emulsione
inferiore (m)
Pt emulsão lado de
baixo (f)

**côté émulsion vers le
haut** (m) Fr
De Emulsionsseite oben
(f)
En emulsion-side up
Es lado de la emulsión
hacia arriba (m)
It lato emulsione
superiore (m)
Pt emulsão lado de
cima (f)

côté feutre (m) Fr
De Filzseite (f)
En felt side
Es lado de fieltro (m)
It lato feltro (m)
Pt lado de feltro (m)

côté toilé (m) Fr
De Siebseite (f)
En wire side
Es cara interior (f)
It lato tela (m)
Pt lado da tela (m)

cotización (f) n Es
De Angebot (n)
En quotation (estimate)
Fr prix coté (m)
It quotazione (f)
Pt cotação (f)

cotizar vb Es
De ein Angebot
unterbreiten
En quote (a price)
Fr mentionner
It dare le quotazioni
Pt cotar

couchage du papier (m)
Fr
De Streichen (n)
En coating
Es revestimiento (m)
It rivestimento (m)
Pt revestimento (m)

coulée (f) n Fr
De Giesen (n)
En casting
Es fusión (f)
It fusione (f)
Pt fusão (f)

coupure (f) n Fr
De Trennung (f)
En hyphenation
Es separación con
guiones (f)
It legatura con trattino
(f)
Pt colocação de um
traço de união (f)

coupure de journal (f) Fr
De Presseausschnitt (m)
En press cutting
Es recorte de prensa (m)
It ritaglio di giornale
(m)
Pt recorte de imprensa
(f)

courrier (m) n Fr
De Post (f)
En mail
Es correo (m)
It posta (f)
Pt correio (m)

courrier aérien (m) Fr
De Luftkurier (m)
En air courier
Es estafeta aérea (f)
It corriere aereo (m)
Pt mensageiro aéreo
(m)

**coût, assurance, et fret
(c.a.f.)** Fr
De Kosten,

Versicherung, und
Fracht
En cost, insurance, and
freight (c.i.f.)
Es costo, seguro, y flete
It costo, assicurazione,
e nolo
Pt custo, seguro, e frete

coût de fabrication (m)
Fr
De Herstellungskosten
(pl)
En manufacturing costs
Es costes de fabricación
(m pl)
It costi di lavorazione
(m pl)
Pt custos de produção
(m pl)

**coût du tirage
supplémentaire** (m)
Fr
De Fortdruck-Preis (m)
En run-on price
Es precio de más
ejemplares (m)
It prezzo di
super-tiratura (m)
Pt preço de exemplares
a mais (m)

coût unitaire (m) Fr
De Einheitskosten (pl)
En unit cost
Es coste unitario (m)
It costo unitario (m)
Pt custo unitário (m)

couture dans le pli (f) Fr
De Sattelheftung (f)
En saddle stitching
Es cosido a galápago
(m)
It cucitura in piega (f)
Pt costura com
grampos (f)

couture de côté (f) Fr
De Querheftung (f)
En side-stitching
Es cosido por el costado
(m)
It cucitura laterale (f)
Pt cosido pela lombada
(m)

couture métallique (f) Fr
De Drahtheftung (f)
En wire stitching

Es cosido con alambre
(m)
It cucitura a punti
metallici (f)
Pt costura com arame
(f)

couverture (f) n Fr
De Buchdeckel (m)
En case (bookbinding)
Es tapas (f)
It custodia (f)
Pt capa separada (f)

couvrir ses dépenses Fr
De die Kosten decken
En cover one's costs
Es cubrir los gastos
propios
It coprire i costi
Pt cobrir as despesas

cover one's costs En
De die Kosten decken
Es cubrir los gastos
propios
Fr couvrir ses dépenses
It coprire i costi
Pt cobrir as despesas

cover paper En
De Umschlagpapier (n)
Es papel para cubiertas
(m)
Fr papier à couverture
(m)
It carta per copertine (f)
Pt papel de cobertura
(m)

craft books pl n En
De Handwerksbücher
(pl)
Es libros de trabajos
manuales (m pl)
Fr ouvrages artisanaux
(m pl)
It guide pratiche (f pl)
Pt livros técnicos (m pl)

craftsman n En
De Handwerker (m)
Es artesano (m)
Fr artisan (m)
It artigiano (m)
Pt artesão (m)

cran (m) n Es, Fr
De Signaturrinne (f)
En nick

It tacca (f)
Pt entalhe (m)

crasses (f pl) n Fr
De Krätze (f)
En dross
Es escoria (f)
It scarto (m)
Pt escória (f)

creación (f) n Es
De Entstehungsarbeiten
    (pl)
En origination
Fr source (f)
It origine (f)
Pt criação (f)

cream laid paper En
De mattgelbes geripptes
    Papier (n)
Es papel verjurado
    crema (m)
Fr papier vergé pâle (m)
It carta vergata crema
    (f)
Pt papel rugoso (m)

cream wove paper En
De mattgelbes
    Velinpapier (n)
Es papel avitelado
    crema (m)
Fr vélin crème (m)
It velino cremo (m)
Pt papel tecido
    enrugado (m)

créateur (m) n Fr
De Designer (m)
En designer
Es diseñador (m)
It disegnatore (m)
Pt desenhador (m)

créditos (m pl) Es, Pt
De Anerkennung (f)
En credits pl n
Fr remerciements (m pl)
It ringraziamento (m)

credits pl n En
De Anerkennung (f)
Es créditos (m pl)
Fr remerciements (m pl)
It ringraziamento (m)
Pt créditos (m pl)

crénage (m) n Fr
De Überhang (m)
En kern
Es talud (m)
It sporgenza (f)
Pt saliência do corpo do
    tipo (f)

criação (f) n Pt
De Entstehungsarbeiten
    (pl)
En origination
Es creación (f)
Fr source (f)
It origine (f)

crimp vb En
De kräuseln
Es marcar con rayas
Fr gaufrer
It ondulare
Pt enrugar

critica letteraria (f) It
De Literaturkritik (f)
En literary criticism
Es crítica literaria (f)
Fr critique littéraire (f)
Pt crítica literária (f)

crítica literaria (f) Es
De Literaturkritik (f)
En literary criticism
Fr critique littéraire (f)
It critica letteraria (f)
Pt crítica literária (f)

crítica literária (f) Pt
De Literaturkritik (f)
En literary criticism
Es crítica literaria (f)
Fr critique littéraire (f)
It critica letteraria (f)

critique d'un livre (f) Fr
De Rezension (f)
En review
Es reseña (f)
It recensione (f)
Pt resenha (f)

critique littéraire (f) Fr
De Literaturkritik (f)
En literary criticism
Es crítica literaria (f)
It critica letteraria (f)
Pt crítica literária (f)

croce (f) n It
De Kreuz (n)
En dagger
Es cruz (f)
Fr croix (f)
Pt cruz (f)

croci di registro (m pl) It
De Paßkreuze (pl)
En register marks
Es marcas de registro (f
    pl)
Fr croix de repère (f pl)
Pt marcas de registo (f
    pl)

croix (f) n Fr
De Kreuz (n)
En dagger
Es cruz (f)
It croce (f)
Pt cruz (f)

croix de repère (f pl) Fr
De Paßkreuze (pl)
En register marks
Es marcas de registro (f
    pl)
It croci di registro (m
    pl)
Pt marcas de registo (f
    pl)

cronista (m) n It
De Berichterstatter (m)
En reporter
Es reportero (m)
Fr reporter (m)
Pt reporter (m)

crop vb En
De zurichten
Es recortar
Fr détourer
It scontornare
Pt recortar

croquis (m) n Fr
De Skizze (f)
En rough
Es boceto (m)
It abbozzo (m)
Pt esboço (m)

cross reference En
De Querverweis (m)
Es interreferencia (f)
Fr renvoi (m)
It rimando (m)
Pt nota remissiva (f)

cross section En
De Querschnitt (m)
Es sección transversal (f)
Fr vue en coupe (f)
It sezione trasversale (f)
Pt corte transversal (m)

cruz (f) n Es, Pt
De Kreuz (n)
En dagger
Fr croix (f)
It croce (f)

cuadrado (m) n Es
De Quadrat (n)
En quad
Fr cadrat (m)
It quadrato (m)
Pt quadrado (m)

cuadratín (m) n Es
De Geviert (n)
En em
Fr cadratin (m)
It riga (f)
Pt quadratim (m)

cuadrícula (f) n Es
De kariertes Papier (n)
En quadrille
Fr papier quadrillé (m)
It carta quadrettata (f)
Pt papel quadriculado
    (m)

cuarto oscuro (m) Es
De Dunkelkammer (f)
En darkroom
Fr chambre noire (f)
It camera oscura (f)
Pt câmara escura (f)

cuatricromía (f) n Es
Am four-color printing
De Vierfarbdruck (m)
En four-colour printing
Fr quadrichromie (f)
It stampa a quattro
    colori (f)
Pt impressão a quatro
    cores (f)

**cubrir los gastos
    propios** Es
De die Kosten decken
En cover one's costs
Fr couvrir ses dépenses
It coprire i costi
Pt cobrir as despesas

cucitura a punti metallici *(f)* It
De Drahtheftung *(f)*
En wire stitching
Es cosido con alambre *(m)*
Fr couture métallique *(f)*
Pt costura com arame *(f)*

cucitura a punto saltato *(f)* It
De Holländern *(n)*
En oversewing
Es cosido por el plano *(m)*
Fr point hollandais *(m)*
Pt coser por fora *(m)*

cucitura in piega *(f)* It
De Sattelheftung *(f)*
En saddle stitching
Es cosido a galápago *(m)*
Fr couture dans le pli *(f)*
Pt costura com grampos *(f)*

cucitura laterale *(f)* It
De Querheftung *(f)*
En side-stitching
Es cosido por el costado *(m)*
Fr couture de côté *(f)*
Pt cosido pela lombada *(m)*

cuerpo del tipo *(m)* Es
De Punktgröβe *(f)*
En point size
Fr corps *(m)*
It corpo *(m)*
Pt tamanho de ponto *(m)*

cuerpo de papel *(m)* Es
De Papierdicke *(f)*
En bulk (of paper)
Fr épaisseur de papier *(f)*
It grossezza di carta *(f)*
Pt grossura do papel *(f)*

cul-de-lampe *(m)* n Fr
De Schluβvignette *(f)*
En tailpiece
Es culo de lámpara *(m)*
It finalino *(m)*
Pt vinheta final *(f)*

culo de lámpara *(m)* Es
De Schluβvignette *(f)*
En tailpiece
Fr cul-de-lampe *(m)*
It finalino *(m)*
Pt vinheta final *(f)*

cuña *(f)* n Es
De Keil *(m)*
En quoin
Fr coin *(m)*
It serraforme *(m)*
Pt cunha *(f)*

cunha *(f)* n Pt
De Keil *(m)*
En quoin
Es cuña *(f)*
Fr coin *(m)*
It serraforme *(m)*

cursivas *(f pl)* Es
De Kursivdruck *(m)*
En italics *pl n*
Fr italiques *(m pl)*
It caratteri corsivi *(m pl)*
Pt itálico *(m)*

custodia *(f)* n It
De Buchdeckel *(m)*
En case (bookbinding)
Es tapas *(f)*
Fr couverture *(f)*
Pt capa separada *(f)*

custos de armazém *(m pl)* Pt
De Lagerkosten *(pl)*
En warehousing costs
Es gastos de almacén *(m pl)*
Fr frais d'emmagasinage *(m pl)*
It costi di immagazzinaggio *(m pl)*

custos de envio *(m pl)* Pt
De Verschiffungkosten *(pl)*
En shipping costs
Es gastos de envío *(m pl)*
Fr frais d'expédition *(m pl)*
It costi di spedizione *(m pl)*

custos de produção *(m pl)* Pt
De Herstellungskosten *(pl)*
En manufacturing costs
Es costes de fabricación *(m pl)*
Fr coût de fabrication *(m)*
It costi di lavorazione *(m pl)*

custos de transporte *(m pl)* Pt
De Transportkosten *(pl)*
En transport costs
Es gastos de transporte *(m pl)*
Fr frais de transport *(m pl)*
It costi di trasporto *(m pl)*

custo, seguro, e frete Pt
De Kosten, Versicherung, und Fracht
En cost, insurance, and freight (c.i.f.)
Es costo, seguro, y flete
Fr coût, assurance, et fret (c.a.f.)
It costo, assicurazione, e nolo

custo unitário *(m)* Pt
De Einheitskosten *(pl)*
En unit cost
Es coste unitario *(m)*
Fr coût unitaire *(m)*
It costo unitario *(m)*

cutaway view En
De Schnittbild *(n)*
Es vista en corte *(f)*
Fr scène de coupe *(f)*
It vista in sezione *(f)*
Pt vista recortada *(f)*

cut flush En
De glatt zurichten
Es cortado a ras
Fr composé à l'américaine
It tagliato a filo
Pt recorte raso

cut out En
De Freistellung *(f)*
Es recortado *(m)*
Fr découpage *(m)*

It scontornata *(f)*
Pt recorte *(m)*

cyan n En; Fr *(m)*
De Cyan *(n)*
Es azul verdoso *(m)*
It ciano *(m)*

Cyan *(n)* n De
En cyan
Es azul verdoso *(m)*
Fr cyan *(m)*
It ciano *(m)*
Pt cianogénio *(m)*

cylinder dressing En
De Zylinderaufzug *(m)*
Es rectificado de cilindros *(m)*
Fr habillage *(m)*
It rivestimento per cilindri *(m)*
Pt rectificação de cilindros *(f)*

cylinder machine En
De Schnellpresse *(f)*
Es prensa planocilíndrica *(f)*
Fr machine à forme ronde *(f)*
It rotativa *(f)*
Pt máquina de rolos *(f)*

cyrillic alphabet En
De kyrillisches Alphabet *(n)*
Es alfabeto cirílico *(m)*
Fr alphabet cyrillique *(m)*
It alfabeto cirillico *(m)*
Pt alfabeto cirílico *(m)*

D

dactilógrafa *(f)* n Pt
De Typistin *(f)*
En typist
Es mecanografía *(f)*
Fr dactylographe *(f)*
It dattilografa *(f)*

dactilografado (m) n Pt
De Maschinenschrift (f)
En typescript
Es escrito a máquina (m)
Fr manuscrit
   dactylographié (m)
It dattiloscritto (m)

dactilografia (f) n Pt
De Tippen (n)
En typing
Es mecanografiado (m)
Fr dactylographie (f)
It scrivere a macchina
   (m)

dactylographe (f) n Fr
De Typistin (f)
En typist
Es mecanografía (f)
It dattilografa (f)
Pt dactilógrafa (f)

dactylographie (f) n Fr
De Tippen (n)
En typing
Es mecanografiado (m)
It scrivere a macchina
   (m)
Pt dactilografia (f)

dados (m pl) Pt
De Daten (pl)
En data pl n
Es datos (m pl)
Fr données (f pl)
It dati (m pl)

dados de impressão (m
   pl) Pt
De Impressums-Daten
   (pl)
En imprint data
Es datos a pie de
   imprenta (m pl)
Fr indications d'editeur
   et d'imprimeur (f pl)
It data d'impressa (f)

dados de publicação (m
   pl) Pt
De Veröffent-
   lichungsdaten (pl)
En publication data
Es datos de publicación
   (m pl)
Fr référence de la
   publication (f)
It dati di pubblicazione
   (m pl)

**dados legíveis na
   máquina** (m pl) Pt
De vom Rechner lesbare
   Daten (pl)
En machine-readable
   data
Es datos legibles con
   máquina (m pl)
Fr éléments codés (m
   pl)
It dati leggibili per la
   macchina (m pl)

dagger n En
De Kreuz (n)
Es cruz (f)
Fr croix (f)
It croce (f)
Pt cruz (f)

damper n En
De Feuchtwalze (f)
Es mojador (m)
Fr rouleau mouilleur (m)
It umettatore (m)
Pt molhador (m)

dandy roll En
De Egoutteur (m)
Es rodillo afiligranador
   (m)
Fr rouleau égoutteur
   (m)
It cilindro à filigrana (m)
Pt rolo filigranador (m)

**Dank für die
   Genehmigung von
   Photos** (m) De
En photo credits
Es fotocréditos (m pl)
Fr origine des
   photographies (f)
It indice dei fotografi
   (m pl)
Pt fotocréditos (m pl)

dare le quotazioni It
De ein Angebot
   unterbreiten
En quote (a price)
Es cotizar
Fr mentionner
Pt cotar

darkroom n En
De Dunkelkammer (f)
Es cuarto oscuro (m)
Fr chambre noire (f)
It camera oscura (f)
Pt câmara escura (f)

dash n En
De Gedankenstrich (m)
Es raya (f)
Fr filet (m)
It lineetta (f)
Pt filete (m)

data pl n En
De Daten (pl)
Es datos (m pl)
Fr données (f pl)
It dati (m pl)
Pt dados (m pl)

data bank En
De Datenbank (f)
Es banco de datos (m)
Fr banque de données
   (f)
It banca dei dati (f)
Pt banco de dados (m)

data capture En
De Datenerfassung (f)
Es toma de datos (f)
Fr saisie de données (f)
It cattura dei dati (f)
Pt captação de dados (f)

data de publicação (f) Pt
De Veröffent-
   lichungsdatum (n)
En publication date
Es fecha de publicación
   (f)
Fr date de parution (f)
It data di pubblicazione
   (f)

data d'impressa (f) It
De Impressums-Daten
   (pl)
En imprint data
Es datos a pie de
   imprenta (m pl)
Fr indications d'editeur
   et d'imprimeur (f pl)
Pt dados de impressão
   (m pl)

data di pubblicazione (f)
   It
De Veröffent-
   lichungsdatum (n)
En publication date
Es fecha de publicación
   (f)
Fr date de parution (f)
Pt data de publicação (f)

data file En
De Datenablage (f)
Es fichero de datos (m)
Fr fichier de données
   (m)
It archivio dati (m)
Pt arquivo de dados (m)

data processing En
De Datenverarbeitung (f)
Es proceso de datos (m)
Fr traitement des
   données (m)
It elaborazione di dati
   (f)
Pt tratamento de dados
   (m)

date de parution (f) Fr
De Veröffent-
   lichungsdatum (n)
En publication date
Es fecha de publicación
   (f)
It data di pubblicazione
   (f)
Pt data de publicação (f)

Daten (pl) De
En data pl n
Es datos (m pl)
Fr données (f pl)
It dati (m pl)
Pt dados (m pl)

Datenablage (f) n De
En data file
Es fichero de datos (m)
Fr fichier de données
   (m)
it archivio dati (m)
Pt arquivo de dados (m)

Datenbank (f) n De
En data bank
Es banco de datos (m)
Fr banque de données
   (f)
It banca dei dati (f)
Pt banco de dados (m)

Datenerfassung (f) n De
En data capture
Es toma de datos (f)
Fr saisie de données (f)
It cattura dei dati (f)
Pt captação de dados (f)

Datenverarbeitung (f) n
   De
En data processing

Es proceso de datos *(m)*
Fr traitement des
données *(m)*
It elaborazione di dati
(f)
Pt tratamento de dados
(m)

dati *(m pl)* It
De Daten *(pl)*
En data *pl n*
Es datos *(m pl)*
Fr données *(f pl)*
Pt dados *(m pl)*

dati di pubblicazione *(m
pl)* It
De Veröffent-
lichungsdaten *(pl)*
En publication data
Es datos de publicación
(m pl)
Fr référence de la
publication *(f)*
Pt dados de publicação
(m pl)

**dati leggibili per la
macchina** *(m pl)* It
De vom Rechner lesbare
Daten *(pl)*
En machine-readable
data
Es datos legibles con
máquina *(m pl)*
Fr éléments codés *(m
pl)*
Pt dados legíveis na
máquina *(m pl)*

datore di lavoro *(m)* It
De Arbeitgeber *(m)*
En employer
Es patrón *(m)*
Fr employeur *(m)*
Pt entidade patronal *(f)*

datos *(m pl)* Es
De Daten *(pl)*
En data *pl n*
Fr données *(f pl)*
It dati *(m pl)*
Pt dados *(m pl)*

datos a pie de imprenta
(m pl) Es
De Impressums-Daten
(pl)
En imprint data
Fr indications d'editeur
et d'imprimeur *(f pl)*
It data d'impressa *(f)*

Pt dados de impressão
(m pl)

datos de publicación *(m
pl)* Es
De Veröffent-
lichungsdaten *(pl)*
En publication data
Fr référence de la
publication *(f)*
It dati di pubblicazione
(m pl)
Pt dados de publicação
(m pl)

**datos legibles con
máquina** *(m pl)* Es
De vom Rechner lesbare
Daten *(pl)*
En machine-readable
data
Fr éléments codés *(m
pl)*
It dati leggibili per la
macchina *(m pl)*
Pt dados legíveis na
máquina *(m pl)*

dattilografa *(f)* n It
De Typistin *(f)*
En typist
Es mecanografía *(f)*
Fr dactylographe *(f)*
Pt dactilógrafa *(f)*

dattiloscritto *(m)* n It
De Maschinenschrift *(f)*
En typescript
Es escrito a máquina *(m)*
Fr manuscrit
dactylographié *(m)*
Pt dactilografado *(m)*

Daumenindex *(m)* n De
En thumb index
Es índice recortado *(m)*
Fr index à onglets *(m)*
It indice a rubrica *(m)*
Pt índice com letras
salientes na borda da
página *(m)*

deadline n En
De Stichtag *(m)*
Es plazo *(m)*
Fr limite *(f)*
It scadenza *(f)*
Pt prazo *(m)*

decapitar *vb* Pt
De auseinandertragen
En decollate
Es separar hojas
Fr déliasser
It decollare

décharge *(f)* n Fr
De Drucktuch *(n)*
En blanket (offset litho)
Es mantilla *(f)*
It caucciù *(m)*; tessuto
gommato *(m)*
Pt feltro *(m)*

decimal point En
De Dezimalkomma *(n)*
Es punto decimal *(m)*
Fr virgule *(f)*
It virgola decimale *(f)*
Pt ponto decimal *(m)*

decisão marginal *(f)* Pt
De knappe Entscheidung
(f)
En marginal decision
Es decisión marginal *(f)*
Fr décision marginale *(f)*
It decisione marginale
(f)

decisione marginale *(f)*
It
De knappe Entscheidung
(f)
En marginal decision
Es decisión marginal *(f)*
Fr décision marginale *(f)*
Pt decisão marginal *(f)*

decisión marginal *(f)* Es
De knappe Entscheidung
(f)
En marginal decision
Fr décision marginale *(f)*
It decisione marginale
(f)
Pt decisão marginal *(f)*

décision marginale *(f)* Fr
De knappe Entscheidung
(f)
En marginal decision
Es decisión marginal *(f)*
It decisione marginale
(f)
Pt decisão marginal *(f)*

Deckblatt *(n)* n De
En overlay (on artwork,
etc.)

Es superponible *(m)*
Fr becquet *(m)*
It sovrapposizione *(f)*
Pt coberta *(f)*

deckle edge En
De Büttenrand *(m)*
Es barba *(f)*
Fr barbe *(f)*
It zazzera *(f)*
Pt barba *(f)*

decollare *vb* It
De auseinandertragen
En decollate
Es separar hojas
Fr déliasser
Pt decapitar

decollate *vb* En
De auseinandertragen
Es separar hojas
Fr déliasser
It decollare
Pt decapitar

de cortes dorados Es
De mit Goldschnitt
En gilt-edged
Fr doré sur tranche
It con bordi dorati
Pt dourado nas beiras

découpage *(m)* n Fr
De Freistellung *(f)*
En cut out
Es recortado *(m)*
It scontornata *(f)*
Pt recorte *(m)*

découpure *(f)* n Fr
De Papierabschnitt *(n)*
En offcut
Es papel de recorte *(m)*
It ritaglio di carta *(m)*
Pt papel de recorte *(m)*

dedica *(f)* n It
De Widmung *(f)*
En dedication
Es dedicatoria *(f)*
Fr dédicace *(f)*
Pt dedicatória *(f)*

dédicace *(f)* n Fr
De Widmung *(f)*
En dedication
Es dedicatoria *(f)*
It dedica *(f)*
Pt dedicatória *(f)*

dedication n En
De Widmung (f)
Es dedicatoria (f)
Fr dédicace (f)
It dedica (f)
Pt dedicatória (f)

dedication page En
De Widmungsseite (f)
Es página de dedicatoria (f)
Fr page de dédicace (f)
It pagina di dedica (f)
Pt página de dedicatória (f)

dedicatoria (f) n Es
De Widmung (f)
En dedication
Fr dédicace (f)
It dedica (f)
Pt dedicatória (f)

dedicatória (f) n Pt
De Widmung (f)
En dedication
Es dedicatoria (f)
Fr dédicace (f)
It dedica (f)

deep-etch litho plate En
De Tiefdruck-Offsetplatte (f)
Es plancha al hueco-offset (f)
Fr offset en creux (m)
It lastra litografica a incisione profonda (f)
Pt chapa litográfica de gravação funda (f)

défaut (m) n Fr
De Fehler (m)
En blemish
Es imperfección (f)
It imperfezione (f)
Pt mancha (f)

Defekt (m) n De
En battered type
Es carácter estropeo (m)
Fr caractère endommagé (m)
It carattere avariato (m)
Pt carácter defeituoso (m)

Defektbogen (m) n De
En broke (papermaking)
Es papel roto (m)
Fr cassés (m pl)

It cascame di carta (m)
Pt empastelado (m)

definição (f) n Pt
De Definition (f)
En definition (lexicography)
Es definición (f)
Fr définition (f)
It definizione (f)

definición (f) n Es
De Definition (f)
En definition (lexicography)
Fr définition (f)
It definizione (f)
Pt definição (f)

definition (lexicography) n En
De Definition (f)
Es definición (f)
Fr définition (f)
It definizione (f)
Pt definição (f)

definition (photography) n En
De Bildschärfe (f)
Es claridad (f)
Fr netteté (f)
It nitidezza (f)
Pt nitidez (f)

Definition (f) n De
En definition (lexicography)
Es definición (f)
Fr définition (f)
It definizione (f)
Pt definição (f)

définition (f) n Fr
De Definition (f)
En definition (lexicography)
Es definición (f)
It definizione (f)
Pt definição (f)

definizione (f) n It
De Definition (f)
En definition (lexicography)
Es definición (f)
Fr définition (f)
Pt definição (f)

défraîchi adj Fr
De verschmutzt
En shop-soiled
Es sucio
It sporco
Pt sujado na loja

de interés periodístico Es
De aktuell
En newsworthy
Fr d'intérêt journalistique
It che fa notizia
Pt digno de ser publicado

déjeuner de travail (m) Fr
De geschäftliches Mittagessen (n)
En working lunch
Es comida de trabajo (f)
It pranzo di lavoro (m)
Pt almoço de trabalho (m)

delaminación (f) n Es
De Ableimung (f)
En delamination
Fr séparation des plis (f)
It separazione degli strati (f)
Pt deslaminação (f)

delamination n En
De Ableimung (f)
Es delaminación (f)
Fr séparation des plis (f)
It separazione degli strati (f)
Pt deslaminação (f)

delegato di fabbrica (m) It
De Gewerkschafts-Betriebsobmann (m)
En shop steward
Es dirigente obrero (m)
Fr délégué d'atelier (m)
Pt balconista (m)

délégué d'atelier (m) Fr
De Gewerkschafts-Betriebsobmann (m)
En shop steward
Es dirigente obrero (m)
It delegato di fabbrica (m)
Pt balconista (m)

delete vb En
De streichen
Es suprimir
Fr rayer
It cancellare
Pt apagar

delete mark En
De Tilgungszeichen (n)
Es marca de supresión (f)
Fr marque à supprimer (f)
It segno di cancellatura (m)
Pt marca de eliminação (f)

deletion n En
De Streichung (f)
Es supresión (f)
Fr suppression (f)
It cancellatura (f)
Pt eliminação (f)

deletrear vb Es
De buchstabieren
En spell
Fr épeler
It sillabare
Pt soletrar

deletreo (m) n Es
De Buchstabierung (f)
En spelling
Fr épellation (f)
It compitazione (f)
Pt soletração (f)

deletreo americano (m) Es
De amerikanische Schreibweise (f)
En American spelling
Fr orthographe américaine (f)
It ortografia americana (f)
Pt ortografia americana (f)

deletreo británico (m) Es
De britische Schreibweise (f)
En British spelling
Fr orthographe anglaise (f)
It ortografia britannica (f)
Pt ortografia britânica (f)

déliasser vb Fr
De auseinandertragen
En decollate
Es separar hojas
It decollare
Pt decapitar

déliés (m pl) Fr
De Haarstriche (pl)
En hair lines
Es filetes extrafinos (m pl)
It linee finissime (f pl)
Pt filetes extrafinos (m pl)

delineante (m) n Es
Am draftsman
De Zeichner (m)
En draughtsman
Fr dessinateur-concepteur (m)
It disegnatore (m)
Pt autor de esboço (m)

demi-cadratin (m) n Fr
De Halbgeviert (n)
En en
Es medio cuadratín (m)
It mezza riga (f)
Pt meio quadratim (m)

demi-reliure (f) Fr
De Buchband mit engem Lederrücken (n)
En quarter-bound book
Es libro encuadernado a cuarta piel (m)
It libro rilegato con dorso in pelle (m)
Pt livro in quarto (m)

demi-reliure à petits coins (f) Fr
De Halbfranzband (m)
En half binding
Es encuadernación a media piel (f)
It mezza rilegatura (f)
Pt encadernação a meia pele (f)

densimètre (m) n Fr
De Densitometer (n)
En densitometer
Es densitómetro (m)
It densitometro (m)
Pt densitómetro (m)

densimétrie (f) n Fr
De Densitometrie (f)
En densitometry
Es densitometría (f)
It densitometria (f)
Pt densitometria (f)

densitometer n En
De Densitometer (n)
Es densitómetro (m)
Fr densimètre (m)
It densitometro (m)
Pt densitómetro (m)

Densitometer (n) n De
En densitometer
Es densitómetro (m)
Fr densimètre (m)
It densitometro (m)
Pt densitómetro (m)

densitometria (f) n It, Pt
De Densitometrie (f)
En densitometry
Es densitometría (f)
Fr densimétrie (f)

densitometría (f) n Es
De Densitometrie (f)
En densitometry
Fr densimétrie (f)
It densitometria (f)
Pt densitometria (f)

Densitometrie (f) n De
En densitometry
Es densitometría (f)
Fr densimétrie (f)
It densitometria (f)
Pt densitometria (f)

densitometro (m) n It
De Densitometer (n)
En densitometer
Es densitómetro (m)
Fr densimètre (m)
Pt densitómetro (m)

densitómetro (m) n Es, Pt
De Densitometer (n)
En densitometer
Fr densimètre (m)
It densitometro (m)

densitometry n En
De Densitometrie (f)
Es densitometría (f)
Fr densimétrie (f)

It densitometria (f)
Pt densitometria (f)

dentada adj Pt
De eingerückt
En indented
Es sangrado
Fr dentelé
It dentellato

dentelé adj Fr
De eingerückt
En indented
Es sangrado
It dentellato
Pt dentada

dentellare vb It
De einrücken
En indent
Es sangrar
Fr renforcer
Pt abrir parágrafo

dentellato adj It
De eingerückt
En indented
Es sangrado
Fr dentelé
Pt dentada

departamento de derechos en el extranjero (m) Es
De Auslandsrecht-Abteilung (f)
En foreign-rights department
Fr service des droits à l'étranger (m)
It reparto diritti esteri (m)
Pt departamento de direitos estrangeiros (m)

departamento de direitos estrangeiros (m) Pt
De Auslandsrecht-Abteilung (f)
En foreign-rights department
Es departamento de derechos en el extranjero (m)
Fr service des droits à l'étranger (m)
It reparto diritti esteri (m)

departamento de produção (m) Pt
De Produktionsabteilung (f)
En production department
Es departamento de producción (m)
Fr service production (m)
It reparto produzione (m)

departamento de producción (m) Es
De Produktionsabteilung (f)
En production department
Fr service production (m)
It reparto produzione (m)
Pt departamento de produção (m)

departamento de publicidad (m) Es
De Werbeabteilung (f)
En publicity department
Fr service de la publicité (m)
It reparto pubblicitario (m)
Pt departamento de publicidade (f)

departamento de publicidade (f) Pt
De Werbeabteilung (f)
En publicity department
Es departamento de publicidad (m)
Fr service de la publicité (m)
It reparto pubblicitario (m)

departamento editorial (m) Es, Pt
De Redaktion (f)
En editorial department
Fr rédaction (f)
It redazione (f)

depósito (m) n Es, Pt
De Schriftlager (n)
En magazine (matrix store)
Fr magasin (m)
It caricatore (m)

depth *n* En
De Satzhöhe *(f)*
Es profundidad *(f)*
Fr hauteur *(f)*
It profondità *(f)*
Pt profundidade *(f)*

**derechos
cinematográficos**
(m pl) Es
De Verfilmungsrechte
(pl)
En film rights *pl n*
Fr droits sur le film *(m pl)*
It diritti cinematografici
(m pl)
Pt direitos
cinematográficos *(m pl)*

derechos de autor *(m pl)*
Es
De Tantiemen *(pl)*
En royalties *pl n*
Fr droits d'auteur *(m pl)*
It diritti di licenza *(m pl)*
Pt direitos de autor *(m pl)*

derechos de televisión
(m pl) Es
De Fernsehrechte *(pl)*
En television rights *pl n*
Fr droits de télévision
(m pl)
It diritti televisivi *(m pl)*
Pt direitos de televisão
(m pl)

**derechos en el
extranjero** *(m pl)* Es
De Auslandsrechte *(pl)*
En foreign rights
Fr droits à l'étranger *(m pl)*
It diritti esteri *(m pl)*
Pt direitos estrangeiros
(m pl)

desactualizado *adj* Pt
De veraltet
En out of date
Es anticuado
Fr périmé
It superato

desarrollar *vb* Es
De entwickeln (Planung)
En develop (planning)
Fr exécuter

It elaborare
Pt desenvolver

descascamento *(m) n* Pt
De Kalkschleier *(m)*
En chalking
Es desintegración en
polvo *(f)*
Fr poudrage *(m)*
It sfarinamento *(m)*

descenders (of letter) *pl
n* En
De Unterlängen *(pl)*
Es trazos inferiores *(m pl)*
Fr jambages *(m pl)*
It lettere discendenti *(f pl)*
Pt traços inferiores *(m pl)*

descuadrado *adj* Es
De nicht gerade
En out of square
Fr mal cadré
It fuori squadra
Pt fora do
enquadramento

desenhador *(m) n* Pt
De Designer *(m)*
En designer
Es diseñador *(m)*
Fr créateur *(m)*
It disegnatore *(m)*

desenhador gráfico *(m)*
Pt
De Grafiker *(m)*
En graphic designer
Es diseñador gráfico *(m)*
Fr dessinateur *(m)*
It disegnatore grafico
(m)

desenhador tipográfico
(m) Pt
De Satzgestalter *(m)*
En typographic designer
Es diseñador tipográfico
(m)
Fr concepteur
typographique *(m)*
It disegnatore
tipografico *(m)*

desenhar *vb* Pt
De entwerfen
En design
Es diseñar

Fr concevoir
It concepire

desenho *(m) n* Pt
De Gestaltung *(f)*
En design
Es diseño *(m)*
Fr projet *(m)*
It disegno *(m)*

desenho a lápis *(m)* Pt
De Bleistiftzeichnung *(f)*
En pencil drawing
Es dibujo a lápiz *(m)*
Fr dessin au crayon *(m)*
It disegno a matita *(m)*

desenho a lápis ou pena
(m) Pt
De Strichzeichnung *(f)*
En line drawing
Es dibujo de línea *(m)*
Fr dessin au trait *(m)*
It disegno a tratteggio
(m)

desenho da sobrecapa
(m) Pt
De Umschlagentwurf
(m)
En jacket design
Es diseño de la
sobrecubierta *(m)*
Fr conception de la
jaquette *(f)*
It disegno della
sovracopertina *(m)*

desenho técnico *(m)* Pt
De technische
Zeichnung *(f)*
En technical drawing
Es dibujo técnico *(m)*
Fr dessin industriel *(m)*
It disegno tecnico *(m)*

desenho tipográfico *(m)*
Pt
De Satzgestaltung *(f)*
En typographic design
Es diseño tipográfico
(m)
Fr représentation
typographique *(f)*
It disegno tipografico
(m)

désensibiliser *vb* Fr
De desensibilisieren
En desensitize
Es desensibilizar

It desensibilizzare
Pt dessensibilizar

desensibilisieren *vb* De
En desensitize
Es desensibilizar
Fr désensibiliser
It desensibilizzare
Pt dessensibilizar

desensibilizar *vb* Es
De desensibilisieren
En desensitize
Fr désensibiliser
It desensibilizzare
Pt dessensibilizar

desensibilizzare *vb* It
De desensibilisieren
En desensitize
Es desensibilizar
Fr désensibiliser
Pt dessensibilizar

desensitize *vb* En
De desensibilisieren
Es desensibilizar
Fr désensibiliser
It desensibilizzare
Pt dessensibilizar

desenvolver *vb* Pt
De entwickeln (Planung)
En develop (planning)
Es desarrollar
Fr exécuter
It elaborare

design *vb* En
De entwerfen
Es diseñar
Fr concevoir
It concepire
Pt desenhar

design *n* En
De Gestaltung *(f)*
Es diseño *(m)*
Fr projet *(m)*
It disegno *(m)*
Pt desenho *(m)*

designer *n* En
De Designer *(m)*
Es diseñador *(m)*
Fr créateur *(m)*
It disegnatore *(m)*
Pt desenhador *(m)*

Designer (m) n De
En designer
Es diseñador (m)
Fr créateur (m)
It disegnatore (m)
Pt desenhador (m)

desintegración en polvo
(f) Es
De Kalkschleier (m)
En chalking
Fr poudrage (m)
It sfarinamento (m)
Pt descascamento (m)

desinterlineado adj Es
De kompreß
En solid
Fr à-plat
It sterlineato
Pt macizo

desk encyclopedia En
De Schreibtisch-Lexikon
(n)
Es enciclopedia de
mesa (f)
Fr petite encyclopédie
(f)
It enciclopedia da
tavolo (f)
Pt enciclopédia de
mesa (f)

deslaminação (f) n Pt
De Ableimung (f)
En delamination
Es delaminación (f)
Fr séparation des plis (f)
It separazione degli
strati (f)

de source sure Fr
De autoritativ
En authoritative
Es autorizado
It autorevole
Pt autoritativo

despedir vb Es
De entlassen
En lay off
Fr licencier
It licenziare
Pt dispensar
temporariamente

dessensibilizar vb Pt
De desensibilisieren
En desensitize
Es desensibilizar

Fr désensibiliser
It desensibilizzare

dessin (m) n Fr
De Bild (n)
En image
Es imagen (f)
It immagine (f)
Pt imagem (f)

dessinateur (m) n Fr
De Grafiker (m)
En graphic designer
Es diseñador gráfico (m)
It disegnatore grafico
(m)
Pt desenhador gráfico
(m)

dessinateur-concepteur
(m) n Fr
Am draftsman
De Zeichner (m)
En draughtsman
Es delineante (m)
It disegnatore (m)
Pt autor de esboço (m)

dessin au crayon (m) Fr
De Bleistiftzeichnung (f)
En pencil drawing
Es dibujo a lápiz (m)
It disegno a matita (m)
Pt desenho a lápis (m)

dessin au trait (m) Fr
De Strichzeichnung (f)
En line drawing
Es dibujo de línea (m)
It disegno a tratteggio
(m)
Pt desenho a lápis ou
pena (m)

dessiner vb Fr
De zeichnen
En draw
Es dibujar
It disegnare
Pt traçar

dessiner à l'échelle Fr
De Maßstab festlegen
En scale
Es poner a escala
It graduare
Pt pôr à escala

dessin industriel (m) Fr
De technische
Zeichnung (f)
En technical drawing
Es dibujo técnico (m)
It disegno tecnico (m)
Pt desenho técnico (m)

détaillant (m) n Fr
De Einzelhändler (m)
En retailer
Es minorista (m)
It dettagliante (m)
Pt retalhista (m)

detective novel En
De Kriminalroman (m)
Es novela policíaca (f)
Fr roman policier (m)
It racconto poliziesco
(m)
Pt livro policial (m)

détourer vb Fr
De zurichten
En crop
Es recortar
It scontornare
Pt recortar

dettagliante (m) n It
De Einzelhändler (m)
En retailer
Es minorista (m)
Fr détaillant (m)
Pt retalhista (m)

deux-points (m) n Fr
De Doppelpunkt (m)
En colon
Es dos puntos (m)
It doppiopunto (m)
Pt dois pontos (m)

develop (photography)
vb En
De entwickeln
(Photographie)
Es revelar
Fr développer
It sviluppare
Pt revelar

develop (planning) vb En
De entwickeln (Planung)
Es desarrollar
Fr exécuter
It elaborare
Pt desenvolver

development program
Am
De Entwicklungs-
programm (n)
En development
programme
Es programa de
desarrollo (m)
Fr plan de
développement (m)
It programma di
sviluppo (m)
Pt programa de
desenvolvimento (m)

**development
programme** En
Am development
program
De Entwicklungs-
programm (n)
Es programa de
desarrollo (m)
Fr plan de
développement (m)
It programma di
sviluppo (m)
Pt programa de
desenvolvimento (m)

development project En
De Entwicklungsprojekt
(n)
Es proyecto de
desarrollo (m)
Fr projet de
développement (m)
It progetto di sviluppo
(m)
Pt projecto de
desenvolvimento (m)

développer vb Fr
De entwickeln
(Photographie)
En develop
(photography)
Es revelar
It sviluppare
Pt revelar

devis (m) n Fr
De Kostenvoranschlag
(m)
En estimate
Es estimación (f)
It valutazione (f)
Pt estimativa (f)

devoluciones (f pl) Es
De Rückgüter (pl)
En returns pl n

Fr invendus *(m pl)*
It ritorni *(m pl)*
Pt devoluções *(f pl)*

devoluções *(f pl)* Pt
De Rückgüter *(pl)*
En returns *pl n*
Es devoluciones *(f pl)*
Fr invendus *(m pl)*
It ritorni *(m pl)*

Dezimalkomma *(n) n* De
En decimal point
Es punto decimal *(m)*
Fr virgule *(f)*
It virgola decimale *(f)*
Pt ponto decimal *(m)*

Dia *(n) n* De
En transparency
Es diapositiva *(f)*
Fr diapositive *(f)*
It diapositiva *(f)*
Pt diapositivo *(m)*

diaeresis *n* En
De Diäresis *(f)*
Es diéresis *(f)*
Fr tréma *(m)*
It dieresi *(f)*
Pt diérese *(f)*

diagram *n* En
De Diagramm *(n)*
Es esquema *(m)*
Fr schéma *(m)*
It diagramma *(m)*
Pt diagrama *(m)*

diagrama *(m) n* Es
De Tabelle *(f)*
En chart
Fr diagramme *(m)*
It tabella *(f)*
Pt carta *(f)*

diagrama *(m) n* Pt
De Diagramm *(n)*
En diagram
Es esquema *(m)*
Fr schéma *(m)*
It diagramma *(m)*

diagrama de fluxo *(m)* Pt
De Schaubild *(n)*
En flow chart
Es organigrama *(f)*
Fr schéma de
   fabrication *(m)*
It reograma *(m)*

**diagrama de passo a
   passo** *(m)* Pt
De stufenweises
   Diagramm *(n)*
En step-by-step diagram
Es esquema paso a
   paso *(m)*
Fr schéma progressif
   (m)
It diagramma graduale
   (m)

diagrama esquemático
   (m) Es, Pt
De schematisches
   Diagramm *(n)*
En schematic diagram
Fr schéma de principe
   (m)
It diagramma
   schematico *(m)*

diagramático *adj* Pt
De schematisch
En diagrammatic
Es esquemático
Fr schématique
It schematico

Diagramm *(n) n* De
En diagram
Es esquema *(m)*
Fr schéma *(m)*
It diagramma *(m)*
Pt diagrama *(m)*

diagramma *(m) n* It
De Diagramm *(n)*
En diagram
Es esquema *(m)*
Fr schéma *(m)*
Pt diagrama *(m)*

diagramma graduale *(m)*
   It
De stufenweises
   Diagramm *(n)*
En step-by-step diagram
Es esquema paso a
   paso *(m)*
Fr schéma progressif
   (m)
Pt diagrama de passo a
   passo *(m)*

diagramma schematico
   (m) It
De schematisches
   Diagramm *(n)*
En schematic diagram
Es diagrama
   esquemático *(m)*

Fr schéma de principe
   (m)
Pt diagrama
   esquemático *(m)*

diagrammatic *adj* En
De schematisch
Es esquemático
Fr schématique
It schematico
Pt diagramático

diagramme *(m) n* Fr
De Tabelle *(f)*
En chart
Es diagrama *(m)*
It tabella *(f)*
Pt carta *(f)*

diapositiva *(f) n* Es, It
De Dia *(n)*
En transparency
Fr diapositive *(f)*
Pt diapositivo *(m)*

diapositive *(f) n* Fr
De Dia *(n)*
En transparency
Es diapositiva *(f)*
It diapositiva *(f)*
Pt diapositivo *(m)*

diapositivo *(m) n* Pt
De Dia *(n)*
En transparency
Es diapositiva *(f)*
Fr diapositive *(f)*
It diapositiva *(f)*

Diäresis *(f) n* De
En diaeresis
Es diéresis *(f)*
Fr tréma *(m)*
It dieresi *(f)*
Pt diérese *(f)*

diario *(m) n* Es
De Zeitung *(f)*
En newspaper
Fr journal *(m)*
It giornale quotidiano
   (m)
Pt jornal diário *(m)*

dibujar *vb* Es
De zeichnen
En draw
Fr dessiner
It disegnare
Pt traçar

dibujo a lápiz *(m)* Es
De Bleistiftzeichnung *(f)*
En pencil drawing
Fr dessin au crayon *(m)*
It disegno a matita *(m)*
Pt desenho a lápis *(m)*

dibujo de línea *(m)* Es
De Strichzeichnung *(f)*
En line drawing
Fr dessin au trait *(m)*
It disegno a tratteggio
   (m)
Pt desenho a lápis ou
   pena *(m)*

dibujo técnico *(m)* Es
De technische
   Zeichnung *(f)*
En technical drawing
Fr dessin industriel *(m)*
It disegno tecnico *(m)*
Pt desenho técnico *(m)*

diccionario *(m) n* Es
De Wörterbuch *(n)*
En dictionary
Fr dictionnaire *(m)*
It dizionario *(m)*
Pt dicionário *(m)*

diccionario abreviado
   (m) Es
De Kurzwörterbuch *(n)*
En concise dictionary
Fr dictionnaire abrégé
   (m)
It dizionario conciso
   (m)
Pt dicionário conciso
   (m)

diccionario bilingüe *(m)*
   Es
De zweisprachiges
   Wörterbuch *(n)*
En bilingual dictionary
Fr dictionnaire bilingue
   (m)
It dizionario bilingue
   (m)
Pt dicionário bilíngue
   (m)

diccionario de bolsillo
   (m) Es
De Taschenwörterbüch
   (n)
En pocket dictionary
Fr dictionnaire de poche
   (m)

It dizionario tascabile
(m)
Pt dicionário de bolso
(m)

**diccionario de lengua
extranjera** *(m)* Es
De Fremdsprachen-
Wörterbuch *(n)*
En foreign-language
dictionary
Fr dictionnaire de
langues étrangères
(m)
It dizionario in lingua
straniera *(m)*
Pt dicionário de lingua
estrangeira *(m)*

diccionario multilingue
(m) Es
De Mehrsprachen-
Wörterbuch *(n)*
En multilingual
dictionary
Fr dictionnaire
polyglotte *(m)*
It dizionario multilingue
(m)
Pt dicionário multilingue
(m)

diccionario técnico *(m)*
Es
De technisches
Wörterbuch *(n)*
En technical dictionary
Fr dictionnaire
technique *(m)*
It dizionario tecnico *(m)*
Pt dicionário técnico *(m)*

Dichter *(m)* n De
En poet
Es poeta *(m)*
Fr poète *(m)*
It poeta *(m)*
Pt poeta *(m)*

Dichtung *(f)* n De
En poetry
Es poesía *(f)*
Fr poésie *(f)*
It poesia *(f)*
Pt poesia *(f)*

dicionário *(m)* n Pt
De Wörterbuch *(n)*
En dictionary
Es diccionario *(m)*
Fr dictionnaire *(m)*
It dizionario *(m)*

dicionário bilíngue *(m)*
Pt
De zweisprachiges
Wörterbuch *(n)*
En bilingual dictionary
Es diccionario bilingüe
(m)
Fr dictionnaire bilingue
(m)
It dizionario bilingue
(m)

dicionário conciso *(m)* Pt
De Kurzwörterbuch *(n)*
En concise dictionary
Es diccionario abreviado
(m)
Fr dictionnaire abrégé
(m)
It dizionario conciso
(m)

dicionário de bolso *(m)*
Pt
De Taschenwörterbüch
(n)
En pocket dictionary
Es diccionario de bolsillo
(m)
Fr dictionnaire de poche
(m)
It dizionario tascabile
(m)

**dicionário de lingua
estrangeira** *(m)* Pt
De Fremdsprachen-
Wörterbuch *(n)*
En foreign-language
dictionary
Es diccionario de lengua
extranjera *(m)*
Fr dictionnaire de
langues étrangères
(m)
It dizionario in lingua
straniera *(m)*

dicionário geográfico
(m) Pt
De geographisches
Lexicon *(n)*
En gazetteer
Es gacetero *(m)*
Fr répertoire
géographique *(m)*
It dizionario geografico
(m)

dicionário multilingue
(m) Pt

De Mehrsprachen-
Wörterbuch *(n)*
En multilingual
dictionary
Es diccionario
multilingue *(m)*
Fr dictionnaire
polyglotte *(m)*
It dizionario multilingue
(m)

dicionário técnico *(m)* Pt
De technisches
Wörterbuch *(n)*
En technical dictionary
Es diccionario técnico
(m)
Fr dictionnaire
technique *(m)*
It dizionario tecnico *(m)*

dickes Spatium *(n)* De
En thick space
Es espacio grueso *(m)*
Fr espace forte *(f)*
It spazio grosso *(m)*
Pt espaço grosso *(m)*

dictionary n En
De Wörterbuch *(n)*
Es diccionario *(m)*
Fr dictionnaire *(m)*
It dizionario *(m)*
Pt dicionário *(m)*

dictionnaire *(m)* n Fr
De Wörterbuch *(n)*
En dictionary
Es diccionario *(m)*
It dizionario *(m)*
Pt dicionário *(m)*

dictionnaire abrégé *(m)*
Fr
De Kurzwörterbuch *(n)*
En concise dictionary
Es diccionario abreviado
(m)
It dizionario conciso
(m)
Pt dicionário conciso
(m)

dictionnaire bilingue *(m)*
Fr
De zweisprachiges
Wörterbuch *(n)*
En bilingual dictionary
Es diccionario bilingüe
(m)
It dizionario bilingue
(m)

Pt dicionário bilíngue
(m)

**dictionnaire de langues
étrangères** *(m)* Fr
De Fremdsprachen-
Wörterbuch *(n)*
En foreign-language
dictionary
Es diccionario de lengua
extranjera *(m)*
It dizionario in lingua
straniera *(m)*
Pt dicionário de lingua
estrangeira *(m)*

dictionnaire de poche
(m) Fr
De Taschenwörterbüch
(n)
En pocket dictionary
Es diccionario de bolsillo
(m)
It dizionario tascabile
(m)
Pt dicionário de bolso
(m)

dictionnaire polyglotte
(m) Fr
De Mehrsprachen-
Wörterbuch *(n)*
En multilingual
dictionary
Es diccionario
multilingue *(m)*
It dizionario multilingue
(m)
Pt dicionário multilingue
(m)

dictionnaire technique
(m) Fr
De technisches
Wörterbuch *(n)*
En technical dictionary
Es diccionario técnico
(m)
It dizionario tecnico *(m)*
Pt dicionário técnico *(m)*

didascalia *(f)* n It
De Bildunterschrift *(f)*
En caption
Es encabezamiento *(m)*
Fr inscription *(f)*
Pt epígrafe *(f)*

didone *(f)* n Fr
De moderner Schrifttyp
(m)
En modern face

Es tipo moderno *(m)*
It carattere moderno *(m)*
Pt olho moderno *(m)*

die *n* En
De Prägestock *(m)*
Es troquel *(m)*
Fr étampe *(f)*
It stampo *(m)*
Pt matriz *(f)*

die Kosten decken De
En cover one's costs
Es cubrir los gastos propios
Fr couvrir ses dépenses
It coprire i costi
Pt cobrir as despesas

Dienstleitungsfirma *(f) n* De
En service company
Es compañía de servicios *(f)*
Fr entretien *(m)*
It società di servizio *(f)*
Pt companhia de serviços *(f)*

diérese *(f) n* Pt
De Diäresis *(f)*
En diaeresis
Es diéresis *(f)*
Fr tréma *(m)*
It dieresi *(f)*

dieresi *(f) n* It
De Diäresis *(f)*
En diaeresis
Es diéresis *(f)*
Fr tréma *(m)*
Pt diérese *(f)*

diéresis *(f) n* Es
De Diäresis *(f)*
En diaeresis
Fr tréma *(m)*
It dieresi *(f)*
Pt diérese *(f)*

die stamping En
De Prägestempel *(m)*
Es estampación en relieve *(m)*
Fr repoussage *(m)*
It stampa incavorilievografica *(f)*
Pt estampagem em relevo *(f)*

diffuseur *(m) n* Fr
De Popularisierer *(m)*
En popularizer
Es popularizador *(m)*
It divulgatore *(m)*
Pt vulgarizador *(m)*

digit *n* En
De Stelle *(f)*
Es dígito *(m)*
Fr chiffre *(m)*
It cifra *(f)*
Pt dígito *(m)*

digital computer En
De Digitalcomputer *(m)*
Es ordenador digital *(m)*
Fr calculateur numérique *(m)*
It elaboratore digitale *(m)*
Pt computador digital *(m)*

Digitalcomputer *(m) n* De
En digital computer
Es ordenador digital *(m)*
Fr calculateur numérique *(m)*
It elaboratore digitale *(m)*
Pt computador digital *(m)*

dígito *(m) n* Es, Pt
De Stelle *(f)*
En digit
Fr chiffre *(m)*
It cifra *(f)*

digno de ser publicado Pt
De aktuell
En newsworthy
Es de interés periodístico
Fr d'intérêt journalistique
It che fa notizia

dígrafo *(m) n* Pt
De Digraph *(m)*
En digraph
Es digrama *(m)*
Fr digramme *(m)*
It digramma *(f)*

digrama *(m) n* Es
De Digraph *(m)*
En digraph

Fr digramme *(m)*
It digramma *(f)*
Pt dígrafo *(m)*

digramma *(f) n* It
De Digraph *(m)*
En digraph
Es digrama *(m)*
Fr digramme *(m)*
Pt dígrafo *(m)*

digramme *(m) n* Fr
De Digraph *(m)*
En digraph
Es digrama *(m)*
It digramma *(f)*
Pt dígrafo *(m)*

digraph *n* En
De Digraph *(m)*
Es digrama *(m)*
Fr digramme *(m)*
It digramma *(f)*
Pt dígrafo *(m)*

Digraph *(m) n* De
En digraph
Es digrama *(m)*
Fr digramme *(m)*
It digramma *(f)*
Pt dígrafo *(m)*

diluenti *(m pl)* It
De Zusätze *(pl)*
En reducers *pl n*
Es diluyentes *(m pl)*
Fr réducteurs *(m pl)*
Pt redutores *(m pl)*

diluyentes *(m pl)* Es
De Zusätze *(pl)*
En reducers *pl n*
Fr réducteurs *(m pl)*
It diluenti *(m pl)*
Pt redutores *(m pl)*

dimensione irregolare *(f)* It
De Bastardkegel *(m)*
En bastard size
Es tamaño bastardo *(m)*
Fr format bâtard *(m)*
Pt tamanho bastardo *(m)*

dimensioni D.I.N. *(f pl)* It
De DIN-Größen *(pl)*
En DIN sizes

Es tamaños D.I.N. *(m pl)*
Fr formats D.I.N. *(m pl)*
Pt tamanhos D.I.N. *(m pl)*

dimensioni di pagina rifilata *(f pl)* It
De Beschnittgröße *(f)*
En trimmed page size
Es tamaño de página cortada *(m)*
Fr format fini *(m)*
Pt tamanho de página aparada *(m)*

dimensioni ISO *(f pl)* It
De ISO-Größen *(pl)*
En ISO sizes
Es tamaños ISO *(m pl)*
Fr formats ISO *(m pl)*
Pt tamanhos ISO *(m pl)*

DIN-Größen *(pl)* De
En DIN sizes
Es tamaños D.I.N. *(m pl)*
Fr formats D.I.N. *(m pl)*
It dimensioni D.I.N. *(f pl)*
Pt tamanhos D.I.N. *(m pl)*

d'intérêt journalistique Fr
De aktuell
En newsworthy
Es de interés periodístico
It che fa notizia
Pt digno de ser publicado

dipendente *(m) n* It
De Angestellter *(m)*
En employee
Es empleado *(m)*
Fr employé *(m)*
Pt empregado *(m)*

diphthong *n* En
De Diphthong *(m)*
Es diptongo *(m)*
Fr diphtongue *(f)*
It dittongo *(m)*
Pt ditongo *(m)*

Diphthong *(m) n* De
En diphthong
Es diptongo *(m)*
Fr diphtongue *(f)*

It dittongo *(m)*
Pt ditongo *(m)*

diphtongue *(f)* n Fr
De Diphthong *(m)*
En diphthong
Es diptongo *(m)*
It dittongo *(m)*
Pt ditongo *(m)*

diptongo *(m)* n Es
De Diphthong *(m)*
En diphthong
Fr diphtongue *(f)*
It dittongo *(m)*
Pt ditongo *(m)*

direcção *(f)* n Pt
De Geschäftsleitung *(f)*
En management
Es manejo *(m)*
Fr direction *(f)*
It direzione *(f)*

direcção da máquina *(f)*
Pt
De Laufrichtung *(f)*
En machine direction
Es dirección de máquina
(f)
Fr sens machine *(m)*
It direzione di macchina
(f)

dirección *(f)* n Es
De Adresse *(f)*
En address (computer)
Fr adresse *(f)*
It indirizzo *(m)*
Pt endereço *(m)*

dirección de máquina *(f)*
Es
De Laufrichtung *(f)*
En machine direction
Fr sens machine *(m)*
It direzione di macchina
(f)
Pt direcção da máquina
(f)

direct approach platen
En
De Parallel-
bewegungstiegel *(m)*
Es platina de
aproximación directa
(f)
Fr platine à approche
directe *(f)*

It platina ad approccio
diretto *(f)*
Pt platina de
aproximação directa
(f)

directeur *(m)* n Fr
De Direktor *(m)*
En director
Es director *(m)*
It direttore *(m)*
Pt director *(m)*

directeur artistique *(m)*
Fr
De künstlerischer Leiter
(m)
En art director
Es director gráfico *(m)*
It direttore artistico *(m)*
Pt director artístico *(m)*

directeur commercial
(m) Fr
De Verkaufsdirektor *(m)*
En sales director
Es director de ventas
(m)
It direttore alle vendite
(m)
Pt director de vendas
(m)

**directeur de la
production** *(m)* Fr
De Produktionsleiter *(m)*
En production manager
Es jefe de producción
(m)
It direttore di
produzione *(m)*
Pt director de produção
(m)

**directeur de la
promotion** *(m)* Fr
De Werbefachmann *(m)*
En promotion manager
Es jefe de promoción
(m)
It dirigente dell'attività
promozionale *(m)*
Pt director de promoção
(m)

directeur de la publicité
(m) Fr
De Werbeleiter *(m)*
En publicity manager
Es jefe de publicidad *(m)*
It direttore pubblicitario
(m)

Pt director de
publicidade *(m)*

**directeur de la
rédaction** *(m)* Fr
De Chefredakteur *(m)*
En editorial director
Es director de editorial
(m)
It direttore editoriale
(m)
Pt director editorial *(m)*

**directeur des droits à
l'étranger** *(m)* Fr
De Auslandsrecht-Leiter
(m)
En foreign-rights
manager
Es director de derechos
en el extranjero *(m)*
It dirigente diritti esteri
(m)
Pt director dos direitos
estrangeiros *(m)*

directeur du personnel
(m) Fr
De Personal-
abteilungsleiter *(m)*
En personnel manager
Es jefe de personal *(m)*
It direttore del
personale *(m)*
Pt director do pessoal
(m)

directeur financier *(m)*
Fr
De Finanzdirektor *(m)*
En financial director
Es director financiero
(m)
It direttore finanziario
(m)
Pt director financeiro
(m)

directeur général *(m)* Fr
De Geschäftsführender
Direktor *(m)*
En managing director
Es director gerente *(m)*
It amministratore
delegato *(m)*
Pt director geral *(m)*

direct impression En
De Direktdruck *(m)*
Es impresión directa *(f)*
Fr impression directe *(f)*

It stampa diretta *(f)*
Pt impressão directa *(f)*

direction *(f)* n Fr
De Geschäftsleitung *(f)*
En management
Es manejo *(m)*
It direzione *(f)*
Pt direcção *(f)*

direction générale *(f)* Fr
De Vorstand *(m)*
En board of directors
Es consejo de
administración *(m)*
It comitato direttivo *(m)*
Pt conselho de
administração *(m)*

direct-mail selling En
De Postwurfwerbung *(f)*
Es venta directa por
correo *(f)*
Fr vente directe par
correspondance *(f)*
It vendite per
corrispondenza *(f pl)*
Pt venda por correio *(f)*

direct-mail shot En
De Postwurfsendung *(f)*
Es envío por correo
directo; oferta por
correo *(m f)*
Fr mailing; offre
promotionelle *(m f)*
It invio diretto per
posta; offerta postale
(m f)
Pt publicidade por
correio *(f)*

director n En; Es, Pt *(m)*
De Direktor *(m)*
Fr directeur *(m)*
It direttore *(m)*

director artístico *(m)* Pt
De künstlerischer Leiter
(m)
En art director
Es director gráfico *(m)*
Fr directeur artistique
(m)
It direttore artistico *(m)*

**director de derechos en
el extranjero** *(m)* Es
De Auslandsrecht-Leiter
(m)

En foreign-rights
   manager
Fr directeur des droits à
   l´étranger *(m)*
It dirigente diritti esteri
   (m)
Pt director dos direitos
   estrangeiros *(m)*

director de editorial *(m)*
   Es
De Chefredakteur *(m)*
En editorial director
Fr directeur de la
   rédaction *(m)*
It direttore editoriale
   (m)
Pt director editorial *(m)*

director de produção
   (m) Pt
De Produktionsleiter *(m)*
En production manager
Es jefe de producción
   (m)
Fr directeur de la
   production *(m)*
It direttore di
   produzione *(m)*

director de promoção
   (m) Pt
De Werbefachmann *(m)*
En promotion manager
Es jefe de promoción
   (m)
Fr directeur de la
   promotion *(m)*
It dirigente dell´attività
   promozionale *(m)*

director de publicidade
   (m) Pt
De Werbeleiter *(m)*
En publicity manager
Es jefe de publicidad *(m)*
Fr directeur de la
   publicité *(m)*
It direttore pubblicitario
   (m)

director de vendas *(m)*
   Pt
De Verkaufsdirektor *(m)*
En sales director
Es director de ventas
   (m)
Fr directeur commercial
   (m)
It direttore alle vendite
   (m)

director de ventas *(m)* Es
De Verkaufsdirektor *(m)*
En sales director
Fr directeur commercial
   (m)
It direttore alle vendite
   (m)
Pt director de vendas
   (m)

director do pessoal *(m)*
   Pt
De Personal-
   abteilungsleiter *(m)*
En personnel manager
Es jefe de personal *(m)*
Fr directeur du
   personnel *(m)*
It direttore del
   personale *(m)*

**director dos direitos
   estrangeiros** *(m)* Pt
De Auslandsrecht-Leiter
   (m)
En foreign-rights
   manager
Es director de derechos
   en el extranjero *(m)*
Fr directeur des droits à
   l´étranger *(m)*
It dirigente diritti esteri
   (m)

director editorial *(m)* Pt
De Chefredakteur *(m)*
En editorial director
Es director de editorial
   (m)
Fr directeur de la
   rédaction *(m)*
It direttore editoriale
   (m)

director financiero *(m)*
   Es
De Finanzdirektor *(m)*
En financial director
Fr directeur financier
   (m)
It direttore finanziario
   (m)
Pt director financeiro
   (m)

director financeiro *(m)*
   Pt
De Finanzdirektor *(m)*
En financial director
Es director financiero
   (m)

Fr directeur financier
   (m)
It direttore finanziario
   (m)

director geral *(m)* Pt
De Geschäftsführender
   Direktor *(m)*
En managing director
Es director gerente *(m)*
Fr directeur général *(m)*
It amministratore
   delegato *(m)*

director gerente *(m)* Es
De Geschäftsführender
   Direktor *(m)*
En managing director
Fr directeur général *(m)*
It amministratore
   delegato *(m)*
Pt director geral *(m)*

director gráfico *(m)* Es
De künstlerischer Leiter
   (m)
En art director
Fr directeur artistique
   (m)
It direttore artistico *(m)*
Pt director artístico *(m)*

directorio *(m)* n Es
De Adreßbuch *(n)*
En directory
Fr annuaire *(m)*
It annuario *(m)*
Pt anuário *(m)*

directory n En
De Adreßbuch *(n)*
Es directorio *(m)*
Fr annuaire *(m)*
It annuario *(m)*
Pt anuário *(m)*

direct process En
De Direktverfahren *(n)*
Es reproducción directa
   (f)
Fr procédé direct *(m)*
It procedimento diretto
   (m)
Pt processo directo *(m)*

**direitos
   cinematográficos**
   (m pl) Pt
De Verfilmungsrechte
   (pl)
En film rights *pl n*

Es derechos
   cinematográficos *(m
   pl)*
Fr droits sur le film *(m
   pl)*
It diritti cinematografici
   (m pl)

direitos de autor *(m pl)*
   Pt
De Tantiemen *(pl)*
En royalties *pl n*
Es derechos de autor *(m
   pl)*
Fr droits d´auteur *(m pl)*
It diritti di licenza *(m pl)*

direitos de televisão *(m
   pl)* Pt
De Fernsehrechte *(pl)*
En television rights *pl n*
Es derechos de
   televisión *(m pl)*
Fr droits de télévision
   (m pl)
It diritti televisivi *(m pl)*

direitos estrangeiros *(m
   pl)* Pt
De Auslandsrechte *(pl)*
En foreign rights
Es derechos en el
   extranjero *(m pl)*
Fr droits à l´étranger *(m
   pl)*
It diritti esteri *(m pl)*

Direktdruck *(m)* n De
En direct impression
Es impresión directa *(f)*
Fr impression directe *(f)*
It stampa diretta *(f)*
Pt impressão directa *(f)*

Direktor *(m)* n De
En director
Es director *(m)*
Fr directeur *(m)*
It direttore *(m)*
Pt director *(m)*

Direktverfahren *(n)* n De
En direct process
Es reproducción directa
   (f)
Fr procédé direct *(m)*
It procedimento diretto
   (m)
Pt processo directo *(m)*

Direktzugriffsspeicher
(m) n De
En random-access store
Es memoria de acceso
al azar (f)
Fr mémoire à accés
direct (f)
It memoria ad accesso
casuale (f)
Pt memória de acesso
aleatório (f)

direttore (m) n It
De Direktor (m)
En director
Es director (m)
Fr directeur (m)
Pt director (m)

direttore alle vendite
(m) It
De Verkaufsdirektor (m)
En sales director
Es director de ventas
(m)
Fr directeur commercial
(m)
Pt director de vendas
(m)

direttore artistico (m) It
De künstlerischer Leiter
(m)
En art director
Es director gráfico (m)
Fr directeur artistique
(m)
Pt director artístico (m)

direttore del personale
(m) It
De Personal-
abteilungsleiter (m)
En personnel manager
Es jefe de personal (m)
Fr directeur du
personnel (m)
Pt director do pessoal
(m)

direttore di produzione
(m) It
De Produktionsleiter (m)
En production manager
Es jefe de producción
(m)
Fr directeur de la
production (m)
Pt director de produção
(m)

direttore editoriale (m) It
De Chefredakteur (m)
En editorial director
Es director de editorial
(m)
Fr directeur de la
rédaction (m)
Pt director editorial (m)

direttore finanziario (m)
It
De Finanzdirektor (m)
En financial director
Es director financiero
(m)
Fr directeur financier
(m)
Pt director financeiro
(m)

direttore generale (m) It
De leitende
Führungskraft (f)
En chief executive
Es jefe ejecutivo (m)
Fr administrateur
directeur (m)
Pt executivo principal
(m)

direttore pubblicitario
(m) It
De Werbeleiter (m)
En publicity manager
Es jefe de publicidad (m)
Fr directeur de la
publicité (m)
Pt director de
publicidade (m)

direttore vendite (m) It
De Verkaufsleiter (m)
En sales manager
Es jefe de ventas (m)
Fr chef des ventes (m)
Pt gerente de vendas
(m)

direzione (f) n It
De Geschäftsleitung (f)
En management
Es manejo (m)
Fr direction (f)
Pt direcção (f)

direzione di macchina (f)
It
De Laufrichtung (f)
En machine direction
Es dirección de máquina
(f)
Fr sens machine (m)

Pt direcção da máquina
(f)

dirigente (m) n It
De Geschäftsleiter (m)
En manager
Es gerente (m)
Fr gérant (m)
Pt gerente (m)

**dirigente dell'attività
promozionale** (m) It
De Werbefachmann (m)
En promotion manager
Es jefe de promoción
(m)
Fr directeur de la
promotion (m)
Pt director de promoção
(m)

dirigente diritti esteri
(m) It
De Auslandsrecht-Leiter
(m)
En foreign-rights
manager
Es director de derechos
en el extranjero (m)
Fr directeur des droits à
l'étranger (m)
Pt director dos direitos
estrangeiros (m)

dirigente obrero (m) Es
De Gewerkschafts-
Betriebsobmann (m)
En shop steward
Fr délégué d'atelier (m)
It delegato di fabbrica
(m)
Pt balconista (m)

diritti cinematografici
(m pl) It
De Verfilmungsrechte
(pl)
En film rights pl n
Es derechos
cinematográficos (m
pl)
Fr droits sur le film (m
pl)
Pt direitos
cinematográficos (m
pl)

diritti di licenza (m pl) It
De Tantiemen (pl)
En royalties pl n
Es derechos de autor (m
pl)

Fr droits d'auteur (m pl)
Pt direitos de autor (m
pl)

diritti esteri (m pl) It
De Auslandsrechte (pl)
En foreign rights
Es derechos en el
extranjero (m pl)
Fr droits à l'étranger (m
pl)
Pt direitos estrangeiros
(m pl)

diritti televisivi (m pl) It
De Fernsehrechte (pl)
En television rights pl n
Es derechos de
televisión (m pl)
Fr droits de télévision
(m pl)
Pt direitos de televisão
(m pl)

disco (m) n Es, It, Pt
De Platte (f)
En disk
Fr disque (m)

disco blando (m) Es
De Floppy Disk (m)
En floppy disk
Fr disque souple (m)
It floppy disk (m)
Pt disco floppy (m)

disco flexible (m) Es
De Diskette (f)
En diskette
Fr minidisque (m)
It diskette (m)
Pt disqueta (f)

disco floppy (m) Pt
De Floppy Disk (m)
En floppy disk
Es disco blando (m)
Fr disque souple (m)
It floppy disk (m)

disco magnetico (m) It
De Magnetplatte (f)
En magnetic disk
Es disco magnético (m)
Fr disque magnétique
(m)
Pt disco magnético (m)

disco magnético (m) Es, Pt
De Magnetplatte (f)
En magnetic disk
Fr disque magnétique (m)
It disco magnetico (m)

discretionary hyphen En
De willkürlicher Trennstrich (m)
Es guión discrecional (m)
Fr trait d'union facultatif (m)
It lineetta discrezionale (f)
Pt traço de união discricionário (m)

disegnare vb It
De zeichnen
En draw
Es dibujar
Fr dessiner
Pt traçar

disegnatore (m) n It
Am draftsman
De Zeichner (m)
En designer; draughtsman
Es delineante (m)
Fr dessinateur-concepteur (m)
Pt autor de esboço (m)

disegnatore grafico (m) It
De Grafiker (m)
En graphic designer
Es diseñador gráfico (m)
Fr dessinateur (m)
Pt desenhador gráfico (m)

disegnatore tipografico (m) It
De Satzgestalter (m)
En typographic designer
Es diseñador tipográfico (m)
Fr concepteur typographique (m)
Pt desenhador tipográfico (m)

disegno (m) n It
De Gestaltung (f)
En design
Es diseño (m)

Fr projet (m)
Pt desenho (m)

disegno a matita (m) It
De Bleistiftzeichnung (f)
En pencil drawing
Es dibujo a lápiz (m)
Fr dessin au crayon (m)
Pt desenho a lápis (m)

disegno a tratteggio (m) It
De Strichzeichnung (f)
En line drawing
Es dibujo de línea (m)
Fr dessin au trait (m)
Pt desenho a lápis ou pena (m)

disegno della sovracopertina (m) It
De Umschlagentwurf (m)
En jacket design
Es diseño de la sobrecubierta (m)
Fr conception de la jaquette (f)
Pt desenho da sobrecapa (m)

disegno tecnico (m) It
De technische Zeichnung (f)
En technical drawing
Es dibujo técnico (m)
Fr dessin industriel (m)
Pt desenho técnico (m)

disegno tipografico (m) It
De Satzgestaltung (f)
En typographic design
Es diseño tipográfico (m)
Fr représentation typographique (f)
Pt desenho tipográfico (m)

diseñador (m) n Es
De Designer (m)
En designer
Fr créateur (m)
It disegnatore (m)
Pt desenhador (m)

diseñador gráfico (m) Es
De Grafiker (m)
En graphic designer

Fr dessinateur (m)
It disegnatore grafico (m)
Pt desenhador gráfico (m)

diseñador tipográfico (m) Es
De Satzgestalter (m)
En typographic designer
Fr concepteur typographique (m)
It disegnatore tipografico (m)
Pt desenhador tipográfico (m)

diseñar vb Es
De entwerfen
En design
Fr concevoir
It concepire
Pt desenhar

diseño (m) n Es
De Gestaltung (f)
En design
Fr projet (m)
It disegno (m)
Pt desenho (m)

diseño de la sobrecubierta (m) Es
De Umschlagentwurf (m)
En jacket design
Fr conception de la jaquette (f)
It disegno della sovracopertina (m)
Pt desenho da sobrecapa (m)

diseño tipográfico (m) Es
De Satzgestaltung (f)
En typographic design
Fr représentation typographique (f)
It disegno tipografico (m)
Pt desenho tipográfico (m)

disk n En
De Platte (f)
Es disco (m)
Fr disque (m)
It disco (m)
Pt disco (m)

diskette n En; It (m)
De Diskette (f)
Es disco flexible (m)
Fr minidisque (m)
Pt disqueta (f)

Diskette (f) n De
En diskette
Es disco flexible (m)
Fr minidisque (m)
It diskette (m)
Pt disqueta (f)

dispensar temporariamente Pt
De entlassen
En lay off
Es despedir
Fr licencier
It licenziare

display vb En
De ausstellen
Es exhibir
Fr exhiber
It mostrare
Pt exibir

display n En
De Display (n)
Es exhibición (f)
Fr exposition (f)
It esposizione (f)
Pt exibição (f)

Display (n) n De
En display
Es exhibición (f)
Fr exposition (f)
It esposizione (f)
Pt exibição (f)

display advertisement En
De Displaywerbung (f)
Es anuncio publicitario (m)
Fr grande annonce (f)
It inserzione pubblicitaria (f)
Pt anúncio em majúsculas e ilustrado (m)

display type En
De Auszeichnungssatz (m)
Es tipos titulares (m pl)
Fr caractères vedettes (m pl)

It caratteri di titolo *(m pl)*
Pt tipos de maiúscula *(m pl)*

Displaywerbung *(f) n* De
En display advertisement
Es anuncio publicitario *(m)*
Fr grande annonce *(f)*
It inserzione pubblicitaria *(f)*
Pt anúncio em majúsculas e ilustrado *(m)*

disponer (tipo) Es
De gestalten
En lay out
Fr disposer (caractères)
It disporre (caratteri)
Pt preparar (tipo)

disporre (caratteri) It
De gestalten
En lay out
Es disponer (tipo)
Fr disposer (caractères)
Pt preparar (tipo)

disposer (caractères) Fr
De gestalten
En lay out
Es disponer (tipo)
It disporre (caratteri)
Pt preparar (tipo)

disposição tipográfica *(f)* Pt
De Layout *(n)*
En layout
Es disposición tipográfica *(f)*
Fr disposition typographique *(f)*
It disposizione tipografica *(f)*

disposición tipográfica *(f)* Es
De Layout *(n)*
En layout
Fr disposition typographique *(f)*
It disposizione tipografica *(f)*
Pt disposição tipográfica *(f)*

disposition typographique *(f)* Fr
De Layout *(n)*
En layout
Es disposición tipográfica *(f)*
It disposizione tipografica *(f)*
Pt disposição tipográfica *(f)*

dispositivo explorador *(m)* Pt
De Abtaster *(m)*
En scanner
Es explorador *(m)*
Fr analyseur électronique *(m)*
It scanner *(m)*

disposizione tipografica *(f)* It
De Layout *(n)*
En layout
Es disposición tipográfica *(f)*
Fr disposition typographique *(f)*
Pt disposição tipográfica *(f)*

disque *(m) n* Fr
De Platte *(f)*
En disk
Es disco *(m)*
It disco *(m)*
Pt disco *(m)*

disque magnétique *(m)* Fr
De Magnetplatte *(f)*
En magnetic disk
Es disco magnético *(m)*
It disco magnetico *(m)*
Pt disco magnético *(m)*

disque souple *(m)* Fr
De Floppy Disk *(m)*
En floppy disk
Es disco blando *(m)*
It floppy disk *(m)*
Pt disco floppy *(m)*

disqueta *(f) n* Pt
De Diskette *(f)*
En diskette
Es disco flexible *(m)*
Fr minidisque *(m)*
It diskette *(m)*

distribución *(f) n* Es
De Vertrieb *(m)*
En distribution
Fr distribution *(f)*
It distribuzione *(f)*
Pt distribuição *(f)*

distribución al por mayor *(f)* Es
De Großhandelsvertrieb *(m)*
En wholesale distribution
Fr commerce de gros *(m)*
It distribuzione all'ingrosso *(f)*
Pt distribuição por atacado *(f)*

distribución de tipos *(f)* Es
De Schriftverteilung *(f)*
En type distribution
Fr distribution des caractères *(f)*
It distribuzione del carattere *(m)*
Pt distribuição de tipos *(f)*

distribuer *vb* Fr
De vertreiben
En distribute
Es distribuir
It distribuire
Pt distribuir

distribuição *(f) n* Pt
De Vertrieb *(m)*
En distribution
Es distribución *(f)*
Fr distribution *(f)*
It distribuzione *(f)*

distribuição de tipos *(f)* Pt
De Schriftverteilung *(f)*
En type distribution
Es distribución de tipos *(f)*
Fr distribution des caractères *(f)*
It distribuzione del carattere *(m)*

distribuição por atacado *(f)* Pt
De Großhandelsvertrieb *(m)*
En wholesale distribution

Es distribución al por mayor *(f)*
Fr commerce de gros *(m)*
It distribuzione all'ingrosso *(f)*

distribuidor *(m) n* Es, Pt
De Vertriebsstelle *(f)*
En distributor
Fr distributeur *(m)*
It distributore *(m)*

distribuir *vb* Es, Pt
De vertreiben
En distribute
Fr distribuer
It distribuire

distribuire *vb* It
De vertreiben
En distribute
Es distribuir
Fr distribuer
Pt distribuir

distribute *vb* En
De vertreiben
Es distribuir
Fr distribuer
It distribuire
Pt distribuir

distributeur *(m) n* Fr
De Vertriebsstelle *(f)*
En distributor
Es distribuidor *(m)*
It distributore *(m)*
Pt distribuidor *(m)*

distribution *n* En; Fr *(f)*
De Vertrieb *(m)*
Es distribución *(f)*
It distribuzione *(f)*
Pt distribuição *(f)*

distribution automatique des piles *(f)* Fr
De automatischer Stapelausleger *(m)*
En automatic pile delivery
Es receptor automático de pila de pliegos *(m)*
It avanzamento automatico di pile *(f)*
Pt entrega automática de pilhas *(f)*

**distribution des
caractères** *(f)* Fr
De Schriftverteilung *(f)*
En type distribution
Es distribución de tipos
(f)
It distribuzione del
carattere *(m)*
Pt distribuição de tipos
(f)

distribution network En
De Vertriebsnetz *(n)*
Es red de distribución *(f)*
Fr réseau de
distribution *(m)*
It rete di distribuzione
(f)
Pt rede de distribuição
(f)

distributor *n* En
De Vertriebsstelle *(f)*
Es distribuidor *(m)*
Fr distributeur *(m)*
It distributore *(m)*
Pt distribuidor *(m)*

distributore *(m) n* It
De Vertriebsstelle *(f)*
En distributor
Es distribuidor *(m)*
Fr distributeur *(m)*
Pt distribuidor *(m)*

distribuzione *(f) n* It
De Vertrieb *(m)*
En distribution
Es distribución *(f)*
Fr distribution *(f)*
Pt distribuição *(f)*

**distribuzione
all'ingrosso** *(f)* It
De Großhandelsvertrieb
(m)
En wholesale
distribution
Es distribución al por
mayor *(f)*
Fr commerce de gros
(m)
Pt distribuição por
atacado *(f)*

**distribuzione del
carattere** *(m)* It
De Schriftverteilung *(f)*
En type distribution
Es distribución de tipos
(f)

Fr distribution des
caractères *(f)*
Pt distribuição de tipos
(f)

ditongo *(m) n* Pt
De Diphthong *(m)*
En diphthong
Es diptongo *(m)*
Fr diphtongue *(f)*
It dittongo *(m)*

dittongo *(m) n* It
De Diphthong *(m)*
En diphthong
Es diptongo *(m)*
Fr diphtongue *(f)*
Pt ditongo *(m)*

divisão *(f) n* Pt
De Abteilung *(f)*
En division
Es división *(f)*
Fr division *(f)*
It divisione *(f)*

**divisão de encomendas
por correio** *(f)* Pt
De Versandhaus-
abteilung *(f)*
En mail-order division
Es división de pedidos
por correo *(f)*
Fr service VPC *(m)*
It reparto vendite per
posta *(m)*

division *n* En; Fr *(f)*
De Abteilung *(f)*
Es división *(f)*
It divisione *(f)*
Pt divisão *(f)*

división *(f) n* Es
De Abteilung *(f)*
En division
Fr division *(f)*
It divisione *(f)*
Pt divisão *(f)*

**división de pedidos por
correo** *(f)* Es
De Versandhaus-
abteilung *(f)*
En mail-order division
Fr service VPC *(m)*
It reparto vendite per
posta *(m)*
Pt divisão de
encomendas por
correio *(f)*

divisione *(f) n* It
De Abteilung *(f)*
En division
Es división *(f)*
Fr division *(f)*
Pt divisão *(f)*

divulgatore *(m) n* It
De Popularisierer *(m)*
En popularizer
Es popularizador *(m)*
Fr diffuseur *(m)*
Pt vulgarizador *(m)*

dizionario *(m) n* It
De Wörterbuch *(n)*
En dictionary
Es diccionario *(m)*
Fr dictionnaire *(m)*
Pt dicionário *(m)*

dizionario bilingue *(m)* It
De zweisprachiges
Wörterbuch *(n)*
En bilingual dictionary
Es diccionario bilingüe
(m)
Fr dictionnaire bilingue
(m)
Pt dicionário bilíngue
(m)

dizionario conciso *(m)* It
De Kurzwörterbuch *(n)*
En concise dictionary
Es diccionario abreviado
(m)
Fr dictionnaire abrégé
(m)
Pt dicionário conciso
(m)

dizionario geografico
(m) It
De geographisches
Lexicon *(n)*
En gazetteer
Es gacetero *(m)*
Fr répertoire
géographique *(m)*
Pt dicionário geográfico
(m)

**dizionario in lingua
straniera** *(m)* It
De Fremdsprachen-
Wörterbuch *(n)*
En foreign-language
dictionary
Es diccionario de lengua
extranjera *(m)*
Fr dictionnaire de

langues étrangères
(m)
Pt dicionário de lingua
estrangeira *(m)*

dizionario multilingue
(m) It
De Mehrsprachen-
Wörterbuch *(n)*
En multilingual
dictionary
Es diccionario
multilingue *(m)*
Fr dictionnaire
polyglotte *(m)*
Pt dicionário multilingue
(m)

dizionario tascabile *(m)*
It
De Taschenwörterbüch
(n)
En pocket dictionary
Es diccionario de bolsillo
(m)
Fr dictionnaire de poche
(m)
Pt dicionário de bolso
(m)

dizionario tecnico *(m)* It
De technisches
Wörterbuch *(n)*
En technical dictionary
Es diccionario técnico
(m)
Fr dictionnaire
technique *(m)*
Pt dicionário técnico *(m)*

doble página *(f)* Es
De Doppelseite *(f)*
En double-page spread
Fr double page *(f)*
It doppia pagina *(f)*
Pt página dupla *(f)*

dobrado *(m) n* Pt
De Falzen *(n)*
En folding
Es plegado *(m)*
Fr pliure *(f)*
It piegatura *(f)*

dobradora *(f) n* Pt
De Falzmaschine *(f)*
En folding machine
Es plegadora *(f)*
Fr plieuse *(f)*
It piegatrice meccanica
(f)

doctor blade En
De Rakelmesser *(n)*
Es rasqueta doctor *(f)*
Fr râcle docteur *(f)*
It racle dottore *(f)*
Pt rasqueta doutor *(f)*

dois pontos *(m)* Pt
De Doppelpunkt *(m)*
En colon
Es dos puntos *(m)*
Fr deux-points *(m)*
It doppiopunto *(m)*

données *(f pl)* Fr
De Daten *(pl)*
En data *pl n*
Es datos *(m pl)*
It dati *(m pl)*
Pt dados *(m pl)*

Doppelpunkt *(m)* n De
En colon
Es dos puntos *(m)*
Fr deux-points *(m)*
It doppiopunto *(m)*
Pt dois pontos *(m)*

Doppelseite *(f)* n De
En double-page spread
Es doble página *(f)*
Fr double page *(f)*
It doppia pagina *(f)*
Pt página dupla *(f)*

doppia pagina *(f)* It
De Doppelseite *(f)*
En double-page spread
Es doble página *(f)*
Fr double page *(f)*
Pt página dupla *(f)*

doppiopunto *(m)* n It
De Doppelpunkt *(m)*
En colon
Es dos puntos *(m)*
Fr deux-points *(m)*
Pt dois pontos *(m)*

doradura *(f)* n Es
De Metalldruck *(m)*
En gilding
Fr dorure *(f)*
It doratura *(f)*
Pt douração *(f)*

doratura *(f)* n It
De Metalldruck *(m)*
En gilding
Es doradura *(f)*

Fr dorure *(f)*
Pt douração *(f)*

doré sur tranche Fr
De mit Goldschnitt
En gilt-edged
Es de cortes dorados
It con bordi dorati
Pt dourado nas beiras

dorso *(m)* n It
De Rücken *(m)*
En spine
Es lomo *(m)*
Fr dos *(m)*
Pt lombada *(f)*

dorure *(f)* n Fr
De Metalldruck *(m)*
En gilding
Es doradura *(f)*
It doratura *(f)*
Pt douração *(f)*

dorure à froid *(f)* Fr
De Blindprägung *(f)*
En blind embossing
Es gofrado *(m)*
It goffratura cieca *(f)*
Pt gravação em alto
relevo cego *(f)*

dorure à la presse *(f)* Fr
De Goldprägung *(f)*
En gold stamping
Es estampación dorada
(f)
It stampigliatura in oro
(f)
Pt estampagem a ouro
(f)

dos *(m)* n Fr
De Rücken *(m)*
En spine
Es lomo *(m)*
It dorso *(m)*
Pt lombada *(f)*

dos puntos *(m)* Es
De Doppelpunkt *(m)*
En colon
Fr deux-points *(m)*
It doppiopunto *(m)*
Pt dois pontos *(m)*

dot etching En
De Punktätzung *(f)*
Es reducción de los
puntos *(f)*

Fr morsure par
couverture *(f)*
It incisione a punti *(f)*
Pt redução dos pontos
reticulares *(f)*

double page *(f)* Fr
De Doppelseite *(f)*
En double-page spread
Es doble página *(f)*
It doppia pagina *(f)*
Pt página dupla *(f)*

double-page spread En
De Doppelseite *(f)*
Es doble página *(f)*
Fr double page *(f)*
It doppia pagina *(f)*
Pt página dupla *(f)*

douração *(f)* n Pt
De Metalldruck *(m)*
En gilding
Es doradura *(f)*
Fr dorure *(f)*
It doratura *(f)*

dourado nas beiras Pt
De mit Goldschnitt
En gilt-edged
Es de cortes dorados
Fr doré sur tranche
It con bordi dorati

down time En
De Ausfallszeit *(f)*
Es tiempo muerto *(m)*
Fr période d'arrêt *(f)*
It tempo passivo *(m)*
Pt tempo de paragem
(m)

dozavo *(m)* n Es
De Duodezformat *(n)*
En duodecimo
Fr in-douze *(m)*
It in dodicesimo *(m)*
Pt duodécimo *(m)*

draft n En
De Entwurf *(m)*
Es borrador *(m)*
Fr ébauche *(f)*
It minuta *(f)*
Pt rascunho *(m)*

draftsman n Am
De Zeichner *(m)*
En draughtsman
Es delineante *(m)*

Fr dessinateur-
concepteur *(m)*
It disegnatore *(m)*
Pt autor de esboço *(m)*

Drahtheftung *(f)* n De
En wire stitching
Es cosido con alambre
(m)
Fr couture métallique *(f)*
It cucitura a punti
metallici *(f)*
Pt costura com arame
(f)

Drahtmarkierungen *(pl)*
De
En wiremarks *pl n*
Es marcas de tela
metálica *(f pl)*
Fr marques de la toile *(f
pl)*
It segni della tela *(m pl)*
Pt marcas de tela
metálica *(f pl)*

drama n En; Es, Pt *(m)*
De Drama *(n)*
Fr théâtre *(m)*
It dramma *(m)*

Drama *(n)* n De
En drama
Es drama *(m)*
Fr théâtre *(m)*
It dramma *(m)*
Pt drama *(m)*

dramma *(m)* n It
De Drama *(n)*
En drama
Es drama *(m)*
Fr théâtre *(m)*
Pt drama *(m)*

draughtsman n En
Am draftsman
De Zeichner *(m)*
Es delineante *(m)*
Fr dessinateur-
concepteur *(m)*
It disegnatore *(m)*
Pt autor de esboço *(m)*

draw *vb* En
De zeichnen
Es dibujar
Fr dessiner
It disegnare
Pt traçar

dreidimensionaler Druck *(m)* De
En three-dimensional printing
Es impresión tridimensional *(f)*
Fr impression tridimensionnelle *(f)*
It stampa tridimensionale *(f)*
Pt impressão a três dimensões *(f)*

Dreifarbendruck *(m) n* De
Am three-color printing
En three-colour printing
Es tricromía *(f)*
Fr trichromie *(f)*
It stampa a tre colori *(f)*
Pt impressão a três cores *(f)*

dreiviertelgebundenes Buch *(n)* De
En three-quarter bound book
Es libro encuadernado a tres cuartos de piel *(m)*
Fr livre en demi-reliure amateur *(m)*
It libro a tre quarti rilegato *(m)*
Pt livro encadernado a três quartos *(m)*

drier *n* En
De Trockner *(m)*
Es secante *(m)*
Fr sécheur *(m)*
It essiccante *(m)*
Pt secador *(m)*

droits à l'étranger *(m pl)* Fr
De Auslandsrechte *(pl)*
En foreign rights
Es derechos en el extranjero *(m pl)*
It diritti esteri *(m pl)*
Pt direitos estrangeiros *(m pl)*

droits d'auteur *(m pl)* Fr
De Tantiemen *(pl)*
En royalties *pl n*
Es derechos de autor *(m pl)*
It diritti di licenza *(m pl)*
Pt direitos de autor *(m pl)*

droits de télévision *(m pl)* Fr
De Fernsehrechte *(pl)*
En television rights *pl n*
Es derechos de televisión *(m pl)*
It diritti televisivi *(m pl)*
Pt direitos de televisão *(m pl)*

droits sur le film *(m pl)* Fr
De Verfilmungsrechte *(pl)*
En film rights *pl n*
Es derechos cinematográficos *(m pl)*
It diritti cinematografici *(m pl)*
Pt direitos cinematográficos *(m pl)*

dross *n* En
De Krätze *(f)*
Es escoria *(f)*
Fr crasses *(f pl)*
It scarto *(m)*
Pt escória *(f)*

Druck *(m) n* De
En print
Es impresión *(f)*
Fr imprimé *(m)*
It impressione *(f)*
Pt estampa *(f)*

Druckbetriebe *(pl)* De
En trade houses *pl n*
Es casas comerciales *(f pl)*
Fr maisons commerciales *(f pl)*
It case commerciali *(f pl)*
Pt casas comerciais *(f pl)*

Druckbogen *(m)* De
En section
Es pliego *(m)*
Fr cahier *(m)*
It sezione *(f)*
Pt secção *(f)*

drucken *vb* De
En print
Es imprimir
Fr imprimer

It stampare (stampatura)
Pt imprimir

Drucker *(m) n* De
En printer
Es impresor *(m)*
Fr imprimeur *(m)*
It stampatore *(m)*
Pt tipógrafo *(m)*

Druckerei *(f) n* De
En printing house
Es imprenta (casa) *(f)*
Fr imprimerie (maison) *(f)*
It stabilimento tipografico *(m)*
Pt casa tipográfica *(f)*

Druckerei-Korrekturleser *(m) n* De
En printer's reader
Es corrector de imprenta *(m)*
Fr corrigeur *(m)*
It correttore di bozze da stampa *(m)*
Pt leitor de tipografia *(m)*

Druckfarbe *(f) n* De
En ink (printer's)
Es tinta de imprenta *(f)*
Fr encre d'impression *(f)*
It inchiostro da stampa *(m)*
Pt tinta de impressão *(f)*

Druckfehler *(m) n* De
En printer's error
Es errata de imprenta *(f)*
Fr faute d'impression *(f)*
It errore dello stampatore *(m)*
Pt erro de impressão *(m)*

Druckkarren *(m) n* De
En bed (printing machine)
Es platina *(f)*
Fr marbre *(m)*
It piano *(m)*
Pt mesa *(f)*

Druckkunst *(f) n* De
En printing
Es imprenta (arte) *(f)*

Fr imprimerie (art) *(f)*
It stampatura *(f)*
Pt impressão *(f)*

Druckmaschine *(f) n* De
En printing machine
Es máquina de imprimir *(f)*
Fr machine à imprimer *(f)*
It stampatrice *(f)*
Pt máquina de imprimir *(f)*

Druckplatte *(f) n* De
En plate (printing)
Es plancha *(f)*
Fr plaque *(f)*
It lastra *(f)*
Pt placa *(f)*

Druckpresse *(f) n* De
En press (printing)
Es máquina de imprimir *(f)*
Fr presse d'imprimerie *(f)*
It macchina da stampa *(f)*
Pt prensa *(f)*

Drucktuch *(n) n* De
En blanket (offset litho)
Es mantilla *(f)*
Fr décharge *(f)*
It cauccìu *(m)*; tessuto gommato *(m)*
Pt feltro *(m)*

dry laminating En
De Trockenfolien-kaschierung *(f)*
Es laminación en seco *(f)*
Fr stratification à sec *(f)*
It laminazione a secco *(f)*
Pt laminagem a seco *(f)*

dry offset En
De Trockenoffset *(m)*
Es offset seco *(m)*
Fr offset à sec *(m)*
It offset secco *(m)*
Pt offset seco *(m)*

dummy *n* En
De Blindband *(m)*
Es maqueta *(f)*
Fr maquette *(f)*
It menabò *(m)*

Pt maquete *(f)*

Dunkelkammer *(f) n* De
En darkroom
Es cuarto oscuro *(m)*
Fr chambre noire *(f)*
It camera oscura *(f)*
Pt câmara escura *(f)*

Dünndruckpapier *(n) n*
De
En onion-skin paper
Es papel cebolla *(m)*
Fr papier pelure *(m)*
It carta traslucida *(f)*
Pt papel cebola *(m)*

dünnes Spatium *(n)* De
En thin space
Es espacio fino *(m)*
Fr espace fine *(f)*
It spazio sottile *(m)*
Pt espaço fino *(m)*

duodecimo *n* En
De Duodezformat *(n)*
Es dozavo *(m)*
Fr in-douze *(m)*
It in dodicesimo *(m)*
Pt duodécimo *(m)*

duodécimo *(m) n* Pt
De Duodezformat *(n)*
En duodecimo
Es dozavo *(m)*
Fr in-douze *(m)*
It in dodicesimo *(m)*

Duodezformat *(n) n* De
En duodecimo
Es dozavo *(m)*
Fr in-douze *(m)*
It in dodicesimo *(m)*
Pt duodécimo *(m)*

duotipia *(f) n* It, Pt
De Zweifarbenschrift *(f)*
En duotype
Es duotipia bitono *(f)*
Fr duotype *(m)*

duotipia bitono *(f)* Es
De Zweifarbenschrift *(f)*
En duotype
Fr duotype *(m)*
It duotipia *(f)*
Pt duotipia *(f)*

duotone illustration En

De Zweifarbenillustration
(f)
Es ilustración en
bicromía *(f)*
Fr illustration double
ton *(f)*
It illustrazione bicolore
(f)
Pt ilustração
bicromática *(f)*

duotype *n* En; Fr *(m)*
De Zweifarbenschrift *(f)*
Es duotipia bitono *(f)*
It duotipia *(f)*
Pt duotipia *(f)*

duplex paper En
De Duplexpapier *(n)*
Es cartón duplo *(m)*
Fr papier duplex *(m)*
It carta duplex *(f)*
Pt papel duplex *(m)*

Duplexpapier *(n) n* De
En duplex paper
Es cartón duplo *(m)*
Fr papier duplex *(m)*
It carta duplex *(f)*
Pt papel duplex *(m)*

duplicadora *(f) n* Es, Pt
De Vervielfältigungs-
maschine *(f)*
En duplicator
Fr duplicateur *(m)*
It copialettere *(f)*

duplicate blocks *pl n* En
De Duplikatklischees *(pl)*
Es bloques duplicados
(m pl)
Fr cliché en double *(m)*
It cliché duplicati *(m pl)*
Pt blocos duplicados *(m
pl)*

duplicateur *(m) n* Fr
De Vervielfältigungs-
maschine *(f)*
En duplicator
Es duplicadora *(f)*
It copialettere *(f)*
Pt duplicadora *(f)*

duplicator *n* En
De Vervielfältigungs-
maschine *(f)*
Es duplicadora *(f)*
Fr duplicateur *(m)*

It copialettere *(f)*
Pt duplicadora *(f)*

Duplikatklischees *(pl)*
De
En duplicate blocks *pl n*
Es bloques duplicados
(m pl)
Fr cliché en double *(m)*
It cliché duplicati *(m pl)*
Pt blocos duplicados *(m
pl)*

Durchscheinbild *(n) n* De
En ghosting
Es mancha de reflexión
(f)
Fr image fantôme *(f)*
It falsa immagine *(f)*
Pt fantasma *(m)*

Durchscheinen *(n) n* De
En look-through
Es textura a la luz *(f)*
Fr épair *(m)*
It trasparente *(m)*
Pt transparência *(f)*

Durchschießen *(n) n* De
En leading
Es interlineado *(m)*
Fr interlignage *(m)*
It interlineazione *(f)*
Pt interlineado *(m)*

Durchschüsse *(pl)* De
En leads *pl n*
Es interlíneas *(f pl)*
Fr entre-lignes *(f pl)*
It interlinea *(f)*
Pt entrelinhas *(f pl)*

E

earnings *pl n* En
De Einnahmen *(pl)*
Es beneficios *(m pl)*
Fr bénéfices *(m pl)*
It entrate *(f pl)*
Pt rendimentos *(m pl)*

ébarber *vb* Fr
De beschneiden
En trim
Es cortar
It rifilare
Pt aparar

ébauche *(f) n* Fr
De Entwurf *(m)*
En draft
Es borrador *(m)*
It minuta *(f)*
Pt rascunho *(m)*

échantillon *(m) n* Fr
De Muster *(n)*
En swatch
Es muestrario *(m)*
It campione *(m)*
Pt mostruário *(m)*

e comercial *(f)* Pt
De Und-Zeichen *(n)*
En ampersand
Es y abreviada *(f)*
Fr et commercial *(m)*
It congiunzione
commerciale *(f)*

écran *(m) n* Fr
De Raster *(m)*
En screen
Es retícula *(f)*
It retino *(m)*
Pt retícula *(f)*

écran de contact *(m)* Fr
De Kontaktraster *(m)*
En contact screen
Es retícula de contacto
(f)
It retino a contatto *(m)*
Pt retícula de contacto
(f)

écrivassier *(m) n* Fr
De Mietschreiber *(m)*
En hack writer

Es escritor mercenario
(m)
It imbrattacarte *(m)*
Pt escritor comercial
(m)

edição *(f) n* Pt
De Ausgabe *(f)*
En edition
Es edición *(f)*
Fr édition *(f)*
It edizione *(f)*

edição comercial *(f)* Pt
De Fachausgabe *(f)*
En trade edition
Es edición profesional *(f)*
Fr édition
professionnelle *(f)*
It edizione
commerciale *(f)*

edição de bolso *(f)* Pt
De Taschenbuch-
Ausgabe *(f)*
En paperback edition
Es edición de libros en
rústica *(f)*
Fr édition de poche *(f)*
It edizione economica
(f)

**edição de club de
leitores** *(f)* Pt
De Buchclub-Auflage *(f)*
En book-club edition
Es edición de club del
libro *(f)*
Fr édition club du livre
(f)
It edizione club del libro
(f)

edição de lombada dura
(f) Pt
Am hardcover edition
De gebundene Ausgabe
(f)
En hardback edition
Es edición
encuadernada *(f)*
Fr édition reliée *(f)*
It edizione con
copertina rigida *(f)*

edição de tradução *(f)* Pt
De übersetzte Ausgabe
(f)
En translation edition
Es edición de traducción
(f)

Fr édition de
traductions *(f)*
It edizione tradotta *(f)*

edição facsímile *(f)* Pt
De Faksimile-Ausgabe *(f)*
En facsimile edition
Es edición facsímil *(f)*
Fr édition fac-similé *(f)*
It edizione facsimile *(f)*

**edição para encomenda
por correio** *(f)* Pt
De Versandhausausgabe
(f)
En mail-order edition
Es edición para envío
por correo *(f)*
Fr édition vendue par
correspondance *(f)*
It edizione per vendite
per posta *(f)*

**edição revista e
actualizada** *(f)* Pt
De revidierte und
überarbeitete Auflage
(f)
En revised and updated
edition
Es edición corregida y
puesta al día *(f)*
Fr édition révisée et
mise à jour *(f)*
It edizione corretta ed
aggiornata *(f)*

edición *(f) n* Es
De Ausgabe *(f)*
En edition
Fr édition *(f)*
It edizione *(f)*
Pt edição *(f)*

**edición corregida y
puesta al día** *(f)* Es
De revidierte und
überarbeitete Auflage
(f)
En revised and updated
edition
Fr édition révisée et
mise à jour *(f)*
It edizione corretta ed
aggiornata *(f)*
Pt edição revista e
actualizada *(f)*

edición de club del libro
(f) Es
De Buchclub-Auflage *(f)*
En book-club edition

Fr édition club du livre
(f)
It edizione club del libro
(f)
Pt edição de club de
leitores *(f)*

**edición de libros en
rústica** *(f)* Es
De Taschenbuch-
Ausgabe *(f)*
En paperback edition
Fr édition de poche *(f)*
It edizione economica
(f)
Pt edição de bolso *(f)*

edición de traducción *(f)*
Es
De übersetzte Ausgabe
(f)
En translation edition
Fr édition de
traductions *(f)*
It edizione tradotta *(f)*
Pt edição de tradução
(f)

edición encuadernada
(f) Es
Am hardcover edition
De gebundene Ausgabe
(f)
En hardback edition
Fr édition reliée *(f)*
It edizione con
copertina rigida *(f)*
Pt edição de lombada
dura *(f)*

edición facsímil *(f)* Es
De Faksimile-Ausgabe *(f)*
En facsimile edition
Fr édition fac-similé *(f)*
It edizione facsimile *(f)*
Pt edição facsímile *(f)*

**edición para envío por
correo** *(f)* Es
De Versandhausausgabe
(f)
En mail-order edition
Fr édition vendue par
correspondance *(f)*
It edizione per vendite
per posta *(f)*
Pt edição para
encomenda por
correio *(f)*

Fr édition club du livre
(f)
It edizione club del libro
(f)
Pt edição de club de
leitores *(f)*

edición profesional *(f)*
Es
De Fachausgabe *(f)*
En trade edition
Fr édition
professionnelle *(f)*
It edizione
commerciale *(f)*
Pt edição comercial *(f)*

editar *vb* Pt
De Manuskript
revidieren
En copy-edit
Es corregir originales
Fr éditer un texte
It correggere originali

éditer un texte Fr
De Manuskript
revidieren
En copy-edit
Es corregir originales
It correggere originali
Pt editar

éditeur *(m) n* Fr
De Verleger *(m)*
En publisher (person)
Es editor *(m)*
It editore *(m)*
Pt editor *(m)*

**éditeur de livres à gros
tirage** *(m)* Fr
De Massenabsatz-
Verleger *(m)*
En mass-market
publisher
Es editor para el
mercado de masas
(m)
It editore per il mercato
di massa *(m)*
Pt editor para mercado
de massas *(m)*

**éditeur de livres de
poche** *(m)* Fr
De Taschenbuch-
Verleger *(m)*
En paperback publisher
Es editor de libros en
rústica *(m)*
It editore di collane
economiche *(m)*
Pt editor de livros de
bolso *(m)*

éditeur de romans *(m)* Fr
De Romanverleger *(m)*
En fiction publisher

Es editor de novelas *(m)*
It editore di narrativa *(m)*
Pt editorial de ficção *(f)*

éditeur d'ouvrages de référence *(m)* Fr
De Nachschlagewerk-Verleger *(m)*
En reference-book publisher
Es editor de obras de consulta *(m)*
It editore di libri di consultazione *(m)*
Pt editor de livros de consulta *(m)*

éditeur d'ouvrages généraux *(m)* Fr
De Sachliteratur-Verleger *(m)*
En non-fiction publisher
Es editor de libros no novelescos *(m)*
It editore di saggistica *(m)*
Pt editor de não ficção *(m)*

éditeur d'ouvrages médicaux *(m)* Fr
De Verleger von medizinischen Veröffentlichungen *(m)*
En medical publisher
Es editora de libros de medicina *(f)*
It editore di testi medici *(m)*
Pt editor de livros de medicina *(m)*

éditeur d'ouvrages spécialisés *(m)* Fr
De Spezial-Verleger *(m)*
En specialist publisher
Es editor de obras especializadas *(m)*
It editore di opere specialistiche *(m)*
Pt editora de obras especiais *(m)*

edition *n* En
De Ausgabe *(f)*
Es edición *(f)*
Fr édition *(f)*
It edizione *(f)*
Pt edição *(f)*

édition *(f)* *n* Fr
De Ausgabe *(f)*
En edition
Es edición *(f)*
It edizione *(f)*
Pt edição *(f)*

édition club du livre *(f)* Fr
De Buchclub-Auflage *(f)*
En book-club edition
Es edición de club del libro *(f)*
It edizione club del libro *(f)*
Pt edição de club de leitores *(f)*

édition de poche *(f)* Fr
De Taschenbuch-Ausgabe *(f)*
En paperback edition
Es edición de libros en rústica *(f)*
It edizione economica *(f)*
Pt edição de bolso *(f)*

édition de traductions *(f)* Fr
De übersetzte Ausgabe *(f)*
En translation edition
Es edición de traducción *(f)*
It edizione tradotta *(f)*
Pt edição de tradução *(f)*

édition fac-similé *(f)* Fr
De Faksimile-Ausgabe *(f)*
En facsimile edition
Es edición facsímil *(f)*
It edizione facsimile *(f)*
Pt edição facsímil *(f)*

édition originale *(f)* Fr
De erste Auflage *(f)*
En first edition
Es primera edición *(f)*
It prima edizione *(f)*
Pt primeira edição *(f)*

édition professionnelle *(f)* Fr
De Fachausgabe *(f)*
En trade edition
Es edición profesional *(f)*
It edizione commerciale *(f)*
Pt edição comercial *(f)*

édition reliée *(f)* Fr
Am hardcover edition
De gebundene Ausgabe *(f)*
En hardback edition
Es edición encuadernada *(f)*
It edizione con copertina rigida *(f)*
Pt edição de lombada dura *(f)*

édition révisée et mise à jour *(f)* Fr
De revidierte und überarbeitete Auflage *(f)*
En revised and updated edition
Es edición corregida y puesta al día *(f)*
It edizione corretta ed aggiornata *(f)*
Pt edição revista e actualizada *(f)*

édition vendue par correspondance *(f)* Fr
De Versandhausausgabe *(f)*
En mail-order edition
Es edición para envío por correo *(f)*
It edizione per vendite per posta *(f)*
Pt edição para encomenda por correio *(f)*

editor *(m)* *n* Es, Pt
De Verleger *(m)*
En publisher (person)
Fr éditeur *(m)*
It editore *(m)*

editor (de libros) *(m)* *n* Es
De Herausgeber *(m)*
En editor (publisher's)
Fr rédacteur *(m)*
It editore (di libri) *(m)*
Pt editor (de livros) *(m)*

editor (de livros) *(m)* *n* Pt
De Herausgeber *(m)*
En editor (publisher's)
Es editor (de libros) *(m)*
Fr rédacteur *(m)*
It editore (di libri) *(m)*

editor (newspaper) *n* En
De Redakteur *(m)*
Es redactor *(m)*
Fr rédacteur en chef *(m)*
It redattore *(m)*
Pt redactor *(m)*

editor (publisher's) *n* En
De Herausgeber *(m)*
Es editor (de libros) *(m)*
Fr rédacteur *(m)*
It editore (di libri) *(m)*
Pt editor (de livros) *(m)*

editora de libros de medicina *(f)* Es
De Verleger von medizinischen Veröffentlichungen *(m)*
En medical publisher
Fr éditeur d'ouvrages médicaux *(m)*
It editore di testi medici *(m)*
Pt editor de livros de medicina *(m)*

editora de obras especiais *(m)* Pt
De Spezial-Verleger *(m)*
En specialist publisher
Es editor de obras especializadas *(m)*
Fr éditeur d'ouvrages spécialisés *(m)*
It editore di opere specialistiche *(m)*

editor adjunto *(m)* Pt
De stellvertretender Redakteur *(m)*
En assistant editor
Es redactor adjunto *(m)*
Fr rédacteur adjoint *(m)*
It assistente editore *(m)*

editor artístico *(m)* Pt
De Kunst-Redakteur *(m)*
En art editor
Es redactor gráfico *(m)*
Fr rédacteur artistique *(m)*
It editore artistico *(m)*

editor de libros en rústica *(m)* Es
De Taschenbuch-Verleger *(m)*
En paperback publisher
Fr éditeur de livres de poche *(m)*

It editore di collane
   economiche (m)
Pt editor de livros de
   bolso (m)

**editor de libros no
   novelescos** (m) Es
De Sachliteratur-
   Verleger (m)
En non-fiction publisher
Fr éditeur d'ouvrages
   généraux (m)
It editore di saggistica
   (m)
Pt editor de não ficção
   (m)

editor de livros de bolso
   (m) Pt
De Taschenbuch-
   Verleger (m)
En paperback publisher
Es editor de libros en
   rústica (m)
Fr éditeur de livres de
   poche (m)
It editore di collane
   economiche (m)

**editor de livros de
   consulta** (m) Pt
De Nachschlagewerk-
   Verleger (m)
En reference-book
   publisher
Es editor de obras de
   consulta (m)
Fr éditeur d'ouvrages
   de référence (m)
It editore di libri di
   consultazione (m)

**editor de livros de
   medicina** (m) Pt
De Verleger von
   medizinischen
   Veröffentlichungen
   (m)
En medical publisher
Es editora de libros de
   medicina (f)
Fr éditeur d'ouvrages
   médicaux (m)
It editore di testi medici
   (m)

editor de não ficção (m)
   Pt
De Sachliteratur-
   Verleger (m)
En non-fiction publisher

Es editor de libros no
   novelescos (m)
Fr éditeur d'ouvrages
   généraux (m)
It editore di saggistica
   (m)

editor de novelas (m) Es
De Romanverleger (m)
En fiction publisher
Fr éditeur de romans
   (m)
It editore di narrativa
   (m)
Pt editorial de ficção (f)

**editor de obras de
   consulta** (m) Es
De Nachschlagewerk-
   Verleger (m)
En reference-book
   publisher
Fr éditeur d'ouvrages
   de référence (m)
It editore di libri di
   consultazione (m)
Pt editor de livros de
   consulta (m)

**editor de obras
   especializadas** (m)
   Es
De Spezial-Verleger (m)
En specialist publisher
Fr éditeur d'ouvrages
   spécialisés (m)
It editore di opere
   specialistiche (m)
Pt editora de obras
   especiais (m)

editore (m) n It
De Verleger (m)
En publisher (person)
Es editor (de libros) (m)
Fr éditeur (m)
Pt editor (de livros) (m)

editore (di libri) (m) n It
De Herausgeber (m)
En editor (publisher's)
Es editor (de libros) (m)
Fr rédacteur (m)
Pt editor (de livros) (m)

editore artístico (m) It
De Kunst-Redakteur (m)
En art editor
Es redactor gráfico (m)
Fr rédacteur artistique
   (m)
Pt editor artístico (m)

editore di coedizione
   (m) It
De Verleger einer
   gemeinsamen
   Ausgabe (m)
En co-edition publisher
Es editorial de
   coediciones (f)
Fr co-éditeur (m)
Pt editorial de coedição
   (f)

**editore di collane
   economiche** (m) It
De Taschenbuch-
   Verleger (m)
En paperback publisher
Es editor de libros en
   rústica (m)
Fr éditeur de livres de
   poche (m)
Pt editor de livros de
   bolso (m)

**editore di libri di
   consultazione** (m) It
De Nachschlagewerk-
   Verleger (m)
En reference-book
   publisher
Es editor de obras de
   consulta (m)
Fr éditeur d'ouvrages
   de référence (m)
Pt editor de livros de
   consulta (m)

editore di narrativa (m)
   It
De Romanverleger (m)
En fiction publisher
Es editor de novelas (m)
Fr éditeur de romans
   (m)
Pt editorial de ficção (f)

**editore di opere
   specialistiche** (m) It
De Spezial-Verleger (m)
En specialist publisher
Es editor de obras
   especializadas (m)
Fr éditeur d'ouvrages
   spécialisés (m)
Pt editora de obras
   especiais (m)

editore di saggistica (m)
   It
De Sachliteratur-
   Verleger (m)

En non-fiction publisher
Es editor de libros no
   novelescos (m)
Fr éditeur d'ouvrages
   généraux (m)
Pt editor de não ficção
   (m)

editore di testi medici
   (m) Pt
Es Verleger von
   medizinischen
   Veröffentlichungen
   (m)
En medical publisher
Fr editora de libros de
   medicina (f)
It éditeur d'ouvrages
   médicaux (m)
Pt editor de livros de
   medicina (m)

**editore per il mercato di
   massa** (m) It
De Massenabsatz-
   Verleger (m)
En mass-market
   publisher
Es editor para el
   mercado de masas
   (m)
Fr éditeur de livres à
   gros tirage (m)
Pt editor para mercado
   de massas (m)

editore senior (m) It
De leitender Redakteur
   (m)
En senior editor
Es redactor jefe (m)
Fr rédacteur gérant (m)
Pt editor senior (m)

editoria (f) n It
De Verlagswesen (n)
En publishing
Es editorial (f)
Fr commerce de
   l'édition (m)
Pt negocio de
   publicação (m)

editorial (f) n Es
De Verlagswesen (n)
En publishing
Fr publication (f)
It editoria (f)
Pt publicação (f)

editorial agency En
De Redaktionsagentur (f)
Es agemcia editorial (f)
Fr agence de rédaction (f)
It agenzia editoriale (f)
Pt agência editorial (f)

editorial assistant En
De Redaktionsassistent (m)
Es ayudante de editorial (m)
Fr secrétaire de rédaction (m)
It assistente editoriale (m)
Pt ajudante editorial (m)

editorial de coedição (f) Pt
De Verleger einer gemeinsamen Ausgabe (m)
En co-edition publisher
Es editorial de coediciones (f)
Fr co-éditeur (m)
It editore di coedizione (m)

editorial de coediciones (f) Es
De Verleger einer gemeinsamen Ausgabe (m)
En co-edition publisher
Fr co-éditeur (m)
It editore di coedizione (m)
Pt editorial de coedição (f)

editorial de ficção (f) Pt
De Romanverleger (m)
En fiction publisher
Es editor de novelas (m)
Fr éditeur de romans (m)
It editore di narrativa (m)

editorial department En
De Redaktion (f)
Es departamento editorial (m)
Fr rédaction (f)
It redazione (f)
Pt departamento editorial (m)

editorial director En
De Chefredakteur (m)
Es director de editorial (m)
Fr directeur de la rédaction (m)
It direttore editoriale (m)
Pt director editorial (m)

editorial services pl n En
De Redaktionsdienste (pl)
Es servicios editoriales (m pl)
Fr services rédactionnels (m pl)
It servizi editoriali (m pl)
Pt serviços editoriais (m pl)

editor para el mercado de masas (m) Es
De Massenabsatz-Verleger (m)
En mass-market publisher
Fr éditeur de livres à gros tirage (m)
It editore per il mercato di massa (m)
Pt editor para mercado de massas (m)

editor para mercado de massas (m) Pt
De Massenabsatz-Verleger (m)
En mass-market publisher
Es editor para el mercado de masas (m)
Fr éditeur de livres à gros tirage (m)
It editore per il mercato di massa (m)

editor por encargo (m) Es
De Auftragvergabe-Redakteur (m)
En commissioning editor
Fr rédacteur chargé des commandes (m)
It redattore commissioni (m)
Pt editor que encomenda a obra (m)

editor que encomenda a obra (m) Pt
De Auftragvergabe-Redakteur (m)
En commissioning editor
Es editor por encargo (m)
Fr rédacteur chargé des commandes (m)
It redattore commissioni (m)

editor senior (m) Pt
De leitender Redakteur (m)
En senior editor
Es redactor jefe (m)
Fr rédacteur gérant (m)
It editore senior (m)

edizione (f) n It
De Ausgabe (f)
En edition
Es edición (f)
Fr édition (f)
Pt edição (f)

edizione club del libro (f) It
De Buchclub-Auflage (f)
En book-club edition
Es edición de club del libro (f)
Fr édition club du livre (f)
Pt edição de club de leitores (f)

edizione commerciale (f) It
De Fachausgabe (f)
En trade edition
Es edición profesional (f)
Fr édition professionnelle (f)
Pt edição comercial (f)

edizione con copertina rigida (f) It
Am hardcover edition
De gebundene Ausgabe (f)
En hardback edition
Es edición encuadernada (f)
Fr édition reliée (f)
Pt edição de lombada dura (f)

edizione corretta ed aggiornata (f) It
De revidierte und überarbeitete Auflage (f)
En revised and updated edition
Es edición corregida y puesta al día (f)
Fr édition révisée et mise à jour (f)
Pt edição revista e actualizada (f)

edizione economica (f) It
De Taschenbuch-Ausgabe (f)
En paperback edition
Es edición de libros en rústica (f)
Fr édition de poche (f)
Pt edição de bolso (f)

edizione facsimile (f) It
De Faksimile-Ausgabe (f)
En facsimile edition
Es edición facsímil (f)
Fr édition fac-similé (f)
Pt edição facsímile (f)

edizione per vendite per posta (f) It
De Versandhausausgabe (f)
En mail-order edition
Es edición para envío por correo (f)
Fr édition vendue par correspondance (f)
Pt edição para encomenda por correio (f)

edizione tradotta (f) It
De übersetzte Ausgabe (f)
En translation edition
Es edición de traducción (f)
Fr édition de traductions (f)
Pt edição de tradução (f)

educational books pl n En
De Erziehungsbücher (pl)
Es libros educativos (m pl)
Fr livres éducatifs (m pl)
It libri pedagogici (m pl)
Pt livros educacionais (m pl)

**efecto de piel de
naranja** *(m)* Es
De Apfelsinenschalen-
Effekt *(m)*
En orange-peel effect
Fr effet pelure d´orange
(m)
It effetto a buccia
d´arancia *(m)*
Pt efeito casca de
laranja *(m)*

efectos de escritorio *(m
pl)* Es
De Briefpapier *(n)*
En stationery
Fr papeterie de détail *(f)*
It cartoleria *(f)*
Pt papel e artigos de
escritório *(m)*

efeito casca de laranja
(m) Pt
De Apfelsinenschalen-
Effekt *(m)*
En orange-peel effect
Es efecto de piel de
naranja *(m)*
Fr effet pelure d´orange
(m)
It effetto a buccia
d´arancia *(m)*

efeito moiré *(m)* Pt
De Schnürlmoiré *(n)*
En moiré effect
Es moiré *(m)*
Fr moiré *(m)*
It effetto moiré *(m)*

effacer *vb* Fr
De löschen
En erase
Es borrar
It cassare
Pt apagar

effet pelure d'orange
(m) Fr
De Apfelsinenschalen-
Effekt *(m)*
En orange-peel effect
Es efecto de piel de
naranja *(m)*
It effetto a buccia
d´arancia *(m)*
Pt efeito casca de
laranja *(m)*

**effetto a buccia
d'arancia** *(m)* It

De Apfelsinenschalen-
Effekt *(m)*
En orange-peel effect
Es efecto de piel de
naranja *(m)*
Fr effet pelure d´orange
(m)
Pt efeito casca de
laranja *(m)*

effetto moiré *(m)* It
De Schnürlmoiré *(n)*
En moiré effect
Es moiré *(m)*
Fr moiré *(m)*
Pt efeito moiré *(m)*

Egoutteur *(m)* n De
En dandy roll
Es rodillo afiligranador
(m)
Fr rouleau égoutteur
(m)
It cilindro à filigrana *(m)*
Pt rolo filigranador *(m)*

**ein Angebot
unterbreiten** De
En quote (a price)
Es cotizar
Fr mentionner
It dare le quotazioni
Pt cotar

einbändiges Werk *(n)*
De
En single-volume work
Es obra de un solo
volumen *(f)*
Fr oeuvre en un volume
(f)
It opera in un solo
volume *(f)*
Pt obra num só volume
(f)

einfarbig *adj* De
En monochrome
Es monocromo
Fr monochrome
It monocromatico
Pt monocrómico

einfarbige illustration *(f)*
De
En monochrome
illustration
Es ilustración
monocroma *(f)*
Fr illustration
monochrome *(f)*

It illustrazione
monocromatica *(f)*
Pt ilustração
monocrómica *(f)*

einfügen *vb* De
En insert
Es encartar
Fr insérer
It inserire
Pt inserir

Einführung *(f)* n De
En guide
Es guía *(f)*
Fr guide *(m)*
It guida *(f)*
Pt guia *(m)*

Eingabe *(f)* n De
En input
Es entrada *(f)*
Fr entrée *(f)*
It input *(m)*
Pt entrada *(f)*

eingerückt *adj* De
En indented
Es sangrado
Fr dentelé
It dentellato
Pt dentada

Einhängen *(n)* n De
En casing-in
Es metido en tapas *(m)*
Fr cartonnage *(m)*
It messa in custodia *(f)*
Pt colocação em capa
separada *(f)*

Einheitskosten *(pl)* n De
En unit cost
Es coste unitario *(m)*
Fr coût unitaire *(m)*
It costo unitario *(m)*
Pt custo unitário *(m)*

Einkommen *(n)* n De
En revenue
Es ingresos *(m pl)*
Fr recette *(f)*
It entrata *(f)*
Pt receita *(f)*

Einleger *(m)* n De
En feeder
Es alimentador *(m)*
Fr margeur *(m)*

It alimentatore *(m)*
Pt alimentadora *(f)*

einleiten *vb* De
En preface
Es prologar
Fr préfacer
It fare una prefazione
Pt redigir um prefácio

Einleitung *(f)* n De
En introduction
Es introducción *(f)*
Fr introduction *(f)*
It introduzione *(f)*
Pt introdução *(f)*

Einnahmen *(pl)* De
En earnings *pl n*
Es beneficios *(m pl)*
Fr bénéfices *(m pl)*
It entrate *(f pl)*
Pt rendimentos *(m pl)*

Einpassung *(f)* n De
Am register (color
printing)
En register (colour
printing)
Es registro (imprenta en
color) *(m)*
Fr repérage *(m)*
It registro (stampatura
a colori) *(m)*
Pt registo (impressão a
cores) *(m)*

einrücken *vb* De
En indent
Es sangrar
Fr renforcer
It dentellare
Pt abrir parágrafo

Einsatz *(m)* n De
En insert
Es encarte *(m)*
Fr encartage *(m)*
It inserto *(m)*
Pt inserção *(f)*

Einsetzen *(n)* n De
En insetting
Es encuadre *(m)*
Fr mise en place *(f)*
It incorniciatura *(f)*
Pt intercalagem *(f)*

Einstufenätzverfahren
    (n) n De
En powderless etching
Es grabado rápido *(m)*
Fr gravure sans poudre
    (f)
It incisione senza
    polvere *(f)*
Pt gravura sem pó *(f)*

eintasten *vb* De
En keyboard
Es introducir desde
    teclado
Fr introduire par clavier
It introdurre mediante
    la tastiera
Pt introduzir desde
    teclado

Eintrag *(m) n* De
En entry
Es artículo *(m)*
Fr entrée *(f)*
It voce *(f)*
Pt entrada *(f)*

Eintragsliste *(f) n* De
En entry list
Es relación de artículos
    (f)
Fr liste des entrées *(f)*
It elenco di voci *(m)*
Pt lista de inscrição *(f)*

Einzelhandels-Verkäufe
    (pl) De
En retail sales
Es ventas al por menor *(f*
    pl)
Fr vente au détail *(f)*
It vendite al minuto *(f*
    pl)
Pt vendas a retalho *(f pl)*

Einzelhändler *(m) n* De
En retailer
Es minorista *(m)*
Fr détaillant *(m)*
It dettagliante *(m)*
Pt retalhista *(m)*

ejemplar de obsequio
    (m) Es
De Gratisexemplar *(n)*
En complimentary copy
Fr exemplaire en
    hommage *(m)*
It copia omaggio *(f)*
Pt exemplar de oferta
    (m)

ejemplares de obsequio
    del autor *(m pl)* Es
De Autorexemplare *(pl)*
En author's free copies
    pl n
Fr exemplaires gratuits
    pour l'auteur *(m pl)*
It copie gratuite
    dell'autore *(f pl)*
Pt exemplares grátis
    para o autor *(m pl)*

ejemplares para reseña
    (m pl) Es
De Vorausexemplare *(pl)*
En advance copies *pl n*
Fr exemplaires de
    lancement *(m pl)*
It copie in anteprima *(f*
    pl)
Pt provas tipográficas *(f*
    pl)

ejemplar mucho
    enmendada *(m)* Es
De stark revidiertes
    Manuskript *(n)*
En heavily edited copy
Fr texte très corrigé *(m)*
It copia molto
    emendata *(f)*
Pt exemplar muito
    corrigido *(m)*

ejemplar para reseña
    (m) Es
De Rezensions-Exemplar
    (n)
En review copy
Fr exemplaire de service
    de presse *(m)*
It copia di recensione
    (f)
Pt exemplar para
    resenha *(m)*

elaborare *vb* It
De entwickeln (Planung)
En develop (planning)
Es desarrollar
Fr exécuter
Pt desenvolver

elaboratore digitale *(m)*
    It
De Digitalcomputer *(m)*
En digital computer
Es ordenador digital *(m)*
Fr calculateur
    numérique *(m)*
Pt computador digital
    (m)

elaborazione di dati *(f)* It
De Datenverarbeitung *(f)*
En data processing
Es proceso de datos *(m)*
Fr traitement des
    données *(m)*
Pt tratamento de dados
    (m)

elaborazione
    elettronica dei dati
    (f) It
De elektronische
    Datenverarbeitung *(f)*
En electronic data
    processing
Es proceso electrónico
    de datos *(m)*
Fr traitement
    électronique de
    l'information *(m)*
Pt tratamento
    electrónico de dados
    (m)

electricidade estática *(f)*
    Pt
De statische Elektrizität
    (f)
En static electricity
Es electricidad estática
    (f)
Fr électricité statique *(f)*
It elettricità statica *(f)*

electricidad estática *(f)*
    Es
De statische Elektrizität
    (f)
En static electricity
Fr électricité statique *(f)*
It elettricità statica *(f)*
Pt electricidade estática
    (f)

électricité statique *(f)* Fr
De statische Elektrizität
    (f)
En static electricity
Es electricidad estática
    (f)
It elettricità statica *(f)*
Pt electricidade estática
    (f)

electronic data
    processing En
De elektronische
    Datenverarbeitung *(f)*
Es proceso electrónico
    de datos *(m)*
Fr traitement

électronique de
    l'information *(m)*
It elaborazione
    elettronica dei dati *(f)*
Pt tratamento
    electrónico de dados
    (m)

electronic engraving En
De elektronische
    Gravierung *(f)*
Es grabado electrónico
    (m)
Fr gravure électronique
    (f)
It incisione elettronica
    (f)
Pt gravura electrónica
    (f)

electronic scanning En
De elektronische
    Abtastung *(f)*
Es selección electrónica
    (f)
Fr exploration
    électronique *(f)*
It scanning elettronico
    (m)
Pt seleccionadora
    electrónica de cores
    (f)

electrotipo *(m) n* Es, Pt
De Galvano *(n)*
En electrotype
Fr électrotype *(m)*
It elettrotipo *(m)*

electrotype *n* En
De Galvano *(n)*
Es electrotipo *(m)*
Fr électrotype *(m)*
It elettrotipo *(m)*
Pt electrotipo *(m)*

électrotype *(m) n* Fr
De Galvano *(n)*
En electrotype
Es electrotipo *(m)*
It elettrotipo *(m)*
Pt electrotipo *(m)*

électrotype par dessin
    sur métal paraffiné
    (m) Fr
De Wachsgravieren *(n)*
En wax engraving
Es cerotipia *(f)*
It incisione a cera *(f)*
Pt cerotipia *(f)*

elektronische Abtastung *(f)* De
En electronic scanning
Es selección electrónica *(f)*
Fr exploration électronique *(f)*
It scanning elettronico *(m)*
Pt seleccionadora electrónica de cores *(f)*

elektronische Datenverarbeitung *(f)* De
En electronic data processing
Es proceso electrónico de datos *(m)*
Fr traitement électronique de l'information *(m)*
It elaborazione elettronica dei dati *(f)*
Pt tratamento electrónico de dados *(m)*

elektronische Gravierung *(f)* De
En electronic engraving
Es grabado electrónico *(m)*
Fr gravure électronique *(f)*
It incisione elettronica *(f)*
Pt gravura electrónica *(f)*

elemento mobile *(m)* It
De Mobilé *(n)*
En mobile
Es hastidor móvil *(m)*
Fr mobile *(m)*
Pt mobile *(m)*

éléments codés *(m pl)* Fr
De vom Rechner lesbare Daten *(pl)*
En machine-readable data
Es datos legibles con máquina *(m pl)*
It dati leggibili per la macchina *(m pl)*
Pt dados legíveis na máquina *(m pl)*

elenco *(m) n* It
De Liste *(f)*
En list (publisher's)
Es lista *(f)*
Fr liste *(f)*
Pt lista *(f)*

elenco d'autunno *(m)* It
De Herbstliste *(f)*
En autumn list
Es catálogo de otoño *(m)*
Fr catalogue de la rentrée *(m)*
Pt lista de outono *(f)*

elenco di narrativa *(m)* It
De Romanliteratur-Liste *(f)*
En fiction list
Es catálogo de novelas *(m)*
Fr catalogue des romans *(m)*
Pt lista de ficção *(f)*

elenco di parole principali *(m)* It
De Liste der haupten Wörter *(f)*
En headword list
Es lista de palabras principales *(f)*
Fr liste des mots en-têtes *(f)*
Pt lista de palavras-índice *(f)*

elenco di primavera *(m)* It
De Frühjahrsliste *(f)*
En spring list
Es catálogo de primavera *(m)*
Fr catalogue de printemps *(m)*
Pt lista de Primavera *(f)*

elenco di voci *(m)* It
De Eintragsliste *(f)*
En entry list
Es relación de artículos *(f)*
Fr liste des entrées *(f)*
Pt lista de inscrição *(f)*

elettricità statica *(f)* It
De statische Elektrizität *(f)*
En static electricity
Es electricidad estática *(f)*

Fr électricité statique *(f)*
Pt electricidade estática *(f)*

elettrotipo *(m) n* It
De Galvano *(n)*
En electrotype
Es electrotipo *(m)*
Fr électrotype *(m)*
Pt electrotipo *(m)*

elevador reunidor *(m)* Es
De Sammler *(m)*
En assembler
Fr assembleur *(m)*
It raccoglitore *(m)*
Pt ajustadora *(f)*

Elfenbeinkarton *(m) n* De
En ivory board
Es cartulina marfil *(f)*
Fr carton invoire *(m)*
It cartone avorio *(m)*
Pt cartão marfim *(m)*

eliminação *(f) n* Pt
De Streichung *(f)*
En deletion
Es supresión *(f)*
Fr suppression *(f)*
It cancellatura *(f)*

elzévir *(m) n* Fr
De Mediäval *(n)*
En old face
Es estilo antiguo *(m)*
It carattere elzeviro *(m)*
Pt tipo de estilo antigo *(m)*

em *n* En
De Geviert *(n)*
Es cuadratín *(m)*
Fr cadratin *(m)*
It riga *(f)*
Pt quadratim *(m)*

embalagem de encolher *(f)* Pt
De Schrumpfverpackung *(f)*
En shrink-wrapping
Es envoltura por contracción *(f)*
Fr emballage serré *(m)*
It confezionamento a restringimento *(m)*

embalar *vb* Es, Pt
De packen
En pack
Fr emballer
It imballare

emballage *(m) n* Fr
De Klebenindung *(f)*
En wrappering
Es sobrecubierta *(f)*
It mettitura le sovracopertine *(f)*
Pt colocação de sobrecapa *(f)*

emballage serré *(m)* Fr
De Schrumpfverpackung *(f)*
En shrink-wrapping
Es envoltura por contracción *(f)*
It confezionamento a restringimento *(m)*
Pt embalagem de encolher *(f)*

emballer *vb* Fr
De packen
En pack
Es embalar
It imballare
Pt embalar

embossing *n* En
De Prägedruck *(m)*
Es estampado en relieve *(m)*
Fr gaufrage *(m)*
It goffratura *(f)*
Pt gravação em relevo *(f)*

embossing ink En
De Prägedruckfarbe *(f)*
Es tinta de estampación *(f)*
Fr encre à gaufrer *(f)*
It inchiostro per goffratura *(m)*
Pt tinta de estampagem *(f)*

em itálico Pt
De kursiv gedruckt
En in italics
Es en cursiva
Fr en italiques
It in corsivo

empacotar *vb* Pt
De verpacken
En package
Es empaquetar
Fr empaqueter
It impaccare

empaquetar *vb* Es
De verpacken
En package
Fr empaqueter
It impaccare
Pt empacotar

empaqueter *vb* Fr
De verpacken
En package
Es empaquetar
It impaccare
Pt empacotar

emparejamiento de hojas *(m)* Es
De Aufstoβen *(n)*
En knocking-up (of paper)
Fr taquage des feuilles *(m)*
It uniformazione di foglie *(f)*
Pt empilhamento de folhas *(m)*

empastelado *(m)* *n* Pt
De Defektbogen *(m)*
En broke (papermaking)
Es papel roto *(m)*
Fr cassés *(m pl)*
It cascame di carta *(m)*

empâtement *(m)* *n* Fr
De Serif *(m)*
En serif
Es bigotillo *(m)*
It terminazione *(f)*
Pt remate *(m)*

empilhamento de folhas *(m)* Pt
De Aufstoβen *(n)*
En knocking-up (of paper)
Es emparejamiento de hojas *(m)*
Fr taquage des feuilles *(m)*
It uniformazione di foglie *(f)*

empleado *(m)* *n* Es
De Angestellter *(m)*
En employee
Fr employé *(m)*
It dipendente *(m)*
Pt empregado *(m)*

employé *(m)* *n* Fr
De Angestellter *(m)*
En employee
Es empleado *(m)*
It dipendente *(m)*
Pt empregado *(m)*

employee *n* En
De Angestellter *(m)*
Es empleado *(m)*
Fr employé *(m)*
It dipendente *(m)*
Pt empregado *(m)*

employer *n* En
De Arbeitgeber *(m)*
Es patrón *(m)*
Fr employeur *(m)*
It datore di lavoro *(m)*
Pt entidade patronal *(f)*

employeur *(m)* *n* Fr
De Arbeitgeber *(m)*
En employer
Es patrón *(m)*
It datore di lavoro *(m)*
Pt entidade patronal *(f)*

empregado *(m)* *n* Pt
De Angestellter *(m)*
En employee
Es empleado *(m)*
Fr employé *(m)*
It dipendente *(m)*

empreinte *(f)* *n* Fr
Am mold (papermaking)
De Guβform *(f)*
En mould (papermaking)
Es molde *(m)*
It stampo (industria cartiera) *(m)*
Pt molde *(m)*

empreinte sur plomb *(f)* Fr
Am lead mold
De Bleiform *(f)*
En lead mould
Es molde de plomo *(m)*
It stampo di piombo *(m)*
Pt molde de chumbo *(m)*

empresa de composição *(f)* Pt
De Schriftsetzerei *(f)*
En typesetter (company)
Es taller de composición *(m)*
Fr maison de composition *(f)*
It compositoria *(f)*

em rule En
De Geviertstrich *(m)*
Es pleca-cuadratín *(f)*
Fr tiret sur cadratin *(m)*
It lineato a quadratone *(m)*
Pt filete de quadratim *(m)*

em trânsito Pt
De im Transit befindlich
En in transit
Es en tránsito
Fr en transit
It in transito

emulsão *(f)* *n* Pt
De Emulsion *(f)*
En emulsion
Es emulsión *(f)*
Fr émulsion *(f)*
It emulsione *(f)*

emulsão lado de baixo *(f)* Pt
De Emulsionsseite unten *(f)*
En emulsion-side down
Es lado de la emulsión hacia abajo *(m)*
Fr côté émulsion vers le bas *(m)*
It lato emulsione inferiore *(m)*

emulsão lado de cima *(f)* Pt
De Emulsionsseite oben *(f)*
En emulsion-side up
Es lado de la emulsión hacia arriba *(m)*
Fr côté émulsion vers le haut *(m)*
It lato emulsione superiore *(m)*

emulsion *n* En
De Emulsion *(f)*
Es emulsión *(f)*
Fr émulsion *(f)*
It emulsione *(f)*
Pt emulsão *(f)*

Emulsion *(f)* *n* De
En emulsion
Es emulsión *(f)*
Fr émulsion *(f)*
It emulsione *(f)*
Pt emulsão *(f)*

émulsion *(f)* *n* Fr
De Emulsion *(f)*
En emulsion
Es emulsión *(f)*
It emulsione *(f)*
Pt emulsão *(f)*

emulsión *(f)* *n* Es
De Emulsion *(f)*
En emulsion
Fr émulsion *(f)*
It emulsione *(f)*
Pt emulsão *(f)*

emulsione *(f)* *n* It
De Emulsion *(f)*
En emulsion
Es emulsión *(f)*
Fr émulsion *(f)*
Pt emulsão *(f)*

emulsion-side down En
De Emulsionsseite unten *(f)*
Es lado de la emulsión hacia abajo *(m)*
Fr côté émulsion vers le bas *(m)*
It lato emulsione inferiore *(m)*
Pt emulsão lado de baixo *(f)*

emulsion-side up En
De Emulsionsseite oben *(f)*
Es lado de la emulsión hacia arriba *(m)*
Fr côté émulsion vers le haut *(m)*
It lato emulsione superiore *(m)*
Pt emulsão lado de cima *(f)*

Emulsionsseite unten *(f)* De
En emulsion-side down
Es lado de la emulsión hacia abajo *(m)*

Fr côté émulsion vers le
   bas *(m)*
It lato emulsione
   inferiore *(m)*
Pt emulsão lado de
   baixo *(f)*

Emulsionsseite oben *(f)*
   De
En emulsion-side up
Es lado de la emulsión
   hacia arriba *(f)*
Fr côté émulsion vers le
   haut *(m)*
It lato emulsione
   superiore *(m)*
Pt emulsão lado de
   cima *(f)*

en *n* En
De Halbgeviert *(n)*
Es medio cuadratín *(m)*
Fr demi-cadratin *(m)*
It mezza riga *(f)*
Pt meio quadratim *(m)*

enamel paper En
De Hochglanzpapier *(n)*
Es papel esmaltado *(m)*
Fr papier émaillé *(m)*
It carta smaltata *(f)*
Pt papel esmalte *(m)*

encabezamiento *(m) n*
   Es
De Bildunterschrift *(f)*
En caption
Fr inscription *(f)*
It didascalia *(f)*
Pt epígrafe *(f)*

encabezamiento de
   capítulo *(m)* Es
De Kapitelüberschrift *(f)*
En chapter heading
Fr tête de chapitre *(f)*
It titolo del capitolo *(m)*
Pt título do capítulo *(m)*

encadernação *(f) n* Pt
De Buchbinden *(n)*
En bookbinding
Es encuadernación de
   libros *(f)*
Fr reliure *(f)*
It rilegatura *(f)*

encadernação à
   máquina *(f)* Pt
De Maschinenbinden *(n)*
En machine binding

Es encuadernación a
   machina *(f)*
Fr reliure à machine *(f)*
It rilegatura a macchina
   (f)

encadernação a meia
   pele *(f)* Pt
De Halbfranzband *(m)*
En half binding
Es encuadernación a
   media piel *(f)*
Fr demi-reliure à petits
   coins *(f)*
It mezza rilegatura *(f)*

encadernação com
   anilhas *(f)* Pt
De Ringbindung *(f)*
En ring binding
Es encuadernación con
   anillas *(f)*
Fr reliure à anneaux *(f)*
It legatura ad anelli *(f)*

encadernação de folhas
   soltas *(f)* Pt
De Loseblattbindung *(f)*
En loose-leaf binding
Es encuadernación de
   hojas sueltas *(f)*
Fr reliure à feuillets
   mobiles *(f)*
It legatura a fogli sciolti
   (f)

encadernação em
   espiral *(f)* Pt
De Spiralbindung *(f)*
En spiral binding
Es encuadernación en
   espiral *(f)*
Fr reliure spirale *(f)*
It rilegatura a spirale *(f)*

encadernação flexível
   (f) Pt
De flexibles Binden *(n)*
En flexible binding
Es encuadernación
   flexible *(f)*
Fr reliure souple *(f)*
It rilegatura flessibile *(f)*

encadernação mecânica
   (f) Pt
De mechanische
   Bindung *(f)*
En mechanical binding
Es encuadernación
   mecánica *(f)*
Fr reliure mécanique *(f)*

It legatura meccanica
   (f)

encadernação não
   cosida *(f)* Pt
De nicht geheftete
   Bindung *(f)*
En unsewn binding
Es encuadernación sin
   coser *(f)*
Fr reliure sans couture
   (f)
It rilegatura non cucita
   (f)

encadernação
   ornamentada *(f)* Pt
De Punzenbindung *(f)*
En tooled binding
Es encuadernación
   repujada *(f)*
Fr reliure ciselée *(f)*
It rilegatura con attrezzi
   (f)

encadernação para
   escritório *(f)* Pt
De Briefpapier-Binden
   (n)
En stationery binding
Es acuñado de material
   de escritorio *(m)*
Fr reliure papeterie *(f)*
It rilegatura da
   cartoleria *(f)*

encadernação sem
   costura *(f)* Pt
De Klebebindung *(f)*
En perfect binding
Es encuadernación sin
   cosido *(f)*
Fr reliure parfaite *(f)*
It rilegatura perfetta *(f)*

encadernação
   tipográfica *(f)* Pt
De Buchdruck-Binden
   (n)
En letterpress binding
Es acuñado tipográfico
   (m)
Fr reliure imprimerie *(f)*
It legatura da tipografia
   (f)

encadernado a carneira
   Pt
De gebunden in
   Kalbleder
En calfbound

Es encuadernado en piel
   de becerro
Fr relié en veau
It rilegato in pelle

encadernador *(m) n* Pt
De Buchbinder *(m)*
En binder
Es encuadernador *(m)*
Fr relieur *(m)*
It rilegatore *(m)*

encadernadora *(f) n* Pt
De Bindemaschine *(f)*
En binding machine
Es encuadernadora *(f)*
Fr machine à relier *(f)*
It macchina legatrice *(f)*

encadernar *vb* Pt
De binden
En bind
Es encuadernar
Fr relier
It rilegare

encargar *vb* Es
De in Auftrag geben
En commission
Fr commander
It commissionare
Pt encomendar

encargo *(m) n* Es
De Kommission *(f)*
En commission
Fr commission *(f)*
It commissione *(f)*
Pt comissão *(f)*

encartage *(m) n* Fr
De Einsatz *(m)*
En insert
Es encarte *(m)*
It inserto *(m)*
Pt inserção *(f)*

encartar *vb* Es
De einfügen
En insert
Fr insérer
It inserire
Pt inserir

encarte *(m) n* Es
De Einsatz *(m)*
En insert
Fr encartage *(m)*
It inserto *(m)*
Pt inserção *(f)*

enciclopedia *(f) n* Es, It
De Enzyklopädie *(f)*
En encyclopedia
Fr encyclopédie *(f)*
Pt enciclopédia *(f)*

enciclopédia *(f) n* Pt
De Enzyklopädie *(f)*
En encyclopedia
Es enciclopedia *(f)*
Fr encyclopédie *(f)*
It enciclopedia *(f)*

enciclopedia da tavolo
(f) It
De Schreibtisch-Lexikon
(n)
En desk encyclopedia
Es enciclopedia de
mesa *(f)*
Fr petite encyclopédie
(f)
Pt enciclopédia de
mesa *(f)*

enciclopedia de mesa *(f)*
Es
De Schreibtisch-Lexikon
(n)
En desk encyclopedia
Fr petite encyclopédie
(f)
It enciclopedia da
tavolo *(f)*
Pt enciclopédia de
mesa *(f)*

enciclopédia de mesa *(f)*
Pt
De Schreibtisch-Lexikon
(n)
En desk encyclopedia
Es enciclopedia de
mesa *(f)*
Fr petite encyclopédie
(f)
It enciclopedia da
tavolo *(f)*

enciclopedico *adj* It
De enzyklopädisch
En encyclopedic
Es enciclopédico
Fr encyclopédique
Pt enciclopédico

enciclopédico *adj* Es, Pt
De enzyklopädisch
En encyclopedic
Fr encyclopédique
It enciclopedico

encolado *(m) n* Es
De Leimung *(f)*
En sizing
Fr encollage *(m)*
It collaggio *(m)*
Pt encolamento *(m)*

encolamento *(m) n* Pt
De Leimung *(f)*
En sizing
Es encolado *(m)*
Fr encollage *(m)*
It collaggio *(m)*

encollage *(m) n* Fr
De Leimung *(f)*
En sizing
Es encolado *(m)*
It collaggio *(m)*
Pt encolamento *(m)*

encoller *vb* Fr
De klebeumbrechen
En paste up
Es montar
It incollare
Pt montar

encomenda por correio
(f) Pt
De Versandhausauftrag
(m)
En mail order
Es pedido por correo
(m)
Fr vente par
correspondance *(f)*
It vendite per posta *(f)*

encomendar *vb* Pt
De in Auftrag geben
En commission
Es encargar
Fr commander
It commissionare

encordoamento *(m) n* Pt
De Verschnüren *(n)*
En cording
Es encordonado *(m)*
Fr nerf *(m)*
It imputaggio *(m)*

encordonado *(m) n* Es
De Verschnüren *(n)*
En cording
Fr nerf *(m)*
It imputaggio *(m)*
Pt encordoamento *(m)*

en couleurs Fr
Am in full color
De in voller Farbe
En in full colour
Es a todo color
It a colori
Pt a toda a cor

encrage *(m) n* Fr
De Farbauftrag *(m)*
En inking
Es entintaje *(f)*
It inchiostrazione *(f)*
Pt tintura *(f)*

encrassement *(m) n* Fr
De Pelzen *(n)*
En piling
Es espesamiento *(m)*
It ammassamento *(m)*
Pt espessamento de
tinta *(m)*

encre à gaufrer *(f)* Fr
De Prägedruckfarbe *(f)*
En embossing ink
Es tinta de estampación
(f)
It inchiostro per
goffratura *(m)*
Pt tinta de estampagem
(f)

encre à l'aniline *(f)* Fr
De Anilinfarbe *(f)*
En aniline ink
Es tinta de anilina *(f)*
It inchiostro all'anilina
(m)
Pt tinta de anilina *(f)*

encre d'impression *(f)* Fr
De Druckfarbe *(f)*
En ink (printer's)
Es tinta de imprenta *(f)*
It inchiostro da stampa
(m)
Pt tinta de impressão *(f)*

encre liée *(f)* Fr
De gebundene Farbe *(f)*
En bonded ink
Es tinta adherida *(f)*
It inchiostro aderente
(m)
Pt tinta aglutinada *(f)*

encre magnétique *(f)* Fr
De Magnettinte *(f)*
En magnetic ink
Es tinta magnética *(f)*

It inchiostro magnetico
(m)
Pt tinta magnética *(f)*

encre métallique *(f)* Fr
Am aluminum ink
De Aluminiumfarbe *(f)*
En aluminium ink
Es tinta plateada *(f)*
It inchiostro
all'alluminio *(m)*
Pt tinta de alumínio *(f)*

encres métalliques *(f pl)*
Fr
De Bronzedrucktinten
(pl)
En metallic inks
Es tintas metálicas *(f pl)*
It inchiostri metallici *(m
pl)*
Pt tintas metálicas *(f pl)*

encrier *(m) n* Fr
De Farbkanal *(m)*
En ink duct
Es tintero de la prensa
(m)
It condotto per
inchiostro *(m)*
Pt canal de tinta *(m)*

**encuadernación a
media piel** *(f)* Es
De Halbfranzband *(m)*
En half binding
Fr demi-reliure à petits
coins *(f)*
It mezza rilegatura *(f)*
Pt encadernação a meia
pele *(f)*

**encuadernación a
machina** *(f)* Es
De Maschinenbinden *(n)*
En machine binding
Fr reliure à machine *(f)*
It rilegatura a macchina
(f)
Pt encadernação à
máquina *(f)*

**encuadernación con
anillas** *(f)* Es
De Ringbindung *(f)*
En ring binding
Fr reliure à anneaux *(f)*
It legatura ad anelli *(f)*
Pt encadernação com
anilhas *(f)*

encuadernación de
hojas sueltas *(f)* Es
De Loseblattbindung *(f)*
En loose-leaf binding
Fr reliure à feuillets
mobiles *(f)*
It legatura a fogli sciolti
(f)
Pt encadernação de
folhas soltas *(f)*

encuadernación de
libros *(f)* Es
De Buchbinden *(n)*
En bookbinding
Fr reliure *(f)*
It rilegatura *(f)*
Pt encadernação *(f)*

encuadernación en
espiral *(f)* Es
De Spiralbindung *(f)*
En spiral binding
Fr reliure spirale *(f)*
It rilegatura a spirale *(f)*
Pt encadernação em
espiral *(f)*

encuadernación flexible
(f) Es
De flexibles Binden *(n)*
En flexible binding
Fr reliure souple *(f)*
It rilegatura flessibile *(f)*
Pt encadernação flexivel
(f)

encuadernación
mecánica *(f)* Es
De mechanische
Bindung *(f)*
En mechanical binding
Fr reliure mécanique *(f)*
It legatura meccanica
(f)
Pt encadernação
mecânica *(f)*

encuadernación
repujada *(f)* Es
De Punzenbindung *(f)*
En tooled binding
Fr reliure ciselée *(f)*
It rilegatura con attrezzi
(f)
Pt encadernação
ornamentada *(f)*

encuadernación sin
coser *(f)* Es
De nicht geheftete
Bindung *(f)*

En unsewn binding
Fr reliure sans couture
(f)
It rilegatura non cucita
(f)
Pt encadernação não
cosida *(f)*

encuadernación sin
cosido *(f)* Es
De Klebebindung *(f)*
En perfect binding
Fr reliure parfaite *(f)*
It rilegatura perfetta *(f)*
Pt encadernação sem
costura *(f)*

encuadernado en piel
de becerro Es
De gebunden in
Kalbleder
En calfbound
Fr relié en veau
It rilegato in pelle
Pt encadernado a
carneira

encuadernador *(m) n* Es
De Buchbinder *(m)*
En binder
Fr relieur *(m)*
It rilegatore *(m)*
Pt encadernador *(m)*

encuadernadora *(f) n* Es
De Bindemaschine *(f)*
En binding machine
Fr machine à relier *(f)*
It macchina legatrice *(f)*
Pt encadernadora *(f)*

encuadernar *vb* Es
De binden
En bind
Fr relier
It rilegare
Pt encadernar

encuadre *(m) n* Es
De Einsetzen *(n)*
En insetting
Fr mise en place *(f)*
It incorniciatura *(f)*
Pt intercalagem *(f)*

en cursiva Es
De kursiv gedruckt
En in italics
Fr en italiques
It in corsivo
Pt em itálico

encyclopedia *n* En
De Enzyklopädie *(f)*
Es enciclopedia *(f)*
Fr encyclopédie *(f)*
It enciclopedia *(f)*
Pt enciclopédia *(f)*

encyclopedic *adj* En
De enzyklopädisch
Es enciclopédico
Fr encyclopédique
It enciclopedico
Pt enciclopédico

encyclopédie *(f) n* Fr
De Enzyklopädie *(f)*
En encyclopedia
Es enciclopedia *(f)*
It enciclopedia *(f)*
Pt enciclopédia *(f)*

encyclopédique *adj* Fr
De enzyklopädisch
En encyclopedic
Es enciclopédico
It enciclopedico
Pt enciclopédico

endereço *(m) n* Pt
De Adresse *(f)*
En address (computer)
Es dirección *(f)*
Fr adresse *(f)*
It indirizzo *(m)*

end-of-line hyphen En
De Zeilenende-
Trennstrich *(m)*
Es guión de final de
línea *(m)*
Fr trait d'union de fin de
ligne *(m)*
It trattino di fine linea
(m)
Pt traço de união de fim
de linha *(m)*

endossure *(f) n* Fr
De Abpressen *(n)*
En backing
Es formación de cajos *(f)*
It rinforzo *(m)*
Pt colocação de
lombada *(f)*

endpapers *pl n* En
De Vorsatzpapiere *(pl)*
Es guardas *(f pl)*
Fr papiers de garde *(m
pl)*
It risguardi *(m pl)*

Pt folhas de contracapa
(f pl)

engine-sized paper En
De Maschinengröβe *(f)*
Es papel encolado a
máquina *(m)*
Fr papier collé en pâte
(m)
It carta tagliata a
macchina *(f)*
Pt papel encolado à
máquina *(m)*

engrave *vb* En
De gravieren
Es grabar
Fr graver
It incidere
Pt gravar

engraving (print) *n* En
De Gravur *(f)*
Es grabado (estampa)
(m)
Fr estampe *(f)*
It incisione *(f)*
Pt gravura (estampa) *(f)*

engraving (process) *n* En
De Gravierung *(f)*
Es grabado (proceso)
(m)
Fr gravure *(f)*
It arte dell'incisione *(f)*
Pt gravura (processo) *(f)*

engrudo *(m) n* Es
De Kleister *(m)*
En paste
Fr colle *(f)*
It colla *(f)*
Pt cola *(f)*

en impression Fr
De gedruckt
En in print
Es publicado
It in corso di stampa
Pt impresso e publicado

en italiques Fr
De kursiv gedruckt
En in italics
Es en cursiva
It in corsivo
Pt em itálico

enlarge *vb* En
De vergrößern
Es ampliar
Fr agrandir
It ingrandire
Pt ampliar

enlarger *n* En
De Vergrößerungsgerät
(n)
Es ampliadora (f)
Fr agrandisseur (m)
It ingranditore (m)
Pt ampliadora (f)

enlazar *vb* Es
De in Kontakt stehen
En liaise
Fr garder contact
It collegarsi
Pt ligar

enlumineur *(m) n* Fr
De Kolorierer (m)
En illuminator
Es iluminador (m)
It illuminatore (m)
Pt iluminador (m)

enluminure *(f) n* Fr
De Illuminierung (f)
En illumination
Es iluminación (f)
It illuminazione (f)
Pt iluminura (f)

enmascarado *(m) n* Es
De Abdeckung (f)
En masking
Fr masquage (m)
It mascheratura (f)
Pt máscara (f)

enmascarar *vb* Es
De abdecken
En mask
Fr oblitérer
It mascherare
Pt mascarar

**enmienda con
sobreimpresión** *(f)*
Es
De Abdecken (n)
En blocking out
Fr oblitération (f)
It mascheratura con
vernice coprente (f)
Pt cobrimento (m)

en octavo *(m)* Es
De Oktavformat (n)
En octavo
Fr in-octavo (m)
It in ottavo (m)
Pt octavo (m)

enramado *(m) n* Pt
De Schließen (n)
En locking-up
Es acuñado (m)
Fr serrage (m)
It serramento (m)

enrugamento *(m) n* Pt
De Kräuseln (n)
En cockling
Es amartillamiento (m)
Fr gondolage (m)
It arricciatura (f)

enrugar *vb* Pt
De kräuseln
En crimp
Es marcar con rayas
Fr gaufrer
It ondulare

en rule En
De Halbgeviertstrich (m)
Es pleca de medio
cuadratín (f)
Fr tiret sur
demi-cadratin (m)
It lineato a
demi-quadratone (m)
Pt filete de meio
quadratim (m)

entalhe *(m) n* Pt
De Signaturrinne (f)
En nick
Es cran (m)
Fr cran (m)
It tacca (f)

en-tête *(m)* Fr
De haupt Wort (n)
En headword
Es palabra principal (f)
It parola principale (f)
Pt palavra-índice (f)

entidade patronal *(f)* Pt
De Arbeitgeber (m)
En employer
Es patrón (m)
Fr employeur (m)
It datore di lavoro (m)

entintado en caliente
(m) Es
De Warmwalzen (n)
En hot rolling
Fr laminage à chaud (m)
It calandratura a caldo
(f)
Pt laminação a quente
(f)

entintaje *(f) n* Es
De Farbauftrag (m)
En inking
Fr encrage (m)
It inchiostrazione (f)
Pt tintura (f)

entlassen *vb* De
En lay off
Es despedir
Fr licencier
It licenziare
Pt dispensar
temporariamente

Entlassung *(f) n* De
En redundancy
Es redundancia (f)
Fr chomage partiel (m)
It ridondanza (f)
Pt redundância (f)

Entlassungsgeld *(n) n* De
En redundancy payment
Es pago redundante (m)
Fr indemnité de
chômage (f)
It pagamento di
ridondanza (m)
Pt pagamento de
redundância (m)

entrada *(f) n* Es, Pt
De Eingabe (f)
En input; entry
Fr entrée (f)
It input; voce (m f)

en transit Fr
De im Transit befindlich
En in transit
Es en tránsito
It in transito
Pt em trânsito

en tránsito Es
De im Transit befindlich
En in transit
Fr en transit
It in transito
Pt em trânsito

entrata *(f) n* It
De Einkommen (n)
En revenue
Es ingresos (m pl)
Fr recette (f)
Pt receita (f)

entrate *(f pl)* It
De Einnahmen (pl)
En earnings pl n
Es beneficios (m pl)
Fr bénéfices (m pl)
Pt rendimentos (m pl)

entrée *(f) n* Fr
De Eingabe (f)
En input
Es entrada (f)
It input (m)
Pt entrada (f)

**entrega automática de
pilhas** *(f)* Pt
De automatischer
Stapelausleger (m)
En automatic pile
delivery
Es receptor automático
de pila de pliegos (m)
Fr distribution
automatique des
piles (f)
It avanzamento
automatico di pile (f)

entre-lignes *(f pl)* Fr
De Durchschüsse (pl)
En leads pl n
Es interlíneas (f pl)
It interlinea (f)
Pt entrelinhas (f pl)

entrelinhas *(f pl)* Pt
De Durchschüsse (pl)
En leads pl n
Es interlíneas (f pl)
Fr entre-lignes (f pl)
It interlinea (f)

entre parênteses Pt
De in Klammern
En in parentheses
Es entre paréntesis
Fr entre parenthèses
It tra parentesi

entre paréntesis Es
De in Klammern
En in parentheses
Fr entre parenthèses

It tra parentesi
Pt entre parênteses

entre parenthèses Fr
De in Klammern
En in parentheses
Es entre paréntesis
It tra parentesi
Pt entre parênteses

entreposer *vb* Fr
De lagern
En store
Es almacenar
It immagazzinare
Pt armazenar

entrepôt *(m) n* Fr
De Lagerhaus *(n)*
En warehouse
Es almacén *(m)*
It magazzino *(m)*
Pt armazém *(m)*

entrepôts *(m pl)* Fr
De Speicherungs-
   möglichkeiten *(pl)*
En storage facilities
Es almacenes *(m pl)*
It servizi di
   immagazzinaggio *(m pl)*
Pt instalações de
   armazenamento *(f pl)*

**entreprise de
l'emballage** *(f)* Fr
De Verpackungsfirma *(f)*
En packaging company
Es compañía
   empaquetadora *(f)*
It società
   confezionamento *(m)*
Pt sociedade
   empacotadora *(f)*

entretien *(m) n* Fr
De Dienstleitungsfirma
   (f)
En service company
Es compañía de
   servicios *(f)*
It società di servizio *(f)*
Pt companhia de
   serviços *(f)*

entry *n* En
De Eintrag *(m)*
Es artículo *(m)*
Fr entrée *(f)*

It voce *(f)*
Pt entrada *(f)*

entry list En
De Eintragsliste *(f)*
Es relación de artículos
   (f)
Fr liste des entrées *(f)*
It elenco di voci *(m)*
Pt lista de inscrição *(f)*

Entstehungsarbeiten
   (pl) n De
En origination
Es creación *(f)*
Fr source *(f)*
It origine *(f)*
Pt criação *(f)*

entwerfen *vb* De
En design
Es diseñar
Fr concevoir
It concepire
Pt desenhar

entwickeln
   (Photographie) *vb*
   De
En develop
   (photography)
Es revelar
Fr développer
It sviluppare
Pt revelar

entwickeln (Planung) *vb*
   De
En develop (planning)
Es desarrollar
Fr exécuter
It elaborare
Pt desenvolver

**Entwicklungs-
programm** *(n) n* De
Am development
   program
En development
   programme
Es programa de
   desarrollo *(m)*
Fr plan de
   développement *(m)*
It programma di
   sviluppo *(m)*
Pt programa de
   desenvolvimento *(m)*

Entwicklungsprojekt *(n)*
   n De
En development project
Es proyecto de
   desarrollo *(m)*
Fr projet de
   développement *(m)*
It progetto di sviluppo
   (m)
Pt projecto de
   desenvolvimento *(m)*

Entwurf *(m) n* De
En draft
Es borrador *(m)*
Fr ébauche *(f)*
It minuta *(f)*
Pt rascunho *(m)*

enviar *vb* Pt
De versenden
En forward
Es expedir
Fr expédier
It spedire

enviar por correo Es
De mit der Post schicken
En mail
Fr envoyer par la poste
It spedire per posta
Pt enviar por correio

enviar por correio Pt
De mit der Post schicken
En mail
Es enviar por correo
Fr envoyer par la poste
It spedire per posta

envio *(m) n* Pt
De Verschiffung *(f)*
En shipping
Es envío *(m)*
Fr expédition *(f)*
It spedizione *(f)*

envío *(m) n* Es
De Verschiffung *(f)*
En shipping
Fr expédition *(f)*
It spedizione *(f)*
Pt envio *(m)*

envío por correo directo
   (m) Es
De Postwurfsendung *(f)*
En direct-mail shot
Fr mailing; offre
   promotionnelle *(m f)*
It invio diretto per

posta; offerta postale
   (m f)
Pt publicidade por
   correio *(f)*

**envoltura por
contracción** *(f)* Es
De Schrumpfverpackung
   (f)
En shrink-wrapping
Fr emballage serré *(m)*
It confezionamento a
   restringimento *(m)*
Pt embalagem de
   encolher *(f)*

envoyer par la poste Fr
De mit der Post schicken
En mail
Es enviar por correo
It spedire per posta
Pt enviar por correio

Enzyklopädie *(f) n* De
En encyclopedia
Es enciclopedia *(f)*
Fr encyclopédie *(f)*
It enciclopedia *(f)*
Pt enciclopédia *(f)*

enzyklopädisch *adj* De
En encyclopedic
Es enciclopédico
Fr encyclopédique
It enciclopedico
Pt enciclopédico

épair *(m) n* Fr
De Durchscheinen *(n)*
En look-through
Es textura a la luz *(f)*
It trasparente *(m)*
Pt transparência *(f)*

épaisseur de papier *(f)*
   Fr
De Papierdicke *(f)*
En bulk (of paper)
Es cuerpo de papel *(m)*
It grossezza di carta *(f)*
Pt grossura do papel *(f)*

épaisseur d'un livre *(f)*
   Fr
De Masse *(f)*
En bulk (of a book)
Es grueso de libro *(m)*
It grossezza del libro *(f)*
Pt espessura dum livro
   (f)

épeler *vb* Fr
De buchstabieren
En spell
Es deletrear
It sillabare
Pt soletrar

épellation *(f) n* Fr
De Buchstabierung *(f)*
En spelling
Es deletreo *(m)*
It compitazione *(f)*
Pt soletração *(f)*

epígrafe *(f) n* Pt
De Bildunterschrift *(f)*
En caption
Es encabezamiento *(m)*
Fr inscription *(f)*
It didascalia *(f)*

épreuve *(f) n* Fr
De Abzug *(m)*
En proof
Es prueba *(f)*
It bozza *(f)*
Pt prova *(f)*

épreuve au net *(f)* Fr
De sauberer Abzug *(m)*
En clean proof
Es prueba limpia *(f)*
It bozza nitida *(f)*
Pt prova limpa *(f)*

épreuve couleurs *(f)* Fr
Am color proof
De Farbabzug *(m)*
En colour proof
Es prueba en colores *(f)*
It bozza a colori *(f)*
Pt prova a cores *(f)*

épreuve d'auteur *(f)* Fr
De Autor-Korrekturabzug *(m)*
En author's proof
Es prueba de autor *(f)*
It bozza dell'autore *(f)*
Pt prova do autor *(f)*

épreuve de reproduction *(f)* Fr
De Repro-Abzug *(m)*
En reproduction proof
Es prueba de reproducción *(f)*
It prova di fotoriproduzione *(f)*
Pt prova de reprodução *(f)*

épreuve en pages *(f)* Fr
De Korrektur *(f)*
En page proof
Es prueba de página *(f)*
It bozza impaginata *(f)*
Pt prova de página *(f)*

épreuve en placard *(f)* Fr
De Korrekturfahne *(f)*
En galley proof
Es prueba de galeradas *(f)*
It bozza in colonna *(f)*
Pt prova de galé *(f)*

épreuves de révision *(f pl)* Fr
De revidierter Abzug *(m)*
En revised proofs
Es pruebas corregidas *(f pl)*
It bozze corrette *(f pl)*
Pt provas revistas *(f pl)*

épreuves-gammes *(f pl)* Fr
De Farbandrucke *(pl)*
En progressive proofs
Es pruebas de gama *(f pl)*
It bozze progressive *(f pl)*
Pt provas progressivas *(f pl)*

épuisé *adj* Fr
De vergriffen
En out of print
Es agotado
It esaurito
Pt esgotado

equilibrare la composizione It
De berechnen
En cast off
Es calibrar la composición
Fr calibrer un texte
Pt calibrar a composição

equipo instruccional *(m)* Es
De Software *(f)*
En software
Fr logiciel *(m)*
It software *(m)*
Pt software *(m)*

erase *vb* En
De löschen
Es borrar
Fr effacer
It cassare
Pt apagar

errata *n pl* Es, Pt *(f)*; En; Fr *(m)*
De Errata *(pl)*
It errata corrige *(m)*

Errata *(pl)* De
En errata *pl n*
Es errata *(f)*
Fr errata *(m)*
It errata corrige *(m)*
Pt errata *(f)*

errata corrige *(m)* It
De Errata *(pl)*
En errata *pl n*
Es errata *(f)*
Fr errata *(m)*
Pt errata *(f)*

errata de imprenta *(f)* Es
De Druckfehler *(m)*
En printer's error
Fr faute d'impression *(f)*
It errore dello stampatore *(m)*
Pt erro de impressão *(m)*

errata literal *(f)* Pt
De Setzfehler *(m)*
En literal
Es error de imprenta *(m)*
Fr coquille *(f)*
It errore di stampa *(m)*

erreur typographique *(f)* Fr
De typographischer Fehler *(m)*
En typographical error
Es error tipográfico *(m)*
It errore tipografico *(m)*
Pt erro tipográfico *(m)*

erro de impressão *(m)* Pt
De Druckfehler *(m)*
En printer's error
Es errata de imprenta *(f)*
Fr faute d'impression *(f)*
It errore dello stampatore *(m)*

error de imprenta *(m)* Es
De Setzfehler *(m)*
En literal
Fr coquille *(f)*
It errore di stampa *(m)*
Pt errata literal *(f)*

errore dello stampatore *(m)* It
De Druckfehler *(m)*
En printer's error
Es errata de imprenta *(f)*
Fr faute d'impression *(f)*
Pt erro de impressão *(m)*

errore di stampa *(m)* It
De Setzfehler *(m)*
En literal
Es error de imprenta *(m)*
Fr coquille *(f)*
Pt errata literal *(f)*

errore tipografico *(m)* It
De typographischer Fehler *(m)*
En typographical error
Es error tipográfico *(m)*
Fr erreur typographique *(f)*
Pt erro tipográfico *(m)*

error tipográfico *(m)* Es
De typographischer Fehler *(m)*
En typographical error
Fr erreur typographique *(f)*
It errore tipografico *(m)*
Pt erro tipográfico *(m)*

erro tipográfico *(m)* Pt
De typographischer Fehler *(m)*
En typographical error
Es error tipográfico *(m)*
Fr erreur typographique *(f)*
It errore tipografico *(m)*

erste Auflage *(f)* De
En first edition
Es primera edición *(f)*
Fr édition originale *(f)*
It prima edizione *(f)*
Pt primeira edição *(f)*

erster Korrekturabzug *(m)* De
En first proof
Es primera prueba *(f)*

Fr première épreuve *(f)*
It prima bozza *(f)*
Pt primeira prova *(f)*

erudito *adj* Es, It
De gelehrt
En scholarly
Fr savant
Pt sábio

Erziehungsbücher *(pl) n*
De
En educational books
Es libros educativos *(m pl)*
Fr livres éducatifs *(m pl)*
It libri pedagogici *(m pl)*
Pt livros educacionais *(m pl)*

esaurito *adj* It
De vergriffen; ausverkauft
En out of print; sold out
Es agotado
Fr épuisé; liquidé
Pt esgotado

esboço *(m) n* Pt
De Skizze *(f)*
En rough
Es boceto *(m)*
Fr croquis *(m)*
It abbozzo *(m)*

escala de tipos *(f)* Es
De Schriftsatz-Lineal *(n)*
En typescale
Fr typomètre *(m)*
It tipometro *(m)*
Pt tipómetro *(m)*

escalpelo *(m) n* Es
De Skalpell *(n)*
En scalpel
Fr scalpel *(m)*
It bisturi ad un solo taglio *(m)*
Pt bisturí *(m)*

escoria *(f) n* Es
De Krätze *(f)*
En dross
Fr crasses *(f pl)*
It scarto *(m)*
Pt escória *(f)*

escória *(f) n* Pt
De Krätze *(f)*
En dross

Es escoria *(f)*
Fr crasses *(f pl)*
It scarto *(m)*

escrito a mano Es
De handgeschrieben
En hand-written
Fr manuscrit
It scritto a mano
Pt escrito à mão

escrito à mão Pt
De handgeschrieben
En hand-written
Es escrito a mano
Fr manuscrit
It scritto a mano

escrito a máquina *(m)* Es
De Maschinenschrift *(f)*
En typescript
Fr manuscrit dactylographié *(m)*
It dattiloscritto *(m)*
Pt dactilografado *(m)*

escritor comercial *(m)* Pt
De Mietschreiber *(m)*
En hack writer
Es escritor mercenario *(m)*
Fr écrivassier *(m)*
It imbrattacarte *(m)*

escritor fantasma *(m)* Es
De Schattenautor *(m)*
En ghost writer
Fr nègre *(m)*
It collaboratore anonimo *(m)*
Pt colaborador anónimo *(m)*

escritor mercenario *(m)* Es
De Mietschreiber *(m)*
En hack writer
Fr écrivassier *(m)*
It imbrattacarte *(m)*
Pt escritor comercial *(m)*

esgotado *adj* Pt
De vergriffen; ausverkauft
En out of print; sold out
Es agotado
Fr épuisé; liquidé
It esaurito

esgotado em armazém Pt
De nicht vorrätig
En out of stock
Es sin existencias
Fr non disponible
It sprovvisto

espaçamento *(m) n* Pt
De Abstand *(m)*
En spacing
Es espaciado *(m)*
Fr espacement *(m)*
It spaziatura *(f)*

espaçamento óptico de letras *(m)* Pt
De optischer Buchstabenabstand *(m)*
En optical letterspacing
Es espaciado óptico entre letras *(m)*
Fr interlettrage optique *(m)*
It spaziatura ottica tra le lettere *(f)*

espace *(m) n* Fr
De Ausschluβstück *(m)*
En space
Es espacio *(m)*
It spazio *(m)*
Pt espaço *(m)*

espace entre deux lignes *(m)* Fr
De Zeilenabstand *(m)*
En line space
Es espacio entre líneas *(m)*
It spazio tra le righe *(m)*
Pt espaço entre linhas *(m)*

espace fine *(f)* Fr
De dünnes Spatium *(n)*
En thin space
Es espacio fino *(m)*
It spazio sottile *(m)*
Pt espaço fino *(m)*

espace forte *(f)* Fr
De dickes Spatium *(n)*
En thick space
Es espacio grueso *(m)*
It spazio grosso *(m)*
Pt espaço grosso *(m)*

espacement *(m) n* Fr
De Abstand *(m)*
En spacing
Es espaciado *(m)*
It spaziatura *(f)*
Pt espaçamento *(m)*

espacement entre caractère *(m)* Fr
De Buchstabenabstand *(m)*
En letter spacing
Es espaciado entre letras *(m)*
It spaziatura tra le lettere *(f)*
Pt espaço entre letras *(m)*

espace variable *(m)* Fr
De variabler Abstand *(m)*
En variable space
Es espacio variable *(m)*
It spazio variabile *(m)*
Pt espaço variável *(m)*

espaciado *(m) n* Es
De Abstand *(m)*
En spacing
Fr espacement *(m)*
It spaziatura *(f)*
Pt espaçamento *(m)*

espaciado entre letras *(m)* Es
De Buchstabenabstand *(m)*
En letter spacing
Fr espacement entre caractère *(m)*
It spaziatura tra le lettere *(f)*
Pt espaço entre letras *(m)*

espaciado óptico entre letras *(m)* Es
De optischer Buchstabenabstand *(m)*
En optical letterspacing
Fr interlettrage optique *(m)*
It spaziatura ottica tra le lettere *(f)*
Pt espaçamento óptico de letras *(m)*

espacio *(m) n* Es
De Ausschluβstück *(m)*
En space
Fr espace *(m)*

It spazio (m)
Pt espaço (m)

espacio entre líneas (m) Es
De Zeilenabstand (m)
En line space
Fr espace entre deux lignes (m)
It spazio tra le righe (m)
Pt espaço entre linhas (m)

espacio fino (m) Es
De dünnes Spatium (n)
En thin space
Fr espace fine (f)
It spazio sottile (m)
Pt espaço fino (m)

espacio grueso (m) Es
De dickes Spatium (n)
En thick space
Fr espace forte (f)
It spazio grosso (m)
Pt espaço grosso (m)

espacio variable (m) Es
De variabler Abstand (m)
En variable space
Fr espace variable (m)
It spazio variabile (m)
Pt espaço variável (m)

espaço (m) n Pt
De Ausschluβstück (m)
En space
Es espacio (m)
Fr espace (m)
It spazio (m)

espaço defeituoso (m) Pt
De weiβer Streifen im Satz (m)
En river
Es calle (f)
Fr rue (f)
It spaziatura difettosa (f)

espaço entre letras (m) Pt
De Buchstabenabstand (m)
En letter spacing
Es espaciado entre letras (m)
Fr espacement entre caractère (m)

It spaziatura tra le lettere (f)

espaço entre linhas (m) Pt
De Zeilenabstand (m)
En line space
Es espacio entre líneas (m)
Fr espace entre deux lignes (m)
It spazio tra le righe (m)

espaço fino (m) Pt
De dünnes Spatium (n)
En thin space
Es espacio fino (m)
Fr espace fine (f)
It spazio sottile (m)

espaço grosso (m) Pt
De dickes Spatium (n)
En thick space
Es espacio grueso (m)
Fr espace forte (f)
It spazio grosso (m)

espaço variável (m) Pt
De variabler Abstand (m)
En variable space
Es espacio variable (m)
Fr espace variable (m)
It spazio variabile (m)

esparto (m) n Es, Pt
De Esparto (n)
En esparto grass
Fr alfa (m)
It sparto (m)

Esparto (n) n De
En esparto grass
Es esparto (m)
Fr alfa (m)
It sparto (m)
Pt esparto (m)

esparto grass En
De Esparto (n)
Es esparto (m)
Fr alfa (m)
It sparto (m)
Pt esparto (m)

especialista (m) n Es, Pt
De Spezialist (m)
En specialist
Fr spécialiste (m)
It specialista (m/f)

especializar vb Es, Pt
De spezialisieren
En specialize
Fr se spécialiser
It specializzare

especificação (f) n Pt
De Spezifikation (f)
En specification
Es especificación (f)
Fr caractéristiques (f pl)
It specifiche (f pl)

especificación (f) n Es
De Spezifikation (f)
En specification
Fr caractéristiques (f pl)
It specifiche (f pl)
Pt especificação (f)

espesamiento (m) n Es
De Pelzen (n)
En piling
Fr encrassement (m)
It ammassamento (m)
Pt espessamento de tinta (m)

espessamento de tinta (m) Pt
De Pelzen (n)
En piling
Es espesamiento (m)
Fr encrassement (m)
It ammassamento (m)

espessura dum livro (f) Pt
De Masse (f)
En bulk (of a book)
Es grueso de libro (m)
Fr épaisseur d'un livre (f)
It grossezza del libro (f)

esporre vb It
De belichten
En expose
Es exponer
Fr exposer
Pt expor

espositore (m) n It
De Aussteller (m)
En exhibitor
Es expositor (m)
Fr exposant (m)
Pt expositor (m)

esposizione (f) n It
De Display (n)
En display
Es exhibición (f)
Fr exposition (f)
Pt exibição (f)

esquema (m) n Es
De Diagramm (n)
En diagram
Fr schéma (m)
It diagramma (m)
Pt diagrama (m)

esquema paso a paso (m) Es
De stufenweises Diagramm (n)
En step-by-step diagram
Fr schéma progressif (m)
It diagramma graduale (m)
Pt diagrama de passo a passo (m)

esquemático adj Es
De schematisch
En diagrammatic
Fr schématique
It schematico
Pt diagramático

essiccante (m) n It
De Trockner (m)
En drier
Es secante (m)
Fr sécheur (m)
Pt secador (m)

essiccata ad aria It
De luftgetrocknet
En air-dried
Es secado al aire
Fr séché à l'air
Pt seco ao ar

estafeta aérea (f) Es
De Luftkurier (m)
En air courier
Fr courrier aérien (m)
It corriere aereo (m)
Pt mensageiro aéreo (m)

estampa (f) n Pt
De Druck (m)
En print
Es impresión (f)
Fr imprimé (m)
It impressione (f)

estampación (f) n Es
De Prägen (n)
En stamping
Fr timbrage (m)
It stampaggio (m)
Pt estampagem (f)

estampación dorada (f)
Es
De Goldprägung (f)
En gold stamping
Fr dorure à la presse (f)
It stampigliatura in oro
(f)
Pt estampagem a ouro
(f)

estampación en relieve
(f) Es
De Prägestempel (m)
En die stamping
Fr repoussage (m)
It stampa
incavorilievografica
(f)
Pt estampagem em
relevo (f)

estampado en relieve
(m) Es
De Prägedruck (m)
En embossing
Fr gaufrage (m)
It goffratura (f)
Pt gravação em relevo
(f)

estampagem (f) n Pt
De Prägen (n)
En stamping
Es estampación (f)
Fr timbrage (m)
It stampaggio (m)

estampagem a ouro (f)
Pt
De Goldprägung (f)
En gold stamping
Es estampación dorada
(f)
Fr dorure à la presse (f)
It stampigliatura in oro
(f)

estampagem em relevo
(f) Pt
De Prägestempel (m)
En die stamping
Es estampación en
relieve (f)
Fr repoussage (m)
It stampa

incavorilievografica
(f)

estampe (f) n Fr
De Gravur (f)
En engraving (print)
Es grabado (estampa)
(m)
It incisione (f)
Pt gravura (estampa) (f)

estencil de tela (m) Pt
De Gewebeschablone (f)
En tissue stencil
Es matriz de papel de
seda (f)
Fr stencil de duplication
(m)
It matrice in carta di
seta (f)

estensione (m) n It
De Seitenzahl (f)
En extent
Es amplitud (f)
Fr nombre de pages (m)
Pt extensão (f)

estereo-niquelado (m) Pt
De Nickelstereo (n)
En nickel stereo
Es estereotipia
niquelada (f)
Fr stéréo nickel (m)
It stereo-nichel (m)

estereo-rotativa (f) Pt
De Rotationsstereo (n)
En rotary stereo
Es estereotipia rotativa
(f)
Fr stéréo courbe (f)
It stereo rotatorio (m)

estereos de borracha (m
pl) Pt
De Gummiklischees (pl)
En rubber stereos
Es estereotipos de
caucho (m pl)
Fr stéréos caoutchouc
(m pl)
It stereos di gomma (m
pl)

estereotipia (f) n Es, Pt
De Stereotypie (f)
En stereotyping
Fr stéréotypie (f)
It stereotipizzazione (f)

estereotipia niquelada
(f) Es
De Nickelstereo (n)
En nickel stereo
Fr stéréo nickel (m)
It stereo-nichel (m)
Pt estereo-niquelado
(m)

estereotipia rotativa (f)
Es
De Rotationsstereo (n)
En rotary stereo
Fr stéréo courbe (f)
It stereo rotatorio (m)
Pt estereo-rotativa (f)

estereotipo (m) n Es
De Stereo (n)
En stereotype
Fr stéréotype (m)
It stereotipo (m)
Pt estereótipo (m)

estereótipo (m) n Pt
De Stereo (n)
En stereotype
Es estereotipo (m)
Fr stéréotype (m)
It stereotipo (m)

estereotipos de caucho
(m pl) Es
De Gummiklischees (pl)
En rubber stereos
Fr stéréos caoutchouc
(m pl)
It stereos di gomma (m
pl)
Pt estereos de borracha
(m pl)

estilete (m) n Es, Pt
De Feder (f)
En stylus
Fr imprimante à stylets
(f)
It stilo (m)

estilo (m) n Es, Pt
De Stil (m)
En style
Fr style (f)
It stile (m)

estilo antiguo (m) Es
De Mediäval (n)
En old face
Fr elzévir (m)
It carattere elzeviro (m)

Pt tipo de estilo antigo
(m)

estilo da casa (m) Pt
De Hausstil (m)
En house style
Es estilo de reglamento
(m)
Fr style maison (m)
It stile di casa (m)

estilo de reglamento (m)
Es
De Hausstil (m)
En house style
Fr style maison (m)
It stile di casa (m)
Pt estilo da casa (m)

**estilo de tipo
condensado** (m) Pt
De schmaler Schrifttyp
(m)
En condensed typeface
Es tipo estrecho (m)
Fr caractère effilé (m)
It carattere allungato
(m)

estimación (f) n Es
De Kostenvoranschlag
(m)
En estimate
Fr devis (m)
It valutazione (f)
Pt estimativa (f)

estimate n En
De Kostenvoranschlag
(m)
Es estimación (f)
Fr devis (m)
It valutazione (f)
Pt estimativa (f)

estimativa (f) n Pt
De Kostenvoranschlag
(m)
En estimate
Es estimación (f)
Fr devis (m)
It valutazione (f)

estojo de livro (m) Pt
De Schuber (m)
En slip case
Es estuche (m)
Fr étui (m)
It astuccio del libro (m)

estuche (m) n Es
De Schuber (m)
En slip case
Fr étui (m)
It astuccio del libro (m)
Pt estojo de livro (m)

étampe (f) n Fr
De Prägestock (m)
En die
Es troquel (m)
It stampo (m)
Pt matriz (f)

etching n En
De Radierung (f)
Es grabado al agua
  fuerte (f)
Fr gravure à l'eau forte
  (f)
It incisione
  all'acquaforte (f)
Pt gravura a áqua-forte
  (f)

et commercial (m) Fr
De Und-Zeichen (n)
En ampersand
Es y abreviada (f)
It congiunzione
  commerciale (f)
Pt e comercial (f)

etichette (f pl) It
De Bezeichnungen (pl)
En labels (on diagram) pl
  n
Es rótulos (m pl)
Fr étiquettes (f pl)
Pt legendas (f pl)

etimologia (f) n It, Pt
De Etymologie (f)
En etymology
Es etimología (f)
Fr étymologie (f)

etimología (f) n Es
De Etymologie (f)
En etymology
Fr étymologie (f)
It etimologia (f)
Pt etimologia (f)

étiquettes (f pl) Fr
De Bezeichnungen (pl)
En labels (on diagram) pl
  n
Es rótulos (m pl)
It etichette (f pl)
Pt legendas (f pl)

étui (m) n Fr
De Schuber (m)
En slip case
Es estuche (m)
It astuccio del libro (m)
Pt estojo de livro (m)

Etymologie (f) n De
En etymology
Es etimología (f)
Fr étymologie (f)
It etimologia (f)
Pt etimologia (f)

étymologie (f) n Fr
De Etymologie (f)
En etymology
Es etimología (f)
It etimologia (f)
Pt etimologia (f)

etymology n En
De Etymologie (f)
Es etimología (f)
Fr étymologie (f)
It etimologia (f)
Pt etimologia (f)

exclamation mark En
De Ausrufungszeichen
  (n)
Es signo de admiración
  (m)
Fr point d'exclamation
  (m)
It punto esclamativo
  (m)
Pt ponto de exclamação
  (m)

exécuter vb Fr
De entwickeln (Planung)
En develop (planning)
Es desarrollar
It elaborare
Pt desenvolver

exécution des ombres
  (f) Fr
De Schattierung (f)
En shading
Es sombreado (m)
It ombreggiatura (f)
Pt tracejado (m)

executivo principal (m)
  Pt
De leitende
  Führungskraft (f)
En chief executive
Es jefe ejecutivo (m)

Fr administrateur
  directeur (m)
It direttore generale (m)

**exemplaire de service
  de presse** (m) Fr
De Rezensions-Exemplar
  (n)
En review copy
Es ejemplar para reseña
  (m)
It copia di recensione
  (f)
Pt exemplar para
  resenha (m)

**exemplaire en
  hommage** (m) Fr
De Gratisexemplar (n)
En complimentary copy
Es ejemplar de obsequio
  (m)
It copia omaggio (f)
Pt exemplar de oferta
  (m)

**exemplaires de
  lancement** (m pl) Fr
De Vorausexemplare (pl)
En advance copies pl n
Es ejemplares para
  reseña (m pl)
It copie in anteprima (f
  pl)
Pt provas tipográficas (f
  pl)

**exemplaires gratuits
  pour l'auteur** (m pl)
  Fr
De Autorexemplare (pl)
En author's free copies
  pl n
Es ejemplares de
  obsequio del autor
  (m pl)
It copie gratuite
  dell'autore (f pl)
Pt exemplares grátis
  para o autor (m pl)

exemplar a limpo (m) Pt
De sauberer Text (m)
En clean copy
Es original limpio (m)
Fr copie au net (f)
It copia nitida (f)

exemplar de leitura (m)
  Pt
De Lesebuch (n)
En reader (book)

Es libro de lectura (m)
Fr livre de lecture (m)
It libro di lettura (m)

exemplar de oferta (m)
  Pt
De Gratisexemplar (n)
En complimentary copy
Es ejemplar de obsequio
  (m)
Fr exemplaire en
  hommage (m)
It copia omaggio (f)

**exemplares grátis para
  o autor** (m pl) Pt
De Autorexemplare (pl)
En author's free copies
  pl n
Es ejemplares de
  obsequio del autor
  (m pl)
Fr exemplaires gratuits
  pour l'auteur (m pl)
It copie gratuite
  dell'autore (f pl)

exemplar ilegível (m) Pt
De schlechtes
  Manuskript (n)
En bad copy
Es original malo (m)
Fr mauvaise copie (f)
It copia illeggibile (f)

**exemplar muito
  corrigido** (m) Pt
De stark revidiertes
  Manuskript (n)
En heavily edited copy
Es ejemplar mucho
  enmendada (m)
Fr texte très corrigé (m)
It copia molto
  emendata (f)

exemplar para resenha
  (m) Pt
De Rezensions-Exemplar
  (n)
En review copy
Es ejemplar para reseña
  (m)
Fr exemplaire de service
  de presse (m)
It copia di recensione
  (f)

**exemplar pronto para a
  máquina
  fotográfica** (m) Pt

De kamerafertige
  Vorlage *(f)*
En camera-ready copy
Es original preparado
  para la cámara *(m)*
Fr copie prête à
  photographier *(f)*
It copia pronta per
  fotografia *(f)*

exento de ácido Es
De säurefrei
En acid-free
Fr sans acide
It privo di acidi
Pt isento de ácido

exhiber *vb* Fr
De ausstellen
En display
Es exhibir
It mostrare
Pt exibir

exhibición *(f) n* Es
De Display *(n)*
En display
Fr exposition *(f)*
It esposizione *(f)*
Pt exibição *(f)*

exhibir *vb* Es
De ausstellen
En display
Fr exhiber
It mostrare
Pt exibir

exhibitor *n* En
De Aussteller *(m)*
Es expositor *(m)*
Fr exposant *(m)*
It espositore *(m)*
Pt expositor *(m)*

exibição *(f) n* Pt
De Display *(n)*
En display
Es exhibición *(f)*
Fr exposition *(f)*
It esposizione *(f)*

exibir *vb* Pt
De ausstellen
En display
Es exhibir
Fr exhiber
It mostrare

existencias *(f pl) n* Es
De Vorrat *(m)*
En stock (books)
Fr stock *(m)*
It scorta *(f)*
Pt existências *(f pl)*

existências *(f pl) n* Pt
De Vorrat *(m)*
En stock (books)
Es existencias *(f pl)*
Fr stock *(m)*
It scorta *(f)*

existencias excesivas *(f pl)* Es
De Übervorrat *(m)*
En overstocks *pl n*
Fr stock excessif *(m)*
It giacenze *(f pl)*
Pt existências que
  sobram *(f pl)*

existências que sobram *(f pl)* Pt
De Übervorrat *(m)*
En overstocks *pl n*
Es existencias excesivas
  (f pl)
Fr stock excessif *(m)*
It giacenze *(f pl)*

ex libris *(m)* Es
De Bücherzeichen *(n)*
En bookplate
Fr ex-libris *(m)*
It ex-libris *(m)*
Pt ex-libris *(m)*

ex-libris *(m) n* Fr, It, Pt
De Bücherzeichen *(n)*
En bookplate
Es ex libris *(m)*

expanded typeface En
De breiter Schrifttyp *(m)*
Es tipo de ojo ancho *(m)*
Fr oeil plus grand que la
  normale *(m)*
It carattere largo (m)
Pt tipo de olho largo *(m)*

expédier *vb* Fr
De versenden
En forward
Es expedir
It spedire
Pt enviar

expedir *vb* Es
De versenden
En forward
Fr expédier
It spedire
Pt enviar

expédition *(f) n* Fr
De Verschiffung *(f)*
En shipping
Es envío *(m)*
It spedizione *(f)*
Pt envio *(m)*

explorador *(m) n* Es
De Abtaster *(m)*
En scanner
Fr analyseur
  électronique *(m)*
It scanner *(m)*
Pt dispositivo
  explorador *(m)*

explorar direita Pt
De rechts in Linie
  bringen
En range right
Es alinear al margen
  derecho
Fr aligner à droite
It allineare
  verticalmente a
  destra

explorar esquerda Pt
De links in Linie bringen
En range left
Es alinear al margen
  izquierdo
Fr aligner à gauche
It allineare
  verticalmente a
  sinistra

**exploration
  électronique** *(f)* Fr
De elektronische
  Abtastung *(f)*
En electronic scanning
Es selección electrónica
  (f)
It scanning elettronico
  (m)
Pt seleccionadora
  electrónica de cores
  (f)

exponentes *(m pl)* Es
De hochstehende
  Buchstaben *(pl)*
En superior characters
  pl n

Fr caractères supérieurs
  (m pl)
It caratteri superiori *(m
  pl)*
Pt caracteres superiores
  (m pl)

exponer *vb* Es
De belichten
En expose
Fr exposer
It esporre
Pt expor

expor *vb* Pt
De belichten
En expose
Es exponer
Fr exposer
It esporre

exposant *(m) n* Fr
De Aussteller *(m)*
En exhibitor
Es expositor *(m)*
It espositore *(m)*
Pt expositor *(m)*

expose *vb* En
De belichten
Es exponer
Fr exposer
It esporre
Pt expor

exposer *vb* Fr
De belichten
En expose
Es exponer
It esporre
Pt expor

exposição *(f) n* Pt
De Belichtung *(f)*
En exposure
  (photographic)
Es exposición *(f)*
Fr pose *(f)*
It posa *(f)*

exposición *(f) n* Es
De Belichtung *(f)*
En exposure
  (photographic)
Fr pose *(f)*
It posa *(f)*
Pt exposição *(f)*

exposition *(f) n* Fr
De Display *(n)*
En display
Es exhibición *(f)*
It esposizione *(f)*
Pt exibição *(f)*

expositor *(m) n* Es, Pt
De Aussteller *(m)*
En exhibitor
Fr exposant *(m)*
It espositore *(m)*

exposure (photographic)
n En
De Belichtung *(f)*
Es exposición *(f)*
Fr pose *(f)*
It posa *(f)*
Pt exposição *(f)*

extensão *(f) n* Pt
De Seitenzahl *(f)*
En extent
Es amplitud *(f)*
Fr nombre de pages *(m)*
It estensione *(m)*

extent *n* En
De Seitenzahl *(f)*
Es amplitud *(f)*
Fr nombre de pages *(m)*
It estensione *(m)*
Pt extensão *(f)*

F

fabbricazione *(f) n* It
De Herstellung *(f)*
En manufacture
Es fabricación *(f)*
Fr fabrication *(f)*
Pt manufactura *(f)*

fabbricazione di carta *(f)*
It
De Papierherstellung *(f)*
En papermaking
Es fabricación de papel
(f)
Fr papeterie *(f)*
Pt produção de papel *(f)*

fabricación *(f) n* Es
De Herstellung *(f)*
En manufacture
Fr fabrication *(f)*
It fabbricazione *(f)*
Pt manufactura *(f)*

fabricación de papel *(f)*
Es
De Papierherstellung *(f)*
En papermaking
Fr papeterie *(f)*
It fabbricazione di carta
(f)
Pt produção de papel *(f)*

fábrica de papel *(f)* Es, Pt
De Papierfabrik *(f)*
En paper mill
Fr fabrique de papier *(f)*
It cartiera *(f)*

fabricant *(m) n* Fr
De Hersteller *(m)*
En manufacturer
Es fabricante *(m)*
It produttore *(m)*
Pt produtor *(m)*

fabricante *(m) n* Es
De Hersteller *(m)*
En manufacturer
Fr fabricant *(m)*
It produttore *(m)*
Pt produtor *(m)*

fabricar *vb* Es
De herstellen
En manufacture
Fr fabriquer
It produrre
Pt produzir

fabrication *(f) n* Fr
De Herstellung *(f)*
En manufacture
Es fabricación *(f)*
It fabbricazione *(f)*
Pt manufactura *(f)*

Fabrik *(f) n* De
En shop (in industry)
Es taller *(m)*
Fr atelier *(m)*
It officina *(f)*
Pt oficina *(f)*

fabrique de papier *(f)* Fr
De Papierfabrik *(f)*
En paper mill

Es fábrica de papel *(f)*
It cartiera *(f)*
Pt fábrica de papel *(f)*

fabriquer *vb* Fr
De herstellen
En manufacture
Es fabricar
It produrre
Pt produzir

Fachausgabe *(f) n* De
En trade edition
Es edición profesional *(f)*
Fr édition
professionnelle *(f)*
It edizione
commerciale *(f)*
Pt edição comercial *(f)*

Fachbuch *(n) n* De
En trade book
Es libro profesional *(m)*
Fr livre professionnel
(m)
It libro commerciale
(m)
Pt livro de ofícios *(m)*

Fach-Taschenbuch *(n)*
De
En trade paperback
Es libro profesional en
rústica *(m)*
Fr fascicule
professionnel *(m)*
It libro economico
commerciale *(m)*
Pt livro de bolso
comercial *(m)*

Fachzeitschrift *(f) n* De
En trade journal
Es revista profesional *(f)*
Fr revue professionnelle
(f)
It rivista commerciale
(f)
Pt revista comercial *(f)*

facsímil *(m) n* Es
De Faksimile *(n)*
En facsimile
Fr fac-similé *(m)*
It facsimile *(m)*
Pt facsímile *(m)*

facsimile *n* En; It *(m)*
De Faksimile *(n)*
Es facsímil *(m)*

Fr fac-similé *(m)*
Pt facsímile *(m)*

fac-similé *(m) n* Fr
De Faksimile *(n)*
En facsimile
Es facsímil *(m)*
It facsimile *(m)*
Pt facsímile *(m)*

facsímile *(m) n* Pt
De Faksimile *(n)*
En facsimile
Es facsímil *(m)*
Fr fac-similé *(m)*
It facsimile *(m)*

facsimile edition En
De Faksimile-Ausgabe *(f)*
Es edición facsímil *(f)*
Fr édition fac-similé *(f)*
It edizione facsimile *(f)*
Pt edição facsímile *(f)*

factura *(f) n* Es, Pt
De Rechnung *(f)*
En invoice
Fr facture *(f)*
It fattura *(f)*

facturar *vb* Es, Pt
De in Rechnung stellen
En invoice
Fr facturer
It fatturare

facture *(f) n* Fr
De Rechnung *(f)*
En invoice
Es factura *(f)*
It fattura *(f)*
Pt factura *(f)*

facturer *vb* Fr
De in Rechnung stellen
En invoice
Es facturar
It fatturare
Pt facturar

failli *(m) n* Fr
De Bankerotteur *(m)*
En bankrupt
Es quebrado *(m)*
It fallito *(m)*
Pt falido *(m)*

faillite *(f) n* Fr
De Bankerott *(m)*
En bankruptcy

Es bancarrota (f)
It bancarotta (f)
Pt falência (f)

faire de la publicité pour Fr
De werben
En advertise
Es anunciar
It pubblicizzare
Pt anunciar

faire des tirages supplémentaires Fr
De fortdrucken
En run on (printing)
Es proseguir la tirada
It imprimir una super-tiratura (f)
Pt continuar a imprimir

faire un reportage Fr
De berichten
En report
Es informar
It relazionare
Pt informar

Faksimile (n) n De
En facsimile
Es facsímil (m)
Fr fac-similé (m)
It facsimile (m)
Pt facsímile (m)

Faksimile-Ausgabe (f) De
En facsimile edition
Es edición facsímil (f)
Fr édition fac-similé (f)
It edizione facsimile (f)
Pt edição facsímile (f)

falência (f) n Pt
De Bankerott (m)
En bankruptcy
Es bancarrota (f)
Fr faillite (f)
It bancarotta (f)

falido (m) n Pt
De Bankerotteur (m)
En bankrupt
Es quebrado (m)
Fr failli (m)
It fallito (m)

falir vb Pt
De bankerott machen
En bankrupt

Es quebrar
Fr mettre en faillite
It far bancarotta

fallito (m) n It
De Bankerotteur (m)
En bankrupt
Es quebrado (m)
Fr failli (m)
Pt falido (m)

falsa immagine (f) It
De Durchscheinbild (n)
En ghosting
Es mancha de reflexión (f)
Fr image fantôme (f)
Pt fantasma (m)

falscher Buchstabe (m) De
Am wrong font
En wrong fount
Es letra de otro tipo (f)
Fr lettre d'une autre fonte (f)
It testina sbagliata (f)
Pt letra de outro tipo (f)

falscher Schrifttyp (m) De
En wrong typeface
Es ojo de tipo incorrecto (m)
Fr lettre d'un autre oeil (f)
It carattere sbagliato (m)
Pt olho de tipo errado (m)

falsches Maß (n) De
En wrong measure
Es medida incorrecta (f)
Fr justification incorrecte (f)
It misura sbagliata (f)
Pt medida errada (f)

Falzen (n) n De
En folding
Es plegado (m)
Fr pliure (f)
It piegatura (f)
Pt dobrado (m)

Falzmaschine (f) n De
En folding machine
Es plegadora (f)
Fr plieuse (f)

It piegatrice meccanica (f)
Pt dobradora (f)

Falzrahmen (m) n De
En folding chase
Es rama dúplex (f)
Fr châssis de pliage (m)
It telaio di piegafoglio (m)
Pt rama duplex (f)

fantascienza (f) n It
De Science-fiction (f)
En science fiction
Es ciencia-ficción (f)
Fr science-fiction (f)
Pt ficção científica (f)

fantasma (m) n Pt
De Durchscheinbild (n)
En ghosting
Es mancha de reflexión (f)
Fr image fantôme (f)
It falsa immagine (f)

Farbabzug (m) n De
Am color proof
En colour proof
Es prueba en colores (f)
Fr épreuve couleurs (f)
It bozza a colori (f)
Pt prova a cores (f)

far bancarotta It
De bankerott machen
En bankrupt
Es quebrar
Fr mettre en faillite
Pt falir

Farbandrucke (pl) De
En progressive proofs
Es pruebas de gama (f pl)
Fr épreuves-gammes (f pl)
It bozze progressive (f pl)
Pt provas progressivas (f pl)

Farbauftrag (m) n De
En inking
Es entintaje (f)
Fr encrage (m)
It inchiostrazione (f)
Pt tintura (f)

Farbbeilage (f) n De
Am color supplement
En colour supplement
Es suplemento en color (m)
Fr supplément en couleurs (m)
It supplemento a colori (m)
Pt suplemento a cores (m)

Farbillustration (f) n De
Am color illustration
En colour illustration
Es ilustración en color (f)
Fr illustration en couleurs (f)
It illustrazione a colori (f)
Pt ilustração a cores (f)

Farbkanal (m) n De
En ink duct
Es tintero de la prensa (m)
Fr encrier (m)
It condotto per inchiostro (m)
Pt canal de tinta (m)

Farbkorrektur (f) n De
Am color correction
En colour correction
Es rectificación cromática (f)
Fr correction des couleurs (f)
It correzione di colore (f)
Pt correcção de cor (f)

Farbmischen (n) n De
En knocking-up (of printing ink)
Es mezclando de tinta (m)
Fr mélange de l'encre (m)
It mischiante d'inchiostro (m)
Pt mistura de tinta (f)

Farbphoto (n) n De
Am color photograph
En colour photograph
Es fotografía en colores (f)
Fr photographie en couleurs (f)
It fotografia a colori (f)
Pt fotografia a cores (f)

Farbreiber *(m) n* De
En brayer
Es rodillo batidor *(m)*
Fr rouleau à main *(m)*
It rullo inchiostratore a
   mano *(m)*
Pt rolo de mão *(m)*

Farbstreifen *(pl)* De
Am color bars
En colour bars
Es franjas de color *(f pl)*
Fr bandes des couleurs
   (f pl)
It barre di colore *(f pl)*
Pt franjas de cor *(f pl)*

Farbtafeln *(pl)* De
Am color plates
En colour plates
Es láminas en color *(f pl)*
Fr planches en couleurs
   (f pl)
It tavole a colori *(f pl)*
Pt páginas a cores *(f pl)*

Farbtrennung *(f) n* De
Am color separation
En colour separation
Es selección
   fotomecánica de
   colores *(f)*
Fr séparation des
   couleurs *(f)*
It selezione di colore *(f)*
Pt separação de cores
   (f)

Farbwalzen *(pl)* De
En ink rollers
Es rodillos de imprenta
   (m pl)
Fr rouleaux encreurs *(m
   pl)*
It rulli per inchiostro *(m
   pl)*
Pt rolos de dar tinta *(m
   pl)*

fare una prefazione It
De einleiten
En preface
Es prologar
Fr préfacer
Pt redigir um prefácio

fascicule professionnel
   (m) Fr
De Fach-Taschenbuch
   (n)
En trade paperback

Es libro profesional en
   rústica *(m)*
It libro economico
   commerciale *(m)*
Pt livro de bolso
   comercial *(m)*

fastness (to light) *n* En
De Lichtbeständigkeit *(f)*
Es solidez a la luz *(f)*
Fr solidité à la lumière
   (f)
It stabilità alla luce *(f)*
Pt inalterabilidade à luz
   (f)

fattura *(f) n* It
De Rechnung *(f)*
En invoice
Es factura *(f)*
Fr facture *(f)*
Pt factura *(f)*

fatturare *vb* It
De in Rechnung stellen
En invoice
Es facturar
Fr facturer
Pt facturar

fatturato *(m) n* It
De Umsatz *(m)*
En turnover
Es cifra de negocios *(f)*
Fr chiffre d'affaires *(m)*
Pt movimento *(m)*

fausse page *(f)* Fr
De linke Seite *(f)*
En left-hand page
Es página izquierda *(f)*
It pagina di sinistra *(f)*
Pt página de esquerda
   (f)

faute d'impression *(f)* Fr
De Druckfehler *(m)*
En printer's error
Es errata de imprenta *(f)*
It errore dello
   stampatore *(m)*
Pt erro de impressão
   (m)

faux-titre *(m) n* Fr
De Innentitel *(m)*
En half title
Es anteportada *(f)*
It titolo abbreviato *(m)*
Pt anteportada *(f)*

fazer a revisão de Pt
De revidieren
En revise
Es refundir
Fr reviser
It revisionare

featherweight paper En
De Federleichtpapier *(n)*
Es papel ligero *(m)*
Fr papier bouffant *(m)*
It carta piuma *(f)*
Pt papel peso pena *(m)*

fecha de publicación *(f)*
   Es
De Veröffent-
   lichungsdatum *(n)*
En publication date
Fr date de parution *(f)*
It data di pubblicazione
   (f)
Pt data de publicação *(f)*

Feder *(f) n* De
En stylus
Es estilete *(m)*
Fr imprimante à stylets
   (f)
It stilo *(m)*
Pt estilete *(m)*

Federleichtpapier *(n) n*
   De
En featherweight paper
Es papel ligero *(m)*
Fr papier bouffant *(m)*
It carta piuma *(f)*
Pt papel peso pena *(m)*

Federlinierung *(f) n* De
En pen ruling
Es rayado a pluma *(m)*
Fr réglure au crayon *(f)*
It sottolineatura a
   penna *(f)*
Pt linhas à pena *(m)*

feed edges *pl n* En
De Anlagekanten *(pl)*
Es orillas de entrada *(f
   pl)*
Fr côté des marges *(m)*
It margini di entrata *(m
   pl)*
Pt bordos de entrada *(m
   pl)*

feeder *n* En
De Einleger *(m)*
Es alimentador *(m)*

Fr margeur *(m)*
It alimentatore *(m)*
Pt alimentadora *(f)*

Fehler *(m) n* De
En blemish
Es imperfección *(f)*
Fr défaut *(m)*
It imperfezione *(f)*
Pt mancha *(f)*

fehlerhaftes Register
   De
En out of register
Es fuera de registro
Fr mal registré
It fuori registro
Pt fora de registo

Feinätzung *(f) n* De
En fine etching
Es aguafuerte fina *(f)*
Fr gravure à l'eau-forte
   très mordancé *(m)*
It acquafortista
   raffinata *(f)*
Pt gravado fino *(m)*

feiner Raster *(m)* De
En fine screen
Es trama fina *(f)*
Fr trame fine *(f)*
It retino fine *(m)*
Pt retícula fina *(f)*

Feinstrich *(m) n* De
En fine rule
Es regla fina *(f)*
Fr filet maigre *(m)*
It riga sottile *(f)*
Pt rilete fino *(m)*

feints *pl n* En
De blaue Linien *(pl)*
Es rayas en azul *(f pl)*
Fr règles en bleu clair *(f
   pl)*
It righi finti *(m pl)*
Pt linhas pautadas a
   azul-claro *(f pl)*

feira do livro *(f)* Pt
De Büchermesse *(f)*
En book fair
Es feria del libro *(f)*
Fr foire du livre *(f)*
It fiera del libro *(m)*

Feira do Livro de Francfort *(f)* Pt
De Frankfurter Buchmesse *(f)*
En Frankfurt Book Fair
Es Fería del Libro de Frankfurt *(f)*
Fr foire de Francfort *(f)*
It Fiera del Libro di Francoforte *(f)*

feltro *(m)* n Pt
De Drucktuch *(n)*
En blanket (offset litho)
Es mantilla *(f)*
Fr décharge *(f)*
It caucciù *(m)*: tessuto gommato *(m)*

felt side En
De Filzseite *(f)*
Es lado de fieltro *(m)*
Fr côté feutre *(m)*
It lato feltro *(m)*
Pt lado de feltro *(m)*

feria del libro *(f)* Es
De Büchermesse *(f)*
En book fair
Fr foire du livre *(f)*
It fiera del libro *(m)*
Pt feira do livro *(f)*

Fería del Libro de Frankfurt *(f)* Es
De Frankfurter Buchmesse *(f)*
En Frankfurt Book Fair
Fr foire de Francfort *(f)*
It Fiera del Libro di Francoforte *(f)*
Pt Feira do Livro de Francfort *(f)*

Fernsehrechte *(pl)* De
En television rights
Es derechos de televisión *(m pl)*
Fr droits de télévision *(m pl)*
It diritti televisivi *(m pl)*
Pt direitos de televisão *(m pl)*

ferramenta de encadernação *(f)* Pt
De Buchbinder-Werkzeuge *(pl)*
En binder's tools
Es herramientas de encuadernación *(f pl)*
Fr outils de reliure *(m pl)*

It attrezzi da rilegatore *(m pl)*

fett *adj* De
En bold
Es negrita
Fr mi-gras
It neretto
Pt negrito

fetter Schrifttyp *(m)* De
En boldface type
Es tipo negrilla *(m)*
Fr caractères gras *(m pl)*
It carattere in neretto *(m)*
Pt tipo cheio *(m)*

feuchte Platte *(f)* De
En wet plate
Es placa húmeda *(f)*
Fr plaque humide *(f)*
It lastra al collodio *(f)*
Pt chapa molhada *(f)*

Feuchtwalze *(f)* n De
En damper
Es mojador *(m)*
Fr rouleau mouilleur *(m)*
It umettatore *(m)*
Pt molhador *(m)*

feuille de garde *(f)* Fr
De Respektblatt *(n)*
En flyleaf
Es cortesía *(f)*
It risguardo *(m)*
Pt folha em branco *(f)*

feuille d'or *(f)* Fr
De Goldfolie *(f)*
En gold leaf
Es pan de oro *(m)*
It oro in fogli *(m)*
Pt folha de ouro *(f)*

feuille-échantillon *(f)* n Fr
De Musterseite *(f)*
En specimen page
Es página de muestra *(f)*
It pagina campione *(f)*
Pt página amostra *(f)*

feuille quadrillée *(f)* Fr
De Layoutbogen *(m)*
En grid sheet
Es hoja cuadriculada *(f)*
It foglio a griglia *(m)*
Pt folha quadriculada *(f)*

feuilles de roulement *(f pl)* Fr
De folgende Bogen *(pl)*
En running sheets
Es hojas sucesivas *(f pl)*
It fogli successivi *(m pl)*
Pt folhas sucessivas *(f pl)*

feuilles liminaires *(f pl)* Fr
De Vortext *(m)*
En front matter
Es principios del libro *(m pl)*
It preliminari del libro *(m pl)*
Pt princípio do livro *(m)*

feuilles machine *(f pl)* Fr
De Pressebögen *(pl)*
En press sheets
Es pliegos de prensa *(m pl)*
It fogli di stampa *(m pl)*
Pt folhas de imprensa *(f pl)*

feuillet *(m)* n Fr
De Blatt *(n)*
En leaf
Es hoja *(f)*
It foglio *(m)*
Pt folha *(f)*

feuille volante *(f)* Fr
De Merkblatt *(n)*
En leaflet
Es prospecto *(m)*
It volantino a stampa *(m)*
Pt folheto *(m)*

fibra *(f)* n Es
De Körnung *(f)*
En grain
Fr grain *(m)*
It grana *(f)*
Pt grão *(m)*

ficção *(f)* n Pt
De Romanliteratur *(f)*
En fiction
Es literatura novelesca *(f)*
Fr romans *(m pl)*
It narrativa *(f)*

ficção científica *(f)* Pt
De Science-fiction *(f)*
En science fiction

Es ciencia-ficción *(f)*
Fr science-fiction *(f)*
It fantascienza *(f)*

ficção popular *(f)* Pt
De volkstümliche Romanliteratur *(f)*
En popular fiction
Es literatura popular *(f)*
Fr romans populaires *(m pl)*
It narrativa popolare *(f)*

ficha magnética *(f)* Es, Pt
De Magnetkarte *(f)*
En magnetic card
Fr carte magnétique *(f)*
It scheda magnetica *(f)*

ficha perfurada *(f)* Pt
De Lochkarte *(f)*
En punched card
Es tarjeta perforada *(f)*
Fr carte perforée *(f)*
It scheda perforata *(f)*

fichas de arquivo *(f pl)* Pt
De Karteikarten *(pl)*
En index cards
Es tarjetas de ficheros *(f pl)*
Fr fiches *(f pl)*
It schede *(f pl)*

fichero de datos *(m)* Es
De Datenablage *(f)*
En data file
Fr fichier de données *(m)*
It archivio dati *(m)*
Pt arquivo de dados *(m)*

fiches *(f pl)* Fr
De Karteikarten *(pl)*
En index cards
Es tarjetas de ficheros *(f pl)*
It schede *(f pl)*
Pt fichas de arquivo *(f pl)*

fichier de données *(m)* Fr
De Datenablage *(f)*
En data file
Es fichero de datos *(m)*
It archivio dati *(m)*
Pt arquivo de dados *(m)*

fiction *n* En
De Romanliteratur *(f)*
Es literatura novelesca
(f)
Fr romans *(m pl)*
It narrativa *(f)*
Pt ficção *(f)*

fiction list En
De Romanliteratur-Liste
(f)
Es catálogo de novelas
(m)
Fr catalogue des
romans *(m)*
It elenco di narrativa
(m)
Pt lista de ficção *(f)*

fiction publisher En
De Romanverleger *(m)*
Es editor de novelas *(m)*
Fr éditeur de romans
(m)
It editore di narrativa
(m)
Pt editorial de ficção *(f)*

fiera del libro *(m)* It
De Büchermesse *(f)*
En book fair
Es feria del libro *(f)*
Fr foire du livre *(f)*
Pt feira do livro *(f)*

**Fiera del Libro di
Francoforte** *(f)* It
De Frankfurter
Buchmesse *(f)*
En Frankfurt Book Fair
Es Fería del Libro de
Frankfurt *(f)*
Fr foire de Francfort *(f)*
Pt Feira do Livro de
Francfort *(f)*

figura *(f)* *n* It
De Bild *(n)*
En picture
Es imagen *(f)*
Fr image *(f)*
Pt imagem *(f)*

figure spéciale *(f)* Fr
De Spezial-Schrifttyp *(m)*
En special sort
Es suerte especial *(f)*
It tipo speciale *(m)*
Pt sortes especial *(f)*

figures spéciales *(f pl)* Fr
De Handsatz-
Schrifttypen *(pl)*
En pi characters
Es caracteres pi *(m pl)*
It caratteri pi *(m pl)*
Pt caracteres pi *(m pl)*

fijado *(m)* *n* Es
De Fixieren *(n)*
En fixing
Fr fixage *(m)*
It fissaggio *(m)*
Pt fixação *(f)*

fijador *(m)* *n* Es
De Fixativ *(n)*
En fixative
Fr fixateur *(m)*
It fissativo *(m)*
Pt fixador *(m)*

filet *(m)* *n* Fr
De Gedankenstrich *(m)*
En dash
Es raya *(f)*
It lineetta *(f)*
Pt filete *(m)*

**filet d'encadrement
latéral** *(m)* Fr
De Linieneinfassung *(f)*
En box rule
Es filete de marco *(m)*
It filleto di cornice *(m)*
Pt filete de requadro *(m)*

filete *(m)* *n* Pt
De Gedankenstrich *(m)*
En dash
Es raya *(f)*
Fr filet *(m)*
It lineetta *(f)*

fileteado *(m)* *n* Es
De Polieren *(n)*
En burnishing
Fr brunissage *(m)*
It brunitura *(f)*
Pt lustro *(m)*

filete de marco *(m)* Es
De Linieneinfassung *(f)*
En box rule
Fr filet d'encadrement
latéral *(m)*
It filleto di cornice *(m)*
Pt filete de requadro *(m)*

**filete de meio
quadratim** *(m)* Pt
De Halbgeviertstrich *(m)*
En en rule
Es pleca de medio
cuadratín *(f)*
Fr tiret sur
demi-cadratin *(m)*
It lineato a
demi-quadratone *(m)*

filete de quadratim *(m)*
Pt
De Geviertstrich *(m)*
En em rule
Es pleca-cuadratín *(f)*
Fr tiret sur cadratin *(m)*
It lineato a quadratone
(m)

filete de requadro *(m)* Pt
De Linieneinfassung *(f)*
En box rule
Es filete de marco *(m)*
Fr filet d'encadrement
latéral *(m)*
It filleto di cornice *(m)*

filetes extrafinos *(m pl)*
Es, Pt
De Haarstriche *(pl)*
En hair lines
Fr déliés *(m pl)*
It linee finissime *(f pl)*

filetes puntillados *(m pl)*
Es
De Ausführpunkte *(pl)*
En leaders *pl n*
Fr points de conduite
(m pl)
It puntini *(m pl)*
Pt pontos de reticência
(m pl)

filet maigre *(m)* Fr
De Feinstrich *(m)*
En fine rule
Es regla fina *(f)*
It riga sottile *(f)*
Pt rilete fino *(m)*

filetto *(m)* *n* It
De Strich *(m)*
En rule
Es pleca *(f)*
Fr règle *(f)*
Pt linha recta *(f)*

filigrana *(f)* *n* Es, It, Pt
De Wasserzeichen *(n)*
En watermark
Fr filigrane *(m)*

filigrane *(m)* *n* Fr
De Wasserzeichen *(n)*
En watermark
Es filigrana *(f)*
It filigrana *(f)*
Pt filigrana *(f)*

filler *n* En
De Füllerstoff *(m)*
Es material de carga *(m)*
Fr charge *(f)*
It carica *(f)*
Pt carga *(f)*

filleto di cornice *(m)* It
De Linieneinfassung *(f)*
En box rule
Es filete de marco *(m)*
Fr filet d'encadrement
latéral *(m)*
Pt filete de requadro *(m)*

film *n* En; Fr *(m)*
De Film *(m)*
Es película *(f)*
It pellicola *(f)*
Pt película *(f)*

Film *(m)* *n* De
En film
Es película *(f)*
Fr film *(m)*
It pellicola *(f)*
Pt película *(f)*

film à lecture à l'envers
(m) Fr
De seitenverkehrter Film
(m)
En wrong-reading film
Es película de lectura
incorrecta *(f)*
It pellicola a lettura
sbagliata *(f)*
Pt película de leitura do
lado errado *(f)*

film à lecture juste *(m)*
Fr
De seitenrichtiger Film
(m)
En right-reading film
Es película de lectura
correcta *(f)*
It pellicola a lettura
giusta *(f)*

Pt película de leitura do
lado direito *(f)*

film négatif *(m)* Fr
De Negativfilm *(m)*
En negative film
Es película negativa *(f)*
It film negativo *(m)*
Pt película negativa *(f)*

film negativo *(m)* It
De Negativfilm *(m)*
En negative film
Es película negativa *(f)*
Fr film négatif *(m)*
Pt película negativa *(f)*

film noir au blanc *(m)* Fr
De Umkehrfilm *(m)*
En reversal film
Es película reversible *(f)*
It pellicola invertibile *(f)*
Pt película de inversão
(f)

film positif *(m)* Fr
De Positivfilm *(m)*
En positive film
Es película para
positivos *(f)*
It pellicola positiva *(f)*
Pt película positiva *(f)*

film rights *pl n* En
De Verfilmungsrechte
(pl)
Es derechos
cinematográficos *(m*
pl)
Fr droits sur le film *(m*
pl)
It diritti cinematografici
(m pl)
Pt direitos
cinematográficos *(m*
pl)

filmsetter *n* En
De Film-Setzmaschine *(f)*
Es fotocompositor *(m)*
Fr photocomposeuse *(f)*
It fotocompositrice *(f)*
Pt fotocompositor *(m)*

Film-Setzmaschine *(f) n*
De
En filmsetter
Es fotocompositor *(m)*
Fr photocomposeuse *(f)*
It fotocompositrice *(f)*
Pt fotocompositor *(m)*

filter *n* En
De Filter *(n)*
Es filtro *(m)*
Fr filtre *(m)*
It filtro *(m)*
Pt filtro *(m)*

Filter *(n) n* De
En filter
Es filtro *(m)*
Fr filtre *(m)*
It filtro *(m)*
Pt filtro *(m)*

filtre *(m) n* Fr
De Filter *(n)*
En filter
Es filtro *(m)*
It filtro *(m)*
Pt filtro *(m)*

filtro *(m) n* Es, It, Pt
De Filter *(n)*
En filter
Fr filtre *(m)*

Filzseite *(f) n* De
En felt side
Es lado de fieltro *(m)*
Fr côté feutre *(m)*
It lato feltro *(m)*
Pt lado de feltro *(m)*

finalino *(m) n* It
De Schlußvignette *(f)*
En tailpiece
Es culo de lámpara *(m)*
Fr cul-de-lampe *(m)*
Pt vinheta final *(f)*

finanças *(f pl)* Pt
De Finanzen *(pl)*
En finances *pl n*
Es finanzas *(f pl)*
Fr finances *(f pl)*
It finanze *(f pl)*

finance *vb* En
De finanzieren
Es financiar
Fr financer
It finanziare
Pt financiar

financer *vb* Fr
De finanzieren
En finance
Es financiar
It finanziare
Pt financiar

finances *pl n* En; Fr *(f)*
De Finanzen *(pl)*
Es finanzas *(f pl)*
It finanze *(f pl)*
Pt finanças *(f pl)*

financial director En
De Finanzdirektor *(m)*
Es director financiero
(m)
Fr directeur financier
(m)
It direttore finanziario
(m)
Pt director financeiro
(m)

financiar *vb* Es, Pt
De finanzieren
En finance
Fr financer
It finanziare

finanzas *(f pl)* Es
De Finanzen *(pl)*
En finances *pl n*
Fr finances *(f pl)*
It finanze *(f pl)*
Pt finanças *(f pl)*

Finanzdirektor *(m) n* De
En financial director
Es director financiero
(m)
Fr directeur financier
(m)
It direttore finanziario
(m)
Pt director financeiro
(m)

finanze *(f pl)* It
De Finanzen *(pl)*
En finances *pl n*
Es finanzas *(f pl)*
Fr finances *(f pl)*
Pt finanças *(f pl)*

Finanzen *(pl)* De
En finances *pl n*
Es finanzas *(f pl)*
Fr finances *(f pl)*
It finanze *(f pl)*
Pt finanças *(f pl)*

finanziare *vb* It
De finanzieren
En finance
Es financiar
Fr financer
Pt financiar

finanzieren *vb* De
En finance
Es financiar
Fr financer
It finanziare
Pt financiar

fine etching En
De Feinätzung *(f)*
Es aguafuerte fina *(f)*
Fr gravure à l'eau-forte
très mordancé *(m)*
It acquafortista
raffinata *(f)*
Pt gravado fino *(m)*

fine rule En
De Feinstrich *(m)*
Es regla fina *(f)*
Fr filet maigre *(m)*
It riga sottile *(f)*
Pt rilete fino *(m)*

fine screen En
De feiner Raster *(m)*
Es trama fina *(f)*
Fr trame fine *(f)*
It retino fine *(m)*
Pt retícula fina *(f)*

finish *n* En
De Ausrüstung *(f)*
Es acabado *(m)*
Fr apprêt *(m)*
It appretto *(m)*
Pt acabamento *(m)*

finitura cieca *(f)* It
De Blindbearbeitung *(f)*
En blind finishing
Es acabado en seco *(m)*
Fr gaufrage à sec *(m)*
Pt acabamento cego
(m)

firmar *vb* Es
De signieren
En autograph
Fr signer
It autografare
Pt autógrafar

first edition En
De erste Auflage *(f)*
Es primera edición *(f)*
Fr édition originale *(f)*
It prima edizione *(f)*
Pt primeira edição *(f)*

first proof En
De erster Korrekturabzug
   (m)
Es primera prueba (f)
Fr première épreuve (f)
It prima bozza (f)
Pt primeira prova (f)

fissaggio (m) n It
De Fixieren (n)
En fixing
Es fijado (m)
Fr fixage (m)
Pt fixação (f)

fissativo (m) n It
De Fixativ (n)
En fixative
Es fijador (m)
Fr fixateur (m)
Pt fixador (m)

fita de mascarar (f) Pt
De Abdeckband (n)
En masking tape
Es cinta para
   enmascarar (f)
Fr bande de masquage
   (f)
It nastro per
   mascheratura (m)

fita de papel (f) Pt
De Lochstreifen (m)
En paper tape
Es cinta de papel (f)
Fr bande de papier (f)
It nastro di carta (m)

fita de papel perfurado
   (f) Pt
De Lochstreifen (m)
En punched paper tape
Es cinta perforada (f)
Fr bande perforée (f)
It nastro di carta
   perforato (m)

fita magnética (f) Pt
De Magnetband (n)
En magnetic tape
Es cinta magnética (f)
Fr bande magnétique (f)
It nastro magnetico (m)

fixação (f) n Pt
De Fixieren (n)
En fixing
Es fijado (m)
Fr fixage (m)
It fissaggio (m)

fixador (m) n Pt
De Fixativ (n)
En fixative
Es fijador (m)
Fr fixateur (m)
It fissativo (m)

fixage (m) n Fr
De Fixieren (n)
En fixing
Es fijado (m)
It fissaggio (m)
Pt fixação (f)

fixateur (m) n Fr
De Fixativ (n)
En fixative
Es fijador (m)
It fissativo (m)
Pt fixador (m)

Fixativ (n) n De
En fixative
Es fijador (m)
Fr fixateur (m)
It fissativo (m)
Pt fixador (m)

fixative n En
De Fixativ (n)
Es fijador (m)
Fr fixateur (m)
It fissativo (m)
Pt fixador (m)

fixed back book En
De Buch mit festem
   Rücken (n)
Es libro de lomo fijo (m)
Fr livre à dos fixe (m)
It libro a costa fissa (m)
Pt livro de lombada fixa
   (m)

fixer un prix Fr
De Preis festsetzen
En price
Es valorar
It prezzare
Pt marcar o preço

Fixieren (n) n De
En fixing
Es fijado (m)
Fr fixage (m)
It fissaggio (m)
Pt fixação (f)

fixing n En
De Fixieren (n)
Es fijado (m)
Fr fixage (m)
It fissaggio (m)
Pt fixação (f)

Flachdruck (m) n De
En planographic printing
Es impresión
   planográfica (f)
Fr impression à plat (f)
It stampa comune (f)
Pt impressão
   planográfica (f)

flaches Negativ (n) De
En flat negative
Es cliché sin contrastes
   (m)
Fr négatif sans
   contraste (m)
It negativo senza
   contrasti (m)
Pt negativo plano (m)

Fladen (n) n De
En flong
Es flan (m)
Fr flan (m)
It flan (m)
Pt flan (m)

flan (m) n Es, Fr, It, Pt
De Fladen (n)
En flong

flange n En
De Flansch (m)
Es reborde (m)
Fr rebord (m)
It flangia (f)
Pt rebordo (m)

flangia (f) n It
De Flansch (m)
En flange
Es reborde (m)
Fr rebord (m)
Pt rebordo (m)

Flansch (m) n De
En flange
Es reborde (m)
Fr rebord (m)
It flangia (f)
Pt rebordo (m)

flat-back book En
De Buch mit flachen
   Rücken (n)
Es libro de lomo liso (m)
Fr livre à dos plat (m)
It libro a costa piatta
   (m)
Pt livro de lombada
   plana (m)

flat negative En
De flaches Negativ (n)
Es cliché sin contrastes
   (m)
Fr négatif sans
   contraste (m)
It negativo senza
   contrasti (m)
Pt negativo plano (m)

flat-tint plate En
De Tonplatte (f)
Es clisé de media tinta
   (m)
Fr aplat (m)
It lastra a tinta opaca (f)
Pt chapa de meia-tinta
   (f)

flete aéreo (m) Es
De Luftfracht (f)
En airfreight
Fr fret aérien (m)
It trasporto merci per
   via aerea (m)
Pt frete aéreo (m)

fleuron n En; Fr, It (m)
De Blumenornament (n)
Es florón (m)
Pt floreta (f)

flexible binding En
De flexibles Binden (n)
Es encuadernación
   flexible (f)
Fr reliure souple (f)
It rilegatura flessibile (f)
Pt encadernação flexível
   (f)

flexibles Binden (n) De
En flexible binding
Es encuadernación
   flexible (f)
Fr reliure souple (f)
It rilegatura flessibile (f)
Pt encadernação flexível
   (f)

Flexodruck *(m)* *n* De
En flexographic printing
Es flexografía *(f)*
Fr flexographie *(f)*
It stampa flessografica *(f)*
Pt impressão flexográfica *(f)*

flexografía *(f)* *n* Es
De Flexodruck *(m)*
En flexographic printing
Fr flexographie *(f)*
It stampa flessografica *(f)*
Pt impressão flexográfica *(f)*

flexographic printing En
De Flexodruck *(m)*
Es flexografía *(f)*
Fr flexographie *(f)*
It stampa flessografica *(f)*
Pt impressão flexográfica *(f)*

flexographie *(f)* *n* Fr
De Flexodruck *(m)*
En flexographic printing
Es flexografía *(f)*
It stampa flessografica *(f)*
Pt impressão flexográfica *(f)*

floating accent En
De Schwebender Akzent *(m)*
Es acento postizo *(m)*
Fr accent flottant *(m)*
It accento fluttuante *(m)*
Pt acento flutuante *(m)*

flong *n* En
De Fladen *(n)*
Es flan *(m)*
Fr flan *(m)*
It flan *(m)*
Pt flan *(m)*

floppy disk En; It *(m)*
De Floppy Disk *(m)*
Es disco blando *(m)*
Fr disque souple *(m)*
Pt disco floppy *(m)*

Floppy Disk *(m)* De
En floppy disk
Es disco blando *(m)*

Fr disque souple *(m)*
It floppy disk *(m)*
Pt disco floppy *(m)*

floreta *(f)* *n* Pt
De Blumenornament *(n)*
En fleuron
Es florón *(m)*
Fr fleuron *(m)*
It fleuron *(m)*

florilegio *(m)* *n* It
De Thesaurus *(m)*
En thesaurus
Es tesoro *(m)*
Fr thésaurus *(m)*
Pt léxico *(m)*

florón *(m)* *n* Es
De Blumenornament *(n)*
En fleuron
Fr fleuron *(m)*
It fleuron *(m)*
Pt floreta *(f)*

flow chart En
De Schaubild *(n)*
Es organigrama *(f)*
Fr schéma de fabrication *(m)*
It reogramma *(m)*
Pt diagrama de fluxo *(m)*

flüchtig *adj* De
En fugitive
Es fugaz
Fr fugitif
It instabile
Pt instável

Flugschrift *(f)* *n* De
En pamphlet
Es panfleto *(m)*
Fr opuscule *(m)*
It opuscolo *(m)*
Pt panfleto *(m)*

flujo de caja *(m)* Es
De Bargeldfluβ *(m)*
En cash flow
Fr cash-flow *(m)*
It movimento di cassa *(m)*
Pt movimento em dinheiro *(m)*

flush *adj* En
De glatt
Es a ras
Fr ras

It a livello
Pt nivelado

Flüssigkeit *(f)* *n* De
En solvency
Es solvencia *(f)*
Fr solvabilité *(f)*
It solvenza *(f)*
Pt solvência *(f)*

flyleaf *n* En
De Respektblatt *(n)*
Es cortesía *(f)*
Fr feuille de garde *(f)*
It risguardo *(m)*
Pt folha em branco *(f)*

fodera di costa *(f)* It
De Buchrücken-Fütterung *(f)*
En back lining
Es contralomo *(m)*
Fr garniture du dos *(f)*
Pt forro de lombada *(m)*

fogli aggiunti *(m pl)* It
De Zuschuβ *(m)*
En overs *pl* *n*
Es hojas sobrantes *(f pl)*
Fr passe *(f)*
Pt folhas que sobram *(f pl)*

fogli di stampa *(m pl)* It
De Pressebögen *(pl)*
En press sheets
Es pliegos de prensa *(m pl)*
Fr feuilles machine *(f pl)*
Pt folhas de imprensa *(f pl)*

fogli in anticipo *(m pl)* It
De Aushängebogen *(pl)*
En advance sheets
Es hojas por adelantado *(f pl)*
Fr bonnes feuilles *(f pl)*
Pt folhas tipográficas *(f pl)*

foglio *(m)* *n* It
De Blatt *(n)*
En leaf
Es hoja *(f)*
Fr feuillet *(m)*
Pt folha *(f)*

foglio a griglia *(m)* It
De Layoutbogen *(m)*
En grid sheet
Es hoja cuadriculada *(f)*
Fr feuille quadrillée *(f)*
Pt folha quadriculada *(f)*

fogli successivi *(m pl)* It
De folgende Bogen *(pl)*
En running sheets
Es hojas sucesivas *(f pl)*
Fr feuilles de roulement *(f pl)*
Pt folhas sucessivas *(f pl)*

foire de Francfort *(f)* Fr
De Frankfurter Buchmesse *(f)*
En Frankfurt Book Fair
Es Fería del Libro de Frankfurt *(f)*
It Fiera del Libro di Francoforte *(f)*
Pt Feira do Livro de Francfort *(f)*

foire du livre *(f)* Fr
De Büchermesse *(f)*
En book fair
Es feria del libro *(f)*
It fiera del libro *(m)*
Pt feira do livro *(f)*

folding *n* En
De Falzen *(n)*
Es plegado *(m)*
Fr pliure *(f)*
It piegatura *(f)*
Pt dobrado *(m)*

folding chase En
De Falzrahmen *(m)*
Es rama dúplex *(f)*
Fr châssis de pliage *(m)*
It telaio di piegafoglio *(m)*
Pt rama duplex *(f)*

folding machine En
De Falzmaschine *(f)*
Es plegadora *(f)*
Fr plieuse *(f)*
It piegatrice meccanica *(f)*
Pt dobradora *(f)*

folgende Bogen *(pl)* De
En running sheets
Es hojas sucesivas *(f pl)*

Fr feuilles de roulement
  (f pl)
It fogli successivi *(m pl)*
Pt folhas sucessivas *(f
  pl)*

folha *(f) n* Pt
De Blatt *(n)*
En leaf
Es hoja *(f)*
Fr feuillet *(m)*
It foglio *(m)*

folha de ouro *(f)* Pt
De Goldfolie *(f)*
En gold leaf
Es pan de oro *(m)*
Fr feuille d´or *(f)*
It oro in fogli *(m)*

folha em branco *(f)* Pt
De Respektblatt *(n)*
En flyleaf
Es cortesía *(f)*
Fr feuille de garde *(f)*
It risguardo *(m)*

folha quadriculada *(f)* Pt
De Layoutbogen *(m)*
En grid sheet
Es hoja cuadriculada *(f)*
Fr feuille quadrillée *(f)*
It foglio a griglia *(m)*

folhas de contracapa *(f
  pl)* Pt
De Vorsatzpapiere *(pl)*
En endpapers *pl n*
Es guardas *(f pl)*
Fr papiers de garde *(m
  pl)*
It risguardi *(m pl)*

folhas de imprensa *(f pl)*
  Pt
De Pressebögen *(pl)*
En press sheets
Es pliegos de prensa *(m
  pl)*
Fr feuilles machine *(f pl)*
It fogli di stampa *(m pl)*

folhas que sobram *(f pl)*
  Pt
De Zuschuß *(m)*
En overs *pl n*
Es hojas sobrantes *(f pl)*
Fr passe *(f)*
It fogli aggiunti *(m pl)*

folhas sucessivas *(f pl)*
  Pt
De folgende Bogen *(pl)*
En running sheets
Es hojas sucesivas *(f pl)*
Fr feuilles de roulement
  (f pl)
It fogli successivi *(m pl)*

folhas tipográficas *(f pl)*
  Pt
De Aushängebogen *(pl)*
En advance sheets
Es hojas por adelantado
  (f pl)
Fr bonnes feuilles *(f pl)*
It fogli in anticipo *(m pl)*

folheto *(m) n* Pt
De Merkblatt *(n)*
En booklet
Es opúsculo *(m)*
Fr plaquette *(f)*
It volantino a stampa
  (m)

folheto *(m) n* Pt
De Broschüre *(f)*
En leaflet
Es prospecto *(m)*
Fr feuille volante *(f)*
It opuscolo *(m)*

folio *n* En; Es, Fr *(m)*
De Pagina *(f)*
It numero della pagina
  (m)
Pt fólio *(m)*

fólio *(m) n* Pt
De Pagina *(f)*
En folio
Es folio *(m)*
Fr folio *(m)*
It nurnero della pagina
  (m)

Folioformat *(n) n* De
En foolscap
Es papel de oficio *(m)*
Fr papier ministre *(m)*
It carta protocollo *(f)*
Pt papel ministro *(m)*

folleto *(m) n* Es
De Broschüre *(f)*
En brochure
Fr brochure *(f)*
It opuscolo *(m)*
Pt brochura *(f)*

fonderia di caratteri *(f)* It
De Schriftgießerei *(f)*
En type foundry
Es fundición de tipos *(f)*
Fr clicherie *(f)*
Pt fundição de tipos
  (casa) *(f)*

fondeuse à la ligne *(f)* Fr
De Zeilengießmaschine
  (f)
En linecasting machine
Es fundidora de lingotes
  (f)
It macchina fonditrice a
  linea *(f)*
Pt fundidora de lingotes
  (f)

fondos grisados *(m pl)*
  Es
De mechanische Töne
  (pl)
En mechanical tints
Fr coloration
  mécanique *(f)*
It colori di gradazioni
  chiare ottenuti
  meccanicamente *(m
  pl)*
Pt lâminas de acinzentar
  (f pl)

fonetica *(f) n* It
De Phonetik *(f)*
En phonetics
Es fonética *(f)*
Fr phonétique *(f)*
Pt fonética *(f)*

fonética *(f) n* Es, Pt
De Phonetik *(f)*
En phonetics
Fr phonétique *(f)*
It fonetica *(f)*

fonte *(f) n* Fr
De Schriftart *(f)*
En fount
Es fundición *(f)*
It serie di caratteri *(f)*
Pt fundição *(f)*

fonte de caractères *(f)* Fr
De Schriftguß *(m)*
En typecasting
Es composición
  mecanotípica *(f)*
It fusione dei caratteri
  (f)
Pt fundição de tipos
  (processo) *(f)*

fonte luminosa *(f)* It, Pt
De Lichtquelle *(f)*
En light source
Es fuente luminosa *(f)*
Fr source lumineuse *(f)*

foolscap *n* En
De Folioformat *(n)*
Es papel de oficio *(m)*
Fr papier ministre *(m)*
It carta protocollo *(f)*
Pt papel ministro *(m)*

foot *n* En
De Fuß *(m)*
Es pie *(m)*
Fr pied *(m)*
It piede *(m)*
Pt pé *(m)*

footnote *n* En
De Fußnote *(f)*
Es nota al pie de la
  página *(f)*
Fr note en bas de page
  (f)
It nota in calce *(f)*
Pt nota de pé de página
  (f)

fora de registo Pt
De fehlerhaftes Register
En out of register
Es fuera de registro
Fr mal registré
It fuori registro

fora do enquadramento
  Pt
De nicht gerade
En out of square
Es descuadrado
Fr mal cadré
It fuori squadra

fore edge En
De Schnitt *(m)*
Es canto *(m)*
Fr gouttière *(f)*
It bordo anteriore *(m)*
Pt canto dianteiro *(m)*

**foreign-language
  dictionary** En
De Fremdsprachen-
  Wörterbuch *(n)*
Es diccionario de lengua
  extranjera *(m)*
Fr dictionnaire de
  langues étrangères
  (m)

It dizionario in lingua
    straniera *(m)*
Pt dicionário de lingua
    estrangeira *(m)*

foreign rights En
De Auslandsrechte *(pl)*
Es derechos en el
    extranjero *(m pl)*
Fr droits à l'étranger *(m
    pl)*
It diritti esteri *(m pl)*
Pt direitos estrangeiros
    (m pl)

**foreign-rights
    department** En
De Auslandsrecht-
    Abteilung *(f)*
Es departamento de
    derechos en el
    extranjero *(m)*
Fr service des droits à
    l'étranger *(m)*
It reparto diritti esteri
    (m)
Pt departamento de
    direitos estrangeiros
    (m)

foreign-rights manager
    En
De Auslandsrecht-Leiter
    (m)
Es director de derechos
    en el extranjero *(m)*
Fr directeur des droits à
    l'étranger *(m)*
It dirigente diritti esteri
    (m)
Pt director dos direitos
    estrangeiros *(m)*

foreign sales *pl n* En
De Auslandsumsätze *(pl)*
Es ventas extranjeras *(f
    pl)*
Fr ventes à l'étranger *(f
    pl)*
It servizio vendite
    estero *(m)*
Pt vendas no
    estrangeiro *(f pl)*

foreword *n* En
De Vorwort
Es proemio *(m)*
Fr avant-propos *(m)*
It proemio *(m)*
Pt proémio *(m)*

Form *(f) n* De
En forme
Es forma *(f)*
Fr forme *(f)*
It forma *(f)*
Pt forma *(f)*

Form *(f) n* De
En stone (letterpress
    composition)
Es composición de
    imposición *(f)*
Fr marbre de serrage
    (m)
It banco tipografico *(m)*
Pt superfície de
    imposição *(f)*

forma *(f) n* Es, It, Pt
De Form *(f)*
En forme
Fr forme *(f)*

formación *(m) n* Es
De Formatierung *(f)*
En formatting
Fr mise en page *(f)*
It formazione *(f)*
Pt formatação *(f)*

formación de cajos *(f)* Es
De Abpressen *(n)*
En backing
Fr endossure *(f)*
It rinforzo *(m)*
Pt colocação de
    lombada *(f)*

forma interior *(f)* Pt
De innere Form *(f)*
En inner forme
Es plana interior *(f)*
Fr côté de deux *(m)*
It forma interna *(f)*

forma interna *(f)* It
De innere Form *(f)*
En inner forme
Es plana interior *(f)*
Fr côté de deux *(m)*
Pt forma interior *(f)*

Formalgebrauch *(m) n*
    De
En formal usage
Es uso formal *(m)*
Fr bon usage *(m)*
It uso formale *(m)*
Pt utilização formal *(f)*

formal usage En
De Formalgebrauch *(m)*
Es uso formal *(m)*
Fr bon usage *(m)*
It uso formale *(m)*
Pt utilização formal *(f)*

format *n* En; Fr *(m)*
De Format *(n)*
Es formato *(m)*
It veste tipografica *(f)*
Pt formato *(m)*

Format *(n) n* De
En format
Es formato *(m)*
Fr format *(m)*
It veste tipografica *(f)*
Pt formato *(m)*

formatação *(f) n* Pt
De Formatierung *(f)*
En formatting
Es formación *(m)*
Fr mise en page *(f)*
It formazione *(f)*

format à l'italienne *(m)*
    Fr
De Langformat-Papier
    (n)
En oblong paper
Es papel apaisado *(m)*
It carta oblunga *(f)*
Pt papel alongado *(m)*

format bâtard *(m)* Fr
De Bastardkegel *(m)*
En bastard size
Es tamaño bastardo *(m)*
It dimensione
    irregolare *(f)*
Pt tamanho bastardo
    (m)

format en hauteur *(m)* Fr
De Hochformat *(n)*
En portrait page
Es página vertical *(f)*
It pagina verticale *(f)*
Pt página de retrato *(f)*

format fini *(m)* Fr
De Beschnittgröße *(f)*
En trimmed page size
Es tamaño de página
    cortada *(m)*
It dimensioni di pagina
    rifilata *(f pl)*
Pt tamanho de página
    aparada *(m)*

format identique Fr
De gleichgroß
En same size (s/s)
Es igual tamaño
It stessa dimensione
Pt mesmo tamanho

formati di libri *(m pl)* It
De Büchergrößen *(pl)*
En book sizes *pl n*
Es tamaños de libros *(m
    pl)*
Fr formats des livres *(m
    pl)*
Pt formatos de livros *(m
    pl)*

Formatierung *(f) n* De
En formatting
Es formación *(m)*
Fr mise en page *(f)*
It formazione *(f)*
Pt formatação *(f)*

formato *(m) n* Es, Pt
De Format *(n)*
En format
Fr format *(m)*
It veste tipografica *(f)*

format oblong *(m)* Fr
De Querformat-Seite *(f)*
En landscape page
Es página apaisada *(f)*
It pagina orizzontale *(f)*
Pt página horizontal *(f)*

formatos de livros *(m pl)*
    Pt
De Büchergrößen *(pl)*
En book sizes *pl n*
Es tamaños de libros *(m
    pl)*
Fr formats des livres *(m
    pl)*
It formati di libri *(m pl)*

formats D.I.N. *(m pl)* Fr
De DIN-Größen *(pl)*
En DIN sizes
Es tamaños D.I.N. *(m
    pl)*
It dimensioni D.I.N. *(f
    pl)*
Pt tamanhos D.I.N. *(m
    pl)*

formats des livres *(m pl)*
    Fr
De Büchergrößen *(pl)*
En book sizes *pl n*

Es tamaños de libros *(m pl)*
It formati di libri *(m pl)*
Pt formatos de livros *(m pl)*

formats ISO *(m pl)* Fr
De ISO-Größen *(pl)*
En ISO sizes
Es tamaños ISO *(m pl)*
It dimensioni ISO *(f pl)*
Pt tamanhos ISO *(m pl)*

Formatsteg *(m) n* De
En furniture (printers')
Es guanición *(f)*
Fr garniture *(f)*
It fraschetta *(f)*
Pt guarnição *(f)*

formatting *n* En
De Formatierung *(f)*
Es formación *(m)*
Fr mise en page *(f)*
It formazione *(f)*
Pt formatação *(f)*

formazione *(f) n* It
De Formatierung *(f)*
En formatting
Es formación *(m)*
Fr mise en page *(f)*
Pt formatação *(f)*

forme *n* En; Fr *(f)*
De Form *(f)*
Es forma *(f)*
It forma *(f)*
Pt forma *(f)*

fornecedor *(m) n* Pt
De Lieferant *(m)*
En supplier
Es proveedor *(m)*
Fr fournisseur *(m)*
It fornitore *(m)*

fornitore *(m) n* It
De Lieferant *(m)*
En supplier
Es proveedor *(m)*
Fr fournisseur *(m)*
Pt fornecedor *(m)*

forro de lombada *(m)* Pt
De Buchrücken-Fütterung *(f)*
En back lining
Es contralomo *(m)*

Fr garniture du dos *(f)*
It fodera di costa *(f)*

Forschungs-Assistent *(m) n* De
En research assistant
Es ayudante de investigación *(m)*
Fr assistant des recherches *(m)*
It assistente di ricerca *(m)*
Pt ajudante de investigação *(m)*

fortdrucken *vb* De
En run on (printing)
Es proseguir la tirada
Fr faire des tirages supplémentaires
It imprimir una super-tiratura *(f)*
Pt continuar a imprimir

Fortdruck-Preis *(m)* De
En run-on price
Es precio de más ejemplares *(m)*
Fr coût du tirage supplémentaire *(m)*
It prezzo di super-tiratura *(m)*
Pt preço de exemplares a mais *(m)*

forward *vb* En
De versenden
Es expedir
Fr expédier
It spedire
Pt enviar

forwarding agent En
De Spediteur *(m)*
Es agente expedidor *(m)*
Fr transitaire *(m)*
It spedizioniere *(m)*
Pt agente expedidor *(m)*

fotocomposição *(f) n* Pt
De Photosatz *(m)*
En photocomposition; phototypesetting
Es fotocomposición *(f)*
Fr photocomposition *(f)*
It fotocomposizione *(f)*

fotocomposición *(f) n* Es
De Photosatz *(m)*
En photocomposition; phototypesetting

Fr photocomposition *(f)*
It fotocomposizione *(f)*
Pt fotocomposição *(f)*

fotocompositor *(m) n* Es, Pt
De Film-Setzmaschine *(f)*
En filmsetter
Fr photocomposeuse *(f)*
It fotocompositrice *(f)*

fotocompositrice *(f) n* It
De Film-Setzmaschine *(f)*
En filmsetter
Es fotocompositor *(m)*
Fr photocomposeuse *(f)*
Pt fotocompositor *(m)*

fotocomposizione *(f) n* It
De Photosatz *(m)*
En photocomposition; phototypesetting
Es fotocomposición *(f)*
Fr photocomposition *(f)*
Pt fotocomposição *(f)*

fotocopiadora *(f)* Pt
De Photokopier-maschine *(f)*
En photocopying machine
Es máquina fotocopiadora *(f)*
Fr photocopieuse *(f)*
It fotocopiatrice *(f)*

fotocopiatrice *(f)* It
De Photokopier-maschine *(f)*
En photocopying machine
Es máquina fotocopiadora *(f)*
Fr photocopieuse *(f)*
Pt fotocopiadora *(f)*

fotocréditos *(m pl)* Es, Pt
De Dank für die Genehmigung von Photos *(m)*
En photo credits
Fr origine des photographies *(f)*
It indice dei fotografi *(m pl)*

fotogiornalismo *(m) n* It
De Photojournalismus *(m)*
En photojournalism
Es fotoperiodismo *(m)*

Fr photojournalisme *(m)*
Pt fotojornalismo *(m)*

fotograbado *(m) n* Es
De Chemiegraphie *(f)*
En process engraving
Fr photogravure *(f)*
It zincografia *(f)*
Pt fototipogravura *(f)*

fotograbado de línea *(m)* Es
De Strichätzung *(f)*
En line block
Fr cliché au trait *(m)*
It cliché a tratto *(m)*
Pt placa de estereotipia *(f)*

fotograbados esfumados *(m pl)* Es
De Gelegenheitsvignetta *(f)*
En vignetted blocks *pl n*
Fr simili dégradée *(f)*
It clichés à vignette *(m pl)*
Pt blocos de vinheta *(m pl)*

fotografar *vb* Pt
De photographieren
En photograph
Es fotografiar
Fr photographier
It fotografare

fotografare *vb* It
De photographieren
En photograph
Es fotografiar
Fr photographier
Pt fotografar

fotografia (figura) *(f) n* It
De Photo *(n)*
En photograph
Es fotografía (imagen) *(f)*
Fr photographie (image) *(f)*
Pt fotografia (imagem) *(f)*

fotografia (imagem) *(f) n* Pt
De Photo *(n)*
En photograph
Es fotografía (imagen) *(f)*

Fr photographie (image)
(f)
It fotografia (figura) *(f)*

fotografia
(procedimento) *(f) n*
It
De Photographie *(f)*
En photography
Es fotografía (método)
(f)
Fr photographie
(procédé) *(f)*
Pt fotografia (processo)
(f)

fotografia (processo) *(f) n*
Pt
De Photographie *(f)*
En photography
Es fotografía (método)
(f)
Fr photographie
(procédé) *(f)*
It fotografia
(procedimento) *(f)*

fotografía (imagen) *(f) n*
Es
De Photo *(n)*
En photograph
Fr photographie (image)
(f)
It fotografia (figura) *(f)*
Pt fotografia (imagem)
(f)

fotografía (método) *(f) n*
Es
De Photographie *(f)*
En photography
Fr photographie
(procédé) *(f)*
It fotografia
(procedimento) *(f)*
Pt fotografia (processo)
(f)

fotografia a colori *(f)* It
Am color photograph
De Farbphoto *(n)*
En colour photograph
Es fotografía en colores
(f)
Fr photographie en
couleurs *(f)*
Pt fotografia a cores *(f)*

fotografia a cores *(f)* Pt
Am color photograph
De Farbphoto *(n)*
En colour photograph

Es fotografía en colores
(f)
Fr photographie en
couleurs *(f)*
It fotografia a colori *(f)*

fotografía en colores *(f)*
Es
Am color photograph
De Farbphoto *(n)*
En colour photograph
Fr photographie en
couleurs *(f)*
It fotografia a colori *(f)*
Pt fotografia a cores *(f)*

fotografiar *vb* Es
De photographieren
En photograph
Fr photographier
It fotografare
Pt fotografar

fotografo *(m) n* It
De Photograph *(f)*
En photographer
Es fotógrafo *(m)*
Fr photographe *(m)*
Pt fotógrafo *(m)*

fotógrafo *(m) n* Es, Pt
De Photograph *(m)*
En photographer
Fr photographe *(m)*
It fotografo *(m)*

fotogravura *(f) (n)* Pt
De Kupfertiefdruck *(m)*
En photogravure
Es huecograbado *(m)*
Fr héliogravure *(f)*
It fotoincisione *(f)*

fotoincisione *(f) (n)* It
De Kupfertiefdruck *(m)*
En photogravure
Es huecograbado *(m)*
Fr héliogravure *(f)*
Pt fotogravura *(f)*

fotojornalismo *(m) n* Pt
De Photojournalismus
(m)
En photojournalism
Es fotoperiodismo *(m)*
Fr photojournalisme *(m)*
It fotogiornalismo *(m)*

fotolitografía *(f) n* Es
De Photolithographie *(f)*
En photolithography
Fr phototypie *(f)*
It fotolitografia *(f)*
Pt fotolitografia *(f)*

fotolitografia *(f) n* It, Pt
De Photolithographie *(f)*
En photolithography
Es fotolitografía *(f)*
Fr phototypie *(f)*

fotoperiodismo *(m) n* Es
De Photojournalismus
(m)
En photojournalism
Fr photojournalisme *(m)*
It fotogiornalismo *(m)*
Pt fotojornalismo *(m)*

fototipogravura *(f) n* Pt
De Chemiegraphie *(f)*
En process engraving
Es fotograbado *(m)*
Fr photogravure *(f)*
It zincografia *(f)*

fount *n* En
De Schriftart *(f)*
Es fundición *(f)*
Fr fonte *(f)*
It serie di caratteri *(f)*
Pt fundição *(f)*

four-color printing Am
De Vierfarbdruck *(m)*
En four-colour printing
Es cuatricromía *(f)*
Fr quadrichromie *(f)*
It stampa a quattro
colori *(f)*
Pt impressão a quatro
cores *(f)*

four-colour printing En
Am four-color printing
De Vierfarbdruck *(m)*
Es cuatricromía *(f)*
Fr quadrichromie *(f)*
It stampa a quattro
colori *(f)*
Pt impressão a quatro
cores *(f)*

fournisseur *(m) n* Fr
De Lieferant *(m)*
En supplier
Es proveedor *(m)*
It fornitore *(m)*
Pt fornecedor *(m)*

fournitures de dessin *(f*
pl) Fr
De Kunstmaterialien *(pl)*
En artist's materials *pl n*
Es materiales de
dibujante *(m pl)*
It materiale d'arte *(m)*
Pt materiais do artista
(m pl)

Frage *(f) n* De
En query
Es interrogación *(f)*
Fr question *(f)*
It quesito *(m)*
Pt pergunta *(f)*

Fragezeichen *(n) n* De
En question mark
Es signo de
interrogación *(m)*
Fr point d'interrogation
(m)
It punto di domanda
(m)
Pt ponto de
interrogação *(m)*

frais d'emmagasinage
(m pl) Fr
De Lagerkosten *(pl)*
En warehousing costs *pl
n*
Es gastos de almacén
(m pl)
It costi di
immagazzinaggio *(m
pl)*
Pt custos de armazém
(m pl)

frais de transport *(m pl)*
Fr
De Transportkosten *(pl)*
En transport costs *pl n*
Es gastos de transporte
(m pl)
It costi di trasporto *(m
pl)*
Pt custos de transporte
(m pl)

frais d'expédition *(m pl)*
Fr
De Verschiffungkosten
(pl)
En shipping costs
Es gastos de envío *(m
pl)*
It costi di spedizione *(m
pl)*

Pt custos de envio *(m pl)*

fraiseuse *(f) n* Fr
De Fräser *(m)*
En routing machine
Es fresadora *(f)*
It fresatrice *(f)*
Pt fresadora *(f)*

franco à bord Fr
De frei an Bord
En free on board (f.o.b.)
Es franco a bordo
It franco a bordo
Pt franco a bordo

franco a bordo Es, It, Pt
De frei an Bord
En free on board (f.o.b.)
Fr franco à bord

franjas de color *(f pl)* Es
Am color bars
De Farbstreifen *(pl)*
En colour bars
Fr bandes des couleurs *(f pl)*
It barre di colore *(f pl)*
Pt franjas de cor *(f pl)*

franjas de cor *(f pl)* Pt
Am color bars
De Farbstreifen *(pl)*
En colour bars
Es franjas de color *(f pl)*
Fr bandes des couleurs *(f pl)*
It barre di colore *(f pl)*

Frankfurt Book Fair En
De Frankfurter Buchmesse *(f)*
Es Fería del Libro de Frankfurt *(f)*
Fr foire de Francfort *(f)*
It Fiera del Libro di Francoforte *(f)*
Pt Feira do Livro de Francfort *(f)*

Frankfurter Buchmesse *(f)* De
En Frankfurt Book Fair
Es Fería del Libro de Frankfurt *(f)*
Fr foire de Francfort *(f)*
It Fiera del Libro di Francoforte *(f)*
Pt Feira do Livro de Francfort *(f)*

fraschetta *(f) n* It
De Formatsteg *(m)*
En furniture (printers')
Es guanición *(f)*
Fr garniture *(f)*
Pt guarnição *(f)*

frase *(f) n* It, Pt
De Satz *(m)*
En sentence
Es cláusula *(f)*
Fr phrase *(f)*

Fräser *(m) n* De
En routing machine
Es fresadora *(f)*
Fr fraiseuse *(f)*
It fresatrice *(f)*
Pt fresadora *(f)*

freelance *adj* En
De freiberuflich
Es independiente
Fr indépendant
It indipendente
Pt independente

free on board (f.o.b.) En
De frei an Bord
Es franco a bordo
Fr franco à bord
It franco a bordo
Pt franco a bordo

frei an Bord De
En free on board (f.o.b.)
Es franco a bordo
Fr franco à bord
It franco a bordo
Pt franco a bordo

freiberuflich *adj* De
En freelance
Es independiente
Fr indépendant
It indipendente
Pt independente

Freistellung *(f) n* De
En cut out
Es recortado *(m)*
Fr découpage *(m)*
It scontornata *(f)*
Pt recorte *(m)*

Fremdsprachen-Wörterbuch *(n)* De
En foreign-language dictionary

Es diccionario de lengua extranjera *(m)*
Fr dictionnaire de langues étrangères *(m)*
It dizionario in lingua straniera *(m)*
Pt dicionário de lingua estrangeira *(m)*

fresadora *(f) n* Es, Pt
De Fräser *(m)*
En routing machine
Fr fraiseuse *(f)*
It fresatrice *(f)*

fresatrice *(f) n* It
De Fräser *(m)*
En routing machine
Es fresadora *(f)*
Fr fraiseuse *(f)*
Pt fresadora *(f)*

fret aérien *(m)* Fr
De Luftfracht *(f)*
En airfreight
Es flete aéreo *(m)*
It trasporto merci per via aerea *(m)*
Pt frete aéreo *(m)*

frete aéreo *(m)* Pt
De Luftfracht *(f)*
En airfreight
Es flete aéreo *(m)*
Fr fret aérien *(m)*
It trasporto merci per via aerea *(m)*

friso *(m) n* Pt
De Kapitelband *(m)*
En headband
Es cabecera *(f)*
Fr tranchefile *(f)*
It capitello *(m)*

frontespizio *(m) n* It
De Titelseite *(f)*
En title page
Es portada *(f)*
Fr page de titre *(m)*
Pt página de título *(f)*

frontespizio illustrato *(m)* It
De Frontispiz *(n)*
En frontispiece
Es frontispicio *(m)*
Fr frontispice *(m)*
Pt frontispício *(m)*

front flap En
De vordere Umschlagklappe *(f)*
Es solapa delantera *(f)*
Fr rabat avant *(m)*
It risvolto anteriore *(m)*
Pt aleta dianteira *(f)*

frontispice *(m) n* Fr
De Frontispiz *(n)*
En frontispiece
Es frontispicio *(m)*
It frontespizio illustrato *(m)*
Pt frontispício *(m)*

frontispicio *(m) n* Es
De Frontispiz *(n)*
En frontispiece
Fr frontispice *(m)*
It frontespizio illustrato *(m)*
Pt frontispício *(m)*

frontispício *(m) n* Pt
De Frontispiz *(n)*
En frontispiece
Es frontispicio *(m)*
Fr frontispice *(m)*
It frontespizio illustrato *(m)*
Pt frontispício *(m)*

frontispiece *n* En
De Frontispiz *(n)*
Es frontispicio *(m)*
Fr frontispice *(m)*
It frontespizio illustrato *(m)*
Pt frontispício *(m)*

Frontispiz *(n) n* De
En frontispiece
Es frontispicio *(m)*
Fr frontispice *(m)*
It frontespizio illustrato *(m)*
Pt frontispício *(m)*

front matter En
De Vortext *(m)*
Es principios del libro *(m pl)*
Fr feuilles liminaires *(f pl)*
It preliminari del libro *(m pl)*
Pt princípio do livro *(m)*

Frühjahrsliste *(f) n* De
En spring list

Es catálogo de
 primavera *(m)*
Fr catalogue de
 printemps *(m)*
It elenco di primavera
 (m)
Pt lista de Primavera *(f)*

**Frühjahrs-
 Veröffentlichung**
 (f) n De
En spring publication
Es publicación de
 primavera *(f)*
Fr parution de
 printemps *(f)*
It pubblicazione di
 primavera *(f)*
Pt publicação de
 Primavera *(f)*

fuente luminosa *(f)* Es
De Lichtquelle *(f)*
En light source
Fr source lumineuse *(f)*
It fonte luminosa *(f)*
Pt fonte luminosa *(f)*

fuera de registro Es
De fehlerhaftes Register
En out of register
Fr mal registré
It fuori registro
Pt fora de registo

fugaz *adj* Es
De flüchtig
En fugitive
Fr fugitif
It instabile
Pt instável

fugitif *adj* Fr
De flüchtig
En fugitive
Es fugaz
It instabile
Pt instável

fugitive *adj* En
De flüchtig
Es fugaz
Fr fugitif
It instabile
Pt instável

Führungsloch-Vorschub
 (m) De
En advanced sprocket
 feed

Es arrastre por rueda
 dentada *(m)*
Fr perforation
 d'entraînement *(f)*
It alimentazione a
 tamburo dentato
 avanzato *(f)*
Pt alimentação
 avançada do carreto
 (f)

full-color illustration Am
De Vierfarbillustration *(f)*
En full-colour illustration
Es ilustración a todo
 color *(f)*
Fr illustration en tous
 les couleurs *(f)*
It illustrazione a tutti
 colori *(f)*
Pt ilustração a toda a
 cor *(f)*

full-colour illustration
 En
Am full-color illustration
De Vierfarbillustration *(f)*
Es ilustración a todo
 color *(f)*
Fr illustration en tous
 les couleurs *(f)*
It illustrazione a tutti
 colori *(f)*
Pt ilustração a toda a
 cor *(f)*

Füllerstoff *(m) n* De
En filler
Es material de carga *(m)*
Fr charge *(f)*
It carica *(f)*
Pt carga *(f)*

full stop En
Am period
De Punkt *(m)*
Es punto final *(m)*
Fr point final *(m)*
It punto fermo *(m)*
Pt ponto final *(m)*

fully bound En
De voll gebunden
Es totalmente
 encuadernado
Fr reliure pleine
It completamente
 rilegato
Pt completamente
 encadernado

fundição *(f) n* Pt
De Schriftart *(f)*
En fount
Es fundición *(f)*
Fr fonte *(f)*
It serie di caratteri *(f)*

fundição de tipos (casa)
 (f) Pt
De Schriftgieserei *(f)*
En type foundry
Es fundición de tipos *(f)*
Fr clicherie *(f)*
It fonderia di caratteri
 (f)

fundição de tipos
 (processo) *(f)* Pt
De Schriftguβ *(m)*
En typecasting
Es composición
 mecanotípica *(f)*
Fr fonte de caractères
 (f)
It fusione dei caratteri
 (f)

fundición *(f) n* Es
De Schriftart *(f)*
En fount
Fr fonte *(f)*
It serie di caratteri *(f)*
Pt fundição *(f)*

fundición de tipos *(f)* Es
De Schriftgieβerei *(f)*
En type foundry
Fr clicherie *(f)*
It fonderia di caratteri
 (f)
Pt fundição de tipos
 (casa) *(f)*

fundidora de lingotes *(f)*
 Es, Pt
De Zeilengieβmaschine
 (f)
En linecasting machine
Fr fondeuse à la ligne *(f)*
It macchina fonditrice a
 linea *(f)*

fuori registro It
De fehlerhaftes Register
En out of register
Es fuera de registro
Fr mal registré
Pt fora de registo

fuori squadra It
De nicht gerade
En out of square
Es descuadrado
Fr mal cadré
Pt fora do
 enquadramento

furnish *n* En
De Stoffeintrag *(m)*
Es materias primas *(f pl)*
Fr matières premières *(f
 pl)*
It materia prima *(f)*
Pt matérias-primas *(f pl)*

furniture (printers') *n* En
De Formatsteg *(m)*
Es guanición *(f)*
Fr garniture *(f)*
It fraschetta *(f)*
Pt guarnição *(f)*

furos *(m pl)* Pt
De Nadellöcher *(pl)*
En pinholes *pl n*
Es burbujas *(f pl)*
Fr perforation des
 négatifs *(f)*
It mancanza di densità
 (f)

further reading En
De weitere Literatur *(f)*
Es relectura *(f)*
Fr lectures
 complémentaires *(f
 pl)*
It ulteriori letture *(f pl)*
Pt leitura adicional *(f)*

fusão *(f) n* Pt
De Giesen *(n)*
En casting
Es fusión *(f)*
Fr coulée *(f)*
It fusione *(f)*

fusión *(f) n* Es
De Gieβen *(n)*
En casting
Fr coulée *(f)*
It fusione *(f)*
Pt fusão *(f)*

fusione *(f) n* It
De Gieβen *(n)*
En casting
Es fusión *(f)*
Fr coulée *(f)*
Pt fusão *(f)*

fusione dei caratteri (f)
It
De Schriftguß (m)
En typecasting
Es composición mecanotípica (f)
Fr fonte de caractères (f)
Pt fundição de tipos (processo) (f)

Fuß (m) n De
En foot
Es pie (m)
Fr pied (m)
It piede (m)
Pt pé (m)

Fußnote (f) n De
En footnote
Es nota al pie de la página (f)
Fr note en bas de page (f)
It nota in calce (f)
Pt nota de pé de página (f)

G

gacetero (m) n Es
De geographisches Lexicon (n)
En gazetteer
Fr répertoire géographique (m)
It dizionario geografico (m)
Pt dicionário geográfico (m)

galé (f) n Pt
De Satzschiff (n)
En galley
Es galera (f)
Fr galée (f)
It vantaggio (m)

galée (f) n Fr
De Satzschiff (n)
En galley
Es galera (f)
It vantaggio (m)
Pt galé (f)

galera (f) n Es
De Satzschiff (n)
En galley
Fr galée (f)
It vantaggio (m)
Pt galé (f)

galley n En
De Satzschiff (n)
Es galera (f)
Fr galée (f)
It vantaggio (m)
Pt galé (f)

galley press En
De Spaltenabziehpresse (f)
Es prensa para prueba de galeradas (f)
Fr presse à épreuves (f)
It stampa di vantaggio (f)
Pt prensa de galé (f)

galley proof En
De Korrekturfahne (f)
Es prueba de galeradas (f)
Fr épreuve en placard (f)
It bozza in colonna (f)
Pt prova de galé (f)

Galvano (n) n De
En electrotype
Es electrotipo (m)
Fr électrotype (m)
It elettrotipo (m)
Pt electrotipo (m)

galvano-nichel (m) n It
De Nickelgalvano (n)
En nickel electro
Es galvano niquelado (m)
Fr galvano nickel (m)
Pt galvano niquelado (m)

galvano nickel (m) Fr
De Nickelgalvano (n)
En nickel electro
Es galvano niquelado (m)
It galvano-nichel (m)
Pt galvano niquelado (m)

galvano niquelado (m) Es, Pt
De Nickelgalvano (n)
En nickel electro

Fr galvano nickel (m)
It galvano-nichel (m)

gambi (m pl) It
De Säulen (pl)
En stems pl n
Es palos gruesos (m pl)
Fr hastes (f pl)
Pt paus grossos (m pl)

gambo (m) n It
De Stiel (m)
En shank
Es árbol (m)
Fr tige (f)
Pt árvore (f)

garder contact Fr
De in Kontakt stehen
En liaise
Es enlazar
It collegarsi
Pt ligar

garniture (f) n Fr
De Formatsteg (m)
En furniture (printers')
Es guanición (f)
It fraschetta (f)
Pt guarnição (f)

garniture du dos (f) Fr
De Buchrücken-Fütterung (f)
En back lining
Es contralomo (m)
It fodera di costa (f)
Pt forro de lombada (m)

gastos de almacén (m pl) Es
De Lagerkosten (pl)
En warehousing costs pl n
Fr frais d'emmagasinage (m pl)
It costi di immagazzinaggio (m pl)
Pt custos de armazém (m pl)

gastos de envío (m pl) Es
De Verschiffungkosten (pl)
En shipping costs
Fr frais d'expédition (m pl)
It costi di spedizione (m pl)

Pt custos de envio (m pl)

gastos de transporte (m pl) Es
De Transportkosten (pl)
En transport costs pl n
Fr frais de transport (m pl)
It costi di trasporto (m pl)
Pt custos de transporte (m pl)

gather vb En
De zusammentragen
Es reunir
Fr rassembler
It raccogliere
Pt reunir

gathering n En
De Zusammentragen (n)
Es recogida (f)
Fr assemblage (m)
It raccolta (f)
Pt reunião (f)

gaufrage (m) n Fr
De Prägedruck (m)
En embossing
Es estampado en relieve (m)
It goffratura (f)
Pt gravação em relevo (f)

gaufrage à sec (m) Fr
De Blindbearbeitung (f)
En blind finishing
Es acabado en seco (m)
It finitura cieca (f)
Pt acabamento cego (m)

gaufrer vb Fr
De kräuseln
En crimp
Es marcar con rayas
It ondulare
Pt enrugar

gazetteer n En
De geographisches Lexicon (n)
Es gacetero (m)
Fr répertoire géographique (m)
It dizionario geografico (m)

Pt dicionário geográfico
(m)

gebundene Ausgabe (f)
De
Am hardcover edition
En hardback edition
Es edición
encuadernada (f)
Fr édition reliée (f)
It edizione con
copertina rigida (f)
Pt edição de lombada
dura (f)

gebundene Bücher (pl)
De
En bound books
Es libros encuadernados
(m pl)
Fr livres reliés (m pl)
It libri rilegati (m pl)
Pt livros encadernados
(m pl)

gebundene Farbe (f) De
En bonded ink
Es tinta adherida (f)
Fr encre liée (f)
It inchiostro aderente
(m)
Pt tinta aglutinada (f)

gebundenes Buch (n) De
En hardback book
Es libro encuadernado
(m)
Fr livre relié (m)
It libro con copertina
rigida (m)
Pt livro de lombada dura
(m)

gebunden in Kalbleder
De
En calfbound
Es encuadernado en piel
de becerro
Fr relié en veau
It rilegato in pelle
Pt encadernado a
carneira

Gedankenstrich (m) n
De
En dash
Es raya (f)
Fr filet (m)
It lineetta (f)
Pt filete (m)

Gedichtband (m) n De
En poetry book
Es libro do poesías (m)
Fr livre de poésie (m)
It libro di poesia (m)
Pt livro de poesia (m)

gedruckt adj De
En in print
Es publicado
Fr en impression
It in corso di stampa
Pt impresso e publicado

geheftete Arbeit (f) De
En sewn work
Es obra cosida (f)
Fr reliure cousue (f)
It lavoro di cucitura (m)
Pt obra cosida (f)

Gelegenheitsvignetta (f)
De
En vignetted blocks pl n
Es fotograbados
esfumados (m pl)
Fr simili dégradée (f)
It clichés à vignette (m
pl)
Pt blocos de vinheta (m
pl)

gelehrt adj De
En scholarly
Es erudito
Fr savant
It erudito
Pt sábio

gelehrte Bücher (pl) De
En scholarly books
Es libros eruditos (m pl)
Fr livres d'érudition (m
pl)
It libri eruditi (m pl)
Pt livros de estudo (m
pl)

gemeinsame Ausgabe
(f) De
En co-edition
Es coedición (f)
Fr co-édition (f)
It coedizione (f)
Pt coedição (f)

genere (m) n It
De Genre (n)
En genre
Es género (m)

Fr genre (m)
Pt género (m)

género (m) n Es, Pt
De Genre (n)
En genre
Fr genre (m)
It genere (m)

genre n En; Fr (m)
De Genre (n)
Es género (m)
It genere (m)
Pt género (m)

Genre (n) n De
En genre
Es género (m)
Fr genre (m)
It genere (m)
Pt género (m)

**geographisches
Lexicon** (n) De
En gazetteer
Es gacetero (m)
Fr répertoire
géographique (m)
It dizionario geografico
(m)
Pt dicionário geográfico
(m)

gérant (m) n Fr
De Geschäftsleiter (m)
En manager
Es gerente (m)
It dirigente (m)
Pt gerente (m)

gerente (m) n Es, Pt
De Geschäftsleiter (m)
En manager
Fr gérant (m)
It dirigente (m)

gerente de vendas (m)
Pt
De Verkaufsleiter (m)
En sales manager
Es jefe de ventas (m)
Fr chef des ventes (m)
It direttore vendite (m)

gesammelten Werke
(pl) De
En collected works
Es obras reunidas (f pl)
Fr recueil des oeuvres
(m pl)

It raccolta di opere (f pl)
Pt compilação de obras
(f)

**geschäftliches
Mittagessen** (n) De
En working lunch
Es comida de trabajo (f)
Fr déjeuner de travail
(m)
It pranzo di lavoro (m)
Pt almoço de trabalho
(m)

**Geschäftsführender
Direktor** (m) De
En managing director
Es director gerente (m)
Fr directeur général (m)
It amministratore
delegato (m)
Pt director geral (m)

Geschäftsleiter (m) n De
En manager
Es gerente (m)
Fr gérant (m)
It dirigente (m)
Pt gerente (m)

Geschäftsleitung (f) n
De
En management
Es manejo (m)
Fr direction (f)
It direzione (f)
Pt direcção (f)

gestalten vb De
En lay out
Es disponer (tipo)
Fr disposer (caractères)
It disporre (caratteri)
Pt preparar (tipo)

Gestaltung (f) n De
En design
Es diseño (m)
Fr projet (m)
It disegno (m)
Pt desenho (m)

gestrichener Text (m)
De
En cancelled matter
Es composición
suprimida (f)
Fr texte annulé (m)
It testo annullato (m)
Pt matéria cancelada (f)

gestrichenes Papier (n)
De
En coated paper
Es papel cuché (m)
Fr papier couché (m)
It carta patinata (f)
Pt papel revestido (m)

getöntes Papier (n) De
En tinted paper
Es papel coloreado (m)
Fr papier de couleur (m)
It carta colorata (f)
Pt papel colorido (m)

Geviert (n) n De
En em
Es cuadratín (m)
Fr cadratin (m)
It riga (f)
Pt quadratim (m)

Geviertstrich (m) n De
En em rule
Es pleca-cuadratín (f)
Fr tiret sur cadratin (m)
It lineato a quadratone
(m)
Pt filete de quadratim
(m)

Gewebeschablone (f) n
De
En tissue stencil
Es matriz de papel de
seda (f)
Fr stencil de duplication
(m)
It matrice in carta di
seta (f)
Pt estencil de tela (m)

Gewerkschaft (f) n De
En trade union
Es sindicato (m)
Fr syndicat (m)
It sindacato (m)
Pt sindicato (m)

**Gewerkschafts-
Betriebsobmann**
(m) n De
En shop steward
Es dirigente obrero (m)
Fr délégué d'atelier (m)
It delegato di fabbrica
(m)
Pt balconista (m)

Gewinnspanne (f) n De
En margin (profit)
Es margen de beneficio
(m)
Fr marge bénéficiaire (f)
It margine di utile (m)
Pt margem de lucro (f)

ghosting n En
De Durchscheinbild (n)
Es mancha de reflexión
(f)
Fr image fantôme (f)
It falsa immagine (f)
Pt fantasma (m)

ghost writer En
De Schattenautor (m)
Es escritor fantasma (m)
Fr nègre (m)
It collaboratore
anonimo (m)
Pt colaborador anónimo
(m)

giacenze (f pl) It
De Übervorrat (m)
En overstocks pl n
Es existencias excesivas
(f pl)
Fr stock excessif (m)
Pt existências que
sobram (f pl)

giallo (m) n It
De Reißer (m)
En thriller
Es novela de misterio (f)
Fr roman à sensation
(m)
Pt policial (m)

giallo di tricromia (m) It
De Verfahrensgelb (n)
En process yellow
Es amarillo de tricromía
(m)
Fr jaune d'impression
couleur (m)
Pt amarelo para
policromia (m)

Gießbach (m) n De
En gutter
Es medianil (m)
Fr petits fonds (m pl)
It scanalatura per sfogo
(f)
Pt medianiz (m)

Gießen (n) n De
En casting
Es fusión (f)
Fr coulée (f)
It fusione (f)
Pt fusão (f)

gilding n En
De Metalldruck (m)
Es doradura (f)
Fr dorure (f)
It doratura (f)
Pt douração (f)

gilt-edged adj En
De mit Goldschnitt
Es de cortes dorados
Fr doré sur tranche
It con bordi dorati
Pt dourado nas beiras

gioco di caratteri (m) It
De Buchstabensatz (m)
En character set
Es juego de caracteres
(m)
Fr jeu de caractères (m)
Pt jogo de caracteres
(m)

giornale (m) n It
De Journal (n)
En journal
Es periódico (m)
Fr revue (f)
Pt jornal (m)

giornale quotidiano (m)
It
De Zeitung (f)
En newspaper
Es diario (m)
Fr journal (m)
Pt jornal diário (m)

giornalismo (m) n It
De Journalismus (m)
En journalism
Es periodismo (m)
Fr journalisme (m)
Pt jornalismo (m)

giornalista (m/f) n It
De Journalist (m)
En journalist
Es periodista (m/f)
Fr journaliste (m/f)
Pt jornalista (m/f)

giuntare vb It
De montieren
En strip in
Es montar inserciones
Fr raccorder
Pt incluir

giustificare vb It
De justieren
En justify
Es justificar
Fr justifier
Pt justificar

giustificato adj It
De justiert
En justified
Es justificado
Fr justifié
Pt justificado

giustificazione (f) n It
De Justierung (f)
En justification
Es justificación (f)
Fr justification (f)
Pt justificação (f)

glanzfolienkaschiert adj
De
En laminated
Es laminado
Fr laminé
It laminato
Pt laminado

Glanzfolienkaschierung
(f) n De
En laminating
Es laminación (f)
Fr contrecollage sous
pression (m)
It laminazione (f)
Pt laminação (f)

Glanzpapier (n) n De
En glazed paper
Es papel lustroso (m)
Fr papier glacé (m)
It carta lucida (f)
Pt papel lustrado (m)

glatt adj De
En flush
Es a ras
Fr ras
It a livello
Pt nivelado

glatt zurichten De
En cut flush
Es cortado a ras
Fr composé à
l'américaine
It tagliato a filo
Pt recorte raso

glazed paper En
De Glanzpapier (n)
Es papel lustroso (m)
Fr papier glacé (m)
It carta lucida (f)
Pt papel lustrado (m)

gleichgroβ De
En same size (s/s)
Es igual tamaño
Fr format identique
It stessa dimensione
Pt mesmo tamanho

glosario (m) n Es
De Glossarium (n)
En glossary
Fr glossaire (m)
It glossario (m)
Pt glossário (m)

glossaire (m) n Fr
De Glossarium (n)
En glossary
Es glosario (m)
It glossario (m)
Pt glossário (m)

glossario (m) n It
De Glossarium (n)
En glossary
Es glosario (m)
Fr glossaire (m)
Pt glossário (m)

glossário (m) n Pt
De Glossarium (n)
En glossary
Es glosario (m)
Fr glossaire (m)
It glossario (m)

Glossarium (n) n De
En glossary
Es glosario (m)
Fr glossaire (m)
It glossario (m)
Pt glossário (m)

glossary n En
De Glossarium (n)
Es glosario (m)

Fr glossaire (m)
It glossario (m)
Pt glossário (m)

goffratura (f) n It
De Prägedruck (m)
En embossing
Es estampado en relieve
(m)
Fr gaufrage (m)
Pt gravação em relevo
(f)

goffratura cieca (f) It
De Blindprägung (f)
En blind embossing
Es gofrado (m)
Fr dorure à froid (f)
Pt gravação em alto
relevo cego (f)

gofrado (m) n Es
De Blindprägung (f)
En blind embossing
Fr dorure à froid (f)
It goffratura cieca (f)
Pt gravação em alto
relevo cego (f)

Goldfolie (f) n De
En gold leaf
Es pan de oro (m)
Fr feuille d'or (f)
It oro in fogli (m)
Pt folha de ouro (f)

gold leaf En
De Goldfolie (f)
Es pan de oro (m)
Fr feuille d'or (f)
It oro in fogli (m)
Pt folha de ouro (f)

Goldprägung (f) n De
En gold stamping
Es estampación dorada
(f)
Fr dorure à la presse (f)
It stampigliatura in oro
(f)
Pt estampagem a ouro
(f)

gold stamping En
De Goldprägung (f)
Es estampación dorada
(f)
Fr dorure à la presse (f)
It stampigliatura in oro
(f)

Pt estampagem a ouro
(f)

gondolage (m) n Fr
De Kräuseln (n)
En cockling
Es amartillamiento (m)
It arricciatura (f)
Pt enrugamento (m)

gothic n En
De Gotisch (f)
Es gótico (m)
Fr gothique (m)
It gotico (m)
Pt gótico (m)

gothique (m) n Fr
De Gotisch (f)
En gothic
Es gótico (m)
It gotico (m)
Pt gótico (m)

gotico (m) n It
De Gotisch (f)
En gothic
Es gótico (m)
Fr gothique (m)
Pt gótico (m)

gótico (m) n Es, Pt
De Gotisch (f)
En gothic
Fr gothique (m)
It gotico (m)

Gotisch (f) n De
En gothic
Es gótico (m)
Fr gothique (m)
It gotico (m)
Pt gótico (m)

gouache n En; Fr (f)
De Gouachegemälde (n)
Es aguada (f)
It guazzo (m)
Pt guache (f)

Gouachegemälde (n) n
De
En gouache
Es aguada (f)
Fr gouache (f)
It guazzo (m)
Pt guache (f)

gouttière (f) n Fr
De Schnitt (m)
En fore edge
Es canto (m)
It bordo anteriore (m)
Pt canto dianteiro (m)

grabado (estampa) (m) n
Es
De Gravur (f)
En engraving (print)
Fr estampe (f)
It incisione (f)
Pt gravura (estampa) (f)

grabado (proceso) (m) n
Es
De Gravierung (f)
En engraving (process)
Fr gravure (f)
It arte dell'incisione (f)
Pt gravura (processo) (f)

grabado al agua fuerte
(m) Es
De Radierung (f)
En etching
Fr gravure à l'eau forte
(f)
It incisione
all'acquaforte (f)
Pt gravura a áqua-forte
(f)

grabado de linóleo (m)
Es
De Linolschnitt (m)
En lino cut
Fr gravure sur linoléum
(f)
It incisione in linoleum
(f)
Pt gravura em linóleo (f)

grabado electrónico (m)
Es
De elektronische
Gravierung (f)
En electronic engraving
Fr gravure électronique
(f)
It incisione elettronica
(f)
Pt gravura electrónica
(f)

grabado mezzotinto (m)
Es
De Mezzotintoverfahren
(n)
En mezzotint
Fr mezzo-tinto (m)

It acquaforte *(m)*
Pt meia-tinta *(f)*

grabador *(m) n* Es
De Klischeeanstalt *(f)*
En blockmaker
Fr photograveur *(m)*
It zincografo *(m)*
Pt gravador *(m)*

grabado rápido *(m)* Es
De Einstufenätzverfahren *(n)*
En powderless etching
Fr gravure sans poudre *(f)*
It incisione senza polvere *(f)*
Pt gravura sem pó *(f)*

grabar *vb* Es
De gravieren
En engrave
Fr graver
It incidere
Pt gravar

gradazione *(f) n* It
De Ton *(m)*
En tint
Es media tinta *(f)*
Fr teinte *(f)*
Pt matiz *(m)*

graduare *vb* It
De Maßstab festlegen
En scale
Es poner a escala
Fr dessiner à l'échelle
Pt pôr à escala

gráfica *(f) n* Es, Pt
De graphisches Gewerbe *(n)*
En graphics *pl n*
Fr graphique *(f)*
It arti grafiche *(f pl)*

grafico *(m) n* It
De Kurve *(f)*
En graph
Es gráfico *(m)*
Fr graphique *(m)*
Pt gráfico *(m)*

grafico *adj* It
De graphisch
En graphic
Es gráfico

Fr graphique
Pt gráfico

gráfico *(m) n* Es, Pt
De Kurve *(f)*
En graph
Fr graphique *(m)*
It grafico *(m)*

gráfico *adj* Es, Pt
De graphisch
En graphic
Fr graphique
It grafico

Grafiker *(m) n* De
En graphic designer
Es diseñador gráfico *(m)*
Fr dessinateur *(m)*
It disegnatore grafico *(m)*
Pt desenhador gráfico *(m)*

grain *n* En; Fr *(m)*
De Körnung *(f)*
Es fibra *(f)*
It grana *(f)*
Pt grão *(m)*

gramagem *(m) n* Pt
De Quadratmetergewicht *(n)*
En substance (of paper)
Es gramaje *(m)*
Fr grammage *(m)*
It grammatura *(f)*

gramaje *(m) n* Es
De Quadratmetergewicht *(n)*
En substance (of paper)
Fr grammage *(m)*
It grammatura *(f)*
Pt gramagem *(m)*

gramática *(f) n* Es, Pt
De Grammatik *(f)*
En grammar
Fr grammaire *(f)*
It grammatica *(f)*

gramatical *adj* Es, Pt
De grammatisch
En grammatical
Fr grammatical
It grammaticale

grammage *(m) n* Fr
De Quadratmetergewicht *(n)*
En substance (of paper)
Es gramaje *(m)*
It grammatura *(f)*
Pt gramagem *(m)*

grammaire *(f) n* Fr
De Grammatik *(f)*
En grammar
Es gramática *(f)*
It grammatica *(f)*
Pt gramática *(f)*

grammar *n* En
De Grammatik *(f)*
Es gramática *(f)*
Fr grammaire *(f)*
It grammatica *(f)*
Pt gramática *(f)*

grammatica *(f) n* It
De Grammatik *(f)*
En grammar
Es gramática *(f)*
Fr grammaire *(f)*
Pt gramática *(f)*

grammatical *adj* En, Fr
De grammatisch
Es gramatical
It grammaticale
Pt gramatical

grammaticale *adj* It
De grammatisch
En grammatical
Es gramatical
Fr grammatical
Pt gramatical

Grammatik *(f) n* De
En grammar
Es gramática *(f)*
Fr grammaire *(f)*
It grammatica *(f)*
Pt gramática *(f)*

grammatisch *adj* De
En grammatical
Es gramatical
Fr grammatical
It grammaticale
Pt gramatical

grammatura *(f) n* It
De Quadratmetergewicht *(n)*
En substance (of paper)

Es gramaje *(m)*
Fr grammage *(m)*
Pt gramagem *(m)*

grana *(f) n* It
De Körnung *(f)*
En grain
Es fibra *(f)*
Fr grain *(m)*
Pt grão *(m)*

grande annonce *(f)* Fr
De Displaywerbung *(f)*
En display advertisement
Es anuncio publicitario *(m)*
It inserzione pubblicitaria *(f)*
Pt anúncio em majúsculas e ilustrado *(m)*

grandes lumières *(f pl)* Fr
De Lichter *(pl)*
En highlights *pl n*
Es blancos *(m pl)*
It alte luci *(f pl)*
Pt partes claras *(f pl)*

grande tiratura *(f)* It
De hohe Druckauflage *(f)*
En long print run
Es tirada grande *(f)*
Fr grand tirage *(m)*
Pt tiragem grande *(f)*

grand tirage *(m)* Fr
De hohe Druckauflage *(f)*
En long print run
Es tirada grande *(f)*
It grande tiratura *(f)*
Pt tiragem grande *(f)*

Granierung *(f) n* De
En stippling
Es punteado *(m)*
Fr grisé *(m)*
It battitura *(f)*
Pt ponteado *(m)*

grão *(m) n* Pt
De Körnung *(f)*
En grain
Es fibra *(f)*
Fr grain *(m)*
It grana *(f)*

graph *n* En
De Kurve *(f)*
Es gráfico *(m)*
Fr graphique *(m)*
It grafico *(m)*
Pt gráfico *(m)*

graphic *adj* En
De graphisch
Es gráfico
Fr graphique
It grafico
Pt gráfico

graphic designer En
De Grafiker *(m)*
Es diseñador gráfico *(m)*
Fr dessinateur *(m)*
It disegnatore grafico *(m)*
Pt desenhador gráfico *(m)*

graphics *pl n* En
De graphisches Gewerbe *(n)*
Es gráfica *(f)*
Fr graphique *(f)*
It arti grafiche *(f pl)*
Pt gráfica *(f)*

graphique *(m) n* Fr
De Kurve *(f)*
En graph
Es gráfico *(m)*
It grafico *(m)*
Pt gráfico *(m)*

graphique *adj* Fr
De graphisch
En graphic
Es gráfico
It grafico
Pt gráfico

graphique *(f) n* Fr
De graphisches Gewerbe *(n)*
En graphics *pl n*
Es gráfica *(f)*
It arti grafiche *(f pl)*
Pt gráfica *(f)*

graphisch *adj* De
En graphic
Es gráfico
Fr graphique
It grafico
Pt gráfico

graphisches Gewerbe *(n)* De
En graphics *pl n*
Es gráfica *(f)*
Fr graphique *(f)*
It arti grafiche *(f pl)*
Pt gráfica *(f)*

Gratisexemplar *(n) n* De
En complimentary copy
Es ejemplar de obsequio *(m)*
Fr exemplaire en hommage *(m)*
It copia omaggio *(f)*
Pt exemplar de oferta *(m)*

gravação em alto relevo cego *(f)* Pt
De Blindprägung *(f)*
En blind embossing
Es gofrado *(m)*
Fr dorure à froid *(f)*
It goffratura cieca *(f)*

gravação em relevo *(f)* Pt
De Prägedruck *(m)*
En embossing
Es estampado en relieve *(m)*
Fr gaufrage *(m)*
It goffratura *(f)*

gravado fino *(m)* Pt
De Feinätzung *(f)*
En fine etching
Es aguafuerte fina *(f)*
Fr gravure à l´eau-forte très mordancé *(m)*
It acquafortista raffinata *(f)*

gravador *(m) n* Pt
De Klischeeanstalt *(f)*
En blockmaker
Es grabador *(m)*
Fr photograveur *(m)*
It zincografo *(m)*

gravar *vb* Pt
De gravieren
En engrave
Es grabar
Fr graver
It incidere

grave accent En
De Gravis *(m)*
Es acento grave *(m)*
Fr accent grave *(m)*
It accento grave *(m)*
Pt acento grave *(m)*

graver *vb* Fr
De gravieren
En engrave
Es grabar
It incidere
Pt gravar

gravieren *vb* De
En engrave
Es grabar
Fr graver
It incidere
Pt gravar

Gravierung *(f) n* De
En engraving (process)
Es grabado (proceso) *(m)*
Fr gravure *(f)*
It arte dell´incisione *(f)*
Pt gravura (processo) *(f)*

Gravis *(m) n* De
En grave accent
Es acento grave *(m)*
Fr accent grave *(m)*
It accento grave *(m)*
Pt acento grave *(m)*

Gravur *(f) n* De
En engraving (print)
Es grabado (estampa) *(m)*
Fr estampe *(f)*
It incisione *(f)*
Pt gravura (estampa) *(f)*

gravura *(f) n* Pt
De Tafel *(f)*
En plate (picture)
Es lámina *(f)*
Fr planche *(f)*
It tavola *(f)*

gravura (estampa) *(f) n* Pt
De Gravur *(f)*
En engraving (print)
Es grabado (estampa) *(m)*
Fr estampe *(f)*
It incisione *(f)*

gravura (processo) *(f) n* Pt
De Gravierung *(f)*
En engraving (process)

Es grabado (proceso) *(m)*
Fr gravure *(f)*
It arte dell´incisione *(f)*

gravura a áqua-forte *(f)* Pt
De Radierung *(f)*
En etching
Es grabado al agua fuerte *(m)*
Fr gravure à l´eau forte *(f)*
It incisione all´acquaforte *(f)*

gravura electrónica *(f)* Pt
De elektronische Gravierung *(f)*
En electronic engraving
Es grabado electrónico *(m)*
Fr gravure électronique *(f)*
It incisione elettronica *(f)*

gravura em linóleo *(f)* Pt
De Linolschnitt *(m)*
En lino cut
Es grabado de linóleo *(m)*
Fr gravure sur linoléum *(f)*
It incisione in linoleum *(f)*

gravura sem pó *(f)* Pt
De Einstufenätzverfahren *(n)*
En powderless etching
Es grabado rápido *(m)*
Fr gravure sans poudre *(f)*
It incisione senza polvere *(f)*

gravure *(f) n* Fr
De Gravierung *(f)*
En engraving (process)
Es grabado (proceso) *(m)*
It arte dell´incisione *(f)*
Pt gravura (processo) *(f)*

gravure à l´eau forte *(f)* Fr
De Radierung *(f)*
En etching
Es grabado al agua fuerte *(m)*

It incisione
all´acquaforte *(f)*
Pt gravura a áqua-forte
(f)

**gravure à l'eau-forte
très mordancé** *(m)*
Fr
De Feinätzung *(f)*
En fine etching
Es aguafuerte fina *(f)*
It acquafortista
raffinata *(f)*
Pt gravado fino *(m)*

gravure électronique *(f)*
Fr
De elektronische
Gravierung *(f)*
En electronic engraving
Es grabado electrónico
(m)
It incisione elettronica
(f)
Pt gravura electrónica
(f)

gravure sans poudre *(f)*
Fr
De Einstufenätzverfahren
(n)
En powderless etching
Es grabado rápido *(m)*
It incisione senza
polvere *(f)*
Pt gravura sem pó *(f)*

gravure sur bois *(f)* Fr
De Xylographie *(f)*
En wood engraving
Es xilografía *(f)*
It incisione su legno
(m)
Pt xilografia *(f)*

gravure sur cuivre *(f)* Fr
De Kupferdruck *(m)*
En copper-plate printing
Es impresión en hueco
(f)
It stampa a calcografia
(f)
Pt impressão com
chapa de cobre *(f)*

gravure sur linoléum *(f)*
Fr
De Linolschnitt *(m)*
En lino cut
Es grabado de linóleo
(m)

It incisione in linoleum
(f)
Pt gravura em linóleo *(f)*

Greifer *(m)* n De
En gripper
Es pinza *(f)*
Fr pince *(f)*
It pinza *(f)*
Pt agarrador *(m)*

Greifkanten *(f)* n De
En gripper edge
Es orilla de entrada *(f)*
Fr côté des pinces *(m)*
It lato pinza *(m)*
Pt margem dianteira *(f)*

grid paper En
De Koordinatenpapier
(n)
Es papel milimétrico *(m)*
Fr papier millimétrique
(m)
It carta millimetrata *(f)*
Pt papel milimétrico *(m)*

grid sheet En
De Layoutbogen *(m)*
Es hoja cuadriculada *(f)*
Fr feuille quadrillée *(f)*
It foglio a griglia *(m)*
Pt folha quadriculada *(f)*

Griffkante *(f)* n De
En grip
Es margen de agarre *(m)*
Fr prise de pinces *(f)*
It presa *(f)*
Pt margem de agarre *(f)*

grip n En
De Griffkante *(f)*
Es margen de agarre *(m)*
Fr prise de pinces *(f)*
It presa *(f)*
Pt margem de agarre *(f)*

gripper n En
De Greifer *(m)*
Es pinza *(f)*
Fr pince *(f)*
It pinza *(f)*
Pt agarrador *(m)*

gripper edge En
De Greifkanten *(f)*
Es orilla de entrada *(f)*
Fr côté des pinces *(m)*

It lato pinza *(m)*
Pt margem dianteira *(f)*

grisé *(m)* n Fr
De Granierung *(f)*
En stippling
Es punteado *(m)*
It battitura *(f)*
Pt ponteado *(m)*

grober Raster *(m)* De
En coarse screen
Es trama gruesa *(f)*
Fr trame à gros grains
(f)
It a grana grossa *(f)*
Pt retícula grossa *(f)*

Großbuchstaben *(pl)* De
En capitals (caps) *pl n*
Es mayúsculas *(f pl)*
Fr majuscules *(f pl)*
It maiuscole *(f pl)*
Pt maiusculas *(f pl)*

großer Buchstabe *(m)*
De
En upper-case letter
Es letra mayúscula *(f)*
Fr lettre de haut de
casse *(f)*
It lettera maiuscola *(f)*
Pt letra de caixa alta *(f)*

grossezza del libro *(f)* It
De Masse *(f)*
En bulk (of a book)
Es grueso de libro *(m)*
Fr épaisseur d´un livre
(f)
Pt espessura dum livro
(f)

grossezza di carta *(f)* It
De Papierdicke *(f)*
En bulk (of paper)
Es cuerpo de papel *(m)*
Fr épaisseur de papier
(f)
Pt grossura do papel *(f)*

Großhandelsvertrieb
(m) n De
En wholesale
distribution
Es distribución al por
mayor *(f)*
Fr commerce de gros
(m)
It distribuzione
all´ingrosso *(f)*

Pt distribuição por
atacado *(f)*

Großhändier *(m)* n De
En wholesaler
Es mayorista *(m)*
Fr grossiste *(m)*
It grossista *(m)*
Pt armazenista *(m)*

grossista *(m)* n It
De Großhändler *(m)*
En wholesaler
Es mayorista *(m)*
Fr grossiste *(m)*
Pt armazenista *(m)*

grossiste *(m)* n Fr
De Großhändler *(m)*
En wholesaler
Es mayorista *(m)*
It grossista *(m)*
Pt armazenista *(m)*

grossura do papel *(f)* Pt
De Papierdicke *(f)*
En bulk (of paper)
Es cuerpo de papel *(m)*
Fr épaisseur de papier
(f)
It grossezza di carta *(f)*

großzügig illustriert De
En lavishly illustrated
Es profusamente
ilustrado
Fr abondamment
illustré
It riccamente illustrato
Pt profusamente
ilustrado

Grotesk-Schrifttyp *(m)*
n De
En sans-serif typeface
Es tipo sin remate *(m)*
Fr caractère antique
(sans empâtement)
(m)
It bastone *(m)*
Pt olho de tipo sem
remate *(m)*

grueso de libro *(m)* Es
De Masse *(f)*
En bulk (of a book)
Fr épaisseur d´un livre
(f)
It grossezza del libro *(f)*
Pt espessura dum livro
(f)

guache *(f)* n Pt
De Gouachegemälde *(n)*
En gouache
Es aguada *(f)*
Fr gouache *(f)*
It guazzo *(m)*

guanición *(f)* n Es
De Formatsteg *(m)*
En furniture (printers´)
Fr garniture *(f)*
It fraschetta *(f)*
Pt guarnição *(f)*

guardas *(f pl)* Es
De Vorsatzpapiere *(pl)*
En endpapers *pl n*
Fr papiers de garde *(m pl)*
It risguardi *(m pl)*
Pt folhas de contracapa *(f pl)*

guarnição *(f)* n Pt
De Formatsteg *(m)*
En furniture (printers´)
Es guanición *(f)*
Fr garniture *(f)*
It fraschetta *(f)*

guazzo *(m)* n It
De Gouachegemälde *(n)*
En gouache
Es aguada *(f)*
Fr gouache *(f)*
Pt guache *(f)*

guia *(m)* n Pt
De Einführung *(f)*
En guide
Es guía *(f)*
Fr guide *(m)*
It guida *(f)*

guía *(f)* n Es
De Einführung *(f)*
En guide
Fr guide *(m)*
It guida *(f)*
Pt guia *(m)*

guia de estilo *(m)* Pt
De Stilmuster *(n)*
En style guide
Es guía del estilo *(f)*
Fr consignes de conception *(f pl)*
It guida di stile *(f)*

guía del estilo *(f)* Es
De Stilmuster *(n)*
En style guide
Fr consignes de conception *(f pl)*
It guida di stile *(f)*
Pt guia de estilo *(m)*

guía de viajes *(f)* Es
De Reiseleitfaden *(m)*
En travel guide
Fr guide touristique *(m)*
It guida turistica *(f)*
Pt guia turístico *(m)*

guia turístico *(m)* Pt
De Reiseleitfaden *(m)*
En travel guide
Es guía de viajes *(f)*
Fr guide touristique *(m)*
It guida turistica *(f)*

guida *(f)* n It
De Einführung *(f)*
En guide
Es guía *(f)*
Fr guide *(m)*
Pt guia *(m)*

guida di stile *(f)* It
De Stilmuster *(n)*
En style guide
Es guía del estilo *(f)*
Fr consignes de conception *(f pl)*
Pt guia de estilo *(m)*

guida turistica *(f)* It
De Reiseleitfaden *(m)*
En travel guide
Es guía de viajes *(f)*
Fr guide touristique *(m)*
Pt guia turístico *(m)*

guide *n* En; Fr *(m)*
De Einführung *(f)*
Es guía *(f)*
It guida *(f)*
Pt guia *(m)*

guide-âne *(m)* n Fr
De Handbuch *(n)*
En handbook
Es compendio *(m)*
It manualetto *(m)*
Pt compêndio *(m)*

guide pratiche *(f pl)* It
De Handwerksbücher *(pl)*

En craft books *pl n*
Es libros de trabajos manuales *(m pl)*
Fr ouvrages artisanaux *(m pl)*
Pt livros técnicos *(m pl)*

guide touristique *(m)* Fr
De Reiseleitfaden *(m)*
En travel guide
Es guía de viajes *(f)*
It guida turistica *(f)*
Pt guia turístico *(m)*

guilhotina *(f)* n Pt
De Schneidemaschine *(f)*
En guillotine
Es guillotina *(f)*
Fr guillotine *(f)*
It tagliacarta *(f)*

guillemets *(m pl)* n Fr
De Anführungszeichen *(pl)*
En quotation marks
Es comillas *(f pl)*
It virgolette *(f pl)*
Pt aspas *(f pl)*

guillotina *(f)* n Es
De Schneidemaschine *(f)*
En guillotine
Fr guillotine *(f)*
It tagliacarta *(f)*
Pt guilhotina *(f)*

guillotine *n* En; Fr *(f)*
De Schneidemaschine *(f)*
Es guillotina *(f)*
It tagliacarta *(f)*
Pt guilhotina *(f)*

guión *(m)* n Es
De Bindestrich *(m)*
En hyphen
Fr trait d´union *(m)*
It trattino di unione *(m)*
Pt traço de união *(m)*

guión de final de línea *(m)* Es
De Zeilenende-Trennstrich *(m)*
En end-of-line hyphen
Fr trait d´union de fin de ligne *(m)*
It trattino di fine linea *(m)*
Pt traço de união de fim de linha *(m)*

guión discrecional *(m)* Es
De willkürlicher Trennstrich *(m)*
En discretionary hyphen
Fr trait d´union facultatif *(m)*
It lineetta discrezionale *(f)*
Pt traço de união discricionário *(m)*

Gummiklischees *(pl)* n De
En rubber stereos
Es estereotipos de caucho *(m pl)*
Fr stéréos caoutchouc *(m pl)*
It stereos di gomma *(m pl)*
Pt estereos de borracha *(m pl)*

Guβform *(f)* n De
Am mold (papermaking)
En mould (papermaking)
Es molde *(m)*
Fr empreinte *(f)*
It stampo (industria cartiera) *(f)*
Pt molde *(m)*

Gussgestrichenes Papier *(n)* De
En cast-coated paper
Es papel de respaldo esmaltado *(m)*
Fr papier couché chrome superbrillant *(m)*
It carta altobrillante *(f)*
Pt papel estereotipado *(m)*

guter Satz *(m)* De
En standing type
Es composición levantada *(f)*
Fr caractères conservés *(m pl)*
It carattere eretto *(m)*
Pt composição levantada *(f)*

gutter *n* En
De Gieβbach *(m)*
Es medianil *(m)*
Fr petits fonds *(m pl)*
It scanalatura per sfogo *(f)*
Pt medianiz *(m)*

gutter margin En
De Straßenkante *(f)*
Es margen del medianil *(m)*
Fr lézarde *(f)*
It margine di scanalatura *(m)*
Pt margem de medianiz *(f)*

H

Haarstriche *(pl)* De
En hair lines
Es filetes extrafinos *(m pl)*
Fr déliés *(m pl)*
It linee finissime *(f pl)*
Pt filetes extrafinos *(m pl)*

habillage *(m)* n Fr
De Zylinderaufzug *(m)*
En cylinder dressing
Es rectificado de cilindros *(m)*
It rivestimento per cilindri *(m)*
Pt rectificação de cilindros *(f)*

hackneyed *adj* En
De abgedroschen
Es común
Fr stéréotypé
It comune
Pt vulgar

hack writer En
De Mietschreiber *(m)*
Es escritor mercenario *(m)*
Fr écrivassier *(m)*
It imbrattacarte *(m)*
Pt escritor comercial *(m)*

Hadernkarton *(m)* n De
En rag board
Es cartón de trapos *(m)*
Fr carton chiffon *(m)*
It cartone di stracci *(m)*
Pt cartão de trapos *(m)*

Hadernpapier *(n)* n De
En rag paper
Es papel de trapos *(m)*
Fr papier de chiffon *(m)*
It carta di stracci *(f)*
Pt papel de trapos *(m)*

hair lines En
De Haarstriche *(pl)*
Es filetes extrafinos *(m pl)*
Fr déliés *(m pl)*
It linee finissime *(f pl)*
Pt filetes extrafinos *(m pl)*

Halbbogendruck *(m)* n De
En half-sheet work
Es imposición e impresión a blanco y vuelta *(f)*
Fr imposition en demi-feuille *(f)*
It lavoro di mezza pagina *(f)*
Pt trabalho a meia folha *(m)*

halbfetter Satz *(m)* De
En semi-bold type
Es seminegrilla *(f)*
Fr caractère mi-gras *(m)*
It carattere semi-grassetto *(m)*
Pt tipo semi-negro *(m)*

Halbfranzband *(m)* n De
En half binding
Es encuadernación a media piel *(f)*
Fr demi-reliure à petits coins *(f)*
It mezza rilegatura *(f)*
Pt encadernação a meia pele *(f)*

halbgebundenes Buch *n* De
En half-bound book
Es libro encuadernado a media piel *(m)*
Fr livre en demi-reliure *(m)*
It libro mezzo rilegato *(m)*
Pt livro encadernado a meia pele *(m)*

Halbgeviert *(n)* n De
En en
Es medio cuadratín *(m)*

Fr demi-cadratin *(m)*
It mezza riga *(f)*
Pt meio quadratim *(m)*

Halbgeviertstrich *(m)* n De
En en rule
Es pleca de medio cuadratín *(f)*
Fr tiret sur demi-cadratin *(m)*
It lineato a demi-quadratone *(m)*
Pt filete de meio quadratim *(m)*

Halbton *(m)* n De
En halftone
Es autotipia *(f)*
Fr simili *(f)*
It mezzatinta *(f)*
Pt autotipia *(f)*

Halbtonraster *(m)* n De
En halftone screen
Es trama de medio tono *(f)*
Fr trame *(f)*
It retino di mezzatinta *(m)*
Pt retítula de autotipia *(f)*

half binding En
De Halbfranzband *(m)*
Es encuadernación a media piel *(f)*
Fr demi-reliure à petits coins *(f)*
It mezza rilegatura *(f)*
Pt encadernação a meia pele *(f)*

half-bound book En
De halbgebundenes Buch *n*
Es libro encuadernado a media piel *(m)*
Fr livre en demi-reliure *(m)*
It libro mezzo rilegato *(m)*
Pt livro encadernado a meia pele *(m)*

half-sheet work En
De Halbbogendruck *(m)*
Es imposición e impresión a blanco y vuelta *(f)*
Fr imposition en demi-feuille *(f)*

It lavoro di mezza pagina *(f)*
Pt trabalho a meia folha *(m)*

half title En
De Innentitel *(m)*
Es anteportada *(f)*
Fr faux-titre *(m)*
It titolo abbreviato *(m)*
Pt anteportada *(f)*

halftone *n* En
De Halbton *(m)*
Es autotipia *(f)*
Fr simili *(f)*
It mezzatinta *(f)*
Pt autotipia *(f)*

halftone screen En
De Halbtonraster *(m)*
Es trama de medio tono *(f)*
Fr trame *(f)*
It retino di mezzatinta *(m)*
Pt retítula de autotipia *(f)*

Haltzylinderpresse *(f)* n De
En stop-cylinder press
Es prensa de cilindro de parada *(f)*
Fr machine à arrêt du cylindre *(f)*
It rotativa con arresto *(f)*
Pt prensa de cilindro de paragem *(f)*

handbook *n* En
De Handbuch *(n)*
Es compendio *(m)*
Fr guide-âne *(m)*
It manualetto *(m)*
Pt compêndio *(m)*

Handbuch *(n)* n De
En handbook
Es compendio *(m)*
Fr guide-âne *(m)*
It manualetto *(m)*
Pt compêndio *(m)*

Handbütten *(n)* n De
En handmade paper
Es papel hecho a mano *(m)*
Fr papier cuve *(m)*

It carta a mano *(f)*
Pt papel feito à mão *(m)*

Handel *(m) n* De
En trade
Es oficio *(m)*
Fr commerce *(m)*
It commercio *(m)*
Pt comércio *(m)*

Handelnder *(m) n* De
En agent
Es agente *(m)*
Fr agent *(m)*
It agente *(m)*
Pt agente *(m)*

Handelsvertreter *(m) n*
De
En representative
Es representante *(m)*
Fr représentant *(m)*
It rappresentante *(m)*
Pt representante *(m)*

handgeschrieben *adj* De
En hand-written
Es escrito a mano
Fr manuscrit
It scritto a mano
Pt escrito à mão

handmade paper En
De Handbütten *(n)*
Es papel hecho a mano
(m)
Fr papier cuve *(m)*
It carta a mano *(f)*
Pt papel feito à mão *(m)*

hand press En
De Handpresse *(f)*
Es prensa manual *(f)*
Fr presse à bras *(f)*
It torchio a mano *(m)*
Pt prensa manual *(f)*

Handpresse *(f) n* De
En hand press
Es prensa manual *(f)*
Fr presse à bras *(f)*
It torchio a mano *(m)*
Pt prensa manual *(f)*

Handsatz *(m) n* De
En hand setting
Es composición a mano
(f)
Fr composition
manuelle *(f)*

It composizione a
mano *(f)*
Pt composição manual
(f)

Handsatz-Schrifttypen
(pl) De
En pi characters
Es caracteres pi *(m pl)*
Fr figures spéciales *(f pl)*
It caratteri pi *(m pl)*
Pt caracteres pi *(m pl)*

hand setting En
De Handsatz *(m)*
Es composición a mano
(f)
Fr composition
manuelle *(f)*
It composizione a
mano *(f)*
Pt composição manual
(f)

Handwerker *(m) n* De
En craftsman
Es artesano *(m)*
Fr artisan *(m)*
It artigiano *(m)*
Pt artesão *(m)*

Handwerksbücher *(pl)*
De
En craft books *pl n*
Es libros de trabajos
manuales *(m pl)*
Fr ouvrages artisanaux
(m pl)
It guide pratiche *(f pl)*
Pt livros técnicos *(m pl)*

hand-written *adj* En
De handgeschrieben
Es escrito a mano
Fr manuscrit
It scritto a mano
Pt escrito à mão

hardback book En
De gebundenes Buch *(n)*
Es libro encuadernado
(m)
Fr livre relié *(m)*
It libro con copertina
rigida *(m)*
Pt livro de lombada dura
(m)

hardback edition En
Am hardcover edition

De gebundene Ausgabe
(f)
Es edición
encuadernada *(f)*
Fr édition reliée *(f)*
It edizione con
copertina rigida *(f)*
Pt edição de lombada
dura *(f)*

hardcover edition Am
De gebundene Ausgabe
(f)
En hardback edition
Es edición
encuadernada *(f)*
Fr édition reliée *(f)*
It edizione con
copertina rigida *(f)*
Pt edição de lombada
dura *(f)*

hard-sized paper En
De Hartleimpapier *(n)*
Es papel de encolado
duro *(m)*
Fr papier très collé *(m)*
It carta molto
imbozzimada *(f)*
Pt papel de
encolamento duro
(m)

Hartleimpapier *(n) n* De
En hard-sized paper
Es papel de encolado
duro *(m)*
Fr papier très collé *(m)*
It carta molto
imbozzimada *(f)*
Pt papel de
encolamento duro
(m)

hastes *(f pl)* Fr
De Säulen *(pl)*
En stems *pl n*
Es palos gruesos *(m pl)*
It gambi *(m pl)*
Pt paus grossos *(m pl)*

hastidor móvil *(m)* Es
De Mobilé *(n)*
En mobile
Fr mobile *(m)*
It elemento mobile *(m)*
Pt mobile *(m)*

haupt Wort *(n)* De
En headword
Es palabra principal *(f)*
Fr mot en-tête *(m)*

It parola principale *(f)*
Pt palavra-índice *(f)*

hausse *(f) n* Fr
De Unterlage *(f)*
En underlay
Es alza bajo el tipo *(f)*
It alzo *(m)*
Pt calço *(m)*

Hausstil *(m) n* De
En house style
Es estilo de reglamento
(m)
Fr style maison *(m)*
It stile di casa *(m)*
Pt estilo da casa *(m)*

haut de casse *(m)* Fr
De Oberkasten *(m)*
En upper case
Es caja alta *(f)*
It alta cassa
Pt caixa alta *(f)*

hauteur *(f) n* Fr
De Satzhöhe *(f)*
En depth
Es profundidad *(f)*
It profondità *(f)*
Pt profundidade *(f)*

hauteur de caractère *(f)*
Fr
De Schrifthöhe *(f)*
En type height
Es altura del tipo *(f)*
It altezza tipografica *(f)*
Pt altura de tipo *(f)*

head (of page) *n* En
De Seitekopf *(m)*
Es blanco *(m)*
Fr tête *(f)*
It testata *(f)*
Pt cabeçalho *(m)*

headband *n* En
De Kapitelband *(m)*
Es cabecera *(f)*
Fr tranchefile *(f)*
It capitello *(m)*
Pt friso *(m)*

headline (of page) *n* En
De Kopfzeile *(f)*
Es título *(m)*
Fr ligne de tête *(f)*
It titolo *(m)*
Pt linha de cabeçalho *(f)*

headline (of newspaper)
n En
De Überschrift *(f)*
Es titular *(m)*
Fr titre *(m)*
It titolo di testa *(m)*
Pt manchete *(m)*

headword En
De haupt Wort *(n)*
Es palabra principal *(f)*
Fr mot en-tête *(m)*
It parola principale *(f)*
Pt palavra-índice *(f)*

headword list En
De Liste der haupten
    Wörter *(f)*
Es lista de palabras
    principales *(f)*
Fr liste des mot en-têtes
    (f)
It elenco di parole
    principali *(m)*
Pt lista de
    palavras-índice *(f)*

heat-set *adj* En
De heißtrocknend
Es solidificado en
    caliente
Fr seché à chaud
It solidificato a caldo
Pt termofixado

heavily edited copy En
De stark revidiertes
    Manuskript *(n)*
Es ejemplar mucho
    enmendada *(m)*
Fr texte très corrigé *(m)*
It copia molto
    emendata *(f)*
Pt exemplar muito
    corrigido *(m)*

Heft *(n) n* De
En booklet
Es opúsculo *(m)*
Fr plaquette *(f)*
It libretto *(m)*
Pt folheto *(m)*

Heftgaze *(f) n* De
En mull
Es muselina *(f)*
Fr mousseline *(f)*
It mussolina *(f)*
Pt musselina *(f)*

heißtrocknend *adj* De
En heat-set
Es solidificado en
    caliente
Fr seché à chaud
It solidificato a caldo
Pt termofixado

héliogravure *(f) (n)* Fr
De Kupfertiefdruck *(m)*
En photogravure
Es huecograbado *(m)*
It fotoincisione *(f)*
Pt fotogravura *(f)*

Herausgabe *(f) n* De
En launch
Es lanzamiento *(m)*
Fr lancement *(m)*
It lancio *(m)*
Pt lançamento *(m)*

herausgeben *vb* De
En launch
Es lanzar
Fr lancer
It lanciare
Pt lançar

Herausgeber *(m) n* De
En editor (publisher's)
Es editor (de libros) *(m)*
Fr rédacteur *(m)*
It editore (di libri) *(m)*
Pt editor (de livros) *(m)*

Herbstausgabe *(f) n* De
En autumn publication
Es publicación de otoño
    (f)
Fr parution de la rentrée
    (f)
It pubblicazione
    d'autunno *(f)*
Pt publicação de outono
    (f)

Herbstliste *(f) n* De
En autumn list
Es catálogo de otoño
    (m)
Fr catalogue de la
    rentrée *(m)*
It elenco d'autunno *(m)*
Pt lista de outono *(f)*

**herramientas de
    encuadernación** *(f
    pl)* Es
De Buchbinder-
    Werkzeuge *(pl)*

En binder's tools
Fr outils de reliure *(m pl)*
It attrezzi da rilegatore
    (m pl)
Pt ferramenta de
    encadernação *(f)*

herstellen *vb* De
En manufacture
Es fabricar
Fr fabriquer
It produrre
Pt produzir

Hersteller *(m) n* De
En manufacturer
Es fabricante *(m)*
Fr fabricant *(m)*
It produttore *(m)*
Pt produtor *(m)*

Herstellung *(f) n* De
En manufacture
Es fabricación *(f)*
Fr fabrication *(f)*
It fabbricazione *(f)*
Pt manufactura *(f)*

Herstellungskosten *(pl)*
    De
En manufacturing costs
Es costes de fabricación
    (m pl)
Fr coût de fabrication
    (m)
It costi di lavorazione
    (m pl)
Pt custos de produção
    (m pl)

highlights *pl n* En
De Lichter *(pl)*
Es blancos *(m pl)*
Fr grandes lumières *(f
    pl)*
It alte luci *(f pl)*
Pt partes claras *(f pl)*

highly illustrated book
    En
De stark illustriertes
    Buch *(n)*
Es libro profusamente
    ilustrado *(m)*
Fr livre abondamment
    illustré *(m)*
It libro riccamente
    illustrato *(m)*
Pt livro muito ilustrado
    (m)

hinaufsetzen *vb* De
En mark up (price)
Es aumentar
Fr augmenter
It aumentare (il prezzo)
Pt aumentar

Hinaufsetzung *(f) n* De
En mark-up (of prices)
Es aumento *(m)*
Fr augmentation *(f)*
It prezzatura *(f)*
Pt aumento *(m)*

**hintere
    Umschlagklappe** *(f)*
    De
En back flap
Es solapa posterior *(f)*
Fr rabat arrière *(m)*
It risvolto di retro *(m)*
Pt contracapa *(f)*

Hochformat *(n) n* De
En portrait page
Es página vertical *(f)*
Fr format en hauteur
    (m)
It pagina verticale *(f)*
Pt página de retrato *(f)*

Hochglanzpapier *(n) n*
    De
En enamel paper
Es papel esmaltado *(m)*
Fr papier émaillé *(m)*
It carta smaltata *(f)*
Pt papel esmalte *(m)*

**hochstehende
    Buchstaben** *(pl)* De
En superior characters
    pl n
Es exponentes *(m pl)*
Fr caractères supérieurs
    (m pl)
It caratteri superiori *(m
    pl)*
Pt caracteres superiores
    (m pl)

hohe Druckauflage *(f)*
    De
En long print run
Es tirada grande *(f)*
Fr grand tirage *(m)*
It grande tiratura *(f)*
Pt tiragem grande *(f)*

hoja *(f) n* Es
De Blatt *(n)*
En leaf
Fr feuillet *(m)*
It foglio *(m)*
Pt folha *(f)*

hoja cuadriculada *(f)* Es
De Layoutbogen *(m)*
En grid sheet
Fr feuille quadrillée *(f)*
It foglio a griglia *(m)*
Pt folha quadriculada *(f)*

hojas por adelantado *(f pl)* Es
De Aushängebogen *(pl)*
En advance sheets
Fr bonnes feuilles *(f pl)*
It fogli in anticipo *(m pl)*
Pt folhas tipográficas *(f pl)*

hojas sobrantes *(f pl)* Es
De Zuschuß *(m)*
En overs *pl n*
Fr passe *(f)*
It fogli aggiunti *(m pl)*
Pt folhas que sobram *(f pl)*

hojas sucesivas *(f pl)* Es
De folgende Bogen *(pl)*
En running sheets
Fr feuilles de roulement *(f pl)*
It fogli successivi *(m pl)*
Pt folhas sucessivas *(f pl)*

Holländern *(n) n* De
En oversewing
Es cosido por el plano *(m)*
Fr point hollandais *(m)*
It cucitura a punto saltato *(f)*
Pt coser por fora *(m)*

hologram *n* En
De Hologramm *(n)*
Es holograma *(f)*
Fr hologramme *(m)*
It ologramma *(m)*
Pt holograma *(m)*

holograma *n* Es *(f)*; Pt *(m)*
De Hologramm *(n)*
En hologram
Fr hologramme *(m)*
It ologramma *(m)*

Hologramm *(n) n* De
En hologram
Es holograma *(f)*
Fr hologramme *(m)*
It ologramma *(m)*
Pt holograma *(m)*

hologramme *(m) n* Fr
De Hologramm *(n)*
En hologram
Es holograma *(f)*
It ologramma *(m)*
Pt holograma *(m)*

Holzfaser *(f) n* De
En lignin
Es lignina *(f)*
Fr lignine *(f)*
It lignina *(f)*
Pt lenhose *(f)*

holzfreier Papierstoff *(m)* De
En wood-free pulp
Es pasta sin madera *(f)*
Fr pâte sans bois *(f)*
It pasta senza legno *(f)*
Pt polpa sem madeira *(f)*

Holzschliff *(m) n* De
En mechanical wood pulp
Es pasta mecánica *(f)*
Fr pâte mécanique *(f)*
It pasta di legno ottenuta meccanicamente *(f)*
Pt polpa de madeira mecânica *(f)*

Holzstoff *(m) n* De
En wood pulp
Es pasta de madera *(f)*
Fr pâte de bois *(f)*
It pasta di legno *(f)*
Pt polpa de madeira *(f)*

homógrafo *(m) n* Es, Pt
De Homograph *(n)*
En homograph
Fr homographe *(m)*
It omografo *(m)*

homograph *n* En
De Homograph *(n)*
Es homógrafo *(m)*
Fr homographe *(m)*
It omografo *(m)*
Pt homógrafo *(m)*

Homograph *(n) n* De
En homograph
Es homógrafo *(m)*
Fr homographe *(m)*
It omografo *(m)*
Pt homógrafo *(m)*

homographe *(m) n* Fr
De Homograph *(n)*
En homograph
Es homógrafo *(m)*
It omografo *(m)*
Pt homógrafo *(m)*

homónimo *(m) n* Es, Pt
De Homonym *(n)*
En homonym
Fr homonyme *(m)*
It omonimo *(m)*

homonym *n* En
De Homonym *(n)*
Es homónimo *(m)*
Fr homonyme *(m)*
It omonimo *(m)*
Pt homónimo *(m)*

Homonym *(n) n* De
En homonym
Es homónimo *(m)*
Fr homonyme *(m)*
It omonimo *(m)*
Pt homónimo *(m)*

homonyme *(m) n* Fr
De Homonym *(n)*
En homonym
Es homónimo *(m)*
It omonimo *(m)*
Pt homónimo *(m)*

hot-metal typesetting En
De Maschinensatz *(m)*
Es composición metálica en caliente *(f)*
Fr composition chaude *(f)*
It composizione a metallo caldo *(f)*
Pt composição de tipos de metal quente *(f)*

hot rolling En
De Warmwalzen *(n)*
Es entintado en caliente *(m)*
Fr laminage à chaud *(m)*
It calandratura a caldo *(f)*

Pt laminação a quente *(f)*

hourly rate En
De Stundentarif *(m)*
Es régimen horario *(m)*
Fr tarif horaire *(m)*
It paga oraria *(f)*
Pt taxa horária *(f)*

house style En
De Hausstil *(m)*
Es estilo de reglamento *(m)*
Fr style maison *(m)*
It stile di casa *(m)*
Pt estilo da casa *(m)*

huecograbado *(m) (n)* Es
De Kupfertiefdruck *(m)*
En photogravure
Fr héliogravure *(f)*
It fotoincisione *(f)*
Pt fotogravura *(f)*

hule *(m) n* Es
De Wachstuch *(n)*
En American cloth
Fr moleskine *(f)*
It tela cerata *(f)*
Pt pano americano *(m)*

hyphen *n* En
De Bindestrich *(m)*
Es guión *(m)*
Fr trait d'union *(m)*
It trattino di unione *(m)*
Pt traço de união *(m)*

hyphenate *vb* En
De trennen
Es separar con guión
Fr mettre un trait d'union
It legare con trattino
Pt pôr um traço de união

hyphenation *n* En
De Trennung *(f)*
Es separación con guiones *(f)*
Fr coupure *(f)*
It legatura con trattino *(f)*
Pt colocação de um traço de união *(f)*

hyphenation program
Am
De Trennungs-
Programm (n)
En hyphenation
programme
Es programa de
separación con
guiones (m)
Fr programme de
division automatique
(f)
It programma di
legatura con trattino
(m)
Pt programa de
hifenação (m)

**hyphenation
programme** En
Am hyphenation program
De Trennungs-
Programm (n)
Es programa de
separación con
guiones (m)
Fr programme de
division automatique
(f)
It programma di
legatura con trattino
(m)
Pt programa de
hifenação (m)

hyphenation rules En
De Trennungsregelb (pl)
Es normas de
separación con
guiones (f pl)
Fr règles de coupure (f
pl)
It regole di legatura con
trattino (f pl)
Pt regras de hifenação (f
pl)

I

ideogram n En
De Begriffszeichen (n)
Es ideograma (m)
Fr idéogramme (m)
It ideogramma (m)
Pt ideograma (m)

ideograma (m) n Es, Pt
De Begriffszeichen (n)
En ideogram
Fr idéogramme (m)
It ideogramma (m)

ideogramma (m) n It
De Begriffszeichen (n)
En ideogram
Es ideograma (m)
Fr idéogramme (m)
Pt ideograma (m)

idéogramme (m) n Fr
De Begriffszeichen (n)
En ideogram
Es ideograma (m)
It ideogramma (m)
Pt ideograma (m)

idle time En
De Leerlaufzeit (f)
Es tiempo de reposo (m)
Fr temps mort (m)
It tempo di
funzionamento a
vuoto (m)
Pt tempo morto (m)

igual tamaño Es
De gleichgroβ
En same size (s/s)
Fr format identique
It stessa dimensione
Pt mesmo tamanho

illumination n En
De Illuminierung (f)
Es iluminación (f)
Fr enluminure (f)
It illuminazione (f)
Pt iluminura (f)

illuminator n En
De Kolorierer (m)
Es iluminador (m)
Fr enlumineur (m)
It illuminatore (m)
Pt iluminador (m)

illuminatore (m) n It
De Kolorierer (m)
En illuminator
Es iluminador (m)
Fr enlumineur (m)
Pt iluminador (m)

illuminazione (f) n It
De Illuminierung (f)
En illumination

Es iluminación (f)
Fr enluminure (f)
Pt iluminura (f)

Illuminierung (f) n De
En illumination
Es iluminación (f)
Fr enluminure (f)
It illuminazione (f)
Pt iluminura (f)

illustrare vb It
De illustrieren
En illustrate
Es ilustrar
Fr illustrer
Pt ilustrar

illustrate vb En
De illustrieren
Es ilustrar
Fr illustrer
It illustrare
Pt ilustrar

illustrated book En
De illustriertes Buch (n)
Es libro ilustrado (m)
Fr livre illustré (m)
It libro illustrato (m)
Pt livro ilustrado (m)

illustrateur (m) n Fr
De Illustrator (m)
En illustrator
Es ilustrador (m)
It illustratore (m)
Pt ilustrador (m)

illustration n En; Fr (f)
De Illustration (f)
Es ilustración (f)
It illustrazione (f)
Pt ilustração (f)

Illustration (f) n De
En illustration
Es ilustración (f)
Fr illustration (f)
It illustrazione (f)
Pt ilustração (f)

**illustration de la
jaquette** (f) Fr
De Umschlag-
Satzmontage (f)
En jacket artwork
Es trabajo artistíco de la
sobrecubierta (m)

It menabò per
sovracopertina (m)
Pt arte da sobrecapa
(m)

illustration double ton
(f) Fr
De Zweifarbenillustration
(f)
En duotone illustration
Es ilustración en
bicromía (f)
It illustrazione bicolore
(f)
Pt ilustração
bicromática (f)

illustration en couleurs
(f) Fr
Am color illustration
De Farbillustration (f)
En colour illustration
Es ilustración en color (f)
It illustrazione a colori
(f)
Pt ilustração a cores (f)

**illustration en noir et
blanc** (f) Fr
De Schwarzweis-
illustration (f)
En black-and-white
illustration
Es ilustración en blanco
y negro (f)
It illustrazione in bianco
e nero (f)
Pt ilustração a branco e
negro (f)

**illustration en tous les
couleurs** (f) Fr
Am full-color illustration
De Vierfarbillustration (f)
En full-colour illustration
Es ilustración a todo
color (f)
It illustrazione a tutti
colori (f)
Pt ilustração a toda a
cor (f)

**illustration
monochrome** (f) Fr
De einfarbige illustration
(f)
En monochrome
illustration
Es ilustración
monocroma (f)
It illustrazione
monocromatica (f)

Pt ilustração
monocrómica *(f)*

**Illustrations-
druckpapier** *(m) n*
De
En super-calendered
paper
Es papel
supercalandrado *(m)*
Fr papier supercalandré
(m)
It carta
supercalandrata *(f)*
Pt papel
supercalandrado *(m)*

illustrator *n* En
De Illustrator *(m)*
Es ilustrador *(m)*
Fr illustrateur *(m)*
It illustratore *(m)*
Pt ilustrador *(m)*

Illustrator *(m) n* De
En illustrator
Es ilustrador *(m)*
Fr illustrateur *(m)*
It illustratore *(m)*
Pt ilustrador *(m)*

illustratore *(m) n* It
De Illustrator *(m)*
En illustrator
Es ilustrador *(m)*
Fr illustrateur *(m)*
Pt ilustrador *(m)*

illustrazione *(f) n* It
De Illustration *(f)*
En illustration
Es ilustración *(f)*
Fr illustration *(f)*
Pt ilustração *(f)*

illustrazione a colori *(f)*
It
Am color illustration
De Farbillustration *(f)*
En colour illustration
Es ilustración en color *(f)*
Fr illustration en
couleurs *(f)*
Pt ilustração a cores *(f)*

**illustrazione a tutti
colori** *(f)* It
Am full-color illustration
De Vierfarbillustration *(f)*
En full-colour illustration

Es ilustración a todo
color *(f)*
Fr illustration en tous
les couleurs *(f)*
Pt ilustração a toda a
cor *(f)*

illustrazione bicolore *(f)*
It
De Zweifarbenillustration
(f)
En duotone illustration
Es ilustración en
bicromía *(f)*
Fr illustration double
ton *(f)*
Pt ilustração
bicromática *(f)*

**illustrazione in bianco e
nero** *(f)* It
De Schwarzweiß-
illustration *(f)*
En black-and-white
illustration
Es ilustración en blanco
y negro *(f)*
Fr illustration en noir et
blanc *(f)*
Pt ilustração a branco e
negro *(f)*

**illustrazione
monocromatica** *(f)*
It
De einfarbige illustration
(f)
En monochrome
illustration
Es ilustración
monocroma *(f)*
Fr illustration
monochrome *(f)*
Pt ilustração
monocrómica *(f)*

illustrer *vb* Fr
De illustrieren
En illustrate
Es ilustrar
It illustrare
Pt ilustrar

illustrieren *vb* De
En illustrate
Es ilustrar
Fr illustrer
It illustrare
Pt ilustrar

illustriertes Buch *(n)* De
En illustrated book
Es libro ilustrado *(m)*
Fr livre illustré *(m)*
It libro illustrato *(m)*
Pt livro ilustrado *(m)*

iluminación *(f) n* Es
De Illuminierung *(f)*
En illumination
Fr enluminure *(f)*
It illuminazione *(f)*
Pt iluminura *(f)*

iluminador *(m) n* Es, Pt
De Kolorierer *(m)*
En illuminator
Fr enlumineur *(m)*
It illuminatore *(m)*

iluminura *(f) n* Pt
De Illuminierung *(f)*
En illumination
Es iluminación *(f)*
Fr enluminure *(f)*
It illuminazione *(f)*

ilustração *(f) n* Pt
De Illustration *(f)*
En illustration
Es ilustración *(f)*
Fr illustration *(f)*
It illustrazione *(f)*

**ilustração a branco e
negro** *(f)* Pt
De Schwarzweiß-
illustration *(f)*
En black-and-white
illustration
Es ilustración en blanco
y negro *(f)*
Fr illustration en noir et
blanc *(f)*
It illustrazione in bianco
e nero *(f)*

ilustração a cores *(f)* Pt
Am color illustration
De Farbillustration *(f)*
En colour illustration
Es ilustración en color *(f)*
Fr illustration en
couleurs *(f)*
It illustrazione a colori
(f)

ilustração a toda a cor
(f) Pt
Am full-color illustration
De Vierfarbillustration *(f)*

En full-colour illustration
Es ilustración a todo
color *(f)*
Fr illustration en tous
les couleurs *(f)*
It illustrazione a tutti
colori *(f)*

ilustração bicromática
(f) Pt
De Zweifarbenillustration
(f)
En duotone illustration
Es ilustración en
bicromía *(f)*
Fr illustration double
ton *(f)*
It illustrazione bicolore
(f)

ilustração monocrómica
(f) Pt
De einfarbige illustration
(f)
En monochrome
illustration
Es ilustración
monocroma *(f)*
Fr illustration
monochrome *(f)*
It illustrazione
monocromatica *(f)*

ilustración *(f) n* Es
De Illustration *(f)*
En illustration
Fr illustration *(f)*
It illustrazione *(f)*
Pt ilustração *(f)*

ilustración a todo color
(f) Es
Am full-color illustration
De Vierfarbillustration *(f)*
En full-colour illustration
Fr illustration en tous
les couleurs *(f)*
It illustrazione a tutti
colori *(f)*
Pt ilustração a toda a
cor *(f)*

ilustración en bicromía
(f) Es
De Zweifarbenillustration
(f)
En duotone illustration
Fr illustration double
ton *(f)*
It illustrazione bicolore
(f)

Pt ilustração
bicromática *(f)*

**ilustración en blanco y
negro** *(f)* Es
De Schwarzweiß-
illustration *(f)*
En black-and-white
illustration
Fr illustration en noir et
blanc *(f)*
It illustrazione in bianco
e nero *(f)*
Pt ilustração a branco e
negro *(f)*

ilustración en color *(f)* Es
Am color illustration
De Farbillustration *(f)*
En colour illustration
Fr illustration en
couleurs *(f)*
It illustrazione a colori
(f)
Pt ilustração a cores *(f)*

ilustración monocroma
(f) Es
De einfarbige illustration
(f)
En monochrome
illustration
Fr illustration
monochrome *(f)*
It illustrazione
monocromatica *(f)*
Pt ilustração
monocrómica *(f)*

ilustrador *(m)* n Es, Pt
De Illustrator *(m)*
En illustrator
Fr illustrateur *(m)*
It illustratore *(m)*

ilustrar *vb* Es, Pt
De illustrieren
En illustrate
Fr illustrer
It illustrare

image *(f)* n En; Fr *(f)*
De Bild *(n)*
Es imagen *(f)*
It figura; immagine *(f)*
Pt imagem *(f)*

image fantôme *(f)* Fr
De Durchscheinbild *(n)*
En ghosting

Es mancha de reflexión
(f)
It falsa immagine *(f)*
Pt fantasma *(m)*

imagem *(f)* n Pt
De Bild *(n)*
En image; picture
Es imagen *(f)*
Fr dessin; image *(m f)*
It immagine; figura *(f)*

**imagem de reserva de
zinco** *(f)* Pt
De Zinkdruck *(m)*
En zinc print
Es imagen de reserva
formada en cinc *(f)*
Fr offset *(m)*
It stampa in zinco *(f)*

imagen *(f)* n Es
De Bild *(n)*
En image; picture
Fr dessin; image *(m f)*
It immagine; figura *(f)*
Pt imagem *(f)*

**imagen de reserva
formada en cinc** *(f)*
Es
De Zinkdruck *(m)*
En zinc print
Fr offset *(m)*
It stampa in zinco *(f)*
Pt imagem de reserva
de zinco *(f)*

imballare *vb* It
De packen
En pack
Es embalar
Fr emballer
Pt embalar

imbianchimento *(m)* n It
De Bleichen *(n)*
En bleaching
Es blanqueo *(m)*
Fr blanchiment *(m)*
Pt branqueamento *(m)*

imbrattacarte *(m)* n It
De Mietschreiber *(m)*
En hack writer
Es escritor mercenario
(m)
Fr écrivassier *(m)*
Pt escritor comercial
(m)

immagazzinaggio *(m)* n
It
De Speicherung *(f)*
En storage
Es almacenamiento *(m)*
Fr stockage *(m)*
Pt armazenamento *(m)*

immagazzinare *vb* It
De lagern
En store
Es almacenar
Fr entreposer
Pt armazenar

immagine *(f)* n It
De Bild *(n)*
En image; picture
Es imagen *(f)*
Fr dessin; image *(m f)*
Pt imagem *(f)*

impaccare *vb* It
De verpacken
En package
Es empaquetar
Fr empaqueter
Pt empacotar

impaginare *vb* It
De paginieren
En paginate
Es paginar
Fr paginer
Pt paginar

impaginatura *(f)* n It
De Satzumbruch *(m)*
En make-up
Es compaginación *(f)*
Fr montage *(m)*
Pt compaginação *(f)*

impaginazione *(f)* n It
De Paginierung *(f)*
En pagination
Es paginación *(f)*
Fr pagination *(f)*
Pt paginação *(f)*

imperfección *(f)* n Es
De Fehler *(m)*
En blemish
Fr défaut *(m)*
It imperfezione *(f)*
Pt mancha *(f)*

imperfezione *(f)* n It
De Fehler *(m)*
En blemish

Es imperfección *(f)*
Fr défaut *(m)*
Pt mancha *(f)*

importância global *(f)* Pt
De Pauschalbetrag *(m)*
En lump sum
Es suma total *(f)*
Fr somme globale *(f)*
It somma globale *(f)*

imposição *(f)* n Pt
De Montage *(f)*
En imposition
Es imposición *(f)*
Fr mise en pages *(f)*
It imposizione *(f)*

imposición *(f)* n Es
De Montage *(f)*
En imposition
Fr mise en pages *(f)*
It imposizione *(f)*
Pt imposição *(f)*

**imposición e impresión
a blanco y vuelta** *(f)*
Es
De Halbbogendruck *(m)*
En half-sheet work
Fr imposition en
demi-feuille *(f)*
It lavoro di mezza
pagina *(f)*
Pt trabalho a meia folha
(m)

imposing surface En
De Schließplatte *(f)*
Es superficie de
imposición *(f)*
Fr marbre de serrage
(m)
It banco tipografico *(m)*
Pt superfície de
imposição *(f)*

imposition n En
De Montage *(f)*
Es imposición *(f)*
Fr mise en pages *(f)*
It imposizione *(f)*
Pt imposição *(f)*

**imposition en
demi-feuille** *(f)* Fr
De Halbbogendruck *(m)*
En half-sheet work
Es imposición e
impresión a blanco y
vuelta *(f)*

It lavoro di mezza
pagina *(f)*
Pt trabalho a meia folha
(m)

imposizione *(f) n* It
De Montage *(f)*
En imposition
Es imposición *(f)*
Fr mise en pages *(f)*
Pt imposição *(f)*

**imposta sul valore
aggiunto (IVA)** *(f)* It
De Mehrwertsteuer
(Mwst) *(f)*
En value-added tax (VAT)
Es impuesto sobre el
valor añadido *(m)*
Fr taxe sur la valeur
ajoutée (TVA) *(f)*
Pt imposto sobre valor
aduzido *(m)*

**imposto sobre valor
aduzido** *(m)* Pt
De Mehrwertsteuer
(Mwst) *(f)*
En value-added tax (VAT)
Es impuesto sobre el
valor añadido *(m)*
Fr taxe sur la valeur
ajoutée (TVA) *(f)*
It imposta sul valore
aggiunto (IVA) *(f)*

imprensa *(f) n* Pt
De Presse *(f)*
En press (journalism)
Es prensa *(f)*
Fr presse *(f)*
It stampa *(f)*

imprensa universitária
(f) Pt
De Universitäts-
Druckerei *(f)*
En university press
Es prensa universitaria
(f)
Fr presse universitaire
(f)
It stampa universitaria
(f)

imprenta (arte) *(f) n* Es
De Druckkunst *(f)*
En printing
Fr imprimerie (art) *(f)*
It stampatura *(f)*
Pt impressão *(f)*

imprenta (casa) *(f) n* Es
De Druckerei *(f)*
En printing house
Fr imprimerie (maison)
(f)
It stabilimento
tipografico *(m)*
Pt casa tipográfica *(f)*

impresión *(f) n* Es
De Druck *(m)*
En print
Fr imprimé *(m)*
It impressione *(f)*
Pt estampa *(f)*

impresión bicolor *(f)* Es
Am two-color printing
De Zweifarbendruck *(m)*
En two-colour printing
Fr bichromie *(f)*
It stampa a due colori
(f)
Pt impressão a duas
cores *(f)*

**impresión con grabados
en hueco** *(f)* Es
De Tiefdruck *(m)*
En intaglio printing
Fr impression en creux
(f)
It stampa ad intaglio *(f)*
Pt impressão intaglio *(f)*

impresión de hojas *(f)* Es
De Bogendruck *(m)*
En sheet-fed printing
Fr impression à
machine à feuilles *(f)*
It stampa a fogli *(f)*
Pt impressão de folhas
(f)

impresión directa *(f)* Es
De Direktdruck *(m)*
En direct impression
Fr impression directe *(f)*
It stampa diretta *(f)*
Pt impressão directa *(f)*

impresión en hueco *(f)*
Es
De Kupferdruck *(m)*
En copper-plate printing
Fr gravure sur cuivre *(f)*
It stampa a calcografia
(f)
Pt impressão com
chapa de cobre *(f)*

impresión en relieve *(f)*
Es
De Reliefdruck *(m)*
En relief printing
Fr impression en relief
(f)
It stampa in rilievo *(f)*
Pt impressão em relevo
(f)

impresión indirecta *(f)*
Es
De indirekter Hochdruck
(m)
En indirect printing
Fr tirage indirect *(m)*
It stampa indiretta *(f)*
Pt impressão indirecta
(f)

impresión planográfica
(f) Es
De Flachdruck *(m)*
En planographic printing
Fr impression à plat *(f)*
It stampa comune *(f)*
Pt impressão
planográfica *(f)*

impresión reprográfica
(f) Es
De Reprographiedruck
(m)
En reprographic printing
Fr reprographie *(f)*
It stampa reprografica
(f)
Pt impressão
reprográfica *(f)*

impresión serigráfica *(f)*
Es
De Siebdruck *(m)*
En silk-screen printing
Fr sérigraphie *(f)*
It stampa serigrafica *(f)*
Pt serigrafia *(f)*

impresión termográfica
(f) Es
De Thermodruck *(m)*
En thermographic
printing
Fr thermogravure *(f)*
It stampa termografica
(f)
Pt impressão
termográfica *(f)*

impresión tipográfica *(f)*
Es
De Buchdruck *(m)*

En letterpress printing
Fr impression
typographique *(f)*
It stampa tipografica *(f)*
Pt impressão tipográfica
(f)

**impresión
tridimensional** *(f)*
Es
De dreidimensionaler
Druck *(m)*
En three-dimensional
printing
Fr impression
tridimensionnelle *(f)*
It stampa
tridimensionale *(f)*
Pt impressão a três
dimensões *(f)*

impresor *(m) n* Es
De Drucker *(m)*
En printer
Fr imprimeur *(m)*
It stampatore *(m)*
Pt tipógrafo *(m)*

impresora de líneas *(f)*
Es
De Zeilendrucker *(m)*
En line printer
Fr imprimante ligne par
ligne *(f)*
It stampatrice per righe
(f)
Pt impressora de linha
(f)

impresor a remiendos
(m) Es
De Akzidenzdrucker *(m)*
En jobbing printer
Fr imprimeur de travaux
de ville *(m)*
It stampatore
comerciale *(m)*
Pt impressor comercial
(m)

impresora xerográphica
(f) Es
De xerographischer
Drucker *(m)*
En xerographic printer
Fr imprimante
xérographique *(f)*
It stampatrice
xerografica *(f)*
Pt impressora
xerográfica *(f)*

impressa editoriale *(f)* It
De Impressum *(n)*
En imprint
Es pie de imprenta *(m)*
Fr marque d'éditeur *(f)*
Pt nome do editor *(m)*

impressão *(f)* n Pt
De Druckkunst *(f)*
En printing
Es imprenta (arte) *(f)*
Fr imprimerie (art) *(f)*
It stampatura *(f)*

impressão a duas cores
(f) Pt
Am two-color printing
De Zweifarbendruck *(m)*
En two-colour printing
Es impresión bicolor *(f)*
Fr bichromie *(f)*
It stampa a due colori
(f)

impressão a quatro
cores *(f)* Pt
Am four-color printing
De Vierfarbdruck *(m)*
En four-colour printing
Es cuatricromía *(f)*
Fr quadrichromie *(f)*
It stampa a quattro
colori *(f)*

impressão a três cores
(f) Pt
Am three-color printing
De Dreifarbendruck *(m)*
En three-colour printing
Es tricromía *(f)*
Fr trichromie *(f)*
It stampa a tre colori *(f)*

impressão a três
dimensões *(f)* Pt
De dreidimensionaler
Druck *(m)*
En three-dimensional
printing
Es impresión
tridimensional *(f)*
Fr impression
tridimensionnelle *(f)*
It stampa
tridimensionale *(f)*

impressão com chapa
de cobre *(f)* Pt
De Kupferdruck *(m)*
En copper-plate printing
Es impresión en hueco
(f)

Fr gravure sur cuivre *(f)*
It stampa a calcografia
(f)

impressão de folhas *(f)*
Pt
De Bogendruck *(m)*
En sheet-fed printing
Es impresión de hojas *(f)*
Fr impression à
machine à feuilles *(f)*
It stampa a fogli *(f)*

impressão directa *(f)* Pt
De Direktdruck *(m)*
En direct impression
Es impresión directa *(f)*
Fr impression directe *(f)*
It stampa diretta *(f)*

impressão em positivo
directo *(f)* Pt
De Ausdruck *(m)*
En printout
Es vaciado a la
impresora *(m)*
Fr sortie d'imprimante
(f)
It printout *(m)*

impressão em relevo *(f)*
Pt
De Reliefdruck *(m)*
En relief printing
Es impresión en relieve
(f)
Fr impression en relief
(f)
It stampa in rilievo *(f)*

impressão flexográfica
(f) Pt
De Flexodruck *(m)*
En flexographic printing
Es flexografía *(f)*
Fr flexographie *(f)*
It stampa flessografica
(f)

impressão indirecta *(f)*
Pt
De indirekter Hochdruck
(m)
En indirect printing
Es impresión indirecta
(f)
Fr tirage indirect *(m)*
It stampa indiretta *(f)*

impressão intaglio *(f)* Pt
De Tiefdruck *(m)*
En intaglio printing
Es impresión con
grabados en hueco
(f)
Fr impression en creux
(f)
It stampa ad intaglio *(f)*

impressão planográfica
(f) Pt
De Flachdruck *(m)*
En planographic printing
Es impresión
planográfica *(f)*
Fr impression à plat *(f)*
It stampa comune *(f)*

impressão reprográfica
(f) Pt
De Reprographiedruck
(m)
En reprographic printing
Es impresión
reprográfica *(f)*
Fr reprographie *(f)*
It stampa reprografica
(f)

impressão roto-offset *(f)*
Pt
De Rollenoffsetdruck *(m)*
En web-offset printing
Es roto-offset *(m)*
Fr impression offset en
continu *(f)*
It stampa offset dal
rotolo *(f)*

impressão simultânea
de ambos lados *(f)*
Pt
De Schön- und
Widerdruck *(m)*
En perfecting
Es retiración *(f)*
Fr retiration *(f)*
It stampa in volta *(f)*

impressão termográfica
(f) Pt
De Thermodruck *(m)*
En thermographic
printing
Es impresión
termográfica *(f)*
Fr thermogravure *(f)*
It stampa termografica
(f)

impressão tipográfica *(f)*
Pt
De Buchdruck *(m)*
En letterpress printing
Es impresión tipográfica
(f)
Fr impression
typographique *(f)*
It stampa tipografica *(f)*

impression n En
De Auflage *(f)*
Es tirada *(f)*
Fr tirage *(m)*
It tiratura *(f)*
Pt tiragem *(m)*

impression à machine à
feuilles *(f)* Fr
De Bogendruck *(m)*
En sheet-fed printing
Es impresión de hojas *(f)*
It stampa a fogli *(f)*
Pt impressão de folhas
(f)

impression à plat *(f)* Fr
De Flachdruck *(m)*
En planographic printing
Es impresión
planográfica *(f)*
It stampa comune *(f)*
Pt impressão
planográfica *(f)*

impression au jet
d'encre *(f)* Fr
De Spritzdruckverfahren
(n)
En jet printing method
Es método de impresión
por chorro *(m)*
It metodo di stampa a
getto *(m)*
Pt método de
impressão a jacto *(m)*

impression directe *(f)* Fr
De Direktdruck *(m)*
En direct impression
Es impresión directa *(f)*
It stampa diretta *(f)*
Pt impressão directa *(f)*

impressione *(f)* n It
De Druck *(m)*
En print
Es impresión *(f)*
Fr imprimé *(m)*
Pt estampa *(f)*

impression en creux *(f)*
Fr
De Tiefdruck *(m)*
En intaglio printing
Es impresión con
grabados en hueco
(f)
It stampa ad intaglio *(f)*
Pt impressão intaglio *(f)*

impression en relief *(f)*
Fr
De Reliefdruck *(m)*
En relief printing
Es impresión en relieve
(f)
It stampa in rilievo *(f)*
Pt impressão em relevo
(f)

**impression offset en
continu** *(f)* Fr
De Rollenoffsetdruck *(m)*
En web-offset printing
Es roto-offset *(m)*
It stampa offset dal
rotolo *(f)*
Pt impressão roto-offset
(f)

**impression
tridimensionnelle**
(f) Fr
De dreidimensionaler
Druck *(m)*
En three-dimensional
printing
Es impresión
tridimensional *(f)*
It stampa
tridimensionale *(f)*
Pt impressão a três
dimensões *(f)*

**impression
typographique** *(f)*
Fr
De Buchdruck *(m)*
En letterpress printing
Es impresión tipográfica
(f)
It stampa tipografica *(f)*
Pt impressão tipográfica
(f)

impresso e publicado Pt
De gedruckt
En in print
Es publicado
Fr en impression
It in corso di stampa

impressora de linha *(f)*
Pt
De Zeilendrucker *(m)*
En line printer
Es impresora de líneas
(f)
Fr imprimante ligne par
ligne *(f)*
It stampatrice per righe
(f)

impressora xerográfica
(f) Pt
De xerographischer
Drucker *(m)*
En xerographic printer
Es impresora
xerográfica *(f)*
Fr imprimante
xérographique *(f)*
It stampatrice
xerografica *(f)*

impressor comercial *(m)*
Pt
De Akzidenzdrucker *(m)*
En jobbing printer
Es impresor a
remiendos *(m)*
Fr imprimeur de travaux
de ville *(m)*
It stampatore
comerciale *(m)*

Impressum *(n)* n De
En imprint
Es pie de imprenta *(m)*
Fr marque d'éditeur *(f)*
It impressa editoriale *(f)*
Pt nome do editor *(m)*

Impressums-Daten *(pl)*
n De
En imprint data
Es datos a pie de
imprenta *(m pl)*
Fr indications d'éditeur
et d'imprimeur *(f pl)*
It data d'impressa *(f)*
Pt dados de impressão
(m pl)

imprimante à stylets *(f)*
Fr
De Feder *(f)*
En stylus
Es estilete *(m)*
It stilo *(m)*
Pt estilete *(m)*

**imprimante ligne par
ligne** *(f)* Fr
De Zeilendrucker *(m)*
En line printer
Es impresora de líneas
(f)
It stampatrice per righe
(f)
Pt impressora de linha
(f)

**imprimante
xérographique** *(f)*
Fr
De xerographischer
Drucker *(m)*
En xerographic printer
Es impresora
xerográfica *(f)*
It stampatrice
xerografica *(f)*
Pt impressora
xerográfica *(f)*

imprimé *(m)* n Fr
De Druck *(m)*
En print
Es impresión *(f)*
It impressione *(f)*
Pt estampa *(f)*

imprimer vb Fr
De drucken
En print
Es imprimir
It stampare
(stampatura)
Pt imprimir

imprimerie (art) *(f)* n Fr
De Druckkunst *(f)*
En printing
Es imprenta (arte) *(f)*
It stampatura *(f)*
Pt impressão *(f)*

imprimerie (maison) *(f)* n
Fr
De Druckerei *(f)*
En printing house
Es imprenta (casa) *(f)*
It stabilimento
tipografico *(m)*
Pt casa tipográfica *(f)*

imprimeur *(m)* n Fr
De Drucker *(m)*
En printer
Es impresor *(m)*
It stampatore *(m)*
Pt tipógrafo *(m)*

**imprimeur de travaux
de ville** *(m)* Fr
De Akzidenzdrucker *(m)*
En jobbing printer
Es impresor a
remiendos *(m)*
It stampatore
comerciale *(m)*
Pt impressor comercial
(m)

imprimeuse *(f)* n Fr
De Tiegel *(m)*
En platen press
Es minerva *(f)*
It macchina da stampa
a platina *(f)*
Pt minerva *(f)*

imprimir vb Es, Pt
De drucken
En print
Fr imprimer
It stampare
(stampatura)

imprimir (por ordenador)
vb Es
De ausdrucken
En print out
Fr sortir
It stampare (per
elaboratore)
Pt imprimir em positivo
directo

**imprimir em positivo
directo** Pt
De ausdrucken
En print out
Es imprimir (por
ordenador)
Fr sortir
It stampare (per
elaboratore)

**imprimir una
super-tiratura** *(f)* It
De fortdrucken
En run on (printing)
Es proseguir la tirada
Fr faire des tirages
supplémentaires
Pt continuar a imprimir

imprint n En
De Impressum *(n)*
Es pie de imprenta *(m)*
Fr marque d'éditeur *(f)*
It impressa editoriale *(f)*
Pt nome do editor *(m)*

imprint data En
De Impressums-Daten
(pl)
Es datos a pie de
imprenta (m pl)
Fr indications d'editeur
et d'imprimeur (f pl)
It data d'impressa (f)
Pt dados de impressão
(m pl)

**impuesto sobre el valor
añadido** (m) Es
De Mehrwertsteuer
(Mwst) (f)
En value-added tax (VAT)
Fr taxe sur la valeur
ajoutée (TVA) (f)
It imposta sul valore
aggiunto (IVA) (f)
Pt imposto sobre valor
aduzido (m)

imputaggio (m) n It
De Verschnüren (n)
En cording
Es encordonado (m)
Fr nerf (m)
Pt encordoamento (m)

im Transit befindlich De
En in transit
Es en tránsito
Fr en transit
It in transito
Pt em trânsito

inalterabilidade à luz (f)
Pt
De Lichtbeständigkeit (f)
En fastness (to light)
Es solidez a la luz (f)
Fr solidité à la lumière
(f)
It stabilità alla luce (f)

in Arbeit befindlich De
En work-in-progress
Es trabajo en ejecución
(m)
Fr travail en cours (m)
It lavoro in corso (m)
Pt progresso de
adaptação ao
trabalho (m)

in Auftrag geben De
En commission
Es encargar
Fr commander
It commissionare
Pt encomendar

inchiostrazione (f) n It
De Farbauftrag (m)
En inking
Es entintaje (f)
Fr encrage (m)
Pt tintura (f)

inchiostri metallici (m
pl) It
De Bronzedrucktinten
(pl)
En metallic inks
Es tintas metálicas (f pl)
Fr encres métalliques (f
pl)
Pt tintas metálicas (f pl)

inchiostro aderente (m)
It
De gebundene Farbe (f)
En bonded ink
Es tinta adherida (f)
Fr encre liée (f)
Pt tinta aglutinada (f)

inchiostro all'alluminio
(m) It
Am aluminum ink
De Aluminiumfarbe (f)
En aluminium ink
Es tinta plateada (f)
Fr encre métallique (f)
Pt tinta de alumínio (f)

inchiostro all'anilina (m)
It
De Anilinfarbe (f)
En aniline ink
Es tinta de anilina (f)
Fr encre à l'aniline (f)
Pt tinta de anilina (f)

inchiostro da stampa
(m) It
De Druckfarbe (f)
En ink (printer's)
Es tinta de imprenta (f)
Fr encre d'impression
(f)
Pt tinta de impressão (f)

inchiostro magnetico
(m) It
De Magnettinte (f)
En magnetic ink
Es tinta magnética (f)
Fr encre magnétique (f)
Pt tinta magnética (f)

**inchiostro per
goffratura** (m) It
De Prägedruckfarbe (f)
En embossing ink
Es tinta de estampación
(f)
Fr encre à gaufrer (f)
Pt tinta de estampagem
(f)

incidere vb It
De gravieren
En engrave
Es grabar
Fr graver
Pt gravar

incisione (f) n It
De Gravur (f)
En engraving (print)
Es grabado (estampa)
(m)
Fr estampe (f)
Pt gravura (estampa) (f)

incisione a cera (f) It
De Wachsgravieren (n)
En wax engraving
Es cerotipia (f)
Fr électrotype par
dessin sur métal
paraffiné (m)
Pt cerotipia (f)

incisione all'acquaforte
(f) It
De Radierung (f)
En etching
Es grabado al agua
fuerte (m)
Fr gravure à l'eau forte
(f)
Pt gravura a áqua-forte
(f)

incisione a punti (f) It
De Punktätzung (f)
En dot etching
Es reducción de los
puntos (f)
Fr morsure par
couverture (f)
Pt redução dos pontos
reticulares (f)

incisione elettronica (f)
It
De elektronische
Gravierung (f)
En electronic engraving
Es grabado electrónico
(m)

Fr gravure électronique
(f)
Pt gravura electrónica
(f)

incisione in linoleum (f)
It
De Linolschnitt (m)
En lino cut
Es grabado de linóleo
(m)
Fr gravure sur linoléum
(f)
Pt gravura em linóleo (f)

incisione senza polvere
(f) It
De Einstufenätzverfahren
(n)
En powderless etching
Es grabado rápido (m)
Fr gravure sans poudre
(f)
Pt gravura sem pó (f)

incisione su legno (m) It
De Xylographie (f)
En wood engraving
Es xilografía (f)
Fr gravure sur bois (f)
Pt xilografia (f)

incluir vb Pt
De montieren
En strip in
Es montar inserciones
Fr raccorder
It giuntare

incollare vb It
De klebeumbrechen
En paste up
Es montar
Fr encoller
Pt montar

incollatura (f) n It
De Klebeumbruch (m)
En paste-up
Es montaje (m)
Fr collage (m)
Pt montagem (f)

incorniciatura (f) n It
De Einsetzen (n)
En insetting
Es encuadre (m)
Fr mise en place (f)
Pt intercalagem (f)

in corsivo It
De kursiv gedruckt
En in italics
Es en cursiva
Fr en italiques
Pt em itálico

in corso di stampa It
De gedruckt
En in print
Es publicado
Fr en impression
Pt impresso e publicado

incumplimiento de contrato (m) Es
De Vertragsbruch (m)
En breach of contract
Fr rupture de contrat (f)
It violazione di contratto (f)
Pt quebra de contrato (f)

indemnité de chômage (f) Fr
De Entlassungsgeld (n)
En redundancy payment
Es pago redundante (m)
It pagamento di ridondanza (m)
Pt pagamento de redundância (m)

indent vb En
De einrücken
Es sangrar
Fr renforcer
It dentellare
Pt abrir parágrafo

indented adj En
De eingerückt
Es sangrado
Fr dentelé
It dentellato
Pt dentada

indentro del paragrafo (m) It
De Paragrapheinrückung (f)
En paragraph indent
Es sangría de párrafo (f)
Fr renfoncé d'alinéa (m)
Pt reentrância de parágrafo (f)

indépendant adj Fr
De freiberuflich
En freelance
Es independiente

It indipendente
Pt independente

independente adj Pt
De freiberuflich
En freelance
Es independiente
Fr indépendant
It indipendente

independiente adj Es
De freiberuflich
En freelance
Fr indépendant
It indipendente
Pt independente

index n En; Fr (m)
De Index (m)
Es índice (m)
It indice (m)
Pt índice (m)

Index (m) n De
En index
Es índice (m)
Fr index (m)
It indice (m)
Pt índice (m)

indexador (m) n Es
De Indexierer (m)
En indexer
Fr auteur de l'index (m)
It compilatore di un indice (m)
Pt indiciador (m)

index à onglets (m) Fr
De Daumenindex (m)
En thumb index
Es índice recortado (m)
It indice a rubrica (m)
Pt índice com letras salientes na borda da página (m)

index à touche (m) Fr
De Buchstabenindex (m)
En tab index
Es índice de pestañas (m)
It indice a striscettine (m)
Pt índice de pestanas (m)

index cards En
De Karteikarten (pl)

Es tarjetas de ficheros (f pl)
Fr fiches (f pl)
It schede (f pl)
Pt fichas de arquivo (f pl)

indexer n En
De Indexierer (m)
Es indexador (m)
Fr auteur de l'index (m)
It compilatore di un indice (m)
Pt indiciador (m)

Indexierer (m) n De
En indexer
Es indexador (m)
Fr auteur de l'index (m)
It compilatore di un indice (m)
Pt indiciador (m)

indications d'editeur et d'imprimeur (f pl) Fr
De Impressums-Daten (pl)
En imprint data
Es datos a pie de imprenta (m pl)
It data d'impressa (f)
Pt dados de impressão (m pl)

indice (m) n It
De Index (m)
En index
Es índice (m)
Fr index (m)
Pt índice (m)

índice (m) n Es, Pt
De Index (m)
En index
Fr index (m)
It indice (m)

indice a rubrica (m) It
De Daumenindex (m)
En thumb index
Es índice recortado (m)
Fr index à onglets (m)
Pt índice com letras salientes na borda da página (m)

indice a striscettine (m) It
De Buchstabenindex (m)
En tab index

Es índice de pestañas (m)
Fr index à touche (m)
Pt índice de pestanas (m)

índice com letras salientes na borda da página (m) Pt
De Daumenindex (m)
En thumb index
Es índice recortado (m)
Fr index à onglets (m)
It indice a rubrica (m)

indice dei fotografi (m pl) It
De Dank für die Genehmigung von Photos (m)
En photo credits
Es fotocréditos (m pl)
Fr origine des photographies (f)
Pt fotocréditos (m pl)

índice de materias (m) Es
De Inhaltsverzeichnis (n)
En table of contents
Fr table des matières (f)
It sommario delle materie (m)
Pt índice dos assuntos (m)

índice de pestanas (m) Pt
De Buchstabenindex (m)
En tab index
Es índico de pestañas (m)
Fr index à touche (m)
It indice a striscettine (m)

índice de pestañas (m) Es
De Buchstabenindex (m)
En tab index
Fr index à touche (m)
It indice a striscettine (m)
Pt índice de pestanas (m)

índice dos assuntos (m) Pt
De Inhaltsverzeichnis (n)
En table of contents
Es índice de materias (m)

Fr table des matières *(f)*
It sommario delle
materie *(m)*

índice recortado *(m)* Es
De Daumenindex *(m)*
En thumb index
Fr index à onglets *(m)*
It indice a rubrica *(m)*
Pt índice com letras
salientes na borda da
página *(m)*

indiciador *(m)* n Pt
De Indexierer *(m)*
En indexer
Es indexador *(m)*
Fr auteur de l'index *(m)*
It compilatore di un
indice *(m)*

indipendente *adj* It
De freiberuflich
En freelance
Es independiente
Fr indépendant
Pt independente

indirect printing En
De indirekter Hochdruck
(m)
Es impresión indirecta
(f)
Fr tirage indirect *(m)*
It stampa indiretta *(f)*
Pt impressão indirecta
(f)

indirect process En
De indirektes Verfahren
(n)
Es tricromía de tramado
indirecto *(f)*
Fr procédé indirect *(m)*
It procedimento
indiretto *(m)*
Pt processo indirecto
(m)

indirekter Hochdruck
(m) De
En indirect printing
Es impresión indirecta
(f)
Fr tirage indirect *(m)*
It stampa indiretta *(f)*
Pt impressão indirecta
(f)

indirektes Verfahren *(n)*
De
En indirect process
Es tricromía de tramado
indirecto *(f)*
Fr procédé indirect *(m)*
It procedimento
indiretto *(m)*
Pt processo indirecto
(m)

indirizzo *(m)* n It
De Adresse *(f)*
En address (computer)
Es dirección *(f)*
Fr adresse *(f)*
Pt endereço *(m)*

in dodicesimo *(m)* It
De Duodezformat *(n)*
En duodecimo
Es dozavo *(m)*
Fr in-douze *(m)*
Pt duodécimo *(m)*

in-douze *(m)* n Fr
De Duodezformat *(n)*
En duodecimo
Es dozavo *(m)*
It in dodicesimo *(m)*
Pt duodécimo *(m)*

inertar nueva copia Es
De neuen Text einfügen
En insert new copy
Fr insérer nouveau texte
It inserire nuovo testo
Pt inserir novo texto

inferior characters En
De tiefstehende
Buchstaben *(pl)*
Es subíndices *(m pl)*
Fr petites lettres
inférieures *(f pl)*
It caratteri inferiori *(m
pl)*
Pt caracteres inferiores
(m pl)

informal usage En
De informeller Gebrauch
(m)
Es uso informal *(m)*
Fr usage familier *(m)*
It uso informale *(m)*
Pt utilização informal *(f)*

informar *vb* Es, Pt
De berichten
En report

Fr faire un reportage
It relazionare

information retrieval En
De Informationszugriff
(m)
Es recuperación de la
información *(f)*
Fr recherche de
l'information *(f)*
It recupero informazioni
(m)
Pt recuperação de
informação *(f)*

Informationszugriff *(m)*
n De
En information retrieval
Es recuperación de la
información *(f)*
Fr recherche de
l'information *(f)*
It recupero informazioni
(m)
Pt recuperação de
informação *(f)*

informe *(m)* n Es
De Bericht *(m)*
En report
Fr reportage *(m)*
It relazione *(f)*
Pt relatório *(m)*

informeller Gebrauch
(m) De
En informal usage
Es uso informal *(m)*
Fr usage familier *(m)*
It uso informale *(m)*
Pt utilização informal *(f)*

**infracção de um
copyright** *(f)* Pt
De Verletzung des
Copyright *(f)*
En infringement of
copyright
Es violación de los
derechos de autor *(f)*
Fr contrefaçon *(f)*
It violazione di
copyright *(f)*

**infringement of
copyright** En
De Verletzung des
Copyright *(f)*
Es violación de los
derechos de autor *(f)*
Fr contrefaçon *(f)*

It violazione di
copyright *(f)*
Pt infracção de um
copyright *(f)*

in full color Am
De in voller Farbe
En in full colour
Es a todo color
Fr en couleurs
It a colori
Pt a toda a cor

in full colour En
Am in full color
De in voller Farbe
Es a todo color
Fr en couleurs
It a colori
Pt a toda a cor

ingrandire *vb* It
De vergrößern
En enlarge
Es ampliar
Fr agrandir
Pt ampliar

ingrandito *adj* It
De vergrößert
En blown up
Es ampliado
Fr agrandi
Pt ampliado

ingranditore *(m)* n It
De Vergrößerungsgerät
(n)
En enlarger
Es ampliadora *(f)*
Fr agrandisseur *(m)*
Pt ampliadora *(f)*

ingranditore fotografico
(m) It
De photographisches
Vergrößerungsgerät
(n)
En photographic
enlarger
Es ampliadora
fotográfica *(f)*
Fr agrandisseur photo
(m)
Pt ampliador fotográfico
(m)

ingresos *(m pl)* n Es
De Einkommen *(n)*
En revenue
Fr recette *(f)*

It entrata (f)
Pt receita (f)

Inhaltsseite (f) n De
En contents page
Es página de índice (f)
Fr page des matières (f)
It pagina indice (f)
Pt página de índice (f)

Inhaltsverzeichnis (n) n De
En table of contents
Es índice de materias (m)
Fr table des matières (f)
It sommario delle materie (m)
Pt índice dos assuntos (m)

inicial n Es (f); Pt (m)
De Initiale (f)
En initial
Fr initiale (f)
It iniziale (f)

in italics En
De kursiv gedruckt
Es en cursiva
Fr en italiques
It in corsivo
Pt em itálico

initial n En
De Initiale (f)
Es inicial (f)
Fr initiale (f)
It iniziale (f)
Pt inicial (m)

initiale (f) n Fr
De Initiale (f)
En initial
Es inicial (f)
It iniziale (f)
Pt inicial (m)

Initiale (f) n De
En initial
Es inicial (f)
Fr initiale (f)
It iniziale (f)
Pt inicial (m)

iniziale (f) n It
De Initiale (f)
En initial
Es inicial (f)

Fr initiale (f)
Pt inicial (m)

ink (printer's) n En
De Druckfarbe (f)
Es tinta de imprenta (f)
Fr encre d'impression (f)
It inchiostro da stampa (m)
Pt tinta de impressão (f)

ink duct En
De Farbkanal (m)
Es tintero de la prensa (m)
Fr encrier (m)
It condotto per inchiostro (m)
Pt canal de tinta (m)

inking n En
De Farbauftrag (m)
Es entintaje (f)
Fr encrage (m)
It inchiostrazione (f)
Pt tintura (f)

in Klammern De
En in parentheses
Es entre paréntesis
Fr entre parenthèses
It tra parentesi
Pt entre parênteses

in Kontakt stehen De
En liaise
Es enlazar
Fr garder contact
It collegarsi
Pt ligar

ink rollers En
De Farbwalzen (pl)
Es rodillos de imprenta (m pl)
Fr rouleaux encreurs (m pl)
It rulli per inchiostro (m pl)
Pt rolos de dar tinta (m pl)

Innentitel (m) n De
En half title
Es anteportada (f)
Fr faux-titre (m)
It titolo abbreviato (m)
Pt anteportada (f)

innere Form (f) De
En inner forme
Es plana interior (f)
Fr côté de deux (m)
It forma interna (f)
Pt forma interior (f)

inner forme En
De innere Form (f)
Es plana interior (f)
Fr côté de deux (m)
It forma interna (f)
Pt forma interior (f)

in-octavo (m) n Fr
De Oktavformat (n)
En octavo
Es en octavo (m)
It in ottavo (m)
Pt octavo (m)

in ottavo (m) It
De Oktavformat (n)
En octavo
Es en octavo (m)
Fr in-octavo (m)
Pt octavo (m)

in parentheses En
De in Klammern
Es entre paréntesis
Fr entre parenthèses
It tra parentesi
Pt entre parênteses

in print En
De gedruckt
Es publicado
Fr en impression
It in corso di stampa
Pt impresso e publicado

input n En; It (m)
De Eingabe (f)
Es entrada (f)
Fr entrée (f)
Pt entrada (f)

in Rechnung stellen De
En invoice
Es facturar
Fr facturer
It fatturare
Pt facturar

inscription (f) n Fr
De Bildunterschrift (f)
En caption
Es encabezamiento (m)

It didascalia (f)
Pt epígrafe (f)

inserção (f) n Pt
De Einsatz (m)
En insert
Es encarte (m)
Fr encartage (m)
It inserto (m)

insérer vb Fr
De einfügen
En insert
Es encartar
It inserire
Pt inserir

insérer nouveau texte Fr
De neuen Text einfügen
En insert new copy
Es inertar nueva copia
It inserire nuovo testo
Pt inserir novo texto

inserir vb Pt
De einfügen
En insert
Es encartar
Fr insérer
It inserire

inserire vb It
De einfügen
En insert
Es encartar
Fr insérer
Pt inserir

inserire nuovo testo It
De neuen Text einfügen
En insert new copy
Es inertar nueva copia
Fr insérer nouveau texte
Pt inserir novo texto

inserir novo texto Pt
De neuen Text einfügen
En insert new copy
Es inertar nueva copia
Fr insérer nouveau texte
It inserire nuovo testo

insert vb En
De einfügen
Es encartar
Fr insérer
It inserire
Pt inserir

insert n En
De Einsatz *(m)*
Es encarte *(m)*
Fr encartage *(m)*
It inserto *(m)*
Pt inserção *(f)*

insert new copy En
De neuen Text einfügen
Es inertar nueva copia
Fr insérer nouveau texte
It inserire nuovo testo
Pt inserir novo texto

inserto *(m)* n It
De Einsatz *(m)*
En insert
Es encarte *(m)*
Fr encartage *(m)*
Pt inserção *(f)*

inserzione pubblicitaria
(f) It
De Displaywerbung *(f)*
En display
advertisement
Es anuncio publicitario
(m)
Fr grande annonce *(f)*
Pt anúncio em
majúsculas e
ilustrado *(m)*

insetting n En
De Einsetzen *(n)*
Es encuadre *(m)*
Fr mise en place *(f)*
It incorniciatura *(f)*
Pt intercalagem *(f)*

instabile adj It
De flüchtig
En fugitive
Es fugaz
Fr fugitif
Pt instável

instalações de
armazenamento *(f*
pl) Pt
De Speicherungs-
möglichkeiten *(pl)*
En storage facilities
Es almacenes *(m pl)*
Fr entrepôts *(m pl)*
It servizi di
immagazzinaggio *(m*
pl)

instável adj Pt
De flüchtig
En fugitive
Es fugaz
Fr fugitif
It instabile

instrução *(f)* n Pt
De Instruktion *(f)*
En instruction
Es instrucción *(f)*
Fr instruction *(f)*
It istruzione *(f)*

instrucción *(f)* n Es
De Instruktion *(f)*
En instruction
Fr instruction *(f)*
It istruzione *(f)*
Pt instrução *(f)*

instruction n En; Fr *(f)*
De Instruktion *(f)*
Es instrucción *(f)*
It istruzione *(f)*
Pt instrução *(f)*

Instruktion *(f)* n De
En instruction
Es instrucción *(f)*
Fr instruction *(f)*
It istruzione *(f)*
Pt instrução *(f)*

intaglio *(m)* n It
De Unterätzung *(f)*
En undercutting
Es sobremordido *(m)*
Fr massicotage *(m)*
Pt sobremordicação *(f)*

intaglio printing En
De Tiefdruck *(m)*
Es impresión con
grabados en hueco
(f)
Fr impression en creux
(f)
It stampa ad intaglio *(f)*
Pt impressão intaglio *(f)*

intercalagem *(f)* n Pt
De Einsetzen *(n)*
En insetting
Es encuadre *(m)*
Fr mise en place *(f)*
It incorniciatura *(f)*

interface n En; Fr, It, Pt
(f)
De Schnittstelle *(f)*
Es interfase *(f)*

interfase *(f)* n Es
De Schnittstelle *(f)*
En interface
Fr interface *(f)*
It interface *(f)*
Pt interface *(f)*

interlettrage optique
(m) Fr
De optischer
Buchstabenabstand
(m)
En optical letterspacing
Es espaciado óptico
entre letras *(m)*
It spaziatura ottica tra
le lettere *(f)*
Pt espaçamento óptico
de letras *(m)*

interlignage *(m)* n Fr
De Durchschießen *(n)*
En leading
Es interlineado *(m)*
It interlineazione *(f)*
Pt interlineado *(m)*

interlinea *(f)* It
De Durchschüsse *(pl)*
En leads *pl* n
Es interlíneas *(f pl)*
Fr entre-lignes *(f pl)*
Pt entrelinhas *(f pl)*

interlineado *(m)* n Es, Pt
De Durchschießen *(n)*
En leading
Fr interlignage *(m)*
It interlineazione *(f)*

interlíneas *(f pl)* Es
De Durchschüsse *(pl)*
En leads *pl* n
Fr entre-lignes *(f pl)*
It interlinea *(f)*
Pt entrelinhas *(f pl)*

interlineazione *(f)* n It
De Durchschießen *(n)*
En leading
Es interlineado *(m)*
Fr interlignage *(m)*
Pt interlineado *(m)*

international co-edition
En
De internationale
Gemeinschafts-
Ausgabe *(f)*
Es coedición
internacional *(f)*
Fr co-édition
internationale *(f)*
It coedizione
internazionale *(f)*
Pt coedição
internacional *(f)*

internationale
Gemeinschafts-
Ausgabe *(f)* De
En international
co-edition
Es coedición
internacional *(f)*
Fr co-édition
internationale *(f)*
It coedizione
internazionale *(f)*
Pt coedição
internacional *(f)*

internationales
Phonetik-Alphabet
(n) De
En international
phonetic alphabet
(IPA)
Es alfabeto fonético
internacional *(m)*
Fr alphabet phonétique
international *(m)*
It alfabeto fonetico
internazionale *(m)*
Pt alfabeto fonético
international *(m)*

international phonetic
alphabet (IPA) En
De internationales
Phonetik-Alphabet *(n)*
Es alfabeto fonético
internacional *(m)*
Fr alphabet phonétique
international *(m)*
It alfabeto fonetico
internazionale *(m)*
Pt alfabeto fonético
international *(m)*

Interpunktionszeichen
(n) n De
En punctuation mark
Es signo de puntuación
(m)
Fr signe de ponctuation
(m)

It segno di
   punteggiatura *(m)*
Pt sinal de pontuação
   (m)

interreferencia *(f) n* Es
De Querverweis *(m)*
En cross reference
Fr renvoi *(m)*
It rimando *(m)*
Pt nota remissiva *(f)*

interrogación *(f) n* Es
De Frage *(f)*
En query
Fr question *(f)*
It quesito *(m)*
Pt pergunta *(f)*

in transit En
De im Transit befindlich
Es en tránsito
Fr en transit
It in transito
Pt em trânsito

in transito It
De im Transit befindlich
En in transit
Es en tránsito
Fr en transit
Pt em trânsito

introdução *(f) n* Pt
De Einleitung *(f)*
En introduction
Es introducción *(f)*
Fr introduction *(f)*
It introduzione *(f)*

introducción *(f) n* Es
De Einleitung *(f)*
En introduction
Fr introduction *(f)*
It introduzione *(f)*
Pt introdução *(f)*

**introducir desde
   teclado** Es
De eintasten
En keyboard
Fr introduire par clavier
It introdurre mediante
   la tastiera
Pt introduzir desde
   teclado

introduction *n* En; Fr *(f)*
De Einleitung *(f)*
Es introducción *(f)*

It introduzione *(f)*
Pt introdução *(f)*

introduire par clavier Fr
De eintasten
En keyboard
Es introducir desde
   teclado
It introdurre mediante
   la tastiera
Pt introduzir desde
   teclado

**introdurre mediante la
   tastiera** It
De eintasten
En keyboard
Es introducir desde
   teclado
Fr introduire par clavier
Pt introduzir desde
   teclado

introduzione *(f) n* It
De Einleitung *(f)*
En introduction
Es introducción *(f)*
Fr introduction *(f)*
Pt introdução *(f)*

**introduzir desde
   teclado** Pt
De eintasten
En keyboard
Es introducir desde
   teclado
Fr introduire par clavier
It introdurre mediante
   la tastiera

invendus *(m pl)* Fr
De Rückgüter *(pl)*
En returns *pl n*
Es devoluciones *(f pl)*
It ritorni *(m pl)*
Pt devoluções *(f pl)*

inversionista *(m) n* Es
De Investor *(m)*
En investor
Fr investisseur *(m)*
It investitore *(m)*
Pt investidor *(m)*

invertir en Es
De investieren
En invest in
Fr investir dans
It investire in
Pt investir em

investidor *(m) n* Pt
De Investor *(m)*
En investor
Es inversionista *(m)*
Fr investisseur *(m)*
It investitore *(m)*

investieren De
En invest in
Es invertir en
Fr investir dans
It investire in
Pt investir em

**investigação do
   mercado** *(f)* Pt
De Marktforschung *(f)*
En market research
Es investigación del
   mercado *(f)*
Fr analyse de marché *(f)*
It ricerca di mercato *(f)*

**investigación del
   mercado** *(f)* Es
De Marktforschung *(f)*
En market research
Fr analyse de marché *(f)*
It ricerca di mercato *(f)*
Pt investigação do
   mercado *(f)*

invest in En
De investieren
Es invertir en
Fr investir dans
It investire in
Pt investir em

investir dans Fr
De investieren
En invest in
Es invertir en
It investire in
Pt investir em

investire in It
De investieren
En invest in
Es invertir en
Fr investir dans
Pt investir em

investir em Pt
De investieren
En invest in
Es invertir en
Fr investir dans
It investire in

investisseur *(m) n* Fr
De Investor *(m)*
En investor
Es inversionista *(m)*
It investitore *(m)*
Pt investidor *(m)*

investitore *(m) n* It
De Investor *(m)*
En investor
Es inversionista *(m)*
Fr investisseur *(m)*
Pt investidor *(m)*

investor *n* En
De Investor *(m)*
Es inversionista *(m)*
Fr investisseur *(m)*
It investitore *(m)*
Pt investidor *(m)*

Investor *(m) n* De
En investor
Es inversionista *(m)*
Fr investisseur *(m)*
It investitore *(m)*
Pt investidor *(m)*

invio diretto per posta
   (m) It
De Postwurfsendung *(f)*
En direct-mail shot
Es envío por correo
   directo; oferta por
   correo *(m f)*
Fr mailing; offre
   promotionelle *(m f)*
Pt publicidade por
   correio *(f)*

invoice *vb* En
De in Rechnung stellen
Es facturar
Fr facturer
It fatturare
Pt facturar

invoice *n* En
De Rechnung *(f)*
Es factura *(f)*
Fr facture *(f)*
It fattura *(f)*
Pt factura *(f)*

in voller Farbe De
Am in full color
En in full colour
Es a todo color
Fr en couleurs
It a colori
Pt a toda a cor

ISBN number En
De ISBN-Nummer *(f)*
Es número ISBN *(m)*
Fr numéro ISBN *(m)*
It numero ISBN *(m)*
Pt número ISBN *(m)*

ISBN-Nummer *(f)* De
En ISBN number
Es número ISBN *(m)*
Fr numéro ISBN *(m)*
It numero ISBN *(m)*
Pt número ISBN *(m)*

isento de ácido Pt
De säurefrei
En acid-free
Es exento de ácido
Fr sans acide
It privo di acidi

ISO-Größen *(pl)* De
En ISO sizes
Es tamaños ISO *(m pl)*
Fr formats ISO *(m pl)*
It dimensioni ISO *(f pl)*
Pt tamanhos ISO *(m pl)*

ISO sizes En
De ISO-Größen *(pl)*
Es tamaños ISO *(m pl)*
Fr formats ISO *(m pl)*
It dimensioni ISO *(f pl)*
Pt tamanhos ISO *(m pl)*

istruzione *(f)* n It
De Instruktion *(f)*
En instruction
Es instrucción *(f)*
Fr instruction *(f)*
Pt instrução *(f)*

itálico *(m)* Pt
De Kursivdruck *(m)*
En italics *pl n*
Es cursivas *(f pl)*
Fr italiques *(m pl)*
It caratteri corsivi *(m pl)*

italics *pl n* En
De Kursivdruck *(m)*
Es cursivas *(f pl)*
Fr italiques *(m pl)*
It caratteri corsivi *(m pl)*
Pt itálico *(m)*

italiques *(m pl)* Fr
De Kursivdruck *(m)*
En italics *pl n*
Es cursivas *(f pl)*

It caratteri corsivi *(m pl)*
Pt itálico *(m)*

**itinerario promozionale
dell'autore** *(m)* It
De Verfasser-Werbetour
(f)
En author promotion
tour
Es viaje de promoción
del autor *(m)*
Fr voyage promotionnel
d'auteur *(m)*
Pt viagem de promoção
de autor *(f)*

ivory board En
De Elfenbeinkarton *(m)*
Es cartulina marfil *(f)*
Fr carton invoire *(m)*
It cartone avorio *(m)*
Pt cartão marfim *(m)*

J

jacket *n* En
De Umschlag *(m)*
Es camisa *(f)*
Fr jaquette *(f)*
It sovracopertina *(f)*
Pt sobrecapa *(f)*

jacket artwork En
De Umschlag-
Satzmontage *(f)*
Es trabajo artistíco de la
sobrecubierta *(m)*
Fr illustration de la
jaquette *(f)*
It menabò per
sovracopertina *(m)*
Pt arte da sobrecapa
(m)

jacket blurb En
De Umschlag-
Reklamestreifen *(m)*
Es reseña en la cubierta
(f)
Fr manchette sur la
jaquette *(f)*
It sommario della
sovracopertina *(m)*

Pt sinopse de
sobrecapa *(f)*

jacket design En
De Umschlagentwurf
(m)
Es diseño de la
sobrecubierta *(m)*
Fr conception de la
jaquette *(f)*
It disegno della
sovracopertina *(m)*
Pt desenho da
sobrecapa *(m)*

jacket flap En
De Umschlagklappe *(f)*
Es solapa de la cubierta
(f)
Fr rabat de la jaquette
(m)
It risvolto della
sovracopertina *(m)*
Pt aba da sobrecapa *(f)*

Jahrbuch *(n)* n De
En year book
Es anuario *(m)*
Fr annuaire *(m)*
It annuario *(m)*
Pt anuário *(m)*

Jahreskonferenz *(f)* n De
En annual conference
Es conferencia anual *(f)*
Fr congrès annuel *(m)*
It conferenza annuale
(f)
Pt conferência anual *(f)*

jambages *(m pl)* Fr
De Unterlängen *(pl)*
En descenders (of letter)
pl n
Es trazos inferiores *(m
pl)*
It lettere discendenti *(f
pl)*
Pt traços inferiores *(m
pl)*

Japanese vellum En
De Japanpapier *(n)*
Es vitela japonesa *(f)*
Fr papier du Japon *(m)*
It pergamena
giapponese *(f)*
Pt papel pergaminho
japonês *(m)*

Japanpapier *(n)* n De
En Japanese vellum
Es vitela japonesa *(f)*
Fr papier du Japon *(m)*
It pergamena
giapponese *(f)*
Pt papel pergaminho
japonês *(m)*

jaquette *(f)* n Fr
De Umschlag *(m)*
En jacket
Es camisa *(f)*
It sovracopertina *(f)*
Pt sobrecapa *(f)*

jaspeado *(m)* n Es
De Marmorierung *(f)*
En marbling
Fr marbrure *(f)*
It marmorizzazione *(f)*
Pt jaspeamento *(m)*

jaspeamento *(m)* n Pt
De Marmorierung *(f)*
En marbling
Es jaspeado *(m)*
Fr marbrure *(f)*
It marmorizzazione *(f)*

**jaune d'impression
couleur** *(m)* Fr
De Verfahrensgelb *(n)*
En process yellow
Es amarillo de tricromía
(m)
It giallo di tricromia *(m)*
Pt amarelo para
policromia *(m)*

jefe de personal *(m)* Es
De Personal-
abteilungsleiter *(m)*
En personnel manager
Fr directeur du
personnel *(m)*
It direttore del
personale *(m)*
Pt director do pessoal
(m)

jefe de producción *(m)*
Es
De Produktionsleiter *(m)*
En production manager
Fr directeur de la
production *(m)*
It direttore di
produzione *(m)*
Pt director de produção
(m)

jefe de promoción *(m)*
Es
De Werbefachmann *(m)*
En promotion manager
Fr directeur de la
  promotion *(m)*
It dirigente dell'attività
  promozionale *(m)*
Pt director de promoção
  (m)

jefe de publicidad *(m)* Es
De Werbeleiter *(m)*
En publicity manager
Fr directeur de la
  publicité *(m)*
It direttore pubblicitario
  (m)
Pt director de
  publicidade *(m)*

jefe de redacción *(m)* Es
De Betriebsredakteur
  (m)
En managing editor
Fr chef de la rédaction
  (m)
It capo redattore *(m)*
Pt chefe de redacção
  (m)

jefe de ventas *(m)* Es
De Verkaufsleiter *(m)*
En sales manager
Fr chef des ventes *(m)*
It direttore vendite *(m)*
Pt gerente de vendas
  (m)

jefe ejecutivo *(m)* Es
De leitende
  Führungskraft *(f)*
En chief executive
Fr administrateur
  directeur *(m)*
It direttore generale *(m)*
Pt executivo principal
  (m)

jet printing method En
De Spritzdruckverfahren
  (n)
Es método de impresión
  por chorro *(m)*
Fr impression au jet
  d'encre *(f)*
It metodo di stampa a
  getto *(m)*
Pt método de
  impressão a jacto *(m)*

jeu de caractères *(m)* Fr
De Buchstabensatz *(m)*
En character set
Es juego de caracteres
  (m)
It gioco di caratteri *(m)*
Pt jogo de caracteres
  (m)

jobbing printer En
De Akzidenzdrucker *(m)*
Es impresor a
  remiendos *(m)*
Fr imprimeur de travaux
  de ville *(m)*
It stampatore
  comerciale *(m)*
Pt impressor comercial
  (m)

jogo de caracteres *(m)*
Pt
De Buchstabensatz *(m)*
En character set
Es juego de caracteres
  (m)
Fr jeu de caractères *(m)*
It gioco di caratteri *(m)*

jornal *(m)* n Pt
De Journal *(n)*
En journal
Es periódico *(m)*
Fr revue *(f)*
It giornale *(m)*

jornal diário *(m)* Pt
De Zeitung *(f)*
En newspaper
Es diario *(m)*
Fr journal *(m)*
It giornale quotidiano
  (m)

jornalismo *(m)* n Pt
De Journalismus *(m)*
En journalism
Es periodismo *(m)*
Fr journalisme *(m)*
It giornalismo *(m)*

jornalista *(m/f)* n Pt
De Journalist *(m)*
En journalist
Es periodista *(m/f)*
Fr journaliste *(m/f)*
It giornalista *(m/f)*

journal n En
De Journal *(n)*
Es periódico *(m)*

Fr revue *(f)*
It giornale *(m)*
Pt jornal *(m)*

journal *(m)* n Fr
De Zeitung *(f)*
En newspaper
Es diario *(m)*
It giornale quotidiano
  (m)
Pt jornal diário *(m)*

Journal *(n)* n De
En journal
Es periódico *(m)*
Fr revue *(f)*
It giornale *(m)*
Pt jornal *(m)*

journalism n En
De Journalismus *(m)*
Es periodismo *(m)*
Fr journalisme *(m)*
It giornalismo *(m)*
Pt jornalismo *(m)*

journalisme *(m)* n Fr
De Journalismus *(m)*
En journalism
Es periodismo *(m)*
It giornalismo *(m)*
Pt jornalismo *(m)*

Journalismus *(m)* n De
En journalism
Es periodismo *(m)*
Fr journalisme *(m)*
It giornalismo *(m)*
Pt jornalismo *(m)*

journalist n En
De Journalist *(m)*
Es periodista *(m/f)*
Fr journaliste *(m/f)*
It giornalista *(m/f)*
Pt jornalista *(m/f)*

Journalist *(m)* n De
En journalist
Es periodista *(m/f)*
Fr journaliste *(m/f)*
It giornalista *(m/f)*
Pt jornalista *(m/f)*

journaliste *(m/f)* n Fr
De Journalist *(m)*
En journalist
Es periodista *(m/f)*
It giornalista *(m/f)*
Pt jornalista *(m/f)*

juego de caracteres *(m)*
Es
De Buchstabensatz *(m)*
En character set
Fr jeu de caractères *(m)*
It gioco di caratteri *(m)*
Pt jogo de caracteres
  (m)

justieren *vb* De
En justify
Es justificar
Fr justifier
It giustificare
Pt justificar

justiert *adj* De
En justified
Es justificado
Fr justifié
It giustificato
Pt justificado

Justierung *(f)* n De
En justification
Es justificación *(f)*
Fr justification *(f)*
It giustificazione *(f)*
Pt justificação *(f)*

Justierungsroutine *(f)* n
De
En justification routine
Es rutina de justificación
  (f)
Fr routine de
  justification *(f)*
It routine di
  giustificazione *(f)*
Pt rotina de justificação
  (f)

Justierungszone *(f)* n De
En justification zone
Es zona de justificación
  (f)
Fr zone de justification
  (f)
It zona di giustificazione
  (f)
Pt zona de justificação
  (f)

justificação *(f)* n Pt
De Justierung *(f)*
En justification
Es justificación *(f)*
Fr justification *(f)*
It giustificazione *(f)*

justificación *(f) n* Es
De Justierung *(f)*
En justification
Fr justification *(f)*
It giustificazione *(f)*
Pt justificação *(f)*

justificado *adj* Es, Pt
De justiert
En justified
Fr justifié
It giustificato

justificar *vb* Es, Pt
De justieren
En justify
Fr justifier
It giustificare

justification *n* En; Fr *(f)*
De Justierung *(f)*
Es justificación *(f)*
It giustificazione *(f)*
Pt justificação *(f)*

justification incorrecte
(f) Fr
De falsches Maß *(n)*
En wrong measure
Es medida incorrecta *(f)*
It misura sbagliata *(f)*
Pt medida errada *(f)*

justification routine En
De Justierungsroutine *(f)*
Es rutina de justificación
(f)
Fr routine de
justification *(f)*
It routine di
giustificazione *(f)*
Pt rotina de justificação
(f)

justification zone En
De Justierungszone *(f)*
Es zona de justificación
(f)
Fr zone de justification
(f)
It zona di giustificazione
(f)
Pt zona de justificação
(f)

justifié *adj* Fr
De justiert
En justified
Es justificado
It giustificato
Pt justificado

justified *adj* En
De justiert
Es justificado
Fr justifié
It giustificato
Pt justificado

justifier *vb* Fr
De justieren
En justify
Es justificar
It giustificare
Pt justificar

justify *vb* En
De justieren
Es justificar
Fr justifier
It giustificare
Pt justificar

K

Kalander *(m) n* De
En calender
Es calandria *(f)*
Fr calandre finisseuse *(f)*
It calandra *(f)*
Pt calandra *(f)*

kalandriertes Papier *(n)*
De
En calendered paper
Es papel caladrando *(m)*
Fr papier calandré *(m)*
It carta calandrata *(f)*
Pt papel calandrado *(m)*

Kalkschleier *(m) n* De
En chalking
Es desintegración en
polvo *(f)*
Fr poudrage *(m)*
It sfarinamento *(m)*
Pt descascamento *(m)*

kalttrocknend *adj* De
En cold-set
Es solidificardo en frio
Fr seché à froid
It solidificato a freddo
(f)
Pt secado a frio *(f)*

kamerafertige Vorlage
(f) De
En camera-ready copy
Es original preparado
para la cámara *(m)*
Fr copie prête à
photographier *(f)*
It copia pronta per
fotografia *(f)*
Pt exemplar pronto para
a máquina
fotográfica *(m)*

Kanal *(m) n* De
En channel
Es canal *(m)*
Fr rainure *(f)*
It canale *(m)*
Pt canal *(m)*

kaolin *(m) n* Fr
De Kaolin *(n)*
En china clay
Es caolín *(m)*
It caolino *(m)*
Pt caolino *(m)*

Kaolin *(n) n* De
En china clay
Es caolín *(m)*
Fr kaolin *(m)*
It caolino *(m)*
Pt caolino *(m)*

Kapitälchen *(pl) n* De
En small capital letters
Es letras versalitas *(f pl)*
Fr petites majuscules *(f
pl)*
It lettere in
maiuscoletto *(f pl)*
Pt maiúsculas pequenas
(f pl)

Kapitel *(n) n* De
En chapter
Es capítulo *(m)*
Fr chapitre *(m)*
It capitolo *(m)*
Pt capítulo *(m)*

Kapitelband *(m) n* De
En headband
Es cabecera *(f)*
Fr tranchefile *(f)*
It capitello *(m)*
Pt friso *(m)*

Kapitelüberschrift *(f) n*
De
En chapter heading

Es encabezamiento de
capítulo *(m)*
Fr tête de chapitre *(f)*
It titolo del capitolo *(m)*
Pt título do capítulo *(m)*

kariertes Papier *(n)* De
En quadrille
Es cuadrícula *(f)*
Fr papier quadrillé *(m)*
It carta quadrettata *(f)*
Pt papel quadriculado
(m)

Karte *(f) n* De
En map
Es mapa *(m)*
Fr carte *(f)*
It mappa *(f)*
Pt mapa *(m)*

Karteikarten *(pl)* De
En index cards
Es tarjetas de ficheros *(f
pl)*
Fr fiches *(f pl)*
It schede *(f pl)*
Pt fichas de arquivo *(f
pl)*

Karton *(m) n* De
En cardboard
Es cartulina *(f)*
Fr carton *(m)*
It cartone *(m)*
Pt cartão *(m)*

**kartoniertes
Glanzpapier** *(n)* De
En board-glazed paper
Es papel satinado *(m)*
Fr papier satiné *(m)*
It cartone satinato *(m)*
Pt papel acetinado *(m)*

Kartuschenpapier *(n) n*
De
En cartridge paper
Es papel para cartuchos
(m)
Fr papier cartouche *(m)*
It carta da disegno *(f)*
Pt papel cartucho *(m)*

Katalog *(m) n* De
Am catalog
En catalogue
Es catálogo *(m)*
Fr catalogue *(m)*
It catalogo *(m)*
Pt catálogo *(m)*

Kauf oder Rückgabe *(m)*
De
En sale-or-return basis
Es base de ventas o
  devoluciones *(f)*
Fr vente avec possibilité
  de rendre *(f)*
It base venduto o reso
  (f)
Pt base de venda ou
  devolução *(f)*

Kegelgröße *(f) n* De
En body size (of type)
Es tamaño del tipo *(m)*
Fr corps d'un caractère
  (m)
It corpo del carattere
  (m)
Pt tamanho de corpo
  (m)

Keil *(m) n* De
En quoin
Es cuña *(f)*
Fr coin *(m)*
It serraforme *(m)*
Pt cunha *(f)*

kern *n* En
De Überhang *(m)*
Es talud *(m)*
Fr crénage *(m)*
It sporgenza *(f)*
Pt saliência do corpo do
  tipo *(f)*

keyboard *vb* En
De eintasten
Es introducir desde
  teclado
Fr introduire par clavier
It introdurre mediante
  la tastiera
Pt introduzir desde
  teclado

keyboard *n* En
De Tastatur *(m)*
Es teclado *(m)*
Fr clavier *(m)*
It tastiera *(f)*
Pt teclado *(m)*

keyboarder *n* En
De Tastatur-Setzer *(m)*
Es operador de teclado
  (m)
Fr claviste *(m)*
It operatore di tastiera
  (m)
Pt mecanotipista *(m)*

keyboarding room En
De Setzraum *(m)*
Es sala de mecanotipia
  (f)
Fr salle de
  photocomposition *(f)*
It sala di
  fotocomposizione *(f)*
Pt sala de mecanotipia
  (f)

Kinderbücher *(pl)* De
En children's books *pl n*
Es libros para niños *(m
  pl)*
Fr livres pour enfants *(m
  pl)*
It libri per bambini *(m
  pl)*
Pt livros infantís *(m pl)*

Klammer *(f) n* De
En parenthesis
Es paréntesis *(m)*
Fr parenthèse *(f)*
It parentese *(f)*
Pt parêntese *(m)*

Klarschriftlesen *(n) n* De
En optical character
  recognition (OCR)
Es reconocimiento
  óptico de caracteres
  (m)
Fr lecture optique *(f)*
It riconoscimento
  ottico dei caratteri
  (m)
Pt reconhecimento
  óptico de caracteres
  (m)

klassische Werke *(pl)*
De
En classics *pl n*
Es clásicos *(m pl)*
Fr classiques *(m pl)*
It classici *(m pl)*
Pt clássicos *(m pl)*

Klebebindung *(f) n* De
En perfect binding
Es encuadernación sin
  cosido *(f)*
Fr reliure parfaite *(f)*
It rilegatura perfetta *(f)*
Pt encadernação sem
  costura *(f)*

klebegebundenes Buch
(n) De
En perfect-bound book

Es libro encuadernado
  sin costura *(m)*
Fr livre relié sans
  couture *(m)*
It libro perfettamente
  rilegato *(m)*
Pt livro encadernado
  sem costura *(m)*

Klebenindung *(f) n* De
En wrappering
Es sobrecubierta *(f)*
Fr emballage *(m)*
It mettitura le
  sovracopertine *(f)*
Pt colocação de
  sobrecapa *(f)*

klebeumbrechen *vb* De
En paste up
Es montar
Fr encoller
It incollare
Pt montar

Klebeumbruch *(m) n* De
En paste-up
Es montaje *(m)*
Fr collage *(m)*
It incollatura *(f)*
Pt montagem *(f)*

Klebeumbruch-Arbeit
  (f) n De
En paste-up work
Es trabajo de montaje
  (m)
Fr travail de collage *(m)*
It lavoro di incollatura
  (m)
Pt trabalho do
  montagem *(m)*

kleiner Buchstabe *(m)*
De
En lower-case letter
Es minúscula *(f)*
Fr caractère de bas de
  caisse *(m)*
It minuscola *(f)*
Pt minúscula *(f)*

Kleister *(m) n* De
En paste
Es engrudo *(m)*
Fr colle *(f)*
It colla *(f)*
Pt cola *(f)*

Klischee *(n) n* De
En block
Es placa impresora *(f)*
Fr cliché *(m)*
It cliché *(m)*
Pt cliché *(f)*

Klischeeanstalt *(f) n* De
En blockmaker
Es grabador *(m)*
Fr photograveur *(m)*
It zincografo *(m)*
Pt gravador *(m)*

knappe Entscheidung *(f)*
De
En marginal decision
Es decisión marginal *(f)*
Fr décision marginale *(f)*
It decisione marginale
  (f)
Pt decisão marginal *(f)*

knocking-up (of paper) *n*
En
De Aufstoßen *(n)*
Es emparejamiento de
  hojas *(m)*
Fr taquage des feuilles
  (m)
It uniformazione di
  foglie *(f)*
Pt empilhamento de
  folhas *(m)*

knocking-up (of printing
  ink) *n* En
De Farbmischen *(n)*
Es mezclando de tinta
  (m)
Fr mélange de l'encre
  (m)
It mischiante
  d'inchiostro *(m)*
Pt mistura de tinta *(f)*

Kochbuch *(n) n* De
En cookery book
Es libro de cocina *(m)*
Fr livre de cuisine *(m)*
It libro di cucina *(m)*
Pt livro de cozinha *(m)*

Kollationierzeichen *(pl)*
De
En collating marks *pl n*
Es señales escalonadas
  de alzado *(f pl)*
Fr repères
  d'assemblage *(m pl)*
It segni di raccoglitura
  (m pl)

Pt marcas de revisão *(f pl)*

Kolorierer *(m)* n De
En illuminator
Es iluminador *(m)*
Fr enlumineur *(m)*
It illuminatore *(m)*
Pt iluminador *(m)*

Komma *(n)* n De
En comma
Es coma *(f)*
Fr virgule *(f)*
It virgola *(f)*
Pt vírgula *(f)*

Kommission *(f)* n De
En commission
Es encargo *(m)*
Fr commission *(f)*
It commissione *(f)*
Pt comissão *(f)*

kompatibel *adj* De
En compatible (of computer systems)
Es compatible
Fr compatible
It compatibile
Pt compatível

Kompatibiltät *(f)* n De
En compatibility (of computer systems)
Es compatibilidad *(f)*
Fr compatibilité *(f)*
It compatibilità *(f)*
Pt compatibilidade *(f)*

kompreß *adj* De
En solid
Es desinterlineado
Fr à-plat
It sterlineato
Pt maciço

Konditionierung *(f)* n De
En conditioning (of paper)
Es acondicionamiento *(m)*
Fr conditionnement *(m)*
It stagionatura *(f)*
Pt condicionamento *(m)*

Kontaktdruck *(m)* n De
En contact print
Es copia por contacto *(f)*
Fr tirage contact *(m)*

It stampa a contatto *(f)*
Pt prova por contacto *(f)*

Kontaktraster *(m)* n De
En contact screen
Es retícula de contacto *(f)*
Fr écran de contact *(m)*
It retino a contatto *(m)*
Pt retícula de contacto *(f)*

kontinuerlich Ton *(m)* De
En continuous tone
Es tono continuo *(m)*
Fr ton en continu *(m)*
It tono continuo *(m)*
Pt tom contínuo *(m)*

Konus *(m)* n De
En bevel
Es bisel *(m)*
Fr biseau *(m)*
It smusso *(m)*
Pt chanfro *(m)*

Koordinatenpapier *(n)* n De
En grid paper
Es papel milimétrico *(m)*
Fr papier millimétrique *(m)*
It carta millimetrata *(f)*
Pt papel milimétrico *(m)*

Kopf (type) *(m)* n De
En beard (of letter)
Es relieve *(m)*
Fr talus *(m)*
It bianco alla base *(m)*
Pt relevo *(m)*

Kopfzeile *(f)* n De
En headline (of page)
Es título *(m)*
Fr ligne de tête *(f)*
It titolo *(m)*
Pt linha de cabeçalho *(f)*

Kopieren *(n)* n De
En platemaking
Es preparación de planchas *(f)*
Fr clichage *(m)*
It preparazione delle matrici *(f)*
Pt preparação de estampas *(f)*

Körnung *(f)* n De
En grain
Es fibra *(f)*
Fr grain *(m)*
It grana *(f)*
Pt grão *(m)*

Korrektur *(f)* n De
En page proof
Es prueba de página *(f)*
Fr épreuve en pages *(f)*
It bozza impaginata *(f)*
Pt prova de página *(f)*

Korrekturen *(pl)* De
En corrections *pl* n
Es correcciones *(f pl)*
Fr corrections *(f pl)*
It correzioni *(f pl)*
Pt correcções *(f pl)*

Korrekturfahne *(f)* n De
En galley proof
Es prueba de galeradas *(f)*
Fr épreuve en placard *(f)*
It bozza in colonna *(f)*
Pt prova de galé *(f)*

korrekturlesen *vb* De
En proofread
Es corregir pruebas
Fr corriger les épreuves
It correggere le bozze
Pt rever provas

Korrekturlesen *(n)* n De
En proofreading
Es corrección de pruebas *(f)*
Fr correction d´épreuves *(f)*
It correzione di bozze *(f)*
Pt revisão de provas *(f)*

Korrekturleser *(m)* n De
En proofreader
Es corrector de pruebas *(m)*
Fr correcteur d´épreuves *(m)*
It correttore di bozze *(m)*
Pt revisor de provas *(m)*

Korrekturzeichen *(pl)* De
En proofreader´s marks
Es signos de corrección *(m pl)*
Fr signes de corrections

typographiques *(m pl)*
It segni del correttore di bozze *(m pl)*
Pt marcas do revisor de provas *(f pl)*

korrigieren *vb* De
En correct
Es corregir
Fr corriger
It correggere
Pt corrigir

Kosten, Versicherung, und Fracht De
En cost, insurance, and freight (c.i.f.)
Es costo, seguro, y flete
Fr coût, assurance, et fret (c.a.f.)
It costo, assicurazione, e nolo
Pt custo, seguro, e frete

Kostenvoranschlag *(m)* n De
En estimate
Es estimación *(f)*
Fr devis *(m)*
It valutazione *(f)*
Pt estimativa *(f)*

kraft paper En
De Kraftpapier *(n)*
Es papel kraft *(m)*
Fr papier Kraft *(m)*
It carta kraft *(f)*
Pt papel kraft *(m)*

Kraftpapier *(n)* n De
En kraft paper
Es papel kraft *(m)*
Fr papier Kraft *(m)*
It carta kraft *(f)*
Pt papel kraft *(m)*

kraft union paper En
De Kraftverbundpapier *(n)*
Es papel kraft union *(m)*
Fr papier kraft doublé-bitumé *(m)*
It carta kraft union *(f)*
Pt papel kraft union *(m)*

Kraftverbundpapier *(n)* n De
En kraft union paper
Es papel kraft union *(m)*

Fr   papier kraft
     doublé-bitumé *(m)*
It   carta kraft union *(f)*
Pt   papel kraft union *(m)*

Krätze *(f) n* De
En   dross
Es   escoria *(f)*
Fr   crasses *(f pl)*
It   scarto *(m)*
Pt   escória *(f)*

kräuseln *vb* De
En   crimp
Es   marcar con rayas
Fr   gaufrer
It   ondulare
Pt   enrugar

Kräuseln *(n) n* De
En   cockling
Es   amartillamiento *(m)*
Fr   gondolage *(m)*
It   arricciatura *(f)*
Pt   enrugamento *(m)*

Kreidezurichten *(n) n* De
En   chalk overlay
Es   alza mecánica de tiza
     (f)
Fr   papier baryté *(m)*
It   carta gessata *(f)*
Pt   calço de giz *(f)*

Kreuz *(n) n* De
En   dagger
Es   cruz *(f)*
Fr   croix *(f)*
It   croce *(f)*
Pt   cruz *(f)*

Kriminalroman *(m) n* De
En   detective novel
Es   novela policíaca *(f)*
Fr   roman policier *(m)*
It   racconto poliziesco
     (m)
Pt   livro policial *(m)*

Kunde *(m) n* De
En   client
Es   cliente *(m)*
Fr   client *(m)*
It   cliente *(m)*
Pt   cliente *(m)*

Kunstbücher *(pl)* De
En   art books *pl n*
Es   libros de arte *(m pl)*
Fr   livres d'art *(m pl)*

It   libri d'arte *(m pl)*
Pt   livros de arte *(m pl)*

Kunstdruckkarton *(m) n*
     De
En   art board
Es   tablero de dibujo *(m)*
Fr   carte couchée *(f)*
It   cartone da disegno
     (m)
Pt   prancha de arte *(f)*

Kunstgewerbebücher
     (pl) De
En   arts and crafts books
     pl n
Es   libros de artes y
     oficios *(m pl)*
Fr   livres artisanaux *(m
     pl)*
It   libri d'arte e
     d'artigianato *(m pl)*
Pt   livros de artes e
     ofícios *(m pl)*

Künstler *(m) n* De
En   artist
Es   artista *(m)*
Fr   artiste *(m)*
It   artista *(m)*
Pt   artista *(m/f)*

künstlerischer Leiter
     (m) De
En   art director
Es   director gráfico *(m)*
Fr   directeur artistique
     (m)
It   direttore artistico *(m)*
Pt   director artístico *(m)*

Kunstmaterialien *(pl)* De
En   artist's materials *pl n*
Es   materiales de
     dibujante *(m pl)*
Fr   fournitures de dessin
     (f pl)
It   materiale d'arte *(m)*
Pt   materiais do artista
     (m pl)

Kunst-Redakteur *(m)* De
En   art editor
Es   redactor gráfico *(m)*
Fr   rédacteur artistique
     (m)
It   editore artistico *(m)*
Pt   editor artístico *(m)*

Kupferdruck *(m) n* De
En   copper-plate printing
Es   impresión en hueco
     (f)
Fr   gravure sur cuivre *(f)*
It   stampa a calcografia
     (f)
Pt   impressão com
     chapa de cobre *(f)*

Kupfertiefdruck *(m) (n)*
     De
En   photogravure
Es   huecograbado *(m)*
Fr   héliogravure *(f)*
It   fotoincisione *(f)*
Pt   fotogravura *(f)*

Kursivdruck *(m)* De
En   italics *pl n*
Es   cursivas *(f pl)*
Fr   italiques *(m pl)*
It   caratteri corsivi *(m pl)*
Pt   itálico *(m)*

kursiv gedruckt De
En   in italics
Es   en cursiva
Fr   en italiques
It   in corsivo
Pt   em itálico

Kurve *(f) n* De
En   graph
Es   gráfico *(m)*
Fr   graphique *(m)*
It   grafico *(m)*
Pt   gráfico *(m)*

Kurzgeschichte *(f) n* De
En   short story
Es   narración *(f)*
Fr   nouvelle *(f)*
It   racconto breve *(m)*
Pt   novela pequena *(f)*

kurzkörniges Papier *(n)*
     De
En   short-grain paper
Es   papel de fibra corta
     (m)
Fr   papier à fibres
     courtes *(m)*
It   carta a grana corta *(f)*
Pt   papel de grão curto
     (m)

Kurzwörterbuch *(n) n*
     De
En   concise dictionary

Es   diccionario abreviado
     (m)
Fr   dictionnaire abrégé
     (m)
It   dizionario conciso
     (m)
Pt   dicionário conciso
     (m)

kyrillisches Alphabet *(n)*
     De
En   cyrillic alphabet
Es   alfabeto cirílico *(m)*
Fr   alphabet cyrillique
     (m)
It   alfabeto cirillico *(m)*
Pt   alfabeto cirílico *(m)*

L

labels (on diagram) *pl n*
     En
De   Bezeichnungen *(pl)*
Es   rótulos *(m pl)*
Fr   étiquettes *(f pl)*
It   etichette *(f pl)*
Pt   legendas *(f pl)*

labor-intensive work
     Am
De   arbeitsintensive
     Aufträge *(pl)*
En   labour-intensive work
Es   trabajo intensivo de
     mano de obra *(m)*
Fr   travail à forte
     main-d'oeuvre *(m)*
It   lavoro ad alto
     contenuto di mano
     d'opera *(m)*
Pt   trabalho com muita
     mão de obra *(m)*

labor relations Am
De   Arbeitgeber-
     Arbeitnehmer-
     Beziehungen *(pl)*
En   labour relations
Es   relaciones laborales *(f
     pl)*
Fr   relations syndicales *(f
     pl)*
It   relazioni di lavoro *(f
     pl)*

Pt relações laborais (f
pl)

labour-intensive work
En
Am labor-intensive work
De arbeitsintensive
Aufträge (pl)
Es trabajo intensivo de
mano de obra (m)
Fr travail à forte
main-d'oeuvre (m)
It lavoro ad alto
contenuto di mano
d'opera (m)
Pt trabalho com muita
mão de obra (m)

labour relations En
Am labor relations
De Arbeitgeber-
Arbeitnehmer-
Beziehungen (pl)
Es relaciones laborales (f
pl)
Fr relations syndicales (f
pl)
It relazioni di lavoro (f
pl)
Pt relações laborais (f
pl)

Lack (m) n De
En varnish
Es barniz (m)
Fr vernis (m)
It vernice (f)
Pt verniz (m)

Laden (m) n De
En shop (retail)
Es tienda (f)
Fr boutique (f)
It negozio (m)
Pt loja (f)

lado da tela (m) Pt
De Siebseite (f)
En wire side
Es cara interior (f)
Fr côté toilé (m)
It lato tela (m)

lado de feltro (m) Pt
De Filzseite (f)
En felt side
Es lado de fieltro (m)
Fr côté feutre (m)
It lato feltro (m)

lado de fieltro (m) Es
De Filzseite (f)
En felt side
Fr côté feutre (m)
It lato feltro (m)
Pt lado de feltro (m)

**lado de la emulsión
hacia abajo** (m) Es
De Emulsionsseite unten
(f)
En emulsion-side down
Fr côté émulsion vers le
bas (m)
It lato emulsione
inferiore (m)
Pt emulsão lado de
baixo (f)

**lado de la emulsión
hacia arriba** (m) Es
De Emulsionsseite oben
(f)
En emulsion-side up
Fr côté émulsion vers le
haut (m)
It lato emulsione
superiore (m)
Pt emulsão lado de
cima (f)

Lagerhaus (n) n De
En warehouse
Es almacén (m)
Fr entrepôt (m)
It magazzino (m)
Pt armazém (m)

Lagerkosten (pl) De
En warehousing costs pl
n
Es gastos de almacén
(m pl)
Fr frais
d'emmagasinage (m
pl)
It costi di
immagazzinaggio (m
pl)
Pt custos de armazém
(m pl)

lagern vb De
En store
Es almacenar
Fr entreposer
It immagazzinare
Pt armazenar

laid lines En
De Wasserlinien (f pl)

Es líneas en papel
verjurado (f pl)
Fr vergeures (f pl)
It vergature (f pl)
Pt linhas enramadas (f
pl)

laid paper En
De Vergépapier (n)
Es papel verjurado (m)
Fr papier vergé (m)
It carta vergata (f)
Pt papel vergé (m)

laiton (m) n Fr
De Messingreglette (f)
En brass (binder's)
Es latón (m)
It ottone (m)
Pt latão (m)

lámina (f) n Es
De Tafel (f)
En plate (picture)
Fr planche (f)
It tavola (f)
Pt gravura (f)

laminação (f) n Pt
De Glanzfolien-
kaschierung (f)
En laminating
Es laminación (f)
Fr contrecollage sous
pression (m)
It laminazione (f)

laminação a quente (f) Pt
De Warmwalzen (n)
En hot rolling
Es entintado en caliente
(m)
Fr laminage à chaud (m)
It calandratura a caldo
(f)

laminación (f) n Es
De Glanzfolien-
kaschierung (f)
En laminating
Fr contrecollage sous
pression (m)
It laminazione (f)
Pt laminação (f)

laminación en seco (f) Es
De Trockenfolien-
kaschierung (f)
En dry laminating
Fr stratification à sec (f)

It laminazione a secco
(f)
Pt laminagem a seco (f)

laminado adj Es, Pt
De glanzfolienkaschiert
En laminated
Fr laminé
It laminato

laminage à chaud (m) Fr
De Warmwalzen (n)
En hot rolling
Es entintado en caliente
(m)
It calandratura a caldo
(f)
Pt laminação a quente
(f)

laminagem a seco (f) Pt
De Trockenfolien-
kaschierung (f)
En dry laminating
Es laminación en seco
(f)
Fr stratification à sec (f)
It laminazione a secco
(f)

lâminas de acinzentar (f
pl) Pt
De mechanische Töne
(pl)
En mechanical tints
Es fondos grisados (m
pl)
Fr coloration
mécanique (f)
It colori di gradazioni
chiare ottenuti
meccanicamente (m
pl)

láminas en color (f pl) Es
Am color plates
De Farbtafeln (pl)
En colour plates pl n
Fr planches en couleurs
(f pl)
It tavole a colori (f pl)
Pt páginas a cores (f pl)

laminated adj En
De glanzfolienkaschiert
Es laminado
Fr laminé
It laminato
Pt laminado

laminating *n* En
De Glanzfolien-
kaschierung *(f)*
Es laminación *(f)*
Fr contrecollage sous
pression *(m)*
It laminazione *(f)*
Pt laminação *(f)*

laminato *adj* It
De glanzfolienkaschiert
En laminated
Es laminado
Fr laminé
Pt laminado

laminazione *(f) n* It
De Glanzfolien-
kaschierung *(f)*
En laminating
Es laminación *(f)*
Fr contrecollage sous
pression *(m)*
Pt laminação *(f)*

laminazione a secco *(f)*
It
De Trockenfolien-
kaschierung *(f)*
En dry laminating
Es laminación en seco
(f)
Fr stratification à sec *(f)*
Pt laminagem a seco *(f)*

laminé *adj* Fr
De glanzfolienkaschiert
En laminated
Es laminado
It laminato
Pt laminado

lançamento *(m) n* Pt
De Herausgabe *(f)*
En launch
Es lanzamiento *(m)*
Fr lancement *(m)*
It lancio *(m)*

lançar *vb* Pt
De herausgeben
En launch
Es lanzar
Fr lancer
It lanciare

lancement *(m) n* Fr
De Herausgabe *(f)*
En launch
Es lanzamiento *(m)*

It lancio *(m)*
Pt lançamento *(m)*

lancer *vb* Fr
De herausgeben
En launch
Es lanzar
It lanciare
Pt lançar

lanciare *vb* It
De herausgeben
En launch
Es lanzar
Fr lancer
Pt lançar

lancio *(m) n* It
De Herausgabe *(f)*
En launch
Es lanzamiento *(m)*
Fr lancement *(m)*
Pt lançamento *(m)*

landscape page En
De Querformat-Seite *(f)*
Es página apaisada *(f)*
Fr format oblong *(m)*
It pagina orizzontale *(f)*
Pt página horizontal *(f)*

**langage de
programmation** *(m)*
Fr
Am program language
De Programmiersprache
(f)
En programme language
Es lenguaje de
programación *(m)*
It linguaggio di
programma *(m)*
Pt linguagem de
programação *(f)*

**langage indépendant du
calculateur** *(m)* Fr
De maschinen-
unabhängige
Sprache *(f)*
En machine-
independent
language
Es lenguaje universal
(m)
It linguaggio universale
(m)
Pt linguagem
independente da
máquina *(f)*

langage machine *(m)* Fr
De Maschinensprache *(f)*
En machine language
Es lenguaje de máquina
(m)
It linguaggio macchina
(m)
Pt linguagem de
máquina *(f)*

Langformat-Papier *(n)*
De
En oblong paper
Es papel apaisado *(m)*
Fr format à l'italienne
(m)
It carta oblunga *(f)*
Pt papel alongado *(m)*

langkörniges Papier *(n)*
De
En long-grain paper
Es papel plegado al hilo
(m)
Fr papier sens machine
sur longueur *(m)*
It carta a grana lunga
(f)
Pt papel de grão
comprido *(m)*

lanzamiento *(m) n* Es
De Herausgabe *(f)*
En launch
Fr lancement *(m)*
It lancio *(m)*
Pt lançamento *(m)*

lanzar *vb* Es
De herausgeben
En launch
Fr lancer
It lanciare
Pt lançar

largeur du dos *(f)* Fr
De Rückendicke *(f)*
En spine width
Es ancho del lomo *(m)*
It larghezza del dorso *(f)*
Pt largura de lombada
(f)

larghezza del dorso *(f)* It
De Rückendicke *(f)*
En spine width
Es ancho del lomo *(m)*
Fr largeur du dos *(f)*
Pt largura de lombada
(f)

largo *(m) n* Es
De Zeilenmaβ *(n)*
En measure
Fr mesure *(f)*
It misura *(f)*
Pt medida *(f)*

largura de lombada *(f)* Pt
De Rückendicke *(f)*
En spine width
Es ancho del lomo *(m)*
Fr largeur du dos *(f)*
It larghezza del dorso *(f)*

larron *(m) n* Fr
De Ätzphase *(f)*
En bite (platemaking)
Es mordido *(m)*
It acidatura *(f)*
Pt mordente *(m)*

laser *n* En; Es, Fr, It, Pt
(m)
De Laser *(m)*

Laser *(m) n* De
En laser
Es laser *(m)*
Fr laser *(m)*
It laser *(m)*
Pt laser *(m)*

lastra *(f) n* It
De Druckplatte *(f)*
En plate (printing)
Es plancha *(f)*
Fr plaque *(f)*
Pt placa *(f)*

lastra al collodio *(f)* It
De feuchte Platte *(f)*
En wet plate
Es placa húmeda *(f)*
Fr plaque humide *(f)*
Pt chapa molhada *(f)*

lastra all'albumina *(f)* It
De Albuminplatte *(f)*
En albumen plate
Es plancha offset a la
albúmina *(f)*
Fr procédé à l'albumine
(m)
Pt chapa de albumina *(f)*

lastra a tinta opaca *(f)* It
De Tonplatte *(f)*
En flat-tint plate
Es clisé de media tinta
(m)

Fr aplat *(m)*
Pt chapa de meia-tinta *(f)*

lastra da stampa ai fotopolimeri *(f)* It
De Photopolymer-Druckplatte *(f)*
En photopolymer printing plate
Es placa impresora de polimerización fotoquímica *(f)*
Fr plaque photopolymère *(f)*
Pt chapa de impressão fotopolimérica *(f)*

lastra litografica a incisione profonda *(f)* It
De Tiefdruck-Offsetplatte *(f)*
En deep-etch litho plate
Es plancha al hueco-offset *(f)*
Fr offset en creux *(m)*
Pt chapa litográfica de gravação funda *(f)*

lastra nera *(f)* It
De Schwarzplatte *(f)*
En black plate
Es plancha negra *(f)*
Fr cliché en noir *(m)*
Pt chapa preta *(f)*

lastre flessibili *(f pl)* It
De Wickelplatten *(pl)*
En wrap-around plates *pl n*
Es planchas arrollables *(f pl)*
Fr plaques circulaires *(f pl)*
Pt placas flexíveis *(f pl)*

latão *(m) n* Pt
De Messingreglette *(f)*
En brass (binder´s)
Es latón *(m)*
Fr laiton *(m)*
It ottone *(m)*

lato emulsione inferiore *(m)* It
De Emulsionsseite unten *(f)*
En emulsion-side down
Es lado de la emulsión hacia abajo *(m)*

Fr côté émulsion vers le bas *(m)*
Pt emulsão lado de baixo *(f)*

lato emulsione superiore *(m)* It
De Emulsionsseite oben *(f)*
En emulsion-side up
Es lado de la emulsión hacia arriba *(m)*
Fr côté émulsion vers le haut *(m)*
Pt emulsão lado de cima *(f)*

lato feltro *(m)* It
De Filzseite *(f)*
En felt side
Es lado de fieltro *(m)*
Fr côté feutre *(m)*
Pt lado de feltro *(m)*

latón *(m) n* Es
De Messingreglette *(f)*
En brass (binder´s)
Fr laiton *(m)*
It ottone *(m)*
Pt latão *(m)*

lato pinza *(m)* It
De Greifkanten *(f)*
En gripper edge
Es orilla de entrada *(f)*
Fr côté des pinces *(m)*
Pt margem dianteira *(f)*

lato tela *(m)* It
De Siebseite *(f)*
En wire side
Es cara interior *(f)*
Fr côté toilé *(m)*
Pt lado da tela *(m)*

Laufrichtung *(f) n* De
En machine direction
Es dirección de máquina *(f)*
Fr sens machine *(m)*
It direzione di macchina *(f)*
Pt direcção da máquina *(f)*

launch *vb* En
De herausgeben
Es lanzar
Fr lancer
It lanciare
Pt lançar

launch *n* En
De Herausgabe *(f)*
Es lanzamiento *(m)*
Fr lancement *(m)*
It lancio *(m)*
Pt lançamento *(m)*

lavishly illustrated En
De groβzügig illustriert
Es profusamente ilustrado
Fr abondamment illustré
It riccamente illustrato
Pt profusamente ilustrado

lavoro *(m) n* It
De Arbeit *(f)*
En work
Es trabajo *(m)*
Fr travail *(m)*
Pt trabalho *(m)*

lavoro ad alto contenuto di mano d'opera *(m)* It
Am labor-intensive work
De arbeitsintensive Aufträge *(pl)*
En labour-intensive work
Es trabajo intensivo de mano de obra *(m)*
Fr travail à forte main-d´oeuvre *(m)*
Pt trabalho com muita mão de obra *(m)*

lavoro di cucitura *(m)* It
De geheftete Arbeit *(f)*
En sewn work
Es obra cosida *(f)*
Fr reliure cousue *(f)*
Pt obra cosida *(f)*

lavoro di incollatura *(m)* It
De Klebeumbruch-Arbeit *(f)*
En paste-up work
Es trabajo de montaje *(m)*
Fr travail de collage *(m)*
Pt trabalho do montagem *(m)*

lavoro di mezza pagina *(f)* It
De Halbbogendruck *(m)*
En half-sheet work
Es imposición e impresión a blanco y vuelta *(f)*
Fr imposition en demi-feuille *(f)*
Pt trabalho a meia folha *(m)*

lavoro esterno *(m)* It
De Auβenarbeit *(n)*
En outwork
Es trabajo externo *(m)*
Fr travail à domicile *(m)*
Pt trabalho externo *(m)*

lavoro in corso *(m)* It
De in Arbeit befindlich
En work-in-progress
Es trabajo en ejecución *(m)*
Fr travail en cours *(m)*
Pt progresso de adaptação ao trabalho *(m)*

lavoro in tandem *(m)* It
De Tandemarbeit *(f)*
En tandem work
Es trabajo en tandem *(m)*
Fr travail en tandem *(m)*
Pt trabalho em tandem *(m)*

lay off En
De entlassen
Es despedir
Fr licencier
It licenziare
Pt dispensar temporariamente

lay out En
De gestalten
Es disponer (tipo)
Fr disposer (caractères)
It disporre (caratteri)
Pt preparar (tipo)

layout *n* En
De Layout *(n)*
Es disposición tipográfica *(f)*
Fr disposition typographique *(f)*
It disposizione tipografica *(f)*
Pt disposição tipográfica *(f)*

Layout (n) n De
En layout
Es disposición
tipográfica (f)
Fr disposition
typographique (f)
It disposizione
tipografica (f)
Pt disposição
tipográfica (f)

Layoutbogen (m) n De
En grid sheet
Es hoja cuadriculada (f)
Fr feuille quadrillée (f)
It foglio a griglia (m)
Pt folha quadriculada (f)

lead (metal) n En
De Blei (n)
Es plomo (m)
Fr plomb (m)
It piombo (m)
Pt chumbo (m)

leaders pl n En
De Ausführpunkte (pl)
Es filetes puntillados (m
pl)
Fr points de conduite
(m pl)
It puntini (m pl)
Pt pontos de reticência
(m pl)

leading n En
De Durchschießen (n)
Es interlineado (m)
Fr interlignage (m)
It interlineazione (f)
Pt interlineado (m)

lead mold Am
De Bleiform (f)
En lead mould
Es molde de plomo (m)
Fr empreinte sur plomb
(f)
It stampo di piombo
(m)
Pt molde de chumbo
(m)

lead mould En
Am lead mold
De Bleiform (f)
Es molde de plomo (m)
Fr empreinte sur plomb
(f)
It stampo di piombo
(m)

Pt molde de chumbo
(m)

leads pl n En
De Durchschüsse (pl)
Es interlíneas (f pl)
Fr entre-lignes (f pl)
It interlinea (f)
Pt entrelinhas (f pl)

leaf n En
De Blatt (n)
Es hoja (f)
Fr feuillet (m)
It foglio (m)
Pt folha (f)

leaflet n En
De Merkblatt (n)
Es prospecto (m)
Fr feuille volante (f)
It volantino a stampa
(m)
Pt folheto (m)

leather boards En
De Lederfaserpappen
(pl)
Es cartones de cuero (m
pl)
Fr carton simili cuir (m)
It cartoni uso cuoio (m
pl)
Pt cartonados a carneira
(m pl)

leather-bound book En
De ledergebundenes
Buch (n)
Es libro encuadernado
en piel (m)
Fr livre relié cuir (m)
It libro rilegato in pelle
(m)
Pt livro encadernado a
carneira (m)

lebender Kolumnentitel
(pl) De
En running heads
Es títulos de página (m
pl)
Fr titres courants (m pl)
It titoletti (m pl)
Pt títulos repetidos (m
pl)

lecteur (m) n Fr
De Leser (m)
En reader (person)
Es lector (m)

It lettore (m)
Pt leitor (m)

**lecteur de bande
perforée** (m) Fr
De Lochstreifen-Leser
(m)
En punched-tape reader
Es lector de cinta
perforada (m)
It lettore di nastro
perforato (m)
Pt leitor de fita
perfurada (m)

lector (m) n Es
De Leser (m)
En reader (person)
Fr lecteur (m)
It lettore (m)
Pt leitor (m)

**lector de cinta
perforada** (m) Es
De Lochstreifen-Leser
(m)
En punched-tape reader
Fr lecteur de bande
perforée (m)
It lettore di nastro
perforato (m)
Pt leitor de fita
perfurada (m)

**lectura de caracteres de
tinta magnética** (f)
Es
De Lesen von
Magnettintenzeichen
(n)
En magnetic-ink
character reading
(MICR)
Fr reconnaissance de
caractères
magnétiques codés
(f)
It lettura caratteri con
inchiostro magnetico
(f)
Pt leitura de caracteres
de tinta magnética (f)

lecture optique (f) Fr
De Klarschriftlesen (n)
En optical character
recognition (OCR)
Es reconocimiento
óptico de caracteres
(m)
It riconoscimento

ottico dei caratteri
(m)
Pt reconhecimento
óptico de caracteres
(m)

**lectures
complémentaires** (f
pl) Fr
De weitere Literatur (f)
En further reading
Es relectura (f)
It ulteriori letture (f pl)
Pt leitura adicional (f)

Lederfaserpappen (pl)
De
En leather boards
Es cartones de cuero (m
pl)
Fr carton simili cuir (m)
It cartoni uso cuoio (m
pl)
Pt cartonados a carneira
(m pl)

ledergebundenes Buch
(n) De
En leather-bound book
Es libro encuadernado
en piel (m)
Fr livre relié cuir (m)
It libro rilegato in pelle
(m)
Pt livro encadernado a
carneira (m)

leer vb Es
De lesen
En read
Fr lire
It leggere
Pt ler

**leer a la vista del
original** Es
De mit dem Manuskript
vergleichen
En read against copy
Fr corriger avec copie
It confrontare
coll'original
Pt ler comparando com
a cópia

Leerlaufzeit (f) n De
En idle time
Es tiempo de reposo (m)
Fr temps mort (m)
It tempo di

funzionamento a
vuoto *(m)*
Pt tempo morto *(m)*

left-hand page En
De linke Seite *(f)*
Es página izquierda *(f)*
Fr fausse page *(f)*
It pagina di sinistra *(f)*
Pt página de esquerda
(f)

lega *(f) n* It
De Legierung *(f)*
En alloy
Es aleación *(f)*
Fr alliage *(m)*
Pt liga *(f)*

legal book En
De Rechtsbuch *(n)*
Es libro de derecho *(m)*
Fr ouvrage juridique *(m)*
It libro legale *(m)*
Pt livro jurídico *(m)*

lega per caratteri *(f)* It
De Schriftmetall *(n)*
En type metal
Es metal de imprenta
(m)
Fr métal d'imprimerie
(m)
Pt metal para tipos *(m)*

legare con trattino It
De trennen
En hyphenate
Es separar con guión
Fr mettre un trait
d'union
Pt pôr um traço de
união

legatoria *(f) n* It
De Buchbinderei *(f)*
En bindery
Es taller de
encuadernación *(f)*
Fr atelier de reliure *(m)*
Pt oficina de
encadernação *(f)*

legatura *(f) n* It
De Ligatur *(f)*
En ligature
Es ligado *(m)*
Fr ligature *(f)*
Pt letras ligadas *(f pl)*

legatura ad anelli *(f)* It
De Ringbindung *(f)*
En ring binding
Es encuadernación con
anillas *(f)*
Fr reliure à anneaux *(f)*
Pt encadernação com
anilhas *(f)*

legatura a fogli sciolti *(f)*
It
De Loseblattbindung *(f)*
En loose-leaf binding
Es encuadernación de
hojas sueltas *(f)*
Fr reliure à feuillets
mobiles *(f)*
Pt encadernação de
folhas soltas *(f)*

legatura con trattino *(f)*
It
De Trennung *(f)*
En hyphenation
Es separación con
guiones *(f)*
Fr coupure *(f)*
Pt colocação de um
traço de união *(f)*

legatura da tipografia *(f)*
It
De Buchdruck-Binden
(n)
En letterpress binding
Es acuñado tipográfico
(m)
Fr reliure imprimerie *(f)*
Pt encadernação
tipográfica *(f)*

legatura meccanica *(f)* It
De mechanische
Bindung *(f)*
En mechanical binding
Es encuadernación
mecánica *(f)*
Fr reliure mécanique *(f)*
Pt encadernação
mecânica *(f)*

legend *n* En
De Legende *(f)*
Es leyenda *(f)*
Fr légende *(f)*
It legenda *(f)*
Pt legenda *(f)*

legenda *(f) n* It, Pt
De Legende *(f)*
En legend

Es leyenda *(f)*
Fr légende *(f)*

legendas *(f pl)* Pt
De Bezeichnungen *(pl)*
En labels (on diagram) *pl*
n
Es rótulos *(m pl)*
Fr étiquettes *(f pl)*
It etichette *(f pl)*

Legende *(f) n* De
En legend
Es leyenda *(f)*
Fr légende *(f)*
It legenda *(f)*
Pt legenda *(f)*

légende *(f) n* Fr
De Legende *(f)*
En legend
Es leyenda *(f)*
It legenda *(f)*
Pt legenda *(f)*

leggere *vb* It
De lesen
En read
Es leer
Fr lire
Pt ler

Legierung *(f) n* De
En alloy
Es aleación *(f)*
Fr alliage *(m)*
It lega *(f)*
Pt liga *(f)*

Lehrbuch *(n) n* De
En textbook
Es libro de texto *(m)*
Fr manuel *(m)*
It libro di testo *(m)*
Pt livro de texto *(m)*

Leimung *(f) n* De
En sizing
Es encolado *(m)*
Fr encollage *(m)*
It collaggio *(m)*
Pt encolamento *(m)*

Leinenbandbuch *(n) n*
De
En cloth-bound book
Es libro encuadernado
en tela *(m)*
Fr livre relié pleine toile
(m)

It libro rilegato in tela
(m)
Pt livro encadernado em
tela *(m)*

leitende Führungskraft
(f) De
En chief executive
Es jefe ejecutivo *(m)*
Fr administrateur
directeur *(m)*
It direttore generale *(m)*
Pt executivo principal
(m)

leitender Redakteur *(m)*
De
En senior editor
Es redactor jefe *(m)*
Fr rédacteur gérant *(m)*
It editore senior *(m)*
Pt editor senior *(m)*

Leitfaden *(m) n* De
En manual
Es manual *(m)*
Fr manuel *(m)*
It manuale *(m)*
Pt manual *(m)*

leitor *(m) n* Pt
De Leser *(m)*
En reader (person)
Es lector *(m)*
Fr lecteur *(m)*
It lettore *(m)*

leitor de fita perfurada
(m) Pt
De Lochstreifen-Leser
(m)
En punched-tape reader
Es lector de cinta
perforada *(m)*
Fr lecteur de bande
perforée *(m)*
It lettore di nastro
perforato *(m)*

leitor de tipografia *(m)*
Pt
De Druckerei-
Korrekturleser *(m)*
En printer's reader
Es corrector de
imprenta *(m)*
Fr corrigeur *(m)*
It correttore di bozze da
stampa *(m)*

leitura adicional *(f)* Pt
De weitere Literatur *(f)*
En further reading
Es relectura *(f)*
Fr lectures
  complémentaires *(f*
  pl)
It ulteriori letture *(f pl)*

leitura de caracteres de
  tinta magnética *(f)*
  Pt
De Lesen von
  Magnettintenzeichen
  (n)
En magnetic-ink
  character reading
  (MICR)
Es lectura de caracteres
  de tinta magnética *(f)*
Fr reconnaissance de
  caractères
  magnétiques codés
  (f)
It lettura caratteri con
  inchiostro magnetico
  (f)

lenguaje de máquina *(m)*
  Es
De Maschinensprache *(f)*
En machine language
Fr langage machine *(m)*
It linguaggio macchina
  (m)
Pt linguagem de
  máquina *(f)*

lenguaje de
  programación *(m)*
  Es
Am program language
De Programmiersprache
  (f)
En programme language
Fr langage de
  programmation *(m)*
It linguaggio di
  programma *(m)*
Pt linguagem de
  programação *(f)*

lenguaje universal *(m)*
  Es
De maschinen-
  unabhängige
  Sprache *(f)*
En machine-
  independent
  language
Fr langage indépendant
  du calculateur *(m)*

It linguaggio universale
  (m)
Pt linguagem
  independente da
  máquina *(f)*

lenhose *(f) n* Pt
De Holzfaser *(f)*
En lignin
Es lignina *(f)*
Fr lignine *(f)*
It lignina *(f)*

ler *vb* Pt
De lesen
En read
Es leer
Fr lire
It leggere

ler comparando com a
  cópia Pt
De mit dem Manuskript
  vergleichen
En read against copy
Es leer a la vista del
  original
Fr corriger avec copie
It confrontare
  coll'original

Lesebuch *(n) n* De
En reader (book)
Es libro de lectura *(m)*
Fr livre de lecture *(m)*
It libro di lettura *(m)*
Pt exemplar de leitura
  (m)

lesen *vb* De
En read
Es leer
Fr lire
It leggere
Pt ler

Lesen von
  Magnettinten-
  zeichen *(n)* De
En magnetic-ink
  character reading
  (MICR)
Es lectura de caracteres
  de tinta magnética *(f)*
Fr reconnaissance de
  caractères
  magnétiques codés
  (f)
It lettura caratteri con
  inchiostro magnetico
  (f)

Pt leitura de caracteres
  de tinta magnética *(f)*

Leser *(m) n* De
En reader (person)
Es lector *(m)*
Fr lecteur *(m)*
It lettore *(m)*
Pt leitor *(m)*

letra *(f) n* Es, Pt
De Buchstabe *(m)*
En letter
Fr lettre *(f)*
It lettera *(f)*

letra de caixa alta *(f)* Pt
De großer Buchstabe
  (m)
En upper-case letter
Es letra mayúscula *(f)*
Fr lettre de haut de
  casse *(f)*
It lettera maiuscola *(f)*

letra de otro tipo *(f)* Es
Am wrong font
De falscher Buchstabe
  (m)
En wrong fount
Fr lettre d'une autre
  fonte *(f)*
It testina sbagliata *(f)*
Pt letra de outro tipo *(f)*

letra de outro tipo *(f)* Pt
Am wrong font
De falscher Buchstabe
  (m)
En wrong fount
Es letra de otro tipo *(f)*
Fr lettre d'une autre
  fonte *(f)*
It testina sbagliata *(f)*

letra mayúscula *(f)* Es
De großer Buchstabe
  (m)
En upper-case letter
Fr lettre de haut de
  casse *(f)*
It lettera maiuscola *(f)*
Pt letra de caixa alta *(f)*

letras de fantasía *(f pl)*
  Es
De Zierbuchstaben *(pl)*
En swash letters *pl n*
Fr lettres ornées *(f pl)*
It lettere inclinate *(f pl)*

Pt letras de fantasia *(f
  pl)*

letras de fantasia *(f pl)*
  Pt
De Zierbuchstaben *(pl)*
En swash letters *pl n*
Es letras de fantasía *(f
  pl)*
Fr lettres ornées *(f pl)*
It lettere inclinate *(f pl)*

letras ligadas *(f pl)* Pt
De Ligatur *(f)*
En ligature
Es ligado *(m)*
Fr ligature *(f)*
It legatura *(f)*

letras por transferência
  (f pl) Pt
De Transfer-Buchstaben
  (pl)
En transfer lettering
Es letrero por
  transferencia *(m)*
Fr lettres-transfert *(f pl)*
It lettere a trasporto *(f
  pl)*

letras unciales *(f pl)* Pt
De Unzialbuchstaben *(pl)*
En uncials *pl n*
Es unciales *(f pl)*
Fr onciales *(f pl)*
It unciali *(m pl)*

letras versalitas *(f pl)* Es
De Kapitälchen *(pl)*
En small capital letters
Fr petites majuscules *(f
  pl)*
It lettere in
  maiuscoletto *(f pl)*
Pt maiúsculas pequenas
  (f pl)

letrero por
  transferencia *(m)*
  Es
De Transfer-Buchstaben
  (pl)
En transfer lettering
Fr lettres-transfert *(f pl)*
It lettere a trasporto *(f
  pl)*
Pt letras por
  transferência *(f pl)*

letter n En
De Buchstabe (m)
Es letra (f)
Fr lettre (f)
It lettera (f)
Pt letra (f)

lettera (f) n It
De Buchstabe (m)
En letter
Es letra (f)
Fr lettre (f)
Pt letra (f)

lettera maiuscola (f) It
De groβer Buchstabe (m)
En upper-case letter
Es letra mayúscula (f)
Fr lettre de haut de casse (f)
Pt letra de caixa alta (f)

letterario adj It
De literarisch
En literary
Es literario
Fr littéraire
Pt literário

letteratura (f) n It
De Literatur (f)
En literature
Es literatura (f)
Fr littérature (f)
Pt literatura (f)

lettere ascendenti (f pl) It
De Buchstaben-Oberlänge (n pl)
En ascenders (of letter) pl n
Es palos altos (m pl)
Fr ascendantes (f pl)
Pt ascendentes (f pl)

lettere a trasporto (f pl) It
De Transfer-Buchstaben (pl)
En transfer lettering
Es letrero por transferencia (m)
Fr lettres-transfert (f pl)
Pt letras por transferência (f pl)

lettere discendenti (f pl) It
De Unterlängen (pl)

En descenders (of letter) pl n
Es trazos inferiores (m pl)
Fr jambages (m pl)
Pt traços inferiores (m pl)

lettere inclinate (f pl) It
De Zierbuchstaben (pl)
En swash letters pl n
Es letras de fantasía (f pl)
Fr lettres ornées (f pl)
Pt letras de fantasia (f pl)

lettere in maiuscoletto (f pl) It
De Kapitälchen (pl)
En small capital letters
Es letras versalitas (f pl)
Fr petites majuscules (f pl)
Pt maiúsculas pequenas (f pl)

letterpress binding En
De Buchdruck-Binden (n)
Es acuñado tipográfico (m)
Fr reliure imprimerie (f)
It legatura da tipografia (f)
Pt encadernação tipográfica (f)

letterpress printing En
De Buchdruck (m)
Es impresión tipográfica (f)
Fr impression typographique (f)
It stampa tipografica (f)
Pt impressão tipográfica (f)

letter spacing En
De Buchstabenabstand (m)
Es espaciado entre letras (m)
Fr espacement entre caractère (m)
It spaziatura tra le lettere (f)
Pt espaço entre letras (m)

lettore (m) n It
De Leser (m)
En reader (person)
Es lector (m)
Fr lecteur (m)
Pt leitor (m)

lettore di nastro perforato (m) It
De Lochstreifen-Leser (m)
En punched-tape reader
Es lector de cinta perforada (m)
Fr lecteur de bande perforée (m)
Pt leitor de fita perfurada (m)

lettre (f) n Fr
De Buchstabe (m)
En letter
Es letra (f)
It lettera (f)
Pt letra (f)

lettre de haut de casse (f) Fr
De groβer Buchstabe (m)
En upper-case letter
Es letra mayúscula (f)
It lettera maiuscola (f)
Pt letra de caixa alta (f)

lettre d'un autre oeil (f) Fr
De falscher Schrifttyp (m)
En wrong typeface
Es ojo de tipo incorrecto (m)
It carattere sbagliato (m)
Pt olho de tipo errado (m)

lettre d'une autre fonte (f) Fr
Am wrong font
De falscher Buchstabe (m)
En wrong fount
Es letra de otro tipo (m)
It testina sbagliata (f)
Pt letra de outro tipo (f)

lettres ornées (f pl) Fr
De Zierbuchstaben (pl)
En swash letters pl n
Es letras de fantasía (f pl)

It lettere inclinate (f pl)
Pt letras de fantasia (f pl)

lettres-transfert (f pl) n Fr
De Transfer-Buchstaben (pl)
En transfer lettering
Es letrero por transferencia (m)
It lettere a trasporto (f pl)
Pt letras por transferência (f pl)

lettura caratteri con inchiostro magnetico (f) It
De Lesen von Magnettintenzeichen (n)
En magnetic-ink character reading (MICR)
Es lectura de caracteres de tinta magnética (f)
Fr reconnaissance de caractères magnétiques codés (f)
Pt leitura de caracteres de tinta magnética (f)

letzte Korrektur (f) De
En press proof
Es prueba de prensa (f)
Fr bon à tirer (m)
It bozza di stampa (f)
Pt prova de imprensa (f)

Leuchtkasten (m) n De
En light box
Es caja de luz (f)
Fr boîte lumineuse (f)
It cassa luminosa (f)
Pt caixa de luz (f)

Leuchttisch (m) n De
En light table
Es mesa de retoque (f)
Fr table lumineuse (f)
It tavolo luminoso (m)
Pt mesa de retoque (f)

léxico (m) n Pt
De Thesaurus (m)
En thesaurus
Es tesoro (m)
Fr thésaurus (m)
It florilegio (m)

leyenda *(f)* *n* Es
De Legende *(f)*
En legend
Fr légende *(f)*
It legenda *(f)*
Pt legenda *(f)*

lézarde *(f)* *n* Fr
De Straβenkante *(f)*
En gutter margin
Es margen del medianil *(m)*
It margine di scanalatura *(m)*
Pt margem de medianiz *(f)*

liaise *vb* En
De in Kontakt stehen
Es enlazar
Fr garder contact
It collegarsi
Pt ligar

libraio *(m)* *n* It
De Buchhändler *(m)*
En bookseller
Es vendedor de libros *(m)*
Fr libraire *(m)*
Pt livreiro *(m)*

libraire *(m)* *n* Fr
De Buchhändler *(m)*
En bookseller
Es vendedor de libros *(m)*
It libraio *(m)*
Pt livreiro *(m)*

librairie *(f)* *n* Fr
De Buchladen *(m)*
En book shop
Es librería *(f)*
It libreria *(f)*
Pt livraria *(f)*

librairie de solde d'éditions *(f)* Fr
De Remittenden-Buchladen *(m)*
En remainder bookshop
Es libreria de restos de edición *(f)*
It libreria di rimanenze *(f)*
Pt livraria de restos de edição *(f)*

librarian *n* En
De Bibliothekar *(m)*
Es bibliotecario *(m)*
Fr bibliothécaire *(m/f)*
It bibliotecario *(m)*
Pt bibliotecário *(m)*

library *n* En
De Bibliothek *(f)*
Es biblioteca *(f)*
Fr bibliothèque *(f)*
It biblioteca *(f)*
Pt biblioteca *(f)*

library-bound book En
De Buch mit Bibliothek-Einband *(n)*
Es libro encuadernado para biblioteca *(m)*
Fr reliure bibliothèque publique *(f)*
It libro rilegato per biblioteca *(m)*
Pt livro encadernado para biblioteca *(m)*

libreria *(f)* *n* It
De Buchladen *(m)*
En book shop
Es librería *(f)*
Fr librairie *(f)*
Pt livraria *(f)*

librería *(f)* *n* Es
De Buchladen *(m)*
En book shop
Fr librairie *(f)*
It libreria *(f)*
Pt livraria *(f)*

libreria de restos de edición *(f)* Es
De Remittenden-Buchladen *(m)*
En remainder bookshop
Fr librairie de solde d'éditions *(f)*
It libreria di rimanenze *(f)*
Pt livraria de restos de edição *(f)*

libreria di rimanenze *(f)* It
De Remittenden-Buchladen *(m)*
En remainder bookshop
Es libreria de restos de edición *(f)*
Fr librairie de solde d'éditions *(f)*

Pt livraria de restos de edição *(f)*

libretto *(m)* *n* It
De Heft *(n)*
En booklet
Es opúsculo *(m)*
Fr plaquette *(f)*
Pt folheto *(m)*

libri accademici *(m pl)* It
De akademische Bücher *(pl)*
En academic books
Es libros académicos *(m pl)*
Fr livres d'étude *(m pl)*
Pt livros académicos *(m pl)*

libri antichi *(m pl)* It
De antiquarische Bücher *(pl)*
En antiquarian books
Es libros antiguos *(m pl)*
Fr livres anciens *(m pl)*
Pt livros de antiquário *(m pl)*

libri automobilistici *(m pl)* It
De Automobilbücher *(n)*
En automotive books
Es libros sobre el automóvil *(m pl)*
Fr livres sur l'automobile *(m pl)*
Pt livros automotores *(m pl)*

libri d'arte *(m pl)* It
De Kunstbücher *(pl)*
En art books
Es libros de arte *(m pl)*
Fr livres d'art *(m pl)*
Pt livros de arte *(m pl)*

libri d'arte e d'artigianato *(m pl)* It
De Kunstgewerbebücher *(pl)*
En arts and crafts books
Es libros de artes y oficios *(m pl)*
Fr livres artisanaux *(m pl)*
Pt livros de artes e ofícios *(m pl)*

libri di saggistica *(m pl)* It
De Sachbücher *(pl)*
En non-fiction books
Es libros no novelescos *(m pl)*
Fr livres généraux *(m pl)*
Pt livros de não ficção *(m pl)*

libri divulgativi di medicina *(m pl)* It
De volkstümliche Medizinbücher *(pl)*
En popular medical books
Es libros médicos populares *(m pl)*
Fr livres de vulgarisation médicale *(m pl)*
Pt livros de medicina popular *(m pl)*

libri eruditi *(m pl)* It
De gelehrte Bücher *(pl)*
En scholarly books
Es libros eruditos *(m pl)*
Fr livres d'érudition *(m pl)*
Pt livros de estudo *(m pl)*

libri pedagogici *(m pl)* It
De Erziehungsbücher *(pl)*
En educational books *pl n*
Es libros educativos *(m pl)*
Fr livres éducatifs *(m pl)*
Pt livros educacionais *(m pl)*

libri per bambini *(m pl)* It
De Kinderbücher *(pl)*
En children's books
Es libros para niños *(m pl)*
Fr livres pour enfants *(m pl)*
Pt livros infantís *(m pl)*

libri pratici *(m pl)* It
De praktische Bücher *(pl)*
En practical books
Es libros prácticos *(m pl)*
Fr ouvrages pratiques *(m pl)*
Pt livros prácticos *(m pl)*

libri prescolastici *(m)* It
De Vorschulbücher *(pl)*
En pre-school books
Es libros preescolares *(m)*
Fr livres préscolaires *(m pl)*
Pt livros pré-escolares *(m)*

libri rilegati *(m pl)* It
De gebundene Bücher *(pl)*
En bound books
Es libros encuadernados *(m pl)*
Fr livres reliés *(m pl)*
Pt livros encadernados *(m pl)*

libri scientifici divulgativi *(m pl)* It
De volkstümliche wissenschaftliche Bücher *(pl)*
En popular scientific books
Es libros científicos populares *(m pl)*
Fr livres de vulgarisation scientifique *(m pl)*
Pt livros científicos populares *(m pl)*

libri scientifici e tecnici *(m pl)* It
De wissenschaftliche und technische Bücher *(pl)*
En scientific and technical books
Es libros científicos y técnicos *(m pl)*
Fr ouvrages scientifiques et techniques *(m pl)*
Pt livros científicos e técnicos *(m pl)*

libri vendite per posta *(m pl)* It
De Versandhausbücher *(pl)*
En mail-order books
Es libros pedidos por correo *(m pl)*
Fr livres vendus par correspondance *(m pl)*
Pt livros para encomenda por correio *(m pl)*

libro *(m) n* Es, It
De Buch *(n)*
En book
Fr livre *(m)*
Pt livro *(m)*

libro a costa fissa *(m)* It
De Buch mit festem Rücken *(n)*
En fixed back book
Es libro de lomo fijo *(m)*
Fr livre à dos fixe *(m)*
Pt livro de lombada fixa *(m)*

libro a costa piatta *(m)* It
De Buch mit flachen Rücken *(n)*
En flat-back book
Es libro de lomo liso *(m)*
Fr livre à dos plat *(m)*
Pt livro de lombada plana *(m)*

libro a tre quarti rilegato *(m)* It
De dreiviertel-gebundenes Buch *(n)*
En three-quarter bound book
Es libro encuadernado a tres cuartos de piel *(m)*
Fr livre en demi-reliure amateur *(m)*
Pt livro encadernado a três quartos *(m)*

libro commerciale *(m)* It
De Fachbuch *(n)*
En trade book
Es libro profesional *(m)*
Fr livre professionnel *(m)*
Pt livro de ofícios *(m)*

libro con copertina rigida *(m)* It
De gebundenes Buch *(n)*
En hardback book
Es libro encuadernado *(m)*
Fr livre relié *(m)*
Pt livro de lombada dura *(m)*

libro de cocina *(m)* Es
De Kochbuch *(n)*
En cookery book
Fr livre de cuisine *(m)*
It libro di cucina *(m)*
Pt livro de cozinha *(m)*

libro de derecho *(m)* Es
De Rechtsbuch *(n)*
En legal book
Fr ouvrage juridique *(m)*
It libro legale *(m)*
Pt livro jurídico *(m)*

libro de lectura *(m)* Es
De Lesebuch *(n)*
En reader (book)
Fr livre de lecture *(m)*
It libro di lettura *(m)*
Pt exemplar de leitura *(m)*

libro de lomo fijo *(m)* Es
De Buch mit festem Rücken *(n)*
En fixed back book
Fr livre à dos fixe *(m)*
It libro a costa fissa *(m)*
Pt livro de lombada fixa *(m)*

libro de lomo liso *(m)* Es
De Buch mit flachen Rücken *(n)*
En flat-back book
Fr livre à dos plat *(m)*
It libro a costa piatta *(m)*
Pt livro de lombada plana *(m)*

libro de mercado de mesas *(m)* Es
De Massenabsatz-Buch *(n)*
En mass-market book
Fr livre à gros tirage *(m)*
It libro per mercato di massa *(m)*
Pt livro para mercado de massas *(m)*

libro de texto *(m)* Es
De Lehrbuch *(n)*
En textbook
Fr manuel *(m)*
It libro di testo *(m)*
Pt livro de texto *(m)*

libro de viajes *(m)* Es
De Reisebuch *(n)*
En travel book
Fr livre touristique *(m)*
It libro di viaggio *(m)*
Pt livro de viagens *(m)*

libro di consultazione *(m)* It
De Nachschlagewerk *(n)*
En reference book
Es obra de consulta *(f)*
Fr livre de référence *(m)*
Pt livro de consulta *(m)*

libro di cucina *(m)* It
De Kochbuch *(n)*
En cookery book
Es libro de cocina *(m)*
Fr livre de cuisine *(m)*
Pt livro de cozinha *(m)*

libro di lettura *(m)* It
De Lesebuch *(n)*
En reader (book)
Es libro de lectura *(m)*
Fr livre de lecture *(m)*
Pt exemplar de leitura *(m)*

libro di poesia *(m)* It
De Gedichtband *(m)*
En poetry book
Es libro do poesías *(m)*
Fr livre de poésie *(m)*
Pt livro de poesia *(m)*

libro di testo *(m)* It
De Lehrbuch *(n)*
En textbook
Es libro de texto *(m)*
Fr manuel *(m)*
Pt livro de texto *(m)*

libro di viaggio *(m)* It
De Reisebuch *(n)*
En travel book
Es libro de viajes *(m)*
Fr livre touristique *(m)*
Pt livro de viagens *(m)*

libro do poesías *(m)* Es
De Gedichtband *(m)*
En poetry book
Fr livre de poésie *(m)*
It libro di poesia *(m)*
Pt livro de poesia *(m)*

libro economico commerciale *(m)* It
De Fach-Taschenbuch *(n)*
En trade paperback
Es libro profesional en rústica *(m)*
Fr fascicule professionnel *(m)*

Pt livro de bolso
comercial *(m)*

libro encuadernado *(m)*
Es
De gebundenes Buch *(n)*
En hardback book
Fr livre relié *(m)*
It libro con copertina
rigida *(m)*
Pt livro de lombada dura
(m)

libro encuadernado a
cuarta piel *(m)* Es
De Buchband mit engem
Lederrücken *(n)*
En quarter-bound book
Fr demi-reliure *(f)*
It libro rilegato con
dorso in pelle *(m)*
Pt livro in quarto *(m)*

libro encuadernado a
media piel *(m)* Es
De halbgebundenes
Buch *(n)*
En half-bound book
Fr livre en demi-reliure
(m)
It libro mezzo rilegato
(m)
Pt livro encadernado a
meia pele *(m)*

libro encuadernado a
tres cuartos de piel
(m) Es
De dreiviertel-
gebundenes Buch *(n)*
En three-quarter bound
book
Fr livre en demi-reliure
amateur *(m)*
It libro a tre quarti
rilegato *(m)*
Pt livro encadernado a
três quartos *(m)*

libro encuadernado en
piel *(m)* Es
De ledergebundenes
Buch *(n)*
En leather-bound book
Fr livre relié cuir *(m)*
It libro rilegato in pelle
(m)
Pt livro encadernado a
carneira *(m)*

libro encuadernado en
tela *(m)* Es
De Leinenbandbuch *(n)*
En cloth-bound book
Fr livre relié pleine toile
(m)
It libro rilegato in tela
(m)
Pt livro encadernado em
tela *(m)*

libro encuadernado para
biblioteca *(m)* Es
De Buch mit
Bibliothek-Einband
(n)
En library-bound book
Fr reliure bibliothèque
publique *(f)*
It libro rilegato per
biblioteca *(m)*
Pt livro encadernado
para biblioteca *(m)*

libro encuadernado sin
costura *(m)* Es
De klebegebundenes
Buch *(n)*
En perfect-bound book
Fr livre relié sans
couture *(m)*
It libro perfettamente
rilegato *(m)*
Pt livro encadernado
sem costura *(m)*

libro en rústica *(m)* Es
De Taschenbuch *(n)*
En paperback book
Fr livre de poche *(m)*
It libro in edizione
economica *(m)*
Pt livro de bolso *(m)*

libro escolar *(m)* Es
De Schulbuch *(n)*
En schoolbook
Fr livre scolaire *(m)*
It testo scolastico *(m)*
Pt livro escolar *(m)*

libro especializado *(m)*
Es
De Spezial-Buch *(n)*
En specialist book
Fr ouvrage spécialisé
(m)
It libro specialistico *(m)*
Pt livro para
especialistas *(m)*

libro illustrato *(m)* It
De illustriertes Buch *(n)*
En illustrated book
Es libro ilustrado *(m)*
Fr livre illustré *(m)*
Pt livro ilustrado *(m)*

libro ilustrado *(m)* Es
De illustriertes Buch *(n)*
En illustrated book
Fr livre illustré *(m)*
It libro illustrato *(m)*
Pt livro ilustrado *(m)*

libro in edizione
economica *(m)* It
De Taschenbuch *(n)*
En paperback book
Es libro en rústica *(m)*
Fr livre de poche *(m)*
Pt livro de bolso *(m)*

libro legale *(m)* It
De Rechtsbuch *(n)*
En legal book
Es libro de derecho *(m)*
Fr ouvrage juridique *(m)*
Pt livro jurídico *(m)*

libro mezzo rilegato *(m)*
It
De halbgebundenes
Buch *n*
En half-bound book
Es libro encuadernado a
media piel *(m)*
Fr livre en demi-reliure
(m)
Pt livro encadernado a
meia pele *(m)*

libro perfettamente
rilegato *(m)* It
De klebegebundenes
Buch *(n)*
En perfect-bound book
Es libro encuadernado
sin costura *(m)*
Fr livre relié sans
couture *(m)*
Pt livro encadernado
sem costura *(m)*

libro per mercato di
massa *(m)* It
De Massenabsatz-Buch
(n)
En mass-market book
Es libro de mercado de
mesas *(m)*
Fr livre à gros tirage *(m)*

Pt livro para mercado de
massas *(m)*

libro profesional *(m)* Es
De Fachbuch *(n)*
En trade book
Fr livre professionnel
(m)
It libro commerciale
(m)
Pt livro de ofícios
(m)

libro profesional en
rústica *(m)* Es
De Fach-Taschenbuch
(n)
En trade paperback
Fr fascicule
professionnel *(m)*
It libro economico
commerciale *(m)*
Pt livro de bolso
comercial *(m)*

libro profusamente
ilustrado *(m)* Es
De stark illustriertes
Buch *(n)*
En highly illustrated
book
Fr livre abondamment
illustré *(m)*
It libro riccamente
illustrato *(m)*
Pt livro muito ilustrado
(m)

libro riccamente
illustrato *(m)* It
De stark illustriertes
Buch *(n)*
En highly illustrated
book
Es libro profusamente
ilustrado *(m)*
Fr livre abondamment
illustré *(m)*
Pt livro muito ilustrado
(m)

libro rilegato con dorso
in pelle *(m)* It
De Buchband mit engem
Lederrücken *(n)*
En quarter-bound book
Es libro encuadernado a
cuarta piel *(m)*
Fr demi-reliure *(f)*
Pt livro in quarto *(m)*

libro rilegato in pelle *(m)*
It
De ledergebundenes
Buch *(n)*
En leather-bound book
Es libro encuadernado
en piel *(m)*
Fr livre relié cuir *(m)*
Pt livro encadernado a
carneira *(m)*

libro rilegato in tela *(m)*
It
De Leinenbandbuch *(n)*
En cloth-bound book
Es libro encuadernado
en tela *(m)*
Fr livre relié pleine toile
(m)
Pt livro encadernado em
tela *(m)*

**libro rilegato per
biblioteca** *(m)* It
De Buch mit
Bibliothek-Einband
(n)
En library-bound book
Es libro encuadernado
para biblioteca *(m)*
Fr reliure bibliothèque
publique *(f)*
Pt livro encadernado
para biblioteca *(m)*

libros académicos *(m pl)*
Es
De akademische Bücher
(pl)
En academic books
Fr livres d'étude *(m pl)*
It libri accademici *(m pl)*
Pt livros académicos *(m
pl)*

libros antiguos *(m pl)* Es
De antiquarische Bücher
(pl)
En antiquarian books
Fr livres anciens *(m pl)*
It libri antichi *(m pl)*
Pt livros de antiquário
(m pl)

**libros científicos
populares** *(m pl)* Es
De volkstümliche
wissenschaftliche
Bücher *(pl)*
En popular scientific
books

Fr livres de vulgarisation
scientifique *(m pl)*
It libri scientifici
divulgativi *(m pl)*
Pt livros científicos
populares *(m pl)*

**libros científicos y
técnicos** *(m pl)* Es
De wissenschaftliche
und technische
Bücher *(pl)*
En scientific and
technical books
Fr ouvrages
scientifiques et
techniques *(m pl)*
It libri scientifici e
tecnici *(m pl)*
Pt livros científicos e
técnicos *(m pl)*

libros de arte *(m pl)* Es
De Kunstbücher *(pl)*
En art books
Fr livres d'art *(m pl)*
It libri d'arte *(m pl)*
Pt livros de arte *(m pl)*

libros de artes y oficios
(m pl) Es
De Kunstgewerbebücher
(pl)
En arts and crafts books
Fr livres artisanaux *(m
pl)*
It libri d'arte e
d'artigianato *(m pl)*
Pt livros de artes e
ofícios *(m pl)*

libros de medicina *(m pl)*
Es
De Medizinbücher *(pl)*
En medical books
Fr ouvrages médicaux
(m pl)
It testi di medicina *(m
pl)*
Pt livros de medicina *(m
pl)*

**libros de trabajos
manuales** *(m pl)* Es
De Handwerksbücher
(pl)
En craft books
Fr ouvrages artisanaux
(m pl)
It guide pratiche *(f pl)*
Pt livros técnicos *(m pl)*

libros educativos *(m pl)*
Es
De Erziehungsbücher *(pl)*
En educational books
Fr livres éducatifs *(m pl)*
It libri pedagogici *(m pl)*
Pt livros educacionais
(m pl)

libros encuadernados
(m pl) Es
De gebundene Bücher
(pl)
En bound books
Fr livres reliés *(m pl)*
It libri rilegati *(m pl)*
Pt livros encadernados
(m pl)

libros eruditos *(m pl)* Es
De gelehrte Bücher *(pl)*
En scholarly books
Fr livres d'érudition *(m
pl)*
It libri eruditi *(m pl)*
Pt livros de estudo *(m
pl)*

**libros médicos
populares** *(m pl)* Es
De volkstümliche
Medizinbücher *(pl)*
En popular medical
books
Fr livres de vulgarisation
médicale *(m pl)*
It libri divulgativi di
medicina *(m pl)*
Pt livros de medicina
popular *(m pl)*

libros no novelescos *(m
pl)* Es
De Sachbücher *(pl)*
En non-fiction books
Fr livres généraux *(m pl)*
It libri di saggistica *(m
pl)*
Pt livros de não ficção
(m pl)

libros para niños *(m pl)*
Es
De Kinderbücher *(pl)*
En children's books
Fr livres pour enfants *(m
pl)*
It libri per bambini *(m
pl)*
Pt livros infantís *(m pl)*

libro specialistico *(m)* It
De Spezial-Buch *(n)*
En specialist book
Es libro especializado
(m)
Fr ouvrage spécialisé
(m)
Pt livro para
especialistas *(m)*

**libros pedidos por
correo** *(m pl)* Es
De Versandhausbücher
(pl)
En mail-order books
Fr livres vendus par
correspondance *(m
pl)*
It libri vendite per posta
(m pl)
Pt livros para
encomenda por
correio *(m pl)*

libros prácticos *(m pl)* Es
De praktische Bücher
(pl)
En practical books
Fr ouvrages pratiques
(m pl)
It libri pratici *(m pl)*
Pt livros prácticos *(m pl)*

libros preescolares *(m)*
Es
De Vorschulbücher *(pl)*
En pre-school books
Fr livres préscolaires *(m
pl)*
It libri prescolastici *(m)*
Pt livros pré-escolares
(m)

**libros sobre el
automóvil** *(m pl)* Es
De Automobilbücher *(n)*
En automotive books
Fr livres sur
l'automobile *(m pl)*
It libri automobilistici
(m pl)
Pt livros automotores
(m pl)

libro tecnico *(m)* It
De technisches Buch *(n)*
En technical book
Es libro técnico *(m)*
Fr ouvrage technique
(m)
Pt livro técnico *(m)*

libro técnico *(m)* Es
De technisches Buch *(n)*
En technical book
Fr ouvrage technique
(m)
It libro tecnico *(m)*
Pt livro técnico *(m)*

licencier *vb* Fr
De entlassen
En lay off
Es despedir
It licenziare
Pt dispensar
temporariamente

licenziare *vb* It
De entlassen
En lay off
Es despedir
Fr licencier
Pt dispensar
temporariamente

Lichtbeständigkeit *(f) n*
De
En fastness (to light)
Es solidez a la luz *(f)*
Fr solidité à la lumière
(f)
It stabilità alla luce *(f)*
Pt inalterabilidade à luz
(f)

Lichtdruck *(m) n* De
En collotype
Es colotipia *(f)*
Fr phototype *(m)*
It collotipia *(f)*
Pt colotipo *(m)*

Lichter *(pl)* De
En highlights *pl n*
Es blancos *(m pl)*
Fr grandes lumières *(f pl)*
It alte luci *(f pl)*
Pt partes claras *(f pl)*

Lichtquelle *(f) n* De
En light source
Es fuente luminosa *(f)*
Fr source lumineuse *(f)*
It fonte luminosa *(f)*
Pt fonte luminosa *(f)*

Lieferant *(m) n* De
En supplier
Es proveedor *(m)*
Fr fournisseur *(m)*

It fornitore *(m)*
Pt fornecedor *(m)*

liga *(f) n* Pt
De Legierung *(f)*
En alloy
Es aleación *(f)*
Fr alliage *(m)*
It lega *(f)*

ligado *(m) n* Es
De Ligatur *(f)*
En ligature
Fr ligature *(f)*
It legatura *(f)*
Pt letras ligadas *(f pl)*

ligar *vb* Pt
De in Kontakt stehen
En liaise
Es enlazar
Fr garder contact
It collegarsi

Ligatur *(f) n* De
En ligature
Es ligado *(m)*
Fr ligature *(f)*
It legatura *(f)*
Pt letras ligadas *(f pl)*

ligature *n* En; Fr *(f)*
De Ligatur *(f)*
Es ligado *(m)*
It legatura *(f)*
Pt letras ligadas *(f pl)*

light box En
De Leuchtkasten *(m)*
Es caja de luz *(f)*
Fr boîte lumineuse *(f)*
It cassa luminosa *(f)*
Pt caixa de luz *(f)*

light source En
De Lichtquelle *(f)*
Es fuente luminosa *(f)*
Fr source lumineuse *(f)*
It fonte luminosa *(f)*
Pt fonte luminosa *(f)*

light table En
De Leuchttisch *(m)*
Es mesa de retoque *(f)*
Fr table lumineuse *(f)*
It tavolo luminoso *(m)*
Pt mesa de retoque *(f)*

ligne *(f) n* Fr
De Zeile *(f)*
En line
Es línea *(f)*
It linea *(f)*
Pt linha *(f)*

ligne de tête *(f)* Fr
De Kopfzeile *(f)*
En headline (of page)
Es título *(m)*
It titolo *(m)*
Pt linha de cabeçalho *(f)*

lignin *n* En
De Holzfaser *(f)*
Es lignina *(f)*
Fr lignine *(f)*
It lignina *(f)*
Pt lenhose *(f)*

lignina *(f) n* Es, It
De Holzfaser *(f)*
En lignin
Fr lignine *(f)*
Pt lenhose *(f)*

lignine *(f) n* Fr
De Holzfaser *(f)*
En lignin
Es lignina *(f)*
It lignina *(f)*
Pt lenhose *(f)*

limite *(f) n* Fr
De Stichtag *(m)*
En deadline
Es plazo *(m)*
It scadenza *(f)*
Pt prazo *(m)*

line *n* En
De Zeile *(f)*
Es línea *(f)*
Fr ligne *(f)*
It linea *(f)*
Pt linha *(f)*

linea *(f) n* It
De Zeile *(f)*
En line
Es línea *(f)*
Fr ligne *(f)*
Pt linha *(f)*

línea *(f) n* Es
De Zeile *(f)*
En line
Fr ligne *(f)*

It linea *(f)*
Pt linha *(f)*

linea e tono It
De Strich und Ton
En line and tone
Es línea y tono
Fr trait-simili
Pt linha e tono

line and tone En
De Strich und Ton
Es línea y tono
Fr trait-simili
It linea e tono
Pt linha e tono

**líneas en papel
verjurado** *(f pl)* Es
De Wasserlinien *(f pl)*
En laid lines
Fr vergeures *(f pl)*
It vergature *(f pl)*
Pt linhas enramadas *(f pl)*

**lineato a
demi-quadratone**
(m) It
De Halbgeviertstrich *(m)*
En en rule
Es pleca de medio
cuadratín *(f)*
Fr tiret sur
demi-cadratin *(m)*
Pt filete de meio
quadratim *(m)*

lineato a quadratone *(m)*
It
De Geviertstrich *(m)*
En em rule
Es pleca-cuadratín *(f)*
Fr tiret sur cadratin *(m)*
Pt filete de quadratim
(m)

línea y tono Es
De Strich und Ton
En line and tone
Fr trait-simili
It linea e tono
Pt linha e tono

line block En
De Strichätzung *(f)*
Es fotograbado de línea
(m)
Fr cliché au trait *(m)*
It cliché a tratto *(m)*

Pt placa de estereotipia
(f)

linecasting machine En
De Zeilengießmaschine
(f)
Es fundidora de lingotes
(f)
Fr fondeuse à la ligne (f)
It macchina fonditrice a
linea (f)
Pt fundidora de lingotes
(f)

line composition En
De Zeilensatz (m)
Es composición por
líneas (f)
Fr photogravure
typographique (f)
It composizione della
linea (f)
Pt composição de
linhas (f)

line drawing En
De Strichzeichnung (f)
Es dibujo de línea (m)
Fr dessin au trait (m)
It disegno a tratteggio
(m)
Pt desenho a lápis ou
pena (m)

linee finissime (f pl) It
De Haarstriche (pl)
En hair lines
Es filetes extrafinos (m
pl)
Fr déliés (m pl)
Pt filetes extrafinos (m
pl)

lineetta (f) n It
De Gedankenstrich (m)
En dash
Es raya (f)
Fr filet (m)
Pt filete (m)

lineetta discrezionale (f)
It
De willkürlicher
Trennstrich (m)
En discretionary hyphen
Es guión discrecional
(m)
Fr trait d'union facultatif
(m)
Pt traço de união
discricionário (m)

line number En
De Zeilenzahl (f)
Es número de líneas (m)
Fr numéro de ligne (m)
It numero di linea (m)
Pt número de linha (m)

line printer En
De Zeilendrucker (m)
Es impresora de líneas
(f)
Fr imprimante ligne par
ligne (f)
It stampatrice per righe
(f)
Pt impressora de linha
(f)

line space En
De Zeilenabstand (m)
Es espacio entre líneas
(m)
Fr espace entre deux
lignes (m)
It spazio tra le righe (m)
Pt espaço entre linhas
(m)

line up En
De ausrichten
Es alinear
Fr parangonner
It allineare
Pt alinhar

lingot (m) n Fr
De Setzmaschinenzeile
(f)
En slug
Es lingote (m)
It riga intera (f)
Pt lingote (m)

lingote (m) n Es, Pt
De Setzmaschinenzeile
(f)
En slug
Fr lingot (m)
It riga intera (f)

**linguagem de
programação** (f) Pt
Am program language
De Programmiersprache
(f)
En programme language
Es lenguaje de
programación (m)
Fr langage de
programmation (m)
It linguaggio di
programma (m)

**linguagem
independente da
máquina** (f) Pt
De maschinen-
unabhängige
Sprache (f)
En machine-
independent
language
Es lenguaje universal
(m)
Fr langage indépendant
du calculateur (m)
It linguaggio universale
(m)

**linguaggio di
programma** (m) It
Am program language
De Programmiersprache
(f)
En programme language
Es lenguaje de
programación (m)
Fr langage de
programmation (m)
Pt linguagem de
programação (f)

linguaggio macchina (m)
It
De Maschinensprache (f)
En machine language
Es lenguaje de máquina
(m)
Fr langage machine (m)
Pt linguagem de
máquina (f)

linguaggio universale
(m) It
De maschinen-
unabhängige
Sprache (f)
En machine-
independent
language
Es lenguaje universal
(m)

linguagem de máquina
(f) Pt
De Maschinensprache (f)
En machine language
Es lenguaje de máquina
(m)
Fr langage machine (m)
It linguaggio macchina
(m)

Fr langage indépendant
du calculateur (m)
Pt linguagem
independente da
máquina (f)

linha (f) n Pt
De Zeile (f)
En line
Es línea (f)
Fr ligne (f)
It linea (f)

linha de cabeçalho (f) Pt
De Kopfzeile (f)
En headline (of page)
Es título (m)
Fr ligne de tête (f)
It titolo (m)

linha e tono Pt
De Strich und Ton
En line and tone
Es línea y tono
Fr trait-simili
It linea e tono

linha recta (f) Pt
De Strich (m)
En rule
Es filete (m)
Fr règle (f)
It filetto (m)

linhas à pena (m) Pt
De Federlinierung (f)
En pen ruling
Es rayado a pluma (m)
Fr réglure au crayon (f)
It sottolineatura a
penna (f)

linhas enramadas (f pl)
Pt
De Wasserlinien (f pl)
En laid lines
Es líneas en papel
verjurado (f pl)
Fr vergeures (f pl)
It vergature (f pl)

**linhas pautadas a
azul-claro** (f pl) Pt
De blaue Linien (pl)
En feints pl n
Es rayas en azul (f pl)
Fr règles en bleu clair (f
pl)
It righi finti (m pl)

Linieneinfassung *(f) n*
De
En box rule
Es filete de marco *(m)*
Fr filet d'encadrement
latéral *(m)*
It filleto di cornice *(m)*
Pt filete de requadro *(m)*

linke Seite *(f)* De
En left-hand page
Es página izquierda *(f)*
Fr fausse page *(f)*
It pagina di sinistra *(f)*
Pt página de esquerda
(f)

links in Linie bringen De
En range left
Es alinear al margen
izquierdo
Fr aligner à gauche
It allineare
verticalmente a
sinistra
Pt explorar esquerda

**links in Linie gebrachte
Überschrift** *(f)* De
En side head
Es titulillo lateral *(m)*
Fr tête latérale *(f)*
It titolo laterale *(m)*
Pt título lateral *(m)*

lino cut En
De Linolschnitt *(m)*
Es grabado de linóleo
(m)
Fr gravure sur linoléum
(f)
It incisione in linoleum
(f)
Pt gravura em linóleo *(f)*

Linolschnitt *(m) n* De
En lino cut
Es grabado de linóleo
(m)
Fr gravure sur linoléum
(f)
It incisione in linoleum
(f)
Pt gravura em linóleo *(f)*

liquidé *adj* Fr
De ausverkauft
En sold out
Es agotado
It esaurito
Pt esgotado

lire *vb* Fr
De lesen
En read
Es leer
It leggere
Pt ler

list (publisher's) *n* En
De Liste *(f)*
Es lista *(f)*
Fr liste *(f)*
It elenco *(m)*
Pt lista *(f)*

lista *(f) n* Es, Pt
De Liste *(f)*
En list (publisher's)
Fr liste *(f)*
It elenco *(m)*

lista de ficção *(f)* Pt
De Romanliteratur-Liste
(f)
En fiction list
Es catálogo de novelas
(m)
Fr catalogue des
romans *(m)*
It elenco di narrativa
(m)

lista de inscrição *(f)* Pt
De Eintragsliste *(f)*
En entry list
Es relación de artículos
(f)
Fr liste des entrées *(f)*
It elenco di voci *(m)*

lista de outono *(f)* Pt
De Herbstliste *(f)*
En autumn list
Es catálogo de otoño
(m)
Fr catalogue de la
rentrée *(m)*
It elenco d'autunno *(m)*

**lista de palabras
principales** *(f)* Es
De Liste der haupten
Wörter *(f)*
En headword list
Fr liste des mots
en-têtes *(f)*
It elenco di parole
principali *(m)*
Pt lista de
palavras-índice *(f)*

lista de palavras-índice
(f) Pt
De Liste der haupten
Wörter *(f)*
En headword list
Es lista de palabras
principales *(f)*
Fr liste des mots
en-têtes *(f)*
It elenco di parole
principali *(m)*

lista de precios *(f)* Es
De Preisliste *(f)*
En price list
Fr prix-courant *(m)*
It listino prezzi *(m)*
Pt lista de preços *(f)*

lista de preços *(f)* Pt
De Preisliste *(f)*
En price list
Es lista de precios *(f)*
Fr prix-courant *(m)*
It listino prezzi *(m)*

lista de Primavera *(f)* Pt
De Frühjahrsliste *(f)*
En spring list
Es catálogo de
primavera *(m)*
Fr catalogue de
printemps *(m)*
It elenco di primavera
(m)

liste *(f) n* Fr
De Liste *(f)*
En list (publisher's)
Es lista *(f)*
It elenco *(m)*
Pt lista *(f)*

Liste *(f) n* De
En list (publisher's)
Es lista *(f)*
Fr liste *(f)*
It elenco *(m)*
Pt lista *(f)*

**Liste der haupten
Wörter** *(f)* De
En headword list
Es lista de palabras
principales *(f)*
Fr liste des mots
en-têtes *(f)*
It elenco di parole
principali *(m)*
Pt lista de
palavras-índice *(f)*

liste des entrées *(f)* Fr
De Eintragsliste *(f)*
En entry list
Es relación de artículos
(f)
It elenco di voci *(m)*
Pt lista de inscrição *(f)*

liste des mots en-têtes
(f) Fr
De Liste der haupten
Wörter *(f)*
En headword list
Es lista de palabras
principales *(f)*
It elenco di parole
principali *(m)*
Pt lista de
palavras-índice *(f)*

listino prezzi *(m)* It
De Preisliste *(f)*
En price list
Es lista de precios *(f)*
Fr prix-courant *(m)*
Pt lista de preços *(f)*

literal *n* En
De Setzfehler *(m)*
Es error de imprenta *(m)*
Fr coquille *(f)*
It errore di stampa *(m)*
Pt errata literal *(f)*

literario *adj* Es
De literarisch
En literary
Fr littéraire
It letterario
Pt literário

literário *adj* Pt
De literarisch
En literary
Es literario
Fr littéraire
It letterario

literarisch *adj* De
En literary
Es literario
Fr littéraire
It letterario
Pt literário

literarische Beilage *(f)*
De
En literary supplement
Es suplemento literario
(m)

Fr supplément littéraire
   (m)
It supplemento
   letterario *(m)*
Pt suplemento literário
   (m)

literary *adj* En
De literarisch
Es literario
Fr littéraire
It letterario
Pt literário

literary agent En
De Literatur-Agentur *(f)*
Es agente literario *(m)*
Fr agent littéraire *(m)*
It agente letterario *(m)*
Pt agente literário *(m)*

literary criticism En
De Literaturkritik *(f)*
Es crítica literaria *(f)*
Fr critique littéraire *(f)*
It critica letteraria *(f)*
Pt crítica literária *(f)*

literary supplement En
De literarische Beilage *(f)*
Es suplemento literario
   (m)
Fr supplément littéraire
   (m)
It supplemento
   letterario *(m)*
Pt suplemento literário
   (m)

Literatur *(f)* n De
En literature
Es literatura *(f)*
Fr littérature *(f)*
It letteratura *(f)*
Pt literatura *(f)*

literatura *(f)* n Es, Pt
De Literatur *(f)*
En literature
Fr littérature *(f)*
It letteratura *(f)*

Literatur-Agentur *(f)* De
En literary agent
Es agente literario *(m)*
Fr agent littéraire *(m)*
It agente letterario *(m)*
Pt agente literário *(m)*

literatura novelesca *(f)*
   Es
De Romanliteratur *(f)*
En fiction
Fr romans *(m pl)*
It narrativa *(f)*
Pt ficção *(f)*

literatura popular *(f)* Es
De volkstümliche
   Romanliteratur *(f)*
En popular fiction
Fr romans populaires
   (m pl)
It narrativa popolare *(f)*
Pt ficção popular *(f)*

literature *n* En
De Literatur *(f)*
Es literatura *(f)*
Fr littérature *(f)*
It letteratura *(f)*
Pt literatura *(f)*

Literaturkritik *(f)* n De
En literary criticism
Es crítica literaria *(f)*
Fr critique littéraire *(f)*
It critica letteraria *(f)*
Pt crítica literária *(f)*

Literaturverzeichnis *(n)*
   n De
En bibliography
Es bibliografía *(f)*
Fr bibliographie *(f)*
It bibliografia *(f)*
Pt bibliografia *(f)*

litho en offset *(f)* Fr
De Offset-
   Lithographiedruck
   (m)
En offset lithography
Es litografía offset *(f)*
It litografia offset *(f)*
Pt litografia offset *(f)*

lithographie *(f)* n Fr
De Lithographie *(f)*
En lithography
Es litografía *(f)*
It litografia *(f)*
Pt litografia *(f)*

Lithographie *(f)* n De
En lithography
Es litografía *(f)*
Fr lithographie *(f)*
It litografia *(f)*
Pt litografia *(f)*

lithography *n* En
De Lithographie *(f)*
Es litografía *(f)*
Fr lithographie *(f)*
It litografia *(f)*
Pt litografia *(f)*

litografia *(f)* n It, Pt
De Lithographie *(f)*
En lithography
Es litografía *(f)*
Fr lithographie *(f)*

litografía *(f)* n Es
De Lithographie *(f)*
En lithography
Fr lithographie *(f)*
It litografia *(f)*
Pt litografia *(f)*

litografia offset *(f)* It, Pt
De Offset-
   Lithographiedruck
   (m)
En offset lithography
Es litografía offset *(f)*
Fr litho en offset *(f)*

litografía offset *(f)* Es
De Offset-
   Lithographiedruck
   (m)
En offset lithography
Fr litho en offset *(f)*
It litografia offset *(f)*
Pt litografia offset *(f)*

littéraire *adj* Fr
De literarisch
En literary
Es literario
It letterario
Pt literário

littérature *(f)* n Fr
De Literatur *(f)*
En literature
Es literatura *(f)*
It letteratura *(f)*
Pt literatura *(f)*

livraria *(f)* n Pt
De Buchladen *(m)*
En book shop
Es librería *(f)*
Fr librairie *(f)*
It libreria *(f)*

**livraria de restos de
   edição** *(f)* Pt
De Remittenden-
   Buchladen *(m)*
En remainder bookshop
Es librería de restos de
   edición *(f)*
Fr librairie de solde
   d'éditions *(f)*
It libreria di rimanenze
   (f)

livre *(m)* n Fr
De Buch *(n)*
En book
Es libro *(m)*
It libro *(m)*
Pt livro *(m)*

**livre abondamment
   illustré** *(m)* Fr
De stark illustriertes
   Buch *(n)*
En highly illustrated
   book
Es libro profusamente
   ilustrado *(m)*
It libro riccamente
   illustrato *(m)*
Pt livro muito ilustrado
   (m)

livre à dos fixe *(m)* Fr
De Buch mit festem
   Rücken *(n)*
En fixed back book
Es libro de lomo fijo *(m)*
It libro a costa fissa *(m)*
Pt livro de lombada fixa
   (m)

livre à dos plat *(m)* Fr
De Buch mit flachen
   Rücken *(n)*
En flat-back book
Es libro de lomo liso *(m)*
It libro a costa piatta
   (m)
Pt livro de lombada
   plana *(m)*

livre à gros tirage *(m)* Fr
De Massenabsatz-Buch
   (n)
En mass-market book
Es libro de mercado de
   mesas *(m)*
It libro per mercato di
   massa *(m)*
Pt livro para mercado de
   massas *(m)*

livre de cuisine *(m)* Fr
De Kochbuch *(n)*
En cookery book
Es libro de cocina *(m)*
It libro di cucina *(m)*
Pt livro de cozinha *(m)*

livre de lecture *(m)* Fr
De Lesebuch *(n)*
En reader (book)
Es libro de lectura *(m)*
It libro di lettura *(m)*
Pt exemplar de leitura *(m)*

livre de poche *(m)* Fr
De Taschenbuch *(n)*
En paperback book
Es libro en rústica *(m)*
It libro in edizione economica *(m)*
Pt livro de bolso *(m)*

livre de poésie *(m)* Fr
De Gedichtband *(m)*
En poetry book
Es libro do poesías *(m)*
It libro di poesia *(m)*
Pt livro de poesia *(m)*

livre de référence *(m)* Fr
De Nachschlagewerk *(n)*
En reference book
Es obra de consulta *(f)*
It libro di consultazione *(m)*
Pt livro de consulta *(m)*

livre en demi-reliure *(m)* Fr
De halbgebundenes Buch *n*
En half-bound book
Es libro encuadernado a media piel *(m)*
It libro mezzo rilegato *(m)*
Pt livro encadernado a meia pele *(m)*

livre en demi-reliure amateur *(m)* Fr
De dreiviertel-gebundenes Buch *(n)*
En three-quarter bound book
Es libro encuadernado a tres cuartos de piel *(m)*
It libro a tre quarti rilegato *(m)*

Pt livro encadernado a três quartos *(m)*

livre illustré *(m)* Fr
De illustriertes Buch *(n)*
En illustrated book
Es libro ilustrado *(m)*
It libro illustrato *(m)*
Pt livro ilustrado *(m)*

livreiro *(m)* n Pt
De Buchhändler *(m)*
En bookseller
Es vendedor de libros *(m)*
Fr libraire *(m)*
It libraio *(m)*

livre professionnel *(m)* Fr
De Fachbuch *(n)*
En trade book
Es libro profesional *(m)*
It libro commerciale *(m)*
Pt livro de ofícios *(m)*

livre relié *(m)* Fr
De gebundenes Buch *(n)*
En hardback book
Es libro encuadernado *(m)*
It libro con copertina rigida *(m)*
Pt livro de lombada dura *(m)*

livre relié cuir *(m)* Fr
De ledergebundenes Buch *(n)*
En leather-bound book
Es libro encuadernado en piel *(m)*
It libro rilegato in pelle *(m)*
Pt livro encadernado a carneira *(m)*

livre relié pleine toile *(m)* Fr
De Leinenbandbuch *(n)*
En cloth-bound book
Es libro encuadernado en tela *(m)*
It libro rilegato in tela *(m)*
Pt livro encadernado em tela *(m)*

livre relié sans couture *(m)* Fr
De klebegebundenes Buch *(n)*
En perfect-bound book
Es libro encuadernado sin costura *(m)*
It libro perfettamente rilegato *(m)*
Pt livro encadernado sem costura *(m)*

livres anciens *(m pl)* Fr
De antiquarische Bücher *(pl)*
En antiquarian books
Es libros antiguos *(m pl)*
It libri antichi *(m pl)*
Pt livros de antiquário *(m pl)*

livres artisanaux *(m pl)* Fr
De Kunstgewerbebücher *(pl)*
En arts and crafts books
Es libros de artes y oficios *(m pl)*
It libri d´arte e d´artigianato *(m pl)*
Pt livros de artes e ofícios *(m pl)*

livre scolaire *(m)* Fr
De Schulbuch *(n)*
En schoolbook
Es libro escolar *(m)*
It testo scolastico *(m)*
Pt livro escolar *(m)*

livres d'art *(m pl)* Fr
De Kunstbücher *(pl)*
En art books
Es libros de arte *(m pl)*
It libri d´arte *(m pl)*
Pt livros de arte *(m pl)*

livres d'érudition *(m pl)* Fr
De gelehrte Bücher *(pl)*
En scholarly books
Es libros eruditos *(m pl)*
It libri eruditi *(m pl)*
Pt livros de estudo *(m pl)*

livres d'étude *(m pl)* Fr
De akademische Bücher *(pl)*
En academic books
Es libros académicos *(m pl)*

It libri accademici *(m pl)*
Pt livros académicos *(m pl)*

livres de vulgarisation médicale *(m pl)* Fr
De volkstümliche Medizinbücher *(pl)*
En popular medical books
Es libros médicos populares *(m pl)*
It libri divulgativi di medicina *(m pl)*
Pt livros de medicina popular *(m pl)*

livres de vulgarisation scientifique *(m pl)* Fr
De volkstümliche wissenschaftliche Bücher *(pl)*
En popular scientific books
Es libros científicos populares *(m pl)*
It libri scientifici divulgativi *(m pl)*
Pt livros científicos populares *(m pl)*

livres éducatifs *(m pl)* Fr
De Erziehungsbücher *(pl)*
En educational books
Es libros educativos *(m pl)*
It libri pedagogici *(m pl)*
Pt livros educacionais *(m pl)*

livres généraux *(m pl)* Fr
De Sachbücher *(pl)*
En non-fiction books
Es libros no novelescos *(m pl)*
It libri di saggistica *(m pl)*
Pt livros de não ficção *(m pl)*

livres pour enfants *(m pl)* Fr
De Kinderbücher *(pl)*
En children´s books
Es libros para niños *(m pl)*
It libri per bambini *(m pl)*
Pt livros infantís *(m pl)*

livres préscolaires *(m pl)*
Fr
De Vorschulbücher *(pl)*
En pre-school books
Es libros preescolares *(m)*
It libri prescolastici *(m)*
Pt livros pré-escolares *(m)*

livres reliés *(m pl)* Fr
De gebundene Bücher *(pl)*
En bound books
Es libros encuadernados *(m pl)*
It libri rilegati *(m pl)*
Pt livros encadernados *(m pl)*

livres sur l'automobile *(m pl)* Fr
De Automobilbücher *(n)*
En automotive books
Es libros sobre el automóvil *(m pl)*
It libri automobilistici *(m pl)*
Pt livros automotores *(m pl)*

livres vendus par correspondance *(m pl)* Fr
De Versandhausbücher *(pl)*
En mail-order books
Es libros pedidos por correo *(m pl)*
It libri vendite per posta *(m pl)*
Pt livros para encomenda por correio *(m pl)*

livre touristique *(m)* Fr
De Reisebuch *(n)*
En travel book
Es libro de viajes *(m)*
It libro di viaggio *(m)*
Pt livro de viagens *(m)*

livro *(m)* n Pt
De Buch *(n)*
En book
Es libro *(m)*
Fr livre *(m)*
It libro *(m)*

livro de bolso *(m)* Pt
De Taschenbuch *(n)*
En paperback book
Es libro en rústica *(m)*
Fr livre de poche *(m)*
It libro in edizione economica *(m)*

livro de bolso comercial *(m)* Pt
De Fach-Taschenbuch *(n)*
En trade paperback
Es libro profesional en rústica *(m)*
Fr fascicule professionnel *(m)*
It libro economico commerciale *(m)*

livro de consulta *(m)* Pt
De Nachschlagewerk *(n)*
En reference book
Es obra de consulta *(f)*
Fr livre de référence *(m)*
It libro di consultazione *(m)*

livro de cozinha *(m)* Pt
De Kochbuch *(n)*
En cookery book
Es libro de cocina *(m)*
Fr livre de cuisine *(m)*
It libro di cucina *(m)*

livro de lombada dura *(m)* Pt
De gebundenes Buch *(n)*
En hardback book
Es libro encuadernado *(m)*
Fr livre relié *(m)*
It libro con copertina rigida *(m)*

livro de lombada fixa *(m)* Pt
De Buch mit festem Rücken *(n)*
En fixed back book
Es libro de lomo fijo *(m)*
Fr livre à dos fixe *(m)*
It libro a costa fissa *(m)*

livro de lombada plana *(m)* Pt
De Buch mit flachen Rücken *(n)*
En flat-back book
Es libro de lomo liso *(m)*
Fr livre à dos plat *(m)*
It libro a costa piatta *(m)*

livro de ofícios *(m)* Pt
De Fachbuch *(n)*
En trade book
Es libro profesional *(m)*
Fr livre professionnel *(m)*
It libro commerciale *(m)*

livro de poesia *(m)* Pt
De Gedichtband *(m)*
En poetry book
Es libro do poesías *(m)*
Fr livre de poésie *(m)*
It libro di poesia *(m)*

livro de texto *(m)* Pt
De Lehrbuch *(n)*
En textbook
Es libro de texto *(m)*
Fr manuel *(m)*
It libro di testo *(m)*

livro de viagens *(m)* Pt
De Reisebuch *(n)*
En travel book
Es libro de viajes *(m)*
Fr livre touristique *(m)*
It libro di viaggio *(m)*

livro encadernado a carneira *(m)* Pt
De ledergebundenes Buch *(n)*
En leather-bound book
Es libro encuadernado en piel *(m)*
Fr livre relié cuir *(m)*
It libro rilegato in pelle *(m)*

livro encadernado a meia pele *(m)* Pt
De halbgebundenes Buch *(n)*
En half-bound book
Es libro encuadernado a media piel *(m)*
Fr livre en demi-reliure *(m)*
It libro mezzo rilegato *(m)*

livro encadernado a três quartos *(m)* Pt
De dreiviertel-gebundenes Buch *(n)*
En three-quarter bound book
Es libro encuadernado a tres cuartos de piel *(m)*
Fr livre en demi-reliure amateur *(m)*
It libro a tre quarti rilegato *(m)*

livro encadernado em tela *(m)* Pt
De Leinenbandbuch *(n)*
En cloth-bound book
Es libro encuadernado en tela *(m)*
Fr livre relié pleine toile *(m)*
It libro rilegato in tela *(m)*

livro encadernado para biblioteca *(m)* Pt
De Buch mit Bibliothek-Einband *(n)*
En library-bound book
Es libro encuadernado para biblioteca *(m)*
Fr reliure bibliothèque publique *(f)*
It libro rilegato per biblioteca *(m)*

livro encadernado sem costura *(m)* Pt
De klebegebundenes Buch *(n)*
En perfect-bound book
Es libro encuadernado sin costura *(m)*
Fr livre relié sans couture *(m)*
It libro perfettamente rilegato *(m)*

livro escolar *(m)* Pt
De Schulbuch *(n)*
En schoolbook
Es libro escolar *(m)*
Fr livre scolaire *(m)*
It testo scolastico *(m)*

livro ilustrado *(m)* Pt
De illustriertes Buch *(n)*
En illustrated book
Es libro ilustrado *(m)*
Fr livre illustré *(m)*
It libro illustrato *(m)*

livro in quarto *(m)* Pt
De Buchband mit engem Lederrücken *(n)*
En quarter-bound book

Es libro encuadernado a cuarta piel *(m)*
Fr demi-reliure *(f)*
It libro rilegato con dorso in pelle *(m)*

livro jurídico *(m)* Pt
De Rechtsbuch *(n)*
En legal book
Es libro de derecho *(m)*
Fr ouvrage juridique *(m)*
It libro legale *(m)*

livro muito ilustrado *(m)* Pt
De stark illustriertes Buch *(n)*
En highly illustrated book
Es libro profusamente ilustrado *(m)*
Fr livre abondamment illustré *(m)*
It libro riccamente illustrato *(m)*

livro para especialistas *(m)* Pt
De Spezial-Buch *(n)*
En specialist book
Es libro especializado *(m)*
Fr ouvrage spécialisé *(m)*
It libro specialistico *(m)*

livro para mercado de massas *(m)* Pt
De Massenabsatz-Buch *(n)*
En mass-market book
Es libro de mercado de mesas *(m)*
Fr livre à gros tirage *(m)*
It libro per mercato di massa *(m)*

livro policial *(m)* Pt
De Kriminalroman *(m)*
En detective novel
Es novela policíaca *(f)*
Fr roman policier *(m)*
It racconto poliziesco *(m)*

livros académicos *(m pl)* Pt
De akademische Bücher *(pl)*
En academic books
Es libros académicos *(m pl)*

Fr livres d'étude *(m pl)*
It libri accademici *(m pl)*

livros automotores *(m pl)* Pt
De Automobilbücher *(n)*
En automotive books
Es libros sobre el automóvil *(m pl)*
Fr livres sur l'automobile *(m pl)*
It libri automobilistici *(m pl)*

livros científicos e técnicos *(m pl)* Pt
De wissenschaftliche und technische Bücher *(pl)*
En scientific and technical books
Es libros científicos y técnicos *(m pl)*
Fr ouvrages scientifiques et techniques *(m pl)*
It libri scientifici e tecnici *(m pl)*

livros científicos populares *(m pl)* Pt
De volkstümliche wissenschaftliche Bücher *(pl)*
En popular scientific books
Es libros científicos populares *(m pl)*
Fr livres de vulgarisation scientifique *(m pl)*
It libri scientifici divulgativi *(m pl)*

livros de antiquário *(m pl)* Pt
De antiquarische Bücher *(pl)*
En antiquarian books
Es libros antiguos *(m pl)*
Fr livres anciens *(m pl)*
It libri antichi *(m pl)*

livros de arte *(m pl)* Pt
De Kunstbücher *(pl)*
En art books
Es libros de arte *(m pl)*
Fr livres d'art *(m pl)*
It libri d'arte *(m pl)*

livros de artes e ofícios *(m pl)* Pt
De Kunstgewerbebücher *(pl)*
En arts and crafts books
Es libros de artes y oficios *(m pl)*
Fr livres artisanaux *(m pl)*
It libri d'arte e d'artigianato *(m pl)*

livros de estudo *(m pl)* Pt
De gelehrte Bücher *(pl)*
En scholarly books
Es libros eruditos *(m pl)*
Fr livres d'érudition *(m pl)*
It libri eruditi *(m pl)*

livros de medicina *(m pl)* Pt
De Medizinbücher *(pl)*
En medical books
Es libros de medicina *(m pl)*
Fr ouvrages médicaux *(m pl)*
It testi di medicina *(m pl)*

livros de medicina popular *(m pl)* Pt
De volkstümliche Medizinbücher *(pl)*
En popular medical books
Es libros médicos populares *(m pl)*
Fr livres de vulgarisation médicale *(m pl)*
It libri divulgativi di medicina *(m pl)*

livros de não ficção *(m pl)* Pt
De Sachbücher *(pl)*
En non-fiction books
Es libros no novelescos *(m pl)*
Fr livres généraux *(m pl)*
It libri di saggistica *(m pl)*

livros educacionais *(m pl)* Pt
De Erziehungsbücher *(pl)*
En educational books
Es libros educativos *(m pl)*
Fr livres éducatifs *(m pl)*
It libri pedagogici *(m pl)*

livros encadernados *(m pl)* Pt
De gebundene Bücher *(pl)*
En bound books
Es libros encuadernados *(m pl)*
Fr livres reliés *(m pl)*
It libri rilegati *(m pl)*

livros infantís *(m pl)* Pt
De Kinderbücher *(pl)*
En children's books
Es libros para niños *(m pl)*
Fr livres pour enfants *(m pl)*
It libri per bambini *(m pl)*

livros para encomenda por correio *(m pl)* Pt
De Versandhausbücher *(pl)*
En mail-order books
Es libros pedidos por correo *(m pl)*
Fr livres vendus par correspondance *(m pl)*
It libri vendite per posta *(m pl)*

livros prácticos *(m pl)* Pt
De praktische Bücher *(pl)*
En practical books
Es libros prácticos *(m pl)*
Fr ouvrages pratiques *(m pl)*
It libri pratici *(m pl)*

livros pré-escolares *(m)* Pt
De Vorschulbücher *(pl)*
En pre-school books
Es libros preescolares *(m)*
Fr livres préscolaires *(m pl)*
It libri prescolastici *(m)*

livros técnicos *(m pl)* Pt
De Handwerksbücher *(pl)*
En craft books
Es libros de trabajos manuales *(m pl)*
Fr ouvrages artisanaux *(m pl)*
It guide pratiche *(f pl)*

livro técnico *(m)* Pt
De technisches Bucn *(n)*
En technical book
Es libro técnico *(m)*
Fr ouvrage technique *(m)*
It libro tecnico *(m)*

loan paper En
De Aktienpapier *(n)*
Es papel para documentos *(m)*
Fr papier pour titres *(m)*
It carta per valori *(f)*
Pt papel de empréstimo *(m)*

Locher *(m)* *n* De
En punch (for hole punching)
Es sacabocados *(m)*
Fr perforeuse *(f)*
It perforatore *(m)*
Pt perfuradora *(f)*

Lochkarte *(f)* *n* De
En punched card
Es tarjeta perforada *(f)*
Fr carte perforée *(f)*
It scheda perforata *(f)*
Pt ficha perfurada *(f)*

Lochstreifen *(m)* *n* De
En paper tape
Es cinta de papel *(f)*
Fr bande perforée *(f)*
It nastro di carta *(m)*
Pt fita de papel *(f)*

Lochstreifen *(m)* *n* De
En punched paper tape
Es cinta perforada *(f)*
Fr bande de papier *(f)*
It nastro di carta perforato *(m)*
Pt fita de papel perfurado *(f)*

Lochstreifen-Leser *(m)* *n* De
En punched-tape reader
Es lector de cinta perforada *(m)*
Fr lecteur de bande perforée *(f)*
It lettore di nastro perforato *(m)*
Pt leitor de fita perfurada *(f)*

locking-up *n* En
De Schließen *(n)*
Es acuñado *(m)*
Fr serrage *(m)*
It serramento *(m)*
Pt enramado *(m)*

loft-dried paper En
De Lufttrokkenes Papier *(n)*
Es papel secado al aire *(m)*
Fr papier séché à l'air *(m)*
It carta seccata all'aria *(f)*
Pt papel secado ao ar *(m)*

logiciel *(m)* *n* Fr
De Software *(f)*
En software
Es equipo instruccional *(m)*
It software *(m)*
Pt software *(m)*

logotipo *(m)* *n* Es, It, Pt
De Logotype *(f)*
En logotype
Fr logotype *(m)*

logotype *n* En; Fr *(m)*
De Logotype *(f)*
Es logotipo *(m)*
It logotipo *(m)*
Pt logotipo *(m)*

Logotype *(f)* *n* De
En logotype
Es logotipo *(m)*
Fr logotype *(m)*
It logotipo *(m)*
Pt logotipo *(m)*

loja *(f)* *n* Pt
De Laden *(m)*
En shop (retail)
Es tienda *(f)*
Fr boutique *(f)*
It negozio *(m)*

lombada *(f)* *n* Pt
De Rücken *(m)*
En spine
Es lomo *(m)*
Fr dos *(m)*
It dorso *(m)*

lomo *(m)* *n* Es
De Rücken *(m)*
En spine
Fr dos *(m)*
It dorso *(m)*
Pt lombada *(f)*

lona *(f)* *n* Es
De Mattgewebe *(n)*
En canvas (bookbinders')
Fr toile *(f)*
It tela *(f)*
Pt tela *(f)*

long-grain paper En
De langkörniges Papier *(n)*
Es papel plegado al hilo *(m)*
Fr papier sens machine sur longueur *(m)*
It carta a grana lunga *(f)*
Pt papel de grão comprido *(m)*

long print run En
De hohe Druckauflage *(f)*
Es tirada grande *(f)*
Fr grand tirage *(m)*
It grande tiratura *(f)*
Pt tiragem grande *(f)*

look-through *n* En
De Durchscheinen *(n)*
Es textura a la luz *(f)*
Fr épair *(m)*
It trasparente *(m)*
Pt transparência *(f)*

loose-leaf binding En
De Loseblattbindung *(f)*
Es encuadernación de hojas sueltas *(f)*
Fr reliure à feuillets mobiles *(f)*
It legatura a fogli sciolti *(f)*
Pt encadernação de folhas soltas *(f)*

löschen *vb* De
En erase
Es borrar
Fr effacer
It cassare
Pt apagar

Löschpapier *(n)* *n* De
En blotting paper
Es papel secante *(m)*
Fr papier buvard *(m)*
It carta assorbente *(f)*
Pt papel mataborrão *(m)*

Loseblattbindung *(f)* *n* De
En loose-leaf binding
Es encuadernación de hojas sueltas *(f)*
Fr reliure à feuillets mobiles *(f)*
It legatura a fogli sciolti *(f)*
Pt encadernação de folhas soltas *(f)*

lower case En
De Unterkasten *(m)*
Es caja baja *(f)*
Fr bas de caisse *(m)*
It bassa cassa *(f)*
Pt caixa baixa *(f)*

lower-case letter En
De kleiner Buchstabe *(m)*
Es minúscula *(f)*
Fr caractère de bas de caisse *(m)*
It minuscola *(f)*
Pt minúscula *(f)*

Luftfracht *(f)* *n* De
En airfreight
Es flete aéreo *(m)*
Fr fret aérien *(m)*
It trasporto merci per via aerea *(m)*
Pt frete aéreo *(m)*

luftgetrocknet *adj* De
En air-dried
Es secado al aire
Fr séché à l'air
It essiccata ad aria
Pt seco ao ar

Luftkurier *(m)* *n* De
En air courier
Es estafeta aérea *(f)*
Fr courrier aérien *(m)*
It corriere aereo *(m)*
Pt mensageiro aéreo *(m)*

Lufttrokkenes Papier *(n)* De
En loft-dried paper

Es papel secado al aire
 (m)
Fr papier séché à l'air
 (m)
It carta seccata all'aria
 (f)
Pt papel secado ao ar
 (m)

lump sum En
De Pauschalbetrag *(m)*
Es suma total *(f)*
Fr somme globale *(f)*
It somma globale *(f)*
Pt importância global *(f)*

lustro *(m) n* Pt
De Polieren *(n)*
En burnishing
Es fileteado *(m)*
Fr brunissage *(m)*
It brunitura *(f)*

M

macchina da scrivere *(f)*
 It
De Schreibmaschine *(f)*
En typewriter
Es mecanógrafa *(f)*
Fr machine à écrire *(f)*
Pt máquina de escrever
 (f)

macchina da stampa *(f)*
 It
De Druckpresse *(f)*
En press (printing)
Es máquina de imprimir
 (f)
Fr presse d'imprimerie
 (f)
Pt prensa *(f)*

macchina da stampa a
 due colori *(f)* It
Am two-color press
De Zweifarbenpresse *(f)*
En two-colour press
Es prensa bicolor *(f)*
Fr presse à bichromie *(f)*
Pt prensa a duas cores
 (f)

macchina da stampa a
 due giri *(f)* It
De Zweitourenmaschine
 (f)
En two-revolution press
Es prensa de doble
 revolución *(f)*
Fr presse à double
 impression *(f)*
Pt prensa a duas
 rotações *(f)*

macchina da stampa a
 platina *(f)* It
De Tiegel *(m)*
En platen press
Es minerva *(f)*
Fr imprimeuse *(f)*
Pt minerva *(f)*

macchina da stampa
 rotativa *(f)* It
De Rotationspresse *(f)*
En rotary press
Es prensa rotativa *(f)*
Fr rotative *(f)*
Pt prensa rotativa *(f)*

macchina fabbricatrice
 di carta *(f)* It
De Papier-
 herstellungs-
 maschine
 (f)
En papermaking
 machine
Es máquina de fabricar
 papel continuo *(f)*
Fr machine à papier *(f)*
Pt máquina de
 produção de papel *(f)*

macchina fonditrice a
 linea *(f)* It
De Zeilengießmaschine
 (f)
En linecasting machine
Es fundidora de lingotes
 (f)
Fr fondeuse à la ligne *(f)*
Pt fundidora de lingotes
 (f)

macchina fotografica
 per riproduzioni
 fotomeccaniche *(f)*
 It
De Reproduktionsgerät
 (n)
En process camera
Es cámara fotomecánica
 (f)

Fr appareil
 photomécanique *(m)*
Pt câmara de
 processamento *(f)*

macchina legatrice *(f)* It
De Bindemaschine *(f)*
En binding machine
Es encuadernadora *(f)*
Fr machine à relier *(f)*
Pt encadernadora *(f)*

macchina per rotoli *(f)* It
De Packmaschine *(f)*
En bundling machine
Es prensadora-
 embaladora de
 pliegos *(f)*
Fr machine à emballer
 (f)
Pt máquina de prensar e
 formar fascículos *(f)*

macchinista *(m) n* It
De Maschinenmeister
 (m)
En machine minder
Es prensista *(m)*
Fr conducteur de
 machine *(m)*
Pt tratador da máquina
 (m)

machine à arrêt du
 cylindre *(f)* Fr
De Haltzylinderpresse *(f)*
En stop-cylinder press
Es prensa de cilindro de
 parada *(f)*
It rotativa con arresto
 (f)
Pt prensa de cilindro de
 paragem *(f)*

machine à composer *(f)*
 Fr
De Setzmaschine *(f)*
En typesetting machine;
 composing machine
Es máquina de
 composición;
 máquina de
 componer *(f)*
It compositrice *(f)*
Pt compositora de
 tipos; máquina de
 composição *(f)*

machine à écrire *(f)* Fr
De Schreibmaschine *(f)*
En typewriter
Es mecanógrafa *(f)*

It macchina da scrivere
 (f)
Pt máquina de escrever
 (f)

machine à emballer *(f)* Fr
De Packmaschine *(f)*
En bundling machine
Es prensadora-
 embaladora de
 pliegos *(f)*
It macchina per rotoli
 (f)
Pt máquina de prensar e
 formar fascículos *(f)*

machine à forme ronde
 (f) Fr
De Schnellpresse *(f)*
En cylinder machine
Es prensa
 planocilíndrica *(f)*
It rotativa *(f)*
Pt máquina de rolos *(f)*

machine à imprimer *(f)*
 Fr
De Druckmaschine *(f)*
En printing machine
Es máquina de imprimir
 (f)
It stampatrice *(f)*
Pt máquina de imprimir
 (f)

machine à papier *(f)* Fr
De Papier-
 herstellungs-
 maschine
 (f)
En papermaking
 machine
Es máquina de fabricar
 papel continuo *(f)*
It macchina
 fabbricatrice di carta
 (f)
Pt máquina de
 produção de papel *(f)*

machine à relier *(f)* Fr
De Bindemaschine *(f)*
En binding machine
Es encuadernadora *(f)*
It macchina legatrice *(f)*
Pt encadernadora *(f)*

machine binding En
De Maschinenbinden *(n)*
Es encuadernación a
 machina *(f)*
Fr reliure à machine *(f)*

It rilegatura a macchina *(f)*
Pt encadernação à máquina *(f)*

machine chase En
De Maschinenrahmen *(m)*
Es rama de máquina *(f)*
Fr châssis machine *(m)*
It telaio di forma chiusa *(m)*
Pt rama de máquina *(f)*

machine-coated paper En
De maschinen- gestrichenes Papier *(n)*
Es papel estucado a máquina *(m)*
Fr papier couché machine *(m)*
It carta patinata a macchina *(f)*
Pt papel revestido à máquina *(m)*

machine direction En
De Laufrichtung *(f)*
Es dirección de máquina *(f)*
Fr sens machine *(m)*
It direzione di macchina *(f)*
Pt direcção da máquina *(f)*

machine-finished paper En
De maschinenglattes Papier *(n)*
Es papel acabado a máquina *(m)*
Fr papier apprêté sur machine *(m)*
It carta finita a macchina *(f)*
Pt papel acabado à máquina *(m)*

machine-independent language En
De maschinen- unabhängige Sprache *(f)*
Es lenguaje universal *(m)*
Fr langage indépendant du calculateur *(m)*
It linguaggio universale *(m)*

Pt linguagem independente da máquina *(f)*

machine language En
De Maschinensprache *(f)*
Es lenguaje de máquina *(m)*
Fr langage machine *(m)*
It linguaggio macchina *(m)*
Pt linguagem de máquina *(f)*

machine minder En
De Maschinenmeister *(m)*
Es prensista *(m)*
Fr conducteur de machine *(m)*
It macchinista *(m)*
Pt tratador da máquina *(m)*

machine-readable data En
De vom Rechner lesbare Daten *(pl)*
Es datos legibles con máquina *(m pl)*
Fr éléments codés *(m pl)*
It dati leggibili per la macchina *(m pl)*
Pt dados legíveis na máquina *(m pl)*

maciço *adj* Pt
De kompreβ
En solid
Es desinterlineado
Fr à-plat
It sterlineato

madurar *vb* Es
De ausreifen
En mature
Fr conditionner
It stagionare
Pt amadurecer

magasin *(m)* *n* Fr
De Schriftlager *(n)*
En magazine (matrix store)
Es depósito *(m)*
It caricatore *(m)*
Pt depósito *(m)*

Magazin *(n)* *n* De
En magazine (journal)
Es revista *(f)*
Fr magazine *(m)*
It rivista *(f)*
Pt revista *(f)*

magazine *(m)* *n* Fr
De Magazin *(n)*
En magazine (journal)
Es revista *(f)*
It rivista *(f)*
Pt revista *(f)*

magazine (journal) *n* En
De Magazin *(n)*
Es revista *(f)*
Fr magazine *(m)*
It rivista *(f)*
Pt revista *(f)*

magazine (matrix store) *n* En
De Schriftlager *(n)*
Es depósito *(m)*
Fr magasin *(m)*
It caricatore *(m)*
Pt depósito *(m)*

magazine d'information *(m)* Fr
De Nachrichtenmagazin *(n)*
En news magazine
Es revista de información *(f)*
It rivista di attualità *(f)*
Pt revista de informação *(f)*

magazzino *(m)* *n* It
De Lagerhaus *(n)*
En warehouse
Es almacén *(m)*
Fr entrepôt *(m)*
Pt armazém *(m)*

magenta *n* En; Es, Fr, It, Pt *(m)*
De Magenta *(n)*

Magenta *(n)* *n* De
En magenta
Es magenta *(m)*
Fr magenta *(m)*
It magenta *(m)*
Pt magenta *(m)*

Magnetband *(n)* *n* De
En magnetic tape
Es cinta magnética *(f)*
Fr bande magnétique *(f)*
It nastro magnetico *(m)*
Pt fita magnética *(f)*

magnetic card En
De Magnetkarte *(f)*
Es ficha magnética *(f)*
Fr carte magnétique *(f)*
It scheda magnetica *(f)*
Pt ficha magnética *(f)*

magnetic disk En
De Magnetplatte *(f)*
Es disco magnético *(m)*
Fr disque magnétique *(m)*
It disco magnetico *(m)*
Pt disco magnético *(m)*

magnetic ink En
De Magnettinte *(f)*
Es tinta magnética *(f)*
Fr encre magnétique *(f)*
It inchiostro magnetico *(m)*
Pt tinta magnética *(f)*

magnetic-ink character reading (MICR) En
De Lesen von Magnettintenzeichen *(n)*
Es lectura de caracteres de tinta magnética *(f)*
Fr reconnaissance de caractères magnétiques codés *(f)*
It lettura caratteri con inchiostro magnetico *(f)*
Pt leitura de caracteres de tinta magnética *(f)*

magnetic tape En
De Magnetband *(n)*
Es cinta magnética *(f)*
Fr bande magnétique *(f)*
It nastro magnetico *(m)*
Pt fita magnética *(f)*

Magnetkarte *(f)* *n* De
En magnetic card
Es ficha magnética *(f)*
Fr carte magnétique *(f)*
It scheda magnetica *(f)*
Pt ficha magnética *(f)*

Magnetplatte (f) n De
En magnetic disk
Es disco magnético (m)
Fr disque magnétique (m)
It disco magnetico (m)
Pt disco magnético (m)

Magnettinte (f) n De
En magnetic ink
Es tinta magnética (f)
Fr encre magnétique (f)
It inchiostro magnetico (m)
Pt tinta magnética (f)

máquina de impressão simultânea de ambos lados (f) Pt
De Schön- und Widerdruckmaschine (f)
En perfector
Es prensa de retiración (f)
Fr presse à retiration (f)
It stampatrice in volta (f)

Mahlmaschine (f) n De
En beating machine
Es batidora (f)
Fr pilon (m)
It raffinatrice (f)
Pt máquina de bater (f)

Mahlung (f) n De
En beating (papermaking)
Es batido (m)
Fr raffinage (m)
It raffinamento (m)
Pt batimento (m)

mail vb En
De mit der Post schicken
Es enviar por correo
Fr envoyer par la poste
It spedire per posta
Pt enviar por correio

mail n En
De Post (f)
Es correo (m)
Fr courrier (m)
It posta (f)
Pt correio (m)

mailing (m) n Fr
De Postwurfsendung (f)
En direct-mail shot

Es envío por correo directo (m)
It invio diretto per posta (m)
Pt publicidade por correio (f)

mail order En
De Versandhausauftrag (m)
Es pedido por correo (m)
Fr vente par correspondance (f)
It vendite per posta (f)
Pt encomenda por correio (f)

mail-order books En
De Versandhausbücher (pl)
Es libros pedidos por correo (m pl)
Fr livres vendus par correspondance (m pl)
It libri vendite per posta (m pl)
Pt livros para encomenda por correio (m pl)

mail-order division En
De Versandhaus- abteilung (f)
Es división de pedidos por correo (f)
Fr service VPC (m)
It reparto vendite per posta (m)
Pt divisão de encomendas por correio (f)

mail-order edition En
De Versandhausausgabe (f)
Es edición para envío por correo (f)
Fr édition vendue par correspondance (f)
It edizione per vendite per posta (f)
Pt edição para encomenda por correio (f)

main de papier (f) Fr
De Buch (25 Bogen) (n)
En quire
Es mano de papel (f)

It mazzetta di 24 fogli (f)
Pt caderno de papel (f)

maison de composition (f) Fr
De Schriftsetzerei (f)
En typesetter (company)
Es taller de composición (m)
It compositoria (f)
Pt empresa de composição (f)

maison d'édition (f) Fr
De Verlag (m)
En publisher (company)
Es casa editorial (f)
It casa editrice (f)
Pt casa editorial (f)

maisons commerciales (f pl) Fr
De Druckbetriebe (pl)
En trade houses pl n
Es casas comerciales (f pl)
It case commerciali (f pl)
Pt casas comerciais (f pl)

maiuscole (f pl) It
De Großbuchstaben (pl)
En capitals (caps) pl n
Es mayúsculas (f pl)
Fr majuscules (f pl)
Pt maiusculas (f pl)

maiusculas (f pl) Pt
De Großbuchstaben (pl)
En capitals (caps) pl n
Es mayúsculas (f pl)
Fr majuscules (f pl)
It maiuscole (f pl)

maiúsculas pequenas (f pl) Pt
De Kapitälchen (pl)
En small capital letters
Es letras versalitas (f pl)
Fr petites majuscules (f pl)
It lettere in maiuscoletto (f pl)

majuscules (f pl) Fr
De Großbuchstaben (pl)
En capitals (caps) pl n
Es mayúsculas (f pl)

It maiuscole (f pl)
Pt maiusculas (f pl)

make up En
De umbrechen
Es compaginar
Fr mettre en pages
It compaginare
Pt compaginar

make-up n En
De Satzumbruch (m)
Es compaginación (f)
Fr montage (m)
It impaginatura (f)
Pt compaginação (f)

mal cadré Fr
De nicht gerade
En out of square
Es descuadrado
It fuori squadra
Pt fora do enquadramento

mal registré Fr
De fehlerhaftes Register
En out of register
Es fuera de registro
It fuori registro
Pt fora de registo

management n En
De Geschäftsleitung (f)
Es manejo (m)
Fr direction (f)
It direzione (f)
Pt direcção (f)

manager n En
De Geschäftsleiter (m)
Es gerente (m)
Fr gérant (m)
It dirigente (m)
Pt gerente (m)

managing director En
De Geschäftsführender Direktor (m)
Es director gerente (m)
Fr directeur général (m)
It amministratore delegato (m)
Pt director geral (m)

managing editor En
De Betriebsredakteur (m)
Es jefe de redacción (m)

Fr chef de la rédaction
(m)
It capo redattore *(m)*
Pt chefe de redacção
(m)

mancanza di densità *(f)*
It
De Nadellöcher *(pl)*
En pinholes *pl n*
Es burbujas *(f pl)*
Fr perforation des
négatifs *(f)*
Pt furos *(m pl)*

mancha *(f) n* Pt
De Fehler *(m)*
En blemish
Es imperfección *(f)*
Fr défaut *(m)*
It imperfezione *(f)*

mancha de reflexión *(f)*
Es
De Durchscheinbild *(n)*
En ghosting
Fr image fantôme *(f)*
It falsa immagine *(f)*
Pt fantasma *(m)*

manchete *(m) n* Pt
De Überschrift *(f)*
En headline (of
newspaper)
Es titular *(m)*
Fr titre *(m)*
It titolo di testa *(m)*

manchette publicitaire
(f) Fr
De Reklamestreifen *(m)*
En blurb
Es bombo *(m)*
It soffietto editoriale
(m)
Pt sinopse *(f)*

**manchette sur la
jaquette** *(f)* Fr
De Umschlag-
Reklamestreifen *(m)*
En jacket blurb
Es reseña en la cubierta
(f)
It sommario della
sovracopertina *(m)*
Pt sinopse de
sobrecapa *(f)*

mangelhaftes Papier *(n)*
De
En retree
Es papel ligeramente
defectuoso *(m)*
Fr papier imparfait *(m)*
It riscelta *(f)*
Pt papel defeituoso *(m)*

manejo *(m) n* Es
De Geschäftsleitung *(f)*
En management
Fr direction *(f)*
It direzione *(f)*
Pt direcção *(f)*

manifesto *(m) n* It
De Poster *(n)*
En poster
Es cartel *(m)*
Fr affiche *(f)*
Pt cartaz *(m)*

manifold paper En
De Vervielfältigungs-
papier *(n)*
Es papel de copias *(m)*
Fr papier pour formules
(m)
It carta per duplicatori
(f)
Pt papel de cópias *(m)*

manila *(m) n* Es, Pt
De Manilapapier *(n)*
En manilla
Fr papier bulle *(m)*
It manilla *(f)*

Manilapapier *(n) n* De
En manilla
Es manila *(m)*
Fr papier bulle *(m)*
It manilla *(f)*
Pt manila *(m)*

manilla *n* En; It *(f)*
De Manilapapier *(n)*
Es manila *(m)*
Fr papier bulle *(m)*
Pt manila *(m)*

mano de papel *(f)* Es
De Buch (25 Bogen) *(n)*
En quire
Fr main de papier *(f)*
It mazzetta di 24 fogli
(f)
Pt caderno de papel *(f)*

manoscritto *(m) n* It
De Manuskript *(n)*
En manuscript
Es manuscrito *(m)*
Fr manuscrit *(m)*
Pt manuscrito *(m)*

mantilla *(f) n* Es
De Drucktuch *(n)*
En blanket (offset litho)
Fr décharge *(f)*
It cauccíù *(m)*; tessuto
gommato *(m)*
Pt feltro *(m)*

manual *n* En; Es, Pt *(m)*
De Leitfaden *(m)*
Fr manuel *(m)*
It manuale *(m)*

manual de estilos *(m)* Pt
De Stil-Handbuch *(n)*
En style manual
Es manual de redacción
(m)
Fr règles de stylisme *(f
pl)*
It manuale di stile *(m)*

manual de redacción *(m)*
Es
De Stil-Handbuch *(n)*
En style manual
Fr règles de stylisme *(f
pl)*
It manuale di stile *(m)*
Pt manual de estilos *(m)*

manuale *(m) n* It
De Leitfaden *(m)*
En manual
Es manual *(m)*
Fr manuel *(m)*
Pt manual *(m)*

manuale di stile *(m)* It
De Stil-Handbuch *(n)*
En style manual
Es manual de redacción
(m)
Fr règles de stylisme *(f
pl)*
Pt manual de estilos *(m)*

manualetto *(m) n* It
De Handbuch *(n)*
En handbook
Es compendio *(m)*
Fr guide -âne *(m)*
Pt compêndio *(m)*

manuel *(m) n* Fr
De Lehrbuch *(n)*
En textbook
Es libro de texto *(m)*
It libro di testo *(m)*
Pt livro de texto *(m)*

manufactura *(f) n* Pt
De Herstellung *(f)*
En manufacture
Es fabricación *(f)*
Fr fabrication *(f)*
It fabbricazione *(f)*

manufacture *vb* En
De herstellen
Es fabricar
Fr fabriquer
It produrre
Pt produzir

manufacture *n* En
De Herstellung *(f)*
Es fabricación *(f)*
Fr fabrication *(f)*
It fabbricazione *(f)*
Pt manufactura *(f)*

manufacturer *n* En
De Hersteller *(m)*
Es fabricante *(m)*
Fr fabricant *(m)*
It produttore *(m)*
Pt produtor *(m)*

manufacturing costs En
De Herstellungskosten
(pl)
Es costes de fabricación
(m pl)
Fr coût de fabrication
(m)
It costi di lavorazione
(m pl)
Pt custos de produção
(m pl)

manuscript *n* En
De Manuskript *(n)*
Es manuscrito *(m)*
Fr manuscrit *(m)*
It manoscritto *(m)*
Pt manuscrito *(m)*

manuscrit *adj* Fr
De handgeschrieben
En hand-written
Es escrito a mano
It scritto a mano
Pt escrito à mão

manuscrit *(m) n* Fr
De Manuskript *(n)*
En manuscript
Es manuscrito *(m)*
It manoscritto *(m)*
Pt manuscrito *(m)*

**manuscrit
dactylographié** *(m)*
Fr
De Maschinenschrift *(f)*
En typescript
Es escrito a máquina *(m)*
It dattiloscritto *(m)*
Pt dactilografado *(m)*

manuscrito *(m) n* Es, Pt
De Manuskript *(n)*
En manuscript
Fr manuscrit *(m)*
It manoscritto *(m)*

Manuskript *(n) n* De
En manuscript
Es manuscrito *(m)*
Fr manuscrit *(m)*
It manoscritto *(m)*
Pt manuscrito *(m)*

Manuskriptredakteur
(m) n De
En copy-editor
Es corrector de
originales *(m)*
Fr annotateur d'un texte
(m)
It correttore di originali
(m)
Pt revisor do original *(m)*

Manuskript revidieren
De
En copy-edit
Es corregir originales
Fr éditer un texte
It correggere originali
Pt editar

Manuskriptrevision *(f) n*
De
En copy-editing
Es corrección de
originales *(f)*
Fr préparation d'un
texte *(f)*
It correzione di originali
(f)
Pt revisão do original *(f)*

map *n* En
De Karte *(f)*
Es mapa *(m)*
Fr carte *(f)*
It mappa *(f)*
Pt mapa *(m)*

mapa *(m) n* Es, Pt
De Karte *(f)*
En map
Fr carte *(f)*
It mappa *(f)*

mappa *(f) n* It
De Karte *(f)*
En map
Es mapa *(m)*
Fr carte *(f)*
Pt mapa *(m)*

maqueta *(f) n* Es
De Blindband *(m)*
En dummy; mock-up
Fr maquette *(f)*
It manichino; menabò
(m)
Pt maquete *(f)*

**maqueta de
encadernação** *(f)* Pt
De Buchbinder-
blindband *(n)*
En binder's dummy
Es molde de
estampación *(m)*
Fr maquette de la
reliure *(f)*
It menabò del
rilegatore *(m)*

maqueta realzada *(f)* Es
De richtige dickes
Blindband *(n)*
En bulked dummy
Fr maquette garnie *(f)*
It menabò di grossezza
preciso *(m)*
Pt maquete engrossada
(f)

maquete *(f) n* Pt
De Blindband *(m)*
En dummy; mock-up
Es maqueta *(f)*
Fr maquette *(f)*
It manichino; menabò
(m)

maquete engrossada *(f)*
Pt

De richtige dickes
Blindband *(n)*
En bulked dummy
Es maqueta realzada *(f)*
Fr maquette garnie *(f)*
It menabò di grossezza
preciso *(m)*

maquette *(f) n* Fr
De Blindband *(m)*
En dummy; mock-up
Es maqueta *(f)*
It manichino; menabò
(m)
Pt maquete *(f)*

maquette de la reliure
(f) Fr
De Buchbinder-
blindband *(n)*
En binder's dummy
Es molde de
estampación *(m)*
It menabò del
rilegatore *(m)*
Pt maqueta de
encadernação *(f)*

maquette garnie *(f)* Fr
De richtige dickes
Blindband *(n)*
En bulked dummy
Es maqueta realzada *(f)*
It menabò di grossezza
preciso *(m)*
Pt maquete engrossada
(f)

máquina de bater *(f)* Pt
De Mahlmaschine *(f)*
En beating machine
Es batidora *(f)*
Fr pilon *(m)*
It raffinatrice *(f)*

máquina de componer
(f) Es
De Setzmaschine *(f)*
En composing machine
Fr composeuse *(f)*
It compositrice *(f)*
Pt máquina de
composição *(f)*

máquina de composição
(f) Pt
De Setzmaschine *(f)*
En composing machine;
typesetting machine
Es máquina de
componer; máquina
de composición *(f)*

Fr composeuse;
machine à composer
(f)
It compositrice *(f)*

**máquina de
composición** *(f)* Es
De Setzmaschine *(f)*
En composing machine;
typesetting machine
Fr composeuse;
machine à composer
(f)
It compositrice *(f)*
Pt compositora de
tipos; máquina de
composição *(f)*

máquina de escrever *(f)*
Pt
De Schreibmaschine *(f)*
En typewriter
Es mecanógrafa *(f)*
Fr machine à écrire *(f)*
It macchina da scrivere
(f)

**máquina de fabricar
papel continuo** *(f)*
Es
De Papierherstellungs-
maschine *(f)*
En papermaking
machine
Fr machine à papier *(f)*
It macchina
fabbricatrice di carta
(f)
Pt máquina de
produção de papel *(f)*

máquina de imprimir *(f)*
Es, Pt
De Druckmaschine;
Druckpresse *(f)*
En press (printing);
printing machine
Fr machine à imprimer;
presse d'imprimerie
(f)
It macchina da stampa;
stampatrice *(f)*

**máquina de prensar e
formar fascículos**
(f) Pt
De Packmaschine *(f)*
En bundling machine
Es prensadora-
embaladora de
pliegos *(f)*

Fr machine à emballer
(f)
It macchina per rotoli
(f)

**máquina de produção
de papel** (f) Pt
De Papierherstellungs-
maschine (f)
En papermaking
machine
Es máquina de fabricar
papel continuo (f)
Fr machine à papier (f)
It macchina
fabbricatrice di carta
(f)

máquina de rolos (f) Pt
De Schnellpresse (f)
En cylinder machine
Es prensa
planocilíndrica (f)
Fr machine à forme
ronde (f)
It rotativa (f)

máquina fotocopiadora
(f) Es
De Photokopier-
maschine (f)
En photocopying
machine
Fr photocopieuse (f)
It fotocopiatrice (f)
Pt fotocopiadora (f)

marbled paper En
De Marmorpapier (n)
Es papel jaspeado (m)
Fr papier marbré (m)
It carta marmorizzata (f)
Pt papel jaspeado (m)

marbling n En
De Marmorierung (f)
Es jaspeado (m)
Fr marbrure (f)
It marmorizzazione (f)
Pt jaspeamento (m)

marbre (m) n Fr
De Druckkarren (m)
En bed (printing
machine)
Es platina (f)
It piano (m)
Pt mesa (f)

marbre de serrage (m) Fr
De Form; Schließplatte
(f)
En imposing surface;
stone (letterpress
composition)
Es superficie de
imposición (f)
It banco tipografico (m)
Pt superfície de
imposição (f)

marbrure (f) n Fr
De Marmorierung (f)
En marbling
Es jaspeado (m)
It marmorizzazione (f)
Pt jaspeamento (m)

marca de eliminação (f)
Pt
De Tilgungszeichen (n)
En delete mark
Es marca de supresión
(f)
Fr marque à supprimer
(f)
It segno di cancellatura
(m)

marca de supresión (f)
Es
De Tilgungszeichen (n)
En delete mark
Fr marque à supprimer
(f)
It segno di cancellatura
(m)
Pt marca de eliminação
(f)

marcar vb Es, Pt
De auszeichnen
En mark up (copy)
Fr annoter
It contrassegnare

marcar con rayas Es
De kräuseln
En crimp
Fr gaufrer
It ondulare
Pt enrugar

marcar o preço Pt
De Preis festsetzen
En price
Es valorar
Fr fixer un prix
It prezzare

marcas de aparar (f pl) Pt
De Beschnitt-
Markierungen (pl)
En trim marks
Es marcas de recorte (f
pl)
Fr repères de rognage
(m pl)
It segni per rifilatura (m
pl)

marcas de recorte (f pl)
Es
De Beschnitt-
Markierungen (pl)
En trim marks
Fr repères de rognage
(m pl)
It segni per rifilatura (m
pl)
Pt marcas de aparar (f
pl)

marcas de registro (f pl)
Es
De Paßkreuze (pl)
En register marks
Fr croix de repère (f pl)
It croci di registro (m
pl)
Pt marcas de registo (f
pl)

marcas de registo (f pl)
Pt
De Paßkreuze (pl)
En register marks
Es marcas de registro (f
pl)
Fr croix de repère (f pl)
It croci di registro (m
pl)

marcas de revisão (f pl)
Pt
De Kollationierzeichen
(pl)
En collating marks pl n
Es señales escalonadas
de alzado (f pl)
Fr repères
d´assemblage (m pl)
It segni di raccoglitura
(m pl)

marcas de tela metálica
(f pl) Es, Pt
De Drahtmarkierungen
(pl)
En wiremarks pl n

Fr marques de la toile (f
pl)
It segni della tela (m pl)

**marcas do revisor de
provas** (f pl) Pt
De Korrekturzeichen (pl)
En proofreader´s marks
Es signos de corrección
(m pl)
Fr signes de corrections
typographiques (m
pl)
It segni del correttore
di bozze (m pl)

marché (m) n Fr
De Markt (m)
En market
Es mercado (m)
It mercato (m)
Pt mercado (m)

**marché produits grande
consommation** (m)
Fr
De Massenabsatz (m)
En mass market
Es mercado de masas
(m)
It mercato di massa (m)
Pt mercado de massas
(m)

marcos (m pl) Es
De Anschlußstücke (pl)
En borders pl n
Fr vignettes (f pl)
It margini (m pl)
Pt bordas (f pl)

marge (f) n Fr
De Rand (m)
En margin (paper)
Es margen (m)
It margine (m)
Pt margem (f)

marge bénéficiaire (f) Fr
De Gewinnspanne (f)
En margin (profit)
Es margen de beneficio
(m)
It margine di utile (m)
Pt margem de lucro (f)

marge de pied (f) Fr
De Unterschlag (m)
En tail (of page)
Es margen inferior (m)

It piede (di pagina) *(m)*
Pt pé (de página) *(m)*

margem *(f) n* Pt
De Rand *(m)*
En margin (paper)
Es margen *(m)*
Fr marge *(f)*
It margine *(m)*

margem de agarre *(f)* Pt
De Griffkante *(f)*
En grip
Es margen de agarre *(m)*
Fr prise de pinces *(f)*
It presa *(f)*

margem de lucro *(f)* Pt
De Gewinnspanne *(f)*
En margin (profit)
Es margen de beneficio
 (m)
Fr marge bénéficiaire *(f)*
It margine di utile *(m)*

margem de medianiz *(f)*
 Pt
De Straßenkante *(f)*
En gutter margin
Es margen del medianil
 (m)
Fr lézarde *(f)*
It margine di
 scanalatura *(m)*

margem dianteira *(f)* Pt
De Greifkanten *(f)*
En gripper edge
Es orilla de entrada *(f)*
Fr côté des pinces *(m)*
It lato pinza *(m)*

margen *(m) n* Es
De Rand *(m)*
En margin (paper)
Fr marge *(f)*
It margine *(m)*
Pt margem *(f)*

margen de agarre *(m)* Es
De Griffkante *(f)*
En grip
Fr prise de pinces *(f)*
It presa *(f)*
Pt margem de agarre *(f)*

margen de beneficio *(m)*
 Es
De Gewinnspanne *(f)*
En margin (profit)

Fr marge bénéficiaire *(f)*
It margine di utile *(m)*
Pt margem de lucro *(f)*

margen del medianil *(m)*
 Es
De Straßenkante *(f)*
En gutter margin
Fr lézarde *(f)*
It margine di
 scanalatura *(m)*
Pt margem de medianiz
 (f)

margen inferior *(m)* Es
De Unterschlag *(m)*
En tail (of page)
Fr marge de pied *(f)*
It piede (di pagina) *(m)*
Pt pé (de página) *(m)*

margeur *(m) n* Fr
De Einleger *(m)*
En feeder
Es alimentador *(m)*
It alimentatore *(m)*
Pt alimentadora *(f)*

margeur à nappe *(m)* Fr
De Schuppenanleger *(m)*
En stream feeder
Es ponepliegos de
 avance continuo *(m)*
It alimentatore di fogli a
 avanzamento
 continuo *(m)*
Pt alimentador de folhas
 de avanço contínuo
 (m)

margeur automatique
 (m) Fr
De automatischer
 Einleger *(m)*
En automatic feeder
Es alimentador
 automático *(m)*
It alimentatore
 automatico *(f)*
Pt alimentador
 automático *(m)*

margeur automatique à
 aspiration *(m)* Fr
De Sauganleger *(m)*
En suction feeder
Es ponepliegos de soplo
 (m)
It alimentatore ad
 aspirazione *(m)*
Pt alimentador por
 sucção *(m)*

margin (paper) *n* En
De Rand *(m)*
Es margen *(m)*
Fr marge *(f)*
It margine *(m)*
Pt margem *(f)*

margin (profit) *n* En
De Gewinnspanne *(f)*
Es margen de beneficio
 (m)
Fr marge bénéficiaire *(f)*
It margine di utile *(m)*
Pt margem de lucro *(f)*

marginal decision En
De knappe Entscheidung
 (f)
Es decisión marginal *(f)*
Fr décision marginale *(f)*
It decisione marginale
 (f)
Pt decisão marginal *(f)*

marginal notes En
De Randbemerkungen
 (pl)
Es notas marginales *(f*
 pl)
Fr notes marginales *(f*
 pl)
It note a margine *(f pl)*
Pt notas marginais *(f pl)*

margine *(m) n* It
De Rand *(m)*
En margin (paper)
Es margen *(m)*
Fr marge *(f)*
Pt margem *(f)*

margine di scanalatura
 (m) It
De Straßenkante *(f)*
En gutter margin
Es margen del medianil
 (m)
Fr lézarde *(f)*
Pt margem de medianiz
 (f)

margine di utile *(m)* It
De Gewinnspanne *(f)*
En margin (profit)
Es margen de beneficio
 (m)
Fr marge bénéficiaire *(f)*
Pt margem de lucro *(f)*

margini *(m pl)* It
De Anschlußstücke *(pl)*
En borders *pl n*
Es marcos *(m pl)*
Fr vignettes *(f pl)*
Pt bordas *(f pl)*

margini di entrata *(m pl)*
 It
De Anlagekanten *(pl)*
En feed edges *pl n*
Es orillas de entrada *(f*
 pl)
Fr côté des marges *(m)*
Pt bordos de entrada *(m*
 pl)

market *n* En
De Markt *(m)*
Es mercado *(m)*
Fr marché *(m)*
It mercato *(m)*
Pt mercado *(m)*

market research En
De Marktforschung *(f)*
Es investigación del
 mercado *(f)*
Fr analyse de marché *(f)*
It ricerca di mercato *(f)*
Pt investigação do
 mercado *(f)*

Markt *(m) n* De
En market
Es mercado *(m)*
Fr marché *(m)*
It mercato *(m)*
Pt mercado *(m)*

Marktforschung *(f) n* De
En market research
Es investigación del
 mercado *(f)*
Fr analyse de marché *(f)*
It ricerca di mercato *(f)*
Pt investigação do
 mercado *(f)*

mark up (copy) En
De auszeichnen
Es marcar
Fr annoter
It contrassegnare
Pt marcar

mark up (price) En
De hinaufsetzen
Es aumentar
Fr augmenter

It aumentare (il prezzo)
Pt aumentar

mark-up (of prices) *n* En
De Hinaufsetzung *(f)*
Es aumento *(m)*
Fr augmentation *(f)*
It prezzatura *(f)*
Pt aumento *(m)*

Marmorierung *(f) n* De
En marbling
Es jaspeado *(m)*
Fr marbrure *(f)*
It marmorizzazione *(f)*
Pt jaspeamento *(m)*

marmorizzazione *(f) n* It
De Marmorierung *(f)*
En marbling
Es jaspeado *(m)*
Fr marbrure *(f)*
Pt jaspeamento *(m)*

Marmorpapier *(n) n* De
En marbled paper
Es papel jaspeado *(m)*
Fr papier marbré *(f)*
It carta marmorizzata *(f)*
Pt papel jaspeado *(m)*

marocchino *(m) n* It
De Maroquin *(n)*
En Morocco (leather)
Es tafilete *(m)*
Fr maroquin *(m)*
Pt marroquim *(m)*

maroquin *(m) n* Fr
De Maroquin *(n)*
En Morocco (leather)
Es tafilete *(m)*
It marocchino *(m)*
Pt marroquim *(m)*

Maroquin *(n) n* De
En Morocco (leather)
Es tafilete *(m)*
Fr maroquin *(m)*
It marocchino *(m)*
Pt marroquim *(m)*

marque à supprimer *(f)*
Fr
De Tilgungszeichen *(n)*
En delete mark
Es marca de supresión
(f)
It segno di cancellatura
(m)

Pt marca de eliminação
(f)

marque d'éditeur *(f)* Fr
De Impressum *(n)*
En imprint
Es pie de imprenta *(m)*
It impressa editoriale *(f)*
Pt nome do editor *(m)*

marques de la toile *(f pl)*
Fr
De Drahtmarkierungen
(pl)
En wiremarks *pl n*
Es marcas de tela
metálica *(f pl)*
It segni della tela *(m pl)*
Pt marcas de tela
metálica *(f pl)*

marroquim *(m) n* Pt
De Maroquin *(n)*
En Morocco (leather)
Es tafilete *(m)*
Fr maroquin *(m)*
It marocchino *(m)*

máscara *(f) n* Pt
De Abdeckung *(f)*
En masking
Es enmascarado *(m)*
Fr masquage *(m)*
It mascheratura *(f)*

mascarar *vb* Pt
De abdecken
En mask
Es enmascarar
Fr oblitérer
It mascherare

mascherare *vb* It
De abdecken
En mask
Es enmascarar
Fr oblitérer
Pt mascarar

mascheratura *(f) n* It
De Abdeckung *(f)*
En masking
Es enmascarado *(m)*
Fr masquage *(m)*
Pt máscara *(f)*

**mascheratura con
vernice coprente** *(f)*
It
De Abdecken *(n)*

En blocking out
Es enmienda con
sobreimpresión *(f)*
Fr oblitération *(f)*
Pt cobrimento *(m)*

Maschinenbinden *(n) n*
De
En machine binding
Es encuadernación a
machina *(f)*
Fr reliure à machine *(f)*
It rilegatura a macchina
(f)
Pt encadernação à
máquina *(f)*

**maschinengestrichenes
Papier** *(n)* De
En machine-coated
paper
Es papel estucado a
máquina *(m)*
Fr papier couché
machine *(m)*
It carta patinata a
macchina *(f)*
Pt papel revestido à
máquina *(m)*

**maschinenglattes
Papier** *(n)* De
En machine-finished
paper; mill-finished
paper
Es papel acabado a
máquina *(m)*
Fr papier apprêté sur
machine *(m)*
It carta finita a
macchina *(f)*
Pt papel acabado à
máquina *(m)*

Maschinengröβe *(f) n* De
En engine-sized paper
Es papel encolado a
máquina *(m)*
Fr papier collé en pâte
(m)
It carta tagliata a
macchina *(f)*
Pt papel encolado à
máquina *(m)*

Maschinenmeister *(m) n*
De
En machine minder
Es prensista *(m)*
Fr conducteur de
machine *(m)*
It macchinista *(m)*

Pt tratador da máquina
(m)

Maschinenrahmen *(m) n*
De
En machine chase
Es rama de máquina *(f)*
Fr châssis machine *(m)*
It telaio di forma chiusa
(m)
Pt rama de máquina *(f)*

Maschinensatz *(m) n* De
En hot-metal typesetting
Es composición
metálica en caliente
(f)
Fr composition chaude
(f)
It composizione a
metallo caldo *(f)*
Pt composição de tipos
de metal quente *(f)*

Maschinenschrift *(f) n*
De
En typescript
Es escrito a máquina *(m)*
Fr manuscrit
dactylographié *(m)*
It dattiloscritto *(m)*
Pt dactilografado *(m)*

Maschinensprache *(f) n*
De
En machine language
Es lenguaje de máquina
(m)
Fr langage machine *(m)*
It linguaggio macchina
(m)
Pt linguagem de
máquina *(f)*

**maschinenunabhängige
Sprache** *(f)* De
En machine-
independent
language
Es lenguaje universal
(m)
Fr langage indépendant
du calculateur *(m)*
It linguaggio universale
(m)
Pt linguagem
independente da
máquina *(f)*

mask *vb* En
De abdecken
Es enmascarar

Fr oblitérer
It mascherare
Pt mascarar

masking n En
De Abdeckung (f)
Es enmascarado (m)
Fr masquage (m)
It mascheratura (f)
Pt máscara (f)

masking tape En
De Abdeckband (n)
Es cinta para
  enmascarar (f)
Fr bande de masquage
  (f)
It nastro per
  mascheratura (m)
Pt fita de mascarar (f)

masquage (m) n Fr
De Abdeckung (f)
En masking
Es enmascarado (m)
It mascheratura (f)
Pt máscara (f)

Masse (f) n De
En bulk (of a book)
Es grueso de libro (m)
Fr épaisseur d'un livre
  (f)
It grossezza del libro (f)
Pt espessura dum livro
  (f)

Massenabsatz (m) n De
En mass market
Es mercado de masas
  (m)
Fr marché produits
  grande
  consommation (m)
It mercato di massa (m)
Pt mercado de massas
  (m)

Massenabsatz-Buch (n)
  De
En mass-market book
Es libro de mercado de
  mesas (m)
Fr livre à gros tirage (m)
It libro per mercato di
  massa (m)
Pt livro para mercado de
  massas (m)

Massenabsatz-Verleger
  (m) De
En mass-market
  publisher
Es editor para el
  mercado de masas
  (m)
Fr éditeur de livres à
  gros tirage (m)
It editore per il mercato
  di massa (m)
Pt editor para mercado
  de massas (m)

massicotage (m) n Fr
De Unterätzung (f)
En undercutting
Es sobremordido (m)
It intaglio (m)
Pt sobremordicação (f)

mass market En
De Massenabsatz (m)
Es mercado de masas
  (m)
Fr marché produits
  grande
  consommation (m)
It mercato di massa (m)
Pt mercado de massas
  (m)

mass-market book En
De Massenabsatz-Buch
  (n)
Es libro de mercado de
  mesas (m)
Fr livre à gros tirage (m)
It libro per mercato di
  massa (m)
Pt livro para mercado de
  massas (m)

mass-market publisher
  En
De Massenabsatz-
  Verleger (m)
Es editor para el
  mercado de masas
  (m)
Fr éditeur de livres à
  gros tirage (m)
It editore per il mercato
  di massa (m)
Pt editor para mercado
  de massas (m)

Maßstab festlegen De
En scale
Es poner a escala
Fr dessiner à l'échelle

It graduare
Pt pôr à escala

mat adj Fr
De matt
En matt
Es mate
It opaco
Pt mate

mate adj Es, Pt
De matt
En matt
Fr mat
It opaco

matéria cancelada (f) Pt
De gestrichener Text (m)
En cancelled matter
Es composición
  suprimida (f)
Fr texte annulé (m)
It testo annullato (m)

materia de papel (f) Es
De Papiertyp (m)
En stock (paper)
Fr matière de papier (f)
It materia di carta (f)
Pt matéria de papel (f)

matéria de papel (f) Pt
De Papiertyp (m)
En stock (paper)
Es materia de papel (f)
Fr matière de papier (f)
It materia di carta (f)

materia di carta (f) It
De Papiertyp (m)
En stock (paper)
Es materia de papel (f)
Fr matière de papier (f)
Pt matéria de papel (f)

materiais do artista (m
  pl) Pt
De Kunstmaterialien (pl)
En artist's materials pl n
Es materiales de
  dibujante (m pl)
Fr fournitures de dessin
  (f pl)
It materiale d'arte (m)

material de carga (m) Es
De Füllerstoff (m)
En filler
Fr charge (f)

It carica (f)
Pt carga (f)

matérial de PLV (m) Fr
De Verkaufstellen-
  Material (n)
En point-of-sale material
Es material para punto
  de venta (m)
It materiale per punto
  di vendita (m)
Pt material de ponto de
  venda (m)

**material de ponto de
  venda** (m) Pt
De Verkaufstellen-
  Material (n)
En point-of-sale material
Es material para punto
  de venta (m)
Fr matérial de PLV (m)
It materiale per punto
  di vendita (m)

materiale d'arte (m) It
De Kunstmaterialien (pl)
En artist's materials pl n
Es materiales de
  dibujante (m pl)
Fr fournitures de dessin
  (f pl)
Pt materiais do artista
  (m pl)

**materiale per punto di
  vendita** (m) It
De Verkaufstellen-
  Material (n)
En point-of-sale material
Es material para punto
  de venta (m)
Fr matérial de PLV (m)
Pt material de ponto de
  venda (m)

materiales de dibujante
  (m pl) Es
De Kunstmaterialien (pl)
En artist's materials pl n
Fr fournitures de dessin
  (f pl)
It materiale d'arte (m)
Pt materiais do artista
  (m pl)

**material para punto de
  venta** (m) Es
De Verkaufstellen-
  Material (n)
En point-of-sale material
Fr matérial de PLV (m)

It materiale per punto di vendita *(m)*
Pt material de ponto de venda *(m)*

material sobrante *(m)* Es
De überlanger Satz *(m)*
En overmatter
Fr surimpression *(f)*
It composizione sovrastante *(f)*
Pt matéria que sobra *(f)*

materia prima *(f)* It
De Stoffeintrag *(m)*
En furnish
Es materias primas *(f pl)*
Fr matières premières *(f pl)*
Pt matérias-primas *(f pl)*

matéria que sobra *(f)* Pt
De überlanger Satz *(m)*
En overmatter
Es material sobrante *(m)*
Fr surimpression *(f)*
It composizione sovrastante *(f)*

materias primas *(f pl)* Es
De Stoffeintrag *(m)*
En furnish
Fr matières premières *(f pl)*
It materia prima *(f)*
Pt matérias-primas *(f pl)*

matérias-primas *(f pl)* n Pt
De Stoffeintrag *(m)*
En furnish
Es materias primas *(f pl)*
Fr matières premières *(f pl)*
It materia prima *(f)*

matière de papier *(f)* Fr
De Papiertyp *(m)*
En stock (paper)
Es materia de papel *(f)*
It materia di carta *(f)*
Pt matéria de papel *(f)*

matières premières *(f pl)* Fr
De Stoffeintrag *(m)*
En furnish
Es materias primas *(f pl)*
It materia prima *(f)*
Pt matérias-primas *(f pl)*

matiz *(m)* n Pt
De Ton *(m)*
En tint
Es media tinta *(f)*
Fr teinte *(f)*
It gradazione *(f)*

matrice *(f)* n Fr, It
Am mold (typesetting)
De Matrize *(f)*
En matrix; mould
Es matriz *(f)*
Pt matriz *(f)*

matrice in carta di seta *(f)* It
De Gewebeschablone *(f)*
En tissue stencil
Es matriz de papel de seda *(f)*
Fr stencil de duplication *(m)*
Pt estencil de tela *(m)*

matrix n En
De Matrize *(f)*
Es matriz *(f)*
Fr matrice *(f)*
It matrice *(f)*
Pt matriz *(f)*

matriz *(f)* n Es, Pt
Am mold (typesetting)
De Matrize; Prägestock *(f m)*
En die; matrix; mould
Fr étampe *(f)*
It matrice; stampo *(f m)*

matriz de papel de seda *(f)* Es
De Gewebeschablone *(f)*
En tissue stencil
Fr stencil de duplication *(m)*
It matrice in carta di seta *(f)*
Pt estencil de tela *(m)*

Matrize *(f)* n De
Am mold (typesetting)
En matrix; mould (typesetting)
Es matriz *(f)*
Fr matrice *(f)*
It matrice *(f)*
Pt matriz *(f)*

matt adj De, En
Es mate
Fr mat

It opaco
Pt mate

matt art paper En
De Mattkunstdruck- papier *(n)*
Es papel cuché mate *(m)*
Fr papier couché mat *(m)*
It carta patinata opaca *(f)*
Pt papel artístico mate *(m)*

mattgelbes geripptes Papier *(n)* De
En cream laid paper
Es papel verjurado crema *(m)*
Fr papier vergé pâle *(m)*
It carta vergata crema *(f)*
Pt papel rugoso *(m)*

mattgelbes Velinpapier *(n)* De
En cream wove paper
Es papel avitelado crema *(m)*
Fr vélin crème *(m)*
It velino cremo *(m)*
Pt papel tecido enrugado *(m)*

Mattgewebe *(n)* n De
En canvas (bookbinders´)
Es lona *(f)*
Fr toile *(f)*
It tela *(f)*
Pt tela *(f)*

Mattkunstdruckpapier *(n)* n De
En matt art paper
Es papel cuché mate *(m)*
Fr papier couché mat *(m)*
It carta patinata opaca *(f)*
Pt papel artístico mate *(m)*

Mattkunstgewebe *(n)* n De
En art canvas
Es tela de arte *(f)*
Fr toile pour reliure *(f)*
It tela d´arte *(f)*
Pt tela de arte *(f)*

mature vb En
De ausreifen
Es madurar
Fr conditionner
It stagionare
Pt amadurecer

mauvaise copie *(f)* Fr
De schlechtes Manuskript *(n)*
En bad copy
Es original malo *(m)*
It copia illeggibile *(f)*
Pt exemplar ilegível *(m)*

mayorista *(m)* n Es
De Großhändler *(m)*
En wholesaler
Fr grossiste *(m)*
It grossista *(m)*
Pt armazenista *(m)*

mayúsculas *(f pl)* Es
De Großbuchstaben *(pl)*
En capitals (caps) pl n
Fr majuscules *(f pl)*
It maiuscole *(f pl)*
Pt maiusculas *(f pl)*

mazzetta di 24 fogli *(f)* It
De Buch (25 Bogen) *(n)*
En quire
Es mano de papel *(f)*
Fr main de papier *(f)*
Pt caderno de papel *(f)*

measure n En
De Zeilenmaß *(n)*
Es largo *(m)*
Fr mesure *(f)*
It misura *(f)*
Pt medida *(f)*

mecanógrafa *(f)* n Es
De Schreibmaschine *(f)*
En typewriter
Fr machine à écrire *(f)*
It macchina da scrivere *(f)*
Pt máquina de escrever *(f)*

mecanografía *(f)* n Es
De Typistin *(f)*
En typist
Fr dactylographe *(f)*
It dattilografa *(f)*
Pt dactilógrafa *(f)*

mecanografiado *(m) n* Es
De Tippen *(n)*
En typing
Fr dactylographie *(f)*
It scrivere a macchina *(m)*
Pt dactilografia *(f)*

mecanotipista *(m) n* Pt
De Tastatur-Setzer *(m)*
En keyboarder
Es operador de teclado *(m)*
Fr claviste *(m)*
It operatore di tastiera *(m)*

mechanical binding En
De mechanische Bindung *(f)*
Es encuadernación mecánica *(f)*
Fr reliure mécanique *(f)*
It legatura meccanica *(f)*
Pt encadernação mecânica *(f)*

mechanical composition En
De mechanischer Satz *(m)*
Es composición mecánica *(f)*
Fr composition mécanique *(f)*
It composizione meccanica *(f)*
Pt composição mecânica *(f)*

mechanical overlay En
De mechanische Zurichtung *(f)*
Es alza mecánica *(f)*
Fr mise en train mécanique *(f)*
It sovrapposizione meccanica *(f)*
Pt corte mecânico *(m)*

mechanical tints En
De mechanische Töne *(pl)*
Es fondos grisados *(m pl)*
Fr coloration mécanique *(f)*
It colori di gradazioni chiare ottenuti meccanicamente *(m pl)*
Pt lâminas de acinzentar *(f pl)*

mechanical wood pulp En
De Holzschliff *(m)*
Es pasta mecánica *(f)*
Fr pâte mécanique *(f)*
It pasta di legno ottenuta meccanicamente *(f)*
Pt polpa de madeira mecânica *(f)*

mechanische Bindung *(f)* De
En mechanical binding
Es encuadernación mecánica *(f)*
Fr reliure mécanique *(f)*
It legatura meccanica *(f)*
Pt encadernação mecânica *(f)*

mechanischer Satz *(m)* De
En mechanical composition
Es composición mecánica *(f)*
Fr composition mécanique *(f)*
It composizione meccanica *(f)*
Pt composição mecânica *(f)*

mechanische Töne *(pl)* De
En mechanical tints
Es fondos grisados *(m pl)*
Fr coloration mécanique *(f)*
It colori di gradazioni chiare ottenuti meccanicamente *(m pl)*
Pt lâminas de acinzentar *(f pl)*

mechanische Zurichtung *(f)* De
En mechanical overlay
Es alza mecánica *(f)*
Fr mise en train mécanique *(f)*
It sovrapposizione meccanica *(f)*
Pt corte mecânico *(m)*

medianil *(m) n* Es
De Gießbach *(m)*
En gutter
Fr petits fonds *(m pl)*
It scanalatura per sfogo *(f)*
Pt medianiz *(m)*

medianiz *(m) n* Pt
De Gießbach *(m)*
En gutter
Es medianil *(m)*
Fr petits fonds *(m pl)*
It scanalatura per sfogo *(f)*

media tinta *(f)* Es
De Ton *(m)*
En tint
Fr teinte *(f)*
It gradazione *(f)*
Pt matiz *(m)*

Mediäval *(n) n* De
En old face
Es estilo antiguo *(m)*
Fr elzévir *(m)*
It carattere elzeviro *(m)*
Pt tipo de estilo antigo *(m)*

medical books En
De Medizinbücher *(pl)*
Es libros de medicina *(m pl)*
Fr ouvrages médicaux *(m pl)*
It testi di medicina *(m pl)*
Pt livros de medicina *(m pl)*

medical publisher En
De Verleger von medizinischen Veröffentlichungen *(m)*
Es editora de libros de medicina *(f)*
Fr éditeur d'ouvrages médicaux *(m)*
It editore di testi medici *(m)*
Pt editor de livros de medicina *(m)*

medida *(f) n* Pt
De Zeilenmaß *(n)*
En measure
Es largo *(m)*
Fr mesure *(f)*
It misura *(f)*

medida errada *(f)* Pt
De falsches Maß *(n)*
En wrong measure
Es medida incorrecta *(f)*
Fr justification incorrecte *(f)*
It misura sbagliata *(f)*

medida incorrecta *(f)* Es
De falsches Maß *(n)*
En wrong measure
Fr justification incorrecte *(f)*
It misura sbagliata *(f)*
Pt medida errada *(f)*

medio cuadratín *(m)* Es
De Halbgeviert *(n)*
En en
Fr demi-cadratin *(m)*
It mezza riga *(f)*
Pt meio quadratim *(m)*

Medizinbücher *(pl)* De
En medical books
Es libros de medicina *(m pl)*
Fr ouvrages médicaux *(m pl)*
It testi di medicina *(m pl)*
Pt livros de medicina *(m pl)*

mehrbändiges Werk *(n)* De
En multi-volume work
Es obra de varios volúmenes *(f)*
Fr oeuvre en plusieurs volumes *(f)*
It opera in più volumi *(f)*
Pt obra de muitos volumes *(f)*

Mehrsprachen-Wörterbuch *(n) n* De
En multilingual dictionary
Es diccionario multilingue *(m)*
Fr dictionnaire polyglotte *(m)*
It dizionario multilingue *(m)*
Pt dicionário multilingue *(m)*

Mehrwertsteuer (Mwst) *(f)* De
En value-added tax (VAT)

Es impuesto sobre el
valor añadido *(m)*
Fr taxe sur la valeur
ajoutée (TVA) *(f)*
It imposta sul valore
aggiunto (IVA) *(f)*
Pt imposto sobre valor
aduzido *(m)*

meia-tinta *(f) n* Pt
De Mezzotintoverfahren
(n)
En mezzotint
Es grabado mezzotinto
(m)
Fr mezzo-tinto *(m)*
It acquaforte *(m)*

meio quadratim *(m)* Pt
De Halbgeviert *(n)*
En en
Es medio cuadratín *(m)*
Fr demi-cadratin *(m)*
It mezza riga *(f)*

mélange de l'encre *(m)*
Fr
De Farbmischen *(n)*
En knocking-up (of
printing ink)
Es mezclando de tinta
(m)
It mischiante
d'inchiostro *(m)*
Pt mistura de tinta *(f)*

mémoire *(f) n* Fr
De speichern
En store
Es memoria *(f)*
It memoria *(f)*
Pt memória *(f)*

mémoire à accés direct
(f) Fr
De Direktzugriffsspeicher
(m)
En random-access store
Es memoria de acceso
al azar *(f)*
It memoria ad accesso
casuale *(f)*
Pt memória de acesso
aleatório *(f)*

memoria *(f) n* Es, It
De speichern
En store
Fr mémoire *(f)*
Pt memória *(f)*

memória *(f) n* Pt
De speichern
En store
Es memoria *(f)*
Fr mémoire *(f)*
It memoria *(f)*

**memoria ad accesso
casuale** *(f)* It
De Direktzugriffsspeicher
(m)
En random-access store
Es memoria de acceso
al azar *(f)*
Fr mémoire à accés
direct *(f)*
Pt memória de acesso
aleatório *(f)*

**memoria de acceso al
azar** *(f)* Es
De Direktzugriffsspeicher
(m)
En random-access store
Fr mémoire à accés
direct *(f)*
It memoria ad accesso
casuale *(f)*
Pt memória de acesso
aleatório *(f)*

**memória de acesso
aleatório** *(f)* Pt
De Direktzugriffsspeicher
(m)
En random-access store
Es memoria de acceso
al azar *(f)*
Fr mémoire à accés
direct *(f)*
It memoria ad accesso
casuale *(f)*

menabò *(m) n* It
De Blindband *(m)*
En dummy
Es maqueta *(f)*
Fr maquette *(f)*
Pt maquete *(f)*

menabò del rilegatore
(m) It
De Buchbinder-
blindband *(n)*
En binder's dummy
Es molde de
estampación *(m)*
Fr maquette de la
reliure *(f)*
Pt maqueta de
encadernação *(f)*

**menabò di grossezza
preciso** *(m)* It
De richtige dickes
Blindband *(n)*
En bulked dummy
Es maqueta realzada *(f)*
Fr maquette garnie *(f)*
Pt maquete engrossada
(f)

**menabò per
sovracopertina** *(m)*
It
De Umschlag-
Satzmontage *(f)*
En jacket artwork
Es trabajo artístíco de la
sobrecubierta *(m)*
Fr illustration de la
jaquette *(f)*
Pt arte da sobrecapa
(m)

mensageiro aéreo *(m)* Pt
De Luftkurier *(m)*
En air courier
Es estafeta aérea *(f)*
Fr courrier aérien *(m)*
It corriere aereo *(m)*

mentionner *vb* Fr
De ein Angebot
unterbreiten
En quote (a price)
Es cotizar
It dare le quotazioni
Pt cotar

mercado *(m) n* Es, Pt
De Markt *(m)*
En market
Fr marché *(m)*
It mercato *(m)*

mercado de masas *(m)*
Es
De Massenabsatz *(m)*
En mass market
Fr marché produits
grande
consommation *(m)*
It mercato di massa *(m)*
Pt mercado de massas
(m)

mercado de massas *(m)*
Pt
De Massenabsatz *(m)*
En mass market
Es mercado de masas
(m)
Fr marché produits

grande
consommation *(m)*
It mercato di massa *(m)*

mercato *(m) n* It
De Markt *(m)*
En market
Es mercado *(m)*
Fr marché *(m)*
Pt mercado *(m)*

mercato di massa *(m)* It
De Massenabsatz *(m)*
En mass market
Es mercado de masas
(m)
Fr marché produits
grande
consommation *(m)*
Pt mercado de massas
(m)

Merkblatt *(n) n* De
En leaflet
Es prospecto *(m)*
Fr feuille volante *(f)*
It volantino a stampa
(m)
Pt folheto *(m)*

mesa *(f) n* Pt
De Druckkarren *(m)*
En bed (printing
machine)
Es platina *(f)*
Fr marbre *(m)*
It piano *(m)*

mesa de retoque *(f)* Es,
Pt
De Leuchttisch *(m)*
En light table
Fr table lumineuse *(f)*
It tavolo luminoso *(m)*

mesmo tamanho Pt
De gleichgroβ
En same size (s/s)
Es igual tamaño
Fr format identique
It stessa dimensione

messa in custodia *(f)* It
De Einhängen *(n)*
En casing-in
Es metido en tapas *(m)*
Fr cartonnage *(m)*
Pt colocação em capa
separada *(f)*

Messingreglette *(f) n* De
En brass (binder's)
Es latón *(m)*
Fr laiton *(m)*
It ottone *(m)*
Pt latão *(m)*

mesure *(f) n* Fr
De Zeilenmas *(n)*
En measure
Es largo *(m)*
It misura *(f)*
Pt medida *(f)*

metal de imprenta *(m)* Es
De Schriftmetall *(n)*
En type metal
Fr métal d'imprimerie
   (m)
It lega per caratteri *(f)*
Pt metal para tipos *(m)*

métal d'imprimerie *(m)*
   Fr
De Schriftmetall *(n)*
En type metal
Es metal de imprenta
   (m)
It lega per caratteri *(f)*
Pt metal para tipos *(m)*

Metalldruck *(m) n* De
En gilding
Es doradura *(f)*
Fr dorure *(f)*
It doratura *(f)*
Pt douração *(f)*

metallic inks En
De Bronzedrucktinten
   (pl)
Es tintas metálicas *(f pl)*
Fr encres métalliques *(f
   pl)*
It inchiostri metallici *(m
   pl)*
Pt tintas metálicas *(f pl)*

métallisation *(f) n* Fr
De Bronzieren *(n)*
En bronzing (printing)
Es bronceado *(m)*
It bronzatura *(f)*
Pt bronzeamento *(m)*

metal para tipos *(m)* Pt
De Schriftmetall *(n)*
En type metal
Es metal de imprenta
   (m)

Fr métal d'imprimerie
   (m)
It lega per caratteri *(f)*

metido en tapas *(m)* Es
De Einhängen *(n)*
En casing-in
Fr cartonnage *(m)*
It messa in custodia *(f)*
Pt colocação em capa
   separada *(f)*

**método de impresión
   por chorro** *(m)* Es
De Spritzdruckverfahren
   (n)
En jet printing method
Fr impression au jet
   d'encre *(f)*
It metodo di stampa a
   getto *(m)*
Pt método de
   impressão a jacto *(m)*

**método de impressão a
   jacto** *(m)* Pt
De Spritzdruckverfahren
   (n)
En jet printing method
Es método de impresión
   por chorro *(m)*
Fr impression au jet
   d'encre *(f)*
It metodo di stampa a
   getto *(m)*

**metodo di stampa a
   getto** *(m)* It
De Spritzdruckverfahren
   (n)
En jet printing method
Es método de impresión
   por chorro *(m)*
Fr impression au jet
   d'encre *(f)*
Pt método de
   impressão a jacto *(m)*

mettant en retiration *(f)*
   Fr
De Widerdruck *(m)*
En backing-up
Es respaldado *(m)*
It supporto *(m)*
Pt apoio *(m)*

**mettitura le
   sovracopertine** *(f)*
   It
De Klebenindung *(f)*
En wrappering
Es sobrecubierta *(f)*

Fr emballage *(m)*
Pt colocação de
   sobrecapa *(f)*

mettre à jour Fr
De überarbeiten
En update
Es actualizar
It aggiornare
Pt actualizar

mettre au point Fr
De unter der Leitung
   eines Redakteurs
   herausgeben
En subedit
Es redactar
It redigere
Pt subcorrigir

mettre en faillite Fr
De bankerott machen
En bankrupt
Es quebrar
It far bancarotta
Pt falir

mettre en pages Fr
De umbrechen
En make up
Es compaginar
It compaginare
Pt compaginar

mettre un trait d'union
   Fr
De trennen
En hyphenate
Es separar con guión
It legare con trattino
Pt pôr um traço de
   união

mezclando de tinta *(m)*
   Es
De Farbmischen *(n)*
En knocking-up (of
   printing ink)
Fr mélange de l'encre
   (m)
It mischiante
   d'inchiostro *(m)*
Pt mistura de tinta *(f)*

mezza riga *(f)* It
De Halbgeviert *(n)*
En en
Es medio cuadratín *(m)*
Fr demi-cadratin *(m)*
Pt meio quadratim *(m)*

mezza rilegatura *(f)* It
De Halbfranzband *(m)*
En half binding
Es encuadernación a
   media piel *(f)*
Fr demi-reliure à petits
   coins *(f)*
Pt encadernação a meia
   pele *(f)*

mezzatinta *(f) n* It
De Halbton *(m)*
En halftone
Es autotipia *(f)*
Fr simili *(f)*
Pt autotipia *(f)*

mezzotint *n* En
De Mezzotintoverfahren
   (n)
Es grabado mezzotinto
   (m)
Fr mezzo-tinto *(m)*
It acquaforte *(m)*
Pt meia-tinta *(f)*

mezzo-tinto *(m) n* Fr
De Mezzotintoverfahren
   (n)
En mezzotint
Es grabado mezzotinto
   (m)
It acquaforte *(m)*
Pt meia-tinta *(f)*

Mezzotintoverfahren
   (n) n De
En mezzotint
Es grabado mezzotinto
   (m)
Fr mezzo-tinto *(m)*
It acquaforte *(m)*
Pt meia-tinta *(f)*

microficha *(f) n* Es, Pt
De Mikrofiche *(n)*
En microfiche
Fr microfiche *(f)*
It microfiche *(f)*

microfiche *n* En; Fr, It *(f)*
De Mikrofiche *(n)*
Es microficha *(f)*
Pt microficha *(f)*

microfilm *n* En; Es, Fr, It
   (m)
De Mikrofilm *(m)*
Pt microfilme *(m)*

microfilme *(m) n* Pt
De Mikrofilm *(m)*
En microfilm
Es microfilm *(m)*
Fr microfilm *(m)*
It microfilm *(m)*

Mietschreiber *(m) n* De
En hack writer
Es escritor mercenario *(m)*
Fr écrivassier *(m)*
It imbrattacarte *(m)*
Pt escritor comercial *(m)*

mi-gras *adj* Fr
De fett
En bold
Es negrita
It neretto
Pt negrito

Mikrofiche *(n) n* De
En microfiche
Es microficha *(f)*
Fr microfiche *(f)*
It microfiche *(f)*
Pt microficha *(f)*

Mikrofilm *(m) n* De
En microfilm
Es microfilm *(m)*
Fr microfilm *(m)*
It microfilm *(m)*
Pt microfilme *(m)*

mill board En
De Pappdeckel *(m)*
Es cartón grueso *(m)*
Fr carton gris à reliure *(m)*
It cartone forte *(m)*
Pt cartão grosso *(m)*

mill-finished paper En
De maschinenglattes Papier *(n)*
Es papel calandrado *(m)*
Fr papier apprêté machine *(m)*
It carta lisciata a macchina *(f)*
Pt papel de acabamento à máquina *(m)*

minerva *(f) n* Es, Pt
De Tiegel *(m)*
En platen press
Fr imprimeuse *(f)*

It macchina da stampa a platina *(f)*

minidisque *(m) n* Fr
De Diskette *(f)*
En diskette
Es disco flexible *(m)*
It diskette *(m)*
Pt disqueta *(f)*

minorista *(m) n* Es
De Einzelhändler *(m)*
En retailer
Fr détaillant *(m)*
It dettagliante *(m)*
Pt retalhista *(m)*

minuscola *(f) n* It
De kleiner Buchstabe *(m)*
En lower-case letter
Es minúscula *(f)*
Fr caractère de bas de caisse *(m)*
Pt minúscula *(f)*

minúscula *(f) n* Es, Pt
De kleiner Buchstabe *(m)*
En lower-case letter
Fr caractère de bas de caisse *(m)*
It minuscola *(f)*

minuta *(f) n* It
De Entwurf *(m)*
En draft
Es borrador *(m)*
Fr ébauche *(f)*
Pt rascunho *(m)*

mis à jour Fr
De überarbeitet
En updated
Es actualizado
It aggiornato
Pt actualizado

mischiante d'inchiostro *(m)* It
De Farbmischen *(n)*
En knocking-up (of printing ink)
Es mezclando de tinta *(m)*
Fr mélange de l'encre *(m)*
Pt mistura de tinta *(f)*

mise en page *(f)* Fr
De Formatierung *(f)*
En formatting
Es formación *(m)*
It formazione *(f)*
Pt formatação *(f)*

mise en pages *(f)* Fr
De Montage *(f)*
En imposition
Es imposición *(f)*
It imposizione *(f)*
Pt imposição *(f)*

mise en place *(f)* Fr
De Einsetzen *(n)*
En insetting
Es encuadre *(m)*
It incorniciatura *(f)*
Pt intercalagem *(f)*

mise en train mécanique *(f)* Fr
De mechanische Zurichtung *(f)*
En mechanical overlay
Es alza mecánica *(f)*
It sovrapposizione meccanica *(f)*
Pt corte mecânico *(m)*

misregister *n* En
De Paβdifferenz *(f)*
Es registro inexacto *(m)*
Fr repérage défectueux *(m)*
It registro scorretto *(f)*
Pt registo inexacto *(m)*

mistura de tinta *(f)* Pt
De Farbmischen *(n)*
En knocking-up (of printing ink)
Es mezclando de tinta *(m)*
Fr mélange de l'encre *(m)*
It mischiante d'inchiostro *(m)*

misura *(f) n* It
De Zeilenmaβ *(n)*
En measure
Es largo *(m)*
Fr mesure *(f)*
Pt medida *(f)*

misura sbagliata *(f)* It
De falsches Maβ *(n)*
En wrong measure
Es medida incorrecta *(f)*

Fr justification incorrecte *(f)*
Pt medida errada *(f)*

mit dem Manuskript vergleichen De
En read against copy
Es leer a la vista del original
Fr corriger avec copie
It confrontare coll'original
Pt ler comparando com a cópia

mit der Post schicken De
En mail
Es enviar por correo
Fr envoyer par la poste
It spedire per posta
Pt enviar por correio

mit Goldschnitt De
En gilt-edged
Es de cortes dorados
Fr doré sur tranche
It con bordi dorati
Pt dourado nas beiras

mobile *n* En; Fr, Pt *(m)*
De Mobilé *(f)*
Es hastidor móvil *(m)*
It elemento mobile *(m)*

Mobilé *(n) n* De
En mobile
Es hastidor móvil *(m)*
Fr mobile *(m)*
It elemento mobile *(m)*
Pt mobile *(m)*

mock-up *n* En
De Blindband *(m)*
Es maqueta *(f)*
Fr maquette *(f)*
It menabò *(m)*
Pt maquete *(f)*

moderner Schrifttyp *(m)* De
En modern face
Es tipo moderno *(m)*
Fr didone *(f)*
It carattere moderno *(m)*
Pt olho moderno *(m)*

modern face En
De moderner Schrifttyp
   (m)
Es tipo moderno (m)
Fr didone (f)
It carattere moderno
   (m)
Pt olho moderno (m)

moiré (m) n Es, Fr
De Schnürlmoiré (n)
En moiré effect
It effetto moiré (m)
Pt efeito moiré (m)

moiré effect En
De Schnürlmoiré (n)
Es moiré (m)
Fr moiré (m)
It effetto moiré (m)
Pt efeito moiré (m)

mojador (m) n Es
De Feuchtwalze (f)
En damper
Fr rouleau mouilleur (m)
It umettatore (m)
Pt molhador (m)

mold (papermaking) n
   Am
De Guβform (f)
En mould (papermaking)
Es molde (m)
Fr empreinte (f)
It stampo (industria
   cartiera) (m)
Pt molde (m)

mold (typesetting) n Am
De Matrize (f)
En mould (typesetting)
Es matriz (f)
Fr matrice (f)
It matrice (f)
Pt matriz (f)

molde (m) n Es, Pt
Am mold (papermaking)
De Guβform (f)
En mould (papermaking)
Fr empreinte (f)
It stampo (industria
   cartiera) (m)

molde de chumbo (m) Pt
Am lead mold
De Bleiform (f)
En lead mould
Es molde de plomo (m)

Fr empreinte sur plomb
   (f)
It stampo di piombo
   (m)

molde de estampación
   (m) Es
De Buchbinder-
   blindband (n)
En binder's dummy
Fr maquette de la
   reliure (f)
It menabò del
   rilegatore (m)
Pt maqueta de
   encadernação (f)

molde de plomo (m) Es
Am lead mold
De Bleiform (f)
En lead mould
Fr empreinte sur plomb
   (f)
It stampo di piombo
   (m)
Pt molde de chumbo
   (m)

mold-made paper Am
De Büttenwerk-
   druckpapier (n)
En mould-made paper
Es papel de tina (m)
Fr papier moyen âge
   (m)
It carta formata a mano
   (f)
Pt papel moldado (m)

moleskine (f) n Fr
De Wachstuch (n)
En American cloth
Es hule (m)
It tela cerata (f)
Pt pano americano (m)

molhador (m) n Pt
De Feuchtwalze (f)
En damper
Es mojador (m)
Fr rouleau mouilleur (m)
It umettatore (m)

monochrome adj En, Fr
De einfarbig
Es monocromo
It monocromatico
Pt monocrómico

monochrome
   illustration En
De einfarbige illustration
   (f)
Es ilustración
   monocroma (f)
Fr illustration
   monochrome (f)
It illustrazione
   monocromatica (f)
Pt ilustração
   monocrómica (f)

monocromatico adj It
De einfarbig
En monochrome
Es monocromo
Fr monochrome
Pt monocrómico

monocrómico adj Pt
De einfarbig
En monochrome
Es monocromo
Fr monochrome
It monocromatico

monocromo adj Es
De einfarbig
En monochrome
Fr monochrome
It monocromatico
Pt monocrómico

montage (m) n Fr
De Satzumbruch (m)
En make-up
Es compaginación (f)
It impaginatura (f)
Pt compaginação (f)

Montage (f) n De
En imposition
Es imposición (f)
Fr mise en pages (f)
It imposizione (f)
Pt imposição (f)

montage du texte (m) Fr
De Texteinpassung (f)
En copy-fitting
Es ajuste de originales
   (m)
It aggiustamento di
   originali (m)
Pt ajustamento do
   original (m)

montagem (f) n Pt
De Klebeumbruch (m)
En paste-up

Es montaje (m)
Fr collage (m)
It incollatura (f)

montaje (m) n Es
De Klebeumbruch (m)
En paste-up
Fr collage (m)
It incollatura (f)
Pt montagem (f)

montar vb Es, Pt
De klebeumbrechen
En paste up
Fr encoller
It incollare

montar inserciones Es
De montieren
En strip in
Fr raccorder
It giuntare
Pt incluir

montieren vb De
En strip in
Es montar inserciones
Fr raccorder
It giuntare
Pt incluir

mordente (m) n Pt
De Ätzphase (f)
En bite (platemaking)
Es mordido (m)
Fr larron (m)
It acidatura (f)

mordido (m) n Es
De Ätzphase (f)
En bite (platemaking)
Fr larron (m)
It acidatura (f)
Pt mordente (m)

Morocco (leather) n En
De Maroquin (n)
Es tafilete (m)
Fr maroquin (m)
It marocchino (m)
Pt marroquim (m)

morsure par couverture
   (f) Fr
De Punktätzung (f)
En dot etching
Es reducción de los
   puntos (f)
It incisione a punti (f)

Pt redução dos pontos
   reticulares *(f)*

mostrare *vb* It
De ausstellen
En display
Es exhibir
Fr exhiber
Pt exibir

mostruário *(m) n* Pt
De Muster *(n)*
En swatch
Es muestrario *(m)*
Fr échantillon *(m)*
It campione *(m)*

mot en-tête *(m)* Fr
De haupt Wort *(n)*
En headword
Es palabra principal *(f)*
It parola principale *(f)*
Pt palavra-índice *(f)*

mould (papermaking) *n*
   En
Am mold (papermaking)
De Gußform *(f)*
Es molde *(m)*
Fr empreinte *(f)*
It stampo (industria
   cartiera) *(m)*
Pt molde *(m)*

mould (typesetting) *n* En
Am mold (typesetting)
De Matrize *(f)*
Es matriz *(f)*
Fr matrice *(f)*
It matrice *(f)*
Pt matriz *(f)*

mould-made paper En
Am mold-made paper
De Büttenwerk-
   druckpapier *(n)*
Es papel de tina *(m)*
Fr papier moyen âge
   (m)
It carta formata a mano
   (m)
Pt papel moldado *(m)*

mousseline *(f) n* Fr
De Heftgaze *(f)*
En mull
Es muselina *(f)*
It mussolina *(f)*
Pt musselina *(f)*

movable type En
De bewegliche Schrift *(f)*
Es tipos movibles *(m pl)*
Fr caractères mobiles
   (m pl)
It carattere mobile *(m)*
Pt tipo móvel *(m)*

movimento *(m) n* Pt
De Umsatz *(m)*
En turnover
Es cifra de negocios *(f)*
Fr chiffre d'affaires *(m)*
It fatturato *(m)*

movimento di cassa *(m)*
   It
De Bargeldfluß *(m)*
En cash flow
Es flujo de caja *(m)*
Fr cash-flow *(m)*
Pt movimento em
   dinheiro *(m)*

movimento em dinheiro
   (m) Pt
De Bargeldfluß *(m)*
En cash flow
Es flujo de caja *(m)*
Fr cash-flow *(m)*
It movimento di cassa
   (m)

muestrario *(m) n* Es
De Muster *(n)*
En swatch
Fr échantillon *(m)*
It campione *(m)*
Pt mostruário *(m)*

mull *n* En
De Heftgaze *(f)*
Es muselina *(f)*
Fr mousseline *(f)*
It mussolina *(f)*
Pt musselina *(f)*

multilingual dictionary
   En
De Mehrsprachen-
   Wörterbuch *(n)*
Es diccionario
   multilingue *(m)*
Fr dictionnaire
   polyglotte *(m)*
It dizionario multilingue
   (m)
Pt dicionário multilingue
   (m)

multi-volume work En
De mehrbändiges Werk
   (n)
Es obra de varios
   volúmenes *(f)*
Fr oeuvre en plusieurs
   volumes *(f)*
It opera in più volumi *(f)*
Pt obra de muitos
   volumes *(f)*

muselina *(f) n* Es
De Heftgaze *(f)*
En mull
Fr mousseline *(f)*
It mussolina *(f)*
Pt musselina *(f)*

musselina *(f) n* Pt
De Heftgaze *(f)*
En mull
Es muselina *(f)*
Fr mousseline *(f)*
It mussolina *(f)*

mussolina *(f) n* It
De Heftgaze *(f)*
En mull
Es muselina *(f)*
Fr mousseline *(f)*
Pt musselina *(f)*

Muster *(n) n* De
En swatch
Es muestrario *(m)*
Fr échantillon *(m)*
It campione *(m)*
Pt mostruário *(m)*

Musterseite *(f) n* De
En specimen page
Es página de muestra *(f)*
Fr feuille-échantillon *(f)*
It pagina campione *(f)*
Pt página amostra *(f)*

muter *vb* Fr
De transferieren
En transfer
Es trasladar
It trasferire
Pt transferir

N

Nachrichten *(pl)* De
En news *pl n*
Es noticias *(f pl)*
Fr nouvelles *(f pl)*
It notizie *(f pl)*
Pt notícias *(f pl)*

Nachrichtenmagazin *(n)*
   n De
En news magazine
Es revista de
   información *(f)*
Fr magazine
   d'information *(m)*
It rivista di attualità *(f)*
Pt revista de informação
   (f)

Nachschlagewerk *(n) n*
   De
En reference book
Es obra de consulta *(f)*
Fr livre de référence *(m)*.
It libro di consultazione
   (m)
Pt livro de consulta *(m)*

Nachschlagewerk-
   Bücherei *(f) n* De
En reference library
Es biblioteca de
   consulta *(f)*
Fr bibliothèque
   d'ouvrages de
   référence *(f)*
It biblioteca di
   consultazione *(f)*
Pt biblioteca de
   consulta *(f)*

Nachschlagewerk-
   Verleger *(m) n* De
En reference-book
   publisher
Es editor de obras de
   consulta *(m)*
Fr éditeur d'ouvrages
   de référence *(m)*
It editore di libri di
   consultazione *(m)*
Pt editor de livros de
   consulta *(m)*

Nadellöcher *(pl)* De
En pinholes *pl n*
Es burbujas *(f pl)*

Fr perforation des
négatifs *(f)*
It mancanza di densità
(f)
Pt furos *(m pl)*

não gramatical Pt
De nicht grammatisch
En ungrammatical
Es no gramatical
Fr non grammatical
It non grammaticale

narración *(f) n* Es
De Kurzgeschichte *(f)*
En short story
Fr nouvelle *(f)*
It racconto breve *(m)*
Pt novela pequena *(f)*

narrativa *(f) n* It
De Romanliteratur *(f)*
En fiction
Es literatura novelesca
(f)
Fr romans *(m pl)*
Pt ficção *(f)*

narrativa popolare *(f)* It
De volkstümliche
Romanliteratur *(f)*
En popular fiction
Es literatura popular *(f)*
Fr romans populaires
(m pl)
Pt ficção popular *(f)*

nastro di carta *(m)* It
De Lochstreifen *(m)*
En paper tape
Es cinta de papel *(f)*
Fr bande de papier *(f)*
Pt fita de papel *(f)*

**nastro di carta
perforato** *(m)* It
De Lochstreifen *(m)*
En punched paper tape
Es cinta perforada *(f)*
Fr bande perforée *(f)*
Pt fita de papel
perfurado *(f)*

nastro magnetico *(m)* It
De Magnetband *(n)*
En magnetic tape
Es cinta magnética *(f)*
Fr bande magnétique *(f)*
Pt fita magnética *(f)*

**nastro per
mascheratura** *(m)* It
De Abdeckband *(n)*
En masking tape
Es cinta para
enmascarar *(f)*
Fr bande de masquage
(f)
Pt fita de mascarar *(f)*

négatif *(m) n* Fr
De Negativ *(n)*
En negative
Es negativo *(m)*
It negativo *(m)*
Pt negativo *(m)*

négatif sans contraste
(m) Fr
De flaches Negativ *(n)*
En flat negative
Es cliché sin contrastes
(m)
It negativo senza
contrasti *(m)*
Pt negativo plano *(m)*

négatifs sélectionnés
(m pl) Fr
De Teilfarbennegative
(pl)
En separation negatives
Es negativos de
selección *(m pl)*
It negativi da selezione
(m pl)
Pt negativos de
separação *(m pl)*

Negativ *(n) n* De
En negative
Es negativo *(m)*
Fr négatif *(m)*
It negativo *(m)*
Pt negativo *(m)*

negative *n* En
De Negativ *(n)*
Es negativo *(m)*
Fr négatif *(m)*
It negativo *(m)*
Pt negativo *(m)*

negative film En
De Negativfilm *(m)*
Es película negativa *(f)*
Fr film négatif *(m)*
It film negativo *(m)*
Pt película negativa *(f)*

Negativfilm *(m) n* De
En negative film
Es película negativa *(f)*
Fr film négatif *(m)*
It film negativo *(m)*
Pt película negativa *(f)*

negativi da selezione *(m
pl)* It
De Teilfarbennegative
(pl)
En separation negatives
Es negativos de
selección *(m pl)*
Fr négatifs sélectionnés
(m pl)
Pt negativos de
separação *(m pl)*

negativo *(m) n* Es, It, Pt
De Negativ *(n)*
En negative
Fr négatif *(m)*

negativo plano *(m)* Pt
De flaches Negativ *(n)*
En flat negative
Es cliché sin contrastes
(m)
Fr négatif sans
contraste *(m)*
It negativo senza
contrasti *(m)*

negativos de selección
(m pl) Es
De Teilfarbennegative
(pl)
En separation negatives
Fr négatifs sélectionnés
(m pl)
It negativi da selezione
(m pl)
Pt negativos de
separação *(m pl)*

negativos de separação
(m pl) Pt
De Teilfarbennegative
(pl)
En separation negatives
Es negativos de
selección *(m pl)*
Fr négatifs sélectionnés
(m pl)
It negativi da selezione
(m pl)

**negativo senza
contrasti** *(m)* It
De flaches Negativ *(n)*
En flat negative

Es cliché sin contrastes
(m)
Fr négatif sans
contraste *(m)*
Pt negativo plano *(m)*

negocio de publicação
(m) Pt
De Verlagswesen *(n)*
En publishing
Es editorial *(f)*
Fr commerce de
l'édition *(m)*
It editoria *(f)*

negozio *(m) n* It
De Laden *(m)*
En shop (retail)
Es tienda *(f)*
Fr boutique *(f)*
Pt loja *(f)*

nègre *(m) n* Fr
De Schattenautor *(m)*
En ghost writer
Es escritor fantasma *(m)*
It collaboratore
anonimo *(m)*
Pt colaborador anónimo
(m)

negrita *adj* Es
De fett
En bold
Fr mi-gras
It neretto
Pt negrito

negrito *adj* Pt
De fett
En bold
Es negrita
Fr mi-gras
It neretto

neretto *adj* It
De fett
En bold
Es negrita
Fr mi-gras
Pt negrito

nerf *(m) n* Fr
De Verschnüren *(n)*
En cording
Es encordonado *(m)*
It imputaggio *(m)*
Pt encordoamento *(m)*

netteté *(f) n* Fr
De Bildschärfe *(f)*
En definition
    (photography)
Es claridad *(f)*
It nitidezza *(f)*
Pt nitidez *(f)*

Neuauflage *(f) n* De
En reprint
Es reimpresión *(f)*
Fr réimpression *(f)*
It ristampa *(f)*
Pt reimpressão *(f)*

neu auflegen De
En reprint
Es reimprimir
Fr réimprimer
It ristampare
Pt reimprimir

neuen Text einfügen De
En insert new copy
Es inertar nueva copia
Fr insérer nouveau texte
It inserire nuovo testo
Pt inserir novo texto

neu setzen De
En reset
Es componer de nuevo
Fr remanier
It riazzerare
Pt tornar a compor

news *pl n* En
De Nachrichten *(pl)*
Es noticias *(f pl)*
Fr nouvelles *(f pl)*
It notizie *(f pl)*
Pt notícias *(f pl)*

news chase En
De Zeitungsrahmen *(m)*
Es rama de noticias *(f)*
Fr châssis à journal *(m)*
It caccia di notizie *(f)*
Pt rama de notícias *(f)*

news magazine En
De Nachrichtenmagazin
    (n)
Es revista de
    información *(f)*
Fr magazine
    d'information *(m)*
It rivista di attualità *(f)*
Pt revista de informação
    (f)

newspaper *n* En
De Zeitung *(f)*
Es diario *(m)*
Fr journal *(m)*
It giornale quotidiano
    (m)
Pt jornal diário *(m)*

newsprint *n* En
De Rotationsdruckpapier
    (n)
Es papel periódico *(m)*
Fr papier-journal *(m)*
It carta da giornale *(f)*
Pt papel para jornal *(m)*

newsworthy *adj* En
De aktuell
Es de interés
    periodístico
Fr d'intérêt
    journalistique
It che fa notizia
Pt digno de ser
    publicado

**nicht geheftete
    Bindung** *(f)* De
En unsewn binding
Es encuadernación sin
    coser *(f)*
Fr reliure sans couture
    (f)
It rilegatura non cucita
    (f)
Pt encadernação não
    cosida *(f)*

nicht gerade De
En out of square
Es descuadrado
Fr mal cadré
It fuori squadra
Pt fora do
    enquadramento

nicht grammatisch De
En ungrammatical
Es no gramatical
Fr non grammatical
It non grammaticale
Pt não gramatical

nicht vorrätig De
En out of stock
Es sin existencias
Fr non disponible
It sprovvisto
Pt esgotado em
    armazém

nick *n* En
De Signaturrinne *(f)*
Es cran *(m)*
Fr cran *(m)*
It tacca *(f)*
Pt entalhe *(m)*

nickel electro En
De Nickelgalvano *(n)*
Es galvano niquelado
    (m)
Fr galvano nickel *(m)*
It galvano-nichel *(m)*
Pt galvano niquelado
    (m)

Nickelgalvano *(n) n* De
En nickel electro
Es galvano niquelado
    (m)
Fr galvano nickel *(m)*
It galvano-nichel *(m)*
Pt galvano niquelado
    (m)

nickel stereo En
De Nickelstereo *(n)*
Es estereotipia
    niquelada *(f)*
Fr stéréo nickel *(m)*
It stereo-nichel *(m)*
Pt estereo-niquelado
    (m)

Nickelstereo *(n) n* De
En nickel stereo
Es estereotipia
    niquelada *(f)*
Fr stéréo nickel *(m)*
It stereo-nichel *(m)*
Pt estereo-niquelado
    (m)

nitidez *(f) n* Pt
De Bildschärfe *(f)*
En definition
    (photography)
Es claridad *(f)*
Fr netteté *(f)*
It nitidezza *(f)*

nitidezza *(f) n* It
De Bildschärfe *(f)*
En definition
    (photography)
Es claridad *(f)*
Fr netteté *(f)*
Pt nitidez *(f)*

nivelado *adj* Pt
De glatt
En flush
Es a ras
Fr ras
It a livello

niveladores *(m pl)* Pt
De Bestoβhobel *(pl)*
En planes *pl n*
Es asentadores *(m pl)*
Fr rabots *(m pl)*
It pialle *(f pl)*

no gramatical Es
De nicht grammatisch
En ungrammatical
Fr non grammatical
It non grammaticale
Pt não gramatical

nombre de pages *(m)* Fr
De Seitenzahl *(f)*
En extent
Es amplitud *(f)*
It estensione *(m)*
Pt extensão *(f)*

nome do editor *(m)* Pt
De Impressum *(n)*
En imprint
Es pie de imprenta *(m)*
Fr marque d'éditeur *(f)*
It impressa editoriale *(f)*

non disponible Fr
De nicht vorrätig
En out of stock
Es sin existencias
It sprovvisto
Pt esgotado em
    armazém

non-fiction *n* En
De Sachliteratur *(f)*
Es textos no novelescos
    (m pl)
Fr ouvrages généraux
    (m pl)
It saggistica *(f)*
Pt textos de não ficção
    (m pl)

non-fiction books En
De Sachbücher *(pl)*
Es libros no novelescos
    (m pl)
Fr livres généraux *(m pl)*
It libri di saggistica *(m
    pl)*

Pt livros de não ficção
(m pl)

non-fiction publisher En
De Sachliteratur-
Verleger (m)
Es editor de libros no
novelescos (m)
Fr éditeur d'ouvrages
généraux (m)
It editore di saggistica
(m)
Pt editor de não ficção
(m)

non grammatical Fr
De nicht grammatisch
En ungrammatical
Es no gramatical
It non grammaticale
Pt não gramatical

non grammaticale It
De nicht grammatisch
En ungrammatical
Es no gramatical
Fr non grammatical
Pt não gramatical

**normas de separación
con guiones** (f pl) Es
De Trennungsregelb (pl)
En hyphenation rules
Fr règles de coupure (f
pl)
It regole di legatura con
trattino (f pl)
Pt regras de hifenação (f
pl)

nota al pie de la página
(f) Es
De Fußnote (f)
En footnote
Fr note en bas de page
(f)
It nota in calce (f)
Pt nota de pé de página
(f)

nota biográfica (f) Es, Pt
De biographische
Anmerkung (f)
En biographical note
Fr note biographique (f)
It nota biografica (f)

nota biografica (f) It
De biographische
Anmerkung (f)
En biographical note

Es nota biográfica (f)
Fr note biographique (f)
Pt nota biográfica (f)

nota de pé de página (f)
Pt
De Fußnote (f)
En footnote
Es nota al pie de la
página (f)
Fr note en bas de page
(f)
It nota in calce (f)

nota in calce (f) It
De Fußnote (f)
En footnote
Es nota al pie de la
página (f)
Fr note en bas de page
(f)
Pt nota de pé de página
(f)

nota remissiva (f) Pt
De Querverweis (m)
En cross reference
Es interreferencia (f)
Fr renvoi (m)
It rimando (m)

notas (f pl) Es, Pt
De Anmerkungen (pl)
En notes pl n
Fr notes (f pl)
It note (f pl)

notas marginais (f pl) Pt
De Randbemerkungen
(pl)
En marginal notes
Es notas marginales (f
pl)
Fr notes marginales (f
pl)
It note a margine (f pl)

notas marginales (f pl)
Es
De Randbemerkungen
(pl)
En marginal notes
Fr notes marginales (f
pl)
It note a margine (f pl)
Pt notas marginais (f pl)

note (f pl) It
De Anmerkungen (pl)
En notes pl n
Es notas (f pl)

Fr notes (f pl)
Pt notas (f pl)

note a margine (f pl) It
De Randbemerkungen
(pl)
En marginal notes
Es notas marginales (f
pl)
Fr notes marginales (f
pl)
Pt notas marginais (f pl)

note biographique (f) Fr
De biographische
Anmerkung (f)
En biographical note
Es nota biográfica (f)
It nota biografica (f)
Pt nota biográfica (f)

note en bas de page (f)
Fr
De Fußnote (f)
En footnote
Es nota al pie de la
página (f)
It nota in calce (f)
Pt nota de pé de página
(f)

notes n pl En; Fr (f)
De Anmerkungen (pl)
Es notas (f pl)
It note (f pl)
Pt notas (f pl)

notes marginales (f pl) Fr
De Randbemerkungen
(pl)
En marginal notes
Es notas marginales (f
pl)
It note a margine (f pl)
Pt notas marginais (f pl)

noticias (f pl) Es
De Nachrichten (pl)
En news pl n
Fr nouvelles (f pl)
It notizie (f pl)
Pt notícias (f pl)

notícias (f pl) Pt
De Nachrichten (pl)
En news pl n
Es noticias (f pl)
Fr nouvelles (f pl)
It notizie (f pl)

notizie (f pl) It
De Nachrichten (pl)
En news pl n
Es noticias (f pl)
Fr nouvelles (f pl)
Pt notícias (f pl)

nouvelle (f) n Fr
De Kurzgeschichte (f)
En short story
Es narración (f)
It racconto breve (m)
Pt novela pequena (f)

nouvelles (f pl) Fr
De Nachrichten (pl)
En news pl n
Es noticias (f pl)
It notizie (f pl)
Pt notícias (f pl)

novel n En
De Roman (m)
Es novela (f)
Fr roman (m)
It romanzo (m)
Pt romance (m)

novela (f) n Es
De Roman (m)
En novel
Fr roman (m)
It romanzo (m)
Pt romance (m)

novela de misterio (f) Es
De Reißer (m)
En thriller
Fr roman à sensation
(m)
It giallo (m)
Pt policial (m)

novela pequena (f) Pt
De Kurzgeschichte (f)
En short story
Es narración (f)
Fr nouvelle (f)
It racconto breve (m)

novela policíaca (f) Es
De Kriminalroman (m)
En detective novel
Fr roman policier (m)
It racconto poliziesco
(m)
Pt livro policial (m)

novela romántica (f) Es
De romantischer Roman (m)
En romantic novel
Fr roman romanesque (m)
It novella romantica (f)
Pt romance romântico (m)

novelist n En
De Romanschriftsteller (m)
Es novelista (m)
Fr romancier (f)
It romanziere (m)
Pt romancista (m)

novelista (m) n Es
De Romanschriftsteller (m)
En novelist
Fr romancier (f)
It romanziere (m)
Pt romancista (m)

novella romantica (f) It
De romantischer Roman (m)
En romantic novel
Es novela romántica (f)
Fr roman romanesque (m)
Pt romance romântico (m)

numeri arabi (m pl) It
De arabische Ziffern (pl)
En arabic numerals
Es números arábigos (m pl)
Fr chiffres arabes (m pl)
Pt numeros árabes (m pl)

numeri romani (m pl) It
De römische Zahlen (pl)
En roman numerals
Es números romanos (m pl)
Fr chiffres romains (m pl)
Pt números romanos (m pl)

numéro de ligne (m) Fr
De Zeilenzahl (f)
En line number
Es número de líneas (m)
It numero di linea (m)
Pt número de linha (m)

número de líneas (m) Es
De Zeilenzahl (f)
En line number
Fr numéro de ligne (m)
It numero di linea (m)
Pt número de linha (m)

número de linha (m) Pt
De Zeilenzahl (f)
En line number
Es número de líneas (m)
Fr numéro de ligne (m)
It numero di linea (m)

numero della pagina (m) It
De Pagina (f)
En folio
Es folio (m)
Fr folio (m)
Pt fólio (m)

numero di linea (m) It
De Zeilenzahl (f)
En line number
Es número de líneas (m)
Fr numéro de ligne (m)
Pt número de linha (m)

numero ISBN (m) It
De ISBN-Nummer (f)
En ISBN number
Es número ISBN (m)
Fr numéro ISBN (m)
Pt número ISBN (m)

número ISBN (m) Es, Pt
De ISBN-Nummer (f)
En ISBN number
Fr numéro ISBN (m)
It numero ISBN (m)

numéro ISBN (m) Fr
De ISBN-Nummer (f)
En ISBN number
Es número ISBN (m)
It numero ISBN (m)
Pt número ISBN (m)

numeros árabes (m pl) Pt
De arabische Ziffern (pl)
En arabic numerals
Es números arábigos (m pl)
Fr chiffres arabes (m pl)
It numeri arabi (m pl)

números arábigos (m pl) Es
De arabische Ziffern (pl)

En arabic numerals
Fr chiffres arabes (m pl)
It numeri arabi (m pl)
Pt numeros árabes (m pl)

números romanos (m pl) Es, Pt
De römische Zahlen (pl)
En roman numerals
Fr chiffres romains (m pl)
It numeri romani (m pl)

Nutzschwelle (f) n De
En break-even point
Es punto de equilibrio (m)
Fr seuil de rentabilité (m)
It punto di pareggio (m)
Pt ponto de equilíbrio (m)

O

oberflächengeleimtes Papier (n) De
En tub-sized paper
Es papel encolado en tina (m)
Fr papier collé à la cuve (m)
It carta imbozzimata in tino (f)
Pt papel encolado em tina (m)

Oberkasten (m) n De
En upper case
Es caja alta (f)
Fr haut de casse (m)
It alta cassa
Pt caixa alta (f)

oblitération (f) n Fr
De Abdecken (n)
En blocking out
Es enmienda con sobreimpresión (f)
It mascheratura con vernice coprente (f)
Pt cobrimento (m)

oblitérer vb Fr
De abdecken
En mask
Es enmascarar
It mascherare
Pt mascarar

oblong paper En
De Langformat-Papier (n)
Es papel apaisado (m)
Fr format à l'italienne (m)
It carta oblunga (f)
Pt papel alongado (m)

obra cosida (f) Es, Pt
De geheftete Arbeit (f)
En sewn work
Fr reliure cousue (f)
It lavoro di cucitura (m)

obra de consulta (f) Es
De Nachschlagewerk (n)
En reference book
Fr livre de référence (m)
It libro di consultazione (m)
Pt livro de consulta (m)

obra de muitos volumes (f) Pt
De mehrbändiges Werk (n)
En multi-volume work
Es obra de varios volúmenes (f)
Fr oeuvre en plusieurs volumes (f)
It opera in più volumi (f)

obra de un solo volumen (f) Es
De einbändiges Werk (n)
En single-volume work
Fr oeuvre en un volume (f)
It opera in un solo volume (f)
Pt obra num só volume (f)

obra de varios volúmenes (f) Es
De mehrbändiges Werk (n)
En multi-volume work
Fr oeuvre en plusieurs volumes (f)
It opera in più volumi (f)
Pt obra de muitos volumes (f)

obra dramática (f) Es
De Stück (n)
En play
Fr pièce de théâtre (f)
It commedia (f)
Pt peça (f)

obra num só volume (f)
Pt
De einbändiges Werk (n)
En single-volume work
Es obra de un solo
volumen (f)
Fr oeuvre en un volume
(f)
It opera in un solo
volume (f)

obras completas (f pl)
Es, Pt
De sämtliche Werke (pl)
En complete works
Fr oeuvres complètes (f
pl)
It opera completa (f)

obras reunidas (f pl) Es
De gesammelten Werke
(pl)
En collected works
Fr recueil des oeuvres
(m pl)
It raccolta di opere (f pl)
Pt compilação de obras
(f)

occhio del carattere (m)
It
De Schrifttyp (m)
En typeface
Es ojo del tipo (m)
Fr oeil d'un caractère
(m)
Pt olho de tipo (m)

octavo n En; Pt (m)
De Oktavformat (n)
Es en octavo (m)
Fr in-octavo (m)
It in ottavo (m)

oeil d'un caractère (m)
Fr
De Schrifttyp (m)
En typeface
Es ojo del tipo (m)
It occhio del carattere
(m)
Pt olho de tipo (m)

**oeil plus grand que la
normale** (m) Fr
De breiter Schrifttyp (m)
En expanded typeface
Es tipo de ojo ancho (m)
It carattere largo (m)
Pt tipo de olho largo (m)

**oeuvre en plusieurs
volumes** (f) Fr
De mehrbändiges Werk
(n)
En multi-volume work
Es obra de varios
volúmenes (f)
It opera in più volumi (f)
Pt obra de muitos
volumes (f)

oeuvre en un volume (f)
Fr
De einbändiges Werk (n)
En single-volume work
Es obra de un solo
volumen (f)
It opera in un solo
volume (f)
Pt obra num só volume
(f)

oeuvres complètes (f pl)
Fr
De sämtliche Werke (pl)
En complete works
Es obras completas (f pl)
It opera completa (f)
Pt obras completas (f pl)

oferta (f) n Pt
De Prämie (f)
En premium
Es prima (f)
Fr prime (f)
It offerta a premio (f)

oferta por correo (f) Es
De Postwurfsendung (f)
En direct-mail shot
Fr mailing; offre
promotionnelle (m f)
It invio diretto per
posta; offerta postale
(m f)
Pt publicidade por
correio (f)

offcut n En
De Papierabschnitt (n)
Es papel de recorte (m)
Fr découpure (f)
It ritaglio di carta (m)
Pt papel de recorte (m)

öffentlich adj De
En public
Es público
Fr public
It pubblico
Pt público

öffentliche Bibliothek
(f) De
En public library
Es biblioteca pública (f)
Fr bibliothèque
publique (f)
It biblioteca pubblica (f)
Pt biblioteca pública (f)

offerta a premio (f) It
De Prämie (f)
En premium
Es prima (f)
Fr prime (f)
Pt oferta (f)

offerta postale (f) It
De Postwurfsendung (f)
En direct-mail shot
Es envio por correo
directo; oferta por
correo (m f)
Fr mailing; offre
promotionnelle (m f)
Pt publicidade por
correio (f)

officina (f) n It
De Fabrik (f)
En shop (in industry)
Es taller (m)
Fr atelier (m)
Pt oficina (f)

offre promotionnelle (f)
Fr
De Postwurfsendung (f)
En direct-mail shot
Es envio por correo
directo; oferta por
correo (m f)
It invio diretto per
posta; offerta postale
(m f)
Pt publicidade por
correio (f)

offset (m) n Fr
De Zinkdruck (m)
En zinc print
Es imagen de reserva
formada en cinc (f)
It stampa in zinco (f)
Pt imagem de reserva
de zinco (f)

offset à sec (m) Fr
De Trockenoffset (m)
En dry offset
Es offset seco (m)
It offset secco (m)
Pt offset seco (m)

Offset-Buchdruck (m)
De
En offset letterpress
Es tipografía offset (f)
Fr presse offset (f)
It stampa tipografica
offset (f)
Pt prensa offset (f)

offset cartridge paper
En
De Offset-
Kartuschenpapier (n)
Es papel para cartuchos
de offset (m)
Fr papier cartouche
offset (m)
It rotolo di carta per
stampa offset (m)
Pt papel cartucho offset
(m)

offset en creux (m) Fr
De Tiefdruck-Offsetplatte
(f)
En deep-etch litho plate
Es plancha al
hueco-offset (f)
It lastra litografica a
incisione profonda (f)
Pt chapa litográfica de
gravação funda (f)

**Offset-
Kartuschenpapier**
(n) n De
En offset cartridge paper
Es papel para cartuchos
de offset (m)
Fr papier cartouche
offset (m)
It rotolo di carta per
stampa offset (m)
Pt papel cartucho offset
(m)

offset letterpress En
De Offset-Buchdruck (m)
Es tipografía offset (f)
Fr presse offset (f)
It stampa tipografica
offset (f)
Pt prensa offset (f)

offset lithography En
De Offset-
Lithographiedruck
(m)
Es litografía offset *(f)*
Fr litho en offset *(f)*
It litografia offset *(f)*
Pt litografia offset *(f)*

**Offset-
Lithographiedruck**
(m) De
En offset lithography
Es litografía offset *(f)*
Fr litho en offset *(f)*
It litografia offset *(f)*
Pt litografia offset *(f)*

offset secco *(m)* It
De Trockenoffset *(m)*
En dry offset
Es offset seco *(m)*
Fr offset à sec *(m)*
Pt offset seco *(m)*

offset seco *(m)* Es, Pt
De Trockenoffset *(m)*
En dry offset
Fr offset à sec *(m)*
It offset secco *(m)*

oficina *(f)* n Pt
De Fabrik *(f)*
En shop (in industry)
Es taller *(m)*
Fr atelier *(m)*
It officina *(f)*

**oficina de
encadernação** *(f)* Pt
De Buchbinderei *(f)*
En bindery
Es taller de
encuadernación *(f)*
Fr atelier de reliure *(m)*
It legatoria *(f)*

oficio *(m)* n Es
De Handel *(m)*
En trade
Fr commerce *(m)*
It commercio *(m)*
Pt comércio *(m)*

ojo del tipo *(m)* Es
De Schrifttyp *(m)*
En typeface
Fr oeil d'un caractère
(m)

It occhio del carattere
(m)
Pt olho de tipo *(m)*

ojo de tipo incorrecto
(m) Es
De falscher Schrifttyp
(m)
En wrong typeface
Fr lettre d'un autre oeil
(f)
It carattere sbagliato
(m)
Pt olho de tipo errado
(m)

Oktavformat *(n)* n De
En octavo
Es en octavo *(m)*
Fr in-octavo *(m)*
It in ottavo *(m)*
Pt octavo *(m)*

old face En
De Mediäval *(n)*
Es estilo antiguo *(m)*
Fr elzévir *(m)*
It carattere elzeviro *(m)*
Pt tipo de estilo antigo
(m)

olho de tipo *(m)* Pt
De Schrifttyp *(m)*
En typeface
Es ojo del tipo *(m)*
Fr oeil d'un caractère
(m)
It occhio del carattere
(m)

olho de tipo errado *(m)*
Pt
De falscher Schrifttyp
(m)
En wrong typeface
Es ojo de tipo incorrecto
(m)
Fr lettre d'un autre oeil
(f)
It carattere sbagliato
(m)

olho de tipo sem remate
(m) Pt
De Grotesk-Schrifttyp
(m)
En sans-serif typeface
Es tipo sin remate *(m)*
Fr caractère antique
(sans empâtement)
(m)
It bastone *(m)*

olho moderno *(m)* Pt
De moderner Schrifttyp
(m)
En modern face
Es tipo moderno *(m)*
Fr didone *(f)*
It carattere moderno
(m)

ologramma *(m)* n It
De Hologramm *(n)*
En hologram
Es holograma *(f)*
Fr hologramme *(m)*
Pt holograma *(m)*

ombreggiatura *(f)* n It
De Schattierung *(f)*
En shading
Es sombreado *(m)*
Fr exécution des
ombres *(f)*
Pt tracejado *(m)*

omografo *(m)* n It
De Homograph *(n)*
En homograph
Es homógrafo *(m)*
Fr homographe *(m)*
Pt homógrafo *(m)*

omonimo *(m)* n It
De Homonym *(n)*
En homonym
Es homónimo *(m)*
Fr homonyme *(m)*
Pt homónimo *(m)*

onciales *(f pl)* Fr
De Unzialbuchstaben *(pl)*
En uncials *pl n*
Es unciales *(f pl)*
It unciali *(m pl)*
Pt letras unciales *(f pl)*

ondulare *vb* It
De kräuseln
En crimp
Es marcar con rayas
Fr gaufrer
Pt enrugar

onion-skin paper En
De Dünndruckpapier *(n)*
Es papel cebolla *(m)*
Fr papier pelure *(m)*
It carta traslucida *(f)*
Pt papel cebola *(m)*

opacidad *(f)* n Es
De Opazität *(f)*
En opacity
Fr opacité *(m)*
It opacità *(f)*
Pt opacidade *(f)*

opacidade *(f)* n Pt
De Opazität *(f)*
En opacity
Es opacidad *(f)*
Fr opacité *(m)*
It opacità *(f)*

opacità *(f)* n It
De Opazität *(f)*
En opacity
Es opacidad *(f)*
Fr opacité *(m)*
Pt opacidade *(f)*

opacité *(m)* n Fr
De Opazität *(f)*
En opacity
Es opacidad *(f)*
It opacità *(f)*
Pt opacidade *(f)*

opacity n En
De Opazität *(f)*
Es opacidad *(f)*
Fr opacité *(m)*
It opacità *(f)*
Pt opacidade *(f)*

opaco *adj* It
De matt
En matt
Es mate
Fr mat
Pt mate

Opazität *(f)* n De
En opacity
Es opacidad *(f)*
Fr opacité *(m)*
It opacità *(f)*
Pt opacidade *(f)*

opera completa *(f)* It
De sämtliche Werke *(pl)*
En complete works
Es obras completas *(f pl)*
Fr oeuvres complètes *(f
pl)*
Pt obras completas *(f pl)*

operador de teclado *(m)*
Es
De Tastatur-Setzer *(m)*

En keyboarder
Fr claviste *(m)*
It operatore di tastiera *(m)*
Pt mecanotipista *(m)*

opera in più volumi *(f)* It
De mehrbändiges Werk *(n)*
En multi-volume work
Es obra de varios volúmenes *(f)*
Fr oeuvre en plusieurs volumes *(f)*
Pt obra de muitos volumes *(f)*

opera in un solo volume *(f)* It
De einbändiges Werk *(n)*
En single-volume work
Es obra de un solo volumen *(f)*
Fr oeuvre en un volume *(f)*
Pt obra num só volume *(f)*

operatore di tastiera *(m)* It
De Tastatur-Setzer *(m)*
En keyboarder
Es operador de teclado *(m)*
Fr claviste *(m)*
Pt mecanotipista *(m)*

optical character recognition (OCR) En
De Klarschriftlesen *(n)*
Es reconocimiento óptico de caracteres *(m)*
Fr lecture optique *(f)*
It riconoscimento ottico dei caratteri *(m)*
Pt reconhecimento óptico de caracteres *(m)*

optical letterspacing En
De optischer Buchstabenabstand *(m)*
Es espaciado óptico entre letras *(m)*
Fr interlettrage optique *(m)*
It spaziatura ottica tra le lettere *(f)*

Pt espaçamento óptico de letras *(m)*

optischer Buchstabenabstand *(m)* De
En optical letterspacing
Es espaciado óptico entre letras *(m)*
Fr interlettrage optique *(m)*
It spaziatura ottica tra le lettere *(f)*
Pt espaçamento óptico de letras *(m)*

opuscolo *(m)* n It
De Broschüre; Flugschrift *(f)*
En brochure; leaflet; pamphlet
Es folleto; panfleto; prospecto *(m)*
Fr brochure; opuscule *(f m)*
Pt brochura; folheto; panfleto *(f m m)*

opuscule *(m)* n Fr
De Flugschrift *(f)*
En pamphlet
Es panfleto *(m)*
It opuscolo *(m)*
Pt panfleto *(m)*

opúsculo *(m)* n Es
De Heft *(n)*
En booklet
Fr plaquette *(f)*
It libretto *(m)*
Pt folheto *(m)*

orange-peel effect En
De Apfelsinenschalen-Effekt *(m)*
Es efecto de piel de naranja *(m)*
Fr effet pelure d'orange *(m)*
It effetto a buccia d'arancia *(m)*
Pt efeito casca de laranja *(m)*

orario *(m)* n It
De Arbeitsplan *(m)*
En schedule
Es plano *(m)*
Fr prévisions *(f pl)*
Pt plano *(m)*

ordenador *(m)* n Es
De Computer *(m)*
En computer
Fr ordinateur *(m)*
It computer *(m)*
Pt computador *(m)*

ordenador digital *(m)* Es
De Digitalcomputer *(m)*
En digital computer
Fr calculateur numérique *(m)*
It elaboratore digitale *(m)*
Pt computador digital *(m)*

ordinateur *(m)* n Fr
De Computer *(m)*
En computer
Es ordenador *(m)*
It computer *(m)*
Pt computador *(m)*

organigrama *(f)* n Es
De Schaubild *(n)*
En flow chart
Fr schéma de fabrication *(m)*
It reogramma *(m)*
Pt diagrama de fluxo *(m)*

originais *(m pl)* Pt
De Originale *(pl)*
En originals *pl n*
Es originales *(m pl)*
Fr originaux *(m pl)*
It originali *(m pl)*

original *(m)* n Es
De Abschrift *(f)*
En copy
Fr copie *(f)*
It copia *(f)*
Pt cópia *(f)*

Originale *(pl)* De
En originals *pl n*
Es originales *(m pl)*
Fr originaux *(m pl)*
It originali *(m pl)*
Pt originais *(m pl)*

originales *(m pl)* Es
De Originale *(pl)*
En originals *pl n*
Fr originaux *(m pl)*
It originali *(m pl)*
Pt originais *(m pl)*

originali *(m pl)* It
De Originale *(pl)*
En originals *pl n*
Es originales *(m pl)*
Fr originaux *(m pl)*
Pt originais *(m pl)*

original limpio *(m)* Es
De sauberer Text *(m)*
En clean copy
Fr copie au net *(f)*
It copia nitida *(f)*
Pt exemplar a limpo *(m)*

original malo *(m)* Es
De schlechtes Manuskript *(n)*
En bad copy
Fr mauvaise copie *(f)*
It copia illeggibile *(f)*
Pt exemplar ilegível *(m)*

original preparado para la cámara *(m)* Es
De kamerafertige Vorlage *(f)*
En camera-ready copy
Fr copie prête à photographier *(f)*
It copia pronta per fotografia *(f)*
Pt exemplar pronto para a máquina fotográfica *(m)*

originals *pl n* En
De Originale *(pl)*
Es originales *(m pl)*
Fr originaux *(m pl)*
It originali *(m pl)*
Pt originais *(m pl)*

origination n En
De Entstehungsarbeiten *(pl)*
Es creación *(f)*
Fr source *(f)*
It origine *(f)*
Pt criação *(f)*

originaux *(m pl)* Fr
De Originale *(pl)*
En originals *pl n*
Es originales *(m pl)*
It originali *(m pl)*
Pt originais *(m pl)*

origine *(f)* n It
De Entstehungsarbeiten *(pl)*
En origination

Es creación (f)
Fr source (f)
Pt criação (f)

origine des
photographies (f) Fr
De Dank für die
Genehmigung von
Photos (m)
En photo credits
Es fotocréditos (m pl)
It indice dei fotografi
(m pl)
Pt fotocréditos (m pl)

orilla de entrada (f) Es
De Greifkanten (f)
En gripper edge
Fr côté des pinces (m)
It lato pinza (m)
Pt margem dianteira (f)

orillas de entrada (f pl)
Es
De Anlagekanten (pl)
En feed edges pl n
Fr côté des marges (m)
It margini di entrata (m
pl)
Pt bordos de entrada (m
pl)

ornamentações de
impressão (f pl) Pt
De Typenornamente (pl)
En printer's ornaments
Es adornos de imprenta
(m pl)
Fr vignette typo (f)
It ornamenti dello
stampatore (m pl)

ornamenti dello
stampatore (m pl) It
De Typenornamente (pl)
En printer's ornaments
Es adornos de imprenta
(m pl)
Fr vignette typo (f)
Pt ornamentações de
impressão (f pl)

oro in fogli (m) It
De Goldfolie (f)
En gold leaf
Es pan de oro (m)
Fr feuille d'or (f)
Pt folha de ouro (f)

orthochromatic adj En
De orthochromatisch
Es ortocromático
Fr orthochromatique
It ortocromatico
Pt ortocromático

orthochromatique adj Fr
De orthochromatisch
En orthochromatic
Es ortocromático
It ortocromatico
Pt ortocromático

orthochromatisch adj De
En orthochromatic
Es ortocromático
Fr orthochromatique
It ortocromatico
Pt ortocromático

orthographe (f) n Fr
De Orthographie (f)
En orthography
Es ortografía (f)
It ortografia (f)
Pt ortografia (f)

orthographe américaine
(f) Fr
De amerikanische
Schreibweise (f)
En American spelling
Es deletreo americano
(m)
It ortografia americana
(f)
Pt ortografia americana
(f)

orthographe anglaise (f)
Fr
De britische
Schreibweise (f)
En British spelling
Es deletreo británico (m)
It ortografia britannica
(f)
Pt ortografia britânica (f)

Orthographie (f) n De
En orthography
Es ortografía (f)
Fr orthographe (f)
It ortografia (f)
Pt ortografia (f)

orthography n En
De Orthographie (f)
Es ortografía (f)
Fr orthographe (f)

It ortografia (f)
Pt ortografia (f)

ortocromatico adj It
De orthochromatisch
En orthochromatic
Es ortocromático
Fr orthochromatique
Pt ortocromático

ortocromático adj Es, Pt
De orthochromatisch
En orthochromatic
Fr orthochromatique
It ortocromatico

ortografia (f) n It
De Orthographie (f)
En orthography
Es ortografía (f)
Fr orthographe (f)
Pt ortografia (f)

ortografia (f) n Pt
De Orthographie (f)
En orthography
Es ortografía (f)
Fr orthographe (f)
It ortografia (f)

ortografía (f) n Es
De Orthographie (f)
En orthography
Fr orthographe (f)
It ortografia (f)
Pt ortografia (f)

ortografia americana (f)
It, Pt
De amerikanische
Schreibweise (f)
En American spelling
Es deletreo americano
(m)
Fr orthographe
américaine (f)

ortografia britannica (f)
It
De britische
Schreibweise (f)
En British spelling
Es deletreo británico (m)
Fr orthographe anglaise
(f)
Pt ortografia britânica (f)

ortografia britânica (f) Pt
De britische
Schreibweise (f)

En British spelling
Es deletreo británico (m)
Fr orthographe anglaise
It ortografia britannica
(f)

ottone (m) n It
De Messingreglette (f)
En brass (binder's)
Es latón (m)
Fr laiton (m)
Pt latão (m)

outils de reliure (m pl) Fr
De Buchbinder-
Werkzeuge (pl)
En binder's tools
Es herramientas de
encuadernación (f pl)
It attrezzi da rilegatore
(m pl)
Pt ferramenta de
encadernação (f)

out of date En
De veraltet
Es anticuado
Fr périmé
It superato
Pt desactualizado

out of print En
De vergriffen
Es agotado
Fr épuisé
It esaurito
Pt esgotado

out of register En
De fehlerhaftes Register
Es fuera de registro
Fr mal registré
It fuori registro
Pt fora de registo

out of square En
De nicht gerade
Es descuadrado
Fr mal cadré
It fuori squadra
Pt fora do
enquadramento

out of stock En
De nicht vorrätig
Es sin existencias
Fr non disponible
It sprovvisto
Pt esgotado em
armazém

outwork *n* En
De Außenarbeit *(n)*
Es trabajo externo *(m)*
Fr travail à domicile *(m)*
It lavoro esterno *(m)*
Pt trabalho externo *(m)*

ouvrage juridique *(m)* Fr
De Rechtsbuch *(n)*
En legal book
Es libro de derecho *(m)*
It libro legale *(m)*
Pt livro jurídico *(m)*

ouvrages artisanaux *(m pl)* Fr
De Handwerksbücher *(pl)*
En craft books
Es libros de trabajos manuales *(m pl)*
It guide pratiche *(f pl)*
Pt livros técnicos *(m pl)*

ouvrages généraux *(m pl)* Fr
De Sachliteratur *(f)*
En non-fiction
Es textos no novelescos *(m pl)*
It saggistica *(f)*
Pt textos de não ficção *(m pl)*

ouvrages médicaux *(m pl)* Fr
De Medizinbücher *(pl)*
En medical books
Es libros de medicina *(m pl)*
It testi di medicina *(m pl)*
Pt livros de medicina *(m pl)*

ouvrage spécialisé *(m)* Fr
De Spezial-Buch *(n)*
En specialist book
Es libro especializado *(m)*
It libro specialistico *(m)*
Pt livro para especialistas *(m)*

ouvrages pratiques *(m pl)* Fr
De praktische Bücher *(pl)*
En practical books
Es libros prácticos *(m pl)*

It libri pratici *(m pl)*
Pt livros prácticos *(m pl)*

ouvrages scientifiques et techniques *(m pl)* Fr
De wissenschaftliche und technische Bücher *(pl)*
En scientific and technical books
Es libros científicos y técnicos *(m pl)*
It libri scientifici e tecnici *(m pl)*
Pt livros científicos e técnicos *(m pl)*

ouvrage technique *(m)* Fr
De technisches Buch *(n)*
En technical book
Es libro técnico *(m)*
It libro tecnico *(m)*
Pt livro técnico *(m)*

overlay (on artwork, etc.) *n* En
De Deckblatt *(n)*
Es superponible *(m)*
Fr becquet *(m)*
It sovrapposizione *(f)*
Pt coberta *(f)*

overmatter *n* En
De überlanger Satz *(m)*
Es material sobrante *(m)*
Fr surimpression *(f)*
It composizione sovrastante *(f)*
Pt matéria que sobra *(f)*

over-running *n* En
De Umbrechen *(n)*
Es recorrido *(m)*
Fr remaniement *(m)*
It rimaneggiamento *(m)*
Pt acto de recorrer *(m)*

overs *pl n* En
De Zuschuß *(m)*
Es hojas sobrantes *(f pl)*
Fr passe *(f)*
It fogli aggiunti *(m pl)*
Pt folhas que sobram *(f pl)*

oversewing *n* En
De Holländern *(n)*
Es cosido por el plano *(m)*

Fr point hollandais *(m)*
It cucitura a punto saltato *(f)*
Pt coser por fora *(m)*

overstocks *pl n* En
De Übervorrat *(m)*
Es existencias excesivas *(f pl)*
Fr stock excessif *(m)*
It giacenze *(f pl)*
Pt existências que sobram *(f pl)*

P

pacco *(m)* *n* It
De Paket *(n)*
En package
Es paquete *(m)*
Fr colis *(m)*
Pt pacote *(m)*

pack *vb* En
De packen
Es embalar
Fr emballer
It imballare
Pt embalar

package *n* En
De Paket *(n)*
Es paquete *(m)*
Fr colis *(m)*
It pacco *(m)*
Pt pacote *(m)*

package *vb* En
De verpacken
Es empaquetar
Fr empaqueter
It impaccare
Pt empacotar

packaging company En
De Verpackungsfirma *(f)*
Es compañía empaquetadora *(f)*
Fr entreprise de l'emballage *(f)*
It società confezionamento *(m)*

Pt sociedade empacotadora *(f)*

packen *vb* De
En pack
Es embalar
Fr emballer
It imballare
Pt embalar

Packmaschine *(f)* *n* De
En bundling machine
Es prensadora-embaladora de pliegos *(f)*
Fr machine à emballer *(f)*
It macchina per rotoli *(f)*
Pt máquina de prensar e formar fascículos *(f)*

pacote *(m)* *n* Pt
De Paket *(n)*
En package
Es paquete *(m)*
Fr colis *(m)*
It pacco *(m)*

pagamento *(m)* *n* It, Pt
De Zahlung *(f)*
En payment
Es pago *(m)*
Fr paiement *(m)*

pagamento adiantado *(m)* Pt
De Vorauszahlung *(f)*
En payment in advance
Es pago por adelantado *(m)*
Fr payement d'avance *(m)*
It pagamento anticipo *(m)*

pagamento anticipo *(m)* It
De Vorauszahlung *(f)*
En payment in advance
Es pago por adelantado *(m)*
Fr payement d'avance *(m)*
Pt pagamento adiantado *(m)*

pagamento de redundância *(m)* Pt
De Entlassungsgeld *(n)*
En redundancy payment

Es pago redundante *(m)*
Fr indemnité de
  chômage *(f)*
It pagamento di
  ridondanza *(m)*

**pagamento di
  ridondanza** *(m)* It
De Entlassungsgeld *(n)*
En redundancy payment
Es pago redundante *(m)*
Fr indemnité de
  chômage *(f)*
Pt pagamento de
  redundância *(m)*

paga oraria *(f)* It
De Stundentarif *(m)*
En hourly rate
Es régimen horario *(m)*
Fr tarif horaire *(m)*
Pt taxa horária *(f)*

page *n* En; Fr *(f)*
De Seite *(f)*
Es página *(f)*
It pagina *(f)*
Pt página *(f)*

page blanche *(f)* Fr
De Vakantseite *(f)*
En blank page
Es página en blanco *(f)*
It pagina bianca *(f)*
Pt página em branco *(f)*

page de dédicace *(f)* Fr
De Widmungsseite *(f)*
En dedication page
Es página de dedicatoria
  (f)
It pagina di dedica *(f)*
Pt página de dedicatória
  (f)

page des matières *(f)* Fr
De Inhaltsseite *(f)*
En contents page
Es página de índice *(f)*
It pagina indice *(f)*
Pt página de índice *(f)*

page de titre *(m)* Fr
De Titelseite *(f)*
En title page
Es portada *(f)*
It frontespizio *(m)*
Pt página de título *(f)*

page proof En
De Korrektur *(f)*
Es prueba de página *(f)*
Fr épreuve en pages *(f)*
It bozza impaginata *(f)*
Pt prova de página *(f)*

pages de garde *(f pl)* Fr
De Rückseiten *(pl)*
En backing pages
Es páginas de lomo *(f pl)*
It pagine di rinforzo *(f
  pl)*
Pt páginas de lombada
  (f pl)

pages de texte *(f pl)* Fr
De Textseiten *(pl)*
En text pages
Es páginas de texto *(f pl)*
It pagine di testo *(f pl)*
Pt páginas de texto *(f pl)*

pagina *(f)* n It
De Seite *(f)*
En page
Es página *(f)*
Fr page *(f)*
Pt página *(f)*

Pagina *(f)* n De
En folio
Es folio *(m)*
Fr folio *(m)*
It numero della pagina
  (m)
Pt fólio *(m)*

página *(f)* n Es, Pt
De Seite *(f)*
En page
Fr page *(f)*
It pagina *(f)*

página amostra *(f)* Pt
De Musterseite *(f)*
En specimen page
Es página de muestra *(f)*
Fr feuille-échantillon *(f)*
It pagina campione *(f)*

página apaisada *(f)* Es
De Querformat-Seite *(f)*
En landscape page
Fr format oblong *(m)*
It pagina orizzontale *(f)*
Pt página horizontal *(f)*

pagina bianca *(f)* It
De Vakantseite *(f)*
En blank page
Es página en blanco *(f)*
Fr page blanche *(f)*
Pt página em branco *(f)*

pagina campione *(f)* It
De Musterseite *(f)*
En specimen page
Es página de muestra *(f)*
Fr feuille-échantillon *(f)*
Pt página amostra *(f)*

paginação *(f)* n Pt
De Paginierung *(f)*
En pagination
Es paginación *(f)*
Fr pagination *(f)*
It impaginazione *(f)*

paginación *(f)* n Es
De Paginierung *(f)*
En pagination
Fr pagination *(f)*
It impaginazione *(f)*
Pt paginação *(f)*

página da direita *(f)* Pt
De rechte Seite *(f)*
En right-hand page
Es página derecha *(f)*
Fr belle page *(f)*
It pagina di destra *(f)*

página de dedicatoria *(f)*
  Es, Pt
De Widmungsseite *(f)*
En dedication page
Fr page de dédicace *(f)*
It pagina di dedica *(f)*

página de esquerda *(f)*
  Pt
De linke Seite *(f)*
En left-hand page
Es página izquierda *(f)*
Fr fausse page *(f)*
It pagina di sinistra *(f)*

página de índice *(f)* Es,
  Pt
De Inhaltsseite *(f)*
En contents page
Fr page des matières *(f)*
It pagina indice *(f)*

página de muestra *(f)* Es
De Musterseite *(f)*
En specimen page

Fr feuille-échantillon *(f)*
It pagina campione *(f)*
Pt página amostra *(f)*

página derecha *(f)* Es
De rechte Seite *(f)*
En right-hand page
Fr belle page *(f)*
It pagina di destra *(f)*
Pt página da direita *(f)*

página de retrato *(f)* Pt
De Hochformat *(n)*
En portrait page
Es página vertical *(f)*
Fr format en hauteur
  (m)
It pagina verticale *(f)*

página de título *(f)* Pt
De Titelseite *(f)*
En title page
Es portada *(f)*
Fr page de titre *(m)*
It frontespizio *(m)*

pagina di dedica *(f)* It
De Widmungsseite *(f)*
En dedication page
Es página de dedicatoria
  (f)
Fr page de dédicace *(f)*
Pt página de dedicatória
  (f)

pagina di destra *(f)* It
De rechte Seite *(f)*
En right-hand page
Es página derecha *(f)*
Fr belle page *(f)*
Pt página da direita *(f)*

pagina di sinistra *(f)* It
De linke Seite *(f)*
En left-hand page
Es página izquierda *(f)*
Fr fausse page *(f)*
Pt página de esquerda
  (f)

pagina dispari *(f)* It
De rechte Buchseite *(f)*
En recto
Es recto *(m)*
Fr recto *(m)*
Pt recto *(m)*

página dupla *(f)* Pt
De Doppelseite *(f)*
En double-page spread

Es doble página *(f)*
Fr double page *(f)*
It doppia pagina *(f)*

página em branco *(f)* Pt
De Vakantseite *(f)*
En blank page
Es página en blanco *(f)*
Fr page blanche *(f)*
It pagina bianca *(f)*

página en blanco *(f)* Es
De Vakantseite *(f)*
En blank page
Fr page blanche *(f)*
It pagina bianca *(f)*
Pt página em branco *(f)*

página horizontal *(f)* Pt
De Querformat-Seite *(f)*
En landscape page
Es página apaisada *(f)*
Fr format oblong *(m)*
It pagina orizzontale *(f)*

pagina indice *(f)* It
De Inhaltsseite *(f)*
En contents page
Es página de índice *(f)*
Fr page des matières *(f)*
Pt página de índice *(f)*

página izquierda *(f)* Es
De linke Seite *(f)*
En left-hand page
Fr fausse page *(f)*
It pagina di sinistra *(f)*
Pt página de esquerda *(f)*

pagina orizzontale *(f)* It
De Querformat-Seite *(f)*
En landscape page
Es página apaisada *(f)*
Fr format oblong *(m)*
Pt página horizontal *(f)*

paginar *vb* Es, Pt
De paginieren
En paginate
Fr paginer
It impaginare

páginas a cores *(f pl)* Pt
Am color plates
De Farbtafeln *(pl)*
En colour plates
Es láminas en color *(f pl)*

Fr planches en couleurs *(f pl)*
It tavole a colori *(f pl)*

páginas de lombada *(f pl)* Pt
De Rückseiten *(pl)*
En backing pages
Es páginas de lomo *(f pl)*
Fr pages de garde *(f pl)*
It pagine di rinforzo *(f pl)*

páginas de lomo *(f pl)* Es
De Rückseiten *(pl)*
En backing pages
Fr pages de garde *(f pl)*
It pagine di rinforzo *(f pl)*
Pt páginas de lombada *(f pl)*

páginas de texto *(f pl)* Es, Pt
De Textseiten *(pl)*
En text pages
Fr pages de texte *(f pl)*
It pagine di testo *(f pl)*

paginate *vb* En
De paginieren
Es paginar
Fr paginer
It impaginare
Pt paginar

pagination *n* En; Fr *(f)*
De Paginierung *(f)*
Es paginación *(f)*
It impaginazione *(f)*
Pt paginação *(f)*

página vertical *(f)* Es
De Hochformat *(n)*
En portrait page
Fr format en hauteur *(m)*
It pagina verticale *(f)*
Pt página de retrato *(f)*

pagina verticale *(f)* It
De Hochformat *(n)*
En portrait page
Es página vertical *(f)*
Fr format en hauteur *(m)*
Pt página de retrato *(f)*

pagine di rinforzo *(f pl)* It
De Rückseiten *(pl)*
En backing pages
Es páginas de lomo *(f pl)*
Fr pages de garde *(f pl)*
Pt páginas de lombada *(f pl)*

pagine di testo *(f pl)* It
De Textseiten *(pl)*
En text pages
Es páginas de texto *(f pl)*
Fr pages de texte *(f pl)*
Pt páginas de texto *(f pl)*

paginer *vb* Fr
De paginieren
En paginate
Es paginar
It impaginare
Pt paginar

paginieren *vb* De
En paginate
Es paginar
Fr paginer
It impaginare
Pt paginar

Paginierung *(f)* *n* De
En pagination
Es paginación *(f)*
Fr pagination *(f)*
It impaginazione *(f)*
Pt paginação *(f)*

pago *(m)* *n* Es
De Zahlung *(f)*
En payment
Fr paiement *(m)*
It pagamento *(m)*
Pt pagamento *(m)*

pago por adelantado *(m)* Es
De Vorauszahlung *(f)*
En payment in advance
Fr payement d'avance *(m)*
It pagamento anticipo *(m)*
Pt pagamento adiantado *(m)*

pago redundante *(m)* Es
De Entlassungsgeld *(n)*
En redundancy payment
Fr indemnité de chômage *(f)*
It pagamento di ridondanza *(m)*

Pt pagamento de redundância *(m)*

paiement *(m)* *n* Fr
De Zahlung *(f)*
En payment
Es pago *(m)*
It pagamento *(m)*
Pt pagamento *(m)*

Paket *(n)* *n* De
En package
Es paquete *(m)*
Fr colis *(m)*
It pacco *(m)*
Pt pacote *(m)*

palabra principal *(f)* Es
De haupt Wort *(n)*
En headword
Fr mot en-tête *(m)*
It parola principale *(f)*
Pt palavra-índice *(f)*

palavra-índice *(f)* Pt
De haupt Wort *(n)*
En headword
Es palabra principal *(f)*
Fr mot en-tête *(m)*
It parola principale *(f)*

palos altos *(m pl)* Es
De Buchstaben-Oberlänge *(n pl)*
En ascenders (of letter) *pl n*
Fr ascendantes *(f pl)*
It lettere ascendenti *(f pl)*
Pt ascendentes *(f pl)*

palos gruesos *(m pl)* Es
De Säulen *(pl)*
En stems *pl n*
Fr hastes *(f pl)*
It gambi *(m pl)*
Pt paus grossos *(m pl)*

pamphlet *n* En
De Flugschrift *(f)*
Es panfleto *(m)*
Fr opuscule *(m)*
It opuscolo *(m)*
Pt panfleto *(m)*

panchromatic *adj* En
De panchromatisch
Es pancromático
Fr panchromatique

It pancromatico
Pt pancromático

panchromatique *adj* Fr
De panchromatisch
En panchromatic
Es pancromático
It pancromatico
Pt pancromático

panchromatisch *adj* De
En panchromatic
Es pancromático
Fr panchromatique
It pancromatico
Pt pancromático

pancromatico *adj* It
De panchromatisch
En panchromatic
Es pancromático
Fr panchromatique
Pt pancromático

pancromático *adj* Es, Pt
De panchromatisch
En panchromatic
Fr panchromatique
It pancromatico

pan de oro *(m)* Es
De Goldfolie *(f)*
En gold leaf
Fr feuille d´or *(f)*
It oro in fogli *(m)*
Pt folha de ouro *(f)*

panfleto *(m) n* Es, Pt
De Flugschrift *(f)*
En pamphlet
Fr opuscule *(m)*
It opuscolo *(m)*

pano americano *(m)* Pt
De Wachstuch *(n)*
En American cloth
Es hule *(m)*
Fr moleskine *(f)*
It tela cerata *(f)*

papel *(m) n* Es, Pt
De Papier *(n)*
En paper
Fr papier *(m)*
It carta *(f)*

papel absorvente *(m)* Pt
De ungeleimtes Papier *(n)*
En waterleaf

Es papel no encolado *(m)*
Fr papier non collé *(m)*
It carta non imbozzimata *(f)*

papel acabado a máquina *(m)* Es
De maschinenglattes Papier *(n)*
En machine-finished paper; mill-finished paper
Fr papier apprêté sur machine *(m)*
It carta finita a macchina *(f)*
Pt papel acabado à máquina *(m)*

papel acabado à máquina *(m)* Pt
De maschinenglattes Papier *(n)*
En machine-finished paper
Es papel acabado a máquina *(m)*
Fr papier apprêté sur machine *(m)*
It carta finita a macchina *(f)*

papel acetinado *(m)* Pt
De kartoniertes Glanzpapier *(n)*
En board-glazed paper
Es papel satinado *(m)*
Fr papier satiné *(m)*
It cartone satinato *(m)*

papel alongado *(m)* Pt
De Langformat-Papier *(n)*
En oblong paper
Es papel apaisado *(m)*
Fr format à l'italienne *(m)*
It carta oblunga *(f)*

papelão *(m) n* Pt
De Pappe *(f)*
En pasteboard
Es cartón de varias capas *(m)*
Fr carton contre-collé *(m)*
It cartone accoppiato *(m)*

papel apaisado *(m)* Es
De Langformat-Papier
En oblong paper
Fr format à l'italienne *(m)*
It carta oblunga *(f)*
Pt papel alongado *(m)*

papel artístico mate *(m)* Pt
De Mattkunstdruck-papier *(n)*
En matt art paper
Es papel cuché mate *(m)*
Fr papier couché mat *(m)*
It carta patinata opaca *(f)*

papel avitelado *(m)* Es
De Velinpapier *(n)*
En wove paper
Fr papier vélin *(m)*
It carta retinata *(f)*
Pt papel tecido *(m)*

papel avitelado antiguo *(m)* Es
De Antikdruckpapier *(n)*
En antique wove
Fr vélin à l'antique *(m)*
It carta retinata tipo antico *(f)*
Pt tecido estilo antigo *(m)*

papel avitelado crema *(m)* Es
De mattgelbes Velinpapier *(n)*
En cream wove paper
Fr vélin crème *(m)*
It velino cremo *(m)*
Pt papel tecido enrugado *(m)*

papel biblia *(m)* Es
De Bibel(druck)papier *(n)*
En bible paper
Fr papier bible *(m)*
It carta bibbia *(f)*
Pt papel bíblia *(m)*

papel bíblia *(m)* Pt
De Bibel(druck)papier *(n)*
En bible paper
Es papel biblia *(m)*
Fr papier bible *(m)*
It carta bibbia *(f)*

papel bond *(m)* Es, Pt
De Schreibmaschinen-papier *(n)*
En bond paper
Fr papier coquille *(m)*
It carta bond *(f)*

papel caladrando *(m)* Es
De kalandriertes Papier *(n)*
En calendered paper
Fr papier calandré *(m)*
It carta calandrata *(f)*
Pt papel calandrado *(m)*

papel calandrado *(m)* Pt
De kalandriertes Papier *(n)*
En calendered paper
Es papel caladrando *(m)*
Fr papier calandré *(m)*
It carta calandrata *(f)*

papel cartucho *(m)* Pt
De Kartuschenpapier *(n)*
En cartridge paper
Es papel para cartuchos *(m)*
Fr papier cartouche *(m)*
It carta da disegno *(f)*

papel cartucho offset *(m)* Pt
De Offset-Kartuschenpapier *(n)*
En offset cartridge paper
Es papel para cartuchos de offset *(m)*
Fr papier cartouche offset *(m)*
It rotolo di carta per stampa offset *(m)*

papel cebola *(m)* Pt
De Dünndruckpapier *(n)*
En onion-skin paper
Es papel cebolla *(m)*
Fr papier pelure *(m)*
It carta traslucida *(f)*

papel cebolla *(m)* Es
De Dünndruckpapier *(n)*
En onion-skin paper
Fr papier pelure *(m)*
It carta traslucida *(f)*
Pt papel cebola *(m)*

papel centrado em tela *(m)* Pt
Am cloth-centered paper

De Papier mit Stoffmitte
(n)
En cloth-centred paper
Es papel duplex con
alma de lino (m)
Fr papier entre deux
toiles (m)
It carta duplex con
anima di tela (f)

papel coloreado (m) Es
De getöntes Papier (n)
En tinted paper
Fr papier de couleur (m)
It carta colorata (f)
Pt papel colorido (m)

papel colorido (m) Pt
De getöntes Papier (n)
En tinted paper
Es papel coloreado (m)
Fr papier de couleur (m)
It carta colorata (f)

papel cromo (m) Pt
De Chromopapier (n)
En chromo paper
Es papel para
cromolitografía (m)
Fr papier chromo (m)
It carta al cromo (f)

papel cuché (m) Es
De gestrichenes Papier
(n)
En coated paper
Fr papier couché (m)
It carta patinata (f)
Pt papel revestido (m)

papel cuché mate (m) Es
De Mattkunstdruck-
papier (n)
En matt art paper
Fr papier couché mat
(m)
It carta patinata opaca
(f)
Pt papel artístico mate
(m)

**papel de acabamento à
máquina** (m) Pt
De maschinenglattes
Papier (n)
En mill-finished paper
Es papel calandrado (m)
Fr papier apprêté
machine (m)
It carta lisciata a
macchina (f)

papel de calcar (m) Es
De Pauspapier (n)
En tracing paper
Fr papier calque (m)
It carta da lucidi (f)
Pt papel de cópia (m)

papel de cobertura (m)
Pt
De Umschlagpapier (n)
En cover paper
Es papel para cubiertas
(m)
Fr papier à couverture
(m)
It carta per copertine (f)

papel de cópia (m) Pt
De Pauspapier (n)
En tracing paper
Es papel de calcar (m)
Fr papier calque (m)
It carta da lucidi (f)

papel de copias (m) Es
De Vervielfältigungs-
papier (n)
En manifold paper
Fr papier pour formules
(m)
It carta per duplicatori
(f)
Pt papel de cópias (m)

papel de cópias (m) Pt
De Vervielfältigungs-
papier (n)
En manifold paper
Es papel de copias (m)
Fr papier pour formules
(m)
It carta per duplicatori
(f)

papel de empréstimo
(m) Pt
De Aktienpapier (n)
En loan paper
Es papel para
documentos (m)
Fr papier pour titres (m)
It carta per valori (f)

papel de encolado duro
(m) Es
De Hartleimpapier (n)
En hard-sized paper
Fr papier très collé (m)
It carta molto
imbozzimada (f)
Pt papel de

encolamento duro
(m)

**papel de encolamento
duro** (m) Pt
De Hartleimpapier (n)
En hard-sized paper
Es papel de encolado
duro (m)
Fr papier très collé (m)
It carta molto
imbozzimada (f)

papel defeituoso (m) Pt
De mangelhaftes Papier
(n)
En retree
Es papel ligeramente
defectuoso (m)
Fr papier imparfait (m)
It riscelta (f)

papel de fibra corta (m)
Es
De kurzkörniges Papier
(n)
En short-grain paper
Fr papier à fibres
courtes (m)
It carta a grana corta (f)
Pt papel de grão curto
(m)

papel de grão comprido
(m) Pt
De langkörniges Papier
(n)
En long-grain paper
Es papel plegado al hilo
(m)
Fr papier sens machine
sur longueur (m)
It carta a grana lunga
(f)

papel de grão curto (m)
Pt
De kurzkörniges Papier
(n)
En short-grain paper
Es papel de fibra corta
(m)
Fr papier à fibres
courtes (m)
It carta a grana corta (f)

papel de hilo puro (m) Es
De Vollhadernpapier (n)
En all-rag paper
Fr papier pur chiffon (m)
It carta di cenci (f)

Pt papel inteiramente
de trapos (m)

papel de mapa (m) Pt
De Registrierpapier (n)
En chart paper
Es papel gráfico (m)
Fr papier pour
graphiques (m)
It carta da grafici (f)

papel de oficio (m) Es
De Folioformat (n)
En foolscap
Fr papier ministre (m)
It carta protocollo (f)
Pt papel ministro (m)

papel de recorte (m) Es,
Pt
De Papierabschnitt (n)
En offcut
Fr découpure (f)
It ritaglio di carta (m)

**papel de respaldo
esmaltado** (m) Es
De Gussgestrichenes
Papier (n)
En cast-coated paper
Fr papier couché
chrome superbrillant
(m)
It carta altobrillante (f)
Pt papel estereotipado
(m)

papel de seda (m) Es, Pt
De Seidenpapier (n)
En tissue paper
Fr papier mousseline
(m)
It carta velina (f)

papel de tina (m) Es
Am mold-made paper
De Büttenwerk-
druckpapier (n)
En mould-made paper
Fr papier moyen âge
(m)
It carta formata a mano
(f)
Pt papel moldado (m)

papel de trapos (m) Es,
Pt
De Hadernpapier (n)
En rag paper
Fr papier de chiffon (m)
It carta di stracci (f)

papel duplex *(m)* Pt
De Duplexpapier *(n)*
En duplex paper
Es cartón duplo *(m)*
Fr papier duplex *(m)*
It carta duplex *(f)*

papel duplex con alma de lino *(m)* Es
Am cloth-centered paper
De Papier mit Stoffmitte *(n)*
En cloth-centred paper
Fr papier entre deux toiles *(m)*
It carta duplex con anima di tela *(f)*
Pt papel centrado em tela *(m)*

papel e artigos de escritório *(m)* Pt
De Briefpapier *(n)*
En stationery
Es efectos de escritorio *(m pl)*
Fr papeterie de détail *(f)*
It cartoleria *(f)*

papel encolado a máquina *(m)* Es
De Maschinengröße *(f)*
En engine-sized paper
Fr papier collé en pâte *(m)*
It carta tagliata a macchina *(f)*
Pt papel encolado à máquina *(m)*

papel encolado à máquina *(m)* Pt
De Maschinengröße *(f)*
En engine-sized paper
Es papel encolado a máquina *(m)*
Fr papier collé en pâte *(m)*
It carta tagliata a macchina *(f)*

papel encolado em tina *(m)* Pt
De oberflächengeleimtes Papier *(n)*
En tub-sized paper
Es papel encolado en tina *(m)*
Fr papier collé à la cuve *(m)*
It carta imbozzimata in tino *(f)*

papel encolado en tina *(m)* Es
De oberflächengeleimtes Papier *(n)*
En tub-sized paper
Fr papier collé à la cuve *(m)*
It carta imbozzimata in tino *(f)*
Pt papel encolado em tina *(m)*

papel en cuarto *(m)* Es
De Quartformat *(n)*
En quarto
Fr quart *(m)*
It quarto *(m)*
Pt quartos *(m)*

papel esmaltado *(m)* Es
De Hochglanzpapier *(n)*
En enamel paper
Fr papier émaillé *(m)*
It carta smaltata *(f)*
Pt papel esmalte *(m)*

papel esmalte *(m)* Pt
De Hochglanzpapier *(n)*
En enamel paper
Es papel esmaltado *(m)*
Fr papier émaillé *(m)*
It carta smaltata *(f)*

papel estereotipado *(m)* Pt
De Gussgestrichenes Papier *(n)*
En cast-coated paper
Es papel de respaldo esmaltado *(m)*
Fr papier couché chrome superbrillant *(m)*
It carta altobrillante *(f)*

papel estucado a brocha *(m)* Es
De bürstengestrichenes Papier *(n)*
En brush-coated paper
Fr papier couché à la brosse *(m)*
It carta coperta a spazzola *(f)*
Pt papel revestido com pincel *(m)*

papel estucado a máquina *(m)* Es
De maschinen-gestrichenes Papier *(n)*

En machine-coated paper
Fr papier couché machine *(m)*
It carta patinata a macchina *(f)*
Pt papel revestido à máquina *(m)*

papel feito à mão *(m)* Pt
De Handbütten *(n)*
En handmade paper
Es papel hecho a mano *(m)*
Fr papier cuve *(m)*
It carta a mano *(f)*

papel forrado a tela *(m)* Pt
De stoffüberzogenes Papier *(n)*
En cloth-lined paper
Es papel forrado de tela *(m)*
Fr papier entoilé une face *(m)*
It carta rivestita in tela *(f)*

papel forrado de tela *(m)* Es
De stoffüberzogenes Papier *(n)*
En cloth-lined paper
Fr papier entoilé une face *(m)*
It carta rivestita in tela *(f)*
Pt papel forrado a tela *(m)*

papel gráfico *(m)* Es
De Registrierpapier *(n)*
En chart paper
Fr papier pour graphiques *(m)*
It carta da grafici *(f)*
Pt papel de mapa *(m)*

papel hecho a mano *(m)* Es
De Handbütten *(n)*
En handmade paper
Fr papier cuve *(m)*
It carta a mano *(f)*
Pt papel feito à mão *(m)*

papel inteiramente de trapos *(m)* Pt
De Vollhadernpapier *(n)*
En all-rag paper

Es papel de hilo puro *(m)*
Fr papier pur chiffon *(m)*
It carta di cenci *(f)*

papel jaspeado *(m)* Es, Pt
De Marmorpapier *(n)*
En marbled paper
Fr papier marbré *(m)*
It carta marmorizzata *(f)*

papel kraft *(m)* Es, Pt
De Kraftpapier *(n)*
En kraft paper
Fr papier Kraft *(m)*
It carta kraft *(f)*

papel kraft union *(m)* Es, Pt
De Kraftverbundpapier *(n)*
En kraft union paper
Fr papier kraft doublé-bitumé *(m)*
It carta kraft union *(f)*

papel ligeramente defectuoso *(m)* Es
De mangelhaftes Papier *(n)*
En retree
Fr papier imparfait *(m)*
It riscelta *(f)*
Pt papel defeituoso *(m)*

papel ligero *(m)* Es
De Federleichtpapier *(n)*
En featherweight paper
Fr papier bouffant *(m)*
It carta piuma *(f)*
Pt papel peso pena *(m)*

papel lustrado *(m)* Pt
De Glanzpapier *(n)*
En glazed paper
Es papel lustroso *(m)*
Fr papier glacé *(m)*
It carta lucida *(f)*

papel lustrado à prancha *(m)* Pt
De bogenkalander-bearbeitetes Papier *(n)*
En plate-finished paper
Es papel satinado a plancha *(m)*
Fr papier laminé à la plaque *(m)*
It carta rifinita *(f)*

papel lustroso *(m)* Es
De Glanzpapier *(n)*
En glazed paper
Fr papier glacé *(m)*
It carta lucida *(f)*
Pt papel lustrado *(m)*

papel mataborrão *(m)* Pt
De Löschpapier *(n)*
En blotting paper
Es papel secante *(m)*
Fr papier buvard *(m)*
It carta assorbente *(f)*

papel milimétrico *(m)* Es, Pt
De Koordinatenpapier *(n)*
En grid paper
Fr papier millimétrique *(m)*
It carta millimetrata *(f)*

papel ministro *(m)* Pt
De Folioformat *(n)*
En foolscap
Es papel de oficio *(m)*
Fr papier ministre *(m)*
It carta protocollo *(f)*

papel moldado *(m)* Pt
Am mold-made paper
De Büttenwerk-druckpapier *(n)*
En mould-made paper
Es papel de tina *(m)*
Fr papier moyen âge *(m)*
It carta formata a mano *(f)*

papel no encolado *(m)* Es
De ungeleimtes Papier *(n)*
En waterleaf
Fr papier non collé *(m)*
It carta non imbozzimata *(f)*
Pt papel absorvente *(m)*

papel para cartuchos *(m)* Es
De Kartuschenpapier *(n)*
En cartridge paper
Fr papier cartouche *(m)*
It carta da disegno *(f)*
Pt papel cartucho *(m)*

papel para cartuchos de offset *(m)* Es
De Offset-Kartuschenpapier *(n)*
En offset cartridge paper
Fr papier cartouche offset *(m)*
It rotolo di carta per stampa offset *(m)*
Pt papel cartucho offset *(m)*

papel para cromolitografía *(m)* Es
De Chromopapier *(n)*
En chromo paper
Fr papier chromo *(m)*
It carta al cromo *(f)*
Pt papel cromo *(m)*

papel para cubiertas *(m)* Es
De Umschlagpapier *(n)*
En cover paper
Fr papier à couverture *(m)*
It carta per copertine *(f)*
Pt papel de cobertura *(m)*

papel para documentos *(m)* Es
De Aktienpapier *(n)*
En loan paper
Fr papier pour titres *(m)*
It carta per valori *(f)*
Pt papel de empréstimo *(m)*

papel para jornal *(m)* Pt
De Rotationsdruckpapier *(n)*
En newsprint
Es papel periódico *(m)*
Fr papier-journal *(m)*
It carta da giornale *(f)*

papel pergaminho japonês *(m)* Pt
De Japanpapier *(n)*
En Japanese vellum
Es vitela japonesa *(f)*
Fr papier du Japon *(m)*
It pergamena giapponese *(f)*

papel periódico *(m)* Es
De Rotationsdruckpapier *(n)*
En newsprint
Fr papier-journal *(m)*

It carta da giornale *(f)*
Pt papel para jornal *(m)*

papel peso pena *(m)* Pt
De Federleichtpapier *(n)*
En featherweight paper
Es papel ligero *(m)*
Fr papier bouffant *(m)*
It carta piuma *(f)*

papel pigmento *(m)* Es
De Ätzpigmentpapier *(n)*
En carbon tissue
Fr papier au carbone *(m)*
It carta al carbone *(f)*
Pt tecido carbono *(m)*

papel plegado al hilo *(m)* Es
De langkörniges Papier *(n)*
En long-grain paper
Fr papier sens machine sur longueur *(m)*
It carta a grana lunga *(f)*
Pt papel de grão comprido *(m)*

papel quadriculado *(m)* Pt
De kariertes Papier *(n)*
En quadrille
Es cuadrícula *(f)*
Fr papier quadrillé *(m)*
It carta quadrettata *(f)*

papel revestido *(m)* Pt
De gestrichenes Papier *(n)*
En coated paper
Es papel cuché *(m)*
Fr papier couché *(m)*
It carta patinata *(f)*

papel revestido à máquina *(m)* Pt
De maschinen-gestrichenes Papier *(n)*
En machine-coated paper
Es papel estucado a máquina *(m)*
Fr papier couché machine *(m)*
It carta patinata a macchina *(f)*

papel revestido com pincel *(m)* Pt
De bürstengestrichenes Papier *(n)*
En brush-coated paper
Es papel estucado a brocha *(m)*
Fr papier couché à la brosse *(m)*
It carta coperta a spazzola *(f)*

papel roto *(m)* Es
De Defektbogen *(m)*
En broke (papermaking)
Fr cassés *(m pl)*
It cascame di carta *(m)*
Pt empastelado *(m)*

papel rugoso *(m)* Pt
De mattgelbes geripptes Papier *(n)*
En cream laid paper
Es papel verjurado crema *(m)*
Fr papier vergé pâle *(m)*
It carta vergata crema *(f)*

papel satinado *(m)* Es
De kartoniertes Glanzpapier *(n)*
En board-glazed paper
Fr papier satiné *(m)*
It cartone satinato *(m)*
Pt papel acetinado *(m)*

papel satinado a plancha *(m)* Es
De bogenkalander-bearbeitetes Papier *(n)*
En plate-finished paper
Fr papier laminé à la plaque *(m)*
It carta rifinita *(f)*
Pt papel lustrado à prancha *(m)*

papel secado al aire *(m)* Es
De Lufttrokkenes Papier *(n)*
En loft-dried paper
Fr papier séché à l'air *(m)*
It carta seccata all'aria *(f)*
Pt papel secado ao ar *(m)*

papel secado ao ar *(m)*
Pt
De Lufttrokkenes Papier
(n)
En loft-dried paper
Es papel secado al aire
(m)
Fr papier séché à l'air
(m)
It carta seccata all'aria
(f)

papel secante *(m)* Es
De Löschpapier *(n)*
En blotting paper
Fr papier buvard *(m)*
It carta assorbente *(f)*
Pt papel mataborrão *(m)*

papel supercalandrado
(m) Es, Pt
De Illustrations-
druckpapier *(m)*
En super-calendered
paper
Fr papier supercalandré
(m)
It carta
supercalandrata *(f)*

papel tecido *(m)* Pt
De Velinpapier *(n)*
En wove paper
Es papel avitelado *(m)*
Fr papier vélin *(m)*
It carta retinata *(f)*

papel tecido enrugado
(m) Pt
De mattgelbes
Velinpapier *(n)*
En cream wove paper
Es papel avitelado
crema *(m)*
Fr vélin crème *(m)*
It velino cremo *(m)*

papel vergé *(m)* Pt
De Vergépapier *(n)*
En laid paper
Es papel verjurado *(m)*
Fr papier vergé *(m)*
It carta vergata *(f)*

papel verjurado *(m)* Es
De Vergépapier *(n)*
En laid paper
Fr papier vergé *(m)*
It carta vergata *(f)*
Pt papel vergé *(m)*

papel verjurado crema
(m) Es
De mattgelbes geripptes
Papier *(n)*
En cream laid paper
Fr papier vergé pâle *(m)*
It carta vergata crema
(f)
Pt papel rugoso *(m)*

paper *n* En
De Papier *(n)*
Es papel *(m)*
Fr papier *(m)*
It carta *(f)*
Pt papel *(m)*

paperback book En
De Taschenbuch *(n)*
Es libro en rústica *(m)*
Fr livre de poche *(m)*
It libro in edizione
economica *(m)*
Pt livro de bolso *(m)*

paperback edition En
De Taschenbuch-
Ausgabe *(f)*
Es edición de libros en
rústica *(f)*
Fr édition de poche *(f)*
It edizione economica
(f)
Pt edição de bolso *(f)*

paperback publisher En
De Taschenbuch-
Verleger *(m)*
Es editor de libros en
rústica *(m)*
Fr éditeur de livres de
poche *(m)*
It editore di collane
economiche *(m)*
Pt editor de livros de
bolso *(m)*

papermaking *n* En
De Papierherstellung *(f)*
Es fabricación de papel
(f)
Fr papeterie *(f)*
It fabbricazione di carta
(f)
Pt produção de papel *(f)*

papermaking machine
En
De Papierherstellungs-
maschine *(f)*
Es máquina de fabricar
papel continuo *(f)*

Fr machine à papier *(f)*
It macchina
fabbricatrice di carta
(f)
Pt máquina de
produção de papel *(f)*

paper mill En
De Papierfabrik *(f)*
Es fábrica de papel *(f)*
Fr fabrique de papier *(f)*
It cartiera *(f)*
Pt fábrica de papel *(f)*

paper tape En
De Lochstreifen *(m)*
Es cinta de papel *(f)*
Fr bande de papier *(f)*
It nastro di carta *(m)*
Pt fita de papel *(f)*

papeterie *(f)* *n* Fr
De Papierherstellung *(f)*
En papermaking
Es fabricación de papel
(f)
It fabbricazione di carta
(f)
Pt produção de papel *(f)*

papeterie de détail *(f)* Fr
De Briefpapier *(n)*
En stationery
Es efectos de escritorio
(m pl)
It cartoleria *(f)*
Pt papel e artigos de
escritório *(m)*

papier *(m)* *n* Fr
De Papier *(n)*
En paper
Es papel *(m)*
It carta *(f)*
Pt papel *(m)*

Papier *(n)* *n* De
En paper
Es papel *(m)*
Fr papier *(m)*
It carta *(f)*
Pt papel *(m)*

Papierabschnitt *(n)* *n* De
En offcut
Es papel de recorte *(m)*
Fr découpure *(f)*
It ritaglio di carta *(m)*
Pt papel de recorte *(m)*

papier à couverture *(m)*
Fr
De Umschlagpapier *(n)*
En cover paper
Es papel para cubiertas
(m)
It carta per copertine *(f)*
Pt papel de cobertura
(m)

papier à fibres courtes
(m) Fr
De kurzkörniges Papier
(n)
En short-grain paper
Es papel de fibra corta
(m)
It carta a grana corta *(f)*
Pt papel de grão curto
(m)

papier apprêté machine
(m) Fr
De maschinenglattes
Papier *(n)*
En mill-finished paper
Es papel calandrado *(m)*
It carta lisciata a
macchina *(f)*
Pt papel de acabamento
à máquina *(m)*

**papier apprêté sur
machine** *(m)* Fr
De maschinenglattes
Papier *(n)*
En machine-finished
paper
Es papel acabado a
máquina *(m)*
It carta finita a
macchina *(f)*
Pt papel acabado à
máquina *(m)*

papier au bromure *(m)* Fr
De Bromsilberabzug *(m)*
En bromide
Es bromuro *(m)*
It copia al bromuro *(f)*
Pt brometo *(m)*

papier au carbone *(m)* Fr
De Ätzpigmentpapier *(n)*
En carbon tissue
Es papel pigmento *(m)*
It carta al carbone *(f)*
Pt tecido carbono *(m)*

papier baryté *(m)* Fr
De Kreidezurichten *(n)*
En chalk overlay

Es alza mecánica de tiza
(f)
It carta gessata (f)
Pt calço de giz (f)

papier bible (m) Fr
De Bibel(druck)papier (n)
En bible paper
Es papel biblia (m)
It carta bibbia (f)
Pt papel bíblia (m)

papier bouffant (m) Fr
De Federleichtpapier (n)
En featherweight paper
Es papel ligero (m)
It carta piuma (f)
Pt papel peso pena (m)

papier bulle (m) Fr
De Manilapapier (n)
En manilla
Es manila (m)
It manilla (f)
Pt manila (m)

papier buvard (m) Fr
De Löschpapier (n)
En blotting paper
Es papel secante (m)
It carta assorbente (f)
Pt papel mataborrão (m)

papier calandré (m) Fr
De kalandriertes Papier
(n)
En calendered paper
Es papel caladrando (m)
It carta calandrata (f)
Pt papel calandrado (m)

papier calque (m) Fr
De Pauspapier (n)
En tracing paper
Es papel de calcar (m)
It carta da lucidi (f)
Pt papel de cópia (m)

papier cartouche (m) Fr
De Kartuschenpapier (n)
En cartridge paper
Es papel para cartuchos
(m)
It carta da disegno (f)
Pt papel cartucho (m)

papier cartouche offset
(m) Fr
De Offset-
Kartuschenpapier (n)

En offset cartridge paper
Es papel para cartuchos
de offset (m)
It rotolo di carta per
stampa offset (m)
Pt papel cartucho offset
(m)

papier chromo (m) Fr
De Chromopapier (n)
En chromo paper
Es papel para
cromolitografía (m)
It carta al cromo (f)
Pt papel cromo (m)

papier collé à la cuve
(m) Fr
De oberflächengeleimtes
Papier (n)
En tub-sized paper
Es papel encolado en
tina (m)
It carta imbozzimata in
tino (f)
Pt papel encolado em
tina (m)

papier collé en pâte (m)
Fr
De Maschinengröße (f)
En engine-sized paper
Es papel encolado a
máquina (m)
It carta tagliata a
macchina (f)
Pt papel encolado à
máquina (m)

papier coquille (m) Fr
De Schreibmaschinen-
papier (n)
En bond paper
Es papel bond (m)
It carta bond (f)
Pt papel bond (m)

papier couché (m) Fr
De gestrichenes Papier
(n)
En coated paper
Es papel cuché (m)
It carta patinata (f)
Pt papel revestido (m)

**papier couché à la
brosse** (m) Fr
De bürstengestrichenes
Papier (n)
En brush-coated paper
Es papel estucado a
brocha (m)

It carta coperta a
spazzola (f)
Pt papel revestido com
pincel (m)

**papier couché chrome
superbrillant** (m) Fr
De Gussgestrichenes
Papier (n)
En cast-coated paper
Es papel de respaldo
esmaltado (m)
It carta altobrillante (f)
Pt papel estereotipado
(m)

papier couché machine
(m) Fr
De maschinen-
gestrichenes Papier
(n)
En machine-coated
paper
Es papel estucado a
máquina (m)
It carta patinata a
macchina (f)
Pt papel revestido à
máquina (m)

papier couché mat (m)
Fr
De Mattkunstdruck-
papier (n)
En matt art paper
Es papel cuché mate
(m)
It carta patinata opaca
(f)
Pt papel artístico mate
(m)

papier cuve (m) Fr
De Handbütten (n)
En handmade paper
Es papel hecho a mano
(m)
It carta a mano (f)
Pt papel feito à mão (m)

papier de chiffon (m) Fr
De Hadernpapier (n)
En rag paper
Es papel de trapos (m)
It carta di stracci (f)
Pt papel de trapos (m)

papier de couleur (m) Fr
De getöntes Papier (n)
En tinted paper
Es papel coloreado (m)

It carta colorata (f)
Pt papel colorido (m)

Papierdicke (f) n De
En bulk (of paper)
Es cuerpo de papel (m)
Fr épaisseur de papier
(f)
It grossezza di carta (f)
Pt grossura do papel (f)

papier du Japon (m) Fr
De Japanpapier (n)
En Japanese vellum
Es vitela japonesa (f)
It pergamena
giapponese (f)
Pt papel pergaminho
japonês (m)

papier duplex (m) Fr
De Duplexpapier (n)
En duplex paper
Es cartón duplo (m)
It carta duplex (f)
Pt papel duplex (m)

papier émaillé (m) Fr
De Hochglanzpapier (n)
En enamel paper
Es papel esmaltado (m)
It carta smaltata (f)
Pt papel esmalte (m)

papier entoilé une face
(m) Fr
De stoffüberzogenes
Papier (n)
En cloth-lined paper
Es papel forrado de tela
(m)
It carta rivestita in tela
(f)
Pt papel forrado a tela
(m)

papier entre deux toiles
(m) Fr
Am cloth-centered paper
De Papier mit Stoffmitte
(n)
En cloth-centred paper
Es papel duplex con
alma de lino (m)
It carta duplex con
anima di tela (f)
Pt papel centrado em
tela (m)

Papierfabrik *(f)* *n* De
En paper mill
Es fábrica de papel *(f)*
Fr fabrique de papier *(f)*
It cartiera *(f)*
Pt fábrica de papel *(f)*

papier glacé *(m)* Fr
De Glanzpapier *(n)*
En glazed paper
Es papel lustroso *(m)*
It carta lucida *(f)*
Pt papel lustrado *(m)*

Papierherstellung *(f)* *n*
De
En papermaking
Es fabricación de papel
(f)
Fr papeterie *(f)*
It fabbricazione di carta
(f)
Pt produção de papel *(f)*

**Papierherstellungs-
maschine** *(f)* *n* De
En papermaking
machine
Es máquina de fabricar
papel continuo *(f)*
Fr machine à papier *(f)*
It macchina
fabbricatrice di carta
(f)
Pt máquina de
produção de papel *(f)*

papier imparfait *(m)* Fr
De mangelhaftes Papier
(n)
En retree
Es papel ligeramente
defectuoso *(m)*
It riscelta *(f)*
Pt papel defeituoso *(m)*

papier-journal *(m)* *n* Fr
De Rotationsdruckpapier
(n)
En newsprint
Es papel periódico *(m)*
It carta da giornale *(f)*
Pt papel para jornal *(m)*

papier Kraft *(m)* Fr
De Kraftpapier *(n)*
En kraft paper
Es papel kraft *(m)*
It carta kraft *(f)*
Pt papel kraft *(m)*

**papier kraft
doublé-bitumé** *(m)*
Fr
De Kraftverbundpapier
(n)
En kraft union paper
Es papel kraft union *(m)*
It carta kraft union *(f)*
Pt papel kraft union *(m)*

**papier laminé à la
plaque** *(m)* Fr
De bogenkalander-
bearbeitetes Papier
(n)
En plate-finished paper
Es papel satinado a
plancha *(m)*
It carta rifinita *(f)*
Pt papel lustrado à
prancha *(m)*

papier marbré *(m)* Fr
De Marmorpapier *(n)*
En marbled paper
Es papel jaspeado *(m)*
It carta marmorizzata *(f)*
Pt papel jaspeado *(m)*

Papiermasse *(f)* *n* De
En stuff
Es pasta de papel *(f)*
Fr pâte à papier *(f)*
It pasta di carta *(f)*
Pt polpa de papel *(f)*

papier millimétrique *(m)*
Fr
De Koordinatenpapier
(n)
En grid paper
Es papel milimétrico *(m)*
It carta millimetrata *(f)*
Pt papel milimétrico *(m)*

papier ministre *(m)* Fr
De Folioformat *(n)*
En foolscap
Es papel de oficio *(m)*
It carta protocollo *(f)*
Pt papel ministro *(m)*

Papier mit Stoffmitte
(n) De
Am cloth-centered paper
En cloth-centred paper
Es papel duplex con
alma de lino *(m)*
Fr papier entre deux
toiles *(m)*
It carta duplex con
anima di tela *(f)*

Pt papel centrado em
tela *(m)*

papier mousseline *(m)* Fr
De Seidenpapier *(n)*
En tissue paper
Es papel de seda *(m)*
It carta velina *(f)*
Pt papel de seda *(m)*

papier moyen âge *(m)* Fr
Am mold-made paper
De Büttenwerk-
druckpapier *(n)*
En mould-made paper
Es papel de tina *(m)*
It carta formata a mano
(f)
Pt papel moldado *(m)*

papier non collé *(m)* Fr
De ungeleimtes Papier
(n)
En waterleaf
Es papel no encolado
(m)
It carta non
imbozzimata *(f)*
Pt papel absorvente *(m)*

papier pelure *(m)* Fr
De Dünndruckpapier *(n)*
En onion-skin paper
Es papel cebolla *(m)*
It carta traslucida *(f)*
Pt papel cebola *(m)*

papier pour formules
(m) Fr
De Vervielfältigungs-
papier *(n)*
En manifold paper
Es papel de copias *(m)*
It carta per duplicatori
(f)
Pt papel de cópias *(m)*

papier pour graphiques
(m) Fr
De Registrierpapier *(n)*
En chart paper
Es papel gráfico *(m)*
It carta da grafici *(f)*
Pt papel de mapa *(m)*

papier pour titres *(m)* Fr
De Aktienpapier *(n)*
En loan paper
Es papel para
documentos *(m)*
It carta per valori *(f)*

Pt papel de empréstimo
(m)

papier pur chiffon *(m)* Fr
De Vollhadernpapier *(n)*
En all-rag paper
Es papel de hilo puro
(m)
It carta di cenci *(f)*
Pt papel inteiramente
de trapos *(m)*

papier quadrillé *(m)* Fr
De kariertes Papier *(n)*
En quadrille
Es cuadrícula *(f)*
It carta quadrettata *(f)*
Pt papel quadriculado
(m)

papier satiné *(m)* Fr
De kartoniertes
Glanzpapier *(n)*
En board-glazed paper
Es papel satinado *(m)*
It cartone satinato *(m)*
Pt papel acetinado *(m)*

papiers de garde *(m pl)*
Fr
De Vorsatzpapiere *(pl)*
En endpapers *pl* *n*
Es guardas *(f pl)*
It risguardi *(m pl)*
Pt folhas de contracapa
(f pl)

papier séché à l'air *(m)*
Fr
De Lufttrokkenes Papier
(n)
En loft-dried paper
Es papel secado al aire
(m)
It carta seccata all'aria
(f)
Pt papel secado ao ar
(m)

**papier sens machine sur
longueur** *(m)* Fr
De langkörniges Papier
(n)
En long-grain paper
Es papel plegado al hilo
(m)
It carta a grana lunga
(f)
Pt papel de grão
comprido *(m)*

papier supercalandré
(m) Fr
De Illustrations-
druckpapier *(m)*
En super-calendered
paper
Es papel
supercalandrado *(m)*
It carta
supercalandrata *(f)*
Pt papel
supercalandrado *(m)*

papier très collé *(m)* Fr
De Hartleimpapier *(n)*
En hard-sized paper
Es papel de encolado
duro *(m)*
It carta molto
imbozzimada *(f)*
Pt papel de
encolamento duro
(m)

Papiertyp *(m) n* De
En stock (paper)
Es materia de papel *(f)*
Fr matière de papier *(f)*
It materia di carta *(f)*
Pt matéria de papel *(f)*

papier vélin *(m)* Fr
De Velinpapier *(n)*
En wove paper
Es papel avitelado *(m)*
It carta retinata *(f)*
Pt papel tecido *(m)*

papier vergé *(m)* Fr
De Vergépapier *(n)*
En laid paper
Es papel verjurado *(m)*
It carta vergata *(f)*
Pt papel vergé *(m)*

papier vergé pâle *(m)* Fr
De mattgelbes geripptes
Papier *(n)*
En cream laid paper
Es papel verjurado
crema *(m)*
It carta vergata crema
(f)
Pt papel rugoso *(m)*

papiro *(m) n* Es, It, Pt
De Papyrus *(m)*
En papyrus
Fr papyrus *(m)*

Pappdeckel *(m) n* De
En mill board
Es cartón grueso *(m)*
Fr carton gris à reliure
(m)
It cartone forte *(m)*
Pt cartão grosso *(m)*

Pappe *(f) n* De
En pasteboard
Es cartón de varias
capas *(m)*
Fr carton contre-collé
(m)
It cartone accoppiato
(m)
Pt papelão *(m)*

papyrus *n* En; Fr *(m)*
De Papyrus *(m)*
Es papiro *(m)*
It papiro *(m)*
Pt papiro *(m)*

Papyrus *(m) n* De
En papyrus
Es papiro *(m)*
Fr papyrus *(m)*
It papiro *(m)*
Pt papiro *(m)*

paquete *(m) n* Es
De Paket *(n)*
En package
Fr colis *(m)*
It pacco *(m)*
Pt pacote *(m)*

paragrafo *(m) n* It
De Paragraph *(m)*
En paragraph
Es párrafo *(m)*
Fr alinéa *(m)*
Pt parágrafo *(m)*

parágrafo *(m) n* Pt
De Paragraph *(m)*
En paragraph
Es párrafo *(m)*
Fr alinéa *(m)*
It paragrafo *(m)*

paragraph *n* En
De Paragraph *(m)*
Es párrafo *(m)*
Fr alinéa *(m)*
It paragrafo *(m)*
Pt parágrafo *(m)*

Paragraph *(m) n* De
En paragraph
Es párrafo *(m)*
Fr alinéa *(m)*
It paragrafo *(m)*
Pt parágrafo *(m)*

Paragrapheinrückung *(f)*
n De
En paragraph indent
Es sangría de párrafo *(f)*
Fr renfoncé d´alinéa *(m)*
It indentro del
paragrafo *(m)*
Pt reentrância de
parágrafo *(f)*

paragraph indent En
De Paragrapheinrückung
(f)
Es sangría de párrafo *(f)*
Fr renfoncé d´alinéa *(m)*
It indentro del
paragrafo *(m)*
Pt reentrância de
parágrafo *(f)*

**Parallel-
bewegungstiegel**
(m) n De
En direct approach
platen
Es platina de
aproximación directa
(f)
Fr platine à approche
directe *(f)*
It platina ad approccio
diretto *(f)*
Pt platina de
aproximação directa
(f)

parangonner *vb* Fr
De ausrichten
En line up
Es alinear
It allineare
Pt alinhar

parchemin *(m) n* Fr
De Pergament *(n)*
En parchment
Es pergamino *(m)*
It pergamena *(f)*
Pt pergaminho *(m)*

parchment *n* En
De Pergament *(n)*
Es pergamino *(m)*
Fr parchemin *(m)*

It pergamena *(f)*
Pt pergaminho *(m)*

parentese *(f) n* It
De Klammer *(f)*
En parenthesis
Es paréntesis *(m)*
Fr parenthèse *(f)*
Pt parêntese *(m)*

parêntese *(m) n* Pt
De Klammer *(f)*
En parenthesis
Es paréntesis *(m)*
Fr parenthèse *(f)*
It parentese *(f)*

paréntesis *(m) n* Es
De Klammer *(f)*
En parenthesis
Fr parenthèse *(f)*
It parentese *(f)*
Pt parêntese *(m)*

parenthèse *(f) n* Fr
De Klammer *(f)*
En parenthesis
Es paréntesis *(m)*
It parentese *(f)*
Pt parêntese *(m)*

parenthesis *n* En
De Klammer *(f)*
Es paréntesis *(m)*
Fr parenthèse *(f)*
It parentese *(f)*
Pt parêntese *(m)*

parola principale *(f)* It
De haupt Wort *(n)*
En headword
Es palabra principal *(f)*
Fr mot en-tête *(m)*
Pt palavra-índice *(f)*

párrafo *(m) n* Es
De Paragraph *(m)*
En paragraph
Fr alinéa *(m)*
It paragrafo *(m)*
Pt parágrafo *(m)*

parte *(f) n* Es, It, Pt
De Partner *(m)*
En party
Fr partie *(f)*

partes claras *(f pl)* Pt
De Lichter *(pl)*
En highlights *pl n*

Es blancos *(m pl)*
Fr grandes lumières *(f pl)*
It alte luci *(f pl)*

partie *(f) n* Fr
De Partner *(m)*
En party
Es parte *(f)*
It parte *(f)*
Pt parte *(f)*

Partner *(m) n* De
En party
Es parte *(f)*
Fr partie *(f)*
It parte *(f)*
Pt parte *(f)*

part-title *n* En
De Schmutztitel *(m)*
Es título de parte *(m)*
Fr titre partiel *(m)*
It titolo parziale *(m)*
Pt título parcial *(m)*

party *n* En
De Partner *(m)*
Es parte *(f)*
Fr partie *(f)*
It parte *(f)*
Pt parte *(f)*

parution de la rentrée *(f)* Fr
De Herbstausgabe *(f)*
En autumn publication
Es publicación de otoño *(f)*
It pubblicazione d´autunno *(f)*
Pt publicação de outono *(f)*

parution de printemps *(f)* Fr
De Frühjahrs-Veröffentlichung *(f)*
En spring publication
Es publicación de primavera *(f)*
It pubblicazione di primavera *(f)*
Pt publicação de Primavera *(f)*

parution en feuilleton *(f)* Fr
De Veröffentlichung in Fortsetzungen *(f)*
En serialization

Es publicación por entregas *(f)*
It riduzione in serie *(f)*
Pt publicação em série *(f)*

Paßdifferenz *(f) n* De
En misregister
Es registro inexacto *(m)*
Fr repérage défectueux *(m)*
It registro scorretto *(f)*
Pt registo inexacto *(m)*

Paßkreuze *(pl) n* De
En register marks
Es marcas de registro *(f pl)*
Fr croix de repère *(f pl)*
It croci di registro *(m pl)*
Pt marcas de registo *(f pl)*

passe *(f) n* Fr
De Zuschuß *(m)*
En overs *(pl)*
Es hojas sobrantes *(f pl)*
It fogli aggiunti *(m pl)*
Pt folhas que sobram *(f pl)*

pasta *(f) n* Es, It
De Zellstoff *(m)*
En pulp
Fr pâte *(f)*
Pt polpa *(f)*

pasta de madera *(f)* Es
De Holzstoff *(m)*
En wood pulp
Fr pâte de bois *(f)*
It pasta di legno *(f)*
Pt polpa de madeira *(f)*

pasta de madera al sulfato *(f)* Es
Am sulfate wood pulp
De Sulfat-Holzstoff *(m)*
En sulphate wood pulp
Fr pâte de bois au sulfate *(f)*
It pasta di legno al solfato *(f)*
Pt polpa de madeira sulfatada *(f)*

pasta de papel *(f)* Es
De Papiermasse *(f)*
En stuff
Fr pâte à papier *(f)*

It pasta di carta *(f)*
Pt polpa de papel *(f)*

pasta di carta *(f) It*
De Papiermasse *(f)*
En stuff
Es pasta de papel *(f)*
Fr pâte à papier *(f)*
Pt polpa de papel *(f)*

pasta di legno *(f)* It
De Holzstoff *(m)*
En wood pulp
Es pasta de madera *(f)*
Fr pâte de bois *(f)*
Pt polpa de madeira *(f)*

pasta di legno al solfato *(f)* It
Am sulfate wood pulp
De Sulfat-Holzstoff *(m)*
En sulphate wood pulp
Es pasta de madera al sulfato *(f)*
Fr pâte de bois au sulfate *(f)*
Pt polpa de madeira sulfatada *(f)*

pasta di legno ottenuta meccanicamente *(f)* It
De Holzschliff *(m)*
En mechanical wood pulp
Es pasta mecánica *(f)*
Fr pâte mécanique *(f)*
Pt polpa de madeira mecânica *(f)*

pasta mecánica *(f)* Es
De Holzschliff *(m)*
En mechanical wood pulp
Fr pâte mécanique *(f)*
It pasta di legno ottenuta meccanicamente *(f)*
Pt polpa de madeira mecânica *(f)*

pasta senza legno *(f)* It
De holzfreier Papierstoff *(m)*
En wood-free pulp
Es pasta sin madera *(f)*
Fr pâte sans bois *(f)*
Pt polpa sem madeira *(f)*

pasta sin madera *(f)* Es
De holzfreier Papierstoff *(m)*
En wood-free pulp
Fr pâte sans bois *(f)*
It pasta senza legno *(f)*
Pt polpa sem madeira *(f)*

paste *n* En
De Kleister *(m)*
Es engrudo *(m)*
Fr colle *(f)*
It colla *(f)*
Pt cola *(f)*

pasteboard *n* En
De Pappe *(f)*
Es cartón de varias capas *(m)*
Fr carton contre-collé *(m)*
It cartone accoppiato *(m)*
Pt papelão *(m)*

paste up En
De klebeumbrechen
Es montar
Fr encoller
It incollare
Pt montar

paste-up *n* En
De Klebeumbruch *(m)*
Es montaje *(m)*
Fr collage *(m)*
It incollatura *(f)*
Pt montagem *(f)*

paste-up work En
De Klebeumbruch-Arbeit *(f)*
Es trabajo de montaje *(m)*
Fr travail de collage *(m)*
It lavoro di incollatura *(m)*
Pt trabalho do montagem *(m)*

pâte *(f) n* Fr
De Zellstoff *(m)*
En pulp
Es pasta *(f)*
It pasta *(f)*
Pt polpa *(f)*

pâte à papier *(f)* Fr
De Papiermasse *(f)*
En stuff
Es pasta de papel *(f)*

It pasta di carta (f)
Pt polpa de papel (f)

pâte de bois (f) Fr
De Holzstoff (m)
En wood pulp
Es pasta de madera (f)
It pasta di legno (f)
Pt polpa de madeira (f)

pâte de bois au sulfate
    (f) Fr
Am sulfate wood pulp
De Sulfat-Holzstoff (m)
En sulphate wood pulp
Es pasta de madera al
    sulfato (f)
It pasta di legno al
    solfato (f)
Pt polpa de madeira
    sulfatada (f)

pâte mécanique (f) Fr
De Holzschliff (m)
En mechanical wood
    pulp
Es pasta mecánica (f)
It pasta di legno
    ottenuta
    meccanicamente (f)
Pt polpa de madeira
    mecânica (f)

pâte sans bois (f) Fr
De holzfreier Papierstoff
    (m)
En wood-free pulp
Es pasta sin madera (f)
It pasta senza legno (f)
Pt polpa sem madeira (f)

patrón (m) n Es
De Arbeitgeber (m)
En employer
Fr employeur (m)
It datore di lavoro (m)
Pt entidade patronal (f)

Pauschalbetrag (m) n De
En lump sum
Es suma total (f)
Fr somme globale (f)
It somma globale (f)
Pt importância global (f)

paus grossos (m pl) Pt
De Säulen (pl)
En stems pl n
Es palos gruesos (m pl)
Fr hastes (f pl)
It gambi (m pl)

Pauspapier (n) n De
En tracing paper
Es papel de calcar (m)
Fr papier calque (m)
It carta da lucidi (f)
Pt papel de cópia (m)

payement d'avance (m)
    Fr
De Vorauszahlung (f)
En payment in advance
Es pago por adelantado
    (m)
It pagamento anticipo
    (m)
Pt pagamento
    adiantado (m)

payment n En
De Zahlung (f)
Es pago (m)
Fr paiement (m)
It pagamento (m)
Pt pagamento (m)

payment in advance En
De Vorauszahlung (f)
Es pago por adelantado
    (m)
Fr payement d'avance
    (m)
It pagamento anticipo
    (m)
Pt pagamento
    adiantado (m)

pé (m) n Pt
De Fuß (m)
En foot
Es pie (m)
Fr pied (m)
It piede (m)

pé (de página) (m) n Pt
De Unterschlag (m)
En tail (of page)
Es margin inferior (m)
Fr marge de pied (f)
It piede (di pagina) (m)

peça (f) n Pt
De Stück (n)
En play
Es obra dramática (f)
Fr pièce de théâtre (f)
It commedia (f)

pedido por correo (m) Es
De Versandhausauftrag
    (m)
En mail order

Fr vente par
    correspondance (f)
It vendite per posta (f)
Pt encomenda por
    correio (f)

película (f) n Es, Pt
De Film (m)
En film
Fr film (m)
It pellicola (f)

película de inversão (f)
    Pt
De Umkehrfilm (m)
En reversal film
Es película reversible (f)
Fr film noir au blanc (m)
It pellicola invertibile (f)

**película de lectura
    correcta** (f) Es
De seitenrichtiger Film
    (m)
En right-reading film
Fr film à lecture juste
    (m)
It pellicola a lettura
    giusta (f)
Pt película de leitura do
    lado direito (f)

**película de lectura
    incorrecta** (f) Es
De seitenverkehrter Film
    (m)
En wrong-reading film
Fr film à lecture à
    l'envers (m)
It pellicola a lettura
    sbagliata (f)
Pt película de leitura do
    lado errado (f)

**película de leitura do
    lado direito** (f) Pt
De seitenrichtiger Film
    (m)
En right-reading film
Es película de lectura
    correcta (f)
Fr film à lecture juste
    (m)
It pellicola a lettura
    giusta (f)

**película de leitura do
    lado errado** (f) Pt
De seitenverkehrter Film
    (m)
En wrong-reading film

Es película de lectura
    incorrecta (f)
Fr film à lecture à
    l'envers (m)
It pellicola a lettura
    sbagliata (f)

película negativa (f) Es,
    Pt
De Negativfilm (m)
En negative film
Fr film négatif (m)
It film negativo (m)

película para positivos
    (f) Es
De Positivfilm (m)
En positive film
Fr film positif (m)
It pellicola positiva (f)
Pt película positiva (f)

película positiva (f) Pt
De Positivfilm (m)
En positive film
Es película para
    positivos (f)
Fr film positif (m)
It pellicola positiva (f)

película reversible (f) Es
De Umkehrfilm (m)
En reversal film
Fr film noir au blanc (m)
It pellicola invertibile (f)
Pt película de inversão
    (f)

pellicola (f) n It
De Film (m)
En film
Es película (f)
Fr film (m)
Pt película (f)

pellicola a lettura giusta
    (f) It
De seitenrichtiger Film
    (m)
En right-reading film
Es película de lectura
    correcta (f)
Fr film à lecture juste
    (m)
Pt película de leitura do
    lado direito (f)

**pellicola a lettura
    sbagliata** (f) It
De seitenverkehrter Film
    (m)

En wrong-reading film
Es película de lectura
incorrecta *(f)*
Fr film à lecture à
l'envers *(m)*
Pt película de leitura do
lado errado *(f)*

pellicola invertibile *(f)* It
De Umkehrfilm *(m)*
En reversal film
Es película reversible *(f)*
Fr film noir au blanc *(m)*
Pt película de inversão
(f)

pellicola positiva *(f)* It
De Positivfilm *(m)*
En positive film
Es película para
positivos *(f)*
Fr film positif *(m)*
Pt película positiva *(f)*

Pelzen *(n)* n De
En piling
Es espesamiento *(m)*
Fr encrassement *(m)*
It ammassamento *(m)*
Pt espessamento de
tinta *(m)*

pencil drawing En
De Bleistiftzeichnung *(f)*
Es dibujo a lápiz *(m)*
Fr dessin au crayon *(m)*
It disegno a matita *(m)*
Pt desenho a lápis *(m)*

pen ruling En
De Federlinierung *(f)*
Es rayado a pluma *(m)*
Fr réglure au crayon *(f)*
It sottolineatura a
penna *(f)*
Pt linhas à pena *(m)*

perfect binding En
De Klebebindung *(f)*
Es encuadernación sin
cosido *(f)*
Fr reliure parfaite *(f)*
It rilegatura perfetta *(f)*
Pt encadernação sem
costura *(f)*

perfect-bound book En
De klebegebundenes
Buch *(n)*
Es libro encuadernado
sin costura *(m)*

Fr livre relié sans
couture *(m)*
It libro perfettamente
rilegato *(m)*
Pt livro encadernado
sem costura *(m)*

perfecting n En
De Schön- und
Widerdruck *(m)*
Es retiración *(f)*
Fr retiration *(f)*
It stampa in volta *(f)*
Pt impressão
simultânea de ambos
lados *(f)*

perfector n En
De Schön- und
Widerdruckmaschine
(f)
Es prensa de retiración
(f)
Fr presse à retiration *(f)*
It stampatrice in volta
(f)
Pt máquina de
impressão
simultânea de ambos
lados *(f)*

perforación *(f)* n Es
De Perforierung *(f)*
En perforation
Fr perforation *(f)*
It perforazione *(f)*
Pt perfuração *(f)*

perforadora *(f)* n Es
De Perforiermaschine *(f)*
En perforator
Fr perforeuse *(f)*
It perforatore *(m)*
Pt perfuradora *(f)*

perforar vb Es
De perforieren
En perforate
Fr perforer
It perforare
Pt perfurar

perforare vb It
De perforieren
En perforate
Es perforar
Fr perforer
Pt perfurar

perforate vb En
De perforieren
Es perforar
Fr perforer
It perforare
Pt perfurar

perforation n En; Fr *(f)*
De Perforierung *(f)*
Es perforación *(f)*
It perforazione *(f)*
Pt perfuração *(f)*

**perforation
d'entraînement** *(f)*
Fr
De Führungsloch-
Vorschub *(m)*
En advanced sprocket
feed
Es arrastre por rueda
dentada *(m)*
It alimentazione a
tamburo dentato
avanzato *(f)*
Pt alimentação
avançada do carreto
(f)

perforation des négatifs
(f) Fr
De Nadellöcher *(pl)*
En pinholes pl n
Es burbujas *(f pl)*
It mancanza di densità
(f)
Pt furos *(m pl)*

perforator n En
De Perforiermaschine *(f)*
Es perforadora *(f)*
Fr perforeuse *(f)*
It perforatore *(m)*
Pt perfuradora *(f)*

perforatore *(m)* n It
De Locher;
Perforiermaschine *(m
f)*
En perforator; punch
Es perforadora;
sacabocados *(f m)*
Fr perforeuse *(f)*
Pt perfuradora *(f)*

perforazione *(f)* n It
De Perforierung *(f)*
En perforation
Es perforación *(f)*
Fr perforation *(f)*
Pt perfuração *(f)*

perforer vb Fr
De perforieren
En perforate
Es perforar
It perforare
Pt perfurar

perforeuse *(f)* n Fr
De Locher;
Perforiermaschine *(m
f)*
En perforator; punch
Es perforadora;
sacabocados *(f m)*
It perforatore *(m)*
Pt perfuradora *(f)*

perforieren vb De
En perforate
Es perforar
Fr perforer
It perforare
Pt perfurar

Perforiermaschine *(f)* n
De
En perforator
Es perforadora *(f)*
Fr perforeuse *(f)*
It perforatore *(m)*
Pt perfuradora *(f)*

Perforierung *(f)* n De
En perforation
Es perforación *(f)*
Fr perforation *(f)*
It perforazione *(f)*
Pt perfuração *(f)*

perfuração *(f)* n Pt
De Perforierung *(f)*
En perforation
Es perforación *(f)*
Fr perforation *(f)*
It perforazione *(f)*

perfuradora *(f)* n Pt
De Locher;
Perforiermaschine *(m
f)*
En perforator; punch
Es perforadora;
sacabocados *(f m)*
Fr perforeuse *(f)*
It perforatore *(m)*

perfurar vb Pt
De perforieren
En perforate
Es perforar

Fr perforer
It perforare

pergamena *(f) n* It
De Pergament *(n)*
En parchment
Es pergamino *(m)*
Fr parchemin *(m)*
Pt pergaminho *(m)*

pergamena giapponese
(f) It
De Japanpapier *(n)*
En Japanese vellum
Es vitela japonesa *(f)*
Fr papier du Japon *(m)*
Pt papel pergaminho
japonês *(m)*

Pergament *(n) n* De
En parchment
Es pergamino *(m)*
Fr parchemin *(m)*
It pergamena *(f)*
Pt pergaminho *(m)*

pergaminho *(m) n* Pt
De Pergament *(n)*
En parchment
Es pergamino *(m)*
Fr parchemin *(m)*
It pergamena *(f)*

pergamino *(m) n* Es
De Pergament *(n)*
En parchment
Fr parchemin *(m)*
It pergamena *(f)*
Pt pergaminho *(m)*

pergunta *(f) n* Pt
De Frage *(f)*
En query
Es interrogación *(f)*
Fr question *(f)*
It quesito *(m)*

périmé *adj* Fr
De veraltet
En out of date
Es anticuado
It superato
Pt desactualizado

period *n* Am
De Punkt *(m)*
En full stop
Es punto final *(m)*
Fr point final *(m)*

It punto fermo *(m)*
Pt ponto final *(m)*

période d'arrêt *(f)* Fr
De Ausfallszeit *(f)*
En down time
Es tiempo muerto *(m)*
It tempo passivo *(m)*
Pt tempo de paragem
(m)

periodical *n* En
De Zeitschrift *(f)*
Es periódico *(m)*
Fr périodique *(m)*
It periodico *(m)*
Pt periódico *(m)*

periodico *(m) n* It
De Zeitschrift *(f)*
En periodical
Es periódico *(m)*
Fr périodique *(m)*
Pt periódico *(m)*

periódico *(m) n* Es, Pt
De Journal; Zeitschrift *(n
f)*
En journal; periodical
Fr periodique; revue *(m
f)*
It giornale; periodico
(m)
Pt jornal; revista *(m f)*

périodique *(m) n* Fr
De Zeitschrift *(f)*
En periodical
Es periódico *(m)*
It periodico *(m)*
Pt periódico *(m)*

periodismo *(m) n* Es
De Journalismus *(m)*
En journalism
Fr journalisme *(m)*
It giornalismo *(m)*
Pt jornalismo *(m)*

periodista *(m/f) n* Es
De Journalist *(m)*
En journalist
Fr journaliste *(m/f)*
It giornalista *(m/f)*
Pt jornalista *(m/f)*

permeabilidad *(f) n* Es
De Permeabilität *(f)*
En permeability
Fr perméabilité *(f)*

It permeabilità *(f)*
Pt permeabilidade *(f)*

permeabilidade *(f) n* Pt
De Permeabilität *(f)*
En permeability
Es permeabilidad *(f)*
Fr perméabilité *(f)*
It permeabilità *(f)*

permeabilità *(f) n* It
De Permeabilität *(f)*
En permeability
Es permeabilidad *(f)*
Fr perméabilité *(f)*
Pt permeabilidade *(f)*

Permeabilität *(f) n* De
En permeability
Es permeabilidad *(f)*
Fr perméabilité *(f)*
It permeabilità *(f)*
Pt permeabilidade *(f)*

perméabilité *(f) n* Fr
De Permeabilität *(f)*
En permeability
Es permeabilidad *(f)*
It permeabilità *(f)*
Pt permeabilidade *(f)*

permeability *n* En
De Permeabilität *(f)*
Es permeabilidad *(f)*
Fr perméabilité *(f)*
It permeabilità *(f)*
Pt permeabilidade *(f)*

personal *(m) n* Es
De Personal *(n)*
En personnel; staff
Fr personnel *(m)*
It personale *(m)*
Pt pessoal *(m)*

Personal *(n) n* De
En personnel; staff
Es personal *(m)*
Fr personnel *(m)*
It personale *(m)*
Pt pessoal *(m)*

Personal-
abteilungsleiter *(m)*
n De
En personnel manager
Es jefe de personal *(m)*
Fr directeur du
personnel *(m)*

It direttore del
personale *(m)*
Pt director do pessoal
(m)

personal assistant En
De persönlicher
Assistent *(m)*
Es ayudante personal
(m)
Fr adjoint *(m)*
It assistente personale
(m)
Pt ajudante pessoal *(m)*

personale *(m) n* It
De Personal *(n)*
En personnel; staff
Es personal *(m)*
Fr personnel *(m)*
Pt pessoal *(m)*

persönlicher Assistent
(m) De
En personal assistant
Es ayudante personal
(m)
Fr adjoint *(m)*
It assistente personale
(m)
Pt ajudante pessoal *(m)*

personnel *n* En; Fr *(m)*
De Personal *(n)*
Es personal *(m)*
It personale *(m)*
Pt pessoal *(m)*

personnel manager En
De Personal-
abteilungsleiter *(m)*
Es jefe de personal *(m)*
Fr directeur du
personnel *(m)*
It direttore del
personale *(m)*
Pt director do pessoal
(m)

peso del carattere *(m)* It
De Schriftgewicht *(n)*
En type weight
Es peso del tipo *(m)*
Fr poids de caractère
(m)
Pt peso de tipo *(m)*

peso del tipo *(m)* Es
De Schriftgewicht *(n)*
En type weight

Fr poids de caractère
(m)
It peso del carattere
(m)
Pt peso de tipo *(m)*

peso de tipo *(m)* Pt
De Schriftgewicht *(n)*
En type weight
Es peso del tipo *(m)*
Fr poids de caractère
(m)
It peso del carattere
(m)

pessoal *(m) n* Pt
De Personal *(n)*
En personnel; staff
Es personal *(m)*
Fr personnel *(m)*
It personale *(m)*

petite encyclopédie *(f)*
Fr
De Schreibtisch-Lexikon
(n)
En desk encyclopedia
Es enciclopedia de
mesa *(f)*
It enciclopedia da
tavolo *(f)*
Pt enciclopédia de
mesa *(f)*

**petites lettres
inférieures** *(f pl)* Fr
De tiefstehende
Buchstaben *(pl)*
En inferior characters
Es subíndices *(m pl)*
It caratteri inferiori *(m
pl)*
Pt caracteres inferiores
(m pl)

petites majuscules *(f pl)*
Fr
De Kapitälchen *(pl)*
En small capital letters
Es letras versalitas *(f pl)*
It lettere in
maiuscoletto *(f pl)*
Pt maiúsculas pequenas
(f pl)

petits fonds *(m pl)* Fr
De Gießbach *(m)*
En gutter
Es medianil *(m)*
It scanalatura per sfogo
(f)
Pt medianiz *(m)*

phonetics *n* En
De Phonetik *(f)*
Es fonética *(f)*
Fr phonétique *(f)*
It fonetica *(f)*
Pt fonética *(f)*

phonetic symbols En
De Phonetikzeichen *(pl)*
Es signos fonéticos *(m
pl)*
Fr symboles
phonétiques *(m pl)*
It simboli fonetici *(m pl)*
Pt símbolos fonéticos
(m pl)

Phonetik *(f) n* De
En phonetics
Es fonética *(f)*
Fr phonétique *(f)*
It fonetica *(f)*
Pt fonética *(f)*

Phonetikzeichen *(pl) n*
De
En phonetic symbols
Es signos fonéticos *(m
pl)*
Fr symboles
phonétiques *(m pl)*
It simboli fonetici *(m pl)*
Pt símbolos fonéticos
(m pl)

phonétique *(f) n* Fr
De Phonetik *(f)*
En phonetics
Es fonética *(f)*
It fonetica *(f)*
Pt fonética *(f)*

Photo *(n) n* De
En photograph
Es fotografía (imagen) *(f)*
Fr photographie (image)
(f)
It fotografia (figura) *(f)*
Pt fotografia (imagem)
(f)

Photobezug *(m) n* De
En photographic
reference
Es referencia fotográfica
(f)
Fr référence
photographique *(f)*
It riferimento
fotografico *(m)*
Pt referência fotográfica
(f)

photocomposeuse *(f) n*
Fr
De Film-Setzmaschine *(f)*
En filmsetter
Es fotocompositor *(m)*
It fotocompositrice *(f)*
Pt fotocompositor *(m)*

photocomposition *n* En;
Fr *(f)*
De Photosatz *(m)*
Es fotocomposición *(f)*
It fotocomposizione *(f)*
Pt fotocomposição *(f)*

photocopieuse *(f)* Fr
De Photokopier-
maschine *(f)*
En photocopying
machine
Es máquina
fotocopiadora *(f)*
It fotocopiatrice *(f)*
Pt fotocopiadora *(f)*

photocopying machine
En
De Photokopier-
maschine *(f)*
Es máquina
fotocopiadora *(f)*
Fr photocopieuse *(f)*
It fotocopiatrice *(f)*
Pt fotocopiadora *(f)*

photo credits En
De Dank für die
Genehmigung von
Photos *(m)*
Es fotocréditos *(m pl)*
Fr origine des
photographies *(f)*
It indice dei fotografi
(m pl)
Pt fotocréditos *(m pl)*

Photodisplay-Gerät *(n)*
n De
En photodisplay unit
Es unidad de
fotopresentación *(f)*
Fr unité de photodisplay
(f)
It unità di photodisplay
(f)
Pt unidade de
foto-display *(f)*

photodisplay unit En
De Photodisplay-Gerät
(n)

Es unidad de
fotopresentación *(f)*
Fr unité de photodisplay
(f)
It unità di photodisplay
(f)
Pt unidade de
foto-display *(f)*

photograph *vb* En
De photographieren
Es fotografiar
Fr photographier
It fotografare
Pt fotografar

photograph *n* En
De Photo *(n)*
Es fotografía (imagen) *(f)*
Fr photographie (image)
(f)
It fotografia (figura) *(f)*
Pt fotografia (imagem)
(f)

Photograph *(m) n* De
En photographer
Es fotógrafo *(m)*
Fr photographe *(m)*
It fotografo *(m)*
Pt fotógrafo *(m)*

photographe *(m) n* Fr
De Photograph *(m)*
En photographer
Es fotógrafo *(m)*
It fotografo *(m)*
Pt fotógrafo *(m)*

photographer *n* En
De Photograph *(m)*
Es fotógrafo *(m)*
Fr photographe *(m)*
It fotografo *(m)*
Pt fotógrafo *(m)*

photographic enlarger
En
De photographisches
Vergrößerungsgerät
(n)
Es ampliadora
fotográfica *(f)*
Fr agrandisseur photo
(m)
It ingranditore
fotografico *(m)*
Pt ampliador fotográfico
(m)

photographic reference
En
De Photobezug *(m)*
Es referencia fotográfica *(f)*
Fr référence photographique *(f)*
It riferimento fotografico *(m)*
Pt referência fotográfica *(f)*

photographie (image) *(f) n* Fr
De Photo *(n)*
En photograph
Es fotografía (imagen) *(f)*
It fotografia (figura) *(f)*
Pt fotografia (imagem) *(f)*

photographie (procédé) *(f) n* Fr
De Photographie *(f)*
En photography
Es fotografía (método) *(f)*
It fotografia (procedimento) *(f)*
Pt fotografia (processo) *(f)*

Photographie *(f) n* De
En photography
Es fotografía (método) *(f)*
Fr photographie (procédé) *(f)*
It fotografia (procedimento) *(f)*
Pt fotografia (processo) *(f)*

photographie en couleurs *(f)* Fr
Am color photograph
De Farbphoto *(n)*
En colour photograph
Es fotografía en colores *(f)*
It fotografia a colori *(f)*
Pt fotografia a cores *(f)*

photographier *vb* Fr
De photographieren
En photograph
Es fotografiar
It fotografare
Pt fotografar

photographieren *vb* De
En photograph
Es fotografiar
Fr photographier
It fotografare
Pt fotografar

photographisches Vergrößerungsgerät
(n) De
En photographic enlarger
Es ampliadora fotográfica *(f)*
Fr agrandisseur photo *(m)*
It ingranditore fotografico *(m)*
Pt ampliador fotográfico *(m)*

photography *n* En
De Photographie *(f)*
Es fotografía (método) *(f)*
Fr photographie (procédé) *(f)*
It fotografia (procedimento) *(f)*
Pt fotografia (processo) *(f)*

photograveur *(m) n* Fr
De Klischeeanstalt *(f)*
En blockmaker
Es grabador *(m)*
It zincografo *(m)*
Pt gravador *(m)*

photogravure *(n)* En
De Kupfertiefdruck *(m)*
Es huecograbado *(m)*
Fr héliogravure *(f)*
It fotoincisione *(f)*
Pt fotogravura *(f)*

photogravure *(f) n* Fr
De Chemiegraphie *(f)*
En process engraving
Es fotograbado *(m)*
It zincografia *(f)*
Pt fototipogravura *(f)*

photogravure typographique *(f)* Fr
De Zeilensatz *(m)*
En line composition
Es composición por líneas *(f)*

It composizione della linea *(f)*
Pt composição de linhas *(f)*

photojournalism *n* En
De Photojournalismus *(m)*
Es fotoperiodismo *(m)*
Fr photojournalisme *(m)*
It fotogiornalismo *(m)*
Pt fotojornalismo *(m)*

photojournalisme *(m) n* Fr
De Photojournalismus *(m)*
En photojournalism
Es fotoperiodismo *(m)*
It fotogiornalismo *(m)*
Pt fotojornalismo *(m)*

Photojournalismus *(m) n* De
En photojournalism
Es fotoperiodismo *(m)*
Fr photojournalisme *(m)*
It fotogiornalismo *(m)*
Pt fotojornalismo *(m)*

Photokopiermaschine *(f)* De
En photocopying machine
Es máquina fotocopiadora *(f)*
Fr photocopieuse *(f)*
It fotocopiatrice *(f)*
Pt fotocopiadora *(f)*

Photolithographie *(f) n* De
En photolithography
Es fotolitografía *(f)*
Fr phototypie *(f)*
It fotolitografia *(f)*
Pt fotolitografia *(f)*

photolithography *n* En
De Photolithographie *(f)*
Es fotolitografía *(f)*
Fr phototypie *(f)*
It fotolitografia *(f)*
Pt fotolitografia *(f)*

Photopolymer-Druckplatte *(f) n* De
En photopolymer printing plate
Es placa impresora de

polimerización fotoquímica *(f)*
Fr plaque photopolymère *(f)*
It lastra da stampa ai fotopolimeri *(f)*
Pt chapa de impressão fotopolimérica *(f)*

photopolymer printing plate En
De Photopolymer-Druckplatte *(f)*
Es placa impresora de polimerización fotoquímica *(f)*
Fr plaque photopolymère *(f)*
It lastra da stampa ai fotopolimeri *(f)*
Pt chapa de impressão fotopolimérica *(f)*

Photosatz *(m) n* De
En photocomposition; phototypesetting
Es fotocomposición *(f)*
Fr photocomposition *(f)*
It fotocomposizione *(f)*
Pt fotocomposição *(f)*

phototype *(m) n* Fr
De Lichtdruck *(m)*
En collotype
Es colotipia *(f)*
It collotipia *(f)*
Pt colotipo *(m)*

phototypesetting *n* En
De Photosatz *(m)*
Es composición fotomecánica *(f)*
Fr photocomposition *(f)*
It fotocomposizione *(f)*
Pt fotocomposição *(f)*

phototypie *(f) n* Fr
De Photolithographie *(f)*
En photolithography
Es fotolitografía *(f)*
It fotolitografia *(f)*
Pt fotolitografia *(f)*

phrase *(f) n* Fr
De Satz *(m)*
En sentence
Es cláusula *(f)*
It frase *(f)*
Pt frase *(f)*

pialle *(f pl)* It
De Bestoβhobel *(pl)*
En planes *pl n*
Es asentadores *(m pl)*
Fr rabots *(m pl)*
Pt niveladores *(m pl)*

piano *(m) n* It
De Druckkarren *(m)*
En bed (printing machine)
Es platina *(f)*
Fr marbre *(m)*
Pt mesa *(f)*

picado *(m) n* Es, Pt
De Rupfen *(n)*
En plucking
Fr arrachage *(m)*
It strappatura *(f)*

pi characters En
De Handsatz-Schrifttypen *(pl)*
Es caracteres pi *(m pl)*
Fr figures spéciales *(f pl)*
It caratteri pi *(m pl)*
Pt caracteres pi *(m pl)*

picture *n* En
De Bild *(n)*
Es imagen *(f)*
Fr image *(f)*
It figura *(f)*
Pt imagem *(f)*

pie *(m) n* Es
De Fuβ *(m)*
En foot
Fr pied *(m)*
It piede *(m)*
Pt pé *(m)*

pièce de théâtre *(f)* Fr
De Stück *(n)*
En play
Es obra dramática *(f)*
It commedia *(f)*
Pt peça *(f)*

pied *(m) n* Fr
De Fuβ *(m)*
En foot
Es pie *(m)*
It piede *(m)*
Pt pé *(m)*

piede *(m) n* It
De Fuβ *(m)*
En foot

Es pie *(m)*
Fr pied *(m)*
Pt pé *(m)*

piede (di pagina) *(m)* It
De Unterschlag *(m)*
En tail (of page)
Es margen inferior *(m)*
Fr marge de pied *(f)*
Pt pé (de página) *(m)*

pie de imprenta *(m)* Es
De Impressum *(n)*
En imprint
Fr marque d'éditeur *(f)*
It impressa editoriale *(f)*
Pt nome do editor *(m)*

piedra *(f) n* Es
De Stein *(m)*
En stone (lithography)
Fr pierre calcaire *(f)*
It pietra litografica *(f)*
Pt càlcário da Bavária *(m)*

piegatrice meccanica *(f)* It
De Falzmaschine *(f)*
En folding machine
Es plegadora *(f)*
Fr plieuse *(f)*
Pt dobradora *(f)*

piegatura *(f) n* It
De Falzen *(n)*
En folding
Es plegado *(m)*
Fr pliure *(f)*
Pt dobrado *(m)*

pierre calcaire *(f)* Fr
De Stein *(m)*
En stone (lithography)
Es piedra *(f)*
It pietra litografica *(f)*
Pt càlcário da Bavária *(m)*

pietra litografica *(f)* It
De Stein *(m)*
En stone (lithography)
Es piedra *(f)*
Fr pierre calcaire *(f)*
Pt càlcário da Bavária *(m)*

pigment *n* En; Fr *(m)*
De Pigment *(n)*
Es pigmento *(m)*

It pigmento *(m)*
Pt pigmento *(m)*

Pigment *(n) n* De
En pigment
Es pigmento *(m)*
Fr pigment *(m)*
It pigmento *(m)*
Pt pigmento *(m)*

pigmento *(m) n* Es, It, Pt
De Pigment *(n)*
En pigment
Fr pigment *(m)*

piling *n* En
De Pelzen *(n)*
Es espesamiento *(m)*
Fr encrassement *(m)*
It ammassamento *(m)*
Pt espessamento de tinta *(m)*

pilon *(m) n* Fr
De Mahlmaschine *(f)*
En beating machine
Es batidora *(f)*
It raffinatrice *(f)*
Pt máquina de bater *(f)*

pince *(f) n* Fr
De Greifer *(m)*
En gripper
Es pinza *(f)*
It pinza *(f)*
Pt agarrador *(m)*

pinceau pneumatique *(m)* Fr
De Retuschierapparat *(m)*
En airbrush
Es pistola pulverizadora *(f)*
It polverizzatrice ad aria compressa *(f)*
Pt pistola pulverizadora *(f)*

pinholes *pl n* En
De Nadellöcher *(pl)*
Es burbujas *(f pl)*
Fr perforation des négatifs *(f)*
It mancanza di densità *(f)*
Pt furos *(m pl)*

pinza *(f) n* Es, It
De Greifer *(m)*
En gripper
Fr pince *(f)*
Pt agarrador *(m)*

piombo *(m) n* It
De Blei *(n)*
En lead (metal)
Es plomo *(m)*
Fr plomb *(m)*
Pt chumbo *(m)*

pistola pulverizadora *(f)* Es, Pt
De Retuschierapparat *(m)*
En airbrush
Fr pinceau pneumatique *(m)*
It polverizzatrice ad aria compressa *(f)*

placa *(f) n* Pt
De Druckplatte *(f)*
En plate (printing)
Es plancha *(f)*
Fr plaque *(f)*
It lastra *(f)*

placa de estereotipia *(f)* Pt
De Strichätzung *(f)*
En line block
Es fotograbado de línea *(m)*
Fr cliché au trait *(m)*
It cliché a tratto *(m)*

placa húmeda *(f)* Es
De feuchte Platte *(f)*
En wet plate
Fr plaque humide *(f)*
It lastra al collodio *(f)*
Pt chapa molhada *(f)*

placa impresora *(f)* Es
De Klischee *(n)*
En block
Fr cliché *(m)*
It cliché *(m)*
Pt cliché *(f)*

placa impresora de polimerización fotoquímica *(f)* Es
De Photopolymer-Druckplatte *(f)*
En photopolymer printing plate

Fr plaque
photopolymère (f)
It lastra da stampa ai
fotopolimeri (f)
Pt chapa de impressão
fotopolimérica (f)

placas flexíveis (f pl) Pt
De Wickelplatten (pl)
En wrap-around plates
pl n
Es planchas arrollables
(f pl)
Fr plaques circulaires (f
pl)
It lastre flessibili (f pl)

plana interior (f) Es
De innere Form (f)
En inner forme
Fr côté de deux (m)
It forma interna (f)
Pt forma interior (f)

plancha (f) n Es
De Druckplatte (f)
En plate (printing)
Fr plaque (f)
It lastra (f)
Pt placa (f)

plancha al hueco-offset
(f) Es
De Tiefdruck-Offsetplatte
(f)
En deep-etch litho plate
Fr offset en creux (m)
It lastra litografica a
incisione profonda (f)
Pt chapa litográfica de
gravação funda (f)

plancha negra (f) Es
De Schwarzplatte (f)
En black plate
Fr cliché en noir (m)
It lastra nera (f)
Pt chapa preta (f)

plancha offset a la
albúmina (f) Es
De Albuminplatte (f)
En albumen plate
Fr procédé à l'albumine
(m)
It lastra all'albumina (f)
Pt chapa de albumina (f)

planchas arrollables (f
pl) Es
De Wickelplatten (pl)

En wrap-around plates
pl n
Fr plaques circulaires (f
pl)
It lastre flessibili (f pl)
Pt placas flexíveis (f pl)

planche (f) n Fr
De Tafel (f)
En plate (picture)
Es lámina (f)
It tavola (f)
Pt gravura (f)

planches en couleurs (f
pl) Fr
Am color plates
De Farbtafeln (pl)
En colour plates
Es láminas en color (f pl)
It tavole a colori (f pl)
Pt páginas a cores (f pl)

plan de développement
(m) Fr
Am development
program
De Entwicklungs-
programm (n)
En development
programme
Es programa de
desarrollo (m)
It programma di
sviluppo (m)
Pt programa de
desenvolvimento (m)

planear vb Pt
De planen
En schedule
Es proyectar
Fr projeter
It progettare

planen vb De
En schedule
Es proyectar
Fr projeter
It progettare
Pt planear

planes pl n En
De Bestoßhobel (pl)
Es asentadores (m pl)
Fr rabots (m pl)
It pialle (f pl)
Pt niveladores (m pl)

plano (m) n Es, Pt
De Arbeitsplan (m)
En schedule
Fr prévisions (f pl)
It orario (m)

planographic printing
En
De Flachdruck (m)
Es impresión
planográfica (f)
Fr impression à plat (f)
It stampa comune (f)
Pt impressão
planográfica (f)

plaque (f) n Fr
De Druckplatte (f)
En plate (printing)
Es plancha (f)
It lastra (f)
Pt placa (f)

plaque humide (f) Fr
De feuchte Platte (f)
En wet plate
Es placa húmeda (f)
It lastra al collodio (f)
Pt chapa molhada (f)

plaque photopolymère
(f) Fr
De Photopolymer-
Druckplatte (f)
En photopolymer
printing plate
Es placa impresora de
polimerización
fotoquímica (f)
It lastra da stampa ai
fotopolimeri (f)
Pt chapa de impressão
fotopolimérica (f)

plaques circulaires (f pl)
Fr
De Wickelplatten (pl)
En wrap-around plates
pl n
Es planchas arrollables
(f pl)
It lastre flessibili (f pl)
Pt placas flexíveis (f pl)

plaquette (f) n Fr
De Heft (n)
En booklet
Es opúsculo (m)
It libretto (m)
Pt folheto (m)

plate (picture) n En
De Tafel (f)
Es lámina (f)
Fr planche (f)
It tavola (f)
Pt gravura (f)

plate (printing) n En
De Druckplatte (f)
Es plancha (f)
Fr plaque (f)
It lastra (f)
Pt placa (f)

plate-finished paper En
De bogenkalander-
bearbeitetes Papier
(n)
Es papel satinado a
plancha (m)
Fr papier laminé à la
plaque (m)
It carta rifinita (f)
Pt papel lustrado à
prancha (m)

platemaking n En
De Kopieren (n)
Es preparación de
planchas (f)
Fr clichage (m)
It preparazione delle
matrici (f)
Pt preparação de
estampas (f)

platen press En
De Tiegel (m)
Es minerva (f)
Fr imprimeuse (f)
It macchina da stampa
a platina (f)
Pt minerva (f)

platina (f) n Es
De Druckkarren (m)
En bed (printing
machine)
Fr marbre (m)
It piano (m)
Pt mesa (f)

platina ad approccio
diretto (f) It
De Parallel-
bewegungsstiegel (m)
En direct approach
platen
Es platina de
aproximación directa
(f)

Fr platine à approche
directe *(f)*
Pt platina de
aproximação directa
(f)

**platina de aproximação
directa** *(f)* Pt
De Parallel-
bewegungstiegel *(m)*
En direct approach
platen
Es platina de
aproximación directa
(f)
Fr platine à approche
directe *(f)*
It platina ad approccio
diretto *(f)*

**platina de aproximación
directa** *(f)* Es
De Parallel-
bewegungstiegel *(m)*
En direct approach
platen
Fr platine à approche
directe *(f)*
It platina ad approccio
diretto *(f)*
Pt platina de
aproximação directa
(f)

**platine à approche
directe** *(f)* Fr
De Parallel-
bewegungstiegel *(m)*
En direct approach
platen
Es platina de
aproximación directa
(f)
It platina ad approccio
diretto *(f)*
Pt platina de
aproximação directa
(f)

Platte *(f)* n De
En disk
Es disco *(m)*
Fr disque *(m)*
It disco *(m)*
Pt disco *(m)*

play n En
De Stück *(n)*
Es obra dramática *(f)*
Fr pièce de théâtre *(f)*
It commedia *(f)*
Pt peça *(f)*

plazo *(m)* n Es
De Stichtag *(m)*
En deadline
Fr limite *(f)*
It scadenza *(f)*
Pt prazo *(m)*

pleca *(f)* n Es
De Strich *(m)*
En rule
Fr règle *(f)*
It riga *(f)*
Pt linha recta *(f)*

pleca-cuadratín *(f)* n Es
De Geviertstrich *(m)*
En em rule
Fr tiret sur cadratin *(m)*
It lineato a quadratone
(m)
Pt filete de quadratim
(m)

**pleca de medio
cuadratín** *(f)* Es
De Halbgeviertstrich *(m)*
En en rule
Fr tiret sur
demi-cadratin *(m)*
It lineato a
demi-quadratone *(m)*
Pt filete de meio
quadratim *(m)*

plegado *(m)* n Es
De Falzen *(n)*
En folding
Fr pliure *(f)*
It piegatura *(f)*
Pt dobrado *(m)*

plegadora *(f)* n Es
De Falzmaschine *(f)*
En folding machine
Fr plieuse *(f)*
It piegatrice meccanica
(f)
Pt dobradora *(f)*

pliego *(m)* Es
De Druckbogen *(m)*
En section
Fr cahier *(m)*
It sezione *(f)*
Pt secção *(f)*

pliegos de prensa *(m pl)*
Es
De Pressebögen *(pl)*
En press sheets
Fr feuilles machine *(f pl)*

It fogli di stampa *(m pl)*
Pt folhas de imprensa *(f
pl)*

plieuse *(f)* n Fr
De Falzmaschine *(f)*
En folding machine
Es plegadora *(f)*
It piegatrice meccanica
(f)
Pt dobradora *(f)*

pliure *(f)* n Fr
De Falzen *(n)*
En folding
Es plegado *(m)*
It piegatura *(f)*
Pt dobrado *(m)*

plomb *(m)* n Fr
De Blei *(n)*
En lead (metal)
Es plomo *(m)*
It piombo *(m)*
Pt chumbo *(m)*

plomo *(m)* n Es
De Blei *(n)*
En lead (metal)
Fr plomb *(m)*
It piombo *(m)*
Pt chumbo *(m)*

plucking n En
De Rupfen *(n)*
Es picado *(m)*
Fr arrachage *(m)*
It strappatura *(f)*
Pt picado *(m)*

pocket dictionary En
De Taschenwörterbüch
(n)
Es diccionario de bolsillo
(m)
Fr dictionnaire de poche
(m)
It dizionario tascabile
(m)
Pt dicionário de bolso
(m)

poesia *(f)* n It, Pt
De Dichtung *(f)*
En poetry
Es poesía *(f)*
Fr poésie *(f)*

poesía *(f)* n Es
De Dichtung *(f)*
En poetry
Fr poésie *(f)*
It poesia *(f)*
Pt poesia *(f)*

poésie *(f)* n Fr
De Dichtung *(f)*
En poetry
Es poesía *(f)*
It poesia *(f)*
Pt poesia *(f)*

poet n En
De Dichter *(m)*
Es poeta *(m)*
Fr poète *(m)*
It poeta *(m)*
Pt poeta *(m)*

poeta *(m)* n Es, It, Pt
De Dichter *(m)*
En poet
Fr poète *(m)*

poète *(m)* n Fr
De Dichter *(m)*
En poet
Es poeta *(m)*
It poeta *(m)*
Pt poeta *(m)*

poetry n En
De Dichtung *(f)*
Es poesía *(f)*
Fr poésie *(f)*
It poesia *(f)*
Pt poesia *(f)*

poetry book En
De Gedichtband *(m)*
Es libro do poesías *(m)*
Fr livre de poésie *(m)*
It libro di poesia *(m)*
Pt livro de poesia *(m)*

poids de caractère *(m)*
Fr
De Schriftgewicht *(n)*
En type weight
Es peso del tipo *(m)*
It peso del carattere
(m)
Pt peso de tipo *(m)*

poinçon *(m)* n Fr
De Stempel *(m)*
En punch (for
typefounding)

Es punzón *(m)*
It punzone *(m)*
Pt punção *(m)*

point *n* En; Fr *(m)*
De Punkt *(m)*
Es punto *(m)*
It punto *(m)*
Pt ponto *(m)*

point de vente *(m)* Fr
De Verkaufsstelle *(f)*
En point of sale
Es punto de venta *(m)*
It punto di vendita *(m)*
Pt ponto de venda *(m)*

point d'exclamation *(m)*
Fr
De Ausrufungszeichen
(n)
En exclamation mark
Es signo de admiración
(m)
It punto esclamativo
(m)
Pt ponto de exclamação
(m)

point d'interrogation
(m) Fr
De Fragezeichen *(n)*
En question mark
Es signo de
interrogación *(m)*
It punto di domanda
(m)
Pt ponto de
interrogação *(m)*

point final *(m)* Fr
Am period
De Punkt *(m)*
En full stop
Es punto final *(m)*
It punto fermo *(m)*
Pt ponto final *(m)*

point hollandais *(m)* Fr
De Holländern *(n)*
En oversewing
Es cosido por el plano
(m)
It cucitura a punto
saltato *(f)*
Pt coser por fora *(m)*

point of sale En
De Verkaufsstelle *(f)*
Es punto de venta *(m)*
Fr point de vente *(m)*

It punto di vendita *(m)*
Pt ponto de venda *(m)*

point-of-sale material
En
De Verkaufstellen-
Material *(n)*
Es material para punto
de venta *(m)*
Fr matériel de PLV *(m)*
It materiale per punto
di vendita *(m)*
Pt material de ponto de
venda *(m)*

points de conduite *(m*
pl) Fr
De Ausführpunkte *(pl)*
En leaders *pl n*
Es filetes puntillados *(m*
pl)
It puntini *(m pl)*
Pt pontos de reticência
(m pl)

point size En
De Punktgröβe *(f)*
Es cuerpo del tipo *(m)*
Fr corps *(m)*
It corpo *(m)*
Pt tamanho de ponto
(m)

point-virgule *(m)* *n* Fr
De Semikolon *(n)*
En semicolon
Es punto y coma *(m)*
It punto e virgola *(m)*
Pt ponto e vírgula *(m)*

policial *(m)* *n* Pt
De Reiβer *(m)*
En thriller
Es novela de misterio *(f)*
Fr roman à sensation
(m)
It giallo *(m)*

Polieren *(n)* *n* De
En burnishing
Es fileteado *(m)*
Fr brunissage *(m)*
It brunitura *(f)*
Pt lustro *(m)*

polpa *(f)* *n* Pt
De Zellstoff *(m)*
En pulp
Es pasta *(f)*
Fr pâte *(f)*
It pasta *(f)*

polpa de madeira *(f)* Pt
De Holzstoff *(m)*
En wood pulp
Es pasta de madera *(f)*
Fr pâte de bois *(f)*
It pasta di legno *(f)*

polpa de madeira
mecânica *(f)* Pt
De Holzschliff *(m)*
En mechanical wood
pulp
Es pasta mecánica *(f)*
Fr pâte mécanique *(f)*
It pasta di legno
ottenuta
meccanicamente *(f)*

polpa de madeira
sulfatada *(f)* Pt
Am sulfate wood pulp
De Sulfat-Holzstoff *(m)*
En sulphate wood pulp
Es pasta de madera al
sulfato *(f)*
Fr pâte de bois au
sulfate *(f)*
It pasta di legno al
solfato *(f)*

polpa de papel *(f)* Pt
De Papiermasse *(f)*
En stuff
Es pasta de papel *(f)*
Fr pâte à papier *(f)*
It pasta di carta *(f)*

polpa sem madeira *(f)* Pt
De holzfreier Papierstoff
(m)
En wood-free pulp
Es pasta sin madera *(f)*
Fr pâte sans bois *(f)*
It pasta senza legno *(f)*

polverizzatrice ad aria
compressa *(f)* It
De Retuschierapparat
(m)
En airbrush
Es pistola pulverizadora
(f)
Fr pinceau
pneumatique *(m)*
Pt pistola pulverizadora
(f)

polychromie *(f)* *n* Fr
Am process colors
De Verfahrensfarben *(pl)*
En process colours

Es colores para
policromía *(m pl)*
It colori per policromia
(m pl)
Pt cores para policromia
(f pl)

ponctuation *(f)* *n* Fr
De Zeichensetzung *(f)*
En punctuation
Es puntuación *(f)*
It punteggiatura *(f)*
Pt pontuação *(f)*

ponctuer *vb* Fr
De Zeichen setzen
En punctuate
Es puntuar
It punteggiare
Pt pontuar

ponepliegos de avance
continuo *(m)* Es
De Schuppenanleger *(m)*
En stream feeder
Fr margeur à nappe *(m)*
It alimentatore di fogli a
avanzamento
continuo *(m)*
Pt alimentador de folhas
de avanço contínuo
(m)

ponepliegos de soplo
(m) Es
De Sauganleger *(m)*
En suction feeder
Fr margeur
automatique à
aspiration *(m)*
It alimentatore ad
aspirazione *(m)*
Pt alimentador por
sucção *(m)*

poner a escala Es
De Maβstab festlegen
En scale
Fr dessiner à l'échelle
It graduare
Pt pôr à escala

ponteado *(m)* *n* Pt
De Granierung *(f)*
En stippling
Es punteado *(m)*
Fr grisé *(m)*
It battitura *(f)*

ponto *(m)* *n* Pt
De Punkt *(m)*
En point
Es punto *(m)*
Fr point *(m)*
It punto *(m)*

ponto decimal *(m)* Pt
De Dezimalkomma *(n)*
En decimal point
Es punto decimal *(m)*
Fr virgule *(f)*
It virgola decimale *(f)*

ponto de equilíbrio *(m)*
Pt
De Nutzschwelle *(f)*
En break-even point
Es punto de equilibrio
    (m)
Fr seuil de rentabilité
    (m)
It punto di pareggio *(m)*

ponto de exclamação
(m) Pt
De Ausrufungszeichen
    (n)
En exclamation mark
Es signo de admiración
    (m)
Fr point d'exclamation
    (m)
It punto esclamativo
    (m)

ponto de interrogação
(m) Pt
De Fragezeichen *(n)*
En question mark
Es signo de
    interrogación *(m)*
Fr point d'interrogation
    (m)
It punto di domanda
    (m)

ponto de venda *(m)* Pt
De Verkaufsstelle *(f)*
En point of sale
Es punto de venta *(m)*
Fr point de vente *(m)*
It punto di vendita *(m)*

ponto e vírgula *(m)* Pt
De Semikolon *(n)*
En semicolon
Es punto y coma *(m)*
Fr point-virgule *(m)*
It punto e virgola *(m)*

ponto final *(m)* Pt
Am period
De Punkt *(m)*
En full stop
Es punto final *(m)*
Fr point final *(m)*
It punto fermo *(m)*

pontos de reticência *(m*
pl) Pt
De Ausführpunkte *(pl)*
En leaders *pl n*
Es filetes puntillados *(m*
    pl)
Fr points de conduite
    (m pl)
It puntini *(m pl)*

pontuação *(f)* *n* Pt
De Zeichensetzung *(f)*
En punctuation
Es puntuación *(f)*
Fr ponctuation *(f)*
It punteggiatura *(f)*

pontuar *vb* Pt
De Zeichen setzen
En punctuate
Es puntuar
Fr ponctuer
It punteggiare

popolarizzare *vb* It
De popularisieren
En popularize
Es popularizar
Fr vulgariser
Pt vulgarizar

popular fiction En
De volkstümliche
    Romanliteratur *(f)*
Es literatura popular *(f)*
Fr romans populaires
    (m pl)
It narrativa popolare *(f)*
Pt ficção popular *(f)*

popularisieren *vb* De
En popularize
Es popularizar
Fr vulgariser
It popolarizzare
Pt vulgarizar

Popularisierer *(m)* *n* De
En popularizer
Es popularizador *(m)*
Fr diffuseur *(m)*
It divulgatore *(m)*
Pt vulgarizador *(m)*

popularizador *(m)* *n* Es
De Popularisierer *(m)*
En popularizer
Fr diffuseur *(m)*
It divulgatore *(m)*
Pt vulgarizador *(m)*

popularizar *vb* Es
De popularisieren
En popularize
Fr vulgariser
It popolarizzare
Pt vulgarizar

popularize *vb* En
De popularisieren
Es popularizar
Fr vulgariser
It popolarizzare
Pt vulgarizar

popularizer *n* En
De Popularisierer *(m)*
Es popularizador *(m)*
Fr diffuseur *(m)*
It divulgatore *(m)*
Pt vulgarizador *(m)*

popular medical books
En
De volkstümliche
    Medizinbücher *(pl)*
Es libros médicos
    populares *(m pl)*
Fr livres de vulgarisation
    médicale *(m pl)*
It libri divulgativi di
    medicina *(m pl)*
Pt livros de medicina
    popular *(m pl)*

popular press En
De volkstümliche Presse
    (f)
Es prensa popular *(f)*
Fr presse populaire *(f)*
It stampa popolare *(f)*
Pt prensa popular *(f)*

popular scientific books
En
De volkstümliche
    wissenschaftliche
    Bücher *(pl)*
Es libros científicos
    populares *(m pl)*
Fr livres de vulgarisation
    scientifique *(m pl)*
It libri scientifici
    divulgativi *(m pl)*
Pt livros científicos
    populares *(m pl)*

pôr à escala Pt
De Maßstab festlegen
En scale
Es poner a escala
Fr dessiner à l'échelle
It graduare

porre in disparte It
De aufschieben
En shelve
Es postergar
    indefinidamente
Fr ajourner
Pt arquivar

portada *(f)* *n* Es
De Titelseite *(f)*
En title page
Fr page de titre *(m)*
It frontespizio *(m)*
Pt página de título *(f)*

portrait *n* En; Fr *(m)*
De Portrait *(n)*
Es retrato *(m)*
It ritratto *(m)*
Pt retrato *(m)*

Portrait *(n)* *n* De
En portrait
Es retrato *(m)*
Fr portrait *(m)*
It ritratto *(m)*
Pt retrato *(m)*

portrait page En
De Hochformat *(n)*
Es página vertical *(f)*
Fr format en hauteur
    (m)
It pagina verticale *(f)*
Pt página de retrato *(f)*

pôr um traço de união Pt
De trennen
En hyphenate
Es separar con guión
Fr mettre un trait
    d'union
It legare con trattino

posa *(f)* *n* It
De Belichtung *(f)*
En exposure
    (photographic)
Es exposición *(f)*
Fr pose *(f)*
Pt exposição *(f)*

pose (f) n Fr
De Belichtung (f)
En exposure
   (photographic)
Es exposición (f)
It posa (f)
Pt exposição (f)

positif (m) n Fr
De Positiv (n)
En positive
Es positivo (m)
It positivo (m)
Pt positivo (m)

Positiv (n) n De
En positive
Es positivo (m)
Fr positif (m)
It positivo (m)
Pt positivo (m)

positive n En
De Positiv (n)
Es positivo (m)
Fr positif (m)
It positivo (m)
Pt positivo (m)

positive film En
De Positivfilm (m)
Es película para
   positivos (f)
Fr film positif (m)
It pellicola positiva (f)
Pt película positiva (f)

Positivfilm (m) n De
En positive film
Es película para
   positivos (f)
Fr film positif (m)
It pellicola positiva (f)
Pt película positiva (f)

positivo (m) n Es, It, Pt
De Positiv (n)
En positive
Fr positif (m)

Post (f) n De
En mail
Es correo (m)
Fr courrier (m)
It posta (f)
Pt correio (m)

posta (f) n It
De Post (f)
En mail

Es correo (m)
Fr courrier (m)
Pt correio (m)

poster n En
De Poster (n)
Es cartel (m)
Fr affiche (f)
It manifesto (m)
Pt cartaz (m)

Poster (n) n De
En poster
Es cartel (m)
Fr affiche (f)
It manifesto (m)
Pt cartaz (m)

**postergar
   indefinidamente** Es
De aufschieben
En shelve
Fr ajourner
It porre in disparte
Pt arquivar

Postwurfsendung (f) n
   De
En direct-mail shot
Es envío por correo
   directo; oferta por
   correo (m f)
Fr mailing; offre
   promotionnelle (m f)
It invio diretto per
   posta; offerta postale
   (m f)
Pt publicidade por
   correio (f)

Postwurfwerbung (f) n
   De
En direct-mail selling
Es venta directa por
   correo (f)
Fr vente directe par
   correspondance (f)
It vendite per
   corrispondenza (f pl)
Pt venda por correio (f)

poudrage (m) n Fr
De Kalkschleier (m)
En chalking
Es desintegración en
   polvo (f)
It sfarinamento (m)
Pt descascamento (m)

powderless etching En
De Einstufenätzverfahren
   (n)
Es grabado rápido (m)
Fr gravure sans poudre
   (f)
It incisione senza
   polvere (f)
Pt gravura sem pó (f)

practical books En
De praktische Bücher
   (pl)
Es libros prácticos (m pl)
Fr ouvrages pratiques
   (m pl)
It libri pratici (m pl)
Pt livros prácticos (m pl)

Prägedruck (m) n De
En embossing
Es estampado en relieve
   (m)
Fr gaufrage (m)
It goffratura (f)
Pt gravação em relevo
   (f)

Prägedruckfarbe (f) n De
En embossing ink
Es tinta de estampación
   (f)
Fr encre à gaufrer (f)
It inchiostro per
   goffratura (m)
Pt tinta de estampagem
   (f)

Prägen (n) n De
En stamping
Es estampación (f)
Fr timbrage (m)
It stampaggio (m)
Pt estampagem (f)

Prägestempel (m) n De
En die stamping
Es estampación en
   relieve (f)
Fr repoussage (m)
It stampa
   incavorilievografica
   (f)
Pt estampagem em
   relevo (f)

Prägestock (m) n De
En die
Es troquel (m)
Fr étampe (f)
It stampo (m)
Pt matriz (f)

praktische Bücher (pl)
   De
En practical books
Es libros prácticos (m pl)
Fr ouvrages pratiques
   (m pl)
It libri pratici (m pl)
Pt livros prácticos (m pl)

Prämie (f) n De
En premium
Es prima (f)
Fr prime (f)
It offerta a premio (f)
Pt oferta (f)

prancha de arte (f) Pt
De Kunstdruckkarton (m)
En art board
Es tablero de dibujo (m)
Fr carte couchée (f)
It cartone da disegno
   (m)

pranzo di lavoro (m) It
De geschäftliches
   Mittagessen (n)
En working lunch
Es comida de trabajo (f)
Fr déjeuner de travail
   (m)
Pt almoço de trabalho
   (m)

Präsident (m) n De
En president
Es presidente (m)
Fr président (m)
It presidente (m)
Pt presidente (m)

prazo (m) n Pt
De Stichtag (m)
En deadline
Es plazo (m)
Fr limite (f)
It scadenza (f)

preavviamento (m) n It
De Vorzurichtung (f)
En pre-makeready
Es arreglo preliminar (m)
Fr pré-mise en train (f)
Pt arranjo preliminar (m)

precio (m) n Es
De Preis (m)
En price
Fr prix (m)
It prezzo (m)
Pt preço (m)

precio de más ejemplares *(m)* Es
De Fortdruck-Preis *(m)*
En run-on price
Fr coût du tirage supplémentaire *(m)*
It prezzo di super-tiratura *(m)*
Pt preço de exemplares a mais *(m)*

précis *vb* En
De zusammenfassen
Es resumir
Fr résumer
It riassumere
Pt resumir

précis *n* En; Fr *(m)*
De Übersicht *(f)*
Es resumen *(m)*
It riassunto *(m)*
Pt resumo *(m)*

preço *(m) n* Pt
De Preis *(m)*
En price
Es precio *(m)*
Fr prix *(m)*
It prezzo *(m)*

preço de exemplares a mais *(m)* Pt
De Fortdruck-Preis *(m)*
En run-on price
Es precio de más ejemplares *(m)*
Fr coût du tirage supplémentaire *(m)*
It prezzo di super-tiratura *(m)*

preface *vb* En
De einleiten
Es prologar
Fr préfacer
It fare una prefazione
Pt redigir um prefácio

preface *n* En
De Vorrede *(f)*
Es prefacio *(m)*
Fr préface *(f)*
It prefazione *(f)*
Pt prefácio *(m)*

préface *(f) n* Fr
De Vorrede *(f)*
En preface
Es prefacio *(m)*

It prefazione *(f)*
Pt prefácio *(m)*

préfacer *vb* Fr
De einleiten
En preface
Es prologar
It fare una prefazione
Pt redigir um prefácio

prefacio *(m) n* Es
De Vorrede *(f)*
En preface
Fr préface *(f)*
It prefazione *(f)*
Pt prefácio *(m)*

prefácio *(m) n* Pt
De Vorrede *(f)*
En preface
Es prefacio *(m)*
Fr préface *(f)*
It prefazione *(f)*

prefazione *(f) n* It
De Vorrede *(f)*
En preface
Es prefacio *(m)*
Fr préface *(f)*
Pt prefácio *(m)*

Preis *(m) n* De
En price
Es precio *(m)*
Fr prix *(m)*
It prezzo *(m)*
Pt preço *(m)*

Preis festsetzen De
En price
Es valorar
Fr fixer un prix
It prezzare
Pt marcar o preço

Preisliste *(f) n* De
En price list
Es lista de precios *(f)*
Fr prix-courant *(m)*
It listino prezzi *(m)*
Pt lista de preços *(f)*

preliminari del libro *(m pl)* It
De Vortext *(m)*
En front matter
Es principios del libro *(m pl)*

It prefazione *(f)*
Pt prefácio *(m)*

Fr feuilles liminaires *(f pl)*
Pt princípio do livro *(m)*

pre-makeready *n* En
De Vorzurichtung *(f)*
Es arreglo preliminar *(m)*
Fr pré-mise en train *(f)*
It preavviamento *(m)*
Pt arranjo preliminar *(m)*

première épreuve *(f)* Fr
De erster Korrekturabzug *(m)*
En first proof
Es primera prueba *(f)*
It prima bozza *(f)*
Pt primeira prova *(f)*

pré-mise en train *(f)* Fr
De Vorzurichtung *(f)*
En pre-makeready
Es arreglo preliminar *(m)*
It preavviamento *(m)*
Pt arranjo preliminar *(m)*

premium *n* En
De Prämie *(f)*
Es prima *(f)*
Fr prime *(f)*
It offerta a premio *(f)*
Pt oferta *(f)*

prensa *(f) n* Pt
De Druckpresse *(f)*
En press (printing)
Es máquina de imprimir *(f)*
Fr presse d'imprimerie *(f)*
It macchina da stampa *(f)*

prensa *(f) n* Es
De Presse *(f)*
En press (journalism)
Fr presse *(f)*
It stampa *(f)*
Pt imprensa *(f)*

prensa a duas cores *(f)* Pt
Am two-color press
De Zweifarbenpresse *(f)*
En two-colour press
Es prensa bicolor *(f)*
Fr presse à bichromie *(f)*
It macchina da stampa a due colori *(f)*

prensa a duas rotações *(f)* Pt
De Zweitourenmaschine *(f)*
En two-revolution press
Es prensa de doble revolución *(f)*
Fr presse à double impression *(f)*
It macchina da stampa a due giri *(f)*

prensa al vacío *(f)* Es
De Vakuumrahmen *(m)*
En vacuum frame
Fr chassis pneumatique *(m)*
It telaio a vuoto *(m)*
Pt caixilho de vácuo *(m)*

prensa bicolor *(f)* Es
Am two-color press
De Zweifarbenpresse *(f)*
En two-colour press
Fr presse à bichromie *(f)*
It macchina da stampa a due colori *(f)*
Pt prensa a duas cores *(f)*

prensa de cilindro de parada *(f)* Es
De Haltzylinderpresse *(f)*
En stop-cylinder press
Fr machine à arrêt du cylindre *(f)*
It rotativa con arresto *(f)*
Pt prensa de cilindro de paragem *(f)*

prensa de cilindro de paragem *(f)* Pt
De Haltzylinderpresse *(f)*
En stop-cylinder press
Es prensa de cilindro de parada *(f)*
Fr machine à arrêt du cylindre *(f)*
It rotativa con arresto *(f)*

prensa de doble revolución *(f)* Es
De Zweitourenmaschine *(f)*
En two-revolution press
Fr presse à double impression *(f)*
It macchina da stampa a due giri *(f)*

Pt prensa a duas
rotações (f)

prensa de galé (f) Pt
De Spaltenabziehpresse
(f)
En galley press
Es prensa para prueba
de galeradas (f)
Fr presse à épreuves (f)
It stampa di vantaggio
(f)

prensa de retiración (f)
Es
De Schön- und
Widerdruckmaschine
(f)
En perfector
Fr presse à retiration (f)
It stampatrice in volta
(f)
Pt máquina de
impressão
simultânea de ambos
lados (f)

prensado (m) n Es
De Abpressen (n)
En pressing
Fr pressage (m)
It stiratura (f)
Pt compressão (f)

**prensadora-embaladora
de pliegos** (f) Es
De Packmaschine (f)
En bundling machine
Fr machine à emballer
(f)
It macchina per rotoli
(f)
Pt máquina de prensar e
formar fascículos (f)

prensa manual (f) Es, Pt
De Handpresse (f)
En hand press
Fr presse à bras (f)
It torchio a mano (m)

prensa offset (f) Pt
De Offset-Buchdruck (m)
En offset letterpress
Es tipografía offset (f)
Fr presse offset (f)
It stampa tipografica
offset (f)

**prensa para prueba de
galeradas** (f) Es
De Spaltenabziehpresse
(f)
En galley press
Fr presse à épreuves (f)
It stampa di vantaggio
(f)
Pt prensa de galé (f)

prensa para tirar provas
(f) Pt
De Abziehapparat (m)
En proofing press
Es prensa sacapruebas
(f)
Fr presse pour tirer les
épreuves (f)
It tirabozze (m)

prensa planocilíndrica
(f) Es
De Schnellpresse (f)
En cylinder machine
Fr machine à forme
ronde (f)
It rotativa (f)
Pt máquina de rolos (f)

prensa popular (f) Es, Pt
De volkstümliche Presse
(f)
En popular press
Fr presse populaire (f)
It stampa popolare (f)

prensa rotativa (f) Es, Pt
De Rotationspresse (f)
En rotary press
Fr rotative (f)
It macchina da stampa
rotativa (f)

prensa sacapruebas (f)
Es
De Abziehapparat (m)
En proofing press
Fr presse pour tirer les
épreuves (f)
It tirabozze (m)
Pt prensa para tirar
provas (f)

prensa universitaria (f)
Es
De Universitäts-
Druckerei (f)
En university press
Fr presse universitaire
(f)
It stampa universitaria
(f)

Pt imprensa
universitária (f)

prensista (m) n Es
De Maschinenmeister
(m)
En machine minder
Fr conducteur de
machine (m)
It macchinista (m)
Pt tratador da máquina
(m)

**preparação de
estampas** (f) Pt
De Kopieren (n)
En platemaking
Es preparación de
planchas (f)
Fr clichage (m)
It preparazione delle
matrici (f)

**preparación de
planchas** (f) Es
De Kopieren (n)
En platemaking
Fr clichage (m)
It preparazione delle
matrici (f)
Pt preparação de
estampas (f)

preparar (tipo) vb Pt
De gestalten
En lay out
Es disponer (tipo)
Fr disposer (caractères)
It disporre (caratteri)

préparation d'un texte
(f) Fr
De Manuskriptrevision (f)
En copy-editing
Es corrección de
originales (f)
It correzione di originali
(f)
Pt revisão do original (f)

**preparazione delle
matrici** (f) It
De Kopieren (n)
En platemaking
Es preparación de
planchas (f)
Fr clichage (m)
Pt preparação de
estampas (f)

presa (f) n It
De Griffkante (f)
En grip
Es margen de agarre (m)
Fr prise de pinces (f)
Pt margem de agarre (f)

pre-school books En
De Vorschulbücher (pl)
Es libros preescolares
(m)
Fr livres préscolaires (m
pl)
It libri prescolastici (m)
Pt livros pré-escolares
(m)

president n En
De Präsident (m)
Es presidente (m)
Fr président (m)
It presidente (m)
Pt presidente (m)

président (m) n Fr
De Präsident;
Vorsitzender (m)
En chairman; president
Es presidente (m)
It presidente (m)
Pt presidente (m)

presidente (m) n Es, It, Pt
De Präsident;
Vorsitzender (m)
En chairman; president
Fr président (m)

press (journalism) n En
De Presse (f)
Es prensa (f)
Fr presse (f)
It stampa (f)
Pt imprensa (f)

press (printing) n En
De Druckpresse (f)
Es máquina de imprimir
(f)
Fr presse d'imprimerie
(f)
It macchina da stampa
(f)
Pt prensa (f)

pressage (m) n Fr
De Abpressen (n)
En pressing
Es prensado (m)
It stiratura (f)
Pt compressão (f)

press conference En
De Pressekonferenz (f)
Es conferencia de
prensa (f)
Fr conférence de presse
(f)
It conferenza stampa (f)
Pt conferência de
imprensa (f)

press cutting En
De Presseausschnitt (m)
Es recorte de prensa (m)
Fr coupure de journal (f)
It ritaglio di giornale
(m)
Pt recorte de imprensa
(f)

presse (f) n Fr
De Presse (f)
En press (journalism)
Es prensa (f)
It stampa (f)
Pt imprensa (f)

Presse (f) n De
En press (journalism)
Es prensa (f)
Fr presse (f)
It stampa (f)
Pt imprensa (f)

presse à bichromie (f) Fr
Am two-color press
De Zweifarbenpresse (f)
En two-colour press
Es prensa bicolor (f)
It macchina da stampa
a due colori (f)
Pt prensa a duas cores
(f)

presse à bras (f) Fr
De Handpresse (f)
En hand press
Es prensa manual (f)
It torchio a mano (m)
Pt prensa manual (f)

**presse à double
impression** (f) Fr
De Zweitourenmaschine
(f)
En two-revolution press
Es prensa de doble
revolución (f)
It macchina da stampa
a due giri (f)
Pt prensa a duas
rotações (f)

presse à épreuves (f) Fr
De Spaltenabziehpresse
(f)
En galley press
Es prensa para prueba
de galeradas (f)
It stampa di vantaggio
(f)
Pt prensa de galé (f)

presse à retiration (f) Fr
De Schön- und
Widerdruckmaschine
(f)
En perfector
Es prensa de retiración
(f)
It stampatrice in volta
(f)
Pt máquina de
impressão
simultânea de ambos
lados (f)

Presseausschnitt (m) n
De
En press cutting
Es recorte de prensa (m)
Fr coupure de journal (f)
It ritaglio di giornale
(m)
Pt recorte de imprensa
(f)

Pressebögen (pl) De
En press sheets
Es pliegos de prensa (m
pl)
Fr feuilles machine (f pl)
It fogli di stampa (m pl)
Pt folhas de imprensa (f
pl)

presse d'imprimerie (f)
Fr
De Druckpresse (f)
En press (printing)
Es máquina de imprimir
(f)
It macchina da stampa
(f)
Pt prensa (f)

Pressekonferenz (f) n De
En press conference
Es conferencia de
prensa (f)
Fr conférence de presse
(f)
It conferenza stampa (f)
Pt conferência de
imprensa (f)

presse offset (f) Fr
De Offset-Buchdruck (m)
En offset letterpress
Es tipografía offset (f)
It stampa tipografica
offset (f)
Pt prensa offset (f)

presse populaire (f) Fr
De volkstümliche Presse
(f)
En popular press
Es prensa popular (f)
It stampa popolare (f)
Pt prensa popular (f)

**presse pour tirer les
épreuves** (f) Fr
De Abziehapparat (m)
En proofing press
Es prensa sacapruebas
(f)
It tirabozze (m)
Pt prensa para tirar
provas (f)

Pressesaal (m) n De
En press room
Es sala de máquinas (f)
Fr atelier d'imprimerie
(m)
It sala stampa (f)
Pt sala de imprensa (f)

presse universitaire (f)
Fr
De Universitäts-
Druckerei (f)
En university press
Es prensa universitaria
(f)
It stampa universitaria
(f)
Pt imprensa
universitária (f)

Presseveröffentlichung
(f) n De
En press release
Es boletín informativo
(m)
Fr communiqué de
presse (m)
It comunicato stampa
(m)
Pt comunicado de
imprensa (f)

pressing n En
De Abpressen (n)
Es prensado (m)
Fr pressage (m)

It stiratura (f)
Pt compressão (f)

press proof En
De letzte Korrektur (f)
Es prueba de prensa (f)
Fr bon à tirer (m)
It bozza di stampa (f)
Pt prova de imprensa (f)

press release En
De Presseveröffent-
lichung (f)
Es boletín informativo
(m)
Fr communiqué de
presse (m)
It comunicato stampa
(m)
Pt comunicado de
imprensa (f)

press room En
De Pressesaal (m)
Es sala de máquinas (f)
Fr atelier d'imprimerie
(m)
It sala stampa (f)
Pt sala de imprensa (f)

press sheets En
De Pressebögen (pl)
Es pliegos de prensa (m
pl)
Fr feuilles machine (f pl)
It fogli di stampa (m pl)
Pt folhas de imprensa (f
pl)

prévisions (f pl) n Fr
De Arbeitsplan (m)
En schedule
Es plano (m)
It orario (m)
Pt plano (m)

prezzare vb It
De Preis festsetzen
En price
Es valorar
Fr fixer un prix
Pt marcar o preço

prezzatura (f) n It
De Hinaufsetzung (f)
En mark-up (of prices)
Es aumento (m)
Fr augmentation (f)
Pt aumento (m)

prezzo *(m) n* It
De Preis *(m)*
En price
Es precio *(m)*
Fr prix *(m)*
Pt preço *(m)*

prezzo di super-tiratura
(m) It
De Fortdruck-Preis *(m)*
En run-on price
Es precio de más
ejemplares *(m)*
Fr coût du tirage
supplémentaire *(m)*
Pt preço de exemplares
a mais *(m)*

price *vb* En
De Preis festsetzen
Es valorar
Fr fixer un prix
It prezzare
Pt marcar o preço

price *n* En
De Preis *(m)*
Es precio *(m)*
Fr prix *(m)*
It prezzo *(m)*
Pt preço *(m)*

price list En
De Preisliste *(f)*
Es lista de precios *(f)*
Fr prix-courant *(m)*
It listino prezzi *(m)*
Pt lista de preços *(f)*

prima *(f) n* Es
De Prämie *(f)*
En premium
Fr prime *(f)*
It offerta a premio *(f)*
Pt oferta *(f)*

prima bozza *(f)* It
De erster Korrekturabzug
(m)
En first proof
Es primera prueba *(f)*
Fr première épreuve *(f)*
Pt primeira prova *(f)*

prima edizione *(f)* It
De erste Auflage *(f)*
En first edition
Es primera edición *(f)*
Fr édition originale *(f)*
Pt primeira edição *(f)*

prime *(f) n* Fr
De Prämie *(f)*
En premium
Es prima *(f)*
It offerta a premio *(f)*
Pt oferta *(f)*

primeira edição *(f)* Pt
De erste Auflage *(f)*
En first edition
Es primera edición *(f)*
Fr édition originale *(f)*
It prima edizione *(f)*

primeira prova *(f)* Pt
De erster Korrekturabzug
(m)
En first proof
Es primera prueba *(f)*
Fr première épreuve *(f)*
It prima bozza *(f)*

primera edición *(f)* Es
De erste Auflage *(t)*
En first edition
Fr édition originale *(f)*
It prima edizione *(f)*
Pt primeira edição *(f)*

primera prueba *(f)* Es
De erster Korrekturabzug
(m)
En first proof
Fr première épreuve *(f)*
It prima bozza *(f)*
Pt primeira prova *(f)*

princípio do livro *(m)* Pt
De Vortext *(m)*
En front matter
Es principios del libro *(m*
pl)
Fr feuilles liminaires *(f*
pl)
It preliminari del libro
(m pl)

principios del libro *(m*
pl) Es
De Vortext *(m)*
En front matter
Fr feuilles liminaires *(f*
pl)
It preliminari del libro
(m pl)
Pt princípio do livro *(m)*

print *vb* En
De drucken
Es imprimir
Fr imprimer

It stampare
(stampatura)
Pt imprimir

print *n* En
De Druck *(m)*
Es impresión *(f)*
Fr imprimé *(m)*
It impressione *(f)*
Pt estampa *(f)*

printer *n* En
De Drucker *(m)*
Es impresor *(m)*
Fr imprimeur *(m)*
It stampatore *(m)*
Pt tipógrafo *(m)*

printer's error En
De Druckfehler *(m)*
Es errata de imprenta *(f)*
Fr faute d'impression *(f)*
It errore dello
stampatore *(m)*
Pt erro de impressão
(m)

printer's ornaments En
De Typenornamente *(pl)*
Es adornos de imprenta
(m pl)
Fr vignette typo *(f)*
It ornamenti dello
stampatore *(m pl)*
Pt ornamentações de
impressão *(f pl)*

printer's reader En
De Druckerei-
Korrekturleser *(m)*
Es corrector de
imprenta *(m)*
Fr corrigeur *(m)*
It correttore di bozze da
stampa *(m)*
Pt leitor de tipografia
(m)

printing *n* En
De Druckkunst *(f)*
Es imprenta (arte) *(f)*
Fr imprimerie (art) *(f)*
It stampatura *(f)*
Pt impressão *(f)*

printing house En
De Druckerei *(f)*
Es imprenta (casa) *(f)*
Fr imprimerie (maison)
(f)

It stabilimento
tipografico *(m)*
Pt casa tipográfica *(f)*

printing machine En
De Druckmaschine *(f)*
Es máquina de imprimir
(f)
Fr machine à imprimer
(f)
It stampatrice *(f)*
Pt máquina de imprimir
(f)

print out En
De ausdrucken
Es imprimir (por
ordenador)
Fr sortir
It stampare (per
elaboratore)
Pt imprimir em positivo
directo

printout *n* En; It *(m)*
De Ausdruck *(m)*
Es vaciado a la
impresora *(m)*
Fr sortie d'imprimante
(f)
Pt impressão em
positivo directo *(f)*

prise de pinces *(f)* Fr
De Griffkante *(f)*
En grip
Es margen de agarre *(m)*
It presa *(f)*
Pt margem de agarre *(f)*

privo di acidi It
De säurefrei
En acid-free
Es exento de ácido
Fr sans acide
Pt isento de ácido

prix *(m) n* Fr
De Preis *(m)*
En price
Es precio *(m)*
It prezzo *(m)*
Pt preço *(m)*

prix coté *(m)* Fr
De Angebot *(n)*
En quotation (estimate)
Es cotización *(f)*
It quotazione *(f)*
Pt cotação *(f)*

prix-courant *(m) n* Fr
De Preisliste *(f)*
En price list
Es lista de precios *(f)*
It listino prezzi *(m)*
Pt lista de preços *(f)*

procédé *(m) n* Fr
De Verfahren *(n)*
En process
Es procedimiento *(m)*
It procedimento *(m)*
Pt processo *(m)*

procédé à l'albumine
(m) Fr
De Albuminplatte *(f)*
En albumen plate
Es plancha offset a la
albúmina *(f)*
It lastra all'albumina *(f)*
Pt chapa de albumina *(f)*

procédé autographique
(m) Fr
De autographischer
Transferdruck *(m)*
En autographic transfer
Es transferencia
autográfica *(f)*
It trasferimento
autografico *(m)*
Pt transferência
autográfica *(f)*

procédé direct *(m)* Fr
De Direktverfahren *(n)*
En direct process
Es reproducción directa
(f)
It procedimento diretto
(m)
Pt processo directo *(m)*

procédé indirect *(m)* Fr
De indirektes Verfahren
(n)
En indirect process
Es tricromía de tramado
indirecto *(f)*
It procedimento
indiretto *(m)*
Pt processo indirecto
(m)

procedimento *(m) n* It
De Verfahren *(n)*
En process
Es procedimiento *(m)*
Fr procédé *(m)*
Pt processo *(m)*

procedimento diretto
(m) It
De Direktverfahren *(n)*
En direct process
Es reproducción directa
(f)
Fr procédé direct *(m)*
Pt processo directo *(m)*

procedimento indiretto
(m) It
De indirektes Verfahren
(n)
En indirect process
Es tricromía de tramado
indirecto *(f)*
Fr procédé indirect *(m)*
Pt processo indirecto
(m)

procedimiento *(m) n* Es
De Verfahren *(n)*
En process
Fr procédé *(m)*
It procedimento *(m)*
Pt processo *(m)*

procesar *vb* Es
De verarbeiten
En process
Fr traiter
It trattare
Pt tratar

proceso automático de
datos *(m)* Es
De automatische
Datenverarbeitung *(f)*
En automatic data
processing (ADP)
Fr traitement
automatique de
l'information *(m)*
It processazione
automatica dati *(f)*
Pt tratamento
automático de dados
(m)

proceso de datos *(m)* Es
De Datenverarbeitung *(f)*
En data processing
Fr traitement des
données *(m)*
It elaborazione di dati
(f)
Pt tratamento de dados
(m)

proceso electrónico de
datos *(m)* Es

De elektronische
Datenverarbeitung *(f)*
En electronic data
processing
Fr traitement
électronique de
l'information *(m)*
It elaborazione
elettronica dei dati *(f)*
Pt tratamento
electrónico de dados
(m)

process *vb* En
De verarbeiten
Es procesar
Fr traiter
It trattare
Pt tratar

process *n* En
De Verfahren *(n)*
Es procedimiento *(m)*
Fr procédé *(m)*
It procedimento *(m)*
Pt processo *(m)*

processazione
automatica dati *(f)*
It
De automatische
Datenverarbeitung *(f)*
En automatic data
processing (ADP)
Es proceso automático
de datos *(m)*
Fr traitement
automatique de
l'information *(m)*
Pt tratamento
automático de dados
(m)

process blue En
De Verfahrensblau *(n)*
Es azul de tricromía *(m)*
Fr bleu d'impression
couleur *(m)*
It azzurro di tricromia
(m)
Pt azul para policromia
(m)

process camera En
De Reproduktionsgerät
(n)
Es cámara fotomecánica
(f)
Fr appareil
photomécanique *(m)*
It macchina fotografica

per riproduzioni
fotomeccaniche *(f)*
Pt câmara de
processamento *(f)*

process colors Am
De Verfahrensfarben *(pl)*
En process colours
Es colores para
policromía *(m pl)*
Fr polychromie *(f)*
It colori per policromia
(m pl)
Pt cores para policromia
(f pl)

process colours En
Am process colors
De Verfahrensfarben *(pl)*
Es colores para
policromía *(m pl)*
Fr polychromie *(f)*
It colori per policromia
(m pl)
Pt cores para policromia
(f pl)

process engraving En
De Chemiegraphie *(f)*
Es fotograbado *(m)*
Fr photogravure *(f)*
It zincografia *(f)*
Pt fototipogravura *(f)*

processo *(m) n* Pt
De Verfahren *(n)*
En process
Es procedimiento *(m)*
Fr procédé *(m)*
It procedimento *(m)*

processo directo *(m)* Pt
De Direktverfahren *(n)*
En direct process
Es reproducción directa
(f)
Fr procédé direct *(m)*
It procedimento diretto
(m)

processo indirecto *(m)*
Pt
De indirektes Verfahren
(n)
En indirect process
Es tricromía de tramado
indirecto *(f)*
Fr procédé indirect *(m)*
It procedimento
indiretto *(m)*

process red En
De Verfahrensrot *(n)*
Es rojo de tricromía *(m)*
Fr rouge d'impression
couleur *(m)*
It rosso di tricromia *(m)*
Pt vermelho para
policromia *(m)*

process yellow En
De Verfahrensgelb *(n)*
Es amarillo de tricromía
(m)
Fr jaune d'impression
couleur *(m)*
It giallo di tricromia *(m)*
Pt amarelo para
policromia *(m)*

produção *(f)* n Pt
De Produktion *(f)*
En production
Es producción *(f)*
Fr production *(f)*
It produzione *(f)*

produção de papel *(f)* Pt
De Papierherstellung *(f)*
En papermaking
Es fabricación de papel
(f)
Fr papeterie *(f)*
It fabbricazione di carta
(f)

producción *(f)* n Es
De Produktion *(f)*
En production
Fr production *(f)*
It produzione *(f)*
Pt produção *(f)*

production n En; Fr *(f)*
De Produktion *(f)*
Es producción *(f)*
It produzione *(f)*
Pt produção *(f)*

production assistant En
De Produktionsassistent
(m)
Es ayudante de
producción *(m)*
Fr assistant de
production *(m)*
It assistente di
produzione *(m)*
Pt assistente de
produção *(m)*

production department
En
De Produktionsabteilung
(f)
Es departamento de
producción *(m)*
Fr service production
(m)
It reparto produzione
(m)
Pt departamento de
produção *(m)*

production manager En
De Produktionsleiter *(m)*
Es jefe de producción
(m)
Fr directeur de la
production *(m)*
It direttore di
produzione *(m)*
Pt director de produção
(m)

Produktion *(f)* n De
En production
Es producción *(f)*
Fr production *(f)*
It produzione *(f)*
Pt produção *(f)*

Produktionsabteilung
(f) n De
En production
department
Es departamento de
producción *(m)*
Fr service production
(m)
It reparto produzione
(m)
Pt departamento de
produção *(m)*

Produktionsassistent
(m) n De
En production assistant
Es ayudante de
producción *(m)*
Fr assistant de
production *(m)*
It assistente di
produzione *(m)*
Pt assistente de
produção *(m)*

Produktionsleiter *(m)* n
De
En production manager
Es jefe de producción
(m)

Fr directeur de la
production *(m)*
It direttore di
produzione *(m)*
Pt director de produção
(m)

produrre vb It
De herstellen
En manufacture
Es fabricar
Fr fabriquer
Pt produzir

produtor *(m)* n Pt
De Hersteller *(m)*
En manufacturer
Es fabricante *(m)*
Fr fabricant *(m)*
It produttore *(m)*

produttore *(m)* n It
De Hersteller *(m)*
En manufacturer
Es fabricante *(m)*
Fr fabricant *(m)*
Pt produtor *(m)*

produzione *(f)* n It
De Produktion *(f)*
En production
Es producción *(f)*
Fr production *(f)*
Pt produção *(f)*

produzir vb Pt
De herstellen
En manufacture
Es fabricar
Fr fabriquer
t produrre

proemio *(m)* n Es, It
De Vorwort
En foreword
Fr avant-propos *(m)*
Pt proémio *(m)*

proémio *(m)* n Pt
De Vorwort
En foreword
Es proemio *(m)*
Fr avant-propos *(m)*
It proemio *(m)*

profondeur *(f)* n Fr
De Schrifttiefe *(f)*
En type depth
Es profundidad del tipo
(f)

It profondità del
carattere *(f)*
Pt profundidade de tipo
(f)

profondità *(f)* n It
De Satzhöhe *(f)*
En depth
Es profundidad *(f)*
Fr hauteur *(f)*
Pt profundidade *(f)*

profondità del carattere
(f) It
De Schrifttiefe *(f)*
En type depth
Es profundidad del tipo
(f)
Fr profondeur *(f)*
Pt profundidade de tipo
(f)

profundidad *(f)* n Es
De Satzhöhe *(f)*
En depth
Fr hauteur *(f)*
It profondità *(f)*
Pt profundidade *(f)*

profundidad del tipo *(f)*
Es
De Schrifttiefe *(f)*
En type depth
Fr profondeur *(f)*
It profondità del
carattere *(f)*
Pt profundidade de tipo
(f)

profundidade *(f)* n Pt
De Satzhöhe *(f)*
En depth
Es profundidad *(f)*
Fr hauteur *(f)*
It profondità *(f)*

profundidade de tipo *(f)*
Pt
De Schrifttiefe *(f)*
En type depth
Es profundidad del tipo
(f)
Fr profondeur *(f)*
It profondità del
carattere *(f)*

profusamente ilustrado
Es, Pt
De großzügig illustriert
En lavishly illustrated

Fr abondamment
illustré
It riccamente illustrato

progettare *vb* It
De planen
En schedule
Es proyectar
Fr projeter
Pt planear

progetto di sviluppo *(m)*
It
De Entwicklungsprojekt
(n)
En development project
Es proyecto de
desarrollo *(m)*
Fr projet de
développement *(m)*
Pt projecto de
desenvolvimento *(m)*

program *vb* Am
De programmieren
En programme
Es programar
Fr programmer
It programmare
Pt programar

program *n* Am
De Programm *(n)*
En programme
Es programa *(m)*
Fr programme *(m)*
It programma *(m)*
Pt programa *(m)*

programa *(m)* *n* Es, Pt
Am program
De Programm *(n)*
En programme
Fr programme *(m)*
It programma *(m)*

programa de desarrollo
(m) Es
Am development
program
De Entwicklungs-
programm *(n)*
En development
programme
Fr plan de
développement *(m)*
It programma di
sviluppo *(m)*
Pt programa de
desenvolvimento *(m)*

programa de
desenvolvimento
(m) Pt
Am development
program
De Entwicklungs-
programm *(n)*
En development
programme
Es programa de
desarrollo *(m)*
Fr plan de
développement *(m)*
It programma di
sviluppo *(m)*

programa de edição *(m)*
Pt
Am publishing program
De Veröffentlichungs-
programm *(n)*
En publishing
programme
Es programa de
publicaciones *(m)*
Fr calendrier des
parutions *(m)*
It programma editoriale
(m)

programa de hifenação
(m) Pt
Am hyphenation program
De Trennungs-
Programm *(n)*
En hyphenation
programme
Es programa de
separación con
guiones *(m)*
Fr programme de
division automatique
(f)
It programma di
legatura con trattino
(m)

programa de
publicaciones *(m)*
Es
Am publishing program
De Veröffentlichungs-
programm *(n)*
En publishing
programme
Fr calendrier des
parutions *(m)*
It programma editoriale
(m)
Pt programa de edição
(m)

programa de separación
con guiones *(m)* Es
Am hyphenation program
De Trennungs-
Programm *(n)*
En hyphenation
programme
Fr programme de
division automatique
(f)
It programma di
legatura con trattino
(m)
Pt programa de
hifenação *(m)*

programador *(m)* *n* Es, Pt
De Programmierer *(m)*
En programmer
Fr programmeur *(m)*
It programmatore *(m)*

programar *vb* Es, Pt
Am program
De programmieren
En programme
Fr programmer
It programmare

program language Am
De Programmiersprache
(f)
En programme language
Es lenguaje de
programación *(m)*
Fr langage de
programmation *(m)*
It linguaggio di
programma *(m)*
Pt linguagem de
programação *(f)*

Programm *(n)* *n* De
Am program
En programme
Es programa *(m)*
Fr programme *(m)*
It programma *(m)*
Pt programa *(m)*

programma *(m)* *n* It
Am program
De Programm *(n)*
En programme
Es programa *(m)*
Fr programme *(m)*
Pt programa *(m)*

programma di legatura
con trattino *(m)* It
Am hyphenation program

De Trennungs-
Programm *(n)*
En hyphenation
programme
Es programa de
separación con
guiones *(m)*
Fr programme de
division automatique
(f)
Pt programa de
hifenação *(m)*

programma di sviluppo
(m) It
Am development
program
De Entwicklungs-
programm *(n)*
En development
programme
Es programa de
desarrollo *(m)*
Fr plan de
développement *(m)*
Pt programa de
desenvolvimento *(m)*

programma editoriale
(m) It
* Am publishing program
De Veröffentlichungs-
programm *(n)*
En publishing
programme
Es programa de
publicaciones *(m)*
Fr calendrier des
parutions *(m)*
Pt programa de edição
(m)

programmare *vb* It
Am program
De programmieren
En programme
Es programar
Fr programmer
Pt programar

programmatore *(m)* *n* It
De Programmierer *(m)*
En programmer
Es programador *(m)*
Fr programmeur *(m)*
Pt programador *(m)*

programme *vb* En
Am program
De programmieren
Es programar
Fr programmer

It programmare
Pt programar

programme n En; Fr (m)
Am program
De Programm (n)
Es programa (m)
It programma (m)
Pt programa (m)

programme de division automatique (f) Fr
Am hyphenation program
De Trennungs-Programm (n)
En hyphenation programme
Es programa de separación con guiones (m)
It programma di legatura con trattino (m)
Pt programa de hifenação (m)

programme language En
Am program language
De Programmiersprache (f)
Es lenguaje de programación (m)
Fr langage de programmation (m)
It linguaggio di programma (m)
Pt linguagem de programação (f)

programmer vb Fr
Am program
De programmieren
En programme
Es programar
It programmare
Pt programar

programmer n En
De Programmierer (m)
Es programador (m)
Fr programmeur (m)
It programmatore (m)
Pt programador (m)

programmeur (m) n Fr
De Programmierer (m)
En programmer
Es programador (m)
It programmatore (m)
Pt programador (m)

programmieren vb De
Am program
En programme
Es programar
Fr programmer
It programmare
Pt programar

Programmierer (m) n De
En programmer
Es programador (m)
Fr programmeur (m)
It programmatore (m)
Pt programador (m)

Programmiersprache (f) n De
Am program language
En programme language
Es lenguaje de programación (m)
Fr langage de programmation (m)
It linguaggio di programma (m)
Pt linguagem de programação (f)

progressive proofs En
De Farbandrucke (pl)
Es pruebas de gama (f pl)
Fr épreuves-gammes (f pl)
It bozze progressive (f pl)
Pt provas progressivas (f pl)

progresso de adaptação ao trabalho (m) Pt
De in Arbeit befindlich
En work-in-progress
Es trabajo en ejecución (m)
Fr travail en cours (m)
It lavoro in corso (m)

projecto de desenvolvimento (m) Pt
De Entwicklungsprojekt (n)
En development project
Es proyecto de desarrollo (m)
Fr projet de développement (m)
It progetto di sviluppo (m)

projet (m) n Fr
De Gestaltung (f)
En design
Es diseño (m)
It disegno (m)
Pt desenho (m)

projet de développement (m) Fr
De Entwicklungsprojekt (n)
En development project
Es proyecto de desarrollo (m)
It progetto di sviluppo (m)
Pt projecto de desenvolvimento (m)

projeter vb Fr
De planen
En schedule
Es proyectar
It progettare
Pt planear

prologar vb Es
De einleiten
En preface
Fr préfacer
It fare una prefazione
Pt redigir um prefácio

promoção (f) n Pt
De Werbung (f)
En promotion
Es promoción (f)
Fr promotion (f)
It promozione (f)

promoción (f) n Es
De Werbung (f)
En promotion
Fr promotion (f)
It promozione (f)
Pt promoção (f)

promotion n En; Fr (f)
De Werbung (f)
Es promoción (f)
It promozione (f)
Pt promoção (f)

promotional campaign En
De Werbekampagne (f)
Es campaña de promoción (f)
Fr campagne publicitaire (f)

It campagna promozionale (f)
Pt campanha de promoção (f)

promotion manager En
De Werbefachmann (m)
Es jefe de promoción (m)
Fr directeur de la promotion (m)
It dirigente dell'attività promozionale (m)
Pt director de promoção (m)

promozione (f) n It
De Werbung (f)
En promotion
Es promoción (f)
Fr promotion (f)
Pt promoção (f)

prononciation (f) n Fr
De Aussprache (f)
En pronunciation
Es pronunciación (f)
It pronuncia (f)
Pt pronunciação (f)

pronuncia (f) n It
De Aussprache (f)
En pronunciation
Es pronunciación (f)
Fr prononciation (f)
Pt pronunciação (f)

pronunciação (f) n Pt
De Aussprache (f)
En pronunciation
Es pronunciación (f)
Fr prononciation (f)
It pronuncia (f)

pronunciación (f) n Es
De Aussprache (f)
En pronunciation
Fr prononciation (f)
It pronuncia (f)
Pt pronunciação (f)

pronunciation n En
De Aussprache (f)
Es pronunciación (f)
Fr prononciation (f)
It pronuncia (f)
Pt pronunciação (f)

proof *n* En
De Abzug *(m)*
Es prueba *(f)*
Fr épreuve *(f)*
It bozza *(f)*
Pt prova *(f)*

proofing *n* En
De Andrucken *(n)*
Es tirada de pruebas *(f)*
Fr tirage d´épreuves *(m)*
It tiratura di prova *(f)*
Pt tiragem de provas *(f)*

proofing press En
De Abziehapparat *(m)*
Es prensa sacapruebas *(f)*
Fr presse pour tirer les épreuves *(f)*
It tirabozze *(m)*
Pt prensa para tirar provas *(f)*

proofread *vb* En
De korrekturlesen
Es corregir pruebas
Fr corriger les épreuves
It correggere le bozze
Pt rever provas

proofreader *n* En
De Korrekturleser *(m)*
Es corrector de pruebas *(m)*
Fr correcteur d´épreuves *(m)*
It correttore di bozze *(m)*
Pt revisor de provas *(m)*

proofreader's marks En
De Korrekturzeichen *(pl)*
Es signos de corrección *(m pl)*
Fr signes de corrections typographiques *(m pl)*
It segni del correttore di bozze *(m pl)*
Pt marcas do revisor de provas *(f pl)*

proofreading *n* En
De Korrekturlesen *(n)*
Es corrección de pruebas *(f)*
Fr correction d´épreuves *(f)*
It correzione di bozze *(f)*
Pt revisão de provas *(f)*

propiedad literaria *(f)* Es
De Copyright *(n)*
En copyright
Fr copyright *(m)*
It copyright *(m)*
Pt copyright *(m)*

prosa *(f)* *n* Es, It, Pt
De Prosa *(f)*
En prose
Fr prose *(f)*

Prosa *(f)* *n* De
En prose
Es prosa *(f)*
Fr prose *(f)*
It prosa *(f)*
Pt prosa *(f)*

prose *n* En; Fr *(f)*
De Prosa *(f)*
Es prosa *(f)*
It prosa *(f)*
Pt prosa *(f)*

proseguir la tirada Es
De fortdrucken
En run on (printing)
Fr faire des tirages supplémentaires
It imprimir una super-tiratura *(f)*
Pt continuar a imprimir

prospecto *(m)* *n* Es
De Merkblatt *(n)*
En leaflet
Fr feuille volante *(f)*
It volantino a stampa *(m)*
Pt folheto *(m)*

prova *(f)* *n* Pt
De Abzug *(m)*
En proof
Es prueba *(f)*
Fr épreuve *(f)*
It bozza *(f)*

prova a cores *(f)* Pt
Am color proof
De Farbabzug *(m)*
En colour proof
Es prueba en colores *(f)*
Fr épreuve couleurs *(f)*
It bozza a colori *(f)*

prova de galé *(f)* Pt
De Korrekturfahne *(f)*
En galley proof

Es prueba de galeradas *(f)*
Fr épreuve en placard *(f)*
It bozza in colonna *(f)*

prova de imprensa *(f)* Pt
De letzte Korrektur *(f)*
En press proof
Es prueba de prensa *(f)*
Fr bon à tirer *(m)*
It bozza di stampa *(f)*

prova de página *(f)* Pt
De Korrektur *(f)*
En page proof
Es prueba de página *(f)*
Fr épreuve en pages *(f)*
It bozza impaginata *(f)*

prova de reprodução *(f)* Pt
De Repro-Abzug *(m)*
En reproduction proof
Es prueba de reproducción *(f)*
Fr épreuve de reproduction *(f)*
It prova di fotoriproduzione *(f)*

prova di fotoriproduzione *(f)* It
De Repro-Abzug *(m)*
En reproduction proof
Es prueba de reproducción *(f)*
Fr épreuve de reproduction *(f)*
Pt prova de reprodução *(f)*

prova do autor *(f)* Pt
De Autor-Korrekturabzug *(m)*
En author's proof
Es prueba de autor *(f)*
Fr épreuve d´auteur *(f)*
It bozza dell´autore *(f)*

prova limpa *(f)* Pt
De sauberer Abzug *(m)*
En clean proof
Es prueba limpia *(f)*
Fr épreuve au net *(f)*
It bozza nitida *(f)*

prova por contacto *(f)* Pt
De Kontaktdruck *(m)*
En contact print
Es copia por contacto *(f)*

Fr tirage contact *(m)*
It stampa a contatto *(f)*

provas progressivas *(f pl)* Pt
De Farbandrucke *(pl)*
En progressive proofs
Es pruebas de gama *(f pl)*
Fr épreuves-gammes *(f pl)*
It bozze progressive *(f pl)*

provas revistas *(f pl)* Pt
De revidierter Abzug *(m)*
En revised proofs
Es pruebas corregidas *(f pl)*
Fr épreuves de révision *(f pl)*
It bozze corrette *(f pl)*

provas tipográficas *(f pl)* Pt
De Vorausexemplare *(pl)*
En advance copies
Es ejemplares para reseña *(m pl)*
Fr exemplaires de lancement *(m pl)*
It copie in anteprima *(f pl)*

proveedor *(m)* *n* Es
De Lieferant *(m)*
En supplier
Fr fournisseur *(m)*
It fornitore *(m)*
Pt fornecedor *(m)*

proyectar *vb* Es
De planen
En schedule
Fr projeter
It progettare
Pt planear

proyecto de desarrollo *(m)* Es
De Entwicklungsprojekt *(n)*
En development project
Fr projet de développement *(m)*
It progetto di sviluppo *(m)*
Pt projecto de desenvolvimento *(m)*

prueba (f) n Es
De Abzug (m)
En proof
Fr épreuve (f)
It bozza (f)
Pt prova (f)

prueba de autor (f) Es
De Autor-Korrekturabzug (m)
En author's proof
Fr épreuve d'auteur (f)
It bozza dell'autore (f)
Pt prova do autor (f)

prueba de galeradas (f) Es
De Korrekturfahne (f)
En galley proof
Fr épreuve en placard (f)
It bozza in colonna (f)
Pt prova de galé (f)

prueba de página (f) Es
De Korrektur (f)
En page proof
Fr épreuve en pages (f)
It bozza impaginata (f)
Pt prova de página (f)

prueba de prensa (f) Es
De letzte Korrektur (f)
En press proof
Fr bon à tirer (m)
It bozza di stampa (f)
Pt prova de imprensa (f)

prueba de reproducción (f) Es
De Repro-Abzug (m)
En reproduction proof
Fr épreuve de reproduction (f)
It prova di fotoriproduzione (f)
Pt prova de reprodução (f)

prueba en colores (f) Es
Am color proof
De Farbabzug (m)
En colour proof
Fr épreuve couleurs (f)
It bozza a colori (f)
Pt prova a cores (f)

prueba limpia (f) Es
De sauberer Abzug (m)
En clean proof
Fr épreuve au net (f)

It bozza nitida (f)
Pt prova limpa (f)

pruebas corregidas (f pl) Es
De revidierter Abzug (m)
En revised proofs
Fr épreuves de révision (f pl)
It bozze corrette (f pl)
Pt provas revistas (f pl)

pruebas de gama (f pl) Es
De Farbandrucke (pl)
En progressive proofs
Fr épreuves-gammes (f pl)
It bozze progressive (f pl)
Pt provas progressivas (f pl)

pseudonimo (m) n It
De Pseudonym (n)
En pseudonym
Es seudónimo (m)
Fr pseudonyme (m)
Pt pseudónimo (m)

pseudónimo (m) n Pt
De Pseudonym (n)
En pseudonym
Es seudónimo (m)
Fr pseudonyme (m)
It pseudonimo (m)

pseudonym n En
De Pseudonym (n)
Es seudónimo (m)
Fr pseudonyme (m)
It pseudonimo (m)
Pt pseudónimo (m)

Pseudonym (n) n De
En pseudonym
Es seudónimo (m)
Fr pseudonyme (m)
It pseudonimo (m)
Pt pseudónimo (m)

pseudonyme (m) n Fr
De Pseudonym (n)
En pseudonym
Es seudónimo (m)
It pseudonimo (m)
Pt pseudónimo (m)

pubblicare vb It
De verlegen
En publish

Es publicar
Fr publier
Pt publicar

pubblicazione (f) n It
De Veröffentlichung (f)
En publication
Es publicación (f)
Fr publication (f)
Pt publicação (f)

pubblicazione d'autunno (f) It
De Herbstausgabe (f)
En autumn publication
Es publicación de otoño (f)
Fr parution de la rentrée (f)
Pt publicação de outono (f)

pubblicazione di primavera (f) It
De Frühjahrs-Veröffentlichung (f)
En spring publication
Es publicación de primavera (f)
Fr parution de printemps (f)
Pt publicação de Primavera (f)

pubblicità (f) n It
De Werbung (f)
En advertising; publicity
Es publicidad (f)
Fr publicité (f)
Pt publicidade (f)

pubblicizzare vb It
De werben
En advertise
Es anunciar
Fr faire de la publicité pour
Pt anunciar

pubblico adj It
De öffentlich
En public
Es público
Fr public
Pt público

public adj En, Fr
De öffentlich
Es público
It pubblico
Pt público

publicação (f) n Pt
De Veröffentlichung (f)
En publication
Es publicación (f)
Fr publication (f)
It pubblicazione (f)

publicação de outono (f) Pt
De Herbstausgabe (f)
En autumn publication
Es publicación de otoño (f)
Fr parution de la rentrée (f)
It pubblicazione d'autunno (f)

publicação de Primavera (f) Pt
De Frühjahrs-Veröffentlichung (f)
En spring publication
Es publicación de primavera (f)
Fr parution de printemps (f)
It pubblicazione di primavera (f)

publicação em série (f) Pt
De Veröffentlichung in Fortsetzungen (f)
En serialization
Es publicación por entregas (f)
Fr parution en feuilleton (f)
It riduzione in serie (f)

publicación (f) n Es
De Veröffentlichung (f)
En publication
Fr publication (f)
It pubblicazione (f)
Pt publicação (f)

publicación de otoño (f) Es
De Herbstausgabe (f)
En autumn publication
Fr parution de la rentrée (f)
It pubblicazione d'autunno (f)
Pt publicação de outono (f)

publicación de primavera (f) Es

De Frühjahrs-
Veröffentlichung *(f)*
En spring publication
Fr parution de
printemps *(f)*
It pubblicazione di
primavera *(f)*
Pt publicação de
Primavera *(f)*

**publicación por
entregas** *(f)* Es
De Veröffentlichung in
Fortsetzungen *(f)*
En serialization
Fr parution en feuilleton
(f)
It riduzione in serie *(f)*
Pt publicação em série
(f)

publicado *adj* Es
De gedruckt
En in print
Fr en impression
It in corso di stampa
Pt impresso e publicado

publicar *vb* Es, Pt
De verlegen
En publish
Fr publier
It pubblicare

publication *n* En; Fr *(f)*
De Veröffentlichung *(f)*
Es publicación *(f)*
It pubblicazione *(f)*
Pt publicação *(f)*

publication data En
De Veröffent-
lichungsdaten *(pl)*
Es datos de publicación
(m pl)
Fr référence de la
publication *(f)*
It dati di pubblicazione
(m pl)
Pt dados de publicação
(m pl)

publication date En
De Veröffent-
lichungsdatum *(n)*
Es fecha de publicación
(f)
Fr date de parution *(f)*
It data di pubblicazione
(f)
Pt data de publicação *(f)*

publicidad *(f)* *n* Es
De Werbung *(f)*
En advertising; publicity
Fr publicité *(f)*
It pubblicità *(f)*
Pt publicidade *(f)*

publicidade *(f)* *n* Pt
De Werbung *(f)*
En advertising; publicity
Es publicidad *(f)*
Fr publicité *(f)*
It pubblicità *(f)*

publicidade por correio
(f) Pt
De Postwurfsendung *(f)*
En direct-mail shot
Es envío por correo
directo; oferta por
correo *(m f)*
Fr mailing; offre
promotionnelle *(m f)*
It invio diretto per
posta; offerta postale
(m f)

publicité *(f)* *n* Fr
De Werbung *(f)*
En advertising; publicity
Es publicidad *(f)*
It pubblicità *(f)*
Pt publicidade *(f)*

publicity *n* En
De Werbung *(f)*
Es publicidad *(f)*
Fr publicité *(f)*
It pubblicità *(f)*
Pt publicidade *(f)*

publicity department En
De Werbeabteilung *(f)*
Es departamento de
publicidad *(m)*
Fr service de la publicité
(m)
It reparto pubblicitario
(m)
Pt departamento de
publicidade *(f)*

publicity manager En
De Werbeleiter *(m)*
Es jefe de publicidad *(m)*
Fr directeur de la
publicité *(m)*
It direttore pubblicitario
(m)
Pt director de
publicidade *(m)*

public library En
De öffentliche Bibliothek
(f)
Es biblioteca pública *(f)*
Fr bibliothèque
publique *(f)*
It biblioteca pubblica *(f)*
Pt biblioteca pública *(f)*

público *adj* Es, Pt
De öffentlich
En public
Fr public
It pubblico

publier *vb* Fr
De verlegen
En publish
Es publicar
It pubblicare
Pt publicar

publish *vb* En
De verlegen
Es publicar
Fr publier
It pubblicare
Pt publicar

publisher (company) *n* En
De Verlag *(m)*
Es casa editorial *(f)*
Fr maison d'édition *(f)*
It casa editrice *(f)*
Pt casa editorial *(f)*

publisher (person) *n* En
De Verleger *(m)*
Es editor *(m)*
Fr éditeur *(m)*
It editore *(m)*
Pt editor *(m)*

publishing *n* En
De Verlagswesen *(n)*
Es editorial *(f)*
Fr commerce de
l'édition *(m)*
It editoria *(f)*
Pt negocio de
publicação *(m)*

publishing program Am
De Veröffentlichungs-
programm *(n)*
En publishing
programme
Es programa de
publicaciones *(m)*
Fr calendrier des
parutions *(m)*

It programma editoriale
(m)
Pt programa de edição
(m)

publishing programme
En
Am publishing program
De Veröffentlichungs-
programm *(n)*
Es programa de
publicaciones *(m)*
Fr calendrier des
parutions *(m)*
It programma editoriale
(m)
Pt programa de edição
(m)

pulp *n* En
De Zellstoff *(m)*
Es pasta *(f)*
Fr pâte *(f)*
It pasta *(f)*
Pt polpa *(f)*

pulp board En
De Zellstoff-Karton *(m)*
Es cartón de pasta *(m)*
Fr carton-pâte *(m)*
It cartone di pasta di
legno *(m)*
Pt cartão de polpa *(m)*

punção *(m)* *n* Pt
De Stempel *(m)*
En punch (for
typefounding)
Es punzón *(m)*
Fr poinçon *(m)*
It punzone *(m)*

punch (for hole
punching) *n* En
De Locher *(m)*
Es sacabocados *(m)*
Fr perforeuse *(f)*
It perforatore *(m)*
Pt perfuradora *(f)*

punch (for typefounding)
n En
De Stempel *(m)*
Es punzón *(m)*
Fr poinçon *(m)*
It punzone *(m)*
Pt punção *(m)*

punched card En
De Lochkarte *(f)*
Es tarjeta perforada *(f)*

Fr carte perforée *(f)*
It scheda perforata *(f)*
Pt ficha perfurada *(f)*

punched paper tape En
De Lochstreifen *(m)*
Es cinta perforada *(f)*
Fr bande perforée *(f)*
It nastro di carta
   perforato *(m)*
Pt fita de papel
   perfurado *(f)*

punched-tape reader En
De Lochstreifen-Leser
   (m)
Es lector de cinta
   perforada *(m)*
Fr lecteur de bande
   perforée *(f)*
It lettore di nastro
   perforato *(m)*
Pt leitor de fita
   perfurada *(m)*

punctuate *vb* En
De Zeichen setzen
Es puntuar
Fr ponctuer
It punteggiare
Pt pontuar

punctuation *n* En
De Zeichensetzung *(f)*
Es puntuación *(f)*
Fr ponctuation *(f)*
It punteggiatura *(f)*
Pt pontuação *(f)*

punctuation mark En
De Interpunktions-
   zeichen *(n)*
Es signo de puntuación
   (m)
Fr signe de ponctuation
   (m)
It segno di
   punteggiatura *(m)*
Pt sinal de pontuação
   (m)

Punkt *(m)* *n* De
Am period
En full stop; point
Es punto; punto final *(m)*
Fr point; point final *(m)*
It punto; punto fermo
   (m)
Pt ponto; ponto final *(m)*

Punktätzung *(f)* *n* De
En dot etching
Es reducción de los
   puntos *(f)*
Fr morsure par
   couverture *(f)*
It incisione a punti *(f)*
Pt redução dos pontos
   reticulares *(f)*

Punktgröße *(f)* *n* De
En point size
Es cuerpo del tipo *(m)*
Fr corps *(m)*
It corpo *(m)*
Pt tamanho de ponto
   (m)

punteado *(m)* *n* Es
De Granierung *(f)*
En stippling
Fr grisé *(m)*
It battitura *(f)*
Pt ponteado *(m)*

punteggiare *vb* It
De Zeichen setzen
En punctuate
Es puntuar
Fr ponctuer
Pt pontuar

punteggiatura *(f)* *n* It
De Zeichensetzung *(f)*
En punctuation
Es puntuación *(f)*
Fr ponctuation *(f)*
Pt pontuação *(f)*

puntini *(m pl)* It
De Ausführpunkte *(pl)*
En leaders *pl n*
Es filetes puntillados *(m
   pl)*
Fr points de conduite
   (m pl)
Pt pontos de reticência
   (m pl)

punto *(m)* *n* Es, It
De Punkt *(m)*
En point
Fr point *(m)*
Pt ponto *(m)*

punto decimal *(m)* Es
De Dezimalkomma *(n)*
En decimal point
Fr virgule *(f)*
It virgola decimale *(f)*
Pt ponto decimal *(m)*

punto de equilibrio *(m)*
   Es
De Nutzschwelle *(f)*
En break-even point
Fr seuil de rentabilité
   (m)
It punto di pareggio *(m)*
Pt ponto de equilíbrio
   (m)

punto de venta *(m)* Es
De Verkaufsstelle *(f)*
En point of sale
Fr point de vente *(m)*
It punto di vendita *(m)*
Pt. ponto de venda *(m)*

punto di domanda *(m)* It
De Fragezeichen *(n)*
En question mark
Es signo de
   interrogación *(m)*
Fr point d'interrogation
   (m)
Pt ponto de
   interrogação *(m)*

punto di pareggio *(m)* It
De Nutzschwelle *(f)*
En break-even point
Es punto de equilibrio
   (m)
Fr seuil de rentabilité
   (m)
Pt ponto de equilíbrio
   (m)

punto di vendita *(m)* It
De Verkaufsstelle *(f)*
En point of sale
Es punto de venta *(m)*
Fr point de vente *(m)*
Pt ponto de venda *(m)*

punto esclamativo *(m)* It
De Ausrufungszeichen
   (n)
En exclamation mark
Es signo de admiración
   (m)
Fr point d'exclamation
   (m)
Pt ponto de exclamação
   (m)

punto e virgola *(m)* It
De Semikolon *(n)*
En semicolon
Es punto y coma *(m)*
Fr point-virgule *(m)*
Pt ponto e vírgula *(m)*

punto fermo *(m)* It
Am period
De Punkt *(m)*
En full stop
Es punto final *(m)*
Fr point final *(m)*
Pt ponto final *(m)*

punto final *(m)* Es
Am period
De Punkt *(m)*
En full stop
Fr point final *(m)*
It punto fermo *(m)*
Pt ponto final *(m)*

punto y coma *(m)* Es
De Semikolon *(n)*
En semicolon
Fr point-virgule *(m)*
It punto e virgola *(m)*
Pt ponto e vírgula *(m)*

puntuación *(f)* *n* Es
De Zeichensetzung *(f)*
En punctuation
Fr ponctuation *(f)*
It punteggiatura *(f)*
Pt pontuação *(f)*

puntuar *vb* Es
De Zeichen setzen
En punctuate
Fr ponctuer
It punteggiare
Pt pontuar

Punzenbindung *(f)* *n* De
En tooled binding
Es encuadernación
   repujada *(f)*
Fr reliure ciselée *(f)*
It rilegatura con attrezzi
   (f)
Pt encadernação
   ornamentada *(f)*

punzón *(m)* *n* Es
De Stempel *(m)*
En punch (for
   typefounding)
Fr poinçon *(m)*
It punzone *(m)*
Pt punção *(m)*

punzone *(m)* *n* It
De Stempel *(m)*
En punch (for
   typefounding)
Es punzón *(m)*

Q

Fr poinçon *(m)*
Pt punção *(m)*

quad *n* En
De Quadrat *(n)*
Es cuadrado *(m)*
Fr cadrat *(m)*
It quadrato *(m)*
Pt quadrado *(m)*

quadrado *(m) n* Pt
De Quadrat *(n)*
En quad
Es cuadrado *(m)*
Fr cadrat *(m)*
It quadrato *(m)*

Quadrat *(n) n* De
En quad
Es cuadrado *(m)*
Fr cadrat *(m)*
It quadrato *(m)*
Pt quadrado *(m)*

quadratim *(m) n* Pt
De Geviert *(n)*
En em
Es cuadratín *(m)*
Fr cadratin *(m)*
It riga *(f)*

Quadratmetergewicht
(n) n De
En substance (of paper)
Es gramaje *(m)*
Fr grammage *(m)*
It grammatura *(f)*
Pt gramagem *(m)*

quadrato *(m) n* It
De Quadrat *(n)*
En quad
Es cuadrado *(m)*
Fr cadrat *(m)*
Pt quadrado *(m)*

quadrichromie *(f) n* Fr
Am four-color printing
De Vierfarbdruck *(m)*
En four-colour printing
Es cuatricromía *(f)*

It stampa a quattro
colori *(f)*
Pt impressão a quatro
cores *(f)*

quadrille *n* En
De kariertes Papier *(n)*
Es cuadrícula *(f)*
Fr papier quadrillé *(m)*
It carta quadrettata *(f)*
Pt papel quadriculado
(m)

quart *(m) n* Fr
De Quartformat *(n)*
En quarto
Es papel en cuarto *(m)*
It quarto *(m)*
Pt quartos *(m)*

quarter-bound book En
De Buchband mit engem
Lederrücken *(n)*
Es libro encuadernado a
cuarta piel *(m)*
Fr demi-reliure *(f)*
It libro rilegato con
dorso in pelle *(m)*
Pt livro in quarto *(m)*

Quartformat *(n) n* De
En quarto
Es papel en cuarto *(m)*
Fr quart *(m)*
It quarto *(m)*
Pt quartos *(m)*

quarto *n* En; It *(m)*
De Quartformat *(n)*
Es papel en cuarto *(m)*
Fr quart *(m)*
Pt quartos *(m)*

quartos *(m) n* Pt
De Quartformat *(n)*
En quarto
Es papel en cuarto *(m)*
Fr quart *(m)*
It quarto *(m)*

quebra de contrato *(f)* Pt
De Vertragsbruch *(m)*
En breach of contract
Es incumplimiento de
contrato *(m)*
Fr rupture de contrat *(f)*
It violazione di
contratto *(f)*.

quebrado *(m) n* Es
De Bankerotteur *(m)*
En bankrupt
Fr failli *(m)*
It fallito *(m)*
Pt falido *(m)*

quebrar *vb* Es
De bankerott machen
En bankrupt
Fr mettre en faillite
It far bancarotta
Pt falir

Querformat-Seite *(f)* De
En landscape page
Es página apaisada *(f)*
Fr format oblong *(m)*
It pagina orizzontale *(f)*
Pt página horizontal *(f)*

Querheftung *(f) n* De
En side-stitching
Es cosido por el costado
(m)
Fr couture de côté *(f)*
It cucitura laterale *(f)*
Pt cosido pela lombada
(m)

Querschnitt *(m) n* De
En cross section
Es sección transversal *(f)*
Fr vue en coupe *(f)*
It sezione trasversale *(f)*
Pt corte transversal *(m)*

Querverweis *(m) n* De
En cross reference
Es interreferencia *(f)*
Fr renvoi *(m)*
It rimando *(m)*
Pt nota remissiva *(f)*

query *n* En
De Frage *(f)*
Es interrogación *(f)*
Fr question *(f)*
It quesito *(m)*
Pt pergunta *(f)*

quesito *(m) n* It
De Frage *(f)*
En query
Es interrogación *(f)*
Fr question *(f)*
Pt pergunta *(f)*

question *(f) n* Fr
De Frage *(f)*
En query
Es interrogación *(f)*
It quesito *(m)*
Pt pergunta *(f)*

question mark En
De Fragezeichen *(n)*
Es signo de
interrogación *(m)*
Fr point d'interrogation
(m)
It punto di domanda
(m)
Pt ponto de
interrogação *(m)*

quire *n* En
De Buch (25 Bogen) *(n)*
Es mano de papel *(f)*
Fr main de papier *(f)*
It mazzetta di 24 fogli
(f)
Pt caderno de papel *(f)*

quoin *n* En
De Keil *(m)*
Es cuña *(f)*
Fr coin *(m)*
It serraforme *(m)*
Pt cunha *(f)*

quotation (estimate) *n* En
De Angebot *(n)*
Es cotización *(f)*
Fr prix coté *(m)*
It quotazione *(f)*
Pt cotação *(f)*

quotation (extract) *n* En
De Zitat *(n)*
Es cita *(f)*
Fr citation *(f)*
It citazione *(f)*
Pt citação *(f)*

quotation marks En
De Anführungszeichen
(pl)
Es comillas *(f pl)*
Fr guillemets *(m pl)*
It virgolette *(f pl)*
Pt aspas *(f pl)*

quotazione *(f) n* It
De Angebot *(n)*
En quotation (estimate)
Es cotización *(f)*
Fr prix coté *(m)*
Pt cotação *(f)*

quote (an extract) *vb* En
De zitieren
Es citar
Fr citer
It citare tra virgolette
Pt citar

quote (a price) *vb* En
De ein Angebot
    unterbreiten
Es cotizar
Fr mentionner
It dare le quotazioni
Pt cotar

R

rabat arrière (m) Fr
De hintere
    Umschlagklappe (f)
En back flap
Es solapa posterior (f)
It risvolto di retro (m)
Pt contracapa (f)

rabat avant (m) Fr
De vordere
    Umschlagklappe (f)
En front flap
Es solapa delantera (f)
It risvolto anteriore (m)
Pt aleta dianteira (f)

rabat de la jaquette (m)
    Fr
De Umschlagklappe (f)
En jacket flap
Es solapa de la cubierta
    (f)
It risvolto della
    sovracopertina (m)
Pt aba da sobrecapa (f)

rabots (m pl) Fr
De Bestoβhobel (pl)
En planes pl n
Es asentadores (m pl)
It pialle (f pl)
Pt niveladores (m pl)

raccogliere *vb* It
De zusammentragen
En gather

Es reunir
Fr rassembler
Pt reunir

raccoglitore (m) n It
De Sammler (m)
En assembler
Es. elevador reunidor (m)
Fr assembleur (m)
Pt ajustadora (f)

raccoglitura (f) n It
De Zusammentragung (f)
En collating
Es alzado (m)
Fr assemblage (m)
Pt revisão (f)

raccolta (f) n It
De Zusammentragen (n)
En gathering
Es recogida (f)
Fr assemblage (m)
Pt reunião (f)

raccolta di opere (f pl) It
De gesammelten Werke
    (pl)
En collected works
Es obras reunidas (f pl)
Fr recueil des oeuvres
    (m pl)
Pt compilação de obras
    (f)

racconto breve (m) It
De Kurzgeschichte (f)
En short story
Es narración (f)
Fr nouvelle (f)
Pt novela pequena (f)

racconto poliziesco (m)
    It
De Kriminalroman (m)
En detective novel
Es novela policíaca (f)
Fr roman policier (m)
Pt livro policial (m)

raccorder *vb* Fr
De montieren
En strip in
Es montar inserciones
It giuntare
Pt incluir

râcle docteur (f) Fr
De Rakelmesser (n)
En doctor blade

Es rasqueta doctor (f)
It racle dottore (f)
Pt rasqueta doutor (f)

racle dottore (f) It
De Rakelmesser (n)
En doctor blade
Es rasqueta doctor (f)
Fr râcle docteur (f)
Pt rasqueta doutor (f)

Radierung (f) n De
En etching
Es grabado al agua
    fuerte (f)
Fr gravure à l'eau forte
    (f)
It incisione
    all'acquaforte (f)
Pt gravura a áqua-forte
    (f)

raffinage (m) n Fr
De Mahlung (f)
En beating
    (papermaking)
Es batido (m)
It raffinamento (m)
Pt batimento (m)

raffinamento (m) n It
De Mahlung (f)
En beating
    (papermaking)
Es batido (m)
Fr raffinage (m)
Pt batimento (m)

raffinatrice (f) n It
De Mahlmaschine (f)
En beating machine
Es batidora (f)
Fr pilon (m)
Pt máquina de bater (f)

rag board En
De Hadernkarton (m)
Es cartón de trapos (m)
Fr carton chiffon (m)
It cartone di stracci (m)
Pt cartão de trapos (m)

rag paper En
De Hadernpapier (n)
Es papel de trapos (m)
Fr papier de chiffon (m)
It carta di stracci (f)
Pt papel de trapos (m)

Rahmen (m) n De
En chase (letterpress)
Es rama (f)
Fr châssis (m)
It telaio (m)
Pt rama (f)

rainure (f) n Fr
De Kanal (m)
En channel
Es canal (m)
It canale (m)
Pt canal (m)

Rakelmesser (n) n De
En doctor blade
Es rasqueta doctor (f)
Fr râcle docteur (f)
It racle dottore (f)
Pt rasqueta doutor (f)

rama (f) n Es, Pt
De Rahmen (m)
En chase (letterpress)
Fr châssis (m)
It telaio (m)

rama de máquina (f) Es,
    Pt
De Maschinenrahmen
    (m)
En machine chase
Fr châssis machine (m)
It telaio di forma chiusa
    (m)

rama de noticias (f) Es
De Zeitungsrahmen (m)
En news chase
Fr châssis à journal (m)
It caccia di notizie (f)
Pt rama de notícias (f)

rama de notícias (f) Pt
De Zeitungsrahmen (m)
En news chase
Es rama de noticias (f)
Fr châssis à journal (m)
It caccia di notizie (f)

rama duplex (f) Pt
De Falzrahmen (m)
En folding chase
Es rama dúplex (f)
Fr châssis de pliage (m)
It telaio di piegafoglio
    (m)

rama dúplex *(f)* Es
De Falzrahmen *(m)*
En folding chase
Fr châssis de pliage *(m)*
It telaio di piegafoglio *(m)*
Pt rama duplex *(f)*

rame de papier *(f)* Fr
De Ries *(n)*
En ream
Es resma *(f)*
It risma *(f)*
Pt resma *(f)*

Rand *(m)* n De
En margin (paper)
Es margen *(m)*
Fr marge *(f)*
It margine *(m)*
Pt margem *(f)*

Randbemerkungen *(pl)* De
En marginal notes
Es notas marginales *(f pl)*
Fr notes marginales *(f pl)*
It note a margine *(f pl)*
Pt notas marginais *(f pl)*

randlos drucken De
En bleed
Es correrse la tinta
Fr rogner
It refilare
Pt ressumbrar

random-access store En
De Direktzugriffsspeicher *(m)*
Es memoria de acceso al azar *(f)*
Fr mémoire à accés direct *(f)*
It memoria ad accesso casuale *(f)*
Pt memória de acesso aleatório *(f)*

range left En
De links in Linie bringen
Es alinear al margen izquierdo
Fr aligner à gauche
It allineare verticalmente a sinistra
Pt explorar esquerda

range right En
De rechts in Linie bringen
Es alinear al margen derecho
Fr aligner à droite
It allineare verticalmente a destra
Pt explorar direita

rappezzi *(m pl)* It
De Schriftgarnitur *(f)*
En sorts *pl n*
Es suertes *(f pl)*
Fr assortiment *(m)*
Pt sortes *(f pl)*

rappresentante *(m)* n It
De Handelsvertreter *(m)*
En representative
Es representante *(m)*
Fr représentant *(m)*
Pt representante *(m)*

rappresentante commissione *(m)* It
De Auftragsvertreter *(m)*
En commission representative
Es representante a comisión *(m)*
Fr représentant chargé des commandes *(m)*
Pt representante à comissão *(m)*

ras *adj* Fr
De glatt
En flush
Es a ras
It a livello
Pt nivelado

rascunho *(m)* n Pt
De Entwurf *(m)*
En draft
Es borrador *(m)*
Fr ébauche *(f)*
It minuta *(f)*

rasqueta doctor *(f)* Es
De Rakelmesser *(n)*
En doctor blade
Fr râcle docteur *(f)*
It racle dottore *(f)*
Pt rasqueta doutor *(f)*

rasqueta doutor *(f)* Pt
De Rakelmesser *(n)*
En doctor blade

Es rasqueta doctor *(f)*
Fr râcle docteur *(f)*
It racle dottore *(f)*

rassembler *vb* Fr
De zusammentragen
En gather
Es reunir
It raccogliere
Pt reunir

Raster *(m)* n De
En screen
Es retícula *(f)*
Fr écran *(m)*
It retino *(m)*
Pt retícula *(f)*

raya *(f)* n Es
De Gedankenstrich *(m)*
En dash
Fr filet *(m)*
It lineetta *(f)*
Pt filete *(m)*

rayado a pluma *(m)* Es
De Federlinierung *(f)*
En pen ruling
Fr réglure au crayon *(f)*
It sottolineatura a penna *(f)*
Pt linhas à pena *(m)*

rayas en azul *(f pl)* Es
De blaue Linien *(pl)*
En feints *pl n*
Fr règles en bleu clair *(f pl)*
It righi finti *(m pl)*
Pt linhas pautadas a azul-claro *(f pl)*

rayer *vb* Fr
De streichen
En delete
Es suprimir
It cancellare
Pt apagar

read *vb* En
De lesen
Es leer
Fr lire
It leggere
Pt ler

read against copy En
De mit dem Manuskript vergleichen

Es leer a la vista del original
Fr corriger avec copie
It confrontare coll´original
Pt ler comparando com a cópia

reader (book) *n* En
De Lesebuch *(n)*
Es libro de lectura *(m)*
Fr livre de lecture *(m)*
It libro di lettura *(m)*
Pt exemplar de leitura *(m)*

reader (person) *n* En
De Leser *(m)*
Es lector *(m)*
Fr lecteur *(m)*
It lettore *(m)*
Pt leitor *(m)*

ream *n* En
De Ries *(n)*
Es resma *(f)*
Fr rame de papier *(f)*
It risma *(f)*
Pt resma *(f)*

rebord *(m)* n Fr
De Flansch *(m)*
En flange
Es reborde *(m)*
It flangia *(f)*
Pt rebordo *(m)*

reborde *(m)* n Es
De Flansch *(m)*
En flange
Fr rebord *(m)*
It flangia *(f)*
Pt rebordo *(m)*

rebordo *(m)* n Pt
De Flansch *(m)*
En flange
Es reborde *(m)*
Fr rebord *(m)*
It flangia *(f)*

receita *(f)* n Pt
De Einkommen *(n)*
En revenue
Es ingresos *(m pl)*
Fr recette *(f)*
It entrata *(f)*

recensione *(f)* *n* It
De Rezension *(f)*
En review
Es reseña *(f)*
Fr critique d'un livre *(f)*
Pt resenha *(f)*

receptor automático de pila de pliegos *(m)* Es
De automatischer Stapelausleger *(m)*
En automatic pile delivery
Fr distribution automatique des piles *(f)*
It avanzamento automatico di pile *(f)*
Pt entrega automática de pilhas *(f)*

recette *(f)* *n* Fr
De Einkommen *(n)*
En revenue
Es ingresos *(m pl)*
It entrata *(f)*
Pt receita *(f)*

recherche de l'information *(f)* Fr
De Informationszugriff *(m)*
En information retrieval
Es recuperación de la información *(f)*
It recupero informazioni *(m)*
Pt recuperação de informação *(f)*

Rechnung *(f)* *n* De
En invoice
Es factura *(f)*
Fr facture *(f)*
It fattura *(f)*
Pt factura *(f)*

rechte Buchseite *(f)* De
En recto
Es recto *(m)*
Fr recto *(m)*
It pagina dispari *(f)*
Pt recto *(m)*

rechte Seite *(f)* De
En right-hand page
Es página derecha *(f)*
Fr belle page *(f)*
It pagina di destra *(f)*
Pt página da direita *(f)*

Rechtsbuch *(n)* *n* De
En legal book
Es libro de derecho *(m)*
Fr ouvrage juridique *(m)*
It libro legale *(m)*
Pt livro jurídico *(m)*

rechts in Linie bringen De
En range right
Es alinear al margen derecho
Fr aligner à droite
It allineare verticalmente a destra
Pt explorar direita

recogida *(f)* *n* Es
De Zusammentragen *(n)*
En gathering
Fr assemblage *(m)*
It raccolta *(f)*
Pt reunião *(f)*

reconhecimento óptico de caracteres *(m)* Pt
De Klarschriftlesen *(n)*
En optical character recognition (OCR)
Es reconocimiento óptico de caracteres *(m)*
Fr lecture optique *(f)*
It riconoscimento ottico dei caratteri *(m)*

reconnaissance de caractères magnétiques codés *(f)* Fr
De Lesen von Magnettintenzeichen *(n)*
En magnetic-ink character reading (MICR)
Es lectura de caracteres de tinta magnética *(f)*
It lettura caratteri con inchiostro magnetico *(f)*
Pt leitura de caracteres de tinta magnética *(f)*

reconocimiento óptico de caracteres *(m)* Es
De Klarschriftlesen *(n)*

En optical character recognition (OCR)
Fr lecture optique *(f)*
It riconoscimento ottico dei caratteri *(m)*
Pt reconhecimento óptico de caracteres *(m)*

recorrido *(m)* *n* Es
De Umbrechen *(n)*
En over-running
Fr remaniement *(m)*
It rimaneggiamento *(m)*
Pt acto de recorrer *(m)*

recortado *(m)* *n* Es
De Freistellung *(f)*
En cut out
Fr découpage *(m)*
It scontornata *(f)*
Pt recorte *(m)*

recortar *vb* Es, Pt
De zurichten
En crop
Fr détourer
It scontornare

recorte *(m)* *n* Pt
De Freistellung *(f)*
En cut out
Es recortado *(m)*
Fr découpage *(m)*
It scontornata *(f)*

recorte *(m)* *n* Es
De Beschneiden *(n)*
En trimming
Fr rognage *(m)*
It rifilatura *(f)*
Pt aparagem *(f)*

recorte de imprensa *(f)* Pt
De Presseausschnitt *(m)*
En press cutting
Es recorte de prensa *(m)*
Fr coupure de journal *(f)*
It ritaglio di giornale *(m)*

recorte de prensa *(m)* Es
De Presseausschnitt *(m)*
En press cutting
Fr coupure de journal *(f)*
It ritaglio di giornale *(m)*
Pt recorte de imprensa *(f)*

recorte raso Pt
De glatt zurichten
En cut flush
Es cortado a ras
Fr composé à l'américaine
It tagliato a filo

rectificação de cilindros *(f)* Pt
De Zylinderaufzug *(m)*
En cylinder dressing
Es rectificado de cilindros *(m)*
Fr habillage *(m)*
It rivestimento per cilindri *(m)*

rectificación cromática *(f)* Es
Am color correction
De Farbkorrektur *(f)*
En colour correction
Fr correction des couleurs *(f)*
It correzione di colore *(f)*
Pt correcção de cor *(f)*

rectificado de cilindros *(m)* Es
De Zylinderaufzug *(m)*
En cylinder dressing
Fr habillage *(m)*
It rivestimento per cilindri *(m)*
Pt rectificação de cilindros *(f)*

recto *n* En; Es, Fr, Pt *(m)*
De rechte Buchseite *(f)*
It pagina dispari *(f)*

recueil *(m)* *n* Fr
De Sammlung *(f)*
En collection
Es colección *(f)*
It collezione *(f)*
Pt coleção *(f)*

recueil des oeuvres *(m pl)* Fr
De gesammelten Werke *(pl)*
En collected works
Es obras reunidas *(f pl)*
It raccolta di opere *(f pl)*
Pt compilação de obras *(f)*

recuperação de informação *(f)* Pt
De Informationszugriff *(m)*
En information retrieval
Es recuperación de la información *(f)*
Fr recherche de l'information *(f)*
It recupero informazioni *(m)*

recuperación de la información *(f)* Es
De Informationszugriff *(m)*
En information retrieval
Fr recherche de l'information *(f)*
It recupero informazioni *(m)*
Pt recuperação de informação *(f)*

recupero informazioni *(m)* It
De Informationszugriff *(m)*
En information retrieval
Es recuperación de la información *(f)*
Fr recherche de l'information *(f)*
Pt recuperação de informação *(f)*

redactar *vb* Es
De unter der Leitung eines Redakteurs herausgeben
En subedit
Fr mettre au point
It redigere
Pt subcorrigir

rédacteur *(m) n* Fr
De Herausgeber *(m)*
En editor (publisher's)
És editor (de libros) *(m)*
It editore (di libri) *(m)*
Pt editor (de livros) *(m)*

rédacteur adjoint *(m)* Fr
De stellvertretender Redakteur *(m)*
En assistant editor
Es redactor adjunto *(m)*
It assistente editore *(m)*
Pt editor adjunto *(m)*

rédacteur artistique *(m)* Fr
De Kunst-Redakteur *(m)*
En art editor
Es redactor gráfico *(m)*
It editore artistico *(m)*
Pt editor artístico *(m)*

rédacteur chargé des commandes *(m)* Fr
De Auftragvergabe-Redakteur *(m)*
En commissioning editor
Es editor por encargo *(m)*
It redattore commissioni *(m)*
Pt editor que encomenda a obra *(m)*

rédacteur-concepteur publicitaire *(m)* Fr
De Texter *(m)*
En copywriter
Es redactor de textos publicitarios *(m)*
It redattore pubblicitario *(m)*
Pt redactor de textos publicidades *(m)*

rédacteur en chef *(m)* Fr
De Redakteur *(m)*
En editor (newspaper)
Es redactor *(m)*
It redattore *(m)*
Pt redactor *(m)*

rédacteur gérant *(m)* Fr
De leitender Redakteur *(m)*
En senior editor
Es redactor jefe *(m)*
It editore senior *(m)*
Pt editor senior *(m)*

rédaction *(f) n* Fr
De Redaktion *(f)*
En editorial department
Es departamento editorial *(m)*
It redazione *(f)*
Pt departamento editorial *(m)*

redactor *(m) n* Es, Pt
De Redakteur *(m)*
En editor (newspaper)
Fr rédacteur en chef *(m)*
It redattore *(m)*

redactor adjunto *(m)* Es
De stellvertretender Redakteur *(m)*
En assistant editor
Fr rédacteur adjoint *(m)*
It assistente editore *(m)*
Pt editor adjunto *(m)*

redactor auxiliar *(m)* Pt
De Zweiter Redakteur *(m)*
En subeditor
Es corrector *(m)*
Fr secrétaire de la rédaction *(m)*
It redattore aggiunto *(m)*

redactor de textos publicidades *(m)* Pt
De Texter *(m)*
En copywriter
Es redactor de textos publicitarios *(m)*
Fr rédacteur-concepteur publicitaire *(m)*
It redattore pubblicitario *(m)*

redactor de textos publicitarios *(m)* Es
De Texter *(m)*
En copywriter
Fr rédacteur-concepteur publicitaire *(m)*
It redattore pubblicitario *(m)*
Pt redactor de textos publicidades *(m)*

redactor gráfico *(m)* Es
De Kunst-Redakteur *(m)*
En art editor
Fr rédacteur artistique *(m)*
It editore artistico *(m)*
Pt editor artístico *(m)*

redactor jefe *(m)* Es
De leitender Redakteur *(m)*
En senior editor
Fr rédacteur gérant *(m)*
It editore senior *(m)*
Pt editor senior *(m)*

Redakteur *(m) n* De
En editor (newspaper)
Es redactor *(m)*
Fr rédacteur en chef *(m)*

It redattore *(m)*
Pt redactor *(m)*

Redaktion *(f) n* De
En editorial department
Es departamento editorial *(m)*
Fr rédaction *(f)*
It redazione *(f)*
Pt departamento editorial *(m)*

Redaktionsagentur *(f) n* De
En editorial agency
Es agemcia editorial *(f)*
Fr agence de rédaction *(f)*
It agenzia editoriale *(f)*
Pt agência editorial *(f)*

Redaktionsassistent *(m) n* De
En editorial assistant
Es ayudante de editorial *(m)*
Fr secrétaire de rédaction *(m)*
It assistente editoriale *(m)*
Pt ajudante editorial *(m)*

Redaktionsdienste *(pl)* De
En editorial services *pl n*
Es servicios editoriales *(m pl)*
Fr services rédactionnels *(m pl)*
It servizi editoriali *(m pl)*
Pt serviços editoriais *(m pl)*

redattore *(m) n* It
De Redakteur *(m)*
En editor (newspaper)
Es redactor *(m)*
Fr rédacteur en chef *(m)*
Pt redactor *(m)*

redattore aggiunto *(m)* It
De Zweiter Redakteur *(m)*
En subeditor
Es corrector *(m)*
Fr secrétaire de la rédaction *(m)*
Pt redactor auxiliar *(m)*

redattore commissioni
(m) It
De Auftragvergabe-
Redakteur (m)
En commissioning editor
Es editor por encargo
(m)
Fr rédacteur chargé des
commandes (m)
Pt editor que
encomenda a obra
(m)

redattore pubblicitario
(m) It
De Texter (m)
En copywriter
Es redactor de textos
publicitarios (m)
Fr rédacteur-
concepteur
publicitaire (m)
Pt redactor de textos
publicidades (m)

redazione (f) n It
De Redaktion (f)
En editorial department
Es departamento
editorial (m)
Fr rédaction (f)
Pt departamento
editorial (m)

red de distribución (f) Es
De Vertriebsnetz (n)
En distribution network
Fr réseau de
distribution (m)
It rete di distribuzione
(f)
Pt rede de distribuição
(f)

rede de distribuição (f)
Pt
De Vertriebsnetz (n)
En distribution network
Es red de distribución (f)
Fr réseau de
distribution (m)
It rete di distribuzione
(f)

redigere vb It
De unter der Leitung
eines Redakteurs
herausgeben
En subedit
Es redactar
Fr mettre au point
Pt subcorrigir

redigir um prefácio Pt
De einleiten
En preface
Es prologar
Fr préfacer
It fare una prefazione

**redução dos pontos
reticulares** (f) Pt
De Punktätzung (f)
En dot etching
Es reducción de los
puntos (f)
Fr morsure par
couverture (f)
It incisione a punti (f)

reducción de los puntos
(f) Es
De Punktätzung (f)
En dot etching
Fr morsure par
couverture (f)
It incisione a punti (f)
Pt redução dos pontos
reticulares (f)

reduce vb En
De verkleinern
Es reducir
Fr réduire
It ridurre
Pt reduzir

reducers pl n En
De Zusätze (pl)
Es diluyentes (m pl)
Fr réducteurs (m pl)
It diluenti (m pl)
Pt redutores (m pl)

reducir vb Es
De verkleinern
En reduce
Fr réduire
It ridurre
Pt reduzir

réducteurs (m pl) Fr
De Zusätze (pl)
En reducers pl n
Es diluyentes (m pl)
It diluenti (m pl)
Pt redutores (m pl)

réduire vb Fr
De verkleinern
En reduce
Es reducir
It ridurre
Pt reduzir

redundancia (f) n Es
De Entlassung (f)
En redundancy
Fr chomage partiel (m)
It ridondanza (f)
Pt redundância (f)

redundância (f) n Pt
De Entlassung (f)
En redundancy
Es redundancia (f)
Fr chomage partiel (m)
It ridondanza (f)

redundancy n En
De Entlassung (f)
Es redundancia (f)
Fr chomage partiel (m)
It ridondanza (f)
Pt redundância (f)

redundancy payment En
De Entlassungsgeld (n)
Es pago redundante (m)
Fr indemnité de
chômage (f)
It pagamento di
ridondanza (m)
Pt pagamento de
redundância (m)

redutores (m pl) Pt
De Zusätze (pl)
En reducers pl n
Es diluyentes (m pl)
Fr réducteurs (m pl)
It diluenti (m pl)

reduzir vb Pt
De verkleinern
En reduce
Es reducir
Fr réduire
It ridurre

reel n En
De Spule (f)
Es bobina (f)
Fr bobine (f)
It bobina (f)
Pt bobina (f)

**reentrância de
parágrafo** (f) Pt
De Paragrapheinrückung
(f)
En paragraph indent
Es sangría de párrafo (f)
Fr renfoncé d'alinéa (m)
It indentro del
paragrafo (m)

reference (literary) n En
De Referenz (f)
Es referencia (literaria)
(f)
Fr référence (littéraire)
(f)
It riferimento (m)
Pt referência (literária)
(f)

reference (testimonial) n
En
De Zeugnis (n)
Es referencia
(certificado) (f)
Fr référence (certificat)
(f)
It referenza (f)
Pt referência
(certificado) (f)

reference book En
De Nachschlagewerk (n)
Es obra de consulta (f)
Fr livre de référence (m)
It libro di consultazione
(m)
Pt livro de consulta (m)

**reference-book
publisher** En
De Nachschlagewerk-
Verleger (m)
Es editor de obras de
consulta (m)
Fr éditeur d'ouvrages
de référence (m)
It editore di libri di
consultazione (m)
Pt editor de livros de
consulta (m)

**référence de la
publication** (f) Fr
De Veröffent-
lichungsdaten (pl)
En publication data
Es datos de publicación
(m pl)
It dati di pubblicazione
(m pl)
Pt dados de publicação
(m pl)

référence (certificat) (f)
Fr
De Zeugnis (n)
En reference
(testimonial)
Es referencia
(certificado) (f)
It referenza (f)

Pt referência
(certificado) *(f)*

référence (littéraire) *(f)* Fr
De Referenz *(f)*
En reference (literary)
Es referencia (literaria)
(f)
It riferimento *(m)*
Pt referência (literária)
(f)

reference library En
De Nachschlagewerk-
Bücherei *(f)*
Es biblioteca de
consulta *(f)*
Fr bibliothèque
d'ouvrages de
référence *(f)*
It biblioteca di
consultazione *(f)*
Pt biblioteca de
consulta *(f)*

**référence
photographique** *(f)*
Fr
De Photobezug *(m)*
En photographic
reference
Es referencia fotográfica
(f)
It riferimento
fotografico *(m)*
Pt referência fotográfica
(f)

referencia (certificado) *(f)*
Es
De Zeugnis *(n)*
En reference
(testimonial)
Fr référence (certificat)
(f)
It referenza *(f)*
Pt referência
(certificado) *(f)*

referência (certificado) *(f)*
Pt
De Zeugnis *(n)*
En reference
(testimonial)
Es referencia
(certificado) *(f)*
Fr référence (certificat)
(f)
It referenza *(f)*

referencia fotográfica
(f) Es
De Photobezug *(m)*
En photographic
reference
Fr référence
photographique *(f)*
It riferimento
fotografico *(m)*
Pt referência fotográfica
(f)

referência fotográfica
(f) Pt
De Photobezug *(m)*
En photographic
reference
Es referencia fotográfica
(f)
Fr référence
photographique *(f)*
It riferimento
fotografico *(m)*

referencia (literaria) *(f)* Es
De Referenz *(f)*
En reference (literary)
Fr référence (littéraire)
(f)
It riferimento *(m)*
Pt referência (literária)
(f)

referência (literária) *(f)* Pt
De Referenz *(f)*
En reference (literary)
Es referencia (literaria)
(f)
Fr référence (littéraire)
(f)
It riferimento *(m)*

Referenz *(f)* n De
En reference (literary)
Es referencia (literaria)
(f)
Fr référence (littéraire)
(f)
It riferimento *(m)*
Pt referência (literária)
(f)

referenza *(f)* n It
De Zeugnis *(n)*
En reference
(testimonial)
Es referencia
(certificado) *(f)*
Fr référence (certificat)
(f)
Pt referência
(certificado) *(f)*

refilare *vb* It
De randlos drucken
En bleed
Es correrse la tinta
Fr rogner
Pt ressumbrar

refundir *vb* Es
De revidieren
En revise
Fr reviser
It revisionare
Pt fazer a revisão de

régimen horario *(m)* Es
De Stundentarif *(m)*
En hourly rate
Fr tarif horaire *(m)*
It paga oraria *(f)*
Pt taxa horária *(f)*

register (color printing)
Am
De Einpassung *(f)*
En register (colour
printing)
Es registro (imprenta en
color) *(m)*
Fr repérage *(m)*
It registro (stampatura
a colori) *(m)*
Pt registo (impressão a
cores) *(m)*

register (colour printing)
n En
Am register (color
printing)
De Einpassung *(f)*
Es registro (imprenta en
color) *(m)*
Fr repérage *(m)*
It registro (stampatura
a colori) *(m)*
Pt registo (impressão a
cores) *(m)*

register (printing) *n* En
De Register *(n)*
Es registro (imprenta)
(m)
Fr registre *(m)*
It registro (stampatura)
(m)
Pt registo (impressão)
(m)

Register *(n)* n De
En register (printing)
Es registro (imprenta)
(m)
Fr registre *(m)*

It registro (stampatura)
(m)
Pt registo (impressão)
(m)

register marks En
De Paßkreuze *(pl)*
Es marcas de registro *(f
pl)*
Fr croix de repère *(f pl)*
It croci di registro *(m
pl)*
Pt marcas de registo *(f
pl)*

registo inexacto *(m)* Pt
De Paßdifferenz *(f)*
En misregister
Es registro inexacto *(m)*
Fr repérage défectueux
(m)
It registro scorretto *(f)*

registo (impressão) *(m)* Pt
De Register *(n)*
En register (printing)
Es registro (imprenta)
(m)
Fr registre *(m)*
It registro (stampatura)
(m)

registo (impressão a
cores) *(m)* Pt
Am register (color
printing)
De Einpassung *(f)*
En register (colour
printing)
Es registro (imprenta en
color) *(m)*
Fr repérage *(m)*
It registro (stampatura
a colori) *(m)*

registre *(m)* n Fr
De Register *(n)*
En register (printing)
Es registro (imprenta)
(m)
It registro (stampatura)
(m)
Pt registo (impressão)
(m)

Registrierpapier *(n)* n De
En chart paper
Es papel gráfico *(m)*
Fr papier pour
graphiques *(m)*
It carta da grafici *(f)*
Pt papel de mapa *(m)*

registro (imprenta) *(m)* Es
De Register *(n)*
En register (printing)
Fr registre *(m)*
It registro (stampatura) *(m)*
Pt registo (impressão) *(m)*

registro (imprenta en color) *(m)* Es
Am register (color printing)
De Einpassung *(f)*
En register (colour printing)
Fr repérage *(m)*
It registro (stampatura a colori) *(m)*
Pt registo (impressão a cores) *(m)*

registro inexacto *(m)* Es
De Paβdifferenz *(f)*
En misregister
Fr repérage défectueux *(m)*
It registro scorretto *(f)*
Pt registo inexacto *(m)*

registro scorretto *(f)* It
De Paβdifferenz *(f)*
En misregister
Es registro inexacto *(m)*
Fr repérage défectueux *(m)*
Pt registo inexacto *(m)*

registro (stampatura) *(m)* It
De Register *(n)*
En register (printing)
Es registro (imprenta) *(m)*
Fr registre *(m)*
Pt registo (impressão) *(m)*

registro (stampatura a colori) *(m)* It
Am register (color printing)
De Einpassung *(f)*
En register (colour printing)
Es registro (imprenta en color) *(m)*
Fr repérage *(m)*
Pt registo (impressão a cores) *(m)*

regla fina *(f)* Es
De Feinstrich *(m)*
En fine rule
Fr filet maigre *(m)*
It riga sottile *(f)*
Pt rilete fino *(m)*

règle *(f)* n Fr
De Strich *(m)*
En rule
Es filete *(m)*
It filetto *(m)*
Pt linha recta *(f)*

règles de coupure *(f pl)* Fr
De Trennungsregelb *(pl)*
En hyphenation rules
Es normas de separación con guiones *(f pl)*
It regole di legatura con trattino *(f pl)*
Pt regras de hifenação *(f pl)*

règles de stylisme *(f pl)* Fr
De Stil-Handbuch *(n)*
En style manual
Es manual de redacción *(m)*
It manuale di stile *(m)*
Pt manual de estilos *(m)*

règles en bleu clair *(f pl)* Fr
De blaue Linien *(pl)*
En feints *pl n*
Es rayas en azul *(f pl)*
It righi finti *(m pl)*
Pt linhas pautadas a azul-claro *(f pl)*

réglure au crayon *(f)* Fr
De Federlinierung *(f)*
En pen ruling
Es rayado a pluma *(m)*
It sottolineatura a penna *(f)*
Pt linhas à pena *(m)*

regole di legatura con trattino *(f pl)* It
De Trennungsregelb *(pl)*
En hyphenation rules
Es normas de separación con guiones *(f pl)*
Fr règles de coupure *(f pl)*

Pt regras de hifenação *(f pl)*

regras de hifenação *(f pl)* Pt
De Trennungsregelb *(pl)*
En hyphenation rules
Es normas de separación con guiones *(f pl)*
Fr règles de coupure *(f pl)*
It regole di legatura con trattino *(f pl)*

reimpresión *(f)* n Es
De Neuauflage *(f)*
En reprint
Fr réimpression *(f)*
It ristampa *(f)*
Pt reimpressão *(f)*

reimpressão *(f)* n Pt
De Neuauflage *(f)*
En reprint
Es reimpresión *(f)*
Fr réimpression *(f)*
It ristampa *(f)*

réimpression *(f)* n Fr
De Neuauflage *(f)*
En reprint
Es reimpresión *(f)*
It ristampa *(f)*
Pt reimpressão *(f)*

réimprimer *vb* Fr
De neu auflegen
En reprint
Es reimprimir
It ristampare
Pt reimprimir

reimprimir *vb* Es, Pt
De neu auflegen
En reprint
Fr réimprimer
It ristampare

Reisebuch *(n)* n De
En travel book
Es libro de viajes *(m)*
Fr livre touristique *(m)*
It libro di viaggio *(m)*
Pt livro de viagens *(m)*

Reiseleitfaden *(m)* n De
En travel guide
Es guía de viajes *(f)*
Fr guide touristique *(m)*

Pt guia turístico *(m)*

Reißfestigkeit *(f)* n De
En breaking strength (of paper)
Es resistencia a la rotura *(f)*
Fr résistance à la rupture *(f)*
It resistenza allo sfilacciamento *(f)*
Pt resistência à rotura *(f)*

Reißer *(m)* n De
En thriller
Es novela de misterio *(f)*
Fr roman à sensation *(m)*
It giallo *(m)*
Pt policial *(m)*

Reklamestreifen *(m)* n De
En blurb
Es bombo *(m)*
Fr manchette publicitaire *(f)*
It soffietto editoriale *(m)*
Pt sinopse *(f)*

relación de artículos *(f)* Es
De Eintragsliste *(f)*
En entry list
Fr liste des entrées *(f)*
It elenco di voci *(m)*
Pt lista de inscrição *(f)*

relaciones laborales *(f pl)* Es
Am labor relations
De Arbeitgeber-Arbeitnehmer-Beziehungen *(pl)*
En labour relations
Fr relations syndicales *(f pl)*
It relazioni di lavoro *(f pl)*
Pt relações laborais *(f pl)*

relações laborais *(f pl)* Pt
Am labor relations
De Arbeitgeber-Arbeitnehmer-Beziehungen *(pl)*
En labour relations
Es relaciones laborales *(f pl)*

Fr relations syndicales *(f pl)*
It relazioni di lavoro *(f pl)*

relations syndicales *(f pl)* Fr
Am labor relations
De Arbeitgeber-Arbeitnehmer-Beziehungen *(pl)*
En labour relations
Es relaciones laborales *(f pl)*
It relazioni di lavoro *(f pl)*
Pt relações laborais *(f pl)*

relatório *(m) n* Pt
De Bericht *(m)*
En report
Es informe *(m)*
Fr reportage *(m)*
It relazione *(f)*

relazionare *vb* It
De berichten
En report
Es informar
Fr faire un reportage
Pt informar

relazione *(f) n* It
De Bericht *(m)*
En report
Es informe *(m)*
Fr reportage *(m)*
Pt relatório *(m)*

relazioni di lavoro *(f pl)* It
Am labor relations
De Arbeitgeber-Arbeitnehmer-Beziehungen *(pl)*
En labour relations
Es relaciones laborales *(f pl)*
Fr relations syndicales *(f pl)*
Pt relações laborais *(f pl)*

relectura *(f) n* Es
De weitere Literatur *(f)*
En further reading
Fr lectures complémentaires *(f pl)*
It ulteriori letture *(f pl)*
Pt leitura adicional *(f)*

relevo *(m) n* Pt
De Kopf (type) *(m)*
En beard (of letter)
Es relieve *(m)*
Fr talus *(m)*
It bianco alla base *(m)*

relié en veau Fr
De gebunden in Kalbleder
En calfbound
Es encuadernado en piel de becerro
It rilegato in pelle
Pt encadernado a carneira

Reliefdruck *(m) n* De
En relief printing
Es impresión en relieve *(f)*
Fr impression en relief *(f)*
It stampa in rilievo *(f)*
Pt impressão em relevo *(f)*

relief printing En
De Reliefdruck *(m)*
Es impresión en relieve *(f)*
Fr impression en relief *(f)*
It stampa in rilievo *(f)*
Pt impressão em relevo *(f)*

relier *vb* Fr
De binden
En bind
Es encuadernar
It rilegare
Pt encadernar

relieur *(m) n* Fr
De Buchbinder *(m)*
En binder
Es encuadernador *(m)*
It rilegatore *(m)*
Pt encadernador *(m)*

relieve *(m) n* Es
De Kopf (type) *(m)*
En beard (of letter)
Fr talus *(m)*
It bianco alla base *(m)*
Pt relevo *(m)*

reliure *(f) n* Fr
De Buchbinden *(n)*
En bookbinding

Es encuadernación de libros *(f)*
It rilegatura *(f)*
Pt encadernação *(f)*

reliure à anneaux *(f)* Fr
De Ringbindung *(f)*
En ring binding
Es encuadernación con anillas *(f)*
It legatura ad anelli *(f)*
Pt encadernação com anilhas *(f)*

reliure à feuillets mobiles *(f)* Fr
De Loseblattbindung *(f)*
En loose-leaf binding
Es encuadernación de hojas sueltas *(f)*
It legatura a fogli sciolti *(f)*
Pt encadernação de folhas soltas *(f)*

reliure à machine *(f)* Fr
De Maschinenbinden *(n)*
En machine binding
Es encuadernación a machina *(f)*
It rilegatura a macchina *(f)*
Pt encadernação à máquina *(f)*

reliure bibliothèque publique *(f)* Fr
De Buch mit Bibliothek-Einband *(n)*
En library-bound book
Es libro encuadernado para biblioteca *(m)*
It libro rilegato per biblioteca *(m)*
Pt livro encadernado para biblioteca *(m)*

reliure ciselée *(f)* Fr
De Punzenbindung *(f)*
En tooled binding
Es encuadernación repujada *(f)*
It rilegatura con attrezzi *(f)*
Pt encadernação ornamentada *(f)*

reliure cousue *(f)* Fr
De geheftete Arbeit *(f)*
En sewn work
Es obra cosida *(f)*

It lavoro di cucitura *(m)*
Pt obra cosida *(f)*

reliure imprimerie *(f)* Fr
De Buchdruck-Binden *(n)*
En letterpress binding
Es acuñado tipográfico *(m)*
It legatura da tipografia *(f)*
Pt encadernação tipográfica *(f)*

reliure mécanique *(f)* Fr
De mechanische Bindung *(f)*
En mechanical binding
Es encuadernación mecánica *(f)*
It legatura meccanica *(f)*
Pt encadernação mecânica *(f)*

reliure papeterie *(f)* Fr
De Briefpapier-Binden *(n)*
En stationery binding
Es acuñado de material de escritorio *(m)*
It rilegatura da cartoleria *(f)*
Pt encadernação para escritório *(f)*

reliure parfaite *(f)* Fr
De Klebebindung *(f)*
En perfect binding
Es encuadernación sin cosido *(f)*
It rilegatura perfetta *(f)*
Pt encadernação sem costura *(f)*

reliure pleine Fr
De voll gebunden
En fully bound
Es totalmente encuadernado
It completamente rilegato
Pt completamente encadernado

reliure sans couture *(f)* Fr
De nicht geheftete Bindung *(f)*
En unsewn binding
Es encuadernación sin coser *(f)*

It rilegatura non cucita *(f)*
Pt encadernação não cosida *(f)*

reliure souple *(f)* Fr
De flexibles Binden *(n)*
En flexible binding
Es encuadernación flexible *(f)*
It rilegatura flessibile *(f)*
Pt encadernação flexível *(f)*

reliure spirale *(f)* Fr
De Spiralbindung *(f)*
En spiral binding
Es encuadernación en espirale *(f)*
It rilegatura a spirale *(f)*
Pt encadernação em espiral *(f)*

remainder books En
De Remittenden *(pl)*
Es restos de edición *(m pl)*
Fr solde d'éditions *(m)*
It rimanenze *(f pl)*
Pt restos de edição *(m pl)*

remainder bookshop En
De Remittenden-Buchladen *(m)*
Es libreria de restos de edición *(f)*
Fr librairie de solde d'éditions *(f)*
It libreria di rimanenze *(f)*
Pt livraria de restos de edição *(f)*

remaniement *(m)* n Fr
De Umbrechen *(n)*
En over-running
Es recorrido *(m)*
It rimaneggiamento *(m)*
Pt acto de recorrer *(m)*

remanier *vb* Fr
De neu setzen
En reset
Es componer de nuevo
It riazzerare
Pt tornar a compor

remate *(m)* n Pt
De Serif *(m)*
En serif

Es bigotillo *(m)*
Fr empâtement *(m)*
It terminazione *(f)*

remerciements *(m pl)* Fr
De Anerkennung *(f)*
En acknowledgments; credits *pl n*
Es agradecimientos; créditos *(m pl)*
It ringraziamenti *(m pl)*
Pt agradecimentos; créditos *(m pl)*

Remittenden *(pl)* n De
En remainder books
Es restos de edición *(m pl)*
Fr solde d'éditions *(m)*
It rimanenze *(f pl)*
Pt restos de edição *(m pl)*

Remittenden-Buchladen *(m)* De
En remainder bookshop
Es libreria de restos de edición *(f)*
Fr librairie de solde d'éditions *(f)*
It libreria di rimanenze *(f)*
Pt livraria de restos de edição *(f)*

rendimentos *(m pl)* Pt
De Einnahmen *(pl)*
En earnings *pl n*
Es beneficios *(m pl)*
Fr bénéfices *(m pl)*
It entrate *(f pl)*

renfoncé d'alinéa *(m)* Fr
De Paragrapheinrückung *(f)*
En paragraph indent
Es sangría de párrafo *(f)*
It indentro del paragrafo *(m)*
Pt reentrância de parágrafo *(f)*

renforcer *vb* Fr
De einrücken
En indent
Es sangrar
It dentellare
Pt abrir parágrafo

renvoi *(m)* n Fr
De Querverweis *(m)*
En cross reference
Es interreferencia *(f)*
It rimando *(m)*
Pt nota remissiva *(f)*

renvoi de marge *(m)* Fr
De Auslassungszeichen *(n)*
En caret mark
Es signo de intercalación *(m)*
It segno di rimando *(m)*
Pt sinal de intercalar *(m)*

reogramma *(m)* n It
De Schaubild *(n)*
En flow chart
Es organigrama *(f)*
Fr schéma de fabrication *(m)*
Pt diagrama de fluxo *(m)*

reparto diritti esteri *(m)* It
De Auslandsrecht-Abteilung *(f)*
En foreign-rights department
Es departamento de derechos en el extranjero *(m)*
Fr service des droits à l'étranger *(m)*
Pt departamento de direitos estrangeiros *(m)*

reparto produzione *(m)* It
De Produktionsabteilung *(f)*
En production department
Es departamento de producción *(m)*
Fr service production *(m)*
Pt departamento de produção *(m)*

reparto pubblicitario *(m)* It
De Werbeabteilung *(f)*
En publicity department
Es departamento de publicidad *(m)*
Fr service de la publicité *(m)*
Pt departamento de publicidade *(f)*

reparto vendite per posta *(m)* It
De Versandhaus-abteilung *(f)*
En mail-order division
Es división de pedidos por correo *(f)*
Fr service VPC *(m)*
Pt divisão de encomendas por correio *(f)*

repeat *vb* En
De wiederholen
Es repetir
Fr répéter
It ripetere
Pt repetir

repérage *(m)* n Fr
Am register (color printing)
De Einpassung *(f)*
En register (colour printing)
Es registro (imprenta en color) *(m)*
It registro (stampatura a colori) *(m)*
Pt registo (impressão a cores) *(m)*

repérage défectueux *(m)* Fr
De Paßdifferenz *(f)*
En misregister
Es registro inexacto *(m)*
It registro scorretto *(f)*
Pt registo inexacto *(m)*

repères d'assemblage *(m pl)* Fr
De Kollationierzeichen *(pl)*
En collating marks *pl n*
Es señales escalonadas de alzado *(f pl)*
It segni di raccoglitura *(m pl)*
Pt marcas de revisão *(f pl)*

repères de rognage *(m pl)* Fr
De Beschnitt-Markierungen *(pl)*
En trim marks
Es marcas de recorte *(f pl)*
It segni per rifilatura *(m pl)*

Pt marcas de aparar *(f pl)*

répertoire géographique *(m)* Fr
De geographisches Lexicon *(n)*
En gazetteer
Es gacetero *(m)*
It dizionario geografico *(m)*
Pt dicionário geográfico *(m)*

répéter *vb* Fr
De wiederholen
En repeat
Es repetir
It ripetere
Pt repetir

repetição *(f)* n Pt
De Wiederholung *(f)*
En repetition
Es repetición *(f)*
Fr répétition *(f)*
It ripetizione *(f)*

repetición *(f)* n Es
De Wiederholung *(f)*
En repetition
Fr répétition *(f)*
It ripetizione *(f)*
Pt repetição *(f)*

repetir *vb* Es, Pt
De wiederholen
En repeat
Fr répéter
It ripetere

repetition n En
De Wiederholung *(f)*
Es repetición *(f)*
Fr répétition *(f)*
It ripetizione *(f)*
Pt repetição *(f)*

répétition *(f)* n Fr
De Wiederholung *(f)*
En repetition
Es repetición *(f)*
It ripetizione *(f)*
Pt repetição *(f)*

report n En
De Bericht *(m)*
Es informe *(m)*
Fr reportage *(m)*

It relazione *(f)*
Pt relatório *(m)*

report *vb* En
De berichten
Es informar
Fr faire un reportage
It relazionare
Pt informar

reportage *(m)* n Fr
De Bericht *(m)*
En report
Es informe *(m)*
It relazione *(f)*
Pt relatório *(m)*

reporter n En; Fr, Pt *(m)*
De Berichterstatter *(m)*
Es reportero *(m)*
It cronista *(m)*

reportero *(m)* n Es
De Berichterstatter *(m)*
En reporter
Fr reporter *(m)*
It cronista *(m)*
Pt reporter *(m)*

repoussage *(m)* n Fr
De Prägestempel *(m)*
En die stamping
Es estampación en relieve *(f)*
It stampa incavorilierografica *(f)*
Pt cestampagem em relevo *(f)*

représentant *(m)* n Fr
De Handelsvertreter *(m)*
En representative
Es representante *(m)*
It rappresentante *(m)*
Pt representante *(m)*

représentant chargé des commandes *(m)* Fr
De Auftragsvertreter *(m)*
En commission representative
Es representante a comisión *(f)*
It rappresentante commissione *(m)*
Pt representante à comissão *(m)*

representante *(m)* n Es, Pt
De Handelsvertreter *(m)*
En representative
Fr représentant *(m)*
It rappresentante *(m)*

representante a comisión *(m)* Es
De Auftragsvertreter *(m)*
En commission representative
Fr représentant chargé des commandes *(m)*
It rappresentante commissione *(m)*
Pt representante à comissão *(m)*

representante à comissão *(m)* Pt
De Auftragsvertreter *(m)*
En commission representative
Es representante a comisión *(m)*
Fr représentant chargé des commandes *(m)*
It rappresentante commissione *(m)*

représentation typographique *(f)* Fr
De Satzgestaltung *(f)*
En typographic design
Es diseño tipográfico *(m)*
It disegno tipografico *(m)*
Pt desenho tipográfico *(m)*

representative n En
De Handelsvertreter *(m)*
Es representante *(m)*
Fr représentant *(m)*
It rappresentante *(m)*
Pt representante *(m)*

reprint *vb* En
De neu auflegen
Es reimprimir
Fr réimprimer
It ristampare
Pt reimprimir

reprint n En
De Neuauflage *(f)*
Es reimpresión *(f)*
Fr réimpression *(f)*

It ristampa *(f)*
Pt reimpressão *(f)*

Repro-Abzug *(m)* De
En reproduction proof
Es prueba de reproducción *(f)*
Fr épreuve de reproduction *(f)*
It prova di fotoriproduzione *(f)*
Pt prova de reprodução *(f)*

reprodução *(f)* n Pt
De Reproduktion *(f)*
En reproduction
Es reproducción *(f)*
Fr reproduction *(f)*
It riproduzione *(f)*

reproducción *(f)* n Es
De Reproduktion *(f)*
En reproduction
Fr reproduction *(f)*
It riproduzione *(f)*
Pt reprodução *(f)*

reproducción directa *(f)* Es
De Direktverfahren *(n)*
En direct process
Fr procédé direct *(m)*
It procedimento diretto *(m)*
Pt processo directo *(m)*

reproduce *vb* En
De reproduzieren
Es reproducir
Fr reproduire
It riprodurre
Pt reproduzir

reproducir *vb* Es
De reproduzieren
En reproduce
Fr reproduire
It riprodurre
Pt reproduzir

reproduction n En; Fr *(f)*
De Reproduktion *(f)*
Es reproducción *(f)*
It riproduzione *(f)*
Pt reprodução *(f)*

reproduction proof En
De Repro-Abzug *(m)*

Es prueba de
reproducción *(f)*
Fr épreuve de
reproduction *(f)*
It prova di
fotoriproduzione *(f)*
Pt prova de reprodução
(f)

reproduire *vb* Fr
De reproduzieren
En reproduce
Es reproducir
It riprodurre
Pt reproduzir

Reproduktion *(f) n* De
En reproduction
Es reproducción *(f)*
Fr reproduction *(f)*
It riproduzione *(f)*
Pt reprodução *(f)*

Reproduktionsgerät *(n)*
n De
En process camera
Es cámara fotomecánica
(f)
Fr appareil
photomécanique *(m)*
It macchina fotografica
per riproduzioni
fotomeccaniche *(f)*
Pt câmara de
processamento *(f)*

reproduzieren *vb* De
En reproduce
Es reproducir
Fr reproduire
It riprodurre
Pt reproduzir

reproduzir *vb* Pt
De reproduzieren
En reproduce
Es reproducir
Fr reproduire
It riprodurre

reprographic printing En
De Reprographiedruck
(m)
Es impresión
reprográfica *(f)*
Fr reprographie *(f)*
It stampa reprografica
(f)
Pt impressão
reprográfica *(f)*

reprographie *(f) n* Fr
De Reprographiedruck
(m)
En reprographic printing
Es impresión
reprográfica *(f)*
It stampa reprografica
(f)
Pt impressão
reprográfica *(f)*

Reprographiedruck *(m)*
n De
En reprographic printing
Es impresión
reprográfica *(f)*
Fr reprographie *(f)*
It stampa reprografica
(f)
Pt impressão
reprográfica *(f)*

research assistant En
De Forschungs-
Assistent *(m)*
Es ayudante de
investigación *(m)*
Fr assistant des
recherches *(m)*
It assistente di ricerca
(m)
Pt ajudante de
investigação *(m)*

réseau de distribution
(m) Fr
De Vertriebsnetz *(n)*
En distribution network
Es red de distribución *(f)*
It rete di distribuzione
(f)
Pt rede de distribuição
(f)

reseña *(f) n* Es
De Rezension *(f)*
En review
Fr critique d'un livre *(f)*
It recensione *(f)*
Pt resenha *(f)*

reseña en la cubierta *(f)*
Es
De Umschlag-
Reklamestreifen *(m)*
En jacket blurb
Fr manchette sur la
jaquette *(f)*
It sommario della
sovracopertina *(m)*
Pt sinopse de
sobrecapa *(f)*

resenha *(f) n* Pt
De Rezension *(f)*
En review
Es reseña *(f)*
Fr critique d'un livre *(f)*
It recensione *(f)*

reservados todos los
derechos Es
De alle Rechte
vorbehalten
En all rights reserved
Fr tous droits réservés
It tutti i diritti riservati
Pt todos os direitos
reservados

reset *vb* En
De neu setzen
Es componer de nuevo
Fr remanier
It riazzerare
Pt tornar a compor

résistance à la rupture
(f) Fr
De Reißfestigkeit *(f)*
En breaking strength (of
paper)
Es resistencia a la rotura
(f)
It resistenza allo
sfilacciamento *(f)*
Pt resistência à rotura *(f)*

résistance à
l'éclatement *(f)* Fr
De Berstwiderstand *(m)*
En bursting strength
Es resistencia al
reventamiento *(f)*
It resistenza alla rottura
(f)
Pt resistência ao
arrebentamento *(f)*

résistant à l'acide Fr
De säurebeständig
En acid-resist
Es resistente al ácido
It resistente agli acidi
Pt resistente contra
ácidos

resistencia a la rotura *(f)*
Es
De Reißfestigkeit *(f)*
En breaking strength (of
paper)
Fr résistance à la
rupture *(f)*

It resistenza allo
sfilacciamento *(f)*
Pt resistência à rotura *(f)*

resistencia al
reventamiento *(f)*
Es
De Berstwiderstand *(m)*
En bursting strength
Fr résistance à
l'éclatement *(f)*
It resistenza alla rottura
(f)
Pt resistência ao
arrebentamento *(f)*

resistência ao
arrebentamento *(f)*
Pt
De Berstwiderstand *(m)*
En bursting strength
Es resistencia al
reventamiento *(f)*
Fr résistance à
l'éclatement *(f)*
It resistenza alla rottura
(f)

resistência à rotura *(f)* Pt
De Reißfestigkeit *(f)*
En breaking strength (of
paper)
Es resistencia a la rotura
(f)
Fr résistance à la
rupture *(f)*
It resistenza allo
sfilacciamento *(f)*

resistente agli acidi It
De säurebeständig
En acid-resist
Es resistente al ácido
Fr résistant à l'acide
Pt resistente contra
ácidos

resistente al ácido Es
De säurebeständig
En acid-resist
Fr résistant à l'acide
It resistente agli acidi
Pt resistente contra
ácidos

resistente contra ácidos
Pt
De säurebeständig
En acid-resist
Es resistente al ácido
Fr résistant à l'acide
It resistente agli acidi

resistenza alla rottura (f)
It
De Berstwiderstand (m)
En bursting strength
Es resistencia al
  reventamiento (f)
Fr résistance à
  l'éclatement (f)
Pt resistência ao
  arrebentamento (f)

**resistenza allo
sfilacciamento** (f) It
De Reißfestigkeit (f)
En breaking strength (of
  paper)
Es resistencia a la rotura
  (f)
Fr résistance à la
  rupture (f)
Pt resistência à rotura (f)

resma (f) n Es, Pt
De Ries (n)
En ream
Fr rame de papier (f)
It risma (f)

respaldado (m) n Es
De Widerdruck (m)
En backing-up
Fr mettant en retiration
  (f)
It supporto (m)
Pt apoio (m)

Respektblatt (n) n De
En flyleaf
Es cortesía (f)
Fr feuille de garde (f)
It risguardo (m)
Pt folha em branco (f)

ressumbrar vb Pt
De randlos drucken
En bleed
Es correrse la tinta
Fr rogner
It refilare

restos de edição (m pl)
  Pt
De Remittenden (pl)
En remainder books
Es restos de edición (m
  pl)
Fr solde d'éditions (m)
It rimanenze (f pl)

restos de edición (m pl)
  Es
De Remittenden (pl)
En remainder books
Fr solde d'éditions (m)
It rimanenze (f pl)
Pt restos de edição (m
  pl)

résumé (m) n Fr
De Zusammenfassung (f)
En summary
Es sumario (m)
It sommario (m)
Pt resumo (m)

resumen (m) n Es
De Übersicht (f)
En précis
Fr précis (m)
It riassunto (m)
Pt resumo (m)

résumer vb Fr
De zusammenfassen
En précis
Es resumir
It riassumere
Pt resumir

resumir vb Es, Pt
De zusammenfassen
En précis
Fr résumer
It riassumere

resumo (m) n Pt
De Übersicht (f)
En précis
Es resumen (m)
Fr précis (m)
It riassunto (m)

retailer n En
De Einzelhändler (m)
Es minorista (m)
Fr détaillant (m)
It dettagliante (m)
Pt retalhista (m)

retail sales En
De Einzelhandels-
  Verkäufe (pl)
Es ventas al por menor (f
  pl)
Fr vente au détail (f)
It vendite al minuto (f
  pl)
Pt vendas a retalho (f pl)

retalhista (m) n Pt
De Einzelhändler (m)
En retailer
Es minorista (m)
Fr détaillant (m)
It dettagliante (m)

rete di distribuzione (f)
It
De Vertriebsnetz (n)
En distribution network
Es red de distribución (f)
Fr réseau de
  distribution (m)
Pt rede de distribuição
  (f)

retícula (f) n Es, Pt
De Raster (m)
En screen
Fr écran (m)
It retino (m)

retícula de contacto (f)
  Es, Pt
De Kontaktraster (m)
En contact screen
Fr écran de contact (m)
It retino a contatto (m)

retícula fina (f) Pt
De feiner Raster (m)
En fine screen
Es trama fina (f)
Fr trame fine (f)
It retino fine (m)

retícula grossa (f) Pt
De grober Raster (m)
En coarse screen
Es trama gruesa (f)
Fr trame à gros grains
  (f)
It a grana grossa (f)

retino (m) n It
De Raster (m)
En screen
Es retícula (f)
Fr écran (m)
Pt retícula (f)

retino a contatto (m) It
De Kontaktraster (m)
En contact screen
Es retícula de contacto
  (f)
Fr écran de contact (m)
Pt retícula de contacto
  (f)

retino di mezzatinta (m)
It
De Halbtonraster (m)
En halftone screen
Es trama de medio tono
  (f)
Fr trame (f)
Pt retítula de autotipia
  (f)

retino fine (m) It
De feiner Raster (m)
En fine screen
Es trama fina (f)
Fr trame fine (f)
Pt retícula fina (f)

retiración (f) n Es
De Schön- und
  Widerdruck (m)
En perfecting
Fr retiration (f)
It stampa in volta (f)
Pt impressão
  simultânea de ambos
  lados (f)

retiration (f) n Fr
De Schön- und
  Widerdruck (m)
En perfecting
Es retiración (f)
It stampa in volta (f)
Pt impressão
  simultânea de ambos
  lados (f)

retítula de autotipia (f)
  Pt
De Halbtonraster (m)
En halftone screen
Es trama de medio tono
  (f)
Fr trame (f)
It retino di mezzatinta
  (m)

retocado (m) n Es
De Retuschierung (f)
En retouching
Fr retouche (f)
It ritocco (m)
Pt retoque (m)

retocar vb Es, Pt
De retuschieren
En retouch
Fr retoucher
It ritoccare

retoque (m) n Pt
De Retuschierung (f)
En retouching
Es retocado (m)
Fr retouche (f)
It ritocco (m)

retouch vb En
De retuschieren
Es retocar
Fr retoucher
It ritoccare
Pt retocar

retouche (f) n Fr
De Retuschierung (f)
En retouching
Es retocado (m)
It ritocco (m)
Pt retoque (m)

retoucher vb Fr
De retuschieren
En retouch
Es retocar
It ritoccare
Pt retocar

retouching n En
De Retuschierung (f)
Es retocado (m)
Fr retouche (f)
It ritocco (m)
Pt retoque (m)

retrato (m) n Es, Pt
De Portrait (n)
En portrait
Fr portrait (m)
It ritratto (m)

retree n En
De mangelhaftes Papier
(n)
Es papel ligeramente
defectuoso (m)
Fr papier imparfait (m)
It riscelta (f)
Pt papel defeituoso (m)

returns pl n En
De Rückgüter (pl)
Es devoluciones (f pl)
Fr invendus (m pl)
It ritorni (m pl)
Pt devoluções (f pl)

Retuschierapparat (m) n
De
En airbrush

Es pistola pulverizadora
(f)
Fr pinceau
pneumatique (m)
It polverizzatrice ad aria
compressa (f)
Pt pistola pulverizadora
(f)

retuschieren vb De
En retouch
Es retocar
Fr retoucher
It ritoccare
Pt retocar

Retuschierung (f) n De
En retouching
Es retocado (m)
Fr retouche (f)
It ritocco (m)
Pt retoque (m)

reunião (f) n Pt
De Zusammentragen (n)
En gathering
Es recogida (f)
Fr assemblage (m)
It raccolta (f)

réunion de vente (f) Fr
De Verkaufskonferenz (f)
En sales conference
Es conferencia de
ventas (f)
It conferenza di vendita
(f)
Pt conferência de
vendedores (f)

reunir vb Es, Pt
De zusammentragen
En gather
Fr rassembler
It raccogliere

revelar vb Es, Pt
De entwickeln
(Photographie)
En develop
(photography)
Fr développer
It sviluppare

revenue n En
De Einkommen (n)
Es ingresos (m pl)
Fr recette (f)
It entrata (f)
Pt receita (f)

rever vb Pt
De vergleichen
En collate
Es alzar
Fr assembler
It collazionare

rever provas Pt
De korrekturlesen
En proofread
Es corregir pruebas
Fr corriger les épreuves
It correggere le bozze

reversal film En
De Umkehrfilm (m)
Es película reversible (f)
Fr film noir au blanc (m)
It pellicola invertibile (f)
Pt película de inversão
(f)

reverso (m) n Es
De Rückseite (f)
En verso
Fr verso (m)
It verso (m)
Pt verso (m)

revestimento (m) n Pt
De Streichen (n)
En coating
Es revestimiento (m)
Fr couchage du papier
(m)
It rivestimento (m)

revestimiento (m) n Es
De Streichen (n)
En coating
Fr couchage du papier
(m)
It rivestimento (m)
Pt revestimento (m)

revidieren vb De
En revise
Es refundir
Fr reviser
It revisionare
Pt fazer a revisão de

revidierter Abzug (m) De
En revised proofs
Es pruebas corregidas (f
pl)
Fr épreuves de révision
(f pl)
It bozze corrette (f pl)
Pt provas revistas (f pl)

**revidierte und
überarbeitete
Auflage** (f) De
En revised and updated
edition
Es edición corregida y
puesta al día (f)
Fr édition révisée et
mise à jour (f)
It edizione corretta ed
aggiornata (f)
Pt edição revista e
actualizada (f)

review n En
De Rezension (f)
Es reseña (f)
Fr critique d'un livre (f)
It recensione (f)
Pt resenha (f)

review copy En
De Rezensions-Exemplar
(n)
Es ejemplar para reseña
(m)
Fr exemplaire de service
de presse (m)
It copia di recensione
(f)
Pt exemplar para
resenha (m)

revisão (f) n Pt
De Zusammentragung (f)
En collating
Es alzado (m)
Fr assemblage (m)
It raccoglitura (f)

revisão de provas (f) Pt
De Korrekturlesen (n)
En proofreading
Es corrección de
pruebas (f)
Fr correction
d'épreuves (f)
It correzione di bozze (f)

revisão do original (f) Pt
De Manuskriptrevision (f)
En copy-editing
Es corrección de
originales (f)
Fr préparation d'un
texte (f)
It correzione di originali
(f)

revise vb En
De revidieren
Es refundir

Fr reviser
It revisionare
Pt fazer a revisão de

**revised and updated
edition** En
De revidierte und
überarbeitete Auflage
(f)
Es edición corregida y
puesta al día (f)
Fr édition révisée et
mise à jour (f)
It edizione corretta ed
aggiornata (f)
Pt edição revista e
actualizada (f)

revised proofs En
De revidierter Abzug (m)
Es pruebas corregidas (f
pl)
Fr épreuves de révision
(f pl)
It bozze corrette (f pl)
Pt provas revistas (f pl)

reviser vb Fr
De revidieren
En revise
Es refundir
It revisionare
Pt fazer a revisão de

revisionare vb It
De revidieren
En revise
Es refundir
Fr reviser
Pt fazer a revisão de

revisor de provas (m) Pt
De Korrekturleser (m)
En proofreader
Es corrector de pruebas
(m)
Fr correcteur
d'épreuves (m)
It correttore di bozze
(m)

revisor do original (m) Pt
De Manuskriptredakteur
(m)
En copy-editor
Es corrector de
originales (m)
Fr annotateur d'un texte
(m)
It correttore di originali
(m)

revista (f) n Es, Pt
De Magazin (n)
En magazine (journal)
Fr magazine (m)
It rivista (f)

revista científica (f) Es,
Pt
De wissenschaftliches
Journal (n)
En scientific journal
Fr revue scientifique (f)
It rivista scientifica (f)

revista comercial (f) Pt
De Fachzeitschrift (f)
En trade journal
Es revista profesional (f)
Fr revue professionnelle
(f)
It rivista commerciale
(f)

revista de informação (f)
Pt
De Nachrichtenmagazin
(n)
En news magazine
Es revista de
información (f)
Fr magazine
d'information (m)
It rivista di attualità (f)

revista de información
(f) Es
De Nachrichtenmagazin
(n)
En news magazine
Fr magazine
d'information (m)
It rivista di attualità (f)
Pt revista de informação
(f)

revista especializada (f)
Es
De Spezial-Journal (n)
En specialist journal
Fr revue spécialisée (f)
It rivista specializzata (f)
Pt revista para
especialistas (f)

**revista para
especialistas** (f) Pt
De Spezial-Journal (n)
En specialist journal
Es revista especializada
(f)
Fr revue spécialisée (f)
It rivista specializzata (f)

revista profesional (f) Es
De Fachzeitschrift (f)
En trade journal
Fr revue professionnelle
(f)
It rivista commerciale
(f)
Pt revista comercial (f)

revue (f) n Fr
De Journal (n)
En journal
Es periódico (m)
It giornale (m)
Pt jornal (m)

revue professionnelle
(f) Fr
De Fachzeitschrift (f)
En trade journal
Es revista profesional (f)
It rivista commerciale
(f)
Pt revista comercial (f)

revue scientifique (f) Fr
De wissenschaftliches
Journal (n)
En scientific journal
Es revista científica (f)
It rivista scientifica (f)
Pt revista científica (f)

revue spécialisée (f) Fr
De Spezial-Journal (n)
En specialist journal
Es revista especializada
(f)
It rivista specializzata (f)
Pt revista para
especialistas (f)

Rezension (f) n De
En review
Es reseña (f)
Fr critique d'un livre (f)
It recensione (f)
Pt resenha (f)

Rezensions-Exemplar
(n) n De
En review copy
Es ejemplar para reseña
(m)
Fr exemplaire de service
de presse (m)
It copia di recensione
(f)
Pt exemplar para
resenha (m)

riassumere vb It
De zusammenfassen
En précis
Es resumir
Fr résumer
Pt resumir

riassunto (m) n It
De Übersicht (f)
En précis
Es resumen (m)
Fr précis (m)
Pt resumo (m)

riazzerare vb It
De neu setzen
En reset
Es componer de nuevo
Fr remanier
Pt tornar a compor

riccamente illustrato It
De großzügig illustriert
En lavishly illustrated
Es profusamente
ilustrado
Fr abondamment
illustré
Pt profusamente
ilustrado

ricerca di mercato (f) It
De Marktforschung (f)
En market research
Es investigación del
mercado (f)
Fr analyse de marché (f)
Pt investigação do
mercado (f)

**richtige dickes
Blindband** (n) De
En bulked dummy
Es maqueta realzada (f)
Fr maquette garnie (f)
It menabò di grossezza
preciso (m)
Pt maquete engrossada
(f)

**riconoscimento ottico
dei caratteri** (m) It
De Klarschriftlesen (n)
En optical character
recognition (OCR)
Es reconocimiento
óptico de caracteres
(m)
Fr lecture optique (f)
Pt reconhecimento
óptico de caracteres
(m)

ridondanza *(f) n* It
De Entlassung *(f)*
En redundancy
Es redundancia *(f)*
Fr chomage partiel *(m)*
Pt redundância *(f)*

ridurre *vb* It
De verkleinern
En reduce
Es reducir
Fr réduire
Pt reduzir

riduzione in serie *(f)* It
De Veröffentlichung in
   Fortsetzungen *(f)*
En serialization
Es publicación por
   entregas *(f)*
Fr parution en feuilleton
   (f)
Pt publicação em série
   (f)

Ries *(n) n* De
En ream
Es resma *(f)*
Fr rame de papier *(m)*
It risma *(f)*
Pt resma *(f)*

riferimento *(m) n* It
De Referenz *(f)*
En reference (literary)
Es referencia (literaria)
   (f)
Fr référence (littéraire)
   (f)
Pt referência (literária)
   (f)

riferimento fotografico
   (m) It
De Photobezug *(m)*
En photographic
   reference
Es referencia fotográfica
   (f)
Fr référence
   photographique *(f)*
Pt referência fotográfica
   (f)

rifilare *vb* It
De beschneiden
En trim
Es cortar
Fr ébarber
Pt aparar

rifilatura *(f) n* It
De Beschneiden *(n)*
En trimming
Es recorte *(m)*
Fr rognage *(m)*
Pt aparagem *(f)*

riga *(f) n* It
De Geviert *(n)*
En em
Es cuadratín *(m)*
Fr cadratin *(m)*
Pt quadratim *(m)*

riga intera *(f)* It
De Setzmaschinenzeile
   (f)
En slug
Es lingote *(m)*
Fr lingot *(m)*
Pt lingote *(m)*

riga sottile *(f)* It
De Feinstrich *(m)*
En fine rule
Es regla fina *(f)*
Fr filet maigre *(m)*
Pt rilete fino *(m)*

righi finti *(m pl)* It
De blaue Linien *(pl)*
En feints *pl n*
Es rayas en azul *(f pl)*
Fr règles en bleu clair *(f
   pl)*
Pt linhas pautadas a
   azul-claro *(f pl)*

right-hand page En
De rechte Seite *(f)*
Es página derecha *(f)*
Fr belle page *(f)*
It pagina di destra *(f)*
Pt página da direita *(f)*

right-reading film En
De seitenrichtiger Film
   (m)
Es película de lectura
   correcta *(f)*
Fr film à lecture juste
   (m)
It pellicola a lettura
   giusta *(f)*
Pt película de leitura do
   lado direito *(f)*

rilegare *vb* It
De binden
En bind
Es encuadernar

Fr relier
Pt encadernar

rilegato in pelle It
De gebunden in
   Kalbleder
En calfbound
Es encuadernado en piel
   de becerro
Fr relié en veau
Pt encadernado a
   carneira

rilegatore *(m) n* It
De Buchbinder *(m)*
En binder
Es encuadernador *(m)*
Fr relieur *(m)*
Pt encadernador *(m)*

rilegatura *(f) n* It
De Buchbinden *(n)*
En bookbinding
Es encuadernación de
   libros *(f)*
Fr reliure *(f)*
Pt encadernação *(f)*

rilegatura a macchina *(f)*
   It
De Maschinenbinden *(n)*
En machine binding
Es encuadernación a
   machina *(f)*
Fr reliure à machine *(f)*
Pt encadernação à
   máquina *(f)*

rilegatura a spirale *(f)* It
De Spiralbindung *(f)*
En spiral binding
Es encuadernación en
   espiral *(f)*
Fr reliure spirale *(f)*
Pt encadernação em
   espiral *(f)*

rilegatura con attrezzi
   (f) It
De Punzenbindung *(f)*
En tooled binding
Es encuadernación
   repujada *(f)*
Fr reliure ciselée *(f)*
Pt encadernação
   ornamentada *(f)*

rilegatura da cartoleria
   (f) It
De Briefpapier-Binden
   (n)

En stationery binding
Es acuñado de material
   de escritorio *(m)*
Fr reliure papeterie *(f)*
Pt encadernação para
   escritório *(f)*

rilegatura flessibile *(f)* It
De flexibles Binden *(n)*
En flexible binding
Es encuadernación
   flexible *(f)*
Fr reliure souple *(f)*
Pt encadernação flexível
   (f)

rilegatura non cucita *(f)*
   It
De nicht geheftete
   Bindung *(f)*
En unsewn binding
Es encuadernación sin
   coser *(f)*
Fr reliure sans couture
   (f)
Pt encadernação não
   cosida *(f)*

rilegatura perfetta *(f)* It
De Klebebindung *(f)*
En perfect binding
Es encuadernación sin
   cosido *(f)*
Fr reliure parfaite *(f)*
Pt encadernação sem
   costura *(f)*

rilete fino *(m)* Pt
De Feinstrich *(m)*
En fine rule
Es regla fina *(f)*
Fr filet maigre *(m)*
It riga sottile *(f)*

rimando *(m) n* It
De Querverweis *(m)*
En cross reference
Es interreferencia *(f)*
Fr renvoi *(m)*
Pt nota remissiva *(f)*

rimaneggiamento *(m) n*
   It
De Umbrechen *(n)*
En over-running
Es recorrido *(m)*
Fr remaniement *(m)*
Pt acto de recorrer *(m)*

rimanenze *(f pl)* n It
De Remittenden *(pl)*
En remainder books
Es restos de edición *(m pl)*
Fr solde d'éditions *(m)*
Pt restos de edição *(m pl)*

rinforzo *(m)* n It
De Abpressen *(n)*
En backing
Es formación de cajos *(f)*
Fr endossure *(f)*
Pt colocação de lombada *(f)*

ring binding En
De Ringbindung *(f)*
Es encuadernación con anillas *(f)*
Fr reliure à anneaux *(f)*
It legatura ad anelli *(f)*
Pt encadernação com anilhas *(f)*

Ringbindung *(f)* n De
En ring binding
Es encuadernación con anillas *(f)*
Fr reliure à anneaux *(f)*
It legatura ad anelli *(f)*
Pt encadernação com anilhas *(f)*

ringraziamenti *(m pl)* It
De Anerkennung *(f)*
En acknowledgments pl n
Es agradecimientos *(m pl)*
Fr remerciements *(m pl)*
Pt agradecimentos *(m pl)*

ringraziamento *(m)* It
De Anerkennung *(f)*
En credits pl n
Es créditos *(m pl)*
Fr remerciements *(m pl)*
Pt créditos *(m pl)*

ripetere *vb* It
De wiederholen
En repeat
Es repetir
Fr répéter
Pt repetir

ripetizione *(f)* n It
De Wiederholung *(f)*
En repetition
Es repetición *(f)*
Fr répétition *(f)*
Pt repetição *(f)*

riprodurre *vb* It
De reproduzieren
En reproduce
Es reproducir
Fr reproduire
Pt reproduzir

riproduzione *(f)* n It
De Reproduktion *(f)*
En reproduction
Es reproducción *(f)*
Fr reproduction *(f)*
Pt reprodução *(f)*

riscelta *(f)* n It
De mangelhaftes Papier *(n)*
En retree
Es papel ligeramente defectuoso *(m)*
Fr papier imparfait *(m)*
Pt papel defeituoso *(m)*

risguardi *(m pl)* It
De Vorsatzpapiere *(pl)*
En endpapers pl n
Es guardas *(f pl)*
Fr papiers de garde *(m pl)*
Pt folhas de contracapa *(f pl)*

risguardo *(m)* n It
De Respektblatt *(n)*
En flyleaf
Es cortesía *(f)*
Fr feuille de garde *(f)*
Pt folha em branco *(f)*

risma *(f)* n It
De Ries *(n)*
En ream
Es resma *(f)*
Fr rame de papier *(f)*
Pt resma *(f)*

ristampa *(f)* n It
De Neuauflage *(f)*
En reprint
Es reimpresión *(f)*
Fr réimpression *(f)*
Pt reimpressão *(f)*

ristampare *vb* It
De neu auflegen
En reprint
Es reimprimir
Fr réimprimer
Pt reimprimir

risvolto anteriore *(m)* It
De vordere Umschlagklappe *(f)*
En front flap
Es solapa delantera *(f)*
Fr rabat avant *(m)*
Pt aleta dianteira *(f)*

risvolto della sovracopertina *(m)* It
De Umschlagklappe *(f)*
En jacket flap
Es solapa de la cubierta *(f)*
Fr rabat de la jaquette *(m)*
Pt aba da sobrecapa *(f)*

risvolto di retro *(m)* It
De hintere Umschlagklappe *(f)*
En back flap
Es solapa posterior *(f)*
Fr rabat arrière *(m)*
Pt contracapa *(f)*

ritaglio di carta *(m)* It
De Papierabschnitt *(n)*
En offcut
Es papel de recorte *(m)*
Fr découpure *(f)*
Pt papel de recorte *(m)*

ritaglio di giornale *(m)* It
De Presseausschnitt *(m)*
En press cutting
Es recorte de prensa *(m)*
Fr coupure de journal *(f)*
Pt recorte de imprensa *(f)*

ritoccare *vb* It
De retuschieren
En retouch
Es retocar
Fr retoucher
Pt retocar

ritocco *(m)* n It
De Retuschierung *(f)*
En retouching
Es retocado *(m)*

Fr retouche *(f)*
Pt retoque *(m)*

ritorni *(m pl)* It
De Rückgüter *(pl)*
En returns pl n
Es devoluciones *(f pl)*
Fr invendus *(m pl)*
Pt devoluções *(f pl)*

ritratto *(m)* n It
De Portrait *(n)*
En portrait
Es retrato *(m)*
Fr portrait *(m)*
Pt retrato *(m)*

river n En
De weißer Streifen im Satz *(m)*
Es calle *(f)*
Fr rue *(f)*
It spaziatura difettosa *(f)*
Pt espaço defeituoso *(m)*

rivestimento *(m)* n It
De Streichen *(n)*
En coating
Es revestimiento *(m)*
Fr couchage du papier *(m)*
Pt revestimento *(m)*

rivestimento per cilindri *(m)* It
De Zylinderaufzug *(m)*
En cylinder dressing
Es rectificado de cilindros *(m)*
Fr habillage *(m)*
Pt rectificação de cilindros *(f)*

rivista *(f)* n It
De Magazin *(n)*
En magazine (journal)
Es revista *(f)*
Fr magazine *(m)*
Pt revista *(f)*

rivista commerciale *(f)* It
De Fachzeitschrift *(f)*
En trade journal
Es revista profesional *(f)*
Fr revue professionnelle *(f)*
Pt revista comercial *(f)*

rivista di attualità (f) It
De Nachrichtenmagazin (n)
En news magazine
Es revista de información (f)
Fr magazine d'information (m)
Pt revista de informação (f)

rivista scientifica (f) It
De wissenschaftliches Journal (n)
En scientific journal
Es revista científica (f)
Fr revue scientifique (f)
Pt revista científica (f)

rivista specializzata (f) It
De Spezial-Journal (n)
En specialist journal
Es revista especializada (f)
Fr revue spécialisée (f)
Pt revista para especialistas (f)

rodillo (m) n Es
De Walze (f)
En roller
Fr rouleau (d'impression) (m)
It cilindro (m)
Pt rolo (de impressão) (m)

rodillo afiligranador (m) Es
De Egoutteur (m)
En dandy roll
Fr rouleau égoutteur (m)
It cilindro à filigrana (m)
Pt rolo filigranador (m)

rodillo batidor (m) Es
De Farbreiber (m)
En brayer
Fr rouleau à main (m)
It rullo inchiostratore a mano (m)
Pt rolo de mão (m)

rodillos de imprenta (m pl) Es
De Farbwalzen (pl)
En ink rollers
Fr rouleaux encreurs (m pl)
It rulli per inchiostro (m pl)

Pt rolos de dar tinta (m pl)

rognage (m) n Fr
De Beschneiden (n)
En trimming
Es recorte (m)
It rifilatura (f)
Pt aparagem (f)

rogner vb Fr
De randlos drucken
En bleed
Es correrse la tinta
It refilare
Pt ressumbrar

rojo de tricromía (m) Es
De Verfahrensrot (n)
En process red
Fr rouge d'impression couleur (m)
It rosso di tricromia (m)
Pt vermelho para policromia (m)

roll n En
De Rolle (f)
Es rollo (m)
Fr rouleau (de papier) (m)
It rotolo (m)
Pt rolo (de papel) (m)

Rolle (f) n De
En roll
Es rollo (m)
Fr rouleau (de papier) (m)
It rotolo (m)
Pt rolo (de papel) (m)

Rollenoffsetdruck (m) n De
En web-offset printing
Es roto-offset (m)
Fr impression offset en continu (f)
It stampa offset dal rotolo (f)
Pt impressão roto-offset (f)

roller n En
De Walze (f)
Es rodillo (m)
Fr rouleau (d'impression) (m)
It cilindro (m)
Pt rolo (de impressão) (m)

rollo (m) n Es
De Rolle (f)
En roll
Fr rouleau (de papier) (m)
It rotolo (m)
Pt rolo (de papel) (m)

rolo (de impressão) (m) Pt
De Walze (f)
En roller
Es rodillo (m)
Fr rouleau (d'impression) (m)
It cilindro (m)

rolo (de papel) (m) Pt
De Rolle (f)
En roll
Es rollo (m)
Fr rouleau (de papier) (m)
It rotolo (m)

rolo de mão (m) Pt
De Farbreiber (m)
En brayer
Es rodillo batidor (m)
Fr rouleau à main (m)
It rullo inchiostratore a mano (m)

rolo filigranador (m) Pt
De Egoutteur (m)
En dandy roll
Es rodillo afiligranador (m)
Fr rouleau égoutteur (m)
It cilindro à filigrana (m)

rolos de dar tinta (m pl) Pt
De Farbwalzen (pl)
En ink rollers
Es rodillos de imprenta (m pl)
Fr rouleaux encreurs (m pl)
It rulli per inchiostro (m pl)

romain (m) n Fr
De römische Schrift (f)
En roman type
Es tipo redondo (m)
It carattere romano tondo (m)
Pt tipo romano (m)

roman (m) n Fr
De Roman (m)
En novel
Es novela (f)
It romanzo (m)
Pt romance (m)

Roman (m) n De
En novel
Es novela (f)
Fr roman (m)
It romanzo (m)
Pt romance (m)

roman alphabet En
De römisches Alphabet (n)
Es alfabeto romano (m)
Fr alphabet romain (m)
It alfabeto romano tondo (m)
Pt alfabeto romano (m)

roman à sensation (m) Fr
De Reißer
En thriller
Es novela de misterio (f)
It giallo (m)
Pt policial (m)

romance (m) n Pt
De Roman (m)
En novel
Es novela (f)
Fr roman (m)
It romanzo (m)

romance romântico (m) Pt
De romantischer Roman (m)
En romantic novel
Es novela romántica (f)
Fr roman romanesque (m)
It novella romantica (f)

romancier (f) n Fr
De Romanschriftsteller (m)
En novelist
Es novelista (m)
It romanziere (m)
Pt romancista (m)

romancista (m) n Pt
De Romanschriftsteller (m)
En novelist
Es novelista (m)

Fr romancier *(f)*
It romanziere *(m)*

Romanliteratur *(f) n* De
En fiction
Es literatura novelesca
(f)
Fr romans *(m pl)*
It narrativa *(f)*
Pt ficção *(f)*

Romanliteratur-Liste *(f)*
De
En fiction list
Es catálogo de novelas
(m)
Fr catalogue des
romans *(m)*
It elenco di narrativa
(m)
Pt lista de ficção *(f)*

roman numerals En
De römische Zahlen *(pl)*
Es números romanos *(m
pl)*
Fr chiffres romains *(m
pl)*
It numeri romani *(m pl)*
Pt números romanos *(m
pl)*

roman policier *(m)* Fr
De Kriminalroman *(m)*
En detective novel
Es novela policíaca *(f)*
It racconto poliziesco
(m)
Pt livro policial *(m)*

roman romanesque *(m)*
Fr
De romantischer Roman
(m)
En romantic novel
Es novela romántica *(f)*
It novella romantica *(f)*
Pt romance romântico
(m)

romans *(m pl) n* Fr
De Romanliteratur *(f)*
En fiction
Es literatura novelesca
(f)
It narrativa *(f)*
Pt ficção *(f)*

Romanschriftsteller *(m)*
n De
En novelist

Es novelista *(m)*
Fr romancier *(f)*
It romanziere *(m)*
Pt romancista *(m)*

romans populaires *(m
pl)* Fr
De volkstümliche
Romanliteratur *(f)*
En popular fiction
Es literatura popular *(f)*
It narrativa popolare *(f)*
Pt ficção popular *(f)*

romantic novel En
De romantischer Roman
(m)
Es novela romántica *(f)*
Fr roman romanesque
(m)
It novella romantica *(f)*
Pt romance romântico
(m)

romantischer Roman
(m) De
En romantic novel
Es novela romántica *(f)*
Fr roman romanesque
(m)
It novella romantica *(f)*
Pt romance romântico
(m)

roman type En
De römische Schrift *(f)*
Es tipo redondo *(m)*
Fr romain *(m)*
It carattere romano
tondo *(m)*
Pt tipo romano *(m)*

Romanverleger *(m) n* De
En fiction publisher
Es editor de novelas *(m)*
Fr éditeur de romans
(m)
It editore di narrativa
(m)
Pt editorial de ficção *(f)*

romanziere *(m) n* It
De Romanschriftsteller
(m)
En novelist
Es novelista *(m)*
Fr romancier *(f)*
Pt romancista *(m)*

romanzo *(m) n* It
De Roman *(m)*
En novel
Es novela *(f)*
Fr roman *(m)*
Pt romance *(m)*

römisches Alphabet *(n)*
De
En roman alphabet
Es alfabeto romano *(m)*
Fr alphabet romain *(m)*
It alfabeto romano
tondo *(m)*
Pt alfabeto romano *(m)*

römische Schrift *(f)* De
En roman type
Es tipo redondo *(m)*
Fr romain *(m)*
It carattere romano
tondo *(m)*
Pt tipo romano *(m)*

römische Zahlen *(pl)* De
En roman numerals
Es números romanos *(m
pl)*
Fr chiffres romains *(m
pl)*
It numeri romani *(m pl)*
Pt números romanos *(m
pl)*

rosso di tricromia *(m)* It
De Verfahrensrot *(n)*
En process red
Es rojo de tricromía *(m)*
Fr rouge d'impression
couleur *(m)*
Pt vermelho para
policromia *(m)*

rotary press En
De Rotationspresse *(f)*
Es prensa rotativa *(f)*
Fr rotative *(f)*
It macchina da stampa
rotativa *(f)*
Pt prensa rotativa *(f)*

rotary stereo En
De Rotationsstereo *(n)*
Es estereotipia rotativa
(f)
Fr stéréo courbe *(f)*
It stereo rotatorio *(m)*
Pt estereo-rotativa *(f)*

Rotationsdruckpapier
(n) n De
En newsprint
Es papel periódico *(m)*
Fr papier-journal *(m)*
It carta da giornale *(f)*
Pt papel para jornal *(m)*

Rotationspresse *(f) n* De
En rotary press
Es prensa rotativa *(f)*
Fr rotative *(f)*
It macchina da stampa
rotativa *(f)*
Pt prensa rotativa *(f)*

Rotationsstereo *(n)* De
En rotary stereo
Es estereotipia rotativa
(f)
Fr stéréo courbe *(f)*
It stereo rotatorio *(m)*
Pt estereo-rotativa *(f)*

rotativa *(f) n* It
De Schnellpresse *(f)*
En cylinder machine
Es prensa
planocilíndrica *(f)*
Fr machine à forme
ronde *(f)*
Pt máquina de rolos *(f)*

rotativa con arresto *(f)* It
De Haltzylinderpresse *(f)*
En stop-cylinder press
Es prensa de cilindro de
parada *(f)*
Fr machine à arrêt du
cylindre *(f)*
Pt prensa de cilindro de
paragem *(f)*

rotative *(f) n* Fr
De Rotationspresse *(f)*
En rotary press
Es prensa rotativa *(f)*
It macchina da stampa
rotativa *(f)*
Pt prensa rotativa *(f)*

rotina de justificação *(f)*
Pt
De Justierungsroutine *(f)*
En justification routine
Es rutina de justificación
(f)
Fr routine de
justification *(f)*
It routine di
giustificazione *(f)*

rotolo *(m) n* It
De Rolle *(f)*
En roll
Es rollo *(m)*
Fr rouleau (de papier) *(m)*
Pt rolo (de papel) *(m)*

rotolo di carta per stampa offset *(m)* It
De Offset-Kartuschenpapier *(n)*
En offset cartridge paper
Es papel para cartuchos de offset *(m)*
Fr papier cartouche offset *(m)*
Pt papel cartucho offset *(m)*

roto-offset *(m) n* Es
De Rollenoffsetdruck *(m)*
En web-offset printing
Fr impression offset en continu *(f)*
It stampa offset dal rotolo *(f)*
Pt impressão roto-offset *(f)*

rótulos *(m pl)* Es
De Bezeichnungen *(pl)*
En labels (on diagram) *pl n*
Fr étiquettes *(f pl)*
It etichette *(f pl)*
Pt legendas *(f pl)*

rouge d'impression couleur *(m)* Fr
De Verfahrensrot *(n)*
En process red
Es rojo de tricromía *(m)*
It rosso di tricromia *(m)*
Pt vermelho para policromia *(m)*

rough *n* En
De Skizze *(f)*
Es boceto *(m)*
Fr croquis *(m)*
It abbozzo *(m)*
Pt esboço *(m)*

rouleau (de papier) *(m)* Fr
De Rolle *(f)*
En roll
Es rollo *(m)*
It rotolo *(m)*
Pt rolo (de papel) *(m)*

rouleau (d'impression) *(m)* Fr
De Walze *(f)*
En roller
Es rodillo *(m)*
It cilindro *(m)*
Pt rolo (de impressão) *(m)*

rouleau à main *(m)* Fr
De Farbreiber *(m)*
En brayer
Es rodillo batidor *(m)*
It rullo inchiostratore a mano *(m)*
Pt rolo de mão *(m)*

rouleau égoutteur *(m)* Fr
De Egoutteur *(m)*
En dandy roll
Es rodillo afiligranador *(m)*
It cilindro à filigrana *(m)*
Pt rolo filigranador *(m)*

rouleau mouilleur *(m)* Fr
De Feuchtwalze *(f)*
En damper
Es mojador *(m)*
It umettatore *(m)*
Pt molhador *(m)*

rouleaux encreurs *(m pl)* Fr
De Farbwalzen *(pl)*
En ink rollers
Es rodillos de imprenta *(m pl)*
It rulli per inchiostro *(m pl)*
Pt rolos de dar tinta *(m pl)*

routine de justification *(f)* Fr
De Justierungsroutine *(f)*
En justification routine
Es rutina de justificación *(f)*
It routine di giustificazione *(f)*
Pt rotina de justificação *(f)*

routine di giustificazione *(f)* It
De Justierungsroutine *(f)*
En justification routine
Es rutina de justificación *(f)*
Fr routine de justification *(f)*

Pt rotina de justificação *(f)*

routing machine En
De Fräser *(m)*
Es fresadora *(f)*
Fr fraiseuse *(f)*
It fresatrice *(f)*
Pt fresadora *(f)*

royalties *pl n* En
De Tantiemen *(pl)*
Es derechos de autor *(m pl)*
Fr droits d'auteur *(m pl)*
It diritti di licenza *(m pl)*
Pt direitos de autor *(m pl)*

rubber stereos En
De Gummiklischees *(pl)*
Es estereotipos de caucho *(m pl)*
Fr stéréos caoutchouc *(m pl)*
It stereos di gomma *(m pl)*
Pt estereos de borracha *(m pl)*

Rücken *(m) n* De
En spine
Es lomo *(m)*
Fr dos *(m)*
It dorso *(m)*
Pt lombada *(f)*

Rückendicke *(f) n* De
En spine width
Es ancho del lomo *(m)*
Fr largeur du dos *(f)*
It larghezza del dorso *(f)*
Pt largura de lombada *(f)*

Rückgüter *(pl)* De
En returns *pl n*
Es devoluciones *(f pl)*
Fr invendus *(m pl)*
It ritorni *(m pl)*
Pt devoluções *(f pl)*

Rückseite *(f) n* De
En verso
Es reverso *(m)*
Fr verso *(m)*
It verso *(m)*
Pt verso *(m)*

Rückseiten *(pl)* De
En backing pages *pl n*
Es páginas de lomo *(f pl)*
Fr pages de garde *(f pl)*
It pagine di rinforzo *(f pl)*
Pt páginas de lombada *(f pl)*

rue *(f) n* Fr
De weiser Streifen im Satz *(m)*
En river
Es calle *(f)*
It spaziatura diffetosa *(f)*
Pt espaço defeituoso *(m)*

rule *n* En
De Strich *(m)*
Es filete *(m)*
Fr règle *(f)*
It filetto *(m)*
Pt linha recta *(f)*

rulli per inchiostro *(m pl)* It
De Farbwalzen *(pl)*
En ink rollers
Es rodillos de imprenta *(m pl)*
Fr rouleaux encreurs *(m pl)*
Pt rolos de dar tinta *(m pl)*

rullo inchiostratore a mano *(m)* It
De Farbreiber *(m)*
En brayer
Es rodillo batidor *(m)*
Fr rouleau à main *(m)*
Pt rolo de mão *(m)*

running heads En
De lebender Kolumnentitel *(pl)*
Es títulos de página *(m pl)*
Fr titres courants *(m pl)*
It titoletti *(m pl)*
Pt títulos repetidos *(m pl)*

running sheets En
De folgende Bogen *(pl)*
Es hojas sucesivas *(f pl)*
Fr feuilles de roulement *(f pl)*
It fogli successivi *(m pl)*

Pt folhas sucessivas *(f pl)*

run on (printing) En
De fortdrucken
Es proseguir la tirada
Fr faire des tirages supplémentaires
It imprimir una super-tiratura *(f)*
Pt continuar a imprimir

run on (typesetting) En
De anhängen
Es componer sin punto y aparte
Fr suivre sans alinéa
It scrivere a testo continuo
Pt compor seguido

run-on price En
De Fortdruck-Preis *(m)*
Es precio de más ejemplares *(m)*
Fr coût du tirage supplémentaire *(m)*
It prezzo di super-tiratura *(m)*
Pt preço de exemplares a mais *(m)*

Rupfen *(n)* n De
En plucking
Es picado *(m)*
Fr arrachage *(m)*
It strappatura *(f)*
Pt picado *(m)*

rupture de contrat *(f)* Fr
De Vertragsbruch *(m)*
En breach of contract
Es incumplimiento de contrato *(m)*
It violazione di contratto *(f)*
Pt quebra de contrato *(f)*

rutina de justificación *(f)* Es
De Justierungsroutine *(f)*
En justification routine
Fr routine de justification *(f)*
It routine di giustificazione *(f)*
Pt rotina de justificação *(f)*

S

sábio *adj* Pt
De gelehrt
En scholarly
Es erudito
Fr savant
It erudito

sacabocados *(m)* n Es
De Locher *(m)*
En punch (for hole punching)
Fr perforeuse *(f)*
It perforatore *(m)*
Pt perfuradora *(f)*

Sachbücher *(pl)* De
En non-fiction books
Es libros no novelescos *(m pl)*
Fr livres généraux *(m pl)*
It libri di saggistica *(m pl)*
Pt livros de não ficção *(m pl)*

Sachliteratur *(f)* n De
En non-fiction
Es textos no novelescos *(m pl)*
Fr ouvrages généraux *(m pl)*
It saggistica *(f)*
Pt textos de não ficção *(m pl)*

Sachliteratur-Verleger *(m)* n De
En non-fiction publisher
Es editor de libros no novelescos *(m)*
Fr éditeur d'ouvrages généraux *(m)*
It editore di saggistica *(m)*
Pt editor de não ficção *(m)*

saddle stitching En
De Sattelheftung *(f)*
Es cosido a galápago *(m)*
Fr couture dans le pli *(f)*
It cucitura in piega *(f)*
Pt costura com grampos *(f)*

saggistica *(f)* n It
De Sachliteratur *(f)*
En non-fiction
Es textos no novelescos *(m pl)*
Fr ouvrages généraux *(m pl)*
Pt textos de não ficção *(m pl)*

saisie de données *(f)* Fr
De Datenerfassung *(f)*
En data capture
Es toma de datos *(f)*
It cattura dei dati *(f)*
Pt captação de dados *(f)*

sala composizione *(f)* It
De Setzerei *(f)*
En composing room
Es sala de composición *(f)*
Fr atelier de composition *(m)*
Pt sala de composição *(f)*

sala de composição *(f)* Pt
De Setzerei *(f)*
En composing room
Es sala de composición *(f)*
Fr atelier de composition *(m)*
It sala composizione *(f)*

sala de composición *(f)* Es
De Setzerei *(f)*
En composing room
Fr atelier de composition *(m)*
It sala composizione *(f)*
Pt sala de composição *(f)*

sala de imprensa *(f)* Pt
De Pressesaal *(m)*
En press room
Es sala de máquinas *(f)*
Fr atelier d'imprimerie *(m)*
It sala stampa *(f)*

sala de máquinas *(f)* Es
De Pressesaal *(m)*
En press room
Fr atelier d'imprimerie *(m)*
It sala stampa *(f)*
Pt sala de imprensa *(f)*

sala de mecanotipia *(f)* Es, Pt
De Setzraum *(m)*
En keyboarding room
Fr salle de photocomposition *(f)*
It sala di fotocomposizione *(f)*

sala di fotocomposizione *(f)* It
De Setzraum *(m)*
En keyboarding room
Es sala de mecanotipia *(f)*
Fr salle de photocomposition *(f)*
Pt sala de mecanotipia *(f)*

sala stampa *(f)* It
De Pressesaal *(m)*
En press room
Es sala de máquinas *(f)*
Fr atelier d'imprimerie *(m)*
Pt sala de imprensa *(f)*

saldo ainda não ganhado *(m)* Pt
De Saldo unverdient *(m)*
En unearned balance
Es saldo no devengado *(m)*
Fr solde pas encore gagné *(m)*
It saldo non ancora guadagnato *(m)*

saldo no devengado *(m)* Es
De Saldo unverdient *(m)*
En unearned balance
Fr solde pas encore gagné *(m)*
It saldo non ancora guadagnato *(m)*
Pt saldo ainda não ganhado *(m)*

saldo non ancora guadagnato *(m)* It
De Saldo unverdient *(m)*
En unearned balance
Es saldo no devengado *(m)*
Fr solde pas encore gagné *(m)*
Pt saldo ainda não ganhado *(m)*

Saldo unverdient (m) De
En unearned balance
Es saldo no devengado (m)
Fr solde pas encore gagné (m)
It saldo non ancora guadagnato (m)
Pt saldo ainda não ganhado (m)

sale-or-return basis En
De Kauf oder Rückgabe (m)
Es base de ventas o devoluciones (f)
Fr vente avec possibilité de rendre (f)
It base venduto o reso (f)
Pt base de venda ou devolução (f)

sales pl n En
De Verkauf (m)
Es ventas (f pl)
Fr ventes (f pl)
It vendite (f pl)
Pt vendas (f pl)

sales assistant En
De Verkäufer (m)
Es ayudante de ventas (m)
Fr commis (m)
It commesso (m)
Pt ajudante de vendedor (m)

sales campaign En
De Verkaufskampagne (f)
Es campaña de ventas (f)
Fr campagne de vente (f)
It campagna di vendita (f)
Pt campanha comercial (f)

sales conference En
De Verkaufskonferenz (f)
Es conferencia de ventas (f)
Fr réunion de vente (f)
It conferenza di vendita (f)
Pt conferência de vendedores (f)

sales director En
De Verkaufsdirektor (m)
Es director de ventas (m)
Fr directeur commercial (m)
It direttore alle vendite (m)
Pt director de vendas (m)

salesman n En
De Vertreter (m)
Es vendedor (m)
Fr vendeur (m)
It venditore (m)
Pt vendedor (m)

sales manager En
De Verkaufsleiter (m)
Es jefe de ventas (m)
Fr chef des ventes (m)
It direttore vendite (m)
Pt gerente de vendas (m)

saliência do corpo do tipo (f) Pt
De Überhang (m)
En kern
Es talud (m)
Fr crénage (m)
It sporgenza (f)

salle de photocomposition (f) Fr
De Setzraum (m)
En keyboarding room
Es sala de mecanotipia (f)
It sala di fotocomposizione (f)
Pt sala de mecanotipia (f)

same size (s/s) En
De gleichgroβ
Es igual tamaño
Fr format identique
It stessa dimensione
Pt mesmo tamanho

Sammler (m) n De
En assembler
Es elevador reunidor (m)
Fr assembleur (m)
It raccoglitore (m)
Pt ajustadora (f)

Sammlung (f) n De
En collection
Es colección (f)
Fr recueil (m)
It collezione (f)
Pt coleção (f)

sämtliche Werke (pl) De
En complete works
Es obras completas (f pl)
Fr oeuvres complètes (f pl)
It opera completa (f)
Pt obras completas (f pl)

sangrado adj Es
De eingerückt
En indented
Fr dentelé
It dentellato
Pt dentada

sangrar vb Es
De einrücken
En indent
Fr renforcer
It dentellare
Pt abrir parágrafo

sangría de párrafo (f) Es
De Paragrapheinrückung (f)
En paragraph indent
Fr renfoncé d'alinéa (m)
It indentro del paragrafo (m)
Pt reentrância de parágrafo (f)

sans acide Fr
De säurefrei
En acid-free
Es exento de ácido
It privo di acidi
Pt isento de ácido

sans-serif typeface En
De Grotesk-Schrifttyp (m)
Es tipo sin remate (m)
Fr caractère antique (sans empâtement) (m)
It bastone (m)
Pt olho de tipo sem remate (m)

Sattelheftung (f) n De
En saddle stitching
Es cosido a galápago (m)

Fr couture dans le pli (f)
It cucitura in piega (f)
Pt costura com grampos (f)

Satz (m) n De
En sentence
Es cláusula (f)
Fr phrase (f)
It frase (f)
Pt frase (f)

Satzgestalter (m) n De
En typographic designer
Es diseñador tipográfico (m)
Fr concepteur typographique (m)
It disegnatore tipografico (m)
Pt desenhador tipográfico (m)

Satzgestaltung (f) n De
En typographic design
Es diseño tipográfico (m)
Fr représentation typographique (f)
It disegno tipografico (m)
Pt desenho tipográfico (m)

Satzhöhe (f) n De
En depth
Es profundidad (f)
Fr hauteur (f)
It profondità (f)
Pt profundidade (f)

Satzschiff (n) n De
En galley
Es galera (f)
Fr galée (f)
It vantaggio (m)
Pt galé (f)

Satzumbruch (m) n De
En make-up
Es compaginación (f)
Fr montage (m)
It impaginatura (f)
Pt compaginação (f)

sauberer Abzug (m) De
En clean proof
Es prueba limpia (f)
Fr épreuve au net (f)
It bozza nitida (f)
Pt prova limpa (f)

sauberer Text *(m)* De
En clean copy
Es original limpio *(m)*
Fr copie au net *(f)*
It copia nitida *(f)*
Pt exemplar a limpo *(m)*

Sauganleger *(m)* n De
En suction feeder
Es ponepliegos de soplo *(m)*
Fr margeur automatique à aspiration *(m)*
It alimentatore ad aspirazione *(m)*
Pt alimentador por sucção *(m)*

Säulen *(pl)* De
En stems *pl n*
Es palos gruesos *(m pl)*
Fr hastes *(f pl)*
It gambi *(m pl)*
Pt paus grossos *(m pl)*

säurebeständig *adj* De
En acid-resist
Es resistente al ácido
Fr résistant à l'acide
It resistente agli acidi
Pt resistente contra ácidos

säurefrei *adj* De
En acid-free
Es exento de ácido
Fr sans acide
It privo di acidi
Pt isento de ácido

savant *adj* Fr
De gelehrt
En scholarly
Es erudito
It erudito
Pt sábio

scadenza *(f)* n It
De Stichtag *(m)*
En deadline
Es plazo *(m)*
Fr limite *(f)*
Pt prazo *(m)*

scale *vb* En
De Maßstab festlegen
Es poner a escala
Fr dessiner à l'échelle
It graduare
Pt pôr à escala

scalpel *n* En; Fr *(m)*
De Skalpell *(n)*
Es escalpelo *(m)*
It bisturi ad un solo taglio *(m)*
Pt bisturí *(m)*

scanalatura per sfogo *(f)* It
De Gießbach *(m)*
En gutter
Es medianil *(m)*
Fr petits fonds *(m pl)*
Pt medianiz *(m)*

scanner *n* En; It *(m)*
De Abtaster *(m)*
Es explorador *(m)*
Fr analyseur électronique *(m)*
Pt dispositivo explorador *(m)*

scanning elettronico *(m)* It
De elektronische Abtastung *(f)*
En electronic scanning
Es selección electrónica *(f)*
Fr exploration électronique *(f)*
Pt seleccionadora electrónica de cores *(f)*

scarto *(m)* n It
De Krätze *(f)*
En dross
Es escoria *(f)*
Fr crasses *(f pl)*
Pt escória *(f)*

scène de coupe *(f)* Fr
De Schnittbild *(n)*
En cutaway view
Es vista en corte *(f)*
It vista in sezione *(f)*
Pt vista recortada *(f)*

Schattenautor *(m)* n De
En ghost writer
Es escritor fantasma *(m)*
Fr nègre *(m)*
It collaboratore anonimo *(m)*
Pt colaborador anónimo *(m)*

Schattierung *(f)* n De
En shading
Es sombreado *(m)*
Fr exécution des ombres *(f)*
It ombreggiatura *(f)*
Pt tracejado *(m)*

Schaubild *(n)* n De
En flow chart
Es organigrama *(f)*
Fr schéma de fabrication *(m)*
It reogramma *(m)*
Pt diagrama de fluxo *(m)*

scheda magnetica *(f)* It
De Magnetkarte *(f)*
En magnetic card
Es ficha magnética *(f)*
Fr carte magnétique *(f)*
Pt ficha magnética *(f)*

scheda perforata *(f)* It
De Lochkarte *(f)*
En punched card
Es tarjeta perforada *(f)*
Fr carte perforée *(f)*
Pt ficha perfurada *(f)*

schede *(f pl)* It
De Karteikarten *(pl)*
En index cards
Es tarjetas de fichercs *(f pl)*
Fr fiches *(f pl)*
Pt fichas de arquivo *(f pl)*

schedule *vb* En
De planen
Es proyectar
Fr projeter
It progettare
Pt planear

schedule *n* En
De Arbeitsplan *(m)*
Es plano *(m)*
Fr prévisions *(f pl)*
It orario *(m)*
Pt plano *(m)*

schéma *(m)* n Fr
De Diagramm *(n)*
En diagram
Es esquema *(m)*
It diagramma *(m)*
Pt diagrama *(m)*

schéma de fabrication *(m)* Fr
De Schaubild *(n)*
En flow chart
Es organigrama *(f)*
It reogramma *(m)*
Pt diagrama de fluxo *(m)*

schéma de principe *(m)* Fr
De schematisches Diagramm *(n)*
En schematic diagram
Es diagrama esquemático *(m)*
It diagramma schematico *(m)*
Pt diagrama esquemático *(m)*

schéma progressif *(m)* Fr
De stufenweises Diagramm *(n)*
En step-by-step diagram
Es esquema paso a paso *(m)*
It diagramma graduale *(m)*
Pt diagrama de passo a passo *(m)*

schematic diagram En
De schematisches Diagramm *(n)*
Es diagrama esquemático *(m)*
Fr schéma de principe *(m)*
It diagramma schematico *(m)*
Pt diagrama esquemático *(m)*

schematico *adj* It
De schematisch
En diagrammatic
Es esquemático
Fr schématique
Pt diagramático

schématique *adj* Fr
De schematisch
En diagrammatic
Es esquemático
It schematico
Pt diagramático

schematisch *adj* De
En diagrammatic
Es esquemático
Fr schématique

It schematico
Pt diagramático

**schematisches
Diagramm** *(n)* De
En schematic diagram
Es diagrama
esquemático *(m)*
Fr schéma de principe
(m)
It diagramma
schematico *(m)*
Pt diagrama
esquemático *(m)*

schlechtes Manuskript
(n) De
En bad copy
Es original malo *(m)*
Fr mauvaise copie *(f)*
It copia illeggibile *(f)*
Pt exemplar ilegível *(m)*

Schließen *(n)* n De
En locking-up
Es acuñado *(m)*
Fr serrage *(m)*
It serramento *(m)*
Pt enramado *(m)*

Schließplatte *(f)* n De
En imposing surface
Es superficie de
imposición *(f)*
Fr marbre de serrage
(m)
It banco tipografico *(m)*
Pt superfície de
imposição *(f)*

Schlußvignette *(f)* n De
En tailpiece
Es culo de lámpara *(m)*
Fr cul-de-lampe *(m)*
It finalino *(m)*
Pt vinheta final *(f)*

schmaler Schrifttyp *(m)*
De
En condensed typeface
Es tipo estrecho *(m)*
Fr caractère effilé *(m)*
It carattere allungato
(m)
Pt estilo de tipo
condensado *(m)*

Schmutztitel *(m)* n De
En part-title
Es título de parte *(m)*
Fr titre partiel *(m)*

It titolo parziale *(m)*
Pt título parcial *(m)*

Schnalle *(f)* n De
En blister (on paper)
Es ampolla *(f)*
Fr cloque *(f)*
It bolla *(f)*
Pt bolha *(f)*

Schneidemaschine *(f)* n
De
En guillotine
Es guillotina *(f)*
Fr guillotine *(f)*
It tagliacarta *(f)*
Pt guilhotina *(f)*

Schnellpresse *(f)* n De
En cylinder machine
Es prensa
planocilíndrica *(f)*
Fr machine à forme
ronde *(f)*
It rotativa *(f)*
Pt máquina de rolos *(f)*

Schnitt *(m)* n De
En fore edge
Es canto *(m)*
Fr gouttière *(f)*
It bordo anteriore *(m)*
Pt canto dianteiro *(m)*

Schnittbild *(n)* n De
En cutaway view
Es vista en corte *(f)*
Fr scène de coupe *(f)*
It vista in sezione *(f)*
Pt vista recortada *(f)*

Schnittstelle *(f)* n De
En interface
Es interfase *(f)*
Fr interface *(f)*
It interface *(f)*
Pt interface *(f)*

Schnürlmoiré *(n)* n De
En moiré effect
Es moiré *(m)*
Fr moiré *(m)*
It effetto moiré *(m)*
Pt efeito moiré *(m)*

scholarly *adj* En
De gelehrt
Es erudito
Fr savant

It erudito
Pt sábio

scholarly books En
De gelehrte Bücher *(pl)*
Es libros eruditos *(m pl)*
Fr livres d´érudition *(m
pl)*
It libri eruditi *(m pl)*
Pt livros de estudo *(m
pl)*

Schöne Literatur *(f)* De
En belles-lettres *pl* n
Es bellas letras *(f pl)*
Fr belles-lettres *(f pl)*
It belle lettere *(f pl)*
Pt beletrística *(f)*

Schön- und Widerdruck
(m) De
En perfecting
Es retiración *(f)*
Fr retiration *(f)*
It stampa in volta *(f)*
Pt impressão
simultânea de ambos
lados *(f)*

**Schön- und
Widerdruck-
maschine** *(f)* De
En perfector
Es prensa de retiración
(f)
Fr presse à retiration *(f)*
It stampatrice in volta
(f)
Pt máquina de
impressão
simultânea de ambos
lados *(f)*

schoolbook n En
De Schulbuch *(n)*
Es libro escolar *(m)*
Fr livre scolaire *(m)*
It testo scolastico *(m)*
Pt livro escolar *(m)*

school library En
De Schulbücherei *(f)*
Es biblioteca de colegio
(f)
Fr bibliothèque scolaire
(f)
It biblioteca scolastica
(f)
Pt biblioteca escolar *(f)*

Schrägsatz *(m)* n De
En unjustified text
Es texto sin justificar *(m)*
Fr composition en
drapeau *(f)*
It testo non giustificato
(m)
Pt texto não justificado
(m)

Schreibmaschine *(f)* n
De
En typewriter
Es mecanógrafa *(f)*
Fr machine à écrire *(f)*
It macchina da scrivere
(f)
Pt máquina de escrever
(f)

**Schreibmaschinen-
papier** *(n)* n De
En bond paper
Es papel bond *(m)*
Fr papier coquille *(m)*
It carta bond *(f)*
Pt papel bond *(m)*

Schreibmaschinen-Satz
(m) n De
En typewriter
composition
Es composición
mecanográfica *(f)*
Fr composition à la
machine à écrire *(f)*
It composizione su
macchina da scrivere
(f)
Pt composição com
máquina de escrever
(f)

Schreibtisch-Lexikon
(n) n De
En desk encyclopedia
Es enciclopedia de
mesa *(f)*
Fr petite encyclopédie
(f)
It enciclopedia da
tavolo *(f)*
Pt enciclopédia de
mesa *(f)*

Schrift *(f)* n De
En type
Es tipo *(m)*
Fr caractère
d´imprimerie *(m)*

It carattere tipografico *(m)*
Pt tipo *(m)*

Schriftart *(f)* n De
En fount
Es fundición *(f)*
Fr fonte *(f)*
It serie di caratteri *(f)*
Pt fundição *(f)*

Schriftgarnitur *(f)* De
En sorts *pl* n
Es suertes *(f pl)*
Fr assortiment *(m)*
It rappezzi *(m pl)*
Pt sortes *(f pl)*

Schriftgewicht *(n)* n De
En type weight
Es peso del tipo *(m)*
Fr poids de caractère *(m)*
It peso del carattere *(m)*
Pt peso de tipo *(m)*

Schriftgieβerei *(f)* n De
En type foundry
Es fundición de tipos *(f)*
Fr clicherie *(f)*
It fonderia di caratteri *(f)*
Pt fundição de tipos (casa) *(f)*

Schriftguβ *(m)* n De
En typecasting
Es composición mecanotípica *(f)*
Fr fonte de caractères *(f)*
It fusione dei caratteri *(f)*
Pt fundição de tipos (processo) *(f)*

Schrifthöhe *(f)* n De
En type height
Es altura del tipo *(f)*
Fr hauteur de caractère *(f)*
It altezza tipografica *(f)*
Pt altura de tipo *(f)*

Schriftlager *(n)* n De
En magazine (matrix store)
Es depósito *(m)*
Fr magasin *(m)*

It caricatore *(m)*
Pt depósito *(m)*

Schriftmetall *(n)* n De
En type metal
Es metal de imprenta *(m)*
Fr métal d'imprimerie *(m)*
It lega per caratteri *(f)*
Pt metal para tipos *(m)*

Schriftsatz *(m)* n De
En typesetting
Es composición tipográfica *(f)*
Fr composition typographique *(f)*
It composizione tipografica *(f)*
Pt composição de tipos *(f)*

Schriftsatz-Lineal *(n)* n De
En typescale
Es escala de tipos *(f)*
Fr typomètre *(m)*
It tipometro *(m)*
Pt tipómetro *(m)*

Schriftsetzerei *(f)* n De
En typesetter (company)
Es taller de composición *(m)*
Fr maison de composition *(f)*
It compositoria *(f)*
Pt empresa de composição *(f)*

Schrifttiefe *(f)* n De
En type depth
Es profundidad del tipo *(f)*
Fr profondeur *(f)*
It profondità del carattere *(f)*
Pt profundidade de tipo *(f)*

Schrifttyp *(m)* n De
En typeface
Es ojo del tipo *(m)*
Fr oeil d'un caractère *(m)*
It occhio del carattere *(m)*
Pt olho de tipo *(m)*

Schriftverteilung *(f)* n De
En type distribution
Es distribución de tipos *(f)*
Fr distribution des caractères *(f)*
It distribuzione del carattere *(m)*
Pt distribuição de tipos *(f)*

Schriftzeichen *(n)* n De
En character
Es carácter *(m)*
Fr caractère *(m)*
It carattere *(m)*
Pt carácter *(m)*

Schrumpfverpackung *(f)* n De
En shrink-wrapping
Es envoltura por contracción *(f)*
Fr emballage serré *(m)*
It confezionamento a restringimento *(m)*
Pt embalagem de encolher *(f)*

Schuber *(m)* n De
En slip case
Es estuche *(m)*
Fr étui *(m)*
It astuccio del libro *(m)*
Pt estojo de livro *(m)*

Schulbuch *(n)* n De
En schoolbook
Es libro escolar *(m)*
Fr livre scolaire *(m)*
It testo scolastico *(m)*
Pt livro escolar *(m)*

Schulbücherei *(f)* n De
En school library
Es biblioteca de colegio *(f)*
Fr bibliothèque scolaire *(f)*
It biblioteca scolastica *(f)*
Pt biblioteca escolar *(f)*

Schuppenanleger *(m)* n De
En stream feeder
Es ponepliegos de avance continuo *(m)*
Fr margeur à nappe *(m)*
It alimentatore di fogli a avanzamento continuo *(m)*
Pt alimentador de folhas de avanço contínuo *(m)*

Schwarzplatte *(f)* n De
En black plate
Es plancha negra *(f)*
Fr cliché en noir *(m)*
It lastra nera *(f)*
Pt chapa preta *(f)*

Schwarzweiβ-illustration *(f)* n De
En black-and-white illustration
Es ilustración en blanco y negro *(f)*
Fr illustration en noir et blanc *(f)*
It illustrazione in bianco e nero *(f)*
Pt ilustração a branco e negro *(f)*

Schwebender Akzent *(m)* De
En floating accent
Es acento postizo *(m)*
Fr accent flottant *(m)*
It accento fluttuante *(m)*
Pt acento flutuante *(m)*

science n En; Fr *(f)*
De Wissenschaft *(f)*
Es ciencia *(f)*
It scienza *(f)*
Pt ciência *(f)*

science fiction En
De Science-fiction *(f)*
Es ciencia-ficción *(f)*
Fr science-fiction *(f)*
It fantascienza *(f)*
Pt ficção científica *(f)*

science-fiction *(f)* n Fr
De Science-fiction *(f)*
En science fiction
Es ciencia-ficción *(f)*
It fantascienza *(f)*
Pt ficção científica *(f)*

Science-fiction *(f)* n De
En science fiction
Es ciencia-ficción *(f)*
Fr science-fiction *(f)*
It fantascienza *(f)*
Pt ficção científica *(f)*

scientific and technical books En
De wissenschaftliche und technische Bücher *(pl)*
Es libros científicos y técnicos *(m pl)*
Fr ouvrages scientifiques et techniques *(m pl)*
It libri scientifici e tecnici *(m pl)*
Pt livros científicos e técnicos *(m pl)*

scientific journal En
De wissenschaftliches Journal *(n)*
Es revista científica *(f)*
Fr revue scientifique *(f)*
It rivista scientifica *(f)*
Pt revista científica *(f)*

scienza *(f) n* It
De Wissenschaft *(f)*
En science
Es ciencia *(f)*
Fr science *(f)*
Pt ciência *(f)*

scontornare *vb* It
De zurichten
En crop
Es recortar
Fr détourer
Pt recortar

scontornata *(f) n* It
De Freistellung *(f)*
En cut out
Es recortado *(m)*
Fr découpage *(m)*
Pt recorte *(m)*

scorta *(f) n* It
De Vorrat *(m)*
En stock (books)
Es existencias *(f pl)*
Fr stock *(m)*
Pt existências *(f pl)*

screen *n* En
De Raster *(m)*
Es retícula *(f)*
Fr écran *(m)*
It retino *(m)*
Pt retícula *(f)*

scritto a mano It
De handgeschrieben
En hand-written

Es escrito a mano
Fr manuscrit
Pt escrito à mão

scrivere a macchina *(m)* It
De Tippen *(n)*
En typing
Es mecanografiado *(m)*
Fr dactylographie *(f)*
Pt dactilografia *(f)*

scrivere a testo continuo It
De anhängen
En run on (typesetting)
Es componer sin punto y aparte
Fr suivre sans alinéa
Pt compor seguido

secado a frio *(f)* Pt
De kalttrocknend
En cold-set
Es solidificardo en frio
Fr seché à froid
It solidificato a freddo *(f)*

secado al aire Es
De luftgetrocknet
En air-dried
Fr séché à l'air
It essiccata ad aria
Pt seco ao ar

secador *(m) n* Pt
De Trockner *(m)*
En drier
Es secante *(m)*
Fr sécheur *(m)*
It essiccante *(m)*

secante *(m) n* Es
De Trockner *(m)*
En drier
Fr sécheur *(m)*
It essiccante *(m)*
Pt secador *(m)*

secção *(f)* Pt
De Druckbogen *(m)*
En section
Es pliego *(m)*
Fr cahier *(m)*
It sezione *(f)*

sección transversal *(f)* Es
De Querschnitt *(m)*

En cross section
Fr vue en coupe *(f)*
It sezione trasversale *(f)*
Pt corte transversal *(m)*

seché à chaud Fr
De heißtrocknend
En heat-set
Es solidificado en caliente
It solidificato a caldo
Pt termofixado

seché à froid Fr
De kalttrocknend
En cold-set
Es solidificardo en frio
It solidificato a freddo *(f)*
Pt secado a frio *(f)*

séché à l'air Fr
De luftgetrocknet
En air-dried
Es secado al aire
It essiccata ad aria
Pt seco ao ar

sécheur *(m) n* Fr
De Trockner *(m)*
En drier
Es secante *(m)*
It essiccante *(m)*
Pt secador *(m)*

seco ao ar Pt
De luftgetrocknet
En air-dried
Es secado al aire
Fr séché à l'air
It essiccata ad aria

secrétaire *(m) n* Fr
De Sekretär *(m)*
En secretary
Es secretario *(m)*
It segretario *(m)*
Pt secretário *(m)*

secrétaire de la rédaction *(m)* Fr
De Zweiter Redakteur *(m)*
En subeditor
Es corrector *(m)*
It redattore aggiunto *(m)*
Pt redactor auxiliar *(m)*

secrétaire de rédaction *(m)* Fr
De Redaktionsassistent *(m)*
En editorial assistant
Es ayudante de editorial *(m)*
It assistente editoriale *(m)*
Pt ajudante editorial *(m)*

secretaria *(f) n* Es
De Sekretärin *(f)*
En secretary (female)
Fr secrétaire *(f)*
It segretaria *(f)*
Pt secretária *(f)*

secretária *(f) n* Pt
De Sekretärin *(f)*
En secretary (female)
Es secretaria *(f)*
Fr secrétaire *(f)*
It segretaria *(f)*

secretario *(m) n* Es
De Sekretär *(m)*
En secretary (male)
Fr secrétaire *(m)*
It segretario *(m)*
Pt secretário *(m)*

secretário *(m) n* Pt
De Sekretär *(m)*
En secretary (male)
Es secretario *(m)*
Fr secrétaire *(m)*
It segretario *(m)*

secretary (male) *n* En
De Sekretär *(m)*
Es secretario *(m)*
Fr secrétaire *(m)*
It segretario *(m)*
Pt secretário *(m)*

secretary (female) *n* En
De Sekretärin *(f)*
Es secretaria *(f)*
Fr secrétaire *(f)*
It segretaria *(f)*
Pt secretária *(f)*

section En
De Druckbogen *(m)*
Es pliego *(m)*
Fr cahier *(m)*
It sezione *(f)*
Pt secção *(f)*

segnatura *(f)* It
De Signatur *(f)*
En signature (of a book)
Es signatura *(f)*
Fr signature *(f)*
Pt assinatura *(f)*

segni del correttore di bozze *(m pl)* It
De Korrekturzeichen *(pl)*
En proofreader's marks
Es signos de corrección *(m pl)*
Fr signes de corrections typographiques *(m pl)*
Pt marcas do revisor de provas *(f pl)*

segni della tela *(m pl)* It
De Drahtmarkierungen *(pl)*
En wiremarks *pl n*
Es marcas de tela metálica *(f pl)*
Fr marques de la toile *(f pl)*
Pt marcas de tela metálica *(f pl)*

segni di raccoglitura *(m pl)* It
De Kollationierzeichen *(pl)*
En collating marks *pl n*
Es señales escalonadas de alzado *(f pl)*
Fr repères d'assemblage *(m pl)*
Pt marcas de revisão *(f pl)*

segni per rifilatura *(m pl)* It
De Beschnitt-Markierungen *(pl)*
En trim marks
Es marcas de recorte *(f pl)*
Fr repères de rognage *(m pl)*
Pt marcas de aparar *(f pl)*

segno di cancellatura *(m)* It
De Tilgungszeichen *(n)*
En delete mark
Es marca de supresión *(f)*
Fr marque à supprimer *(f)*

Pt marca de eliminação *(f)*

segno di punteggiatura *(m)* It
De Interpunktions-zeichen *(n)*
En punctuation mark
Es signo de puntuación *(m)*
Fr signe de ponctuation *(m)*
Pt sinal de pontuação *(m)*

segno di rimando *(m)* It
De Auslassungszeichen *(n)*
En caret mark
Es signo de intercalación *(m)*
Fr renvoi de marge *(m)*
Pt sinal de intercalar *(m)*

segretaria *(f)* n It
De Sekretärin *(f)*
En secretary (female)
Es secretaria *(f)*
Fr secrétaire *(f)*
Pt secretária *(f)*

segretario *(m)* n It
De Sekretär *(m)*
En secretary (male)
Es secretario *(m)*
Fr secrétaire *(m)*
Pt secretário *(m)*

Seidenpapier *(n)* n De
En tissue paper
Es papel de seda *(m)*
Fr papier mousseline *(m)*
It carta velina *(f)*
Pt papel de seda *(m)*

Seite *(f)* n De
En page
Es página *(f)*
Fr page *(f)*
It pagina *(f)*
Pt página *(f)*

Seitekopf *(m)* n De
En head (of page)
Es blanco *(m)*
Fr tête *(f)*
It testata *(f)*
Pt cabeçalho *(m)*

seitenrichtiger Film *(m)*
De
En right-reading film
Es película de lectura correcta *(f)*
Fr film à lecture juste *(m)*
It pellicola a lettura giusta *(f)*
Pt película de leitura do lado direito *(f)*

seitenverkehrter Film *(m)* De
En wrong-reading film
Es película de lectura incorrecta *(f)*
Fr film à lecture à l'envers *(m)*
It pellicola a lettura sbagliata *(f)*
Pt película de leitura do lado errado *(f)*

Seitenzahl *(f)* n De
En extent
Es amplitud *(f)*
Fr nombre de pages *(m)*
It estensione *(m)*
Pt extensão *(f)*

Sekretär *(m)* n De
En secretary (male)
Es secretario *(m)*
Fr secrétaire *(m)*
It segretario *(m)*
Pt secretário *(m)*

Sekretärin *(f)* n De
En secretary (female)
Es secretaria *(f)*
Fr secrétaire *(f)*
It segretaria *(f)*
Pt secretária *(f)*

seleccionadora electrónica de cores *(f)* Pt
De elektronische Abtastung *(f)*
En electronic scanning
Es selección electrónica *(f)*
Fr exploration électronique *(f)*
It scanning elettronico *(m)*

selección electrónica *(f)* Es
De elektronische Abtastung *(f)*

En electronic scanning
Fr exploration électronique *(f)*
It scanning elettronico *(m)*
Pt seleccionadora electrónica de cores *(f)*

selección fotomecánica de colores *(f)* Es
Am color separation
De Farbtrennung *(f)*
En colour separation
Fr séparation des couleurs *(f)*
It selezione di colore *(f)*
Pt separação de cores *(f)*

selezione di colore *(f)* It
Am color separation
De Farbtrennung *(f)*
En colour separation
Es selección fotomecánica de colores *(f)*
Fr séparation des couleurs *(f)*
Pt separação de cores *(f)*

semi-bold type En
De halbfetter Satz *(m)*
Es seminegrilla *(f)*
Fr caractère mi-gras *(m)*
It carattere semi-grassetto *(m)*
Pt tipo semi-negro *(m)*

semicolon n En
De Semikolon *(n)*
Es punto y coma *(m)*
Fr point-virgule *(m)*
It punto e virgola *(m)*
Pt ponto e vírgula *(m)*

Semikolon *(n)* n De
En semicolon
Es punto y coma *(m)*
Fr point-virgule *(m)*
It punto e virgola *(m)*
Pt ponto e vírgula *(m)*

seminegrilla *(f)* n Es
De halbfetter Satz *(m)*
En semi-bold type
Fr caractère mi-gras *(m)*
It carattere semi-grassetto *(m)*
Pt tipo semi-negro *(m)*

señales escalonadas de alzado *(f pl)* Es
De Kollationierzeichen *(pl)*
En collating marks *pl n*
Fr repères d'assemblage *(m pl)*
It segni di raccoglitura *(m pl)*
Pt marcas de revisão *(f pl)*

senior editor En
De leitender Redakteur *(m)*
Es redactor jefe *(m)*
Fr rédacteur en chef *(m)*
It editore senior *(m)*
Pt editor senior *(m)*

sens machine *(m)* Fr
De Laufrichtung *(f)*
En machine direction
Es dirección de máquina *(f)*
It direzione di macchina *(f)*
Pt direcção da máquina *(f)*

sentence *n* En
De Satz *(m)*
Es cláusula *(f)*
Fr phrase *(f)*
It frase *(f)*
Pt frase *(f)*

separação de cores *(f)* Pt
Am color separation
De Farbtrennung *(f)*
En colour separation
Es selección fotomecánica de colores *(f)*
Fr séparation des couleurs *(f)*
It selezione di colore *(f)*

separación con guiones *(f)* Es
De Trennung *(f)*
En hyphenation
Fr coupure *(f)*
It legatura con trattino *(f)*
Pt colocação de um traço de união *(f)*

separar con guión Es
De trennen
En hyphenate

Fr mettre un trait d'union
It legare con trattino
Pt pôr um traço de união

separar hojas Es
De auseinandertragen
En decollate
Fr déliasser
It decollare
Pt decapitar

séparation des couleurs *(f)* Fr
Am color separation
De Farbtrennung *(f)*
En colour separation
Es selección fotomecánica de colores *(f)*
It selezione di colore *(f)*
Pt separação de cores *(f)*

séparation des plis *(f)* Fr
De Ableimung *(f)*
En delamination
Es delaminación *(f)*
It separazione degli strati *(f)*
Pt deslaminação *(f)*

separation negatives En
De Teilfarbennegative *(pl)*
Es negativos de selección *(m pl)*
Fr négatifs sélectionnés *(m pl)*
It negativi da selezione *(m pl)*
Pt negativos de separação *(m pl)*

separazione degli strati *(f)* It
De Ableimung *(f)*
En delamination
Es delaminación *(f)*
Fr séparation des plis *(f)*
Pt deslaminação *(f)*

serialization En
De Veröffentlichung in Fortsetzungen *(f)*
Es publicación por entregas *(f)*
Fr parution en feuilleton *(f)*
It riduzione in serie *(f)*

Pt publicação em série *(f)*

serie di caratteri *(f)* It
De Schriftart *(f)*
En fount
Es fundición *(f)*
Fr fonte *(f)*
Pt fundição *(f)*

serif *n* En
De Serif *(m)*
Es bigotillo *(m)*
Fr empâtement *(m)*
It terminazione *(f)*
Pt remate *(m)*

Serif *(m)* *n* De
En serif
Es bigotillo *(m)*
Fr empâtement *(m)*
It terminazione *(f)*
Pt remate *(m)*

serigrafia *(f)* *n* Pt
De Siebdruck *(m)*
En silk-screen printing
Es impresión serigráfica *(f)*
Fr sérigraphie *(f)*
It stampa serigrafica *(f)*

sérigraphie *(f)* *n* Fr
De Siebdruck *(m)*
En silk-screen printing
Es impresión serigráfica *(f)*
It stampa serigrafica *(f)*
Pt serigrafia *(f)*

serraforme *(m)* *n* It
De Keil *(m)*
En quoin
Es cuña *(f)*
Fr coin *(m)*
Pt cunha *(f)*

serrage *(m)* *n* Fr
De Schließen *(n)*
En locking-up
Es acuñado *(m)*
It serramento *(m)*
Pt enramado *(m)*

serramento *(m)* *n* It
De Schliesen *(n)*
En locking-up
Es acuñado *(m)*
Fr serrage *(m)*
Pt enramado *(m)*

service company En
De Dienstleitungsfirma *(f)*
Es compañía de servicios *(f)*
Fr entretien *(m)*
It società di servizio *(f)*
Pt companhia de serviços *(f)*

service de la publicité *(m)* Fr
De Werbeabteilung *(f)*
En publicity department
Es departamento de publicidad *(m)*
It reparto pubblicitario *(m)*
Pt departamento de publicidade *(f)*

service des droits à l'étranger *(m)* Fr
De Auslandsrecht-Abteilung *(f)*
En foreign-rights department
Es departamento de derechos en el extranjero *(m)*
It reparto diritti esteri *(m)*
Pt departamento de direitos estrangeiros *(m)*

service production *(m)* Fr
De Produktionsabteilung *(f)*
En production department
Es departamento de producción *(m)*
It reparto produzione *(m)*
Pt departamento de produção *(m)*

services rédactionnels *(m pl)* Fr
De Redaktionsdienste *(pl)*
En editorial services *pl n*
Es servicios editoriales *(m pl)*
It servizi editoriali *(m pl)*
Pt serviços editoriais *(m pl)*

service VPC *(m)* Fr
De Versandhaus-
abteilung *(f)*
En mail-order division
Es división de pedidos
por correo *(f)*
It reparto vendite per
posta *(m)*
Pt divisão de
encomendas por
correio *(f)*

servicios editoriales *(m*
pl) Es
De Redaktionsdienste
(pl)
En editorial services *pl n*
Fr services
rédactionnels *(m pl)*
It servizi editoriali *(m pl)*·
Pt serviços editoriais *(m*
pl)

serviços editoriais *(m pl)*
Pt
De Redaktionsdienste
(pl)
En editorial services *pl n*
Es servicios editoriales
(m pl)
Fr services
rédactionnels *(m pl)*
It servizi editoriali *(m pl)*

servizi di
immagazzinaggio
(m pl) It
De Speicherungs-
möglichkeiten *(pl)*
En storage facilities
Es almacenes *(m pl)*
Fr entrepôts *(m pl)*
Pt instalações de
armazenamento *(f pl)*

servizi editoriali *(m pl)* It
De Redaktionsdienste
(pl)
En editorial services *pl n*
Es servicios editoriales
(m pl)
Fr services
rédactionnels *(m pl)*
Pt serviços editoriais *(m*
pl)

servizio vendite estero
(m) It
De Auslandsumsätze *(pl)*
En foreign sales *pl n*
Es ventas extranjeras *(f*
pl)

Fr ventes à l'étranger *(f*
pl)
Pt vendas no
estrangeiro *(f pl)*

se spécialiser Fr
De spezialisieren
En specialize
Es especializar
It specializzare
Pt especializar

setzen *vb* De
En compose
Es componer
Fr composer
It comporre
Pt compor

Setzen *(n) n* De
En composition
Es composición *(f)*
Fr composition *(f)*
It composizione *(f)*
Pt composição *(f)*

Setzer *(m) n* De
En compositor
Es compositor *(m)*
Fr typographe *(m)*
It compositore *(m)*
Pt compositor *(m)*

Setzerei *(f) n* De
En composing room
Es sala de composición
(f)
Fr atelier de
composition *(m)*
It sala composizione *(f)*
Pt sala de composição
(f)

Setzfehler *(m) n* De
En literal
Es error de imprenta *(m)*
Fr coquille *(f)*
It errore di stampa *(m)*
Pt errata literal *(f)*

Setzkasten *(m) n* De
En case (typesetting)
Es caja *(f)*
Fr casse *(f)*
It cassa tipografica *(f)*
Pt caixa *(f)*

Setzmaschine *(f) n* De
En typesetting machine

Es máquina de
composición *(f)*
Fr machine à composer
(f)
It compositrice *(f)*
Pt compositora de tipos
(f)

Setzmaschinenzeile *(f)*
n De
En slug
Es lingote *(m)*
Fr lingot *(m)*
It riga intera *(f)*
Pt lingote *(m)*

Setzraum *(m) n* De
En keyboarding room
Es sala de mecanotipia
(f)
Fr salle de
photocomposition *(f)*
It sala di
fotocomposizione *(f)*
Pt sala de mecanotipia
(f)

seudónimo *(m) n* Es
De Pseudonym *(n)*
En pseudonym
Fr pseudonyme *(m)*
It pseudonimo *(m)*
Pt pseudónimo *(m)*

seuil de rentabilité *(m)*
Fr
De Nutzschwelle *(f)*
En break-even point
Es punto de equilibrio
(m)
It punto di pareggio *(m)*
Pt ponto de equilíbrio
(m)

sewn work En
De geheftete Arbeit *(f)*
Es obra cosida *(f)*
Fr reliure cousue *(f)*
It lavoro di cucitura *(m)*
Pt obra cosida *(f)*

sezione *(f)* It
De Druckbogen *(m)*
En section
Es pliego *(m)*
Fr cahier *(m)*
Pt secção *(f)*

sezione trasversale *(f)* It
De Querschnitt *(m)*
En cross section

Es sección transversal *(f)*
Fr vue en coupe *(f)*
Pt corte transversal *(m)*

sfarinamento *(m) n* It
De Kalkschleier *(m)*
En chalking
Es desintegración en
polvo *(f)*
Fr poudrage *(m)*
Pt descascamento *(m)*

shading *n* En
De Schattierung *(f)*
Es sombreado *(m)*
Fr exécution des
ombres *(f)*
It ombreggiatura *(f)*
Pt tracejado *(m)*

shank *n* En
De Stiel *(m)*
Es árbol *(m)*
Fr tige *(f)*
It gambo *(m)*
Pt árvore *(f)*

share *n* En
De Aktie *(f)*
Es acción *(f)*
Fr action *(f)*
It azione *(f)*
Pt acção *(f)*

shareholder *n* En
De Aktionär *(m)*
Es accionista *(m)*
Fr actionnaire *(m)*
It azionista *(m/f)*
Pt accionista *(m)*

sheet-fed printing En
De Bogendruck *(m)*
Es impresión de hojas *(f)*
Fr impression à
machine à feuilles *(f)*
It stampa a fogli *(f)*
Pt impressão de folhas
(f)

shelve *vb* En
De aufschieben
Es postergar
indefinidamente
Fr ajourner
It porre in disparte
Pt arquivar

shipping n En
De Verschiffung (f)
Es envío (m)
Fr expédition (f)
It spedizione (f)
Pt envio (m)

shipping costs En
De Verschiffungkosten (pl)
Es gastos de envío (m pl)
Fr frais d'expédition (m pl)
It costi di spedizione (m pl)
Pt custos de envio (m pl)

shop (in industry) n En
De Fabrik (f)
Es taller (m)
Fr atelier (m)
It officina (f)
Pt oficina (f)

shop (retail) n En
De Laden (m)
Es tienda (f)
Fr boutique (f)
It negozio (m)
Pt loja (f)

shop-soiled adj En
De verschmutzt
Es sucio
Fr défraîchi
It sporco
Pt sujado na loja

shop steward En
De Gewerkschafts-Betriebsobmann (m)
Es dirigente obrero (m)
Fr délégué d'atelier (m)
It delegato di fabbrica (m)
Pt balconista (m)

short-grain paper En
De kurzkörniges Papier (n)
Es papel de fibra corta (m)
Fr papier à fibres courtes (m)
It carta a grana corta (f)
Pt papel de grão curto (m)

short story En
De Kurzgeschichte (f)
Es narración (f)
Fr nouvelle (f)
It racconto breve (m)
Pt novela pequena (f)

shrink-wrapping n En
De Schrumpfverpackung (f)
Es envoltura por contracción (f)
Fr emballage serré (m)
It confezionamento a restringimento (m)
Pt embalagem de encolher (f)

Sichtanzeigegerät (n) n De
En visual-display unit (VDU)
Es unidad de visualización (f)
Fr unité de visualisation (f)
It unità di visualizzazione (f)
Pt unidade de visulização (f)

side head En
De links in Linie gebrachte Überschrift (f)
Es titulillo lateral (m)
Fr tête latérale (f)
It titolo laterale (m)
Pt título lateral (m)

side-stitching n En
De Querheftung (f)
Es cosido por el costado (m)
Fr couture de côté (f)
It cucitura laterale (f)
Pt cosido pela lombada (m)

Siebdruck (m) n De
En silk-screen printing
Es impresión serigráfica (f)
Fr sérigraphie (f)
It stampa serigrafica (f)
Pt serigrafia (f)

Siebseite (f) n De
En wire side
Es cara interior (f)
Fr côté toilé (m)

It lato tela (m)
Pt lado da tela (m)

Signatur (f) De
En signature (of a book)
Es signatura (f)
Fr signature (f)
It segnatura (f)
Pt assinatura (f)

signatura (f) Es
De Signatur (f)
En signature (of a book)
Fr signature (f)
It segnatura (f)
Pt assinatura (f)

signature (of a book) En; Fr (f)
De Signatur (f)
Es signatura (f)
It segnatura (f)
Pt assinatura (f)

Signaturrinne (f) n De
En nick
Es cran (m)
Fr cran (m)
It tacca (f)
Pt entalhe (m)

signe de ponctuation (m) Fr
De Interpunktions-zeichen (n)
En punctuation mark
Es signo de puntuación (m)
It segno di punteggiatura (m)
Pt sinal de pontuação (m)

signer vb Fr
De signieren
En autograph
Es firmar
It autografare
Pt autógrafar

signes de corrections typographiques (m pl) Fr
De Korrekturzeichen (pl)
En proofreader's marks
Es signos de corrección (m pl)
It segni del correttore di bozze (m pl)
Pt marcas do revisor de provas (f pl)

Signet (n) n De
En colophon
Es colofón (m)
Fr colophon (m)
It colofone (m)
Pt colofónio (m)

signieren vb De
En autograph
Es firmar
Fr signer
It autografare
Pt autógrafar

signo de admiración (m) Es
De Ausrufungszeichen (n)
En exclamation mark
Fr point d'exclamation (m)
It punto esclamativo (m)
Pt ponto de exclamação (m)

signo de intercalación (m) Es
De Auslassungszeichen (n)
En caret mark
Fr renvoi de marge (m)
It segno di rimando (m)
Pt sinal de intercalar (m)

signo de interrogación (m) Es
De Fragezeichen (n)
En question mark
Fr point d'interrogation (m)
It punto di domanda (m)
Pt ponto de interrogação (m)

signo de puntuación (m) Es
De Interpunktions-zeichen (n)
En punctuation mark
Fr signe de ponctuation (m)
It segno di punteggiatura (m)
Pt sinal de pontuação (m)

signos de corrección (m pl) Es
De Korrekturzeichen (pl)
En proofreader's marks

Fr signes de corrections
  typographiques *(m
  pl)*
It segni del correttore
  di bozze *(m pl)*
Pt marcas do revisor de
  provas *(f pl)*

signos fonéticos *(m pl)*
  Es
De Phonetikzeichen *(pl)*
En phonetic symbols
Fr symboles
  phonétiques *(m pl)*
It simboli fonetici *(m pl)*
Pt símbolos fonéticos
  (m pl)

silk-screen printing En
De Siebdruck *(m)*
Es impresión serigráfica
  (f)
Fr sérigraphie *(f)*
It stampa serigrafica *(f)*
Pt serigrafia *(f)*

sillabare *vb* It
De buchstabieren
En spell
Es deletrear
Fr épeler
Pt soletrar

simboli fonetici *(m pl)* It
De Phonetikzeichen *(pl)*
En phonetic symbols
Es signos fonéticos *(m
  pl)*
Fr symboles
  phonétiques *(m pl)*
Pt símbolos fonéticos
  (m pl)

simbolo *(m) n* It
De Symbol *(n)*
En symbol
Es símbolo *(m)*
Fr symbole *(m)*
Pt símbolo *(m)*

símbolo *(m) n* Es, Pt
De Symbol *(n)*
En symbol
Fr symbole *(m)*
It simbolo *(m)*

símbolos fonéticos *(m
  pl)* Pt
De Phonetikzeichen *(pl)*
En phonetic symbols

Es signos fonéticos *(m
  pl)*
Fr symboles
  phonétiques *(m pl)*
It simboli fonetici *(m pl)*

simili *(f) n* Fr
De Halbton *(m)*
En halftone
Es autotipia *(f)*
It mezzatinta *(f)*
Pt autotipia *(f)*

simili dégradée *(f)* Fr
De Gelegenheitsvignetta
  (f)
En vignetted blocks *pl n*
Es fotograbados
  esfumados *(m pl)*
It clichés à vignette *(m
  pl)*
Pt blocos de vinheta *(m
  pl)*

sinal de intercalar *(m)* Pt
De Auslassungszeichen
  (n)
En caret mark
Es signo de
  intercalación *(m)*
Fr renvoi de marge *(m)*
It segno di rimando *(m)*

sinal de pontuação *(m)*
  Pt
De Interpunktions-
  zeichen *(n)*
En punctuation mark
Es signo de puntuación
  (m)
Fr signe de ponctuation
  (m)
It segno di
  punteggiatura *(m)*

sindacato *(m) n* It
De Gewerkschaft *(f)*
En trade union
Es sindicato *(m)*
Fr syndicat *(m)*
Pt sindicato *(m)*

sindicato *(m) n* Es, Pt
De Gewerkschaft *(f)*
En trade union
Fr syndicat *(m)*
It sindacato *(m)*

sin existencias Es
De nicht vorrätig
En out of stock

Fr non disponible
It sprovvisto
Pt esgotado em
  armazém

single-volume work En
De einbändiges Werk *(n)*
Es obra de un solo
  volumen *(f)*
Fr oeuvre en un volume
  (f)
It opera in un solo
  volume *(f)*
Pt obra num só volume
  (f)

sinonimo *(m) n* It
De Synonym *(n)*
En synonym
Es sinónimo *(m)*
Fr synonyme *(m)*
Pt sinónimo *(m)*

sinónimo *(m) n* Es, Pt
De Synonym *(n)*
En synonym
Fr synonyme *(m)*
It sinonimo *(m)*

sinopse *(f) n* Pt
De Reklamestreifen *(m)*
En blurb
Es bombo *(m)*
Fr manchette
  publicitaire *(f)*
It soffietto editoriale
  (m)

sinopse *(f) n* Pt
De Synopsis *(f)*
En synopsis
Es sinopsis *(f)*
Fr synopsis *(m)*
It sinopsi *(f)*

sinopse de sobrecapa *(f)*
  Pt
De Umschlag-
  Reklamestreifen *(m)*
En jacket blurb
Es reseña en la cubierta
  (f)
Fr manchette sur la
  jaquette *(f)*
It sommario della
  sovracopertina *(m)*

sinopsi *(f) n* It
De Synopsis *(f)*
En synopsis
Es sinopsis *(f)*

Fr synopsis *(m)*
Pt sinopse *(f)*

sinopsis *(f) n* Es
De Synopsis *(f)*
En synopsis
Fr synopsis *(m)*
It sinopsi *(f)*
Pt sinopse *(f)*

sistema *(m) n* Es, It, Pt
De System *(n)*
En system
Fr système *(m)*

sizing *n* En
De Leimung *(f)*
Es encolado *(m)*
Fr encollage *(m)*
It collaggio *(m)*
Pt encolamento *(m)*

Skalpell *(n) n* De
En scalpel
Es escalpelo *(m)*
Fr scalpel *(m)*
It bisturi ad un solo
  taglio *(m)*
Pt bisturí *(m)*

Skizze *(f) n* De
En rough
Es boceto *(m)*
Fr croquis *(m)*
It abbozzo *(m)*
Pt esboço *(m)*

slip case En
De Schuber *(m)*
Es estuche *(m)*
Fr étui *(m)*
It astuccio del libro *(m)*
Pt estojo de livro *(m)*

slug *n* En
De Setzmaschinenzeile
  (f)
Es lingote *(m)*
Fr lingot *(m)*
It riga intera *(f)*
Pt lingote *(m)*

small capital letters En
De Kapitälchen *(pl)*
Es letras versalitas *(f pl)*
Fr petites majuscules *(f
  pl)*
It lettere in
  maiuscoletto *(f pl)*

Pt maiúsculas pequenas
(f pl)

smusso *(m)* n It
De Konus *(m)*
En bevel
Es bisel *(m)*
Fr biseau *(m)*
Pt chanfro *(m)*

sobrecapa *(f)* n Pt
De Umschlag *(m)*
En jacket
Es camisa *(f)*
Fr jaquette *(f)*
It sovracopertina *(f)*

sobrecubierta *(f)* n Es
De Klebenindung *(f)*
En wrappering
Fr emballage *(m)*
It mettitura le
sovracopertine *(f)*
Pt colocação de
sobrecapa *(f)*

sobremordicação *(f)* n Pt
De Unterätzung *(f)*
En undercutting
Es sobremordido *(m)*
Fr massicotage *(m)*
It intaglio *(m)*

sobremordido *(m)* n Es
De Unterätzung *(f)*
En undercutting
Fr massicotage *(m)*
It intaglio *(m)*
Pt sobremordicação *(f)*

**sociedade
empacotadora** *(f)* Pt
De Verpackungsfirma *(f)*
En packaging company
Es compañía
empaquetadora *(f)*
Fr entreprise de
l'emballage *(f)*
It società
confezionamento *(m)*

**società
confezionamento**
(m) It
De Verpackungsfirma *(f)*
En packaging company
Es compañía
empaquetadora *(f)*
Fr entreprise de
l'emballage *(f)*

Pt sociedade
empacotadora *(f)*

società di servizio *(f)* It
De Dienstleitungsfirma
(f)
En service company
Es compañía de
servicios *(f)*
Fr entretien *(m)*
Pt companhia de
serviços *(f)*

soffietto editoriale *(m)* It
De Reklamestreifen *(m)*
En blurb
Es bombo *(m)*
Fr manchette
publicitaire *(f)*
Pt sinopse *(f)*

software n En; It, Pt *(m)*
De Software *(f)*
Es equipo instruccional
(m)
Fr logiciel *(m)*

Software *(f)* n De
En software
Es equipo instruccional
(m)
Fr logiciel *(m)*
It software *(m)*
Pt software *(m)*

solapa de la cubierta *(f)*
Es
De Umschlagklappe *(f)*
En jacket flap
Fr rabat de la jaquette
(m)
It risvolto della
sovracopertina *(m)*
Pt aba da sobrecapa *(f)*

solapa delantera *(f)* Es
De vordere
Umschlagklappe *(f)*
En front flap
Fr rabat avant *(m)*
It risvolto anteriore *(m)*
Pt aleta dianteira *(f)*

solapa posterior *(f)* Es
De hintere
Umschlagklappe *(f)*
En back flap
Fr rabat arrière *(m)*
It risvolto di retro *(m)*
Pt contracapa *(f)*

solde d'éditions *(m)* Fr
De Remittenden *(pl)*
En remainder books
Es restos de edición *(m
pl)*
It rimanenze *(f pl)*
Pt restos de edição *(m
pl)*

solde pas encore gagné
(m) Fr
De Saldo unverdient *(m)*
En unearned balance
Es saldo no devengado
(m)
It saldo non ancora
guadagnato *(m)*
Pt saldo ainda não
ganhado *(m)*

sold out En
De ausverkauft
Es agotado
Fr liquidé
It esaurito
Pt esgotado

soletração *(f)* n Pt
De Buchstabierung *(f)*
En spelling
Es deletreo *(m)*
Fr épellation *(f)*
It compitazione *(f)*

soletrar vb Pt
De buchstabieren
En spell
Es deletrear
Fr épeler
It sillabare

solid adj En
De kompreβ
Es desinterlineado
Fr à-plat
It sterlineato
Pt maciço

solidez a la luz *(f)* Es
De Lichtbeständigkeit *(f)*
En fastness (to light)
Fr solidité à la lumière
(f)
It stabilità alla luce *(f)*
Pt inalterabilidade à luz
(f)

solidificado en caliente
Es
De heiβtrocknend
En heat-set

Fr seché à chaud
It solidificato a caldo
Pt termofixado

solidificardo en frio Es
De kalttrocknend
En cold-set
Fr seché à froid
It solidificato a freddo
(f)
Pt secado a frio *(f)*

solidificato a caldo It
De heiβtrocknend
En heat-set
Es solidificado en
caliente
Fr seché à chaud
Pt termofixado

solidificato a freddo *(f)*
It
De kalttrocknend
En cold-set
Es solidificardo en frio
Fr seché à froid
Pt secado a frio *(f)*

solidité à la lumière *(f)*
Fr
De Lichtbeständigkeit *(f)*
En fastness (to light)
Es solidez a la luz *(f)*
It stabilità alla luce *(f)*
Pt inalterabilidade à luz
(f)

solvabilité *(f)* n Fr
De Flüssigkeit *(f)*
En solvency
Es solvencia *(f)*
It solvenza *(f)*
Pt solvência *(f)*

solvencia *(f)* n Es
De Flüssigkeit *(f)*
En solvency
Fr solvabilité *(f)*
It solvenza *(f)*
Pt solvência *(f)*

solvência *(f)* n Pt
De Flüssigkeit *(f)*
En solvency
Es solvencia *(f)*
Fr solvabilité *(f)*
It solvenza *(f)*

solvency *n* En
De Flüssigkeit *(f)*
Es solvencia *(f)*
Fr solvabilité *(f)*
It solvenza *(f)*
Pt solvência *(f)*

solvenza *(f) n* It
De Flüssigkeit *(f)*
En solvency
Es solvencia *(f)*
Fr solvabilité *(f)*
Pt solvência *(f)*

sombreado *(m) n* Es
De Schattierung *(f)*
En shading
Fr exécution des
ombres *(f)*
It ombreggiatura *(f)*
Pt tracejado *(m)*

somma globale *(f)* It
De Pauschalbetrag *(m)*
En lump sum
Es suma total *(f)*
Fr somme globale *(f)*
Pt importância global *(f)*

sommario *(m) n* It
De Zusammenfassung *(f)*
En summary
Es sumario *(m)*
Fr résumé *(m)*
Pt sumário *(m)*

**sommario della
sovracopertina** *(m)*
It
De Umschlag-
Reklamestreifen *(m)*
En jacket blurb
Es reseña en la cubierta
(f)
Fr manchette sur la
jaquette *(f)*
Pt sinopse de
sobrecapa *(f)*

sommario delle materie
(m) It
De Inhaltsverzeichnis *(n)*
En table of contents
Es índice de materias
(m)
Fr table des matières *(f)*
Pt índice dos assuntos
(m)

somme globale *(f)* Fr
De Pauschalbetrag *(m)*
En lump sum
Es suma total *(f)*
It somma globale *(f)*
Pt importância global *(f)*

sortes *(f pl)* Pt
De Schriftgarnitur *(f)*
En sorts *pl n*
Es suertes *(f pl)*
Fr assortiment *(m)*
It rappezzi *(m pl)*

sortes especial *(f)* Pt
De Spezial-Schrifttyp *(m)*
En special sort
Es suerte especial *(f)*
Fr figure spéciale *(f)*
It tipo speciale *(m)*

sortie d'imprimante *(f)*
Fr
De Ausdruck *(m)*
En printout
Es vaciado a la
impresora *(m)*
It printout *(m)*
Pt impressão em
positivo directo *(f)*

sortir *vb* Fr
De ausdrucken
En print out
Es imprimir (por
ordenador)
It stampare (per
elaboratore)
Pt imprimir em positivo
directo

sorts *pl n* En
De Schriftgarnitur *(f)*
Es suertes *(f pl)*
Fr assortiment *(m)*
It rappezzi *(m pl)*
Pt sortes *(f pl)*

sottolineare *vb* It
De unterstreichen
En underline
Es subrayar
Fr souligner
Pt subraiar

sottolineatura a penna
(f) It
De Federlinierung *(f)*
En pen ruling
Es rayado a pluma *(m)*

Fr réglure au crayon *(f)*
Pt linhas à pena *(m)*

sottostrato *(m) n* It
De Substrat *(n)*
En substrate
Es substrato *(m)*
Fr substrat *(m)*
Pt substrato *(m)*

sottotitolo *(m) n* It
De Untertitel *(m)*
En subtitle
Es subtítulo *(m)*
Fr sous-titre *(m)*
Pt subtítulo *(m)*

souligner *vb* Fr
De unterstreichen
En underline
Es subrayar
It sottolineare
Pt subraiar

source *(f) n* Fr
De Entstehungsarbeiten
(pl)
En origination
Es creación *(f)*
It origine *(f)*
Pt criação *(f)*

source lumineuse *(f)* Fr
De Lichtquelle *(f)*
En light source
Es fuente luminosa *(f)*
It fonte luminosa *(f)*
Pt fonte luminosa *(f)*

sous-titre *(m) n* Fr
De Untertitel *(m)*
En alternate title;
subtitle
Es subtítulo *(m)*
It sottotitolo; titolo
alternato *(m)*
Pt subtítulo; título
alternativo *(m)*

sovracopertina *(f) n* It
De Umschlag *(m)*
En jacket
Es camisa *(f)*
Fr jaquette *(f)*
Pt sobrecapa *(f)*

sovrapposizione *(f) n* It
De Deckblatt *(n)*
En overlay (on artwork,
etc.)

Es superponible *(m)*
Fr becquet *(m)*
Pt coberta *(f)*

**sovrapposizione
meccanica** *(f)* It
De mechanische
Zurichtung *(f)*
En mechanical overlay
Es alza mecánica *(f)*
Fr mise en train
mécanique *(f)*
Pt corte mecânico *(m)*

space *n* En
De Ausschlußstück *(m)*
Es espacio *(m)*
Fr espace *(m)*
It spazio *(m)*
Pt espaço *(m)*

spacing *n* En
De Abstand *(m)*
Es espaciado *(m)*
Fr espacement *(m)*
It spaziatura *(f)*
Pt espaçamento *(m)*

Spalte *(f) n* De
En column (of text)
Es columna *(f)*
Fr colonne *(f)*
It colonna *(f)*
Pt coluna *(f)*

Spaltenabziehpresse *(f)*
n De
En galley press
Es prensa para prueba
de galeradas *(f)*
Fr presse à épreuves *(f)*
It stampa di vantaggio
(f)
Pt prensa de galé *(f)*

sparto *(m) n* It
De Esparto *(n)*
En esparto grass
Es esparto *(m)*
Fr alfa *(m)*
Pt esparto *(m)*

spaziatura *(f) n* It
De Abstand *(m)*
En spacing
Es espaciado *(m)*
Fr espacement *(m)*
Pt espaçamento *(m)*

spaziatura difettosa *(f)* It
De weiβer Streifen im
  Satz *(m)*
En river
Es calle *(f)*
Fr rue *(f)*
Pt espaço defeituoso
  (m)

**spaziatura ottica tra le
lettere** *(f)* It
De optischer
  Buchstabenabstand
  (m)
En optical letterspacing
Es espaciado óptico
  entre letras *(m)*
Fr interlettrage optique
  (m)
Pt espaçamento óptico
  de letras *(m)*

spaziatura tra le lettere
  (f) It
De Buchstabenabstand
  (m)
En letter spacing
Es espaciado entre
  letras *(m)*
Fr espacement entre
  caractère *(m)*
Pt espaço entre letras
  (m)

spazio *(m)* n It
De Ausschluβstück *(m)*
En space
Es espacio *(m)*
Fr espace *(m)*
Pt espaço *(m)*

spazio grosso *(m)* It
De dickes Spatium *(n)*
En thick space
Es espacio grueso *(m)*
Fr espace forte *(f)*
Pt espaço grosso *(m)*

spazio sottile *(m)* It
De dünnes Spatium *(n)*
En thin space
Es espacio fino *(m)*
Fr espace fine *(f)*
Pt espaço fino *(m)*

spazio tra le righe *(m)* It
De Zeilenabstand *(m)*
En line space
Es espacio entre líneas
  (m)
Fr espace entre deux
  lignes *(m)*

Pt espaço entre linhas
  (m)

spazio variabile *(m)* It
De variabler Abstand *(m)*
En variable space
Es espacio variable *(m)*
Fr espace variable *(m)*
Pt espaço variável *(m)*

specialist n En
De Spezialist *(m)*
Es especialista *(m)*
Fr spécialiste *(m)*
It specialista *(m/f)*
Pt especialista *(m)*

specialista *(m/f)* n It
De Spezialist *(m)*
En specialist
Es especialista *(m)*
Fr spécialiste *(m)*
Pt especialista *(m)*

specialist book En
De Spezial-Buch *(n)*
Es libro especializado
  (m)
Fr ouvrage spécialisé
  (m)
It libro specialistico *(m)*
Pt livro para
  especialistas *(m)*

spécialiste *(m)* n Fr
De Spezialist *(m)*
En specialist
Es especialista *(m)*
It specialista *(m/f)*
Pt especialista *(m)*

specialist journal En
De Spezial-Journal *(n)*
Es revista especializada
  (f)
Fr revue spécialisée *(f)*
It rivista specializzata *(f)*
Pt revista para
  especialistas *(f)*

specialist publisher En
De Spezial-Verleger *(m)*
Es editor de obras
  especializadas *(m)*
Fr éditeur d'ouvrages
  spécialisés *(m)*
It editore di opere
  specialistiche *(m)*
Pt editora de obras
  especiais *(m)*

specialize *vb* En
De spezialisieren
Es especializar
Fr se spécialiser
It specializzare
Pt especializar

specializzare *vb* It
De spezialisieren
En specialize
Es especializar
Fr se spécialiser
Pt especializar

special sort En
De Spezial-Schrifttyp *(m)*
Es suerte especial *(f)*
Fr figure spéciale *(f)*
It tipo speciale *(m)*
Pt sortes especial *(f)*

specification n En
De Spezifikation *(f)*
Es especificación *(f)*
Fr caractéristiques *(f pl)*
It specifiche *(f pl)*
Pt especificação *(f)*

specifiche *(f pl)* n It
De Spezifikation *(f)*
En specification
Es especificación *(f)*
Fr caractéristiques *(f pl)*
Pt especificação *(f)*

specimen page En
De Musterseite *(f)*
Es página de muestra *(f)*
Fr feuille-échantillon *(f)*
It pagina campione *(f)*
Pt página amostra *(f)*

spedire *vb* It
De versenden
En forward
Es expedir
Fr expédier
Pt enviar

spedire per posta It
De mit der Post schicken
En mail
Es enviar por correo
Fr envoyer par la poste
Pt enviar por correio

Spediteur *(m)* n De
En forwarding agent
Es agente expedidor *(m)*
Fr transitaire *(m)*

It spedizioniere *(m)*
Pt agente expedidor *(m)*

spedizione *(f)* n It
De Verschiffung *(f)*
En shipping
Es envío *(m)*
Fr expédition *(f)*
Pt envio *(m)*

spedizioniere *(m)* n It
De Spediteur *(m)*
En forwarding agent
Es agente expedidor *(m)*
Fr transitaire *(m)*
Pt agente expedidor *(m)*

speichern n De
En store
Es memoria *(f)*
Fr mémoire *(f)*
It memoria *(f)*
Pt memória *(f)*

Speicherung *(f)* n De
En storage
Es almacenamiento *(m)*
Fr stockage *(m)*
It immagazzinaggio *(m)*
Pt armazenamento *(m)*

**Speicherungs-
möglichkeiten** *(pl)*
  De
En storage facilities
Es almacenes *(m pl)*
Fr entrepôts *(m pl)*
It servizi di
  immagazzinaggio *(m
  pl)*
Pt instalações de
  armazenamento *(f pl)*

spell *vb* En
De buchstabieren
Es deletrear
Fr épeler
It sillabare
Pt soletrar

spelling n En
De Buchstabierung *(f)*
Es deletreo *(m)*
Fr épellation *(f)*
It compitazione *(f)*
Pt soletração *(f)*

Spezial-Buch *(n)* De
En specialist book

Es libro especializado *(m)*
Fr ouvrage spécialisé *(m)*
It libro specialistico *(m)*
Pt livro para especialistas *(m)*

spezialisieren *vb* De
En specialize
Es especializar
Fr se spécialiser
It specializzare
Pt especializar

Spezialist *(m) n* De
En specialist
Es especialista *(m)*
Fr spécialiste *(m)*
It specialista *(m/f)*
Pt especialista *(m)*

Spezial-Journal *(n)* De
En specialist journal
Es revista especializada *(f)*
Fr revue spécialisée *(f)*
It rivista specializzata *(f)*
Pt revista para especialistas *(f)*

Spezial-Schrifttyp *(m)* De
En special sort
Es suerte especial *(f)*
Fr figure spéciale *(f)*
It tipo speciale *(m)*
Pt sortes especial *(f)*

Spezial-Verleger *(m)* De
En specialist publisher
Es editor de obras especializadas *(m)*
Fr éditeur d'ouvrages spécialisés *(m)*
It editore di opere specialistiche *(m)*
Pt editora de obras especiais *(m)*

Spezifikation *(f) n* De
En specification
Es especificación *(f)*
Fr caractéristiques *(f pl)*
It specifiche *(f pl)*
Pt especificação *(f)*

spine *n* En
De Rücken *(m)*
Es lomo *(m)*
Fr dos *(m)*

It dorso *(m)*
Pt lombada *(f)*

spine width En
De Rückendicke *(f)*
Es ancho del lomo *(m)*
Fr largeur du dos *(f)*
It larghezza del dorso *(f)*
Pt largura de lombada *(f)*

spiral binding En
De Spiralbindung *(f)*
Es encuadernación en espiral *(f)*
Fr reliure spirale *(f)*
It rilegatura a spirale *(f)*
Pt encadernação em espiral *(f)*

Spiralbindung *(f) n* De
En spiral binding
Es encuadernación en espiral *(f)*
Fr reliure spirale *(f)*
It rilegatura a spirale *(f)*
Pt encadernação em espiral *(f)*

sporco *adj* It
De verschmutzt
En shop-soiled
Es sucio
Fr défraîchi
Pt sujado na loja

sporgenza *(f) n* It
De Überhang *(m)*
En kern
Es talud *(m)*
Fr crénage *(m)*
Pt saliência do corpo do tipo *(f)*

spring list En
De Frühjahrsliste *(f)*
Es catálogo de primavera *(m)*
Fr catalogue de printemps *(m)*
It elenco di primavera *(m)*
Pt lista de Primavera *(f)*

spring publication En
De Frühjahrs-Veröffentlichung *(f)*
Es publicación de primavera *(f)*
Fr parution de printemps *(f)*

It pubblicazione di primavera *(f)*
Pt publicação de Primavera *(f)*

Spritzdruckverfahren *(n) n* De
En jet printing method
Es método de impresión por chorro *(m)*
Fr impression au jet d'encre *(f)*
It metodo di stampa a getto *(m)*
Pt método de impressão a jacto *(m)*

sprovvisto *adj* It
De nicht vorrätig
En out of stock
Es sin existencias
Fr non disponible
Pt esgotado em armazém

Spule *(f) n* De
En reel
Es bobina *(f)*
Fr bobine *(f)*
It bobina *(f)*
Pt bobina *(f)*

stabilimento tipografico *(m)* It
De Druckerei *(f)*
En printing house
Es imprenta (casa) *(f)*
Fr imprimerie (maison) *(f)*
Pt casa tipográfica *(f)*

stabilità alla luce *(f)* It
De Lichtbeständigkeit *(f)*
En fastness (to light)
Es solidez a la luz *(f)*
Fr solidité à la lumière *(f)*
Pt inalterabilidade à luz *(f)*

staff *n* En
De Personal *(n)*
Es personal *(m)*
Fr personnel *(m)*
It personale *(m)*
Pt pessoal *(m)*

stagionare *vb* It
De ausreifen
En mature
Es madurar

Fr conditionner
Pt amadurecer

stagionatura *(f) n* It
De Konditionierung *(f)*
En conditioning (of paper)
Es acondicionamiento *(m)*
Fr conditionnement *(m)*
Pt condicionamento *(m)*

stampa *(f) n* It
De Presse *(f)*
En press (journalism)
Es prensa *(f)*
Fr presse *(f)*
Pt imprensa *(f)*

stampa a calcografia *(f)* It
De Kupferdruck *(m)*
En copper-plate printing
Es impresión en hueco *(f)*
Fr gravure sur cuivre *(f)*
Pt impressão com chapa de cobre *(f)*

stampa a contatto *(f)* It
De Kontaktdruck *(m)*
En contact print
Es copia por contacto *(f)*
Fr tirage contact *(m)*
Pt prova por contacto *(f)*

stampa ad intaglio *(f)* It
De Tiefdruck *(m)*
En intaglio printing
Es impresión con grabados en hueco *(f)*
Fr impression en creux *(f)*
Pt impressão intaglio *(f)*

stampa a due colori *(f)* It
Am two-color printing
De Zweifarbendruck *(m)*
En two-colour printing
Es impresión bicolor *(f)*
Fr bichromie *(f)*
Pt impressão a duas cores *(f)*

stampa a fogli *(f)* It
De Bogendruck *(m)*
En sheet-fed printing
Es impresión de hojas *(f)*
Fr impression à machine à feuilles *(f)*

Pt impressão de folhas
(f)

stampa a quattro colori
(f) It
Am four-color printing
De Vierfarbdruck (m)
En four-colour printing
Es cuatricromía (f)
Fr quadrichromie (f)
Pt impressão a quatro
cores (f)

stampa a tre colori (f) It
Am three-color printing
De Dreifarbendruck (m)
En three-colour printing
Es tricromía (f)
Fr trichromie (f)
Pt impressão a três
cores (f)

stampa comune (f) It
De Flachdruck (m)
En planographic printing
Es impresión
planográfica (f)
Fr impression à plat (f)
Pt impressão
planográfica (f)

stampa diretta (f) It
De Direktdruck (m)
En direct impression
Es impresión directa (f)
Fr impression directe (f)
Pt impressão directa (f)

stampa di vantaggio (f)
It
De Spaltenabziehpresse
(f)
En galley press
Es prensa para prueba
de galeradas (f)
Fr presse à épreuves (f)
Pt prensa de galé (f)

stampa flessografica (f)
It
De Flexodruck (m)
En flexographic printing
Es flexografía (f)
Fr flexographie (f)
Pt impressão
flexográfica (f)

stampaggio (m) n It
De Prägen (n)
En stamping
Es estampación (f)

Fr timbrage (m)
Pt estampagem (f)

**stampa incavorilievo-
grafica** (f) It
De Prägestempel (m)
En die stamping
Es estampación en
relieve (f)
Fr repoussage (m)
Pt estampagem em
relevo (f)

stampa indiretta (f) It
De indirekter Hochdruck
(m)
En indirect printing
Es impresión indirecta
(f)
Fr tirage indirect (m)
Pt impressão indirecta
(f)

stampa in rilievo (f) It
De Reliefdruck (m)
En relief printing
Es impresión en relieve
(f)
Fr impression en relief
(f)
Pt impressão em relevo
(f)

stampa in volta (f) It
De Schön- und
Widerdruck (m)
En perfecting
Es retiración (f)
Fr retiration (f)
Pt impressão
simultânea de ambos
lados (f)

stampa in zinco (f) It
De Zinkdruck (m)
En zinc print
Es imagen de reserva
formada en cinc (f)
Fr offset (m)
Pt imagem de reserva
de zinco (f)

stampa offset dal rotolo
(f) It
De Rollenoffsetdruck (m)
En web-offset printing
Es roto-offset (m)
Fr impression offset en
continu (f)
Pt impressão roto-offset
(f)

stampa popolare (f) It
De volkstümliche Presse
(f)
En popular press
Es prensa popular (f)
Fr presse populaire (f)
Pt prensa popular (f)

stampare (stampatura)
vb It
De drucken
En print
Es imprimir
Fr imprimer
Pt imprimir

stampare (per
elaboratore) vb It
De ausdrucken
En print out
Es imprimir (por
ordenador)
Fr sortir
Pt imprimir em positivo
directo

stampa reprografica (f)
It
De Reprographiedruck
(m)
En reprographic printing
Es impresión
reprográfica (f)
Fr reprographie (f)
Pt impressão
reprográfica (f)

stampa serigrafica (f) It
De Siebdruck (m)
En silk-screen printing
Es impresión serigráfica
(f)
Fr sérigraphie (f)
Pt serigrafia (f)

stampa termografica (f)
It
De Thermodruck (m)
En thermographic
printing
Es impresión
termográfica (f)
Fr thermogravure (f)
Pt impressão
termográfica (f)

stampa tipografica (f) It
De Buchdruck (m)
En letterpress printing
Es impresión tipográfica
(f)

Fr impression
typographique (f)
Pt impressão tipográfica
(f)

**stampa tipografica
offset** (f) It
De Offset-Buchdruck (m)
En offset letterpress
Es tipografía offset (f)
Fr presse offset (f)
Pt prensa offset (f)

stampatore (m) n It
De Drucker (m)
En printer
Es impresor (m)
Fr imprimeur (m)
Pt tipógrafo (m)

stampatore commerciale
(m) It
De Akzidenzdrucker (m)
En jobbing printer
Es impresor a
remiendos (m)
Fr imprimeur de travaux
de ville (m)
Pt impressor comercial
(m)

stampatrice (f) n It
De Druckmaschine (f)
En printing machine
Es máquina de imprimir
(f)
Fr machine à imprimer
(f)
Pt máquina de imprimir
(f)

stampatrice in volta (f) It
De Schön- und
Widerdruckmaschine
(f)
En perfector
Es prensa de retiración
(f)
Fr presse à retiration (f)
Pt máquina de
impressão
simultânea de ambos
lados (f)

stampatrice per righe (f)
It
De Zeilendrucker (m)
En line printer
Es impresora de líneas
(f)
Fr imprimante ligne par
ligne (f)

Pt impressora de linha
(f)

stampatrice xerografica
(f) It
De xerographischer
Drucker *(m)*
En xerographic printer
Es impresora
xerográphica *(f)*
Fr imprimante
xérographique *(f)*
Pt impressora
xerográfica *(f)*

stampa tridimensionale
(f) It
De dreidimensionaler
Druck *(m)*
En three-dimensional
printing
Es impresión
tridimensional *(f)*
Fr impression
tridimensionnelle *(f)*
Pt impressão a três
dimensões *(f)*

stampatura *(f)* n It
De Druckkunst *(f)*
En printing
Es imprenta (arte) *(f)*
Fr imprimerie (art) *(f)*
Pt impressão *(f)*

stampa universitaria *(f)*
It
De Universitäts-
Druckerei *(f)*
En university press
Es prensa universitaria
(f)
Fr presse universitaire
(f)
Pt imprensa
universitária *(f)*

stampigliatura in oro *(f)*
It
De Goldprägung *(f)*
En gold stamping
Es estampación dorada
(f)
Fr dorure à la presse *(f)*
Pt estampagem a ouro
(f)

stamping n En
De Prägen *(n)*
Es estampación *(f)*
Fr timbrage *(m)*

It stampaggio *(m)*
Pt estampagem *(f)*

stampo *(m)* n It
De Prägestock *(m)*
En die
Es troquel *(m)*
Fr étampe *(f)*
Pt matriz *(f)*

stampo (industria
cartiera) *(m)* n It
Am mold (papermaking)
De Gusform *(f)*
En mould (papermaking)
Es molde *(m)*
Fr empreinte *(f)*
Pt molde *(m)*

stampo di piombo *(m)* It
Am lead mold
De Bleiform *(f)*
En lead mould
Es molde de plomo *(m)*
Fr empreinte sur plomb
(f)
Pt molde de chumbo
(m)

standing type En
De guter Satz *(m)*
Es composición
levantada *(f)*
Fr caractères conservés
(m pl)
It carattere eretto *(m)*
Pt composição
levantada *(f)*

stark illustriertes Buch
(n) De
En highly illustrated
book
Es libro profusamente
ilustrado *(m)*
Fr livre abondamment
illustré *(m)*
It libro riccamente
illustrato *(m)*
Pt livro muito ilustrado
(m)

stark revidiertes
Manuskript *(n)* De
En heavily edited copy
Es ejemplar mucho
enmendada *(m)*
Fr texte très corrigé *(m)*
It copia molto
emendata *(f)*
Pt exemplar muito
corrigido *(m)*

static electricity En
De statische Elektrizität
(f)
Es electricidad estática
(f)
Fr électricité statique *(f)*
It elettricità statica *(f)*
Pt electricidade estática
(f)

stationery n En
De Briefpapier *(n)*
Es efectos de escritorio
(m pl)
Fr papeterie de détail *(f)*
It cartoleria *(f)*
Pt papel e artigos de
escritório *(m)*

stationery binding En
De Briefpapier-Binden
(n)
Es acuñado de material
de escritorio *(m)*
Fr reliure papeterie *(f)*
It rilegatura da
cartoleria *(f)*
Pt encadernação para
escritório *(f)*

statische Elektrizität *(f)*
De
En static electricity
Es electricidad estática
(f)
Fr électricité statique *(f)*
It elettricità statica *(f)*
Pt electricidade estática
(f)

Stehen lassen De
En stet
Es vale lo tachado
Fr à maintenir
It vive
Pt stet

Stein *(m)* n De
En stone (lithography)
Es piedra *(f)*
Fr pierre calcaire *(f)*
It pietra litografica *(f)*
Pt càlcário da Bavária
(m)

Steinauto *(f)* n De
En autolithography
Es autolitografía *(f)*
Fr autographie *(f)*
It autolitografia *(f)*
Pt autolitografia *(f)*

Stelle *(f)* n De
En digit
Es dígito *(m)*
Fr chiffre *(m)*
It cifra *(f)*
Pt dígito *(m)*

stellvertretender
Redakteur *(m)* De
En assistant editor
Es redactor adjunto *(m)*
Fr rédacteur adjoint *(m)*
It assistente editore *(m)*
Pt editor adjunto *(m)*

Stempel *(m)* n De
En punch (for
typefounding)
Es punzón *(m)*
Fr poinçon *(m)*
It punzone *(m)*
Pt punção *(m)*

stems pl n En
De Säulen *(pl)*
Es palos gruesos *(m pl)*
Fr hastes *(f pl)*
It gambi *(m pl)*
Pt paus grossos *(m pl)*

stencil de duplication
(m) Fr
De Gewebeschablone *(f)*
En tissue stencil
Es matriz de papel de
seda *(f)*
It matrice in carta di
seta *(f)*
Pt estencil de tela *(m)*

step-by-step diagram En
De stufenweises
Diagramm *(n)*
Es esquema paso a
paso *(m)*
Fr schéma progressif
(m)
It diagramma graduale
(m)
Pt diagrama de passo a
passo *(m)*

Stereo *(n)* n De
En stereotype
Es estereotipo *(m)*
Fr stéréotipo *(m)*
It stereotipo *(m)*
Pt estereótipo *(m)*

stéréo courbe *(f)* Fr
De Rotationsstereo *(n)*
En rotary stereo
Es estereotipia rotativa
(f)
It stereo rotatorio *(m)*
Pt estereo-rotativa *(f)*

stereo-nichel *(m) n* It
De Nickelstereo *(n)*
En nickel stereo
Es estereotipia
niquelada *(f)*
Fr stéréo nickel *(m)*
Pt estereo-niquelado
(m)

stéréo nickel *(m)* Fr
De Nickelstereo *(n)*
En nickel stereo
Es estereotipia
niquelada *(f)*
It stereo-nichel *(m)*
Pt estereo-niquelado
(m)

stereo rotatorio *(m)* It
De Rotationsstereo *(n)*
En rotary stereo
Es estereotipia rotativa
(f)
Fr stéréo courbe *(f)*
Pt estereo-rotativa *(f)*

stéréos caoutchouc *(m
pl)* Fr
De Gummiklischees *(pl)*
En rubber stereos
Es estereotipos de
caucho *(m pl)*
It stereos di gomma *(m
pl)*
Pt estereos de borracha
(m pl)

stereos di gomma *(m pl)*
It
De Gummiklischees *(pl)*
En rubber stereos
Es estereotipos de
caucho *(m pl)*
Fr stéréos caoutchouc
(m pl)
Pt estereos de borracha
(m pl)

stereotipizzazione *(f) n*
It
De Stereotypie *(f)*
En stereotyping
Es estereotipia *(f)*

Fr stéréotypie *(f)*
Pt estereotipia *(f)*

stereotipo *(m) n* It
De Stereo *(n)*
En stereotype
Es estereotipo *(m)*
Fr stéréotype *(m)*
Pt estereótipo *(m)*

stereotype *n* En
De Stereo *(n)*
Es estereotipo *(m)*
Fr stéréotype *(m)*
It stereotipo *(m)*
Pt estereótipo *(m)*

stéréotypé *adj* Fr
De abgedroschen
En hackneyed
Es común
It comune
Pt vulgar

stéréotype *(m) n* Fr
De Stereo *(n)*
En stereotype
Es estereotipo *(m)*
It stereotipo *(m)*
Pt estereótipo *(m)*

Stereotypie *(f) n* De
En stereotyping
Es estereotipia *(f)*
Fr stéréotypie *(f)*
It stereotipizzazione *(f)*
Pt estereotipia *(f)*

stéréotypie *(f) n* Fr
De Stereotypie *(f)*
En stereotyping
Es estereotipia *(f)*
It stereotipizzazione *(f)*
Pt estereotipia *(f)*

stereotyping *n* En
De Stereotypie *(f)*
Es estereotipia *(f)*
Fr stéréotypie *(f)*
It stereotipizzazione *(f)*
Pt estereotipia *(f)*

sterlineato *adj* It
De kompreß
En solid
Es desinterlineado
Fr à-plat
Pt maciço

Sternchen *(n) n* De
En asterisk
Es asterisco *(m)*
Fr astérisque *(m)*
It asterisco *(m)*
Pt asterisco *(m)*

stessa dimensione It
De gleichgroß
En same size (s/s)
Es igual tamaño
Fr format identique
Pt mesmo tamanho

stet En, Pt
De Stehen lassen
Es vale lo tachado
Fr à maintenir
It vive

Stichtag *(m) n* De
En deadline
Es plazo *(m)*
Fr limite *(f)*
It scadenza *(f)*
Pt prazo *(m)*

Stiel *(m) n* De
En shank
Es árbol *(m)*
Fr tige *(f)*
It gambo *(m)*
Pt árvore *(f)*

Stil *(m) n* De
En style
Es estilo *(m)*
Fr style *(f)*
It stile *(m)*
Pt estilo *(m)*

stile *(m) n* It
De Stil *(m)*
En style
Es estilo *(m)*
Fr style *(f)*
Pt estilo *(m)*

stile di casa *(m)* It
De Hausstil *(m)*
En house style
Es estilo de reglamento
(m)
Fr style maison *(m)*
Pt estilo da casa *(m)*

Stil-Handbuch *(n) n* De
En style manual
Es manual de redacción
(m)

Fr règles de stylisme *(f
pl)*
It manuale di stile *(m)*
Pt manual de estilos *(m)*

Stilmuster *(n) n* De
En style guide
Es guía del estilo *(f)*
Fr consignes de
conception *(f pl)*
It guida di stile *(f)*
Pt guia de estilo *(m)*

stilo *(m) n* It
De Feder *(f)*
En stylus
Es estilete *(m)*
Fr imprimante à stylets
(f)
Pt estilete *(m)*

stippling *n* En
De Granierung *(f)*
Es punteado *(m)*
Fr grisé *(m)*
It battitura *(f)*
Pt ponteado *(m)*

stiratura *(f) n* It
De Abpressen *(n)*
En pressing
Es prensado *(m)*
Fr pressage *(m)*
Pt compressão *(f)*

stock (paper) *n* En
De Papiertyp *(m)*
Es materia de papel *(f)*
Fr matière de papier *(f)*
It materia di carta *(f)*
Pt matéria de papel *(f)*

stock (books) *n* En; Fr *(m)*
De Vorrat *(m)*
Es existencias *(f pl)*
It scorta *(f)*
Pt existências *(f pl)*

stockage *(m) n* Fr
De Speicherung *(f)*
En storage
Es almacenamiento *(m)*
It immagazzinaggio *(m)*
Pt armazenamento *(m)*

stock excessif *(m)* Fr
De Übervorrat *(m)*
En overstocks *pl n*
Es existencias excesivas
(f pl)

It giacenze *(f pl)*
Pt existências que sobram *(f pl)*

Stoffeintrag *(m) n* De
En furnish
Es materias primas *(f pl)*
Fr matières premières *(f pl)*
It materia prima *(f)*
Pt matérias-primas *(f pl)*

stoffüberzogenes Papier *(n)* De
En cloth-lined paper
Es papel forrado de tela *(m)*
Fr papier entoilé une face *(m)*
It carta rivestita in tela *(f)*
Pt papel forrado a tela *(m)*

stone (letterpress composition) *n* En
De Form *(f)*
Es composición de imposición *(f)*
Fr marbre de serrage *(m)*
It banco tipografico *(m)*
Pt superfície de imposição *(f)*

stone (lithography) *n* En
De Stein *(m)*
Es piedra *(f)*
Fr pierre calcaire *(f)*
It pietra litografica *(f)*
Pt cálcário da Bavária *(m)*

stop-cylinder press En
De Haltzylinderpresse *(f)*
Es prensa de cilindro de parada *(f)*
Fr machine à arrêt du cylindre *(f)*
It rotativa con arresto *(f)*
Pt prensa de cilindro de paragem *(f)*

storage *n* En
De Speicherung *(f)*
Es almacenamiento *(m)*
Fr stockage *(m)*
It immagazzinaggio *(m)*
Pt armazenamento *(m)*

storage facilities En
De Speicherungs- möglichkeiten *(pl)*
Es almacenes *(m pl)*
Fr entrepôts *(m pl)*
It servizi di immagazzinaggio *(m pl)*
Pt instalações de armazenamento *(f pl)*

store *vb* En
De lagern
Es almacenar
Fr entreposer
It immagazzinare
Pt armazenar

store *n* En
De speichern
Es memoria *(f)*
Fr mémoire *(f)*
It memoria *(f)*
Pt memória *(f)*

strappatura *(f) n* It
De Rupfen *(n)*
En plucking
Es picado *(m)*
Fr arrachage *(m)*
Pt picado *(m)*

Straßenkante *(f) n* De
En gutter margin
Es margen del medianil *(m)*
Fr lézarde *(f)*
It margine di scanalatura *(m)*
Pt margem de medianiz *(f)*

stratification à sec *(f)* Fr
De Trockenfolien- kaschierung *(f)*
En dry laminating
Es laminación en seco *(f)*
It laminazione a secco *(f)*
Pt laminagem a seco *(f)*

strawboard *n* En
De Strohkarton *(m)*
Es cartón paja *(m)*
Fr carton paille *(m)*
It cartone-paglia *(m)*
Pt cartão amarelo *(m)*

stream feeder En
De Schuppenanleger *(m)*
Es ponepliegos de avance continuo *(m)*
Fr margeur à nappe *(m)*
It alimentatore di fogli a avanzamento continuo *(m)*
Pt alimentador de folhas de avanço contínuo *(m)*

streichen *vb* De
En delete
Es suprimir
Fr rayer
It cancellare
Pt apagar

Streichen *(n) n* De
En coating
Es revestimiento *(m)*
Fr couchage du papier *(m)*
It rivestimento *(m)* '
Pt revestimento *(m)*

Streichung *(f) n* De
En deletion
Es supresión *(f)*
Fr suppression *(f)*
It cancellatura *(f)*
Pt eliminação *(f)*

Strich *(m) n* De
En rule
Es filete *(m)*
Fr règle *(f)*
It filetto *(m)*
Pt linha recta *(f)*

Strichätzung *(f) n* De
En line block
Es fotograbado de línea *(m)*
Fr cliché au trait *(m)*
It cliché a tratto *(m)*
Pt placa de estereotipia *(f)*

Strich und Ton De
En line and tone
Es línea y tono
Fr trait-simili
It linea e tono
Pt linha e tono

Strichzeichnung *(f) n* De
En line drawing
Es dibujo de línea *(m)*
Fr dessin au trait *(m)*

It disegno a tratteggio *(m)*
Pt desenho a lápis ou pena *(m)*

strip in En
De montieren
Es montar inserciones
Fr raccorder
It giuntare
Pt incluir

Strohkarton *(m) n* De
En strawboard
Es cartón paja *(m)*
Fr carton paille *(m)*
It cartone-paglia *(m)*
Pt cartão amarelo *(m)*

Stück *(n) n* De
En play
Es obra dramática *(f)*
Fr pièce de théâtre *(f)*
It commedia *(f)*
Pt peça *(f)*

stufenweises Diagramm *(n)* De
En step-by-step diagram
Es esquema paso a paso *(m)*
Fr schéma progressif *(m)*
It diagramma graduale *(m)*
Pt diagrama de passo a passo *(m)*

stuff *n* En
De Papiermasse *(f)*
Es pasta de papel *(f)*
Fr pâte à papier *(f)*
It pasta di carta *(f)*
Pt polpa de papel *(f)*

Stundentarif *(m) n* De
En hourly rate
Es régimen horario *(m)*
Fr tarif horaire *(m)*
It paga oraria *(f)*
Pt taxa horária *(f)*

style *n* En; Fr *(f)*
De Stil *(m)*
Es estilo *(m)*
It stile *(m)*
Pt estilo *(m)*

style guide En
De Stilmuster *(n)*
Es guía del estilo *(f)*
Fr consignes de
conception *(f pl)*
It guida di stile *(f)*
Pt guia de estilo *(m)*

style maison *(m)* Fr
De Hausstil *(m)*
En house style
Es estilo de reglamento
(m)
It stile di casa *(m)*
Pt estilo da casa *(m)*

style manual En
De Stil-Handbuch *(n)*
Es manual de redacción
(m)
Fr règles de stylisme *(f
pl)*
It manuale di stile *(m)*
Pt manual de estilos *(m)*

stylus *n* En
De Feder *(f)*
Es estilete *(m)*
Fr imprimante à stylets
(f)
It stilo *(m)*
Pt estilete *(m)*

subcorrigir *vb* Pt
De unter der Leitung
eines Redakteurs
herausgeben
En subedit
Es redactar
Fr mettre au point
It redigere

subedit *vb* En
De unter der Leitung
eines Redakteurs
herausgeben
Es redactar
Fr mettre au point
It redigere
Pt subcorrigir

subeditor *n* En
De Zweiter Redakteur
(m)
Es corrector *(m)*
Fr secrétaire de la
rédaction *(m)*
It redattore aggiunto
(m)
Pt redactor auxiliar *(m)*

subíndices *(m pl)* Es
De tiefstehende
Buchstaben *(pl)*
En inferior characters
Fr petites lettres
inférieures *(f pl)*
It caratteri inferiori *(m
pl)*
Pt caracteres inferiores
(m pl)

subraiar *vb* Pt
De unterstreichen
En underline
Es subrayar
Fr souligner
It sottolineare

subrayar *vb* Es
De unterstreichen
En underline
Fr souligner
It sottolineare
Pt subraiar

substance (of paper) *n* En
De Quadratmeter-
gewicht *(n)*
Es gramaje *(m)*
Fr grammage *(m)*
It grammatura *(f)*
Pt gramagem *(m)*

substrat *(m)* *n* Fr
De Substrat *(n)*
En substrate
Es substrato *(m)*
It sottostrato *(m)*
Pt substrato *(m)*

Substrat *(n)* *n* De
En substrate
Es substrato *(m)*
Fr substrat *(m)*
It sottostrato *(m)*
Pt substrato *(m)*

substrate *n* En
De Substrat *(n)*
Es substrato *(m)*
Fr substrat *(m)*
It sottostrato *(m)*
Pt substrato *(m)*

substrato *(m)* *n* Es, Pt
De Substrat *(n)*
En substrate
Fr substrat *(m)*
It sottostrato *(m)*

subtitle *n* En
De Untertitel *(m)*
Es subtítulo *(m)*
Fr sous-titre *(m)*
It sottotitolo *(m)*
Pt subtítulo *(m)*

subtítulo *(m)* *n* Es, Pt
De Untertitel *(m)*
En alternate title;
subtitle
Fr sous-titre *(m)*
It sottotitolo; titolo
alternato *(m)*

sucio *adj* Es
De verschmutzt
En shop-soiled
Fr défraîchi
It sporco
Pt sujado na loja

suction feeder En
De Saùganleger *(m)*
Es ponepliegos de soplo
(m)
Fr margeur
automatique à
aspiration *(m)*
It alimentatore ad
aspirazione *(m)*
Pt alimentador por
sucção *(m)*

suerte especial *(f)* Es
De Spezial-Schrifttyp *(m)*
En special sort
Fr figure spéciale *(f)*
It tipo speciale *(m)*
Pt sortes especial *(f)*

suertes *(f pl)* Es
De Schriftgarnitur *(f)*
En sorts *pl n*
Fr assortiment *(m)*
It rappezzi *(m pl)*
Pt sortes *(f pl)*

suivre sans alinéa Fr
De anhängen
En run on (typesetting)
Es componer sin punto y
aparte
It scrivere a testo
continuo
Pt compor seguido

sujado na loja Pt
De verschmutzt
En shop-soiled
Es sucio

Fr défraîchi
It sporco

sulfate wood pulp Am
De Sulfat-Holzstoff *(m)*
En sulphate wood pulp
Es pasta de madera al
sulfato *(f)*
Fr pâte de bois au
sulfate *(f)*
It pasta di legno al
solfato *(f)*
Pt polpa de madeira
sulfatada *(f)*

Sulfat-Holzstoff *(m)* De
Am sulfate wood pulp
En sulphate wood pulp
Es pasta de madera al
sulfato *(f)*
Fr pâte de bois au
sulfate *(f)*
It pasta di legno al
solfato *(f)*
Pt polpa de madeira
sulfatada *(f)*

sulphate wood pulp En
Am sulfate wood pulp
De Sulfat-Holzstoff *(m)*
Es pasta de madera al
sulfato *(f)*
Fr pâte de bois au
sulfate *(f)*
It pasta di legno al
solfato *(f)*
Pt polpa de madeira
sulfatada *(f)*

sumario *(m)* *n* Es
De Zusammenfassung *(f)*
En summary
Fr résumé *(m)*
It sommario *(m)*
Pt sumário *(m)*

sumário *(m)* *n* Pt
De Zusammenfassung *(f)*
En summary
Es sumario *(m)*
Fr résumé *(m)*
It sommario *(m)*

suma total *(f)* Es
De Pauschalbetrag *(m)*
En lump sum
Fr somme globale *(f)*
It somma globale *(f)*
Pt importância global *(f)*

summary *n* En
De Zusammenfassung *(f)*
Es sumario *(m)*
Fr résumé *(m)*
It sommario *(m)*
Pt sumário *(m)*

superato *adj* It
De veraltet
En out of date
Es anticuado
Fr périmé
Pt desactualizado

super-calendered paper
En
De Illustrations-
druckpapier *(m)*
Es papel
supercalandrado *(m)*
Fr papier supercalandré
(m)
It carta
supercalandrata *(f)*
Pt papel
supercalandrado *(m)*

superfície de imposição
(f) Pt
De Form; Schliesplatte
(f)
En imposing surface;
stone (letterpress
composition)
Es superficie de
imposición *(f)*
Fr marbre de serrage
(m)
It banco tipografico *(m)*

superficie de
imposición *(f)* Es
De Schliesplatte *(f)*
En imposing surface
Fr marbre de serrage
(m)
It banco tipografico *(m)*
Pt superfície de
imposição *(f)*

superior characters *pl n*
En
De hochstehende
Buchstaben *(pl)*
Es exponentes *(m pl)*
Fr caractères supérieurs
(m pl)
It caratteri superiori *(m
pl)*
Pt caracteres superiores
(m pl)

superponible *(m) n* Es
De Deckblatt *(n)*
En overlay (on artwork,
etc.)
Fr becquet *(m)*
It sovrapposizione *(f)*
Pt coberta *(f)*

suplemento a cores *(m)*
Pt
Am color supplement
De Farbbeilage *(f)*
En colour supplement
Es suplemento en color
(m)
Fr supplément en
couleurs *(m)*
It supplemento a colori
(m)

suplemento en color *(m)*
Es
Am color supplement
De Farbbeilage *(f)*
En colour supplement
Fr supplément en
couleurs *(m)*
It supplemento a colori
(m)
Pt suplemento a cores
(m)

suplemento literario *(m)*
Es
De literarische Beilage *(f)*
En literary supplement
Fr supplément littéraire
(m)
It supplemento
letterario *(m)*
Pt suplemento literário
(m)

suplemento literário *(m)*
Pt
De literarische Beilage *(f)*
En literary supplement
Es suplemento literario
(m)
Fr supplément littéraire
(m)
It supplemento
letterario *(m)*

supplément en couleurs
(m) Fr
Am color supplement
De Farbbeilage *(f)*
En colour supplement
Es suplemento en color
(m)

It supplemento a colori
(m)
Pt suplemento a cores
(m)

supplément littéraire
(m) Fr
De literarische Beilage *(f)*
En literary supplement
Es suplemento literario
(m)
It supplemento
letterario *(m)*
Pt suplemento literário
(m)

supplemento a colori
(m) It
Am color supplement
De Farbbeilage *(f)*
En colour supplement
Es suplemento en color
(m)
Fr supplément en
couleurs *(m)*
Pt suplemento a cores
(m)

supplemento letterario
(m) It
De literarische Beilage *(f)*
En literary supplement
Es suplemento literario
(m)
Fr supplément littéraire
(m)
Pt suplemento literário
(m)

supplier *n* En
De Lieferant *(m)*
Es proveedor *(m)*
Fr fournisseur *(m)*
It fornitore *(m)*
Pt fornecedor *(m)*

supporto *(m) n* It
De Widerdruck *(m)*
En backing-up
Es respaldado *(m)*
Fr mettant en retiration
(f)
Pt apoio *(m)*

suppression *(f) n* Fr
De Streichung *(f)*
En deletion
Es supresión *(f)*
It cancellatura *(f)*
Pt eliminação *(f)*

supresión *(f) n* Es
De Streichung *(f)*
En deletion
Fr suppression *(f)*
It cancellatura *(f)*
Pt eliminação *(f)*

suprimir *vb* Es
De streichen
En delete
Fr rayer
It cancellare
Pt apagar

surimpression *(f) n* Fr
De überlanger Satz *(m)*
En overmatter
Es material sobrante *(m)*
It composizione
sovrastante *(f)*
Pt matéria que sobra *(f)*

sviluppare *vb* It
De entwickeln
(Photographie)
En develop
(photography)
Es revelar
Fr développer
Pt revelar

swash letters *pl n* En
De Zierbuchstaben *(pl)*
Es letras de fantasía *(f
pl)*
Fr lettres ornées *(f pl)*
It lettere inclinate *(f pl)*
Pt letras de fantasia *(f
pl)*

swatch *n* En
De Muster *(n)*
Es muestrario *(m)*
Fr échantillon *(m)*
It campione *(m)*
Pt mostruário *(m)*

symbol *n* En
De Symbol *(n)*
Es símbolo *(m)*
Fr symbole *(m)*
It simbolo *(m)*
Pt símbolo *(m)*

Symbol *(n) n* De
En symbol
Es símbolo *(m)*
Fr symbole *(m)*
It simbolo *(m)*
Pt símbolo *(m)*

It supplemento a colori
(m)
Pt suplemento a cores
(m)

supplément littéraire
(m) Fr
De literarische Beilage *(f)*
En literary supplement
Es suplemento literario
(m)
It supplemento
letterario *(m)*
Pt suplemento literário
(m)

symbole *(m) n* Fr
De Symbol *(n)*
En symbol
Es símbolo *(m)*
It simbolo *(m)*
Pt símbolo *(m)*

symboles phonétiques
(m pl) Fr
De Phonetikzeichen *(pl)*
En phonetic symbols
Es signos fonéticos *(m pl)*
It simboli fonetici *(m pl)*
Pt símbolos fonéticos *(m pl)*

syndicat *(m) n* Fr
De Gewerkschaft *(f)*
En trade union
Es sindicato *(m)*
It sindacato *(m)*
Pt sindicato *(m)*

synonym *n* En
De Synonym *(n)*
Es sinónimo *(m)*
Fr synonyme *(m)*
It sinonimo *(m)*
Pt sinónimo *(m)*

Synonym *(n) n* De
En synonym
Es sinónimo *(m)*
Fr synonyme *(m)*
It sinonimo *(m)*
Pt sinónimo *(m)*

synonyme *(m) n* Fr
De Synonym *(n)*
En synonym
Es sinónimo *(m)*
It sinonimo *(m)*
Pt sinónimo *(m)*

synopsis *n* En; Fr *(m)*
De Synopsis *(f)*
Es sinopsis *(f)*
It sinopsi *(f)*
Pt sinopse *(f)*

Synopsis *(f) n* De
En synopsis
Es sinopsis *(f)*
Fr synopsis *(m)*
It sinopsi *(f)*
Pt sinopse *(f)*

system *n* En
De System *(n)*
Es sistema *(m)*
Fr système *(m)*
It sistema *(m)*
Pt sistema *(m)*

System *(n) n* De
En system
Es sistema *(m)*
Fr système *(m)*
It sistema *(m)*
Pt sistema *(m)*

Systemanalytiker *(m) n* De
En systems analyst
Es analista de sistemas *(m)*
Fr analyste de systèmes *(m/f)*
It analista di sistema *(m/f)*
Pt analista de sistemas *(m)*

système *(m) n* Fr
De System *(n)*
En system
Es sistema *(m)*
It sistema *(m)*
Pt sistema *(m)*

systems analyst En
De Systemanalytiker *(m)*
Es analista de sistemas *(m)*
Fr analyste de systèmes *(m/f)*
It analista di sistema *(m/f)*
Pt analista de sistemas *(m)*

T

tabella *(f) n* It
De Tabelle *(f)*
En chart
Es diagrama *(m)*
Fr diagramme *(m)*
Pt carta *(f)*

Tabelle *(f) n* De
En chart
Es diagrama *(m)*
Fr diagramme *(m)*
It tabella *(f)*
Pt carta *(f)*

tab index En
De Buchstabenindex *(m)*
Es índice de pestañas *(m)*
Fr index à touche *(m)*
It indice a striscettine *(m)*
Pt índice de pestanas *(m)*

table des matières *(f)* Fr
De Inhaltsverzeichnis *(n)*
En table of contents
Es índice de materias *(m)*
It sommario delle materie *(m)*
Pt índice dos assuntos *(m)*

table lumineuse *(f)* Fr
De Leuchttisch *(m)*
En light table
Es mesa de retoque *(f)*
It tavolo luminoso *(m)*
Pt mesa de retoque *(f)*

table of contents En
De Inhaltsverzeichnis *(n)*
Es índice de materias *(m)*
Fr table des matières *(f)*
It sommario delle materie *(m)*
Pt índice dos assuntos *(m)*

tablero de dibujo *(m)* Es
De Kunstdruckkarton *(m)*
En art board
Fr carte couchée *(f)*
It cartone da disegno *(m)*
Pt prancha de arte *(f)*

tacca *(f) n* It
De Signaturrinne *(f)*
En nick
Es cran *(m)*
Fr cran *(m)*
Pt entalhe *(m)*

Tafel *(f) n* De
En plate (picture)
Es lámina *(f)*
Fr planche *(f)*
It tavola *(f)*
Pt gravura *(f)*

tafilete *(m) n* Es
De Maroquin *(n)*
En Morocco (leather)
Fr maroquin *(m)*
It marocchino *(m)*
Pt marroquim *(m)*

tagliacarta *(f) n* It
De Schneidemaschine *(f)*
En guillotine
Es guillotina *(f)*
Fr guillotine *(f)*
Pt guilhotina *(f)*

tagliato a filo It
De glatt zurichten
En cut flush
Es cortado a ras
Fr composé à l'américaine
Pt recorte raso

tail (of page) *n* En
De Unterschlag *(m)*
Es margen inferior *(m)*
Fr marge de pied *(f)*
It piede (di pagina) *(m)*
Pt pé (de página) *(m)*

tailpiece *n* En
De Schlußvignette *(f)*
Es culo de lámpara *(m)*
Fr cul-de-lampe *(m)*
It finalino *(m)*
Pt vinheta final *(f)*

taller *(m) n* Es
De Fabrik *(f)*
En shop (in industry)
Fr atelier *(m)*
It officina *(f)*
Pt oficina *(f)*

taller de composición *(m)* Es
De Schriftsetzerei *(f)*
En typesetter (company)
Fr maison de composition *(f)*
It compositoria *(f)*
Pt empresa de composição *(f)*

taller de
encuadernación *(f)*
Es
De Buchbinderei *(f)*
En bindery
Fr atelier de reliure *(m)*
It legatoria *(f)*
Pt oficina de
encadernação *(f)*

talud *(m) n* Es
De Überhang *(m)*
En kern
Fr crénage *(m)*
It sporgenza *(f)*
Pt saliência do corpo do
tipo *(f)*

talus *(m) n* Fr
De Kopf (type) *(m)*
En beard (of letter)
Es relieve *(m)*
It bianco alla base *(m)*
Pt relevo *(m)*

tamanho bastardo *(m)* Pt
De Bastardkegel *(m)*
En bastard size
Es tamaño bastardo *(m)*
Fr format bâtard *(m)*
It dimensione
irregolare *(f)*

tamanho de corpo *(m)* Pt
De Kegelgröβe *(f)*
En body size (of type)
Es tamaño del tipo *(m)*
Fr corps d'un caractère
(m)
It corpo del carattere
(m)

tamanho de página
aparada *(m)* Pt
De Beschnittgröβe *(f)*
En trimmed page size
Es tamaño de página
cortada *(m)*
Fr format fini *(m)*
It dimensioni di pagina
rifilata *(f pl)*

tamanho de ponto *(m)* Pt
De Punktgröβe *(f)*
En point size
Es cuerpo del tipo *(m)*
Fr corps *(m)*
It corpo *(m)*

tamanhos D.I.N. *(m pl)*
Pt
De DIN-Gröβen *(pl)*
En DIN sizes
Es tamaños D.I.N. *(m
pl)*
Fr formats D.I.N. *(m pl)*
It dimensioni D.I.N. *(f
pl)*

tamanhos ISO *(m pl)* Pt
De ISO-Gröβen *(pl)*
En ISO sizes
Es tamaños ISO *(m pl)*
Fr formats ISO *(m pl)*
It dimensioni ISO *(f pl)*

tamaño bastardo *(m)* Es
De Bastardkegel *(m)*
En bastard size
Fr format bâtard *(m)*
It dimensione
irregolare *(f)*
Pt tamanho bastardo
(m)

tamaño del tipo *(m)* Es
De Kegelgröβe *(f)*
En body size (of type)
Fr corps d'un caractère
(m)
It corpo del carattere
(m)
Pt tamanho de corpo
(m)

tamaño de página
cortada *(m)* Es
De Beschnittgröβe *(f)*
En trimmed page size
Fr format fini *(m)*
It dimensioni di pagina
rifilata *(f pl)*
Pt tamanho de página
aparada *(m)*

tamaños de libros *(m pl)*
Es
De Büchergrösen *(pl)*
En book sizes *pl n*
Fr formats des livres *(m
pl)*
It formati di libri *(m pl)*
Pt formatos de livros *(m
pl)*

tamaños D.I.N. *(m pl)* Es
De DIN-Gröβen *(pl)*
En DIN sizes
Fr formats D.I.N. *(m pl)*
It dimensioni D.I.N. *(f
pl)*

Pt tamanhos D.I.N. *(m
pl)*

tamaños ISO *(m pl)* Es
De ISO-Gröβen *(pl)*
En ISO sizes
Fr formats ISO *(m pl)*
It dimensioni ISO *(f pl)*
Pt tamanhos ISO *(m pl)*

Tandemarbeit *(f) n* De
En tandem work
Es trabajo en tandem
(m)
Fr travail en tandem *(m)*
It lavoro in tandem *(m)*
Pt trabalho em tandem
(m)

tandem work En
De Tandemarbeit *(f)*
Es trabajo en tandem
(m)
Fr travail en tandem *(m)*
It lavoro in tandem *(m)*
Pt trabalho em tandem
(m)

Tantiemen *(pl)* De
En royalties *pl n*
Es derechos de autor *(m
pl)*
Fr droits d'auteur *(m pl)*
It diritti di licenza *(m pl)*
Pt direitos de autor *(m
pl)*

Tantiemenvorschuβ *(m)*
n De
En advance against
royalties
Es anticipo sobre
derechos de autor
(m)
Fr avance sur les droits
d'auteur *(f)*
It anticipo sui diritti di
licenza *(m)*
Pt adiantamento sobre
direitos de autor *(m)*

tapas *(f) n* Es
De Buchdeckel *(m)*
En case (bookbinding)
Fr couverture *(f)*
It custodia *(f)*
Pt capa separada *(f)*

taquage des feuilles *(m)*
Fr
De Aufstoβen *(n)*

Pt tamanhos D.I.N. *(m
pl)*

tamaños ISO *(m pl)* Es
De ISO-Gröβen *(pl)*
En ISO sizes
Fr formats ISO *(m pl)*
It dimensioni ISO *(f pl)*
Pt tamanhos ISO *(m pl)*

Tandemarbeit *(f) n* De
En tandem work
Es trabajo en tandem
(m)
Fr travail en tandem *(m)*
It lavoro in tandem *(m)*
Pt trabalho em tandem
(m)

En knocking-up (of
paper)
Es emparejamiento de
hojas *(m)*
It uniformazione di
foglie *(f)*
Pt empilhamento de
folhas *(m)*

tarif horaire *(m)* Fr
De Stundentarif *(m)*
En hourly rate
Es régimen horario *(m)*
It paga oraria *(f)*
Pt taxa horária *(f)*

tarjeta comercial *(f)* Es
De Visitenkarte *(f)*
En business card
Fr carte de visite
professionnelle *(f)*
It bigliettino da visita
(m)
Pt cartão de visita
profissional *(m)*

tarjeta perforada *(f)* Es
De Lochkarte *(f)*
En punched card
Fr carte perforée *(f)*
It scheda perforata *(f)*
Pt ficha perfurada *(f)*

tarjetas de ficheros *(f pl)*
Es
De Karteikarten *(pl)*
En index cards
Fr fiches *(f pl)*
It schede *(f pl)*
Pt fichas de arquivo *(f
pl)*

Taschenbuch *(n) n* De
En paperback book
Es libro en rústica *(m)*
Fr livre de poche *(m)*
It libro in edizione
economica *(m)*
Pt livro de bolso *(m)*

Taschenbuch-Ausgabe
(f) n De
En paperback edition
Es edición de libros en
rústica *(f)*
Fr édition de poche *(f)*
It edizione economica
(f)
Pt edição de bolso *(f)*

Taschenbuch-Verleger
(m) n De
En paperback publisher
Es editor de libros en
rústica *(m)*
Fr éditeur de livres de
poche *(m)*
It editore di collane
economiche *(m)*
Pt editor de livros de
bolso *(m)*

Taschenwörterbüch *(n)*
n De
En pocket dictionary
Es diccionario de bolsillo
(m)
Fr dictionnaire de poche
(m)
It dizionario tascabile
(m)
Pt dicionário de bolso
(m)

Tastatur *(m) n* De
En keyboard
Es teclado *(m)*
Fr clavier *(m)*
It tastiera *(f)*
Pt teclado *(m)*

Tastatur-Setzer *(m) n* De
En keyboarder
Es operador de teclado
(m)
Fr claviste *(m)*
It operatore di tastiera
(m)
Pt mecanotipista *(m)*

tastiera *(f) n* It
De Tastatur *(m)*
En keyboard
Es teclado *(m)*
Fr clavier *(m)*
Pt teclado *(m)*

tastiera cieca *(f)* It
De Blindtastatur *(f)*
En blind keyboard
Es teclado ciego *(m)*
Fr clavier aveugle *(m)*
Pt teclado cego *(m)*

tautologia *(f) n* It, Pt
De Tautologie *(f)*
En tautology
Es tautología *(f)*
Fr tautologie *(f)*

tautología *(f) n* Es
De Tautologie *(f)*
En tautology
Fr tautologie *(f)*
It tautologia *(f)*
Pt tautologia *(f)*

tautologie *(f) n* Fr
De Tautologie *(f)*
En tautology
Es tautología *(f)*
It tautologia *(f)*
Pt tautologia *(f)*

Tautologie *(f) n* De
En tautology
Es tautología *(f)*
Fr tautologie *(f)*
It tautologia *(f)*
Pt tautologia *(f)*

tautology *n* En
De Tautologie *(f)*
Es tautología *(f)*
Fr tautologie *(f)*
It tautologia *(f)*
Pt tautologia *(f)*

tavola *(f) n* It
De Tafel *(f)*
En plate (picture)
Es lámina *(f)*
Fr planche *(f)*
Pt gravura *(f)*

tavole a colori *(f pl)* It
Am color plates
De Farbtafeln *(pl)*
En colour plates *pl n*
Es láminas en color *(f pl)*
Fr planches en couleurs
(f pl)
Pt páginas a cores *(f pl)*

tavolo luminoso *(m)* It
De Leuchttisch *(m)*
En light table
Es mesa de retoque *(f)*
Fr table lumineuse *(f)*
Pt mesa de retoque *(f)*

taxa horária *(f)* Pt
De Stundentarif *(m)*
En hourly rate
Es régimen horario *(m)*
Fr tarif horaire *(m)*
It paga oraria *(f)*

taxe sur la valeur
ajoutée (TVA) *(f)* Fr
De Mehrwertsteuer
(Mwst) *(f)*
En value-added tax (VAT)
Es impuesto sobre el
valor añadido *(m)*
It imposta sul valore
aggiunto (IVA) *(f)*
Pt imposto sobre valor
aduzido *(m)*

technical book En
De technisches Buch *(n)*
Es libro técnico *(m)*
Fr ouvrage technique
(m)
It libro tecnico *(m)*
Pt livro técnico *(m)*

technical dictionary En
De technisches
Wörterbuch *(n)*
Es diccionario técnico
(m)
Fr dictionnaire
technique *(m)*
It dizionario tecnico *(m)*
Pt dicionário técnico *(m)*

technical drawing En
De technische
Zeichnung *(f)*
Es dibujo técnico *(m)*
Fr dessin industriel *(m)*
It disegno tecnico *(m)*
Pt desenho técnico *(m)*

technisches Buch *(n)* De
En technical book
Es libro técnico *(m)*
Fr ouvrage technique
(m)
It libro tecnico *(m)*
Pt livro técnico *(m)*

technisches
Wörterbuch *(n)* De
En technical dictionary
Es diccionario técnico
(m)
Fr dictionnaire
technique *(m)*
It dizionario tecnico *(m)*
Pt dicionário técnico *(m)*

technische Zeichnung
(f) De
En technical drawing
Es dibujo técnico *(m)*
Fr dessin industriel *(m)*

It disegno tecnico *(m)*
Pt desenho técnico *(m)*

tecido anilado *(m)* Pt
De Azur-Velinpapier *(n)*
En azure wove
Es azul celeste avitelado
(m)
Fr vélin azur *(m)*
It carta retinata azzura
(f)

tecido carbono *(m)* Pt
De Ätzpigmentpapier *(n)*
En carbon tissue
Es papel pigmento *(m)*
Fr papier au carbone
(m)
It carta al carbone *(f)*

tecido estilo antigo *(m)*
Pt
De Antikdruckpapier *(n)*
En antique wove
Es papel avitelado
antiguo *(m)*
Fr vélin à l'antique *(m)*
It carta retinata tipo
antico *(f)*

teclado *(m) n* Es, Pt
De Tastatur *(m)*
En keyboard
Fr clavier *(m)*
It tastiera *(f)*

teclado cego *(m)* Pt
De Blindtastatur *(f)*
En blind keyboard
Es teclado ciego *(m)*
Fr clavier aveugle *(m)*
It tastiera cieca *(f)*

teclado ciego *(m)* Es
De Blindtastatur *(f)*
En blind keyboard
Fr clavier aveugle *(m)*
It tastiera cieca *(f)*
Pt teclado cego *(m)*

Teilfarbennegative *(pl)*
n De
En separation negatives
Es negativos de
selección *(m pl)*
Fr négatifs sélectionnés
(m pl)
It negativi da selezione
(m pl)
Pt negativos de
separação *(m pl)*

teinte (f) n Fr
De Ton (m)
En tint
Es media tinta (f)
It gradazione (f)
Pt matiz (m)

tela (f) n It, Pt
De Mattgewebe (n)
En canvas
   (bookbinders')
Es Iona (f)
Fr toile (f)

tela cerata (f) It
De Wachstuch (n)
En American cloth
Es hule (m)
Fr moleskine (f)
Pt pano americano (m)

tela da fusto (f) It
De Buckram (m)
En buckram
Es bucarán (m)
Fr bougran (m)
Pt bocaxim (m)

tela d'arte (f) It
De Mattkunstgewebe (n)
En art canvas
Es tela de arte (f)
Fr toile pour reliure (f)
Pt tela de arte (f)

tela de arte (f) Es, Pt
De Mattkunstgewebe (n)
En art canvas
Fr toile pour reliure (f)
It tela d'arte (f)

telaio (m) n It
De Rahmen (m)
En chase (letterpress)
Es rama (f)
Fr châssis (m)
Pt rama (f)

telaio a vuoto (m) It
De Vakuumrahmen (m)
En vacuum frame
Es prensa al vacío (f)
Fr chassis pneumatique
   (m)
Pt caixilho de vácuo (m)

telaio di forma chiusa
   (m) It
De Maschinenrahmen
   (m)
En machine chase
Es rama de máquina (f)
Fr châssis machine (m)
Pt rama de máquina (f)

telaio di piegafoglio (m)
   It
De Falzrahmen (m)
En folding chase
Es rama dúplex (f)
Fr châssis de pliage (m)
Pt rama duplex (f)

television rights pl n En
De Fernsehrechte (pl)
Es derechos de
   televisión (m pl)
Fr droits de télévision
   (m pl)
It diritti televisivi (m pl)
Pt direitos de televisão
   (m pl)

tempo de acesso (m) Pt
De Zugriffzeit (f)
En access time
Es tiempo de acceso (m)
Fr temps d'accès (m)
It tempo di accesso (m)

tempo de paragem (m)
   Pt
De Ausfallszeit (f)
En down time
Es tiempo muerto (m)
Fr période d'arrêt (f)
It tempo passivo (m)

tempo di accesso (m) It
De Zugriffzeit (f)
En access time
Es tiempo de acceso (m)
Fr temps d'accès (m)
Pt tempo de acesso (m)

tempo di
   funzionamento a
   vuoto (m) It
De Leerlaufzeit (f)
En idle time
Es tiempo de reposo (m)
Fr temps mort (m)
Pt tempo morto (m)

tempo morto (m) Pt
De Leerlaufzeit (f)
En idle time
Es tiempo de reposo (m)
Fr temps mort (m)
It tempo di
   funzionamento a
   vuoto (m)

tempo passivo (m) It
De Ausfallszeit (f)
En down time
Es tiempo muerto (m)
Fr période d'arrêt (f)
Pt tempo de paragem
   (m)

temps d'accès (m) Fr
De Zugriffzeit (f)
En access time
Es tiempo de acceso (m)
It tempo di accesso (m)
Pt tempo de acesso (m)

temps mort (m) Fr
De Leerlaufzeit (f)
En idle time
Es tiempo de reposo (m)
It tempo di
   funzionamento a
   vuoto (m)
Pt tempo morto (m)

term n En
De Bezeichnung (f)
Es término (m)
Fr terme (m)
It termine (m)
Pt termo (m)

terme (m) n Fr
De Bezeichnung (f)
En term
Es término (m)
It termine (m)
Pt termo (m)

terminazione (f) n It
De Serif (m)
En serif
Es bigotillo (m)
Fr empâtement (m)
Pt remate (m)

termine (m) n It
De Bezeichnung (f)
En term
Es término (m)
Fr terme (m)
Pt termo (m)

término (m) n Es
De Bezeichnung (f)
En term
Fr terme (m)

It termine (m)
Pt termo (m)

termo (m) n Pt
De Bezeichnung (f)
En term
Es término (m)
Fr terme (m)
It termine (m)

termofixado adj Pt
De heißtrocknend
En heat-set
Es solidificado en
   caliente
Fr seché à chaud
It solidificato a caldo

terms (of agreement,
   etc.) pl n En
De Bedingungen (pl)
Es condiciones (f pl)
Fr conditions (f pl)
It condizioni (f pl)
Pt condições (m pl)

tesoro (m) n Es
De Thesaurus (m)
En thesaurus
Fr thésaurus (m)
It florilegio (m)
Pt léxico (m)

testata (f) n It
De Seitekopf (m)
En head (of page)
Es blanco (m)
Fr tête (f)
Pt cabeçalho (m)

testi di medicina (m pl) It
De Medizinbücher (pl)
En medical books
Es libros de medicina (m
   pl)
Fr ouvrages médicaux
   (m pl)
Pt livros de medicina (m
   pl)

testina sbagliata (f) It
Am wrong font
De falscher Buchstabe
   (m)
En wrong fount
Es letra de otro tipo (f)
Fr lettre d'une autre
   fonte (f)
Pt letra de outro tipo (f)

testo *(m)* *n* It
De Text *(m)*
En text
Es texto *(m)*
Fr texte *(m)*
Pt texto *(m)*

testo annullato *(m)* It
De gestrichener Text *(m)*
En cancelled matter
Es composición
   suprimida *(f)*
Fr texte annulé *(m)*
Pt matéria cancelada *(f)*

testo non giustificato
   (m) It
De Schrägsatz *(m)*
En unjustified text
Es texto sin justificar *(m)*
Fr composition en
   drapeau *(f)*
Pt texto não justificado
   (m)

testo scolastico *(m)* It
De Schulbuch *(n)*
En schoolbook
Es libro escolar *(m)*
Fr livre scolaire *(m)*
Pt livro escolar *(m)*

tête *(f)* *n* Fr
De Seitekopf *(m)*
En head (of page)
Es blanco *(m)*
It testata *(f)*
Pt cabeçalho *(m)*

tête de chapitre *(f)* Fr
De Kapitelüberschrift *(f)*
En chapter heading
Es encabezamiento de
   capítulo *(m)*
It titolo del capitolo *(m)*
Pt título do capítulo *(m)*

tête latérale *(f)* Fr
De links in Linie
   gebrachte
   Überschrift *(f)*
En side head
Es titulillo lateral *(m)*
It titolo laterale *(m)*
Pt título lateral *(m)*

text *n* En
De Text *(m)*
Es texto *(m)*
Fr texte *(m)*

It testo *(m)*
Pt texto *(m)*

Text *(m)* *n* De
En text
Es texto *(m)*
Fr texte *(m)*
It testo *(m)*
Pt texto *(m)*

textbook *n* En
De Lehrbuch *(n)*
Es libro de texto *(m)*
Fr manuel *(m)*
It libro di testo *(m)*
Pt livro de texto *(m)*

texte *(m)* *n* Fr
De Text *(m)*
En text
Es texto *(m)*
It testo *(m)*
Pt texto *(m)*

texte annulé *(m)* Fr
De gestrichener Text *(m)*
En cancelled matter
Es composición
   suprimida *(f)*
It testo annullato *(m)*
Pt matéria cancelada *(f)*

Texteinpassung *(f)* *n* De
En copy-fitting
Es ajuste de originales
   (m)
Fr montage du texte *(m)*
It aggiustamento di
   originali *(m)*
Pt ajustamento do
   original *(m)*

Texter *(m)* *n* De
En copywriter
Es redactor de textos
   publicitarios *(m)*
Fr rédacteur-
   concepteur
   publicitaire *(m)*
It redattore
   pubblicitario *(m)*
Pt redactor de textos
   publicidades *(m)*

texte très corrigé *(m)* Fr
De stark revidiertes
   Manuskript *(n)*
En heavily edited copy
Es ejemplar mucho
   enmendada *(m)*

It copia molto
   emendata *(f)*
Pt exemplar muito
   corrigido *(m)*

texto *(m)* *n* Es, Pt
De Text *(m)*
En text
Fr texte *(m)*
It testo *(m)*

texto não justificado *(m)*
   Pt
De Schrägsatz *(m)*
En unjustified text
Es texto sin justificar *(m)*
Fr composition en
   drapeau *(f)*
It testo non giustificato
   (m)

textos de não ficção *(m*
   pl) Pt
De Sachliteratur *(f)*
En non-fiction
Es textos no novelescos
   (m pl)
Fr ouvrages généraux
   (m pl)
It saggistica *(f)*

texto sin justificar *(m)*
   Es
De Schrägsatz *(m)*
En unjustified text
Fr composition en
   drapeau *(f)*
It testo non giustificato
   (m)
Pt texto não justificado
   (m)

textos no novelescos *(m*
   pl) Es
De Sachliteratur *(f)*
En non-fiction
Fr ouvrages généraux
   (m pl)
It saggistica *(f)*
Pt textos de não ficção
   (m pl)

text pages *pl* *n* En
De Textseiten *(pl)*
Es páginas de texto *(f pl)*
Fr pages de texte *(f pl)*
It pagine di testo *(f pl)*
Pt páginas de texto *(f pl)*

Textseiten *(pl)* De
En text pages *pl* *n*
Es páginas de texto *(f pl)*
Fr pages de texte *(f pl)*
It pagine di testo *(f pl)*
Pt páginas de texto *(f pl)*

textura a la luz *(f)* Es
De Durchscheinen *(n)*
En look-through
Fr épair *(m)*
It trasparente *(m)*
Pt transparência *(f)*

théâtre *(m)* *n* Fr
De Drama *(n)*
En drama
Es drama *(m)*
It dramma *(m)*
Pt drama *(m)*

Thermodruck *(m)* *n* De
En thermographic
   printing
Es impresión
   termográfica *(f)*
Fr thermogravure *(f)*
It stampa termografica
   (f)
Pt impressão
   termográfica *(f)*

thermographic printing
   En
De Thermodruck *(m)*
Es impresión
   termográfica *(f)*
Fr thermogravure *(f)*
It stampa termografica
   (f)
Pt impressão
   termográfica *(f)*

thermogravure *(f)* *n* Fr
De Thermodruck *(m)*
En thermographic
   printing
Es impresión
   termográfica *(f)*
It stampa termografica
   (f)
Pt impressão
   termográfica *(f)*

thesaurus *n* En
De Thesaurus *(m)*
Es tesoro *(m)*
Fr thésaurus *(m)*
It florilegio *(m)*
Pt léxico *(m)*

Thesaurus *(m) n* De
En thesaurus
Es tesoro *(m)*
Fr thésaurus *(m)*
It florilegio *(m)*
Pt léxico *(m)*

thésaurus *(m) n* Fr
De Thesaurus *(m)*
En thesaurus
Es tesoro *(m)*
It florilegio *(m)*
Pt léxico *(m)*

thick space En
De dickes Spatium *(n)*
Es espacio grueso *(m)*
Fr espace forte *(f)*
It spazio grosso *(m)*
Pt espaço grosso *(m)*

thin space En
De dünnes Spatium *(n)*
Es espacio fino *(m)*
Fr espace fine *(f)*
It spazio sottile *(m)*
Pt espaço fino *(m)*

three-color printing Am
De Dreifarbendruck *(m)*
En three-colour printing
Es tricromía *(f)*
Fr trichromie *(f)*
It stampa a tre colori *(f)*
Pt impressão a três
cores *(f)*

three-colour printing En
Am three-color printing
De Dreifarbendruck *(m)*
Es tricromía *(f)*
Fr trichromie *(f)*
It stampa a tre colori *(f)*
Pt impressão a três
cores *(f)*

**three-dimensional
printing** En
De dreidimensionaler
Druck *(m)*
Es impresión
tridimensional *(f)*
Fr impression
tridimensionnelle *(f)*
It stampa
tridimensionale *(f)*
Pt impressão a três
dimensões *(f)*

**three-quarter bound
book** En
De dreiviertel-
gebundenes Buch *(n)*
Es libro encuadernado a
tres cuartos de piel
(m)
Fr livre en demi-reliure
amateur *(m)*
It libro a tre quarti
rilegato *(m)*
Pt livro encadernado a
três quartos *(m)*

thriller *n* En
De Reißer *(m)*
Es novela de misterio *(f)*
Fr roman à sensation
(m)
It giallo *(m)*
Pt policial *(m)*

thumb index En
De Daumenindex *(m)*
Es índice recortado *(m)*
Fr index à onglets *(m)*
It indice a rubrica *(m)*
Pt índice com letras
salientes na borda da
página *(m)*

Tiefdruck *(m) n* De
En intaglio printing
Es impresión con
grabados en hueco
(f)
Fr impression en creux
(f)
It stampa ad intaglio *(f)*
Pt impressão intaglio *(f)*

Tiefdruck-Offsetplatte
(f) De
En deep-etch litho plate
Es plancha al
hueco-offset *(f)*
Fr offset en creux *(m)*
It lastra litografica a
incisione profonda *(f)*
Pt chapa litográfica de
gravação funda *(f)*

**tiefstehende
Buchstaben** *(pl)* De
En inferior characters
Es subíndices *(m pl)*
Fr petites lettres
inférieures *(f pl)*
It caratteri inferiori *(m
pl)*
Pt caracteres inferiores
(m pl)

Tiegel *(m) n* De
En platen press
Es minerva *(f)*
Fr imprimeuse *(f)*
It macchina da stampa
a platina *(f)*
Pt minerva *(f)*

tiempo de acceso *(m)* Es
De Zugriffzeit *(f)*
En access time
Fr temps d´accès *(m)*
It tempo di accesso *(m)*
Pt tempo de acesso *(m)*

tiempo de reposo *(m)* Es
De Leerlaufzeit *(f)*
En idle time
Fr temps mort *(m)*
It tempo di
funzionamento a
vuoto *(m)*
Pt tempo morto *(m)*

tiempo muerto *(m)* Es
De Ausfallszeit *(f)*
En down time
Fr période d´arrêt *(f)*
It tempo passivo *(m)*
Pt tempo de paragem
(m)

tienda *(f) n* Es
De Laden *(m)*
En shop (retail)
Fr boutique *(f)*
It negozio *(m)*
Pt loja *(f)*

Tierleimbindung *(f) n* De
En animal sizing
Es cola animal *(f)*
Fr collage animal *(m)*
It colla animale *(f)*
Pt cola animal *(f)*

tige *(f) n* Fr
De Stiel *(m)*
En shank
Es árbol *(m)*
It gambo *(m)*
Pt árvore *(f)*

Tilgungszeichen *(n) n* De
En delete mark
Es marca de supresión
(f)
Fr marque à supprimer
(f)
It segno di cancellatura
(m)

Pt marca de eliminação
(f)

timbrage *(m) n* Fr
De Prägen *(n)*
En stamping
Es estampación *(f)*
It stampaggio *(m)*
Pt estampagem *(f)*

tint *n* En
De Ton *(m)*
Es media tinta *(f)*
Fr teinte *(f)*
It gradazione *(f)*
Pt matiz *(m)*

tinta adherida *(f)* Es
De gebundene Farbe *(f)*
En bonded ink
Fr encre liée *(f)*
It inchiostro aderente
(m)
Pt tinta aglutinada *(f)*

tinta aglutinada *(f)* Pt
De gebundene Farbe *(f)*
En bonded ink
Es tinta adherida *(f)*
Fr encre liée *(f)*
It inchiostro aderente
(m)

tinta de alumínio *(f)* Pt
Am aluminum ink
De Aluminiumfarbe *(f)*
En aluminium ink
Es tinta plateada *(f)*
Fr encre métallique *(f)*
It inchiostro
all´alluminio *(m)*

tinta de anilina *(f)* Es, Pt
De Anilinfarbe *(f)*
En aniline ink
Fr encre à l´aniline *(f)*
It inchiostro all´anilina
(m)

tinta de estampación *(f)*
Es
De Prägedruckfarbe *(f)*
En embossing ink
Fr encre à gaufrer *(f)*
It inchiostro per
goffratura *(f)*
Pt tinta de estampagem
(f)

tinta de estampagem *(f)*
Pt
De Prägedruckfarbe *(f)*
En embossing ink
Es tinta de estampación
(f)
Fr encre à gaufrer *(f)*
It inchiostro per
goffratura *(m)*

tinta de imprenta *(f)* Es
De Druckfarbe *(f)*
En ink (printer's)
Fr encre d'impression
(f)
It inchiostro da stampa
(m)
Pt tinta de impressão *(f)*

tinta de impressão *(f)* Pt
De Druckfarbe *(f)*
En ink (printer's)
Es tinta de imprenta *(f)*
Fr encre d'impression
(f)
It inchiostro da stampa
(m)

tinta magnética *(f)* Es, Pt
De Magnettinte *(f)*
En magnetic ink
Fr encre magnétique *(f)*
It inchiostro magnetico
(m)

tinta plateada *(f)* Es
Am aluminum ink
De Aluminiumfarbe *(f)*
En aluminium ink
Fr encre métallique *(f)*
It inchiostro
all'alluminio *(m)*
Pt tinta de alumínio *(f)*

tintas metálicas *(f pl)* Es,
Pt
De Bronzedrucktinten
(pl)
En metallic inks
Fr encres métalliques *(f
pl)*
It inchiostri metallici *(m
pl)*

tinted paper En
De getöntes Papier *(n)*
Es papel coloreado *(m)*
Fr papier de couleur *(m)*
It carta colorata *(f)*
Pt papel colorido *(m)*

tintero de la prensa *(m)*
Es
De Farbkanal *(m)*
En ink duct
Fr encrier *(m)*
It condotto per
inchiostro *(m)*
Pt canal de tinta *(m)*

tintura *(f)* n Pt
De Farbauftrag *(m)*
En inking
Es entintaje *(f)*
Fr encrage *(m)*
It inchiostrazione *(f)*

tipo *(m)* n Es, Pt
De Schrift *(f)*
En type
Fr caractère
d'imprimerie *(m)*
It carattere tipografico
(m)

tipo cheio *(m)* Pt
De fetter Schrifttyp *(m)*
En boldface type
Es tipo negrilla *(m)*
Fr caractères gras *(m pl)*
It carattere in neretto
(m)

tipo de estilo antigo *(m)*
Pt
De Mediäval *(n)*
En old face
Es estilo antiguo *(m)*
Fr elzévir *(m)*
It carattere elzeviro *(m)*

tipo de ojo ancho *(m)* Es
De breiter Schrifttyp *(m)*
En expanded typeface
Fr oeil plus grand que la
normale *(m)*
It carattere largo *(m)*
Pt tipo de olho largo *(m)*

tipo de olho largo *(m)* Pt
De breiter Schrifttyp *(m)*
En expanded typeface
Es tipo de ojo ancho *(m)*
Fr oeil plus grand que la
normale *(m)*
It carattere largo *(m)*

tipo estrecho *(m)* Es
De schmaler Schrifttyp
(m)
En condensed typeface
Fr caractère effilé *(m)*

It carattere allungato
(m)
Pt estilo de tipo
condensado *(m)*

tipografia *(f)* n It, Pt
De Typographie *(f)*
En typography
Es tipografía *(f)*
Fr typographie *(f)*

tipografía *(f)* n Es
De Typographie *(f)*
En typography
Fr typographie *(f)*
It tipografia *(f)*
Pt tipografia *(f)*

tipografía offset *(f)* Es
De Offset-Buchdruck *(m)*
En offset letterpress
Fr presse offset *(f)*
It stampa tipografica
offset *(f)*
Pt prensa offset *(f)*

tipógrafo *(m)* n Pt
De Drucker *(m)*
En printer
Es impresor *(m)*
Fr imprimeur *(m)*
It stampatore *(m)*

tipometro *(m)* n It
De Schriftsatz-Lineal *(n)*
En typescale
Es escala de tipos *(f)*
Fr typomètre *(m)*
Pt tipómetro *(m)*

tipómetro *(m)* n Pt
De Schriftsatz-Lineal *(n)*
En typescale
Es escala de tipos *(f)*
Fr typomètre *(m)*
It tipometro *(m)*

tipo moderno *(m)* Es
De moderner Schrifttyp
(m)
En modern face
Fr didone *(f)*
It carattere moderno
(m)
Pt olho moderno *(m)*

tipo móvel *(m)* Pt
De bewegliche Schrift *(f)*
En movable type
Es tipos movibles *(m pl)*

Fr caractères mobiles
(m pl)
It carattere mobile *(m)*

tipo negrilla *(m)* Es
De fetter Schrifttyp *(m)*
En boldface type
Fr caractères gras *(m pl)*
It carattere in neretto
(m)
Pt tipo cheio *(m)*

tipo redondo *(m)* Es
De römische Schrift *(f)*
En roman type
Fr romain *(m)*
It carattere romano
tondo *(m)*
Pt tipo romano *(m)*

tipo romano *(m)* Pt
De römische Schrift *(f)*
En roman type
Es tipo redondo *(m)*
Fr romain *(m)*
It carattere romano
tondo *(m)*

tipos de maiúscula *(m
pl)* Pt
De Auszeichnungssatz
(m)
En display type
Es tipos titulares *(m pl)*
Fr caractères vedettes
(m pl)
It caratteri di titolo *(m
pl)*

tipo semi-negro *(m)* Pt
De halbfetter Satz *(m)*
En semi-bold type
Es seminegrilla *(f)*
Fr caractère mi-gras *(m)*
It carattere
semi-grassetto *(m)*

tipo sin remate *(m)* Es
De Grotesk-Schrifttyp
(m)
En sans-serif typeface
Fr caractère antique
(sans empâtement)
(m)
It bastone *(m)*
Pt olho de tipo sem
remate *(m)*

tipos movibles *(m pl)* Es
De bewegliche Schrift *(f)*
En movable type

Fr caractères mobiles
    (m pl)
It carattere mobile *(m)*
Pt tipo móvel *(m)*

tipo speciale *(m)* It
De Spezial-Schrifttyp *(m)*
En special sort
Es suerte especial *(f)*
Fr figure spéciale *(f)*
Pt sortes especial *(f)*

tipos titulares *(m pl)* Es
De Auszeichnungssatz
    (m)
En display type
Fr caractères vedettes
    (m pl)
It caratteri di titolo *(m*
    pl)
Pt tipos de maiúscula
    (m pl)

Tippen *(n)* n De
En typing
Es mecanografiado *(m)*
Fr dactylographie *(f)*
It scrivere a macchina
    (m)
Pt dactilografia *(f)*

tirabozze *(m)* n It
De Abziehapparat *(m)*
En proofing press
Es prensa sacapruebas
    (f)
Fr presse pour tirer les
    épreuves *(f)*
Pt prensa para tirar
    provas *(f)*

tirada *(f)* n Es
De Auflage *(f)*
En impression
Fr tirage *(m)*
It tiratura *(f)*
Pt tiragem *(m)*

tirada de pruebas *(f)* Es
De Andrucken *(n)*
En proofing
Fr tirage d'épreuves *(m)*
It tiratura di prova *(f)*
Pt tiragem de provas *(f)*

tirada grande *(f)* Es
De hohe Druckauflage *(f)*
En long print run
Fr grand tirage *(m)*
It grande tiratura *(f)*
Pt tiragem grande *(f)*

tirage *(m)* n Fr
De Auflage *(f)*
En impression
Es tirada *(f)*
It tiratura *(f)*
Pt tiragem *(m)*

tirage contact *(m)* Fr
De Kontaktdruck *(m)*
En contact print
Es copia por contacto *(f)*
It stampa a contatto *(f)*
Pt prova por contacto *(f)*

tirage d'épreuves *(m)* Fr
De Andrucken *(n)*
En proofing
Es tirada de pruebas *(f)*
It tiratura di prova *(f)*
Pt tiragem de provas *(f)*

tirage indirect *(m)* Fr
De indirekter Hochdruck
    (m)
En indirect printing
Es impresión indirecta
    (f)
It stampa indiretta *(f)*
Pt impressão indirecta
    (f)

tiragem *(m)* n Pt
De Auflage *(f)*
En impression
Es tirada *(f)*
Fr tirage *(m)*
It tiratura *(f)*

tiragem de provas *(f)* Pt
De Andrucken *(n)*
En proofing
Es tirada de pruebas *(f)*
Fr tirage d'épreuves *(m)*
It tiratura di prova *(f)*

tiragem grande *(f)* Pt
De hohe Druckauflage *(f)*
En long print run
Es tirada grande *(f)*
Fr grand tirage *(m)*
It grande tiratura *(f)*

tiratura *(f)* n It
De Auflage *(f)*
En impression
Es tirada *(f)*
Fr tirage *(m)*
Pt tiragem *(m)*

tiratura di prova *(f)* It
De Andrucken *(n)*
En proofing
Es tirada de pruebas *(f)*
Fr tirage d'épreuves *(m)*
Pt tiragem de provas *(f)*

tiret sur cadratin *(m)* Fr
De Geviertstrich *(m)*
En em rule
Es pleca-cuadratín *(f)*
It lineato a quadratone
    (m)
Pt filete de quadratim
    (m)

tiret sur demi-cadratin
    (m) Fr
De Halbgeviertstrich *(m)*
En en rule
Es pleca de medio
    cuadratín *(f)*
It lineato a
    demi-quadratone *(m)*
Pt filete de meio
    quadratim *(m)*

tissue paper En
De Seidenpapier *(n)*
Es papel de seda *(m)*
Fr papier mousseline
    (m)
It carta velina *(f)*
Pt papel de seda *(m)*

tissue stencil En
De Gewebeschablone *(f)*
Es matriz de papel de
    seda *(f)*
Fr stencil de duplication
    (m)
It matrice in carta di
    seta *(f)*
Pt estencil de tela *(m)*

Titelseite *(f)* n De
En title page
Es portada *(f)*
Fr page de titre *(m)*
It frontespizio *(m)*
Pt página de título *(f)*

title page En
De Titelseite *(f)*
Es portada *(f)*
Fr page de titre *(m)*
It frontespizio *(m)*
Pt página de título *(f)*

tiratura di prova *(f)* It
De Andrucken *(n)*
En proofing
Es tirada de pruebas *(f)*
Fr tirage d'épreuves *(m)*
Pt tiragem de provas *(f)*

titoletti *(m pl)* It
De lebender
    Kolumnentitel *(pl)*
En running heads
Es títulos de página *(m*
    pl)
Fr titres courants *(m pl)*
Pt títulos repetidos *(m*
    pl)

titolo *(m)* n It
De Kopfzeile *(f)*
En headline (of page)
Es título *(m)*
Fr ligne de tête *(f)*
Pt linha de cabeçalho *(f)*

titolo abbreviato *(m)* It
De Innentitel *(m)*
En half title
Es anteportada *(f)*
Fr faux-titre *(m)*
Pt anteportada *(f)*

titolo alternato *(m)* It
De Untertitel *(m)*
En alternate title
Es subtítulo *(m)*
Fr sous-titre *(m)*
Pt título alternativo *(m)*

titolo del capitolo *(m)* It
De Kapitelüberschrift *(f)*
En chapter heading
Es encabezamiento de
    capítulo *(m)*
Fr tête de chapitre *(f)*
Pt título do capítulo *(m)*

titolo di testa *(m)* It
De Überschrift *(f)*
En headline (of
    newspaper)
Es titular *(m)*
Fr titre *(m)*
Pt manchete *(m)*

titolo laterale *(m)* It
De links in Linie
    gebrachte
    Überschrift *(f)*
En side head
Es titulillo lateral *(m)*
Fr tête latérale *(f)*
Pt título lateral *(m)*

titolo parziale *(m)* It
De Schmutztitel *(m)*
En part-title
Es título de parte *(m)*

Fr titre partiel *(m)*
Pt título parcial *(m)*

titre *(m) n* Fr
De Überschrift *(f)*
En headline (of
    newspaper)
Es titular *(m)*
It titolo di testa *(m)*
Pt manchete *(m)*

titre partiel *(m)* Fr
De Schmutztitel *(m)*
En part-title
Es título de parte *(m)*
It titolo parziale *(m)*
Pt título parcial *(m)*

titres courants *(m pl)* Fr
De lebender
    Kolumnentitel *(pl)*
En running heads
Es títulos de página *(m
    pl)*
It titoletti *(m pl)*
Pt títulos repetidos *(m
    pl)*

titular *(m) n* Es
De Überschrift *(f)*
En headline (of
    newspaper)
Fr titre *(m)*
It titolo di testa *(m)*
Pt manchete *(m)*

titulillo lateral *(m)* Es
De links in Linie
    gebrachte
    Überschrift *(f)*
En side head
Fr tête latérale *(f)*
It titolo laterale *(m)*
Pt título lateral *(m)*

título *(m) n* Es
De Kopfzeile *(f)*
En headline (of page)
Fr ligne de tête *(f)*
It titolo *(m)*
Pt linha de cabeçalho *(f)*

título alternativo *(m)* Pt
De Untertitel *(m)*
En alternate title
Es subtítulo *(m)*
Fr sous-titre *(m)*
It titolo alternato *(m)*

título de parte *(m)* Es
De Schmutztitel *(m)*
En part-title
Fr titre partiel *(m)*
It titolo parziale *(m)*
Pt título parcial *(m)*

título do capítulo *(m)* Pt
De Kapitelüberschrift *(f)*
En chapter heading
Es encabezamiento de
    capítulo *(m)*
Fr tête de chapitre *(f)*
It titolo del capitolo *(m)*

título lateral *(m)* Pt
De links in Linie
    gebrachte
    Überschrift *(f)*
En side head
Es titulillo lateral *(m)*
Fr tête latérale *(f)*
It titolo laterale *(m)*

título parcial *(m)* Pt
De Schmutztitel *(m)*
En part-title
Es título de parte *(m)*
Fr titre partiel *(m)*
It titolo parziale *(m)*

títulos de página *(m pl)*
    Es
De lebender
    Kolumnentitel *(pl)*
En running heads
Fr titres courants *(m pl)*
It titoletti *(m pl)*
Pt títulos repetidos *(m
    pl)*

títulos repetidos *(m pl)*
    Pt
De lebender
    Kolumnentitel *(pl)*
En running heads
Es títulos de página *(m
    pl)*
Fr titres courants *(m pl)*
It titoletti *(m pl)*

**todos os direitos
    reservados** Pt
De alle Rechte
    vorbehalten
En all rights reserved
Es reservados todos los
    derechos
Fr tous droits réservés
It tutti i diritti riservati

toile *(f) n* Fr
De Mattgewebe *(n)*
En canvas
    (bookbinders')
Es lona *(f)*
It tela *(f)*
Pt tela *(f)*

toile pour reliure *(f)* Fr
De Mattkunstgewebe *(n)*
En art canvas
Es tela de arte *(f)*
It tela d'arte *(f)*
Pt tela de arte *(f)*

toma de datos *(f)* Es
De Datenerfassung *(f)*
En data capture
Fr saisie de données *(f)*
It cattura dei dati *(f)*
Pt captação de dados *(f)*

tom contínuo *(m)* Pt
De kontinuerlich Ton *(m)*
En continuous tone
Es tono continuo *(m)*
Fr ton en continu *(m)*
It tono continuo *(m)*

Ton *(m) n* De
En tint
Es media tinta *(f)*
Fr teinte *(f)*
It gradazione *(f)*
Pt matiz *(m)*

ton en continu *(m)* Fr
De kontinuerlich Ton *(m)*
En continuous tone
Es tono continuo *(m)*
It tono continuo *(m)*
Pt tom contínuo *(m)*

tono continuo *(m)* Es, It
De kontinuerlich Ton *(m)*
En continuous tone
Fr ton en continu *(m)*
Pt tom contínuo *(m)*

Tonplatte *(f) n* De
En flat-tint plate
Es clisé de media tinta
    (m)
Fr aplat *(m)*
It lastra a tinta opaca *(f)*
Pt chapa de meia-tinta
    (f)

tooled binding En
De Punzenbindung *(f)*
Es encuadernación
    repujada *(f)*
Fr reliure ciselée *(f)*
It rilegatura con attrezzi
    (f)
Pt encadernação
    ornamentada *(f)*

torchio a mano *(m)* It
De Handpresse *(f)*
En hand press
Es prensa manual *(f)*
Fr presse à bras *(f)*
Pt prensa manual *(f)*

tornar a compor Pt
De neu setzen
En reset
Es componer de nuevo
Fr remanier
It riazzerare

**totalmente
    encuadernado** Es
De voll gebunden
En fully bound
Fr reliure pleine
It completamente
    rilegato
Pt completamente
    encadernado

tous droits réservés Fr
De alle Rechte
    vorbehalten
En all rights reserved
Es reservados todos los
    derechos
It tutti i diritti riservati
Pt todos os direitos
    reservados

trabajo *(m) n* Es
De Arbeit *(f)*
En work
Fr travail *(m)*
It lavoro *(m)*
Pt trabalho *(m)*

**trabajo artístico de la
    sobrecubierta** *(m)*
    Es
De Umschlag-
    Satzmontage *(f)*
En jacket artwork
Fr illustration de la
    jaquette *(f)*
It menabò per
    sovracopertina *(m)*

Pt arte da sobrecapa
(m)

trabajo de montaje (m)
Es
De Klebeumbruch-Arbeit
(f)
En paste-up work
Fr travail de collage (m)
It lavoro di incollatura
(m)
Pt trabalho do
montagem (m)

trabajo en ejecución (m)
Es
De in Arbeit befindlich
En work-in-progress
Fr travail en cours (m)
It lavoro in corso (m)
Pt progresso de
adaptação ao
trabalho (m)

trabajo en tandem (m) Es
De Tandemarbeit (f)
En tandem work
Fr travail en tandem (m)
It lavoro in tandem (m)
Pt trabalho em tandem
(m)

trabajo externo (m) Es
De Außenarbeit (n)
En outwork
Fr travail à domicile (m)
It lavoro esterno (m)
Pt trabalho externo (m)

**trabajo intensivo de
mano de obra** (m)
Es
Am labor-intensive work
De arbeitsintensive
Aufträge (pl)
En labour-intensive work
Fr travail à forte
main-d'oeuvre (m)
It lavoro ad alto
contenuto di mano
d'opera (m)
Pt trabalho com muita
mão de obra (m)

trabalho (m) n Pt
De Arbeit (f)
En work
Es trabajo (m)
Fr travail (m)
It lavoro (m)

trabalho a meia folha
(m) Pt
De Halbbogendruck (m)
En half-sheet work
Es imposición e
impresión a blanco y
vuelta (f)
Fr imposition en
demi-feuille (f)
It lavoro di mezza
pagina (f)

**trabalho com muita mão
de obra** (m) Pt
Am labor-intensive work
De arbeitsintensive
Aufträge (pl)
En labour-intensive work
Es trabajo intensivo de
mano de obra (m)
Fr travail à forte
main-d'oeuvre (m)
It lavoro ad alto
contenuto di mano
d'opera (m)

trabalho do montagem
(m) Pt
De Klebeumbruch-Arbeit
(f)
En paste-up work
Es trabajo de montaje
(m)
Fr travail de collage (m)
It lavoro di incollatura
(m)

trabalho em tandem (m)
Pt
De Tandemarbeit (f)
En tandem work
Es trabajo en tandem
(m)
Fr travail en tandem (m)
It lavoro in tandem (m)

trabalho externo (m) Pt
De Außenarbeit (n)
En outwork
Es trabajo externo (m)
Fr travail à domicile (m)
It lavoro esterno (m)

traçar vb Pt
De zeichen
En draw
Es dibujar
Fr dessiner
It disegnare

tracejado (m) n Pt
De Schattierung (f)
En shading
Es sombreado (m)
Fr exécution des
ombres (f)
It ombreggiatura (f)

tracing paper En
De Pauspapier (n)
Es papel de calcar (m)
Fr papier calque (m)
It carta da lucidi (f)
Pt papel de cópia (m)

traço de união (m) Pt
De Bindestrich (m)
En hyphen
Es guión (m)
Fr trait d'union (m)
It trattino di unione (m)

**traço de união de fim de
linha** (m) Pt
De Zeilenende-
Trennstrich (m)
En end-of-line hyphen
Es guión de final de
línea (m)
Fr trait d'union de fin de
ligne (m)
It trattino di fine linea
(m)

**traço de união
discricionário** (m)
Pt
De willkürlicher
Trennstrich (m)
En discretionary hyphen
Es guión discrecional
(m)
Fr trait d'union facultatif
(m)
It lineetta discrezionale
(f)

traços inferiores (m pl)
Pt
De Unterlängen (pl)
En descenders (of letter)
pl n
Es trazos inferiores (m
pl)
Fr jambages (m pl)
It lettere discendenti (f
pl)

trade n En
De Handel (m)
Es oficio (m)
Fr commerce (m)

It commercio (m)
Pt comércio (m)

trade book En
De Fachbuch (n)
Es libro profesional (m)
Fr livre professionnel
(m)
It libro commerciale
(m)
Pt livro de ofícios (m)

trade edition En
De Fachausgabe (f)
Es edición profesional (f)
Fr édition
professionnelle (f)
It edizione
commerciale (f)
Pt edição comercial (f)

trade houses pl n En
De Druckbetriebe (pl)
Es casas comerciales (f
pl)
Fr maisons
commerciales (f pl)
It case commerciali (f
pl)
Pt casas comerciais (f
pl)

trade journal En
De Fachzeitschrift (f)
Es revista profesional (f)
Fr revue professionnelle
(f)
It rivista commerciale
(f)
Pt revista comercial (f)

trade paperback En
De Fach-Taschenbuch
(n)
Es libro profesional en
rústica (m)
Fr fascicule
professionnel (m)
It libro economico
commerciale (m)
Pt livro de bolso
comercial (m)

trade union En
De Gewerkschaft (f)
Es sindicato (m)
Fr syndicat (m)
It sindacato (m)
Pt sindicato (m)

traducão *(f) n* Pt
De Übersetzung *(f)*
En translation
Es traducción *(f)*
Fr traduction *(f)*
It traduzione *(f)*

traducción *(f) n* Es
De Übersetzung *(f)*
En translation
Fr traduction *(f)*
It traduzione *(f)*
Pt tradução *(f)*

traducir *vb* Es
De übersetzen
En translate
Fr traduire
It tradurre
Pt traduzir

traducteur *(m) n* Fr
De Übersetzer *(m)*
En translator
Es traductor *(m)*
It traduttore *(m)*
Pt tradutor *(m)*

traduction *(f) n* Fr
De Übersetzung *(f)*
En translation
Es traducción *(f)*
It traduzione *(f)*
Pt tradução *(f)*

traductor *(m) n* Es
De Übersetzer *(m)*
En translator
Fr traducteur *(m)*
It traduttore *(m)*
Pt tradutor *(m)*

traduire *vb* Fr
De übersetzen
En translate
Es traducir
It tradurre
Pt traduzir

tradurre *vb* It
De übersetzen
En translate
Es traducir
Fr traduire
Pt traduzir

tradutor *(m) n* Pt
De Übersetzer *(m)*
En translator
Es traductor *(m)*

Fr traducteur *(m)*
It traduttore *(m)*

traduttore *(m) n* It
De Übersetzer *(m)*
En translator
Es traductor *(m)*
Fr traducteur *(m)*
Pt tradutor *(m)*

traduzione *(f) n* It
De Übersetzung *(f)*
En translation
Es traducción *(f)*
Fr traduction *(f)*
Pt tradução *(f)*

traduzir *vb* Pt
De übersetzen
En translate
Es traducir
Fr traduire
It tradurre

trait d'union *(m)* Fr
De Bindestrich *(m)*
En hyphen
Es guión *(m)*
It trattino di unione *(m)*
Pt traço de união *(m)*

**trait d'union de fin de
  ligne** *(m)* Fr
De Zeilenende-
   Trennstrich *(m)*
En end-of-line hyphen
Es guión de final de
   línea *(m)*
It trattino di fine linea
   (m)
Pt traço de união de fim
   de linha *(m)*

trait d'union facultatif
   (m) Fr
De willkürlicher
   Trennstrich *(m)*
En discretionary hyphen
Es guión discrecional
   (m)
It lineetta discrezionale
   (f)
Pt traço de união
   discricionário *(m)*

**traitement automatique
  de l'information**
   (m) Fr
De automatische
   Datenverarbeitung *(f)*

En automatic data
   processing (ADP)
Es proceso automático
   de datos *(m)*
It processazione
   automatica dati *(f)*
Pt tratamento
   automático de dados
   (m)

traitement des données
   (m) Fr
De Datenverarbeitung *(f)*
En data processing
Es proceso de datos *(m)*
It elaborazione di dati
   (f)
Pt tratamento de dados
   (m)

**traitement électronique
  de l'information**
   (m) Fr
De elektronische
   Datenverarbeitung *(f)*
En electronic data
   processing
Es proceso electrónico
   de datos *(m)*
It elaborazione
   elettronica dei dati *(f)*
Pt tratamento
   electrónico de dados
   (m)

traiter *vb* Fr
De verarbeiten
En process
Es procesar
It trattare
Pt tratar

trait-simili Fr
De Strich und Ton
En line and tone
Es línea y tono
It linea e tono
Pt linha e tono

trama de medio tono *(f)*
   Es
De Halbtonraster *(m)*
En halftone screen
Fr trame *(f)*
It retino di mezzatinta
   (m)
Pt retítula de autotipia
   (f)

trama fina *(f)* Es
De feiner Raster *(m)*
En fine screen

Fr trame fine *(f)*
It retino fine *(m)*
Pt retícula fina *(f)*

trama gruesa *(f)* Es
De grober Raster *(m)*
En coarse screen
Fr trame à gros grains
   (f)
It a grana grossa *(f)*
Pt retícula grossa *(f)*

trame *(f) n* Fr
De Halbtonraster *(m)*
En halftone screen
Es trama de medio tono
   (f)
It retino di mezzatinta
   (m)
Pt retítula de autotipia
   (f)

trame à gros grains *(f)* Fr
De grober Raster *(m)*
En coarse screen
Es trama gruesa *(f)*
It a grana grossa *(f)*
Pt retícula grossa *(f)*

trame fine *(f)* Fr
De feiner Raster *(m)*
En fine screen
Es trama fina *(f)*
It retino fine *(m)*
Pt retícula fina *(f)*

tranchefile *(f) n* Fr
De Kapitelband *(m)*
En headband
Es cabecera *(f)*
It capitello *(m)*
Pt friso *(m)*

transfer *vb* En
De transferieren
Es trasladar
Fr muter
It trasferire
Pt transferir

Transfer-Buchstaben
   (pl) n De
En transfer lettering
Es letrero por
   transferencia *(m)*
Fr lettres-transfert *(f pl)*
It lettere a trasporto *(f
   pl)*
Pt letras por
   transferência *(f pl)*

**transferencia
autográfica** *(f)* Es
De autographischer
Transferdruck *(m)*
En autographic transfer
Fr procédé
autographique *(m)*
It trasferimento
autografico *(m)*
Pt transferência
autográfica *(f)*

**transferência
autográfica** *(f)* Pt
De autographischer
Transferdruck *(m)*
En autographic transfer
Es transferencia
autográfica *(f)*
Fr procédé
autographique *(m)*
It trasferimento
autografico *(m)*

transferieren *vb* De
En transfer
Es trasladar
Fr muter
It trasferire
Pt transferir

transferir *vb* Pt
De transferieren
En transfer
Es trasladar
Fr muter
It trasferire

transfer lettering En
De Transfer-Buchstaben
(pl)
Es letrero por
transferencia *(m)*
Fr lettres-transfert *(f pl)*
It lettere a trasporto *(f
pl)*
Pt letras por
transferência *(f pl)*

transitaire *(m) n* Fr
De Spediteur *(m)*
En forwarding agent
Es agente expedidor *(m)*
It spedizioniere *(m)*
Pt agente expedidor *(m)*

translate *vb* En
De übersetzen
Es traducir
Fr traduire
It tradurre
Pt traduzir

translation *n* En
De Übersetzung *(f)*
Es traducción *(f)*
Fr traduction *(f)*
It traduzione *(f)*
Pt tradução *(f)*

translation edition En
De übersetzte Ausgabe
(f)
Es edición de traducción
(f)
Fr édition de
traductions *(f)*
It edizione tradotta *(f)*
Pt edição de tradução
(f)

translator *n* En
De Übersetzer *(m)*
Es traductor *(m)*
Fr traducteur *(m)*
It traduttore *(m)*
Pt tradutor *(m)*

transparência *(f) n* Pt
De Durchscheinen *(n)*
En look-through
Es textura a la luz *(f)*
Fr épair *(m)*
It trasparente *(m)*

transparency *n* En
De Dia *(n)*
Es diapositiva *(f)*
Fr diapositive *(f)*
It diapositiva *(f)*
Pt diapositivo *(m)*

Transparentweiß *(n) n*
De
En transparent white
Es blanco transparente
(m)
Fr blanc transparent *(m)*
It bianco trasparente
(m)
Pt branco transparente
(m)

transparent white En
De Transparentweiß *(n)*
Es blanco transparente
(m)
Fr blanc transparent *(m)*
It bianco trasparente
(m)
Pt branco transparente
(m)

transpor *vb* Pt
De austauschen
En transpose
Es trasponer
Fr transposer
It trasporre

transport *n* En; Fr *(m)*
De Transport *(m)*
Es transporte *(m)*
It trasporto *(m)*
Pt transporte *(m)*

Transport *(m) n* De
En transport
Es transporte *(m)*
Fr transport *(m)*
It trasporto *(m)*
Pt transporte *(m)*

transport costs *pl n* En
De Transportkosten *(pl)*
Es gastos de transporte
(m pl)
Fr frais de transport *(m
pl)*
It costi di trasporto *(m
pl)*
Pt custos de transporte
(m pl)

transporte *(m) n* Es, Pt
De Transport *(m)*
En transport
Fr transport *(m)*
It trasporto *(m)*

Transportkosten *(pl)* De
En transport costs *pl n*
Es gastos de transporte
(m pl)
Fr frais de transport *(m
pl)*
It costi di trasporto *(m
pl)*
Pt custos de transporte
(m pl)

transpose *vb* En
De austauschen
Es trasponer
Fr transposer
It trasporre
Pt transpor

transposer *vb* Fr
De austauschen
En transpose
Es trasponer
It trasporre
Pt transpor

tra parentesi It
De in Klammern
En in parentheses
Es entre paréntesis
Fr entre parenthèses
Pt entre parênteses

**trasferimento
autografico** *(m)* It
De autographischer
Transferdruck *(m)*
En autographic transfer
Es transferencia
autográfica *(f)*
Fr procédé
autographique *(m)*
Pt transferência
autográfica *(f)*

trasferire *vb* It
De transferieren
En transfer
Es trasladar
Fr muter
Pt transferir

trasladar *vb* Es
De transferieren
En transfer
Fr muter
It trasferire
Pt transferir

trasparente *(m) n* It
De Durchscheinen *(n)*
En look-through
Es textura a la luz *(f)*
Fr épair *(m)*
Pt transparência *(f)*

trasponer *vb* Es
De austauschen
En transpose
Fr transposer
It trasporre
Pt transpor

trasporre *vb* It
De austauschen
En transpose
Es trasponer
Fr transposer
Pt transpor

trasporto *(m) n* It
De Transport *(m)*
En transport
Es transporte *(m)*
Fr transport *(m)*
Pt transporte *(m)*

trasporto merci per via aerea *(m)* It
De Luftfracht *(f)*
En airfreight
Es flete aéreo *(m)*
Fr fret aérien *(m)*
Pt frete aéreo *(m)*

tratador da máquina *(m)* Pt
De Maschinenmeister *(m)*
En machine minder
Es prensista *(m)*
Fr conducteur de machine *(m)*
t macchinista *(m)*

tratamento automático de dados *(m)* Pt
De automatische Datenverarbeitung *(f)*
En automatic data processing (ADP)
Es proceso automático de datos *(m)*
Fr traitement automatique de l'information *(m)*
It processazione automatica dati *(f)*

tratamento de dados *(m)* Pt
De Datenverarbeitung *(f)*
En data processing
Es proceso de datos *(m)*
Fr traitement des données *(m)*
It elaborazione di dati *(f)*

tratamento electrónico de dados *(m)* Pt
De elektronische Datenverarbeitung *(f)*
En electronic data processing
Es proceso electrónico de datos *(m)*
Fr traitement électronique de l'information *(m)*
It elaborazione elettronica dei dati *(f)*

tratar *vb* Pt
De verarbeiten
En process
Es procesar
Fr traiter
It trattare

trattare *vb* It
De verarbeiten
En process
Es procesar
Fr traiter
Pt tratar

trattino di fine linea *(m)* It
De Zeilenende-Trennstrich *(m)*
En end-of-line hyphen
Es guión de final de línea *(m)*
Fr trait d'union de fin de ligne *(m)*
Pt traço de união de fim de linha *(m)*

trattino di unione *(m)* It
De Bindestrich *(m)*
En hyphen
Es guión *(m)*
Fr trait d'union *(m)*
Pt traço de união *(m)*

travail *(m)* n Fr
De Arbeit *(f)*
En work
Es trabajo *(m)*
It lavoro *(m)*
Pt trabalho *(m)*

travail à domicile *(m)* Fr
De Außenarbeit *(n)*
En outwork
Es trabajo externo *(m)*
It lavoro esterno *(m)*
Pt trabalho externo *(m)*

travail à forte main-d'oeuvre *(m)* Fr
Am labor-intensive work
De arbeitsintensive Aufträge *(pl)*
En labour-intensive work
Es trabajo intensivo de mano de obra *(m)*
It lavoro ad alto contenuto di mano d'opera *(m)*
Pt trabalho com muita mão de obra *(m)*

travail de collage *(m)* Fr
De Klebeumbruch-Arbeit *(f)*
En paste-up work
Es trabajo de montaje

travail en cours *(m)* Fr
De in Arbeit befindlich
En work-in-progress
Es trabajo en ejecución *(m)*
It lavoro in corso *(m)*
Pt progresso de adaptação ao trabalho *(m)*

travail en tandem *(m)* Fr
De Tandemarbeit *(f)*
En tandem work
Es trabajo en tandem *(m)*
It lavoro in tandem *(m)*
Pt trabalho em tandem *(m)*

travel book En
De Reisebuch *(n)*
Es libro de viajes *(m)*
Fr livre touristique *(m)*
It libro di viaggio *(m)*
Pt livro de viagens *(m)*

travel guide En
De Reiseleitfaden *(m)*
Es guía de viajes *(f)*
Fr guide touristique *(m)*
It guida turistica *(f)*
Pt guia turístico *(m)*

trazos inferiores *(m pl)* Es
De Unterlängen *(pl)*
En descenders (of letter) *pl n*
Fr jambages *(m pl)*
It lettere discendenti *(f pl)*
Pt traços inferiores *(m pl)*

tréma *(m)* n Fr
De Diäresis *(f)*
En diaeresis
Es diéresis *(f)*
It dieresi *(f)*
Pt diérese *(f)*

trennen *vb* De
En hyphenate
Es separar con guión
Fr mettre un trait d'union

It legare con trattino
Pt pôr um traço de união

Trennung *(f)* n De
En hyphenation
Es separación con guiones *(f)*
Fr coupure *(f)*
It legatura con trattino *(f)*
Pt colocação de um traço de união *(f)*

Trennungs-Programm *(n)* De
Am hyphenation program
En hyphenation programme
Es programa de separación con guiones *(m)*
Fr programme de division automatique *(f)*
It programma di legatura con trattino *(m)*
Pt programa de hifenação *(m)*

Trennungsregelb *(pl)* De
En hyphenation rules
Es normas de separación con guiones *(f pl)*
Fr règles de coupure *(f pl)*
It regole di legatura con trattino *(f pl)*
Pt regras de hifenação *(f pl)*

trichromie *(f)* n Fr
Am three-color printing
De Dreifarbendruck *(m)*
En three-colour printing
Es tricromía *(f)*
It stampa a tre colori *(f)*
Pt impressão a três cores *(f)*

tricromía *(f)* n Es
Am three-color printing
De Dreifarbendruck *(m)*
En three-colour printing
Fr trichromie *(f)*
It stampa a tre colori *(f)*
Pt impressão a três cores *(f)*

tricromía de tramado indirecto *(f)* Es
De indirektes Verfahren *(n)*
En indirect process
Fr procédé indirect *(m)*
It procedimento indiretto *(m)*
Pt processo indirecto *(m)*

trim *vb* En
De beschneiden
Es cortar
Fr ébarber
It rifilare
Pt aparar

trim marks En
De Beschnitt-Markierungen *(pl)*
Es marcas de recorte *(f pl)*
Fr repères de rognage *(m pl)*
It segni per rifilatura *(m pl)*
Pt marcas de aparar *(f pl)*

trimmed page size En
De Beschnittgröβe *(f)*
Es tamaño de página cortada *(m)*
Fr format fini *(m)*
It dimensioni di pagina rifilata *(f pl)*
Pt tamanho de página aparada *(m)*

trimming *n* En
De Beschneiden *(n)*
Es recorte *(m)*
Fr rognage *(m)*
It rifilatura *(f)*
Pt aparagem *(f)*

Trockenfolien-kaschierung *(f) n* De
En dry laminating
Es laminación en seco *(f)*
Fr stratification à sec *(f)*
It laminazione a secco *(f)*
Pt laminagem a seco *(f)*

Trockenoffset *(m) n* De
En dry offset
Es offset seco *(m)*
Fr offset à sec *(m)*

It offset secco *(m)*
Pt offset seco *(m)*

Trockner *(m) n* De
En drier
Es secante *(m)*
Fr sécheur *(m)*
It essiccante *(m)*
Pt secador *(m)*

troquel *(m) n* Es
De Prägestock *(m)*
En die
Fr étampe *(f)*
It stampo *(m)*
Pt matriz *(f)*

tub-sized paper En
De oberflächengeleimtes Papier *(n)*
Es papel encolado en tina *(m)*
Fr papier collé à la cuve *(m)*
It carta imbozzimata in tino *(f)*
Pt papel encolado em tina *(m)*

turnover *n* En
De Umsatz *(m)*
Es cifra de negocios *(f)*
Fr chiffre d'affaires *(m)*
It fatturato *(m)*
Pt movimento *(m)*

tutti i diritti riservati It
De alle Rechte vorbehalten
En all rights reserved
Es reservados todos los derechos
Fr tous droits réservés
Pt todos os direitos reservados

two-color press Am
De Zweifarbenpresse *(f)*
En two-colour press
Es prensa bicolor *(f)*
Fr presse à bichromie *(f)*
It macchina da stampa a due colori *(f)*
Pt prensa a duas cores *(f)*

two-color printing Am
De Zweifarbendruck *(m)*
En two-colour printing
Es impresión bicolor *(f)*
Fr bichromie *(f)*

It stampa a due colori *(f)*
Pt impressão a duas cores *(f)*

two-colour press En
Am two-color press
De Zweifarbenpresse *(f)*
Es prensa bicolor *(f)*
Fr presse à bichromie *(f)*
It macchina da stampa a due colori *(f)*
Pt prensa a duas cores *(f)*

two-colour printing En
Am two-color printing
De Zweifarbendruck *(m)*
Es impresión bicolor *(f)*
Fr bichromie *(f)*
It stampa a due colori *(f)*
Pt impressão a duas cores *(f)*

two-revolution press En
De Zweitourenmaschine *(f)*
Es prensa de doble revolución *(f)*
Fr presse à double impression *(f)*
It macchina da stampa a due giri *(f)*
Pt prensa a duas rotações *(f)*

type *n* En
De Schrift *(f)*
Es tipo *(m)*
Fr caractère d'imprimerie *(m)*
It carattere tipografico *(m)*
Pt tipo *(m)*

typecasting *n* En
De Schriftguβ *(m)*
Es composición mecanotípica *(f)*
Fr fonte de caractères *(f)*
It fusione dei caratteri *(f)*
Pt fundição de tipos (processo) *(f)*

type depth En
De Schrifttiefe *(f)*
Es profundidad del tipo *(f)*
Fr profondeur *(f)*

It profondità del carattere *(f)*
Pt profundidade de tipo *(f)*

type distribution En
De Schriftverteilung *(f)*
Es distribución de tipos *(f)*
Fr distribution des caractères *(f)*
It distribuzione del carattere *(m)*
Pt distribuição de tipos *(f)*

typeface *n* En
De Schrifttyp *(m)*
Es ojo del tipo *(m)*
Fr oeil d'un caractère *(m)*
It occhio del carattere *(m)*
Pt olho de tipo *(m)*

type foundry En
De Schriftgieβerei *(f)*
Es fundición de tipos *(f)*
Fr clicherie *(f)*
It fonderia di caratteri *(f)*
Pt fundição de tipos (casa) *(f)*

type height En
De Schrifthöhe *(f)*
Es altura del tipo *(f)*
Fr hauteur de caractère *(f)*
It altezza tipografica *(f)*
Pt altura de tipo *(f)*

type metal En
De Schriftmetall *(n)*
Es metal de imprenta *(m)*
Fr métal d'imprimerie *(m)*
It lega per caratteri *(f)*
Pt metal para tipos *(m)*

Typenornamente *(pl) n* De
En printer's ornaments
Es adornos de imprenta *(m pl)*
Fr vignette typo *(f)*
It ornamenti dello stampatore *(m pl)*
Pt ornamentações de impressão *(f pl)*

typescale *n* En
De Schriftsatz-Lineal *(n)*
Es escala de tipos *(f)*
Fr typomètre *(m)*
It tipometro *(m)*
Pt tipómetro *(m)*

typescript *n* En
De Maschinenschrift *(f)*
Es escrito a máquina *(m)*
Fr manuscrit
   dactylographié *(m)*
It dattiloscritto *(m)*
Pt dactilografado *(m)*

typesetter (company) *n*
   En
De Schriftsetzerei *(f)*
Es taller de composición
   (m)
Fr maison de
   composition *(f)*
It compositoria *(f)*
Pt empresa de
   composição *(f)*

typesetting *n* En
De Schriftsatz *(m)*
Es composición
   tipográfica *(f)*
Fr composition
   typographique *(f)*
It composizione
   tipografica *(f)*
Pt composição de tipos
   (f)

typesetting machine En
De Setzmaschine *(f)*
Es máquina de
   composición;
   máquina de
   componer *(f)*
Fr machine à
   composer;
   composeuse *(f)*
It compositrice *(f)*
Pt compositora de
   tipos; máquina de
   composição *(f)*

type weight En
De Schriftgewicht *(n)*
Es peso del tipo *(m)*
Fr poids de caractère
   (m)
It peso del carattere
   (m)
Pt peso de tipo *(m)*

typewriter *n* En
De Schreibmaschine *(f)*
Es mecanógrafa *(f)*
Fr machine à écrire *(f)*
It macchina da scrivere
   (f)
Pt máquina de escrever
   (f)

typewriter composition
   En
De Schreibmaschinen-
   Satz *(m)*
Es composición
   mecanográfica *(f)*
Fr composition à la
   machine à écrire *(f)*
It composizione su
   macchina da scrivere
   (f)
Pt composição com
   máquina de escrever
   (f)

typing *n* En
De Tippen *(n)*
Es mecanografiado *(m)*
Fr dactylographie *(f)*
It scrivere a macchina
   (m)
Pt dactilografia *(f)*

typist *n* En
De Typistin *(f)*
Es mecanografía *(f)*
Fr dactylographe *(f)*
It dattilografa *(f)*
Pt dactilógrafa *(f)*

Typistin *(f) n* De
En typist
Es mecanografía *(f)*
Fr dactylographe *(f)*
It dattilografa *(f)*
Pt dactilógrafa *(f)*

typographe *(m) n* Fr
De Setzer *(m)*
En compositor
Es compositor *(m)*
It compositore *(m)*
Pt compositor *(m)*

typographical error En
De typographischer
   Fehler *(m)*
Es error tipográfico *(m)*
Fr erreur typographique
   (f)
It errore tipografico *(m)*
Pt erro tipográfico *(m)*

typographic design En
De Satzgestaltung *(f)*
Es diseño tipográfico
   (m)
Fr représentation
   typographique *(f)*
It disegno tipografico
   (m)
Pt desenho tipográfico
   (m)

typographic designer En
De Satzgestalter *(m)*
Es diseñador tipográfico
   (m)
Fr concepteur
   typographique *(m)*
It disegnatore
   tipografico *(m)*
Pt desenhador
   tipográfico *(m)*

typographie *(f) n* Fr
De Typographie *(f)*
En typography
Es tipografía *(f)*
It tipografia *(f)*
Pt tipografia *(f)*

Typographie *(f) n* De
En typography
Es tipografía *(f)*
Fr typographie *(f)*
It tipografia *(f)*
Pt tipografia *(f)*

typographischer Fehler
   (m) De
En typographical error
Es error tipográfico *(m)*
Fr erreur typographique
   (f)
It errore tipografico *(m)*
Pt erro tipográfico *(m)*

typography *n* En
De Typographie *(f)*
Es tipografía *(f)*
Fr typographie *(f)*
It tipografia *(f)*
Pt tipografia *(f)*

typomètre *(m) n* Fr
De Schriftsatz-Lineal *(n)*
En typescale
Es escala de tipos *(f)*
It tipometro *(m)*
Pt tipómetro *(m)*

U

überarbeiten *vb* De
En update
Es actualizar
Fr mettre à jour
It aggiornare
Pt actualizar

überarbeitet *adj* De
En updated
Es actualizado
Fr mis à jour
It aggiornato
Pt actualizado

Überhang *(m) n* De
En kern
Es talud *(m)*
Fr crénage *(m)*
It sporgenza *(f)*
Pt saliência do corpo do
   tipo *(f)*

überlanger Satz *(m)* De
En overmatter
Es material sobrante *(m)*
Fr surimpression *(f)*
It composizione
   sovrastante *(f)*
Pt matéria que sobra *(f)*

überprüfen *vb* De
En check
Es comprobar
Fr vérifier
It verificare
Pt verificar

Überschrift *(f) n* De
En headline (of
   newspaper)
Es titular *(m)*
Fr titre *(m)*
It titolo di testa *(m)*
Pt manchete *(m)*

übersetzen *vb* De
En translate
Es traducir
Fr traduire
It tradurre
Pt traduzir

Übersetzer *(m) n* De
En translator
Es traductor *(m)*

Fr traducteur *(m)*
It traduttore *(m)*
Pt tradutor *(m)*

übersetzte Ausgabe *(f)*
    De
En translation edition
Es edición de traducción
    (f)
Fr édition de
    traductions *(f)*
It edizione tradotta *(f)*
Pt edição de tradução
    (f)

Übersetzung *(f)* n De
En translation
Es traducción *(f)*
Fr traduction *(f)*
It traduzione *(f)*
Pt tradução *(f)*

Übersicht *(f)* n De
En précis
Es resumen *(m)*
Fr précis *(m)*
It riassunto *(m)*
Pt resumo *(m)*

Übervorrat *(m)* De
En overstocks *pl* n
Es existencias excesivas
    (f pl)
Fr stock excessif *(m)*
It giacenze *(f pl)*
Pt existências que
    sobram *(f pl)*

ulteriori letture *(f pl)* It
De weitere Literatur *(f)*
En further reading
Es relectura *(f)*
Fr lectures
    complémentaires *(f
    pl)*
Pt leitura adicional *(f)*

umbrechen *vb* De
En make up
Es compaginar
Fr mettre en pages
It compaginare
Pt compaginar

Umbrechen *(n)* n De
En over-running
Es recorrido *(m)*
Fr remaniement *(m)*
It rimaneggiamento *(m)*
Pt acto de recorrer *(m)*

umettatore *(m)* n It
De Feuchtwalze *(f)*
En damper
Es mojador *(m)*
Fr rouleau mouilleur *(m)*
Pt molhador *(m)*

Umkehrfilm *(m)* n De
En reversal film
Es película reversible *(f)*
Fr film noir au blanc *(m)*
It pellicola invertibile *(f)*
Pt película de inversão
    (f)

Umsatz *(m)* n De
En turnover
Es cifra de negocios *(f)*
Fr chiffre d'affaires *(m)*
It fatturato *(m)*
Pt movimento *(m)*

Umschlag *(m)* n De
En jacket
Es camisa *(f)*
Fr jaquette *(f)*
It sovracopertina *(f)*
Pt sobrecapa *(f)*

Umschlagentwurf *(m)* n
    De
En jacket design
Es diseño de la
    sobrecubierta *(m)*
Fr conception de la
    jaquette *(f)*
It disegno della
    sovracopertina *(m)*
Pt desenho da
    sobrecapa *(m)*

Umschlagklappe *(f)* n De
En jacket flap
Es solapa de la cubierta
    (f)
Fr rabat de la jaquette
    (m)
It risvolto della
    sovracopertina *(m)*
Pt aba da sobrecapa *(f)*

Umschlagpapier *(n)* n De
En cover paper
Es papel para cubiertas
    (m)
Fr papier à couverture
    (m)
It carta per copertine *(f)*
Pt papel de cobertura
    (m)

**Umschlag-
    Reklamestreifen**
    (m) n De
En jacket blurb
Es reseña en la cubierta
    (f)
Fr manchette sur la
    jaquette *(f)*
It sommario della
    sovracopertina *(m)*
Pt sinopse de
    sobrecapa *(f)*

Umschlag-Satzmontage
    (f) De
En jacket artwork
Es trabajo artistíco de la
    sobrecubierta *(m)*
Fr illustration de la
    jaquette *(f)*
It menabò per
    sovracopertina *(m)*
Pt arte da sobrecapa
    (m)

unciales *(f pl)* Es
De Unzialbuchstaben *(pl)*
En uncials *pl* n
Fr onciales *(f pl)*
It unciali *(m pl)*
Pt letras unciales *(f pl)*

unciali *(m pl)* It
De Unzialbuchstaben *(pl)*
En uncials *pl* n
Es unciales *(f pl)*
Fr onciales *(f pl)*
Pt letras unciales *(f pl)*

uncials *pl* n En
De Unzialbuchstaben *(pl)*
Es unciales *(f pl)*
Fr onciales *(f pl)*
It unciali *(m pl)*
Pt letras unciales *(f pl)*

undercutting *n* En
De Unterätzung *(f)*
Es sobremordido *(m)*
Fr massicotage *(m)*
It intaglio *(m)*
Pt sobremordicação *(f)*

underlay *n* En
De Unterlage *(f)*
Es alza bajo el tipo *(f)*
Fr hausse *(f)*
It alzo *(m)*
Pt calço *(m)*

underline *vb* En
De unterstreichen
Es subrayar
Fr souligner
It sottolineare
Pt subraiar

Und-Zeichen *(n)* n De
En ampersand
Es y abreviada *(f)*
Fr et commercial *(m)*
It congiunzione
    commerciale *(f)*
Pt e comercial *(f)*

unearned balance En
De Saldo unverdient *(m)*
Es saldo no devengado
    (m)
Fr solde pas encore
    gagné *(m)*
It saldo non ancora
    guadagnato *(m)*
Pt saldo ainda não
    ganhado *(m)*

ungeleimtes Papier *(n)*
    De
En waterleaf
Es papel no encolado
    (m)
Fr papier non collé *(m)*
It carta non
    imbozzimata *(f)*
Pt papel absorvente *(m)*

ungrammatical *adj* En
De nicht grammatisch
Es no gramatical
Fr non grammatical
It non grammaticale
Pt não gramatical

**unidad de
    fotopresentación**
    (f) Es
De Photodisplay-Gerät
    (n)
En photodisplay unit
Fr unité de photodisplay
    (f)
It unità di photodisplay
    (f)
Pt unidade de
    foto-display *(f)*

unidad de visualización
    (f) Es
De Sichtanzeigegerät *(n)*
En visual-display unit
    (VDU)

Fr unité de visualisation
(f)
It unità di
visualizzazione *(f)*
Pt unidade de
visulização *(f)*

unidade de foto-display
(f) Pt
De Photodisplay-Gerät
(n)
En photodisplay unit
Es unidad de
fotopresentación *(f)*
Fr unité de photodisplay
(f)
It unità di photodisplay
(f)

unidade de visulização
(f) Pt
De Sichtanzeigegerät *(n)*
En visual-display unit
(VDU)
Es unidad de
visualización *(f)*
Fr unité de visualisation
(f)
It unità di
visualizzazione *(f)*

uniformazione di foglie
(f) It
De Aufstoβen *(n)*
En knocking-up (of
paper)
Es emparejamiento de
hojas *(m)*
Fr taquage des feuilles
(m)
Pt empilhamento de
folhas *(m)*

unità di photodisplay *(f)*
It
De Photodisplay-Gerät
(n)
En photodisplay unit
Es unidad de
fotopresentación *(f)*
Fr unité de photodisplay
(f)
Pt unidade de
foto-display *(f)*

unità di visualizzazione
(f) It
De Sichtanzeigegerät *(n)*
En visual-display unit
(VDU)
Es unidad de
visualización *(f)*

Fr unité de visualisation
(f)
Pt unidade de
visulização *(f)*

unit cost En
De Einheitskosten *(pl)*
Es coste unitario *(m)*
Fr coût unitaire *(m)*
It costo unitario *(m)*
Pt custo unitário *(m)*

unité de photodisplay *(f)*
Fr
De Photodisplay-Gerät
(n)
En photodisplay unit
Es unidad de
fotopresentación *(f)*
It unità di photodisplay
(f)
Pt unidade de
foto-display *(f)*

unité de visualisation *(f)*
Fr
De Sichtanzeigegerät *(n)*
En visual-display unit
(VDU)
Es unidad de
visualización *(f)*
It unità di
visualizzazione *(f)*
Pt unidade de
visulização *(f)*

universidad *(f)* n Es
De Universität *(f)*
En university
Fr université *(f)*
It università *(f)*
Pt universidade *(f)*

universidade *(f)* n Pt
De Universität *(f)*
En university
Es universidad *(f)*
Fr université *(f)*
It università *(f)*

università *(f)* n It
De Universität *(f)*
En university
Es universidad *(f)*
Fr université *(f)*
Pt universidade *(f)*

Universität *(f)* n De
En university
Es universidad *(f)*
Fr université *(f)*

It università *(f)*
Pt universidade *(f)*

Universitätsbücherei *(f)*
n De
En university library
Es biblioteca de
universidad *(f)*
Fr bibliothèque
universitaire *(f)*
It biblioteca
universitaria *(f)*
Pt biblioteca
universitária *(f)*

Universitäts-Druckerei
(f) n De
En university press
Es prensa universitaria
(f)
Fr presse universitaire
(f)
It stampa universitaria
(f)
Pt imprensa
universitária *(f)*

université *(f)* n Fr
De Universität *(f)*
En university
Es universidad *(f)*
It università *(f)*
Pt universidade *(f)*

university n En
De Universität *(f)*
Es universidad *(f)*
Fr université *(f)*
It università *(f)*
Pt universidade *(f)*

university library En
De Universitätsbücherei
(f)
Es biblioteca de
universidad *(f)*
Fr bibliothèque
universitaire *(f)*
It biblioteca
universitaria *(f)*
Pt biblioteca
universitária *(f)*

university press En
De Universitäts-
Druckerei *(f)*
Es prensa universitaria
(f)
Fr presse universitaire
(f)
It stampa universitaria
(f)

It università *(f)*
Pt universidade *(f)*

Pt imprensa
universitária *(f)*

unjustified text En
De Schrägsatz *(m)*
Es texto sin justificar *(m)*
Fr composition en
drapeau *(f)*
It testo non giustificato
(m)
Pt texto não justificado
(m)

unscharfe Kanten *(pl)*
De
En blurred edges
Es bordes borrosos *(m
pl)*
Fr bords abîmés *(m pl)*
It bordi sfocati *(m pl)*
Pt bordos borrados *(m
pl)*

unsewn binding En
De nicht geheftete
Bindung *(f)*
Es encuadernación sin
coser *(f)*
Fr reliure sans couture
(f)
It rilegatura non cucita
(f)
Pt encadernação não
cosida *(f)*

Unterätzung *(f)* n De
En undercutting
Es sobremordido *(m)*
Fr massicotage *(m)*
It intaglio *(m)*
Pt sobremordicação *(f)*

**unter der Leitung eines
Redakteurs
herausgeben** De
En subedit
Es redactar
Fr mettre au point
It redigere
Pt subcorrigir

Unterkasten *(m)* n De
En lower case
Es caja baja *(f)*
Fr bas de caisse *(m)*
It bassa cassa *(f)*
Pt caixa baixa *(f)*

Unterlage *(f)* n De
En underlay
Es alza bajo el tipo *(f)*

Fr hausse *(f)*
It alzo *(m)*
Pt calço *(m)*

Unterlängen *(pl)* De
En descenders (of letter)
pl n
Es trazos inferiores *(m pl)*
Fr jambages *(m pl)*
It lettere discendenti *(f pl)*
Pt traços inferiores *(m pl)*

Unterschlag *(m) n* De
En tail (of page)
Es margen inferior *(m)*
Fr marge de pied *(f)*
It piede (di pagina) *(m)*
Pt pé (de página) *(m)*

unterstreichen *vb* De
En underline
Es subrayar
Fr souligner
It sottolineare
Pt subraiar

Untertitel *(m) n* De
En alternate title;
subtitle
Es subtítulo *(m)*
Fr sous-titre *(m)*
It sottotitolo; titolo
alternato *(m)*
Pt subtítulo; título
alternativo *(m)*

Unzialbuchstaben *(pl)*
De
En uncials *pl n*
Es unciales *(f pl)*
Fr onciales *(f pl)*
It unciali *(m pl)*
Pt letras unciales *(f pl)*

update *vb* En
De überarbeiten
Es actualizar
Fr mettre à jour
It aggiornare
Pt actualizar

updated *adj* En
De überarbeitet
Es actualizado
Fr mis à jour
It aggiornato
Pt actualizado

upper case En
De Oberkasten *(m)*
Es caja alta *(f)*
Fr haut de casse *(m)*
It alta cassa
Pt caixa alta *(f)*

upper-case letter En
De großer Buchstabe *(m)*
Es letra mayúscula *(f)*
Fr lettre de haut de casse *(f)*
It lettera maiuscola *(f)*
Pt letra de caixa alta *(f)*

usage américain *(m)* Fr
De amerikanischer
Sprachgebrauch *(m)*
En American usage
Es uso americano *(m)*
It uso americano *(m)*
Pt costume americano *(m)*

usage anglais *(m)* Fr
De britischer
Sprachgebrauch *(m)*
En British usage
Es uso británico *(m)*
It uso britannico *(m)*
Pt costume britânico *(m)*

usage familier *(m)* Fr
De informeller Gebrauch *(m)*
En informal usage
Es uso informal *(m)*
It uso informale *(m)*
Pt utilização informal *(f)*

uso americano *(m)* Es, It
De amerikanischer
Sprachgebrauch *(m)*
En American usage
Fr usage américain *(m)*
Pt costume americano *(m)*

uso británico *(m)* Es
De britischer
Sprachgebrauch *(m)*
En British usage
Fr usage anglais *(m)*
It uso britannico *(m)*
Pt costume britânico *(m)*

uso britannico *(m)* It
De britischer
Sprachgebrauch *(m)*
En British usage
Es uso británico *(m)*
Fr usage anglais *(m)*
Pt costume britânico *(m)*

uso formal *(m)* Es
De Formalgebrauch *(m)*
En formal usage
Fr bon usage *(m)*
It uso formale *(m)*
Pt utilização formal *(f)*

uso formale *(m)* It
De Formalgebrauch *(m)*
En formal usage
Es uso formal *(m)*
Fr bon usage *(m)*
Pt utilização formal *(f)*

uso informal *(m)* Es
De informeller Gebrauch *(m)*
En informal usage
Fr usage familier *(m)*
It uso informale *(m)*
Pt utilização informal *(f)*

uso informale *(m)* It
De informeller Gebrauch *(m)*
En informal usage
Es uso informal *(m)*
Fr usage familier *(m)*
Pt utilização informal *(f)*

utilização formal *(f)* Pt
De Formalgebrauch *(m)*
En formal usage
Es uso formal *(m)*
Fr bon usage *(m)*
It uso formale *(m)*

utilização informal *(f)* Pt
De informeller Gebrauch *(m)*
En informal usage
Es uso informal *(m)*
Fr usage familier *(m)*
It uso informale *(m)*

V

vaciado a la impresora *(m)* Es
De Ausdruck *(m)*
En printout
Fr sortie d'imprimante *(f)*
It printout *(m)*
Pt impressão em positivo directo *(f)*

vacuum frame En
De Vakuumrahmen *(m)*
Es prensa al vacío *(f)*
Fr chassis pneumatique *(m)*
It telaio a vuoto *(m)*
Pt caixilho de vácuo *(m)*

Vakantseite *(f) n* De
En blank page
Es página en blanco *(f)*
Fr page blanche *(f)*
It pagina bianca *(f)*
Pt página em branco *(f)*

Vakuumrahmen *(m) n* De
En vacuum frame
Es prensa al vacío *(f)*
Fr chassis pneumatique *(m)*
It telaio a vuoto *(m)*
Pt caixilho de vácuo *(m)*

vale lo tachado Es
De Stehen lassen
En stet
Fr à maintenir
It vive
Pt stet

valorar *vb* Es
De Preis festsetzen
En price
Fr fixer un prix
It prezzare
Pt marcar o preço

value-added tax (VAT) En
De Mehrwertsteuer (Mwst) *(f)*
Es impuesto sobre el valor añadido *(m)*
Fr taxe sur la valeur ajoutée (TVA) *(f)*

It imposta sul valore
    aggiunto (IVA) *(f)*
Pt imposto sobre valor
    aduzido *(m)*

valutazione *(f) n* It
De Kostenvoranschlag
    (m)
En estimate
Es estimación *(f)*
Fr devis *(m)*
Pt estimativa *(f)*

vantaggio *(m) n* It
De Satzschiff *(n)*
En galley
Es galera *(f)*
Fr galée *(f)*
Pt galé *(f)*

variabler Abstand *(m)*
    De
En variable space
Es espacio variable *(m)*
Fr espace variable *(m)*
It spazio variabile *(m)*
Pt espaço variável *(m)*

variable space En
De variabler Abstand *(m)*
Es espacio variable *(m)*
Fr espace variable *(m)*
It spazio variabile *(m)*
Pt espaço variável *(m)*

varnish *n* En
De Lack *(m)*
Es barniz *(m)*
Fr vernis *(m)*
It vernice *(f)*
Pt verniz *(m)*

vélin *(m) n* Fr
De Velinpapier *(n)*
En vellum
Es vitela *(f)*
It cartapecora *(f)*
Pt velino *(m)*

vélin à l'antique *(m)* Fr
De Antikdruckpapier *(n)*
En antique wove
Es papel avitelado
    antiguo *(m)*
It carta retinata tipo
    antico *(f)*
Pt tecido estilo antigo
    (m)

vélin azur *(m)* Fr
De Azur-Velinpapier *(n)*
En azure wove
Es azul celeste avitelado
    (m)
It carta retinata azzura
    (f)
Pt tecido anilado *(m)*

vélin crème *(m)* Fr
De mattgelbes
    Velinpapier *(n)*
En cream wove paper
Es papel avitelado
    crema *(m)*
It velino cremo *(m)*
Pt papel tecido
    enrugado *(m)*

velino *(m) n* Pt
De Velinpapier *(n)*
En vellum
Es vitela *(f)*
Fr vélin *(m)*
It cartapecora *(f)*

velino cremo *(m)* It
De mattgelbes
    Velinpapier *(n)*
En cream wove paper
Es papel avitelado
    crema *(m)*
Fr vélin crème *(m)*
Pt papel tecido
    enrugado *(m)*

Velinpapier *(n) n* De
En vellum; wove paper
Es vitela *(f)*
Fr vélin *(m)*
It cartapecora *(f)*
Pt velino *(m)*

vellum *n* En
De Velinpapier *(n)*
Es vitela *(f)*
Fr vélin *(m)*
It cartapecora *(f)*
Pt velino *(m)*

venda de livros *(f)* Pt
De Buchverkauf *(m)*
En bookselling
Es venta de libros *(f)*
Fr commerce de
    librairie *(m)*
It vendita di libri *(f)*

venda por correio *(f)* Pt
De Postwurfwerbung *(f)*
En direct-mail selling

Es venta directa por
    correo *(f)*
Fr vente directe par
    correspondance *(f)*
It vendite per
    corrispondenza *(f pl)*

vendas *(f pl)* Pt
De Verkauf *(m)*
En sales *pl n*
Es ventas *(f pl)*
Fr ventes *(f pl)*
It vendite *(f pl)*

vendas a retalho *(f pl)* Pt
De Einzelhandels-
    Verkäufe *(pl)*
En retail sales
Es ventas al por menor *(f
    pl)*
Fr vente au détail *(f)*
It vendite al minuto *(f
    pl)*

vendas no estrangeiro *(f
    pl)* Pt
De Auslandsumsätze *(pl)*
En foreign sales *pl n*
Es ventas extranjeras *(f
    pl)*
Fr ventes à l'étranger *(f
    pl)*
It servizio vendite
    estero *(m)*

vendedor *(m) n* Es, Pt
De Vertreter *(m)*
En salesman
Fr vendeur *(m)*
It venditore *(m)*

vendedor de libros *(m)*
    Es
De Buchhändler *(m)*
En bookseller
Fr libraire *(m)*
It libraio *(m)*
Pt livreiro *(m)*

vendeur *(m) n* Fr
De Vertreter *(m)*
En salesman
Es vendedor *(m)*
It venditore *(m)*
Pt vendedor *(m)*

vendita di libri *(f)* It
De Buchverkauf *(m)*
En bookselling
Es venta de libros *(f)*

Fr commerce de
    librairie *(m)*
Pt venda de livros *(f)*

vendite *(f pl)* It
De Verkauf *(m)*
En sales *pl n*
Es ventas *(f pl)*
Fr ventes *(f pl)*
Pt vendas *(f pl)*

vendite al minuto *(f pl)* It
De Einzelhandels-
    Verkäufe *(pl)*
En retail sales
Es ventas al por menor *(f
    pl)*
Fr vente au détail *(f)*
Pt vendas a retalho *(f pl)*

**vendite per
    corrispondenza** *(f
    pl)* It
De Postwurfwerbung *(f)*
En direct-mail selling
Es venta directa por
    correo *(f)*
Fr vente directe par
    correspondance *(f)*
Pt venda por correio *(f)*

vendite per posta *(f)* It
De Versandhausauftrag
    (m)
En mail order
Es pedido por correo
    (m)
Fr vente par
    correspondance *(f)*
Pt encomenda por
    correio *(f)*

venditore *(m) n* It
De Vertreter *(m)*
En salesman
Es vendedor *(m)*
Fr vendeur *(m)*
Pt vendedor *(m)*

venta de libros *(f)* Es
De Buchverkauf *(m)*
En bookselling
Fr commerce de
    librairie *(m)*
It vendita di libri *(f)*
Pt venda de livros *(f)*

venta directa por correo
    (f) Es
De Postwurfwerbung *(f)*
En direct-mail selling

Fr vente directe par
   correspondance *(f)*
It vendite per
   corrispondenza *(f pl)*
Pt venda por correio *(f)*

ventas *(f pl)* Es
De Verkauf *(m)*
En sales *pl n*
Fr ventes *(f pl)*
It vendite *(f pl)*
Pt vendas *(f pl)*

ventas al por menor *(f*
   pl) Es
De Einzelhandels-
   Verkäufe *(pl)*
En retail sales
Fr vente au détail *(f)*
It vendite al minuto *(f*
   pl)
Pt vendas a retalho *(f pl)*

ventas extranjeras *(f pl)*
   Es
De Auslandsumsätze *(pl)*
En foreign sales *pl n*
Fr ventes à l´étranger *(f*
   pl)
It servizio vendite
   estero *(m)*
Pt vendas no
   estrangeiro *(f pl)*

vente au détail *(f)* Fr
De Einzelhandels-
   Verkäufe *(pl)*
En retail sales
Es ventas al por menor *(f*
   pl)
It vendite al minuto *(f*
   pl)
Pt vendas a retalho *(f pl)*

vente avec possibilité
   de rendre *(f)* Fr
De Kauf oder Rückgabe
   (m)
En sale-or-return basis
Es base de ventas o
   devoluciones *(f)*
It base venduto o reso
   (f)
Pt base de venda ou
   devolução *(f)*

vente directe par
   correspondance *(f)*
   Fr
De Postwurfwerbung *(f)*
En direct-mail selling

Es venta directa por
   correo *(f)*
It vendite per
   corrispondenza *(f pl)*
Pt venda por correio *(f)*

vente par
   correspondance *(f)*
   Fr
De Versandhausauftrag
   (m)
En mail order
Es pedido por correo
   (m)
It vendite per posta *(f)*
Pt encomenda por
   correio *(f)*

ventes *(f pl)* Fr
De Verkauf *(m)*
En sales *pl n*
Es ventas *(f pl)*
It vendite *(f pl)*
Pt vendas *(f pl)*

ventes à l'étranger *(f pl)*
   Fr
De Auslandsumsätze *(pl)*
En foreign sales *pl n*
Es ventas extranjeras *(f*
   pl)
It servizio vendite
   estero *(m)*
Pt vendas no
   estrangeiro *(f pl)*

veraltet *adj* De
En out of date
Es anticuado
Fr périmé
It superato
Pt desactualizado

verarbeiten *vb* De
En process
Es procesar
Fr traiter
It trattare
Pt tratar

Verfahren *(n) n* De
En process
Es procedimiento *(m)*
Fr procédé *(m)*
It procedimento *(m)*
Pt processo *(m)*

Verfahrensblau *(n) n* De
En process blue
Es azul de tricromía *(m)*

Fr bleu d´impression
   couleur *(m)*
It azzurro di tricromia
   (m)
Pt azul para policromia
   (m)

Verfahrensfarben *(pl) n*
   De
Am process colors
En process colours
Es colores para
   policromía *(m pl)*
Fr polychromie *(f)*
It colori per policromia
   (m pl)
Pt cores para policromia
   (f pl)

Verfahrensgelb *(n) n* De
En process yellow
Es amarillo de tricromía
   (m)
Fr jaune d´impression
   couleur *(m)*
It giallo di tricromia *(m)*
Pt amarelo para
   policromia *(m)*

Verfahrensrot *(n) n* De
En process red
Es rojo de tricromía *(m)*
Fr rouge d´impression
   couleur *(m)*
It rosso di tricromia *(m)*
Pt vermelho para
   policromia *(m)*

Verfasser *(m) n* De
En author
Es autor *(m)*
Fr auteur *(m)*
It autore *(m)*
Pt autor *(m)*

Verfasservertrag *(m) n*
   De
En author´s agreement
Es contrato de autor *(m)*
Fr contrat d´auteur *(m)*
It accordo coll´autore
   (m)
Pt acordo do autor *(m)*

Verfasser-Werbetour *(f)*
   De
En author promotion
   tour
Es viaje de promoción
   del autor *(m)*
Fr voyage promotionnel
   d´auteur *(m)*

It itinerario
   promozionale
   dell´autore *(m)*
Pt viagem de promoção
   de autor *(f)*

Verfilmungsrechte *(pl)*
   De
En film rights *pl n*
Es derechos
   cinematográficos *(m*
   pl)
Fr droits sur le film *(m*
   pl)
It diritti cinematografici
   (m pl)
Pt direitos
   cinematográficos *(m*
   pl)

vergature *(f pl)* It
De Wasserlinien *(f pl)*
En laid lines
Es líneas en papel
   verjurado *(f pl)*
Fr vergeures *(f pl)*
Pt linhas enramadas *(f*
   pl)

Vergépapier *(n)* De
En laid paper
Es papel verjurado *(m)*
Fr papier vergé *(m)*
It carta vergata *(f)*
Pt papel vergé *(m)*

vergeures *(f pl)* Fr
De Wasserlinien *(f pl)*
En laid lines
Es líneas en papel
   verjurado *(f pl)*
It vergature *(f pl)*
Pt linhas enramadas *(f*
   pl)

vergleichen *vb* De
En collate
Es alzar
Fr assembler
It collazionare
Pt rever

vergriffen *adj* De
En out of print
Es agotado
Fr épuisé
It esaurito
Pt esgotado

vergrößern *vb* De
En enlarge
Es ampliar
Fr agrandir
It ingrandire
Pt ampliar

vergrößert *adj* De
En blown up
Es ampliado
Fr agrandi
It ingrandito
Pt ampliado

Vergrößerungsgerät *(n)*
n De
En enlarger
Es ampliadora *(f)*
Fr agrandisseur *(m)*
It ingranditore *(m)*
Pt ampliadora *(f)*

verificar *vb* Pt
De überprüfen
En check
Es comprobar
Fr vérifier
It verificare

verificare *vb* It
De überprüfen
En check
Es comprobar
Fr vérifier
Pt verificar

vérifier *vb* Fr
De überprüfen
En check
Es comprobar
It verificare
Pt verificar

Verkauf *(m)* De
En sales *pl n*
Es ventas *(f pl)*
Fr ventes *(f pl)*
It vendite *(f pl)*
Pt vendas *(f pl)*

Verkäufer *(m)* n De
En sales assistant
Es ayudante de ventas
(m)
Fr commis *(m)*
It commesso *(m)*
Pt ajudante de
vendedor *(m)*

Verkaufsdirektor *(m)* n
De
En sales director
Es director de ventas
(m)
Fr directeur commercial
(m)
It direttore alle vendite
(m)
Pt director de vendas
(m)

Verkaufskampagne *(f)* n
De
En sales campaign
Es campaña de ventas
(f)
Fr campagne de vente
(f)
It campagna di vendita
(f)
Pt campanha comercial
(f)

Verkaufskonferenz *(f)* n
De
En sales conference
Es conferencia de
ventas *(f)*
Fr réunion de vente *(f)*
It conferenza di vendita
(f)
Pt conferência de
vendedores *(f)*

Verkaufsleiter *(m)* n De
En sales manager
Es jefe de ventas *(m)*
Fr chef des ventes *(m)*
It direttore vendite *(m)*
Pt gerente de vendas
(m)

Verkaufsstelle *(f)* n De
En point of sale
Es punto de venta *(m)*
Fr point de vente *(m)*
It punto di vendita *(m)*
Pt ponto de venda *(m)*

Verkaufstellen-Material
(n) n De
En point-of-sale material
Es material para punto
de venta *(m)*
Fr matériel de PLV *(m)*
It materiale per punto
di vendita *(m)*
Pt material de ponto de
venda *(m)*

verkleinern *vb* De
En reduce
Es reducir
Fr réduire
It ridurre
Pt reduzir

Verlag *(m)* n De
En publisher (company)
Es casa editorial *(f)*
Fr maison d'édition *(f)*
It casa editrice *(f)*
Pt casa editorial *(f)*

Verlagswesen *(n)* n De
En publishing
Es editorial *(f)*
Fr commerce de
l'édition *(m)*
It editoria *(f)*
Pt negocio de
publicação *(m)*

verlegen *vb* De
En publish
Es publicar
Fr publier
It pubblicare
Pt publicar

Verleger *(m)* n De
En publisher (person)
Es editor *(m)*
Fr éditeur *(m)*
It editore *(m)*
Pt editor *(m)*

Verleger einer
gemeinsamen
Ausgabe *(m)* De
En co-edition publisher
Es editorial de
coediciones *(f)*
Fr co-éditeur *(m)*
It editore di coedizione
(m)
Pt editorial de coedição
(f)

Verleger von
medizinischen
Veröffent-
lichungen *(m)* De
En medical publisher
Es editora de libros de
medicina *(f)*
Fr éditeur d'ouvrages
médicaux *(m)*
It editore di testi medici
(m)
Pt editor de livros de
medicina *(m)*

Verletzung des
Copyright *(f)* De
En infringement of
copyright
Es violación de los
derechos de autor *(f)*
Fr contrefaçon *(f)*
It violazione di
copyright *(f)*
Pt infracção de um
copyright *(f)*

vermelho para
policromia *(m)* Pt
De Verfahrensrot *(n)*
En process red
Es rojo de tricromía *(m)*
Fr rouge d'impression
couleur *(m)*
It rosso di tricromia *(m)*

vernice *(f)* n It
De Lack *(m)*
En varnish
Es barniz *(m)*
Fr vernis *(m)*
Pt verniz *(m)*

vernis *(m)* n Fr
De Lack *(m)*
En varnish
Es barniz *(m)*
It vernice *(f)*
Pt verniz *(m)*

verniz *(m)* n Pt
De Lack *(m)*
En varnish
Es barniz *(m)*
Fr vernis *(m)*
It vernice *(f)*

Veröffentlichung *(f)* n
De
En publication
Es publicación *(f)*
Fr publication *(f)*
It pubblicazione *(f)*
Pt publicação *(f)*

Veröffentlichung in
Fortsetzungen *(f)*
De
En serialization
Es publicación por
entregas *(f)*
Fr parution en feuilleton
(f)
It riduzione in serie *(f)*
Pt publicação em série
(f)

Veröffentlichungsdaten
  (pl) n De
En publication data
Es datos de publicación
    (m pl)
Fr référence de la
    publication *(f)*
It dati di pubblicazione
    (m pl)
Pt dados de publicação
    (m pl)

Veröffent-
  lichungsdatum *(n)*
  n De
En publication date
Es fecha de publicación
    (f)
Fr date de parution *(f)*
It data di pubblicazione
    (f)
Pt data de publicação *(f)*

Veröffentlichungs-
  programm *(n) n* De
Am publishing program
En publishing
    programme
Es programa de
    publicaciones *(m)*
Fr calendrier des
    parutions *(m)*
It programma editoriale
    (m)
Pt programa de edição
    (m)

verpacken *vb* De
En package
Es empaquetar
Fr empaqueter
It impaccare
Pt empacotar

Verpackungsfirma *(f) n*
  De
En packaging company
Es compañía
    empaquetadora *(f)*
Fr entreprise de
    l'emballage *(f)*
It società
    confezionamento *(m)*
Pt sociedade
    empacotadora *(f)*

Versandhausabteilung
  (f) n De
En mail-order division
Es división de pedidos
    por correo *(f)*
Fr service VPC *(m)*

It reparto vendite per
    posta *(m)*
Pt divisão de
    encomendas por
    correio *(f)*

Versandhausauftrag *(m)*
  n De
En mail order
Es pedido por correo
    (m)
Fr vente par
    correspondance *(f)*
It vendite per posta *(f)*
Pt encomenda por
    correio *(f)*

Versandhausausgabe *(f)*
  n De
En mail-order edition
Es edición para envío
    por correo *(f)*
Fr édition vendue par
    correspondance *(f)*
It edizione per vendite
    per posta *(f)*
Pt edição para
    encomenda por
    correio *(f)*

Versandhausbücher *(pl)*
  De
En mail-order books
Es libros pedidos por
    correo *(m pl)*
Fr livres vendus par
    correspondance *(m
    pl)*
It libri vendite per posta
    (m pl)
Pt livros para
    encomenda por
    correio *(m pl)*

Verschiffung *(f) n* De
En shipping
Es envío *(m)*
Fr expédition *(f)*
It spedizione *(f)*
Pt envio *(m)*

Verschiffungkosten *(pl)*
  De
En shipping costs
Es gastos de envío *(m
    pl)*
Fr frais d'expédition *(m
    pl)*
It costi di spedizione *(m
    pl)*
Pt custos de envio *(m
    pl)*

verschmutzt *adj* De
En shop-soiled
Es sucio
Fr défraîchi
It sporco
Pt sujado na loja

Verschnüren *(n) n* De
En cording
Es encordonado *(m)*
Fr nerf *(m)*
It imputaggio *(m)*
Pt encordoamento *(m)*

versenden *vb* De
En forward
Es expedir
Fr expédier
It spedire
Pt enviar

verso *n* En; Fr, It, Pt *(m)*
De Rückseite *(f)*
Es reverso *(m)*

Vertrag *(m) n* De
En contract
Es contrato *(m)*
Fr contrat *(m)*
It contratto *(m)*
Pt contrato *(m)*

Vertragsbruch *(m) n* De
En breach of contract
Es incumplimiento de
    contrato *(m)*
Fr rupture de contrat *(f)*
It violazione di
    contratto *(f)*
Pt quebra de contrato *(f)*

vertreiben *vb* De
En distribute
Es distribuir
Fr distribuer
It distribuire
Pt distribuir

Vertreter *(m) n* De
En salesman
Es vendedor *(m)*
Fr vendeur *(m)*
It venditore *(m)*
Pt vendedor *(m)*

Vertrieb *(m) n* De
En distribution
Es distribución *(f)*
Fr distribution *(f)*

It distribuzione *(f)*
Pt distribuição *(f)*

Vertriebsnetz *(n) n* De
En distribution network
Es red de distribución *(f)*
Fr réseau de
    distribution *(m)*
It rete di distribuzione
    (f)
Pt rede de distribuição·
    (f)

Vertriebsstelle *(f) n* De
En distributor
Es distribuidor *(m)*
Fr distributeur *(m)*
It distributore *(m)*
Pt distribuidor *(m)*

Vervielfältigungs-
  maschine *(f) n* De
En duplicator
Es duplicadora *(f)*
Fr duplicateur *(m)*
It copialettere *(f)*
Pt duplicadora *(f)*

Vervielfältigungspapier
  (n) n De
En manifold paper
Es papel de copias *(m)*
Fr papier pour formules
    (m)
It carta per duplicatori
    (f)
Pt papel de cópias *(m)*

veste tipografica *(f)* It
De Format *(n)*
En format
Es formato *(m)*
Fr format *(m)*
Pt formato *(m)*

viagem de promoção de
  autor *(f)* Pt
De Verfasser-Werbetour
    (f)
En author promotion
    tour
Es viaje de promoción
    del autor *(m)*
Fr voyage promotionnel
    d'auteur *(m)*
It itinerario
    promozionale
    dell'autore *(m)*

viaje de promoción del autor *(m)* Es
De Verfasser-Werbetour *(f)*
En author promotion tour
Fr voyage promotionnel d´auteur *(m)*
It itinerario promozionale dell´autore *(m)*
Pt viagem de promoção de autor *(f)*

Vierfarbdruck *(m) n* De
Am four-color printing
En four-colour printing
Es cuatricromía *(f)*
Fr quadrichromie *(f)*
It stampa a quattro colori *(f)*
Pt impressão a quatro cores *(f)*

Vierfarbillustration *(f) n* De
Am full-color illustration
En full-colour illustration
Es ilustración a todo color *(f)*
Fr illustration en tous les couleurs *(f)*
It illustrazione a tutti colori *(f)*
Pt ilustração a toda a cor *(f)*

vignetted blocks *pl n* En
De Gelegenheitsvignetta *(f)*
Es fotograbados esfumados *(m pl)*
Fr simili dégradée *(f)*
It clichés à vignette *(m pl)*
Pt blocos de vinheta *(m pl)*

vignettes *(f pl)* Fr
De Anschlußstücke *(pl)*
En borders *pl n*
Es marcos *(m pl)*
It margini *(m pl)*
Pt bordas *(f pl)*

vignette typo *(f)* Fr
De Typenornamente *(pl)*
En printer´s ornaments
Es adornos de imprenta *(m pl)*
It ornamenti dello stampatore *(m pl)*

Pt ornamentações de impressão *(f pl)*

vinheta final *(f)* Pt
De Schlußvignette *(f)*
En tailpiece
Es culo de lámpara *(m)*
Fr cul-de-lampe *(m)*
It finalino *(m)*

violación de los derechos de autor *(f)* Es
De Verletzung des Copyright *(f)*
En infringement of copyright
Fr contrefaçon *(f)*
It violazione di copyright *(f)*
Pt infracção de um copyright *(f)*

violazione di contratto *(f)* It
De Vertragsbruch *(m)*
En breach of contract
Es incumplimiento de contrato *(m)*
Fr rupture de contrat *(f)*
Pt quebra de contrato *(f)*

violazione di copyright *(f)* It
De Verletzung des Copyright *(f)*
En infringement of copyright
Es violación de los derechos de autor *(f)*
Fr contrefaçon *(f)*
Pt infracção de um copyright *(f)*

virgola *(f) n* It
De Komma *(n)*
En comma
Es coma *(f)*
Fr virgule *(f)*
Pt vírgula *(f)*

virgola decimale *(f)* It
De Dezimalkomma *(n)*
En decimal point
Es punto decimal *(m)*
Fr virgule *(f)*
Pt ponto decimal *(m)*

virgolette *(f pl) n* It
De Anführungszeichen *(pl)*

En quotation marks
Es comillas *(f pl)*
Fr guillemets *(m pl)*
Pt aspas *(f pl)*

vírgula *(f) n* Pt
De Komma *(n)*
En comma
Es coma *(f)*
Fr virgule *(f)*
It virgola *(f)*

virgule *(f) n* Fr
De Dezimalkomma *(n)*
En comma; decimal point
Es coma; punto decimal *(f m)*
It virgola decimale *(f)*
Pt ponto decimal; vírgula *(m f)*

Visitenkarte *(f) n* De
En business card
Es tarjeta comercial *(f)*
Fr carte de visite professionnelle *(f)*
It bigliettino da visita *(m)*
Pt cartão de visita profissional *(m)*

vista en corte *(f)* Es
De Schnittbild *(n)*
En cutaway view
Fr scène de coupe *(f)*
It vista in sezione *(f)*
Pt vista recortada *(f)*

vista in sezione *(f)* It
De Schnittbild *(n)*
En cutaway view
Es vista en corte *(f)*
Fr scène de coupe *(f)*
Pt vista recortada *(f)*

vista recortada *(f)* Pt
De Schnittbild *(n)*
En cutaway view
Es vista en corte *(f)*
Fr scène de coupe *(f)*
It vista in sezione *(f)*

visual-display unit (VDU) En
De Sichtanzeigegerät *(n)*
Es unidad de visualización *(f)*
Fr unité de visualisation *(f)*

It unità di visualizzazione *(f)*
Pt unidade de visulização *(f)*

vitela *(f) n* Es
De Velinpapier *(n)*
En vellum
Fr vélin *(m)*
It cartapecora *(f)*
Pt velino *(m)*

vitela japonesa *(f)* Es
De Japanpapier *(n)*
En Japanese vellum
Fr papier du Japon *(m)*
It pergamena giapponese *(f)*
Pt papel pergaminho japonês *(m)*

vive It
De Stehen lassen
En stet
Es vale lo tachado
Fr à maintenir
Pt stet

volantino a stampa *(m)* It
De Merkblatt *(n)*
En leaflet
Es prospecto *(m)*
Fr feuille volante *(f)*
Pt folheto *(m)*

volkstümliche Medizinbücher *(pl)* De
En popular medical books
Es libros médicos populares *(m pl)*
Fr livres de vulgarisation médicale *(m pl)*
It libri divulgativi di medicina *(m pl)*
Pt livros de medicina popular *(m pl)*

volkstümliche Presse *(f)* De
En popular press
Es prensa popular *(f)*
Fr presse populaire *(f)*
It stampa popolare *(f)*
Pt prensa popular *(f)*

volkstümliche Romanliteratur *(f)* De

En popular fiction
Es literatura popular (f)
Fr romans populaires (m pl)
It narrativa popolare (f)
Pt ficção popular (f)

volkstümliche wissenschaftliche Bücher (pl) De
En popular scientific books
Es libros científicos populares (m pl)
Fr livres de vulgarisation scientifique (m pl)
It libri scientifici divulgativi (m pl)
Pt livros científicos populares (m pl)

voll gebunden De
En fully bound
Es totalmente encuadernado
Fr reliure pleine
It completamente rilegato
Pt completamente encadernado

Vollhadernpapier (n) n De
En all-rag paper
Es papel de hilo puro (m)
Fr papier pur chiffon (m)
It carta di cenci (f)
Pt papel inteiramente de trapos (m)

volume n En; Fr, It, Pt (m)
De Volumen (n)
Es volumen (m)

volumen (m) n Es
De Volumen (n)
En volume
Fr volume (m)
It volume (m)
Pt volume (m)

Volumen (n) n De
En volume
Es volumen (m)
Fr volume (m)
It volume (m)
Pt volume (m)

vom Rechner lesbare Daten (pl) De
En machine-readable data
Es datos legibles con máquina (m pl)
Fr éléments codés (m pl)
It dati leggibili per la macchina (m pl)
Pt dados legíveis na máquina (m pl)

Vorausexemplare (pl) De
En advance copies pl n
Es ejemplares para reseña (m pl)
Fr exemplaires de lancement (m pl)
It copie in anteprima (f pl)
Pt provas tipográficas (f pl)

Vorauszahlung (f) n De
En payment in advance
Es pago por adelantado (m)
Fr payement d'avance (m)
It pagamento anticipo (m)
Pt pagamento adiantado (m)

vordere Umschlagklappe (f) De
En front flap
Es solapa delantera (f)
Fr rabat avant (m)
It risvolto anteriore (m)
Pt aleta dianteira (f)

Vorrat (m) n De
En stock (books)
Es existencias (f pl)
Fr stock (m)
It scorta (f)
Pt existências (f pl)

Vorrede (f) n De
En preface
Es prefacio (m)
Fr préface (f)
It prefazione (f)
Pt prefácio (m)

Vorsatzpapiere (pl) De
En endpapers pl n
Es guardas (f pl)
Fr papiers de garde (m pl)
It risguardi (m pl)
Pt folhas de contracapa (f pl)

Vorschulbücher (pl) n De
En pre-school books
Es libros preescolares (m)
Fr livres préscolaires (m pl)
It libri prescolastici (m)
Pt livros pré-escolares (m)

Vorschuß (m) n De
En advance
Es anticipo (m)
Fr avance (f)
It anticipo (m)
Pt adiantamento (m)

Vorsitzender (m) n De
En chairman
Es presidente (m)
Fr président (m)
It presidente (m)
Pt presidente (m)

Vorstand (m) n De
En board of directors
Es consejo de administración (m)
Fr direction générale (f)
It comitato direttivo (m)
Pt conselho de administração (m)

Vortext (m) n De
En front matter
Es principios del libro (m pl)
Fr feuilles liminaires (f pl)
It preliminari del libro (m pl)
Pt princípio do livro (m)

Vorwort n De
En foreword
Es proemio (m)
Fr avant-propos (m)
It proemio (m)
Pt proémio (m)

Vorzurichtung (f) n De
En pre-makeready
Es arreglo preliminar (m)
Fr pré-mise en train (f)
It preavviamento (m)
Pt arranjo preliminar (m)

voyage promotionnel d'auteur (m) Fr
De Verfasser-Werbetour (f)
En author promotion tour
Es viaje de promoción del autor (m)
It itinerario promozionale dell'autore (m)
Pt viagem de promoção de autor (f)

vue en coupe (f) Fr
De Querschnitt (m)
En cross section
Es sección transversal (f)
It sezione trasversale (f)
Pt corte transversal (m)

vulgar adj Pt
De abgedroschen
En hackneyed
Es común
Fr stéréotypé
It comune

vulgariser vb Fr
De popularisieren
En popularize
Es popularizar
It popolarizzare
Pt vulgarizar

vulgarizador (m) n Pt
De Popularisierer (m)
En popularizer
Es popularizador (m)
Fr diffuseur (m)
It divulgatore (m)

vulgarizar vb Pt
De popularisieren
En popularize
Es popularizar
Fr vulgariser
It popolarizzare

W

Wachsgravieren *(n) n* De
En wax engraving
Es cerotipia *(f)*
Fr électrotype par
dessin sur métal
paraffiné *(m)*
It incisione a cera *(f)*
Pt cerotipia *(f)*

Wachstuch *(n) n* De
En American cloth
Es hule *(m)*
Fr moleskine *(f)*
It tela cerata *(f)*
Pt pano americano *(m)*

Walze *(f) n* De
En roller
Es rodillo *(m)*
Fr rouleau
(d´impression) *(m)*
It cilindro *(m)*
Pt rolo (de impressão)
(m)

warehouse *n* En
De Lagerhaus *(n)*
Es almacén *(m)*
Fr entrepôt *(m)*
It magazzino *(m)*
Pt armazém *(m)*

warehousing costs *pl n*
En
De Lagerkosten *(pl)*
Es gastos de almacén
(m pl)
Fr frais
d´emmagasinage *(m
pl)*
It costi di
immagazzinaggio *(m
pl)*
Pt custos de armazém
(m pl)

Warmwalzen *(n) n* De
En hot rolling
Es entintado en caliente
(m)
Fr laminage à chaud *(m)*
It calandratura a caldo
(f)
Pt laminação a quente
(f)

Wasserlinien *(f pl)* De
En laid lines
Es líneas en papel
verjurado *(f pl)*
Fr vergeures *(f pl)*
It vergature *(f pl)*
Pt linhas enramadas *(f
pl)*

Wasserzeichen *(n) n* De
En watermark
Es filigrana *(f)*
Fr filigrane *(m)*
It filigrana *(f)*
Pt filigrana *(f)*

waterleaf *n* En
De ungeleimtes Papier
(n)
Es papel no encolado
(m)
Fr papier non collé *(m)*
It carta non
imbozzimata *(f)*
Pt papel absorvente *(m)*

watermark *n* En
De Wasserzeichen *(n)*
Es filigrana *(f)*
Fr filigrane *(m)*
It filigrana *(f)*
Pt filigrana *(f)*

wax engraving En
De Wachsgravieren *(n)*
Es cerotipia *(f)*
Fr électrotype par
dessin sur métal
paraffiné *(m)*
It incisione a cera *(f)*
Pt cerotipia *(f)*

web-offset printing En
De Rollenoffsetdruck *(m)*
Es roto-offset *(m)*
Fr impression offset en
continu *(f)*
It stampa offset dal
rotolo *(f)*
Pt impressão roto-offset
(f)

weißer Streifen im Satz
(m) De
En river
Es calle *(f)*
Fr rue *(f)*
It spaziatura difettosa
(f)
Pt espaço defeituoso
(m)

weitere Literatur *(f)* De
En further reading
Es relectura *(f)*
Fr lectures
complémentaires *(f
pl)*
It ulteriori letture *(f pl)*
Pt leitura adicional *(f)*

Werbeabteilung *(f) n* De
En publicity department
Es departamento de
publicidad *(m)*
Fr service de la publicité
(m)
It reparto pubblicitario
(m)
Pt departamento de
publicidade *(f)*

Werbeagentur *(f) n* De
En advertising agency
Es agencia publicitaria
(f)
Fr agence de publicité
(f)
It agenzia pubblicitaria
(f)
Pt agência de
publicidade *(f)*

Werbefachmann *(m) n*
De
En promotion manager
Es jefe de promoción
(m)
Fr directeur de la
promotion *(m)*
It dirigente dell´attività
promozionale *(m)*
Pt director de promoção
(m)

Werbekampagne *(f) n*
De
En promotional
campaign
Es campaña de
promoción *(f)*
Fr campagne
publicitaire *(f)*
It campagna
promozionale *(f)*
Pt campanha de
promoção *(f)*

Werbeleiter *(m) n* De
En publicity manager
Es jefe de publicidad *(m)*
Fr directeur de la
publicité *(m)*

It direttore pubblicitario
(m)
Pt director de
publicidade *(m)*

werben *vb* De
En advertise
Es anunciar
Fr faire de la publicité
pour
It pubblicizzare
Pt anunciar

Werbung *(f) n* De
En advertising;
promotion; publicity
Es promoción;
publicidad *(f)*
Fr promotion; publicité
(f)
It promozione;
pubblicità *(f)*
Pt promoção;
publicidade *(f)*

wet plate En
De feuchte Platte *(f)*
Es placa húmeda *(f)*
Fr plaque humide *(f)*
It lastra al collodio *(f)*
Pt chapa molhada *(f)*

wholesale distribution
En
De Großhandelsvertrieb
(m)
Es distribución al por
mayor *(f)*
Fr commerce de gros
(m)
It distribuzione
all´ingrosso *(f)*
Pt distribuição por
atacado *(f)*

wholesaler *n* En
De Großhändler *(m)*
Es mayorista *(m)*
Fr grossiste *(m)*
It grossista *(m)*
Pt armazenista *(m)*

Wickelplatten *(pl)* De
En wrap-around plates
pl n
Es planchas arrollables
(f pl)
Fr plaques circulaires *(f
pl)*
It lastre flessibili *(f pl)*
Pt placas flexíveis *(f pl)*

Widerdruck *(m) n* De
En backing-up
Es respaldado *(m)*
Fr mettant en retiration
(f)
It supporto *(m)*
Pt apoio *(m)*

Widmung *(f) n* De
En dedication
Es dedicatoria *(f)*
Fr dédicace *(f)*
It dedica *(f)*
Pt dedicatória *(f)*

Widmungsseite *(f) n* De
En dedication page
Es página de dedicatoria
(f)
Fr page de dédicace *(f)*
It pagina di dedica *(f)*
Pt página de dedicatória
(f)

wiederholen *vb* De
En repeat
Es repetir
Fr répéter
It ripetere
Pt repetir

Wiederholung *(f) n* De
En repetition
Es repetición *(f)*
Fr répétition *(f)*
It ripetizione *(f)*
Pt repetição *(f)*

willkürlicher
Trennstrich *(m)* De
En discretionary hyphen
Es guión discrecional
(m)
Fr trait d'union facultatif
(m)
It lineetta discrezionale
(f)
Pt traço de união
discricionário *(m)*

wiremarks *pl n* En
De Drahtmarkierungen
(pl)
Es marcas de tela
metálica *(f pl)*
Fr marques de la toile *(f
pl)*
It segni della tela *(m pl)*
Pt marcas de tela
metálica *(f pl)*

wire side En
De Siebseite *(f)*
Es cara interior *(f)*
Fr côté toilé *(m)*
It lato tela *(m)*
Pt lado da tela *(m)*

wire stitching En
De Drahtheftung *(f)*
Es cosido con alambre
(m)
Fr couture métallique *(f)*
It cucitura a punti
metallici *(f)*
Pt costura com arame
(f)

Wissenschaft *(f) n* De
En science
Es ciencia *(f)*
Fr science *(f)*
It scienza *(f)*
Pt ciência *(f)*

wissenschaftliches
Journal *(n)* De
En scientific journal
Es revista científica *(f)*
Fr revue scientifique *(f)*
It rivista scientifica *(f)*
Pt revista científica *(f)*

wissenschaftliche und
technische Bücher
(pl) De
En scientific and
technical books
Es libros científicos y
técnicos *(m pl)*
Fr ouvrages
scientifiques et
techniques *(m pl)*
It libri scientifici e
tecnici *(m pl)*
Pt livros científicos e
técnicos *(m pl)*

wood engraving En
De Xylographie *(f)*
Es xilografía *(f)*
Fr gravure sur bois *(f)*
It incisione su legno
(m)
Pt xilografia *(f)*

wood-free pulp En
De holzfreier Papierstoff
(m)
Es pasta sin madera *(f)*
Fr pâte sans bois *(f)*
It pasta senza legno *(f)*
Pt polpa sem madeira *(f)*

wood pulp En
De Holzstoff *(m)*
Es pasta de madera *(f)*
Fr pâte de bois *(f)*
It pasta di legno *(f)*
Pt polpa de madeira *(f)*

work *n* En
De Arbeit *(f)*
Es trabajo *(m)*
Fr travail *(m)*
It lavoro *(m)*
Pt trabalho *(m)*

working lunch En
De geschäftliches
Mittagessen *(n)*
Es comida de trabajo *(f)*
Fr déjeuner de travail
(m)
It pranzo di lavoro *(m)*
Pt almoço de trabalho
(m)

work-in-progress En
De in Arbeit befindlich
Es trabajo en ejecución
(m)
Fr travail en cours *(m)*
It lavoro in corso *(m)*
Pt progresso de
adaptação ao
trabalho *(m)*

Wörterbuch *(n) n* De
En dictionary
Es diccionario *(m)*
Fr dictionnaire *(m)*
It dizionario *(m)*
Pt dicionário *(m)*

wove paper En
De Velinpapier *(n)*
Es papel avitelado *(m)*
Fr papier vélin *(m)*
It carta retinata *(f)*
Pt papel tecido *(m)*

wrap-around plates *pl n*
En
De Wickelplatten *(pl)*
Es planchas arrollables
(f pl)
Fr plaques circulaires *(f
pl)*
It lastre flessibili *(f pl)*
Pt placas flexíveis *(f pl)*.

wrappering *n* En
De Klebenindung *(f)*
Es sobrecubierta *(f)*

Fr emballage *(m)*
It mettitura le
sovracopertine *(f)*
Pt colocação de
sobrecapa *(f)*

wrong font Am
De falscher Buchstabe
(m)
En wrong fount
Es letra de otro tipo *(f)*
Fr lettre d'une autre
fonte *(f)*
It testina sbagliata *(f)*
Pt letra de outro tipo *(f)*

wrong fount En
Am wrong font
De falscher Buchstabe
(m)
Es letra de otro tipo *(f)*
Fr lettre d'une autre
fonte *(f)*
It testina sbagliata *(f)*
Pt letra de outro tipo *(f)*

wrong measure En
De falsches Maß *(n)*
Es medida incorrecta *(f)*
Fr justification
incorrecte *(f)*
It misura sbagliata *(f)*
Pt medida errada *(f)*

wrong-reading film En
De seitenverkehrter Film
(m)
Es película de lectura
incorrecta *(f)*
Fr film à lecture à
l'envers *(m)*
It pellicola a lettura
sbagliata *(f)*
Pt película de leitura do
lado errado *(f)*

wrong typeface En
De falscher Schrifttyp
(m)
Es ojo de tipo incorrecto
(m)
Fr lettre d'un autre oeil
(f)
It carattere sbagliato
(m)
Pt olho de tipo errado
(m)

X

xerografia (f) n It, Pt
De Xerographie (f)
En xerography
Es xerografía (f)
Fr xérographie (f)

xerografía (f) n Es
De Xerographie (f)
En xerography
Fr xérographie (f)
It xerografia (f)
Pt xerografia (f)

xerographic printer En
De xerographischer
  Drucker (m)
Es impresora
  xerográphica (f)
Fr imprimante
  xérographique (f)
It stampatrice
  xerografica (f)
Pt impressora
  xerográfica (f)

Xerographie (f) n De
En xerography
Es xerografía (f)
Fr xérographie (f)
It xerografia (f)
Pt xerografia (f)

xérographie (f) n Fr
De Xerographie (f)
En xerography
Es xerografía (f)
It xerografia (f)
Pt xerografia (f)

xerographischer
  Drucker (m) De
En xerographic printer
Es impresora
  xerográphica (f)
Fr imprimante
  xérographique (f)
It stampatrice
  xerografica (f)
Pt impressora
  xerográfica (f)

xerography n En
De Xerographie (f)
Es xerografía (f)
Fr xérographie (f)

It xerografia (f)
Pt xerografia (f)

xilografia (f) Pt
De Xylographie (f)
En wood engraving
Es xilografía (f)
Fr gravure sur bois (f)
It incisione su legno
  (m)

xilografía (f) Es
De Xylographie (f)
En wood engraving
Fr gravure sur bois (f)
It incisione su legno
  (m)
Pt xilografia (f)

Xylographie (f) De
En wood engraving
Es xilografía (f)
Fr gravure sur bois (f)
It incisione su legno
  (m)
Pt xilografia (f)

Y

y abreviada (f) Es
De Und-Zeichen (n)
En ampersand
Fr et commercial (m)
It congiunzione
  commerciale (f)
Pt e comercial (f)

year book En
De Jahrbuch (n)
Es anuario (m)
Fr annuaire (m)
It annuario (m)
Pt anuário (m)

Z

Zahlung (f) n De
En payment
Es pago (m)
Fr paiement (m)
It pagamento (m)
Pt pagamento (m)

zazzera (f) n It
De Büttenrand (m)
En deckle edge
Es barba (f)
Fr barbe (f)
Pt barba (f)

Zeichen setzen De
En punctuate
Es puntuar
Fr ponctuer
It punteggiare
Pt pontuar

Zeichensetzung (f) n De
En punctuation
Es puntuación (f)
Fr ponctuation (f)
It punteggiatura (f)
Pt pontuação (f)

zeichnen vb De
En draw
Es dibujar
Fr dessiner
It disegnare
Pt traçar

Zeichner (m) n De
Am draftsman
En draughtsman
Es delineante (m)
Fr dessinateur-
  concepteur (m)
It disegnatore (m)
Pt autor de esboço (m)

Zeile (f) n De
En line
Es línea (f)
Fr ligne (f)
It linea (f)
Pt linha (f)

Zeilenabstand (m) n De
En line space
Es espacio entre líneas
  (m)

Fr espace entre deux
  lignes (m)
It spazio tra le righe (m)
Pt espaço entre linhas
  (m)

Zeilendrucker (m) n De
En line printer
Es impresora de líneas
  (f)
Fr imprimante ligne par
  ligne (f)
It stampatrice per righe
  (f)
Pt impressora de linha
  (f)

Zeilenende-Trennstrich
  (m) De
En end-of-line hyphen
Es guión de final de
  línea (f)
Fr trait d'union de fin de
  ligne (m)
It trattino di fine linea
  (m)
Pt traço de união de fim
  de linha (m)

Zeilengießmaschine (f)
  n De
En linecasting machine
Es fundidora de lingotes
  (f)
Fr fondeuse à la ligne (f)
It macchina fonditrice a
  linea (f)
Pt fundidora de lingotes
  (f)

Zeilenmaß (n) n De
En measure
Es largo (m)
Fr mesure (f)
It misura (f)
Pt medida (f)

Zeilensatz (m) n De
En line composition
Es composición por
  líneas (f)
Fr photogravure
  typographique (f)
It composizione della
  linea (f)
Pt composição de
  linhas (f)

Zeilenzahl (f) n De
En line number
Es número de líneas (n)
Fr numéro de ligne (m)

It numero di linea *(m)*
Pt número de linha *(m)*

Zeitschrift *(f) n* De
En periodical
Es periódico *(m)*
Fr périodique *(m)*
It periodico *(m)*
Pt periódico *(m)*

Zeitung *(f) n* De
En newspaper
Es diario *(m)*
Fr journal *(m)*
It giornale quotidiano *(m)*
Pt jornal diário *(m)*

Zeitungsrahmen *(m) n* De
En news chase
Es rama de noticias *(f)*
Fr châssis à journal *(m)*
It caccia di notizie *(f)*
Pt rama de notícias *(f)*

Zellstoff *(m) n* De
En pulp
Es pasta *(f)*
Fr pâte *(f)*
It pasta *(f)*
Pt polpa *(f)*

Zellstoff-Karton *(m)* De
En pulp board
Es cartón de pasta *(m)*
Fr carton-pâte *(m)*
It cartone di pasta di legno *(m)*
Pt cartão de polpa *(m)*

Zellulose *(f) n* De
En cellulose
Es celulosa *(f)*
Fr cellulose *(f)*
It cellulosa *(f)*
Pt celulose *(f)*

zentrieren *vb* De
Am center
En centre (typesetting)
Es centrar
Fr centrer
It centrare
Pt centrar

Zeugnis *(n) n* De
En reference (testimonial)

Es referencia (certificado) *(f)*
Fr référence (certificat) *(f)*
It referenza *(f)*
Pt referência (certificado) *(f)*

Zierbuchstaben *(pl)* De
En swash letters *pl n*
Es letras de fantasía *(f pl)*
Fr lettres ornées *(f pl)*
It lettere inclinate *(f pl)*
Pt letras de fantasia *(f pl)*

zincografia *(f) n* It
De Chemiegraphie *(f)*
En process engraving
Es fotograbado *(m)*
Fr photogravure *(f)*
Pt fototipogravura *(f)*

zincografo *(m) n* It
De Klischeeanstalt *(f)*
En blockmaker
Es grabador *(m)*
Fr photograveur *(m)*
Pt gravador *(m)*

zinc print En
De Zinkdruck *(m)*
Es imagen de reserva formada en cinc *(f)*
Fr offset *(m)*
It stampa in zinco *(f)*
Pt imagem de reserva de zinco *(f)*

Zinkdruck *(m) n* De
En zinc print
Es imagen de reserva formada en cinc *(f)*
Fr offset *(m)*
It stampa in zinco *(f)*
Pt imagem de reserva de zinco *(f)*

Zirkumflex *(m) n* De
En circumflex
Es acento circunflejo *(m)*
Fr accent circonflexe *(m)*
It accento circonflesso *(m)*
Pt acento circunflexo *(m)*

Zitat *(n) n* De
En quotation (extract)
Es cita *(f)*
Fr citation *(f)*
It citazione *(f)*
Pt citação *(f)*

zitieren *vb* De
En quote (an extract)
Es citar
Fr citer
It citare tra virgolette
Pt citar

zona de justificação *(f)* Pt
De Justierungszone *(f)*
En justification zone
Es zona de justificación *(f)*
Fr zone de justification *(f)*
It zona di giustificazione *(f)*

zona de justificación *(f)* Es
De Justierungszone *(f)*
En justification zone
Fr zone de justification *(f)*
It zona di giustificazione *(f)*
Pt zona de justificação *(f)*

zona di giustificazione *(f)* It
De Justierungszone *(f)*
En justification zone
Es zona de justificación *(f)*
Fr zone de justification *(f)*
Pt zona de justificação *(f)*

zone de justification *(f)* Fr
De Justierungszone *(f)*
En justification zone
Es zona de justificación *(f)*
It zona di giustificazione *(f)*
Pt zona de justificação *(f)*

Zugriffzeit *(f) n* De
En access time
Es tiempo de acceso *(m)*
Fr temps d'accès *(m)*

It tempo di accesso *(m)*
Pt tempo de acesso *(m)*

zurichten *vb* De
En crop
Es recortar
Fr détourer
It scontornare
Pt recortar

zusammenfassen *vb* De
En précis
Es resumir
Fr résumer
It riassumere
Pt resumir

Zusammenfassung *(f) n* De
En summary
Es sumario *(m)*
Fr résumé *(m)*
It sommario *(m)*
Pt sumário *(m)*

zusammentragen *vb* De
En gather
Es reunir
Fr rassembler
It raccogliere
Pt reunir

Zusammentragen *(n) n* De
En gathering
Es recogida *(f)*
Fr assemblage *(m)*
It raccolta *(f)*
Pt reunião *(f)*

Zusammentragung *(f) n* De
En collating
Es alzado *(m)*
Fr assemblage *(m)*
It raccoglitura *(f)*
Pt revisão *(f)*

Zusätze *(pl)* De
En reducers *pl n*
Es diluyentes *(m pl)*
Fr réducteurs *(m pl)*
It diluenti *(m pl)*
Pt redutores *(m pl)*

Zuschuß *(m)* De
En overs *pl n*
Es hojas sobrantes *(f pl)*
Fr passe *(f)*
It fogli aggiunti *(m pl)*

Pt folhas que sobram *(f pl)*

Zweideutigkeit *(f) n* De
En ambiguity
Es ambigüedad *(f)*
Fr ambiguïté *(f)*
It ambiguità *(f)*
Pt ambiguidade *(f)*

Zweifarbendruck *(m) n* De
Am two-color printing
En two-colour printing
Es impresión bicolor *(f)*
Fr bichromie *(f)*
It stampa a due colori *(f)*
Pt impressão a duas cores *(f)*

Zweifarbenillustration *(f) n* De

En duotone illustration
Es ilustración en bicromía *(f)*
Fr illustration double ton *(f)*
It illustrazione bicolore *(f)*
Pt ilustração bicromática *(f)*

Zweifarbenpresse *(f) n* De
Am two-color press
En two-colour press
Es prensa bicolor *(f)*
Fr presse à bichromie *(f)*
It macchina da stampa a due colori *(f)*
Pt prensa a duas cores *(f)*

Zweifarbenschrift *(f) n* De

En duotype
Es duotipia bitono *(f)*
Fr duotype *(m)*
It duotipia *(f)*
Pt duotipia *(f)*

zweisprachiges Wörterbuch *(n)* De
En bilingual dictionary
Es diccionario bilingüe *(m)*
Fr dictionnaire bilingue *(m)*
It dizionario bilingue *(m)*
Pt dicionário bilíngue *(m)*

Zweiter Redakteur *(m)* De
En subeditor
Es corrector *(m)*
Fr secrétaire de la rédaction *(m)*

It redattore aggiunto *(m)*
Pt redactor auxiliar *(m)*

Zweitourenmaschine *(f) n* De
En two-revolution press
Es prensa de doble revolución *(f)*
Fr presse à double impression *(f)*
It macchina da stampa a due giri *(f)*
Pt prensa a duas rotações *(f)*

Zylinderaufzug *(m) n* De
En cylinder dressing
Es rectificado de cilindros *(m)*
Fr habillage *(m)*
It rivestimento per cilindri *(m)*
Pt rectificação de cilindros *(f)*